THE
BYSTANDER

THE
BYSTANDER

John F. Kennedy
and the
Struggle for Black Equality

NICK BRYANT

BASIC
BOOKS

A Member of the Perseus Books Group
New York

Published by Basic Books
A Member of the Perseus Books Group

Books published by Basic Books are available at special discounts for bulk purchases in the United States by corporations, institutions, and other organizations. For more information, please contact the Special Markets Department at the Perseus Books Group, 11 Cambridge Center, Cambridge MA 02142, or call (617) 252-5298, (800) 255-1514 or e-mail special.markets@perseusbooks.com.

Designed by Brent Wilcox

Library of Congress Cataloging-in-Publication Data
    Bryant, Nick (Nicholas Andrew)
The bystander : John F. Kennedy and the struggle for Black equality / Nick Bryant.
        p.   cm.
    Includes bibliographical references and index.
    ISBN-13: 978-0-465-00826-1 (hardcover : alk. paper)
    ISBN-10: 0-465-00826-7 (hardcover : alk. paper)
    1. Kennedy, John F. (John Fitzgerald), 1917–1963.   2. African Americans—Civil rights—History—20th century.   3. Civil rights movements—United States—History—20th century.
4. United States—Politics and government—1961–1963.   I. Title.
E842.1.B79 2006
973.922092—dc22
                                                                                2005035495

06 07 08 09 / 10 9 8 7 6 5 4 3 2 1

To Colin and Janet Bryant,
my wonderful parents

CONTENTS

INTRODUCTION

༄

Operation Washington

Across America black fury had broken loose. A swirl of protests, touched off by weeks of racial strife in Birmingham, Alabama, now engulfed much of the country. Between May and late August of 1963, there had been 1,340 demonstrations in over 200 cities in thirty-six states. Some were communities long fractured along racial lines. Others had never before been touched by violence. In Cambridge, Maryland, a once-tranquil cannery town on the Eastern Shore, the governor declared martial law in July after black rioters shot and wounded five whites, including two National Guardsmen and a twelve-year-old boy. Fighting had erupted following a prayer vigil outside the local courthouse, and as the black journalist George W. Collins reported, "Only an act of God could have stayed the hand of death during the long night when bullets literally rained on the county seat of Dorchester County."[1]

In Danville, Virginia, a judge presiding over protest-related hearings took to wearing a revolver in his courtroom, fearing that violence would disrupt the proceedings. Even attorneys representing the black activists on trial were frisked at the entrance for knives and guns. In Jackson, Mississippi, 500 protesters were arrested on a single day in June, and then caged behind razor-wire fences in open-air pens. Thelton Henderson, one of only three black attorneys in the Justice Department's Civil Rights Division, warned that the situation was "terribly tense and Negroes are about to shoot." Henderson had personally encountered three young black men brandishing guns, who threatened to attack white policemen and "shoot their brains out." But angry street protesters were not the only problem, Henderson continued. The feeling among leading ministers was that "they should stop preaching non-violence." In Brooklyn, protesters led by a dozen local black preachers blockaded a construction site, to publicize discriminatory hiring practices. After failing to win concessions, they enlisted black schoolchildren, who climbed onto the bulldozers to prevent them from moving.

1

"The streets are going to run red with blood," cried protest leader Gardner Taylor, the pastor of the local Baptist church.[2]

In Chicago, blacks rioted through the South Side in late May after a white police officer shot a fourteen-year-old black boy who was fleeing the scene of a burglary. Several hundred young men took up rooftop positions, pelting police reinforcements with bottles and stones. Shocked by the viciousness of the young rioters, Edwin C. Berry of the National Urban League warned of a complete breakdown in race relations: "My messages from the beer gardens and the barbershops all indicate the fact that the Negro is at war." On July 4, Reverend J. H. Jackson, the head of the National Baptist Convention and the so-called Negro Pope, was chased off the stage by fifty militants at a rally held in the city by the National Association for the Advancement of Colored People (NAACP). "Kill him, kill him," shouted the mob after Jackson had criticized plans for a massive March on Washington planned for the following month.[3]

The violence was unrelenting, and continued deep into the summer. The very randomness of the unrest made it all the more frightening. In August, protesters in Philadelphia campaigning for an end to discriminatory employment practices at a school construction site fought pitched battles with riot police. The violence was especially shocking because the demonstrations were sponsored by the NAACP, traditionally one of the more restrained national civil rights groups. "My basic strength," boasted Cecil Moore, the head of the organization's local chapter, "is those 300,000 lower-class guys who are ready to mob, rob, steal and kill." For Moore, the strategy of nonviolent protest had run its course.[4]

The Reverend Dr. Martin Luther King, Jr. believed that the events of the early summer had transformed the struggle for equality from a "Negro protest" into a "Negro revolution." In late May, he warned the White House of an impending national calamity because of the "snail like pace of desegregation." "We're through with tokenism and gradualism and see-how-far-you've-comeism," he told a rally in Chicago in June. "We're through with we've-done-more-for-your-people-than-anyone-elseism. We can't wait any longer. Now is the time." That same month, in Boston, he cautioned that America had reached the "explosion point." The Reverend James Bevel, one of King's colleagues in the Southern Christian Leadership Conference (SCLC), put it more plainly: · "Some punk who calls himself the President has the audacity to tell people to go slow. I'm not prepared to be humiliated by white trash the rest of my life, including Mr. Kennedy."[5]

Malcolm X, the spokesman for the Nation of Islam, inflamed tensions with his bellicose rhetoric and spread alarm in Washington by rejecting the strategy of nonviolence. He decried the "white devils" and warned that "you cannot integrate the Negroes and the whites without bloodshed." His militant message resonated in particular with young, inner-city blacks. "I've come to the conclusion that the only thing for this Afro-American to do here in this country is to retaliate," one of his Harlem followers told a *CBS Eyewitness Report Special.* "I don't listen to nothing no more but blood."[6]

Anxious voices made themselves heard within the Kennedy administration. Secretary of State Dean Rusk described the racial flare-up as "one of the gravest issues that we have had since 1865." His assistant G. Mennen Williams, the former governor of Michigan and a longtime advocate of civil rights, feared a complete breakdown in law and order: "the possibility that the inter-action of fervent demonstration and brutal repression would reach such a pitch that public peace and safety would be endangered beyond reasonable control." Berl Bernhard, the staff director of the United States Civil Rights Commission (CRC), the body charged with gathering evidence on racial inequality, believed the nation was "torn by racial insurgency." A CRC advisory committee in Alabama warned that the situation had almost reached the "point of civil war." Even the cerebral Kennedy adviser, the economist John Kenneth Galbraith, then serving as ambassador to India, sounded panicked. "This is our last chance to remain in control of matters," he wrote in June, "and of avoiding the most serious eventuality which is the possible need to use force to restrain Negro violence."[7]

Vice President Lyndon Johnson, the administration's highest-ranking southerner and privately a critic of the president's handling of the racial crisis, also sounded the alarm in May. "Progress must come faster because otherwise the tragic headlines which speak of the breakdown of law and order will increase rather than diminish," he warned a group of black reporters. "Issues which are not settled by justice and fair play will sooner or later be settled by force and violence." In a private memorandum circulated at the highest levels of the Kennedy administration, Louis Martin, the vice chairman of the Democratic National Committee (DNC) and President Kennedy's sole black adviser, wrote, "The accelerated tempo of Negro restiveness may create the most critical state of race relations since the Civil War."[8]

Few were more worried by the violent tumble of events than the president's thirty-seven-year-old brother, Attorney General Robert Kennedy, who had monitored the escalating racial crisis more closely than any other high-ranking member of the federal government. During the first two years of the administration, when violence flared during the Freedom Rides and at the University of Mississippi, he had almost become inured to the sight of white segregationists attacking black demonstrators. Much more terrifying were the new images of black-on-white violence during a night of frenzied rioting in Birmingham on May 11. During a tense meeting at the White House nine days later, Robert Kennedy warned the president that "Negroes are now just antagonistic and mad and they're going to be mad at everything. You can't talk to them. . . . My friends all say [even] the Negro maids and servants are getting antagonistic." Burke Marshall, Robert Kennedy's most trusted Justice Department colleague, compared the recent outbreak of violence with past crises in Alabama and Mississippi. "There we had a white mob against a Negro," he noted, with sharp clarity. "Here we have a Negro mob against whites."[9]

President John F. Kennedy grasped the importance of that shift and was alert to its dangers. For much of his time in office, however, civil rights had been only a peripheral concern. Now he realized his presidency might come to be defined by his response to the racial crisis. Speaking at a conference of U.S. mayors in Honolulu on June 9, Kennedy warned of "a moment of moral and constitutional crisis," and added that "the time for token moves and talk is past." Two days later, in a major nationwide television address, he cautioned that "fires of frustration and discord are burning in every city, North and South, where legal remedies are not at hand. Redress is sought in the streets, in demonstrations, parades, and protests which create tensions and threaten violence and threaten lives."[10]

Meeting business leaders on June 4, Kennedy spoke candidly of his fear that disillusioned blacks could easily lose their faith in government. "We lose them," he warned, "and I don't think we are going to get them back." Unless the White House acted in a forthright manner, he told Governor Jimmie Davis of Louisiana, "[i]t's going to be up North. . . . This isn't anymore just a southern matter. . . . It's Philadelphia and it's going to be Washington, D.C., this summer, and we're trying to figure out what we can do to put this stuff in the courts and get it off the street because somebody's going to get killed and it is going to be—"

"It's going to be the bloodiest thing," Davis interrupted. "It's going to be a civil war."[11]

In late August, the threat of violence brought fear to the capital itself. Over 200,000 protesters planned to gather under the brooding statue of Abraham Lincoln in a self-styled "March on Washington." "The capital stage is set for a definitive encounter," wrote black intellectual Louis E. Lomax, "a major battle in the Negro revolt." Jack Elsen of the *Washington Post*, a newspaper filled for weeks with dire predictions of trouble, posed the question in even plainer terms: "Will Washington Negroes accept the leadership that has brought them this far or will they turn to the extremists? Will future historians record that Washington made a successful transition with peace and pride, or will they record a failure that it was marked by turmoil and violence?"[12]

For a White House that prided itself on its skill at crisis management, the prospect of the March on Washington presented a unique challenge. Its first response midway through June was to lobby black leaders into canceling plans for a mass demonstration. In a meeting at the White House on June 22, Kennedy told them he did not want "a big show on the Capitol" nor did he want to provoke a backlash against the civil rights movement by forcing lawmakers to act "at the point of a gun." When attempts at persuasion failed, the administration's efforts centered on ensuring that the march passed off peacefully. This involved a massive, and wholly unprecedented, mobilization of the federal government's security apparatus. Administration officials also tried to wrest control of the protest itself.[13] The president was unequivocal: "They're liable to come down here and shit all over the [Washington] monument," he reportedly told aides. "I've got a civil rights bill to get through. We'll run it."[14]

The FBI responded by mounting a vast surveillance operation. The bureau instructed every field office across the country to provide intelligence on how many local black activists planned to converge on Washington, whether they had any affiliation with communist organizations, and if hate groups, like the KKK, planned to sabotage them. "All divisions have been ordered to alert Klan and hate informants, racial informants, and other sources," noted an internal FBI memorandum in late July, "to obtain specific details concerning the formation of delegates, mode of travel, and other pertinent details," especially on the "possible participation of subversive organizations." The bureau paid particularly close attention to George Lincoln Rockwell, the head of American Nazi Party, whose plans for a counter-demonstration "could be a very explosive situation," according to a secret surveillance report. So wide was its intelligence dragnet that the FBI even received a tip-off from U.S. Army Intelligence that dynamite had been stolen from a construction site in Virginia, which might be used to attack the Lincoln Memorial. FBI agents even kept tabs on Ledger Smith, a professional roller skater, with the stage name "Roller Man," who had glided the 700 miles between his Chicago home to participate in the demonstration.[15]

At a meeting with FBI chiefs on the Sunday before the march, Deputy Attorney General Nicholas Katzenbach expressed fears that two groups in particular could potentially cause serious trouble: the Nation of Islam and communist infiltrators. Katzenbach asked the FBI to maintain "exceptionally close contact with . . . informants." He was worried, too, that a group of subversives might seize control of the public address system and incite the crowd. It was therefore decided that an administration official should sit to the right of the Lincoln Memorial with an automatic cut-off switch, along with a record turntable. If protesters overran the speaker's platform, the sound feed would be cut and replaced by Mahalia Jackson singing "He's Got the Whole World in His Hands."[16]

Almost 150 agents from the Washington field office were assigned to mingle in the crowd, working in tandem with the Secret Service. Other FBI agents were stationed at rooftop observation points on the Lincoln Memorial, Union Station, and the Commerce Department. Security was also tightened at the FBI headquarters, which Director J. Edgar Hoover feared might come under attack from protesters. "It has been suggested to employees," noted an internal memorandum, "that they should remain away from the windows."[17]

For weeks, the prospect of violence preoccupied Washington police chief Robert V. Murray, who had ordered the Metropolitan Police Department onto its highest state of alert. Murray had served thirty-three years on the force, the

past twelve of them in charge. But nothing had prepared him for the biggest
political demonstration in American history. His officers came up with no less
than seventy-two potential disaster scenarios and had plotted a response to each
one. In the event of a riot, Murray hoped to confine it to the event site, especially since the Lincoln Memorial was enclosed on three sides by water. But
under his master plan, every corner of downtown Washington would be protected. On Capitol Hill, a thin blue line of officers, standing five feet apart,
would surround Congress. A policeman or National Guardsman would be stationed on every corner in downtown business district to guard against looting.
Murray mobilized 1,900 of his 2,930 officers, and ordered them to work eighteen-
hour shifts rather than the usual eight. He also drafted in hundreds of additional officers from neighboring suburban forces, who had attended specially
organized riot training courses. Finally, Murray called up 200 scout cars, eighty-
six motorcycles, twenty-four jeeps, several police helicopters, and twenty-three
cranes to move broken-down buses. So many law enforcement resources were
devoted to policing the march, the FBI feared a spate of bank robberies in the
capital's outlying neighborhoods. In the city's courtrooms, a team of local judges
was placed on round-the-clock standby, while 350 inmates from the district jailhouse were evacuated to create space for any disruptive protesters.[18]

Despite this massive mobilization, the department's sixty-nine police dogs
remained in their kennels. Mindful of the ugly images from Birmingham in
May, when police German shepherds had ripped at the flesh of young black activists, Murray feared their appearance could easily incite the crowd. So, too, did
Robert Kennedy, who called a district commissioner to tell him curtly: "No
dogs." In a further attempt to polish the image of the Washington police, Murray also ended his department's long-standing segregationist practices by announcing that white officers would no longer be able to block black policemen
from being assigned to their squad cars.[19]

Since 1,900 officers alone would be incapable of quelling an unruly crowd of
some 200,000 blacks, 2,400 National Guardsmen were sworn in as "special officers" on the eve of the march and granted temporary powers of arrest. They
slept overnight in musty fatigues, billeted on the concrete floor of the D.C. Armory near the Capitol, which in January 1961, had hosted the most lavish of
President Kennedy's inaugural balls. Along with the 2,400 guardsmen, the District of Columbia National Guard made over 100 doctors and nurses available
as well, augmenting the 750 medical personnel already placed on special alert at
the city's hospitals. Elective surgery in the greater Washington area was canceled, so more than 350 beds could be set aside for riot-related emergencies.
The District of Columbia General Hospital even went as far as to activate its
"national disaster plan."[20]

Life in Washington was completely disrupted in the run-up to the march.
Government offices shut down, and federal employees were advised to stay

home. Acting under recently acquired emergency powers, the commissioners is-sued a twenty-four-hour ban on the sale of alcohol. Restaurateurs and bar-tenders were taken completely by surprise—the sale of liquor had not been banned in the nation's capital since Prohibition. Local churches provided emer-gency shelters for protesters stranded overnight, and when national railway workers threatened strike action over a labor dispute commencing at 8:00 P.M. on the evening of the march, the president himself intervened to stop it.[21]

Fears about the violent potential of the march brought about an unprece-dented degree of cooperation between the administration and black leaders. Ba-yard Rustin, who, as deputy march director, was in overall charge of its planning, agreed immediately to bring forward the start time of the march so that protest-ers would not be left wandering the streets after dark. Rustin also promised Jus-tice Department officials that "there would not be any stunts or efforts to ob-struct traffic, such as laying down in the streets, sit-ins or other activities which might irritate or inflame others." Under intense pressure from the Kennedy ad-ministration and pro–civil rights lawmakers on Capitol Hill, Rustin also agreed to a change in venue. The original plan, for a mass protest on the steps of the U.S. Capitol, was quietly shelved. It was replaced with a demonstration at the foot of the Lincoln Memorial, a 180-acre site that was easier to police.[22]

As march day approached, Rustin even agreed to let a Justice Department offi-cial work full-time alongside the organizing committee. The role was filled by John Douglas, an archetypal New Frontiersman, who was chosen by Robert Kennedy partly because he was the son of Senator Paul Douglas of Illinois, one of the civil rights movement's closest congressional allies. Douglas was there to persuade, ca-jole, and threaten—and to make sure the organizers bent to the administration's will. He channeled his energy into changing the focus of the demonstration away from a protest against the president into a rally in support of his controversial civil rights bill. March leaders acquiesced to this shift in emphasis.[23]

After the march, Rustin would complain that Douglas "almost smothered us. We had to keep raising our demands to keep him from getting ahead of us." Yet disagreements were surprisingly rare, since Rustin was determined to turn the entire event into a showcase for nonviolent protest. With black pride so visibly at stake, he worked tirelessly to ensure the demonstration passed off peacefully and understood the value of working so closely with federal officials.[24]

As march day approached, Rustin supplied the Justice Department with the routes of bus convoys heading to Washington from the South, so the FBI could investigate any threats to protesters on the way. Ambushes, or even bus burn-ings, would "change the entire tenor of the whole demonstration." But the Jus-tice Department informed Rustin that the policing of buses heading toward Washington would be impossible, even if they came under attack—a continua-tion of the administration's long-standing policy of not offering federal protec-tion to civil rights protesters.[25]

At one point, however, the Justice Department did consider taking direct action to secure the release of James Farmer, the leader of the Congress of Racial Equality (CORE), who had been jailed following protests in Plaquemine, Louisiana. Administration officials thought that Farmer's presence would have a moderating effect on hard-line protesters. "This is being considered," noted a secret memorandum, "because of information received by the [Justice] Department as to the activities of a left wing element in CORE which has communist leanings, as well as another faction which has a loose affiliation with the Nation of Islam." Roy Wilkins, head of the NAACP, cited another reason why Farmer should attend. He had the loudest voice of any of the civil rights leaders and could be called upon to drown out the chants of disorderly protesters in the event of trouble.[26]

Even after weeks of meticulous planning, administration officials could not rule out the threat of violence. So on march day itself, the District of Columbia was placed under virtual martial law, with the president ordering the biggest peacetime military buildup in American history. By midmorning on August 28, five military bases on the outskirts of the capital were bursting with activity—a heavily armed, 4,000-strong task force, with the code name INSIDE, prepared for deployment. At Fort Myer, Fort Belvoir, Fort Meade, Quantico Marine base, and the Anacostia Naval Station, thirty helicopters had been flown in especially to provide a rapid airlift capability. At Fort Bragg, North Carolina, 15,000 Special Forces troops, dubbed STRICOM, were placed on standby, ready to be airlifted at the first sign of trouble.[27]

In Washington itself, twenty-six teams were assigned to look out for troublemakers. The FBI also hoped that the sight of "cruising jeeps will have a psychological effect on preserving order," in the words of an FBI planning memorandum. "Truck convoys of Regular Army troops and Marines crisscrossed the city—fighting men racing to take up strategic positions," in the words of one reporter. "Overnight, it seemed, the city was transformed from the capital of a nation at peace to a nation at war." "So extensive were the measures taken," wrote another correspondent, "that it would have surprised no one if the helicopters hovering over the March site were carrying a platoon of paratroopers, ready to jump at the first sign of disorder."[28]

The administration was determined not to repeat the mistakes of the past. Only the previous September, during the "Battle of Ole Miss," two people had been killed as the administration blundered in its deployment of troops. This time, in an effort to simplify the chain of command, the Pentagon set up a "war room," with an open telephone line to the White House. The line was patched through to the office of Kenneth O'Donnell, the hard-nosed Bostonian who served as President Kennedy's political enforcer.[29]

If violence flared, speed of deployment was essential. All the necessary presidential proclamations, executive orders, and letters of instruction were prepared in advance. The military would be activated by an executive order entitled "Providing for the Dispersal of an Extraordinary Assemblage in the District of Columbia," while the standby proclamation was to be issued if a situation developed "which constitutes a threat to lives and property." Days before the march, O'Donnell drew up precise rules of engagement in response to a variety of emergency scenarios. If rioting erupted, the White House would issue a presidential proclamation calling on protesters to disperse forthwith. If the violence continued, the president would sign an executive order authorizing Defense Secretary Robert McNamara to take "all appropriate steps" to disperse the crowd. From that point on, the Pentagon would be in the chair. Troops would be airlifted into the center of Washington. Pentagon officials circulated a "Letter of Instruction" stamped "CONFIDENTIAL" to military commanders warning that: "Desire for use of minimum force must not jeopardize successful completion of mission." In response to an escalating situation, troops would first brandish unloaded rifles with bayonets fixed and sheathed, then bare bayonets. If that failed, tear gas could be used, and then loaded rifles with bare bayonets fixed. The mission went by the code name Operation Washington.[30]

Throughout the morning of August 28, as the demonstration took shape outside his windows, President Kennedy remained inside the White House chairing a meeting of foreign policy advisers on Vietnam. Before the march, he had resisted demands from Wilkins, King, and the other leaders of the so-called Big Six civil rights organizations to grant them a presidential meeting that morning, since he was averse to being identified too closely with a demonstration that might become violent. His advisers also worried that black leaders would arrive at the White House with a list of unreasonable demands, which the president would find impossible to meet. If they left the Oval Office upset, the whole tenor of the demonstration could quickly change. Much to Rustin's disappointment, Kennedy even decided against sending protesters a presidential statement, fearing it could spark demonstrations against him on the Mall. Instead, he agreed to host a delegation of black leaders in the Cabinet Room after the march was over, hoping it would soften their rhetoric against him.[31]

At 1:40 P.M., aides wheeled a small television into the Oval Office. Kennedy began to watch just as King, the untitled leader of the civil rights movement, was about to speak. Standing midway up the steps of the most magnificent platform that America could offer, the preacher looked out over a thicket of microphones onto a stirring vista of over 200,000 demonstrators, stretching down either side of the Reflecting Pool, way down the Mall to the shimmering spire of the Washington Monument. Immediately in front of him were rows of dignitaries—lawmakers from Capitol Hill, a handful of administration officials brave enough to venture from their offices, and a small group of black ambassadors from Africa's newly decolonized countries, some wearing business suits, others more colorful tribal dress. The rank and file of the civil rights movement gathered at the foot of the memorial, singing, praying, hugging, laughing, and applauding. Thousands were stretched out on the grass verges, jammed elbow to elbow, while others waded knee-deep in the water to escape the heat. A few were perched in the elm and oak trees, lilting from side to side in the late-afternoon breeze.

Framed by the colonnade of the Lincoln Memorial, King began by telling protesters that their presence in the symbolic shadow of the Great Emancipator offered proof of the marvelous new militancy sweeping the country and warned that the demonstrations of 1963 marked not an end but a beginning in the fight for equality. For too long, he said, black Americans had been exiles in their own land, "crippled by the manacles of segregation and the chains of discrimination." The whirlwinds of revolt would continue to shake the very foundations of the country: "And those who hope that the Negro needed to blow off steam and will now be content will have a rude awakening if the nation returns to business as normal." It would be fatal, he said, for the nation "to overlook the urgency of the moment and to underestimate the determination of the Negro."

At first, the crowd's reaction was muted. King then cast aside his prepared notes and launched extemporaneously into a glorious refrain. "I have a dream that one day this nation will rise up and live out the true meaning of its creed," he shouted, his outstretched right arm reaching toward the sky. "I have a dream that one day even the state of Mississippi, a desert state, sweltering with the heat of injustice and oppression, will be transformed into an oasis of freedom and justice." Now he was hitting his stride, invigorated by the chants and cries of the crowd. "Dream on! Dream on!" they shouted. "Dream on!" His voice echoed off the marble backdrop and thundered down the Mall, as he imagined a future in which his children could "live in a nation where they will not be judged by the color of their skin but by the content of their character." Then he reached his impassioned finale:

> When we let freedom ring, when we let it ring from every village and every hamlet, from every state and every city, we will be able to speed up that day when all of God's children, black men and white men, Jews and Gentiles, Protestants and Catholics, will be able to join hands and sing in the words of the old Negro spiritual, "Free at last! Free at last! Thank God Almighty, we are free at last!"[32]

Watching at the White House, the president was riveted. It was the first time he had heard the thirty-four-year-old preacher deliver a speech in its entirety— the first time he had taken its measure, listened to its cadence. As the speech reached its climax, Kennedy turned to Lee White, his young civil rights adviser, with a wry smile spreading across his face. "He's good," he said. "He's damned good." According to White, the president seemed impressed more by the quality of King's performance than by the power of his message.[33]

But what did King's dream of racial harmony truly ask of the president? What was its meaning for a politician so full of internal contradictions that even long-time aides, like White, found it impossible to penetrate his mind?

When it came to civil rights, Kennedy's personality contained a bewildering range of possibilities. At times, he was capable of genuine acts of compassion and thoughtfulness. On other occasions, he was cold, disparaging, and notoriously unresponsive—and never more so than when blacks criticized the inadequacies of his policies. Even at moments of great crisis, he could display a numbing indifference to violence and bloodshed. But what now, at this point of grave national uncertainty, when so many communities, North and South, were racked with such instability and confusion?

Just five weeks before the March on Washington, Kennedy had placed himself in the vanguard of the struggle for racial equality by unveiling the most far-reaching civil rights bill that a president had ever put before Congress. Casting aside the political advice of many of his closest advisers, he had appeared before the American people on national television to implore them to examine their consciences and to ask how a democratic society founded on the principles of freedom and equality could countenance such extreme racial inequalities. In his June 11 speech, a long overdue but bold attempt to shape the nation's thinking, he had spoken with an intensity and passion few had seen from him before. He even departed from his prepared script to talk extemporaneously about the racial inequities that continued to blight the lives of millions of black Americans. Even more importantly, he lent the moral prestige of his office to the cause of freedom—a move so unpopular in the South that Kennedy claimed it jeopardized his chances of reelection in 1964. Using words that could easily have been spoken by King or Rustin, the president described civil rights as a "moral issue" as "old as the scriptures" and "as clear as the American Constitution."[34]

Yet even as he spoke, it was hard to divine his true motives—difficult to judge whether they were the words of a benevolent, if belated, reformer or a president caught in the clutches of circumstance, struggling to maintain control. Many complained his newfound enthusiasm for civil rights was little more than an attempt to stem the black revolt—that he had only brought the full weight of his office to bear when he had no other choice but to lead.

Kennedy was partly responsible for this crisis in race relations. His mishandling of civil rights over the previous two years had brought America to this point of uncertainty. Handed an historic opportunity at the beginning of the 1960s to map out a trajectory for the country that could have carried millions of black Americans closer to freedom, he decided instead to adopt a policy of inaction. He feared inflaming the South, splintering the Democratic Party and alienating southern oligarchs on Capitol Hill, whom he believed had accumulated enough power to stymie his legislative program.

His was a political miscalculation of immense scale. Kennedy had unintentionally set in motion a chain reaction that had a radicalizing effect on agitators and extremists on both sides of the racial divide. Kennedy's inertia at the outset of his presidency encouraged white supremacists in the Deep South and on Capitol Hill to believe that they could go on defending segregation indefinitely, which provoked tens of thousands of black demonstrators to adopt increasingly militant tactics. Inadvertently, Kennedy had helped nourish a climate in which racial extremists like Governor George Wallace of Alabama grew in stature and support, and in which black demands for further and more rapid reform became increasingly difficult to fulfill.

Toward the end of his presidency, the nation was moving inexorably "toward two societies, one black, one white—separate and unequal," in the words of the Kerner Commission report published later in the decade. The destructive forces that Kennedy had primed through the optimistic promise of his presidential candidacy had escalated beyond his control. At the beginning of 1961, a less painful transition toward a more equal society might have been possible; by the summer of 1963, the problem had grown intractable, and many more troubled—and violent—days lay ahead as America struggled to confront its "Negro problem."[35]

March day proved a welcome anticlimax for Police Chief Murray, who had spent most of it wandering through the crowds, accompanied by Lieutenant Owen N. Davis, his most senior black officer. By dusk, there had been just three arrests, all involving whites. In the end, the only threat to police came not from unruly protesters but the chicken box dinners handed out earlier in the morning, which had not been properly refrigerated. Just after four o'clock, when Chief Murray first received reports of this development, he issued his most important order of the day—that under no circumstances should his men touch the chicken. Afterwards, Murray convened an impromptu press conference and announced to reporters that the demonstration had the feel of a "church picnic"—though not, of course, for his hungry officers. Robert Kennedy also felt a profound sense of relief, and that evening asked John Douglas to prepare a list of all the government officials he should thank. Afterward, the attorney general telephoned each one individually.[36]

At the foot of the Lincoln Memorial, King and his colleagues were bundled into a caravan of government limousines, which then edged slowly through the departing crowds to the White House. Inside, Kennedy met the black leaders with an outstretched hand, and a jaunty reprise of the lilting refrain that had lifted the whole civil rights movement to a new spiritual plane: "I have a dream." With that, he ushered them into the Oval Office.

CHAPTER 1

❧

"Give the Kid a Break"

John F. Kennedy introduced himself to the voters of Massachusetts with a pithy, six-word slogan that neatly encapsulated the youthful appeal of his candidacy and the optimism of postwar America: "The New Generation Offers a Leader." Just twenty-eight years old, with a gaunt, pencil-thin frame and skin yellow from wartime malaria, he hardly looked like a leader of his generation. But he had returned from the South Pacific, where he helped save the lives of the crew of his naval patrol boat, *PT-109,* after it was rammed by a Japanese destroyer, with a tale of marvelous heroism lending substance to the claim. Kennedy formally announced his candidacy for Congress in a radio address on April 22, 1946, with a short speech stressing sacrifice and service, the very themes he would echo at the fruition of his career. "The temper of our times imposes an obligation upon every thinking citizen to work diligently in peace as we served tirelessly in war," said Kennedy, racing breathlessly through the script. "Everyone who is able to should do his utmost in these days of world and national progress to contribute his talents in keeping with his abilities and resources."[1]

By the standards of Massachusetts's Eleventh Congressional District, the speech was unusually elegant and the kind seldom heard from the local hacks who considered it their fief—Irish- and Italian-Americans steeped in the traditions of its rambunctious style of politics. The area that gave birth to these characters was a confusing sprawl of precincts harboring 328,000 voters of thirty-seven different nationalities. It stretched from the shipyards of Charlestown, an urban forest of smokestacks, oil tanks, and freight yards, to the gray, three-decker high-rises of Somerville; from the white turrets of Harvard to the red-bricked tenements of the Italian North End. Thirty years earlier, the district had been represented in Congress by John F. ("Honey Fitz") Fitzgerald, Boston's former mayor and Kennedy's maternal grandfather. Fitzgerald was a political extrovert, famed for ending precinct meetings by bellowing out "Sweet

Adeline" at the top of his voice. In the Eleventh District, such exuberant behavior was considered the norm.

In temperament and style, Jack Kennedy seemed wholly unsuited to represent the Eleventh District. He was bashful, reticent, and, unusually for a member of the Kennedy clan, lacking in self-confidence. He was also still deeply tormented by the tragic death of his elder brother, Joseph P. Kennedy, Jr., who had been killed during the summer of 1944, when the plane he was piloting disintegrated above the English Channel. Charming and sharp-witted, with a gift for politics, Joe had long been the target of his father's political ambitions and had already been earmarked as one of the Democratic Party's most promising stars. By contrast, politics had never come easily to Jack, who considered himself an unqualified substitute for Joe. As he wrote in *As We Remember Joe*, a book published in tribute to his elder brother, "Joe's worldly success was so assured and inevitable that his death seems to have cut into the natural order of things." Had it not been for his brother's death, Jack Kennedy would almost have certainly continued his nascent career as a journalist. Carrying this psychological burden, he embarked on his career in public life on the strict orders of his father, Joseph P. Kennedy, the family's domineering patriarch. By the beginning of 1946, the only unsettled question in Joe Kennedy's mind was which office his son should seek first.[2]

Fearing Jack would be defeated by more experienced politicians in the cauldron of the Eleventh District's Democratic primary, an early setback that could blight his career, Joe Kennedy instead pressed him to seek the lieutenant governorship of Massachusetts. But the ambassador's second cousin, Joseph Kane, a tough-minded local activist much more attuned to Boston politics, disagreed. Kane implored Joe Sr. to "give the kid a break" in the Eleventh District. Eventually, Kennedy relented and gave Kane the go-ahead to begin planning for the primary race. Over the ensuing months, Kane became Jack Kennedy's chief adviser and image maker. He coined his campaign slogan, drew together the planks of a platform, and hatched a series of backroom deals with the district's warring Irish and Italian factions to ease Kennedy's path. Then Kane suggested that it would take three more things to win: money, money, and money. Since failure was unthinkable, Joe Kennedy gladly provided the cash, reportedly commenting, "We're going to sell Jack like soap flakes."[3]

Jack Kennedy needed all the professional help his father could afford, for the intellectual baggage that he carried into that first election was light. Following in the political tradition of his grandfather and embracing the philanthropic tradition of his family, he presented himself to voters as a bread-and-butter liberal. Kennedy happily appropriated policies like broadened social security, increases in the minimum wage, aid to the aged, and low-cost housing, since they all offered blue-collar workers and returning veterans a more abundant life. In foreign affairs, he displayed more ideological certainty. He quickly emerged as a committed internationalist, at a time when isolationism was in vogue. He was also a resolute anticommunist, having become openly distrustful of the Russians while reporting on the inaugural session of the United Nations in 1945. When a local lawyer told him that the central problem facing the Eleventh District was welfare, Kennedy was incredulous. "What about communism?" he asked. Nonetheless, even though his priority interest lay in foreign affairs, his first platform focused primarily on domestic issues. It embraced the core of the New Deal/Fair Deal agenda and called for the enactment of a Veterans Emergency Housing Bill, the continuation of wartime price controls, slum clearance, minimum wage legislation, and new labor laws offering greater workplace protections. The policies reflected, and were geared toward, the interests of the district's low-income constituents.[4]

After the platform went to press, Kennedy decided he should also make a direct appeal to the district's small pocket of black voters, who lived in Cambridgeport, a shabby slum, with ramshackle houses, sandwiched between Massachusetts Avenue and the Charles River. He fashioned a brief civil rights plank, which was later published as an addendum to the main platform. It called for the abolition of the poll tax, an electoral surcharge levied in the South to bar blacks from voting, and new fair employment laws aimed at eliminating workplace discrimination. The plank celebrated the independence movements sweeping though Africa and likened the battle against colonial rule to the anticommunist struggle in Eastern Europe. "Once we have ceased aggressive action on our own part, with respect to foreign lands," said the young veteran, "we will then be in a position to demand that Russia cease its aggression towards Europe." And he commended blacks for their service during the war: "As one who served in the late war and saw the magnificent courage and heroism of all men around me, regardless of their race, color or creed, and of the failure of any of the servicemen to attach any significance to racial origin, I know that the service and the war effort were ultimately stronger. Therefore the elimination through measures such as this, of racial prejudices, will, in like manner, make our country a stronger one."[5]

This was Kennedy's first public statement on the struggle for racial justice—and an eloquent one at that. It placed him firmly on the side of a growing number of reform-minded lawmakers on Capitol Hill, who were pressing for the enactment of the first civil rights act since 1875. The statement also revealed the rudiments of his early thinking on civil rights. First, he readily accepted the prevailing, and intellectually fashionable, postwar liberal view that a nation that professed to stand for freedom could no longer sanction racial apartheid at home. Moreover, since black servicemen had contributed to that victory they were wholly entitled to become full participants in American life—a version of the argument he would use to devastating effect in addressing the so-called Catholic Question when he ran for the presidency. Kennedy placed particular stress on the link between the expansion of freedom at home and the projection of American ideals abroad, which was given added saliency because of the potency of the postwar communist threat. Having already predicted the rise of the Soviet Union and warned of its dire consequences, he was anxious that the Kremlin could easily exploit the country's dismal civil rights record for propaganda purposes as it sought to extend its sphere of influence in the developing world. To counter that threat, he believed, America should lend moral support to African independence movements.

Perhaps most clearly, though, the platform revealed the young candidate's faith in democracy. The very system from which America derived its moral superiority over the Soviet Union would also provide the solution to the civil rights problem. In his policy recommendations, he called for the abolition of the poll tax, believing that if blacks were granted access to the polling booth they themselves would be vested with the democratic wherewithal to achieve first-class citizenship. "You know what's important?" he said to black aide Harold Vaughan. "Voting. It's imperative that your people realize the importance of the ballot." Kennedy also called for moves to combat workplace discrimination, on the grounds that black employees would be able to improve their own economic condition if only given the chance. At a time when American liberalism was defined not by entitlement but self-reliance, Kennedy believed strongly that equality of opportunity offered a route to black empowerment.[6]

While stressing the need for racial reforms, Kennedy notably refrained from prescribing a more forceful role for the federal government in dismantling southern segregation. Nor did his first platform include any explicit criticism of the South. In this, Kennedy's statement anticipated his subsequent career both as a lawmaker and president. He remained chronically uneasy about using federal authority to engineer changes in race relations, much preferring self-correction over government compulsion. And he was also reluctant to demonize segregationists. His 1946 statement provided the first signs of these contradictions. In promoting civil rights, his strongest impulse was to empower blacks rather than dethrone Jim Crow.

There were strong tactical reasons for the platform addendum and for Kennedy's ensuing focus on race issues during his campaign. While black voters were outnumbered heavily by Irish and Italians, Kennedy had good reason to target them, since most lived in Cambridge, the political stronghold of Mike Neville, his main rival. If Kennedy could make inroads in Cambridge, then victory was almost assured. The Kennedy campaign actively solicited black endorsements and featured them with unusual prominence in campaign literature. "When you listen to Kennedy you are naturally impressed by three outstanding traits," noted Leroy Johnson, a carpenter from Cambridge: "character, sincerity and intelligence." Susie Avena, a housewife from Howard Street in Cambridge, commented, "Mr. Kennedy will get my support because I feel that he is not prejudiced to race, creed or color. I am a disabled veteran's wife. I'm sure he will help their cause." With the help of George Taylor, his black driver and valet, he also organized a meeting at a black gathering place in Cambridge, the Dunbar Club, attended by some five hundred black voters. "Jack was very pleased with the meeting," recalled Taylor, "and he was very happy that we had a good showing, a good turnout." Kennedy was so determined to court black voters that he even considered embellishing his saga of wartime heroism by introducing new characters to lend it universal racial allure. "My story about the collision is getting better all the time," he quipped to one of his war comrades. "Now I've got a Jew and a Nigger in the story and with me being a Catholic, that's great." The use of the epithet "nigger" was unfortunate, though not particularly indicative; for it was part of the military vernacular used commonly by white servicemen and carried nowhere near as much malevolence as it came to.[7]

In the magnificent setting of Boston's Faneuil Hall, during an Independence Day oration grandly entitled "Some Elements of the American Character," Kennedy elaborated his views on civil rights. In the speech, he welcomed how the "philosophy of racism" had been met and destroyed on the battlefields of Europe, and called upon Americans to rededicate themselves to the "dignity of man" and "growth of the human spirit." Yet, in a speech larded with historical allusions, his comments on the Civil War were arguably the most illuminating. He rejected the argument that the conflict was primarily an economic battle waged between the industrial North and agricultural South, and suggested finer principles were at play. "Say what they will," he told his audience, "it is an undeniable fact that the Northern Army of Virginia and the Army of the Potomac were inspired by devotion to principle: on the one hand, the right of secession; on the other, the belief that the 'Union must be preserved.'" He did not even mention slavery and suggested Confederates had fought for a cause they considered noble. Even if he did not agree always with southerners, he was respectful of their traditions, which offered some explanation for his ongoing reluctance throughout his career to denounce segregationists.[8]

Civil rights issues were not, however, at the heart of Kennedy's 1946 campaign. When asked to complete a questionnaire by the League of Women Voters about the country's five most pressing problems, he did not list black inequality among them—instead he cited housing, a strong military, social security, a rise in the minimum wage, and the modernization of Congress. Kennedy was diffident on the issue in more personal ways as well. George Taylor recruited a group of black college women to help with the campaign and complained when they were not invited to lunch with the Kennedy sisters along with the white volunteers. "Jack, I think that's bullshit," Taylor told him. "They're all giving their time. They're all human beings. Why segregate in this way?" Taylor recalled that he replied, "George, you're thin-skinned. That's one of the things of the time."[9]

Four other candidates had a realistic claim on the Democratic nomination. John F. Cotter, a Charlestown native and former Speaker of the Massachusetts House, was not only the most experienced politician in the race but also the most well-connected. Cotter's greatest advantage was his close friendship with Boston's most celebrated politician, Mayor James Michael Curley, the famed "Purple Shamrock," who had represented the Eleventh District in Congress during the mid-1940s and was the city's most powerful political chieftain. Joseph Russo, a highly respected North End councilman, also had a realistic chance of victory. But Russo's prospects dimmed sharply when the Kennedy campaign mischievously uncovered another local Italian with the exact same name and paid him to enter the race in a ploy to confuse voters. Of the other six candidates, the most intriguing was the redoubtable Catherine Falvey, a major in the Women's Army Corps, who toured the district in her white ceremonial uniform, chiding Kennedy for being a "poor little rich kid" trying to make a "silver-spoon" ascent. The label stuck and was seized upon by local precinct captains loyal to Neville and Cotter. In their eyes, Kennedy was an opportunistic carpetbagger, who was running on little more than his story of wartime bravery.

On June 18, Kennedy received a total of 22,183 votes, a 42 percent share of the vote and almost double the number of his closest rival, Mike Neville. It is not possible to break down the election returns by race, but in Cambridge, where the black vote was concentrated, Kennedy came in second—with 41 percent to Neville's 49 percent. Winning the Democratic nomination secured Kennedy his seat in Congress, and in the election on November 5, he polled 69,093 votes compared with 26,007 for his rival, Somerville Republican Lester W. Bowen. So complete was the victory that it attracted interest from way beyond New England. "Kennedy Makes Political Bow," read the headline in the *New York Times*, which printed a photograph showing the boyish-looking candidate marching toward the polling station. At twenty-nine, he became America's newest political celebrity. The "Leader of the New Generation" was off to a flying start, a freshman lawmaker in the country's first postwar Congress. A new generation had, indeed, produced a new kind of leader with a new approach to politics.[10]

∾

The new Congress, the nation's eightieth, presided over a country remade by war. After four years of conflict, America had finally become a centralized industrial society, with a belief, nourished by the reforms of the New Deal, that government could improve people's lives. For all the dark predictions of a postwar economic slump, millions of veterans returned home to enjoy an unexpected consumer boom, and the bleak pessimism of the Depression era quickly gave way to a spirit of determined self-confidence.

There were signs, too, that the country's thirteen million blacks might soon taste the spoils of victory, the alluring prospect of an expanded menu of rights. For a country unused to thinking of segregation as a major problem, fighting fascism had once again raised the perennial question of how a country professing to stand for freedom and equality could countenance such glaring racial inequality. During the war, blacks had fought for a democracy where, in many southern states, they were barred even from voting, and in an army that granted German prisoners certain privileges, such as traveling in railway restaurant cars, which they themselves were routinely denied.

Shortly before the end of the war, Gunnar Myrdal, a Swedish economist who spent six years traveling through the South, drew fresh attention to the question in *An American Dilemma*. This monumental 1,400-page study, published to wide acclaim in 1944, highlighted the economic, social, and political inequalities endured by a tenth of the population. In identifying the "Negro problem" as primarily a "white man's problem," Myrdal helped prick the conscience of America's thinking classes and contributed to an intellectual groundswell in favor of reform. Racism had finally touched the chords of American concern.[11]

Nowhere was the "American Dilemma" more deeply rooted than in the eleven states of the Old Confederacy, where the separation of the races was regulated from the cradle to the grave. Blacks were born in segregated hospitals and buried in segregated cemeteries. "Whites only" and "Colored only" signs adorned every place of public accommodation, from lunch counters to hotels, federal buildings to municipal water fountains. Segregation was an idea carried to absurdity. In southern courthouses, whites and blacks took oaths on separate Bibles, and in most southern states, white ambulances were not even allowed to ferry blacks to the hospital, however critical their condition. In North Carolina, it was illegal for white school pupils to use textbooks touched by black hands; in Georgia, it was unlawful for white baseball teams to play within two blocks of a playground where black teams held games.

The strictures of segregation were applied most rigorously in southern schools, such was the fear that any form of racial assimilation during a child's formative years would lead inexorably to the mongrelization of the white race. Fearing that if social barriers were breached, then sexual barriers would soon collapse as well, southerners banned integrated schools in all eleven states of the Old Confederacy, along with the District of Columbia. Blacks and whites were educated in schools which were supposedly "separate but equal," a policy laid down by the Supreme Court in *Plessy v. Ferguson* decision in 1896. But since southern states spent ten times more money on white schoolchildren as blacks, the idea that their dilapidated classrooms and schoolhouses were in any measure "equal" was a cruel fiction.

In most southern states, blacks were even denied the most rudimentary of civil rights, the opportunity to vote. In local, state, and federal elections, a majority

of blacks were barred from the polls, which deprived them of what was fast becoming their most valuable weapon: political leverage. In 1940, only an estimated five percent of eligible black southerners were registered to vote, a figure
that had risen to just twelve percent by 1947. Recalcitrant voting officials
thwarted black applicants at every turn, by levying arbitrary and prohibitive poll
taxes and setting capricious literacy tests, which disenfranchised even the most
highly educated blacks. Blacks also faced economic coercion, physical intimidation, and sometimes violent death. In 1946, the year Kennedy won his first election, five black Georgians were murdered merely for attempting to vote.[12]

By the end of World War II, however, more Americans were beginning to
challenge outdated racial mores and moving toward a more inclusive society. At
the same time, demographic changes had carved out a new social and political
landscape. By far the most portentous development was the "great migration
north" of southern blacks. While at the turn of the century ninety percent of
black Americans lived in Dixie, by the end of the 1940s almost half lived above
the Mason-Dixon line. Over the same period, the black population grew at an
extraordinary rate, increasing between 1940 and 1950 at least five times the rate
of the white populace, creating a new "black belt" cutting through Illinois,
Michigan, Pennsylvania, New Jersey, and New York. The political implications
were obvious: For northern politicians, it would be an act of great folly to ignore
their black constituents.

By the mid-1940s, President Franklin Delano Roosevelt had already engineered an astounding electoral transformation: the defection of black voters
from the GOP, the party of the Great Emancipator, Abraham Lincoln, to the
Democrats, the party of Confederate leader Jefferson Davis. The New Deal had
brought much-needed economic relief to millions of black Americans, and even
though Roosevelt was a reluctant reformer in the field of civil rights his performance easily outstripped that of his predecessors. His record of achievement
was ambiguous. He had, for example, created a new Civil Liberties Division
within the Justice Department in 1940, thereby becoming the first twentieth-
century president to acknowledge that the federal government had a role to play
in the investigation of racial discrimination. And yet he happily turned a blind
eye to the segregationist policies of the New Deal alphabet agencies, many of
which actually reinforced the racial hegemony of southern whites. Still, even his
limited reforms were enough to impress black voters, which revealed the extent
of their political alienation.[13]

Yet even at the height of his popularity, after four consecutive electoral victories, Roosevelt shied away from confronting southern Democrats on Capitol
Hill, a rump of segregationists, whose tight control over committee chairmanships and readiness to launch paralyzing filibusters, gave them the power to
wreck his legislative program. The president was also worried about widening
the chasm within the Democratic Party between the segregationist South and

progressive North. The administration therefore tailored policies to maintain at least a veneer of political unity. And remarkably, against what often seemed overwhelming odds, he succeeded in holding the party together. By the mid-thirties, he had even managed to cement the famed "Roosevelt coalition," an unlikely electoral alliance that brought northern blacks and white southerners under the same electoral tent. To champion civil rights was to rip its delicate fabric in two, an orthodoxy that dominated Democratic thinking for the next three decades.

For blacks, the legacy of Roosevelt's New Deal was a confounding blend of reaction and reform. Nonetheless, he had laid foundations that more enthusiastic reformers built upon in future years. Even seemingly mundane bureaucratic reforms, like new, national standards of wages and hours, had far-reaching consequences, for they ended the economic isolationism of the South and extended the reach of the federal government into the region. More importantly, however, Roosevelt's relief programs began to lift blacks out of poverty and gave them the means to rise further up the economic and social ladder. While most officials in the upper reaches of government continued to regard them as second-class citizens, Roosevelt included, the president had persuaded black Americans he was paying closer heed to their unsettled grievances and that more meaningful reforms were on the horizon.

Economic changes were ultimately more significant than Roosevelt's policies in transforming race relations at midcentury. The wartime economy opened up dramatic new workplace opportunities for blacks. The galloping industrialization of the South drew tens of thousands of black Americans away from the fields of southern plantations into factories in the cities. With "King Cotton" dislodged from his throne, blacks were freed from the land, where many had been virtually enslaved. A "New South" was slowly emerging, with the locus of economic power shifting from the countryside to the cities—changes accelerated by the manpower demands of the war. In the new defense plants that sprung up across the region, chronic labor shortages led to a slackening of restrictive promotion policies and the creation of a pool of skilled black workers. A small handful even became managers. Union membership among blacks grew dramatically, doubling to 1,250,000 by the end of the war. The vibrancy of the southern economy meant black advancement no longer came necessarily at the expense of white workers, softening their resistance.[14]

Over the same period, "New South" cities, like Atlanta and Charlotte, welcomed new arrivals into the region—corporate executives, managers, and white-collar staff who had been raised and educated in the North and were interested more in lining their pockets than perpetuating outdated racial mores. These Yankee immigrants tended to vote Republican, opening up small fissures in the once-solid Democratic South, and gradually loosening the segregationists' iron grip on power.

Unexpectedly, the military was in the forefront of racial change. During the war, officials at the Pentagon recognized that segregation was hampering the war effort, which led them to break with long-standing military traditions separating white troops from black. In the First World War, black units had been deployed only in a supporting capacity, often well away from the fighting. Now they were thrust onto the front line. On the beaches of Normandy in 1944, General George Patton welcomed the 761st "Black Panther" Tank Battalion into his midst, with the stirring battle cry: "I don't care what color you are as long as you go up there and kill those Kraut sons-of-bitches." By the end of the war, there were signs of slow progress in almost every branch of the services. The U.S. military had desegregated its Officer Cadet School, enrolled the first black U.S. marine, and established a formally integrated army unit, the first in American history. Nonetheless, up until the final months of the war, strict racial quotas governed the deployment of personnel, so that no more than 10.6 percent of American forces, the exact proportion of the country's black population, were black. Black troops were offered inadequate training and out-of-date equipment, and even blood banks administered by the American Red Cross were thoroughly segregated so white soldiers would never run the risk of infection from black blood—which was especially galling since blood banks were the brainchild of Charles Drew, a black physician. These indignities heightened racial consciousness among black enlisted personnel. On entering the military, a huge number received basic training at southern camps, where many were confronted by Jim Crow for the first time in their lives. Millions of blacks spent part of the war in southern army camps, naval bases or airfields, where they were barred from local lunch counters, barber shops, and restaurants, isolated in "colored" living quarters and trained in separate units. Shocked by the racial fiats of southern communities, many vowed to fight for racial justice after fighting for their country. "I spent four years in the Army to free a bunch of Dutchmen and Frenchmen," noted a black corporal from Alabama, "and I'm hanged if I'm going to let the Alabama version of the Germans kick me around when I get home. No sireee-bob! I went into the Army a nigger; I'm comin' out a man."[15]

On returning home, a great many veterans became active members of civil rights organizations, which were now hammering at the walls of prejudice. Most startling was the growth of the National Association for the Advancement of Colored People, which saw its membership grow from 50,000 to 500,000 between 1940 and 1946. Dominated by middle-class blacks, the NAACP favored reform through court-based litigation, but other groups sprung up favoring more militant forms of protest. The Congress of Racial Equality (CRC), formed in 1942, focused on demonstrations and economic boycotts, using the untapped power of the "black dollar" to pressure white-owned businesses into integrating their facilities.

Sometimes even just the threat of direct action could precipitate reform, most notably when A. Philip Randolph, the head of the Brotherhood of Sleeping Car Porters and Maids, called for a March on Washington in 1941 to protest the federal government's failure to eliminate discrimination in the workplace and the military. Roosevelt responded by issuing an executive order establishing the Fair Employment Practices Committee (FEPC). Perhaps the most successful civil rights organization of the day was the NAACP Legal Defense and Educational Fund, an offshoot of the NAACP, which centered its activities upon the federal courts and came up with a string of ground-breaking victories that eroded segregation. From the mid-forties onward, in case after landmark case, the United States Supreme Court came down unambiguously on the side of the civil rights movement. In *Smith v. Allwright* (1944), it ruled that the "white primary," in which blacks were barred from participating, was unconstitutional; five years later, in *Sweatt v. Painter* (1950) it ruled against the University of Texas School of Law, which was segregated; in *McLaurin v. Oklahoma* (1950) it forced the University of Oklahoma to integrate its graduate education school.

With racism leaving an increasingly unpleasant stench in their nostrils, white Americans were also more sympathetically disposed toward reform. "One thing, it would seem, is certain," wrote John Gunther in his 1947 best seller *Inside America*. "The days of treating Negroes like sheep are over. They cannot be maintained indefinitely in a submerged position, because they themselves are strong enough to contest this position, [and] because the overwhelming bulk of white Americans are, in the last analysis, decent minded." For many Americans, both black and white, the country seemed to be on the verge of a Second Reconstruction.[16]

∽

At the time he entered Congress, Jack Kennedy had scant firsthand experience of the severity of southern life. There is no record of him ever having visited the Deep South states of Mississippi, Alabama, Louisiana, and Arkansas until 1956, when he was nearly forty, and his experience of Dixie seems to have been limited during his formative years to visits to Washington, the Florida coast, and a four-month spell stationed at the naval shipyard in South Carolina. During his short interlude in Charleston—or "tired old Charleston," as he disdainfully called it—he seemed largely preoccupied by the social oddities of white southerners rather than their racist way of life. "Have I discussed Southerners with you?" he wrote Lem Billings, his childhood friend. "It's not so much that they say 'here' after every god damned remark—'now come and see us Kennedy, here'—but is the aboots and oots—and the rest of the shit that convinces me we should have let the bootucks go." Based on his letters to Billings, he paid little attention to the problems of race. Thereafter, Kennedy never spoke publicly about his experiences in South Carolina, and there is no evidence that they exerted any influence on his early thinking on civil rights. Unlike Hubert Humphrey, an early presidential rival, whose thoughts on racial injustice were shaped by his years as a professor in Baton Rouge, Louisiana, Kennedy seems to have been untouched by his short sojourns in the South. As Robert Kennedy reflected later, "we weren't thinking of the Negroes of Mississippi or Alabama—what should be done for them. We were thinking of what needed to be done in Massachusetts."[17]

Kennedy may have been naïve about race at this stage, but he was certainly no racist. He shared neither the Boston Irish bigotry of many of his Catholic coreligionists nor the anti-Semitism of his father. Growing up in Boston, he was well aware of the indignities faced by his forebears, dubbed the "blacks of Boston," who on arrival in America were confronted by overwhelming discrimination. But only once during his upbringing, it seems, was he himself the direct victim of prejudice, when Groton, a select preparatory school attended by Franklin Roosevelt and other East Coast patricians, rejected his application because of his Irish roots. Still, it amounted to little more than a temporary setback, since he was soon accepted at Choate, another elite institution.[18]

Despite his Catholicism, Kennedy's formative years were remarkably unaffected by religious intolerance. He was no doubt aware that Catholics struggled still to penetrate the highest echelons of American society (in 1928, at the age of eleven, he may have just been old enough to realize that Governor Al Smith of New York had been defeated in that year's presidential election largely because of his Catholicism). But the Kennedy family's immense wealth and access to power inoculated him from discrimination. He spent vacations and holidays not in Boston but on the family compound at Hyannis Port, or in Palm Beach, Florida. By the time Jack graduated from Choate, Joseph Kennedy was the chairman of the Securities and Exchange Commission in Washington, and well on his way to becoming the ambassador to the Court of St. James in London, the most illustrious diplomatic posting a president could confer.

As he matured into adulthood, blatant acts of racism remained outside his experience. Neither at Choate nor Harvard did he befriend any blacks, and up until his mid-twenties, the only black with whom he regularly interacted was George Taylor, his valet. The two enjoyed a surprisingly close and informal relationship. Taylor continually bantered with Kennedy about his appetite for women, and Kennedy poked fun at Taylor's penchant for whisky and Overland cigars. Occasionally, Kennedy even asked Taylor for political advice. "When Jack was running for congressman," Taylor recalled later, "he would ask me what I thought of his speeches. Sometimes he would make a few changes." It was hardly a friendship of equals, however. No blacks managed to penetrate his close circle of friends. Campaigning in 1960, he was asked by a black dentist in San Francisco precisely how many blacks he was acquainted with. "Doctor, I don't know five Negroes of your caliber well enough to call them by their first names," he conceded, shamefacedly. "But I promise to do better."[19]

The handful of black aides who came to know Kennedy personally early in his career were nonetheless struck by his warmth and charm. Unlike many northern politicians, whose support for black causes did not always extend to expressions of friendship toward blacks themselves, Kennedy enjoyed an easy informality in their presence and treated them with respect. "Northern pols were normally stand-offish," said Harold Vaughan, a young lawyer from Boston, who came to know Kennedy in 1948. "But Kennedy would just walk into a beauty salon in a black neighborhood, go right up to the woman below the hair-dryer and say: 'Hi, I'm Jack Kennedy.'"[20]

On occasion, his thoughtfulness was also impressive and set him apart from other politicians. In 1948, when a memorial was unveiled in Cambridge honoring two black war heroes, Kennedy was on hand to deliver the peroration at the dedication ceremony. His decision to attend demonstrated not only a level of courtesy that few northern politicians showed toward black constituents but as well an appreciation of the black contribution to the war effort. Similarly, when compiling *As We Remember Joe,* he made sure a tribute was included from George Taylor, who had served as his elder brother's valet for six years. Of Joe Jr., Taylor wrote, he "had a radiant personality and befriended every one with whom he came in contact—Jew, Negro and Chinaman—irrespective of race, color or creed." He could easily have written the same about Jack Kennedy (and Bobby, too, who invited Taylor to his wedding in June 1950). Unfriendly biographers have sometimes cited Kennedy's failure to tip black porters at Boston's Logan Field as evidence of bigotry. More accurately, it was the product of his legendary tightfistedness and a stubborn refusal ever to carry cash.[21]

Even his friendliest biographers have suggested that civil rights failed to interest Kennedy during the early stages of his political career and touched only the fringes of his consciousness. According to Theodore Sorensen, his close aide from the early 1950s onward, Kennedy "simply did not give much thought" to civil rights and had "no background or association of activity." Columnist Arthur Krock, a family friend, shared this opinion, asserting that his "compassionate spirit was toward the underprivileged community as a whole, without concentration on the civil inequality of Negroes." Even Robert Kennedy corroborated this assessment: "What we did grow up with was the idea that there were a lot of people who were less fortunate and a lot of people who were hungry. White people and Negroes were all put in that same category. One had a social responsibility to do something about it." Like Sorensen, he believed his brother's record of accomplishment on civil rights as a young congressman was meager.[22]

Evidence from his first six years as a lawmaker, however, reveals a very different version of Kennedy's early political life. Far from being unconcerned by the plight of black Americans, Kennedy battled hard for new civil rights legislation and fought tenaciously on behalf of black residents in the District of Columbia, who continued to live with the burden of segregation. From the very outset of his career, he voted unfailingly for civil rights and signaled his intentions early on by lending enthusiastic support to a series of bills calling for the abolition of the poll tax. His vote in favor of the anti–poll tax bill, HR (House Resolution) 29 was among the first he cast as a freshman congressman. Thereafter, he supported an array of other pro–civil rights causes, from the inclusion of an anti-discrimination provision in the Selective Service Act establishing the peacetime draft, to the integration of Spars, the U.S. Women's Coast Guard. In May 1948, he also opposed congressional funding for the Registered College Plan, which financed segregated educational institutions.[23]

When Harry Truman emerged as an unlikely civil rights champion, Kennedy gave the president his full-fledged support. Truman had been spurred into action by a searing report from the Committee on Civil Rights, a blue-ribbon presidential commission established to investigate the "American Dilemma." "We have surveyed the flaws in the nation's record and have found them to be serious," the committee concluded in a 178-page booklet entitled *To Secure These Rights* published in October, 1947. "We believe the time for action is now." Among its recommendations, the committee called for a federal anti-lynching law, the abolition of the poll tax, a ban on discrimination in the armed services, a permanent Fair Employment Practices Committee, and the strengthening of the Civil Rights Section of the Justice Department. Truman tried to mint the proposals into legislation the following year.[24]

Kennedy supported all these initiatives. He also took an unusually prominent role for such an inexperienced congressman in trying to secure their passage into law. As a member of the House Labor Committee, he fought hard for a compulsory fair employment committee with strong enforcement powers. In 1949 he joined forces with the bill's main sponsor, Congressman Adam Clayton Powell, Jr., Harlem's flamboyant black preacher-politician, to discharge it from committee, a fight that put him at odds with leading segregationists on Capitol Hill. In 1950, when the measure finally came before the House, Kennedy cast nine separate roll-call votes for the most robust bill possible and resisted repeated attempts to weaken it. When an amendment was introduced aimed at diluting the administration-backed bill, Kennedy became the only Massachusetts representative to fight for the strongest version. In this case, the interests of black and white constituents in the Eleventh District coincided, largely because fair employment legislation promised to bring southern employment practices into line with those in the North, ending the region's competitive advantage and boosting job prospects in northern factories. Yet he was also voting his conscience—namely his belief, expressed consistently and forcefully from his first congressional campaign, that artificial obstacles impeding black self-improvement should be removed.[25]

Kennedy also fought with particular vigor on behalf of Washington's black residents, whose lives were strictly regulated by an austere code of segregationist laws. The nation's capital was also the gateway to Dixie. Traveling south by train, blacks had to move from integrated into "colored only" carriages upon arriving at Union Station. Even after the war, the only places they were allowed to eat alongside whites were the cafeterias of federal office buildings, a few restaurants in the downtown business district, and the lunch counters at National Airport and Union Station. Restrictive covenants barred them from residing in the city's more affluent neighborhoods. And despite the fact they represented a majority of the city's population, black Washingtonians were completely disenfranchised, as were all other residents. While they could walk down Pennsylvania Avenue and peer through the gates of the White House, they were not allowed to help decide which president should occupy it. Similarly, they could see the gleaming dome of the U.S. Capitol from all over the city, but not a single lawmaker owed the people of Washington his seat. Even the U.S. Congress itself was segregated, with unwritten rules barring black employees from the swimming pool, barber shop, and restaurants. Black journalists were even prevented from covering its proceedings. As the Committee on Civil Rights stated in the year that Kennedy entered Congress, Washington provided "a graphic illustration of a failure of democracy."[26]

To a large extent, Washington's racial problems stemmed from the blatantly undemocratic way in which it was run. With no local council or mayor, the District was governed instead by three commissioners, who received orders from two congressional committees, the House District of Columbia Committee and Senate District of Columbia Committee. Congress exerted extraordinary control over the city's affairs. It set the budget, enacted its tax laws, chose new street names, and even decided when municipal gardeners should start weeding the flowerbeds. To compound this injustice, the House committee was dominated by one of the most notorious segregationists on Capitol Hill, Representative John Lanneau McMillan, an unabashed racist from Mullins, South Carolina, who reveled in his nickname, "The Mayor of D.C." His chief ally on the committee was "Judge" Howard Worth Smith, an archconservative from Virginia, who viewed the District of Columbia as his personal fiefdom. Both were staunch white supremacists, who believed that if Washington remained segregated, so, too, would the rest of the South.

Kennedy, who became a member of the House District of Columbia Committee as soon as he entered Congress, rejected the racism of McMillan and Smith and challenged them on the question of home rule. When the issue came before the House in 1950, he became one of its most energetic and thoughtful advocates. He told a reporter for the *Boston Daily Globe* that there were two broad reasons to support the creation of an eleven-member city council. "The first is a moral reason," he explained. "The thousands of residents of the capital are entitled to a voice in their own government—which they are today denied." The second reason was practical. By granting home rule, Congress would relieve itself of a "huge and time-demanding job." Self-government would mean mundane matters could be decided easily by an elected city council rather than overworked congressmen (under the then-current Byzantine rules, achieving anything at all required the passage of a bill in Congress through twenty-eight separate stages). "Mr. Kennedy is earnest in his plea for Home Rule," the article concluded. "Although he is only 33 . . . he has already earned for himself a reputation as a hard working and conscientious member of the House." This was especially true when it came to civil rights.[27]

Die-hard segregationists were determined to bottle up the bill in the District of Columbia Committee and prevent it from ever being acted upon on the House floor. Under the arcane rules of the House of Representatives, a bill could only be discharged from committee against the wishes of a majority of its members if other lawmakers demanded the chance to vote on it. That required a discharge petition, which could only be successful if a majority of the full House membership lent their support. Kennedy brazenly launched a personal campaign to obtain the 218 signatures needed to release the bill from committee. Lacking the seniority or influence to either strike political deals or bully colleagues, he relied instead upon the force of his arguments. He set them out in a memorandum entered into the House *Congressional Record* on Friday, March 3, tracing the origins of the home rule debate back to the writings of James Madison. Every other city in the United States enjoyed local self-government, noted Kennedy, as did every other capital city in the world (except for Soviet-bloc countries and Canberra, Australia). The absence of self-government in the U.S. capital was a source not only of national shame, but a propaganda victory for the country's Cold War enemies. How could the United States boast the leadership of the free world, he asked pointedly, if citizens of the District of Columbia were disenfranchised and ignored? "Lack of local self-government in the capital city of the world's greatest democracy embarrasses conduct of our foreign relations," he argued, echoing language from his 1946 platform: "Lack of home rule dulls the edge of democracy—weakens the citizen's sense of civic responsibility—atrophies our political faculties for sheer lack of expression."[28]

After months of feverish lobbying, by September 1950, Kennedy's petition was within just twelve votes of the required 218 signatures, which raised fears among southern Democrats that home rule was now a distinct possibility. Galvanized into action, McMillan and Smith quickly browbeat four moderate southerners and seven conservative Republicans into withdrawing their names from the discharge motion. It was enough to halt Kennedy in his tracks. While 198 congressmen ultimately put their names to the petition, Kennedy required additional signatures to overwhelm southern lawmakers. For almost a year,

Kennedy had put up a noble fight against two of Capitol Hill's most intimidating lawmakers, but his personal campaign had come to naught.[29]

Home rule was not the only issue Kennedy championed on behalf of black Washingtonians. Kennedy was also struck by the disturbing levels of poverty in the District and mindful of how they affected blacks more than whites. So in another battle that pitted him against McMillan and Smith, he campaigned ardently for reduced taxes for low-income blacks. On June 8, 1948, in one of his first House speeches, he argued against a new sales tax, because he claimed it would penalize blacks unfairly. Armed with charts and diagrams, he illustrated how the new 3 percent sales tax, "would put the main burden on the people who cannot afford to pay it." In March of the following year, when the sales tax idea was revived, Kennedy spoke out against it once more. If the District needed additional revenue, the more affluent citizens should carry the burden in increased income and property taxes. "The sales tax is most unfair," he argued. "It puts the major burden on the people in the lowest income groups," most of whom were black. Opposition to the new sales tax put him at loggerheads once more with "Judge" Smith, who maintained it was impossible to raise revenues any other way. But Kennedy argued that taxes on property values in the District were much fairer and marshaled an impressive array of economic statistics to buttress his case. Ultimately the attempt failed—the House voted 176–166 to retain the tax—but the young representative's role during the battle brought him admiring reviews in the press. "The congressman who did most to save the District from the burden of a sales tax is a tousle-haired bachelor generally named 'Jack,'" wrote one reporter in a flattering profile for the *Washington Daily News*. "He looks like the *Saturday Evening Post*'s idea of the All-American Boy, and his vote-getting appeal to New England's womenfolk must be terrific. He is also something of a political curiosity . . . born with a silver soup ladle in his mouth, but with the welfare of the humble in his heart."[30]

ↄ

Fair employment legislation, the abolition of the poll tax, and home rule for Washington—Kennedy had quickly become an enthusiastic supporter of three of the major civil rights issues of the immediate postwar years. He boasted a voting record that matched, if not surpassed, those of most northern colleagues. As his aides gleefully pointed out, during his six years in Congress he never missed a single civil rights vote.[31]

Kennedy did not, however, enter into close alliances with the so-called ultra-liberals on Capitol Hill, such as Congressman Hubert Humphrey, who were at the vanguard of the fight for civil rights. This stemmed partly from his aversion to belonging to *any* group or cabal and partly from his personal distaste for overly moralizing politicians, whom he sometimes referred to disdainfully as

"attitudinizing liberals." Fiercely independent, both temperamentally and politically, Kennedy wanted to fight for civil rights on his own terms, in battles of his
own choosing. Though by no means a crusading ideologue, he seemed genuinely to care about the disadvantages faced by blacks, especially those in
Boston and the District of Columbia, and believed political and economic empowerment offered the best solutions. For all this, he was struck during his formative years more by the illogic and irrationality of racism than by its cruelty,
and displayed only a fragmentary awareness of the brutish realities of southern
racism. Perhaps as a result, the whole question seemed to trouble him intellectually rather than arouse him emotionally.[32]

It was by no fault of his own that Kennedy took no part in one the great civil
rights skirmishes of the early postwar years—the fight led by Hubert
Humphrey, the then mayor of Minneapolis, for a toughly worded civil rights
plank at the 1948 Democratic convention. When Humphrey mounted the
podium in Philadelphia and called upon the party "to get out of the shadow of
states rights and walk forthrightly into the bright sunshine of human rights,"
Kennedy was 3,000 miles away in England. He was settling the affairs of his
sister, Kathleen, who had been killed that May in an air crash. "A lot of Massachusetts delegates have been asking for Jack," noted the *Boston Globe*, seemingly
unaware of the reason for his absence. Kennedy would certainly have supported
Humphrey's far-reaching civil rights plank, as did every member of the forty-
four-strong Massachusetts delegation. But it is hard to imagine him getting
caught up in the emotion of the debate, unlike colleagues in the Massachusetts
delegations who, according to one reporter, exchanged "sneering remarks" with
the neighboring Georgia delegation, as "a tense situation developed on the
floor." Nor would he have likely described the civil rights struggle as a "spiritual
crisis," a phrase used in Philadelphia by Humphrey.[33]

Over the course of his first six years on Capitol Hill, Kennedy grew much
more sure of himself, both politically and philosophically. He was now a polished performer with a deft turn of phrase, his initial shyness had given way to
an infectious self-confidence, and the ideas with which he started his career became organized more coherently in his mind. He was quick minded rather than
deep thinking, and speedily grasped the bare essentials of a problem or issue
without examining it with any great penetration. Rational, calm, and phleg-
matic, he approached problems with cool detachment; flashes of anger, remorse,
or any other kind of outward emotion were rare. Occasionally he showed signs
of seriousness, but only intermittently. But despite his notoriously short attention span, he was an avid reader of history. When asked by Walter Cronkite just
prior to becoming president what made him uniquely qualified for the job, he
replied that it was his sense of history.[34]

Kennedy reserved his deepest intellectual passion for the fight against communism. To his credit, he avoided the kind of bullying and histrionic rants that

propelled Richard Nixon, his congressional classmate, to national fame. Nor did he ever succumb to "red baiting," even though many of his Irish Catholic constituents were receptive to that kind of demagoguery. The Cold War nevertheless defined Kennedy's political worldview and animated his ideas about race from the outset. Throughout his life, he would link the fight for equality to the struggle against communism. This pattern emerged in the earliest stages of his career—from his very first political platform, which stressed the importance of lending U.S. support to anti-colonial movements as a bulwark against the spread of communism, to his campaign for home rule in Washington, which sprung partly from a belief that the city's segregation laws were the source of great embarrassment abroad.

During this period, Kennedy's thinking on domestic policy also became more clearly defined. Though no admirer either of Roosevelt or Truman, largely because his father had had fractious relations with both, he agreed with the central tenets of New Deal/Fair Deal thinking, with its emphasis on social justice and practical liberalism. But on certain issues, he was a politician of conservative inclination, wary always of government intrusiveness, and a fervent champion of the freedom of the individual over the primacy of the state. As he said in his Fourth of July speech of 1946, "The right of the individual against the State has ever been one of our most cherished political principles." Later on in his congressional career, he expressed himself more boldly, noting: "I don't believe in big government."[35]

Because of his suspicion of government excess, he believed in strict fiscal discipline, a conservative-leaning stance that sometimes put him at odds with party liberals. That did not worry him, since from his earliest days as a congressman he not only possessed a marked contrarian streak but displayed a strong aversion to being pigeonholed, politically or ideologically. "He seemed like a mixed package," in the words of one reporter, "partly conservative, partly liberal and a little bewildered."[36] Always ready to assert his independence, his relationship with the Democratic Party, both locally and nationally, was strained and was best described as a loose affiliation rather than a close affinity. He was notoriously unwilling to assist other Massachusetts Democrats with his time or money. By the beginning of the 1950s, it had become increasingly clear that he was first and foremost a Kennedy, not a Democrat.

Despite being able to claim impressive progressive credentials, he remained aloof from party liberals, like Chester Bowles of Connecticut (who would become an important ally later on), whom he considered sanctimonious. Famously, in 1953 he boasted to a reporter: "I'm not a liberal at all. I never joined the Americans for Democratic Action or the American Veterans Committee. I'm not comfortable with those people." Despite repeated invitations from Sam Beer, a Harvard academic, he refused even to address the Boston ADA. Often Kennedy felt more at ease in the company of conservatives who, like him, were fun-loving and irreverent. His closest companion was Florida Congressman George Smathers. He also enjoyed the friendship of Mississippi Congressman John Rankin, one of the South's most foul-mouthed demagogues, and Senator Richard Russell of Georgia, the region's most masterful strategist. In the clubby atmosphere of Capitol Hill at midcentury, such allegiances were not uncommon—Congressman Eugene McCarthy, a Minnesota liberal who entered Congress in 1949 with strong civil rights credentials, kept much the same company—and were largely explained by his genial personality and attraction to people who made him laugh. Differences over segregation were quickly papered over and rarely allowed to sour the relationship. Ted Sorensen recalls him once being angered when a southern senator made a "slurring reference" in the presence of Congressman William Dawson, the country's senior black lawmaker. But Sorensen added, in the same breath, that "he found the approach of many single-minded civil rights advocates uncomfortable and unreasonable also." Kennedy treated the politics of segregation in much the same way others treated divergent views on faith: with respect for the customs and history that gave rise to them. Kennedy did not care to scold the South—a moral relativism he hinted at early on in his comments about the Civil War during his first campaign.[37]

Kennedy's awareness of race had served him well in his first campaign. And his adoption of a pro–civil rights stance during his years in the House proved an adroit move. When he decided to run for the Senate in 1952 he was particularly well placed to tap the support of Massachusetts's sizable black electorate. But at this stage of his career, at least, Kennedy's support of civil rights was not primarily motivated by political calculation. Rather, he was concerned that the persistence of racial inequality undercut America's oft-stated claims of moral superiority over the Soviet Union, and he was able to identify common-sense reforms, especially in the economic sphere, to improve the lives of blacks without upsetting the delicate relationship between the federal government and the states.

CHAPTER 2

❧

Blue Blood Against Green

By December 1951, a map of Massachusetts fastened to the wall of John Kennedy's unofficial campaign headquarters on Beacon Hill was a gaudy kaleidoscope of brightly colored pins. Each one represented a village, town, or city where the congressman had delivered a speech. Most weekends that year he had followed the same, exacting routine. He would fly on Thursday evening from Washington to Boston's Logan Field, the first stop in a chaotic round of meetings and engagements at veterans' halls, Gold Star Mothers' groups, Rotary clubs, churches, Masonic temples, fishing sheds, and front porches all over the state. Each weekend, as he was driven from one whitewashed clapboard community to the next, his movements were tracked by campaign aide Dave Powers. By year's end, Powers estimated that Kennedy had spoken in thirty-nine cities and 312 towns.[1]

For a politician suffering from chronic back pain and Addison's disease, the schedule was intense. But Kennedy was eager to swap his seat in the House for a mahogany desk in the Senate. After nearly five years on Capitol Hill, he was bored with the drudgery of committee work and frustrated by his lack of seniority. Life as a senator promised to be more stimulating. It would also enable him to concentrate on foreign affairs, the policy area that most fascinated him. So fierce was his desire that he was prepared even to challenge the commonwealth's popular Republican incumbent, Senator Henry Cabot Lodge, Jr.—an audacious move that threatened to bring a promising career in Washington to an abrupt end.

Lodge was a formidable opponent—urbane, absurdly wealthy, and able to boast a stellar political bloodline. The grandson of former Senator Henry Cabot Lodge, Sr., he first won election to the Senate in 1936, a year when Roosevelt was at the height of his powers, by edging out James Michael Curley, the indefatigable "Purple Shamrock." In subsequent elections, he cemented his reputation as one of New England's favorite political sons. Such was his enduring popularity that Lodge viewed the 1952 election as a formality and spent most of the year orchestrating Dwight D. Eisenhower's insurgent campaign for the presidential nomination. When Eisenhower triumphed at the Republican convention with a staggering first-ballot victory over Senator Robert A. Taft, Lodge became complacent. He felt so certain of reelection that he spent two weeks in the Caribbean vacationing rather than busying himself with his own campaign.

There was a delicious historical irony in Kennedy's decision to run, for in 1916 his maternal grandfather, John F. "Honey Fitz" Fitzgerald had campaigned for the same Senate seat against Lodge's grandfather. The 1952 campaign therefore had the feel of a long-running dynastic feud—a fight between two political princes, one with blue blood, the other with green.

The Kennedy campaign faced a pressing strategic question after Kennedy announced his candidacy on April 6: whether to attack Lodge from the left or the right; or, as Kennedy's new political adviser Lawrence O'Brien framed the question, whether to portray him as "too liberal or too conservative." The Kennedy camp was split. Advisers like O'Brien, a public relations man from Springfield, Massachusetts, urged JFK to run as a bread-and-butter liberal and emphasize issues including his long-held commitment to civil rights. Other advisers, most notably Joe Kennedy, believed Lodge was too progressive to be outflanked on the left. But in a rare break with his father, Jack decided to campaign as a "Roosevelt Democrat." Acting out of conviction as well as calculation, Kennedy believed it would enable him to exploit his pro-labor record, tighten his hold on Boston's blue-collar voters, and hammer home the central theme of his announcement address: that Lodge was blind to Massachusetts's chronic economic distress. "He Can Do More for Massachusetts" became the congressman's campaign slogan. Lodge countered with: "He Has Done the Most for Massachusetts."[2]

Having decided to attack Lodge from the left, the support of Massachusetts's 50,000–70,000 black voters became pivotal for the Kennedy campaign. Anticipating their growing importance and determined to benefit from his long-standing support for civil rights, Kennedy had been raising his profile on the issue since the beginning of the year. Congressional staffers ensured that black journalists were kept abreast of each new initiative. In January, he vociferously condemned the murder of black schoolteachers Harry T. Moore and his wife, Harriet, who had been killed on Christmas night at their home in Mims, Florida, by a bomb planted by segregationists. Moore, the Florida secretary of the NAACP, had campaigned to prosecute a white sheriff for shooting two handcuffed blacks held in custody—a fight that cost him his life. "All of us, I am sure, are incensed by this cold-blooded murder and deplore the fact that the criminals have not yet been brought to justice," said Kennedy in a speech on the House floor, in which he called upon President Truman to launch an immediate federal investigation.

The speech hit its mark. The *Boston Chronicle*, the city's most widely read black newspaper, gave it front-page coverage under the banner headline "Kennedy Backs Bill to Punish Miami Killers." In the spring, Kennedy drew fresh attention to the case, meeting members of the Boston NAACP in the symbolic setting of Faneuil Hall for a progress report on the Florida investigation. Once again, his intervention drew favorable headlines in Boston's black press.[3]

Civil rights provided a crucial opportunity for Kennedy to draw bright lines of distinction between the two campaigns. At the outset, he sent campaign workers a handwritten note instructing them to examine Lodge's record on civil rights. He was confident it was weaker than his own. In particular, Kennedy urged them to study a series of roll calls on Rule XXII, the directive that enshrined the power of the filibuster, the device used by southern Democrats to prevent civil rights bills from ever becoming law. Kennedy, who had long supported moves to weaken the filibuster, suspected Lodge might be vulnerable on the issue, and knew it would damage him. Black voters had grown weary of seeing civil rights bills passed by the House but blocked by a Senate filibuster. "I believe that in 1949, Lodge and 33 other Republicans voted for a rule that would permit a filibuster on a motion to end filibusters," Kennedy told his staff, a move that would have made it all but impossible to revise Rule XXII. "We should also have Nixon's position," he added, suspecting that Eisenhower's vice-presidential running mate might be vulnerable, too. After scouring the congressional record, researchers discovered that Lodge had twice voted against efforts to curb the power of the filibuster. It was precisely the kind of incriminating evidence with which Kennedy could attack his opponent. They also unearthed polling data showing that Lodge had performed poorly in black neighborhoods in previous elections, most notably in 1946, when he won just one out of Boston's six predominantly black wards.[4]

Kennedy was determined to press home his advantage, and approached Joshua Guberman, a lawyer with close ties to Boston's black community, and asked him to "develop civil rights business," as he matter-of-factly put it. Guberman quickly generated a closely argued memorandum that called for Kennedy to adopt a "strong stand on civil rights." Given the size of the black electorate and the willingness of many white voters in Massachusetts to support racial reform, Guberman concluded it "is absolutely essential to have a clear-cut, strong position." He then put forward a thirteen-point civil rights program, the centerpiece of which was the reform of Rule XXII—or the cloture rule, as it was also known. "A candidate must say that he is for laws against lynching, segregation, employment discrimination and all the rest," Guberman argued, "but if he is not in favor of workable cloture rule which will enable the Senate to vote on the various laws which have been proposed, you know that he does not mean what he says." While southerners clung to the filibuster, "the civil rights program will never be anything more than a plank in a party platform." He also

called upon Kennedy to reiterate his support for legislation creating a fair employment practices committee, a ban on lynching, the abolition of the poll tax,
and home rule for Washington, D.C., a "symbol of America" presently "untrue
to American ideals." Finally, he urged Kennedy to call upon the federal government to strengthen the Justice Department's Civil Rights Section, create a permanent Commission on Civil Rights and order the FBI to investigate crimes
against blacks. Guberman suspected Lodge would adopt a strong civil rights
stance himself, largely out of political necessity. Lodge could ill afford to repeat
his dismal showing among black voters from six years earlier. Kennedy became
even more convinced that black voters could provide his margin of victory and
acted quickly on Guberman's advice.[5]

One of his first acts was to sit down with a legal notepad and draft a handwritten speech, which he entitled "Kennedy Fights for Civil Rights." It survives
as a ragged document, peppered with errors, deletions, and marginalia, as he
toyed with various sentences and phrases. The congressman began with a bold,
declarative statement: "There is nothing worse in life than racial bigotry." On
further reflection, though, he decided to cross out the word "bigotry" and replace it with "prejudice." Then he inserted the discarded word into his second
sentence: "There is nothing lower than bigotry." After a few stabs at the next
line, Kennedy settled on a formulation that stressed the strong link between the
struggle for equality and the fight against communism: "Those who view fellow
Americans—regardless of race, color or national origin—as anything other than
fellow Americans are fostering the very climate in which the seeds of communism flourish." Then he underlined the point again: "A strong civil rights program—one that guarantees every American a fairly-earned share of those
opportunities to better oneself and his family which only our country can
offer—is vital to the continued strength and progress of the United States. That
is why in 6 years in Congress I have supported and fought for a compulsory
FEPC—that is why I have stood firmly in favor of good treatment for all Americans in school, in the Armed Services and on the Supreme Court."[6]

Kennedy then turned his attention to Lodge's civil rights record. "My opponent says he is for legislation, too—in fact, he informs us he is going to end filibusters in the Senate single-handed. But the facts just don't back him up." How
was it possible to support civil rights, he pointedly asked, without changing the
filibuster rule? "I want to go to the Senate to join those who are really fighting
for a change in the present Senate rules—which permits empty words to kill all
attempts to protect the constitutional rights of minority groups of Americans. I
want to go to the Senate to continue my fight for Civil Rights legislation."[7]

Never before had Kennedy laid down the case for reform in such detail or
with such force. It was all the more impressive since he drafted the speech himself. Clearly he thought civil rights was sufficiently important to organize and
articulate his own thoughts, rather than leave the task to one of his aides. But

the speech revealed significant limitations in Kennedy's political imagination on the topic of race. In no way did he address the indignities suffered by southern blacks. He merely called for the "good treatment" of all Americans in schools, the armed services, and the Supreme Court, which at that time was being asked by civil rights groups to rule on an expanding docket of cases aimed at ending de jure segregation in Dixie. He did not call for the integration of southern schools or the dismantling of segregation in public accommodations, omissions that reflected his chronic reluctance to advocate federal solutions to problems he thought would be best tackled at the state level. But they also suggested an on-going political naïveté with regard to the extent of the southern race problem.

By early July, Kennedy had decided to make Senate reform his signature issue. That month, as Democrats converged on Chicago for their national convention, he called upon party leaders to issue a strongly worded civil rights plank promising to curb the power of the filibuster to pave the way for new legislation. Kennedy focused his lobbying efforts on Congressman John McCormack, his senior colleague in the Massachusetts delegation and the chairman of the influential platform committee. In a telegram to McCormack, Kennedy argued that the filibuster rule was "un-democratic and indefensible" and in urgent need of change. "I hope the Democratic platform will take a forthright and realistic stand on the question of civil rights," he added. As delegates arrived in Chicago, aides leaked the telegram to black newspaper reporters back home in Boston.[8]

After returning from the Chicago convention, which nominated Illinois Governor Adlai Stevenson and Alabama Senator John Sparkman as the Democratic presidential and vice presidential candidates, Kennedy continued with his efforts to woo black voters, most of whom lived in Roxbury and Dorchester, the two worst slums of Boston. Both neighborhoods were the political fiefdom of Silas "Shag" Taylor, chairman of Boston's NAACP and patriarch of the black community in Massachusetts. Kennedy worked assiduously to cultivate him, though to little effect. Taylor was a close friend of Congressman McCormack, who was deeply mistrustful of the Kennedys, and an even closer associate of James Michael Curley, who hated them. Notoriously cantankerous, Taylor was seemingly immune to Kennedy's much-vaunted charm and signaled at the outset of the campaign that he would offer little in the way of help.[9]

Kennedy was forced to look elsewhere for black support and focused his efforts on younger activists, some of whom had never before been involved in electoral politics. From previous campaigns, Kennedy knew he could rely on the organizational flair of Harold Vaughan, who, as an aide to Boston Mayor John B. Hynes, boasted excellent contacts all over the city. Eager to extend his reach even further into the black community, Kennedy also made contact with NAACP activist Herbert Tucker, whom he had first met four years earlier. Tucker was more contemplative than Vaughan but no less effective. Ruth Batson, a resident of Roxbury with a passion for reform, also volunteered. In later years, Batson emerged as the "conscience" of Kennedy's Boston Black Cabinet. During the 1952 campaign, however, her primary responsibility was to help mobilize the black vote through mail-shots, voter registration drives and word of mouth on the streets of Roxbury, her home community.[10]

From the outset, Vaughan and Tucker were brought into the inner sanctum of the campaign. They worked out of the same headquarters on a fully integrated basis, something that, in the early 1950s, was unusual. They participated in strategy meetings and had regular access to the candidate. Bobby Kennedy, the candidate's twenty-seven-year-old brother, who took charge of his first political campaign, also made sure they received a handsome share of the advertising budget. "If the idea was good," reflected Vaughan, "the money was always there."[11]

With thousands of dollars at his disposal, Vaughan launched a publicity blitz. By the end of the summer, the *Boston Chronicle* was carrying a slew of advertisements targeting black voters, another innovation of the Kennedy campaign. Vaughan subtly changed the main campaign slogan, "Kennedy has done and will do more for us," to appeal directly to black voters: "Kennedy has done and will do more *for more of us.*" To most observers, the change was almost imperceptible. But Vaughan was convinced the words "more of us" conveyed special meaning for black voters, who would appreciate its deliberately inclusive tone. Other advertisements touted the congressman's proud record of accomplishment, such as his repeated calls for the State Department to employ a greater number of black career officers in the Foreign Service and his demand for new fair employment legislation. The campaign also plastered hundreds of posters on billboards in black neighborhoods. One entitled, "Kennedy, Champion of Human Rights," proclaimed that the congressman had "fought courageously" for slum clearance, rent and price controls, fair employment legislation, and more enlightened immigration policies. The goal was to cast Kennedy as a quintessential "Roosevelt Democrat," since, seven years after his death, the former president continued to exert an almost hypnotic hold on black voters.[12]

In early August, Kennedy decided to spend almost an entire day barnstorming through Boston's black wards. The day began with a voter registration drive in Jamaica Plain and then continued with a tour of Roxbury's beauty salons, barber shops, and pool halls. Finally, he addressed over 100 black businessmen at the Professional and Businessmen's Club. Strongly partisan, the speech took aim at the Republican senators who had joined southern Democrats in blocking President Truman's civil rights program and savaged Lodge over his failure to support a change to the filibuster rule.[13]

Local ward captains were astounded that Kennedy had devoted almost an entire day of campaigning to black voters. Even "Shag" Taylor grudgingly conceded the visit had been a success. Taylor, who had been told ahead of time that Kennedy planned to spend the day in Roxbury, doubted he would even show up. As the congressman's motorcade swept into the neighborhood, Vaughan had to drag Taylor unceremoniously from his drugstore on Tremont Street to head up the welcoming committee.[14]

As the election approached, Kennedy launched a new campaign on behalf of Washington's black citizens, which this time seemed partly calculated to boost his standing among black voters at home in Massachusetts. He did so by highlighting the dismal employment record of the Capital Transit Company (CTC), the District's bus and trolley operator. For decades the CTC had resisted pressure to hire black drivers and mechanics and even when faced with chronic labor shortages at the height of the war, preferred to cancel services rather than recruit blacks. Kennedy mounted a searing attack on the company, urging it to launch a recruitment drive in black communities.[15]

Back in Boston, as the campaign reached its climax in the final weeks of October, Kennedy also devoted a second major speech to civil rights, which highlighted the achievements of the Roosevelt and Truman administrations. During the speech, he drew upon his recent trip to Indochina, during which he had not seen a single black American diplomat at any of the U.S. embassies on his itinerary. He urged the Foreign Service to recruit more blacks, a move that would shield America from Soviet criticism, an urgent Cold War concern.[16]

The black campaign reached its apogee a few weeks before Election Day, with the decision to host one of the famed "Kennedy teas" in the heart of Roxbury. A staple of previous campaigns, the teas followed a tested formula. Rose Kennedy, the family's proud matriarch, would march into a hotel ballroom or meeting room, flanked by her glamorous young daughters, draped in fur and daubed in make-up, and launch into a gushing tribute to her son. Embarrassed by her hyperbole, Jack would fidget uncomfortably at the side of the stage, before making a few, more modest comments of his own. Then the audience would be invited on stage, prompting a procession sometimes lasting hours.

Late in the campaign, with the race still too close to call, campaign aides decided that if the teas worked with white women, they would have the same magical effect on blacks. Ruth Batson first heard of the plan when she was stuffing envelopes one day at Kennedy's Bowdoin Street campaign headquarters. "Why don't you hold a party for Jack Kennedy?" asked one of the congressman's staff. Batson, who lived in a cramped two-bedroom apartment on the first floor of a housing project in Roxbury, thought he must be joking.

"D'you think they'd want to come to a housing project?" she asked.

"Of course," said the aide.[17]

Within days, Batson had compiled an invitation list from local church groups, bridge and gardening clubs, and posted hundreds of neatly printed cards. They were slipped inside exactly the same hand-addressed vellum envelopes that were delivered to white housewives. Kennedy himself was unable to attend, but Batson could hardly believe her eyes when his sister Eunice swept into the Orchard Park Housing Project, wearing a billowing felt skirt that had

"Kennedy" emblazoned across it. The Roxbury tea was so successful that Vaughan hurriedly organized a second one, this time at the Copley Plaza, a fashionable hotel in downtown Boston. This time the candidate would attend in person. In the brilliant sunshine of the New England fall, black women arrived from all over the city, dressed in their Sunday finery to hear Kennedy speak. After sandwiches had been served, Kennedy launched into a thoughtful speech, which was much more substantive than the platitudes of his normal tea remarks. Weaving together familiar themes, he began by attacking segregation in Washington, D.C., as a "national disgrace" and called once more upon the city's Capital Transit Company to hire more blacks. Then, he turned to an issue closer to home—his efforts throughout the year to end discriminatory employment practices at a hospital in Concord, in northern Massachusetts, which barred black interns and nurses.[18]

Lodge was drowning in a tidal wave of tea. "I can keep up with the campaign spending," he joked later in the campaign, when he unexpectedly ran into Vaughan. "But damn. I don't have enough brothers and sisters. I'm running against seven Kennedys." The teas were so successful that Vaughan worried black men might feel excluded. To rectify this, he brought together an informal steering group, with ten members drawn from all-male organizations, like the Inter-Denominational Ministerial Alliance, local Masonic groups, the Elks, and veterans groups. "They could not necessarily deliver a vote," said Vaughan, "but they could spread the message. It was a question of knowing which buttons to push."[19]

Kennedy was pioneering a new approach to black electioneering. Traditionally, northern Democrats won the allegiance of black voters by emphasizing pocket-book issues, like better housing and a rise in the minimum wage, and relying on a local black boss to mobilize support. Kennedy focused as much on their social aspirations as their economic needs, through the immense symbolic power of the teas as well as the decision to draw black campaign workers, like Vaughan and Tucker, into his inner circle. For black voters, status symbols could be as important as substantive proposals, a lesson that Kennedy learned early in his career and used to devastating effect during the 1960 presidential election.

As the campaign entered its final weeks, Vaughan had only one complaint: Kennedy's stubborn refusal to join the NAACP, or even lend his name to an informal committee made up of local dignitaries that occasionally sponsored its events. The issue first arose the previous year, when Kennedy was approached by Rheable Edwards, a local NAACP official organizing an event to draw attention to the discrimination suffered by black U.S. servicemen in Korea. Hoping to boost attendance, Edwards wanted him to join a committee of "outstanding Bostonians" to endorse the meeting. Kennedy politely refused. "I have adopted a policy whereby I do not lend my name to any organization, or committee," he explained, "unless I have an opportunity to take an active part in the work of that particular body." When Vaughan later confronted him on the subject, Kennedy said he was afraid of being accused of bias and that his opinions would carry more weight if he remained outside the NAACP. When Herbert Tucker asked him to join, Kennedy said he did not have enough money on him to pay his membership dues—two dollars. Kennedy, who was reflexively distrustful of political organizations, was especially loath to join one that courted so much controversy. The NAACP was also committed to the idea that the federal government was primarily responsible for putting an end to segregation—a stance that Kennedy was not wholly willing to embrace.[20]

By the final weeks of the campaign, black newspapers in the state sensed Lodge was losing the battle for black voters, and their coverage started to betray a decidedly pro-Kennedy slant. In late October, when the *Afro-American Colored Weekly* interviewed both candidates and compared their respective records, the paper came out sharply critical of Lodge. Notably, the editors did not focus on Lodge's record on Senate reform but his failure either to employ blacks in his Washington office or secure federal jobs for prominent Massachusetts blacks. Lodge's explanation that no blacks had ever applied for work did little to assuage them. The editors decided Kennedy's record on a raft of civil rights–related issues was much stronger and described it as a "direct, straightforward approach," which was "unlike your average politician." The *Afro-American Colored Weekly* stopped short of a clear-cut endorsement. But readers were left in little doubt which candidate it preferred.[21]

That both Lodge and Kennedy had agreed to be interviewed at length by the paper's editorial board was, in itself, a portentous development. It underscored the growing influence of the black voting bloc in Massachusetts. As the editors noted, never before in a statewide campaign had blacks been paid such close attention: "Colored supporters are, for the first time in their political lives, issuing statements to the press, giving the records of their candidates to help voters decide whom to cast their votes for."[22]

The final days of campaigning were frenetic, and commentators were reluctant to predict the outcome. By mid-October, Kennedy seemed on the verge of a remarkable victory, but in the final hours of campaigning, Lodge appeared to be narrowing the gap. He was helped by Eisenhower, who, in an attempt to rescue his friend, finished up his presidential campaign in Massachusetts. The former Supreme Allied Commander joined Lodge in a motorcade, which wove through the streets of Boston, in a route carefully planned to drum up black support in Roxbury. Afterwards, both men appeared together in a rally at the Boston Garden, an event thought to have handed Lodge thousands of extra votes.

Ending his campaign more modestly, Kennedy made a few low-key appearances in Gloucester, before heading to Boston to cast his vote. Strolling through the Boston Public Garden on Election Day with his Harvard college friend,

Torbert MacDonald, almost offhandedly he made two predictions: that Eisenhower would become president and that he himself would enter the Senate. When the return came in, Kennedy had beaten Lodge by 70,000 votes.[23]

Black voters made a significant, if not decisive, contribution to Lodge's defeat. In Ward Nine, one of Boston's most populous black enclaves, Kennedy got 72 percent of the vote, while in Roxbury's Ward Twelve his share was 65 percent. His decision to target Massachusetts black voters proved a tactical masterstroke, and he benefited immeasurably from his vigorous support for civil rights during his six years in the House. Never before had a senatorial candidate pursued black voters so aggressively nor drawn together such an accomplished campaign team to help. Guberman produced the policy, Vaughan provided the contacts, Tucker offered a link with the NAACP, and Batson opened up her living room. This division of labor would establish the pattern for future campaigns. From early on, Kennedy relied upon black campaign officials to deliver the vote but entrusted only white campaign officials with shaping policy.[24]

Had Kennedy spent more time exploring and understanding the grievances of black voters with advisers like Tucker and Batson, rather than focusing on the cold practicalities of boosting black turnout, he might have gained a more sophisticated understanding of the struggle for equality. And though he had little difficulty in making a personal connection with black associates and voters, he never made much of an attempt to truly understand them or the sources of their discontent. Partly as a result, he was much more finely attuned to the aspirations of black Americans—their overwhelming desire for social acceptance—than the political sources of their anger.

Above all, the 1952 campaign showed that Kennedy was an adroit tactician, and his decision to highlight Lodge's opposition to Senate reform was a strategic coup de grâce. Kennedy had fought a virtually flawless campaign. From targeted advertising to campaign teas, his campaign was extraordinarily innovative. And at a time when blacks were clamoring for status and recognition, the young congressman provided it in cupfuls. Traditional Democratic promises of improved housing and better-paid jobs were not unimportant. But Kennedy was offering much more: the prospect of truly first-class citizenship.

Kennedy had used civil rights to help define himself politically, in this instance portraying himself as a crusading liberal. Over the coming years, as he sought even greater political prizes, his nimbleness at using the issue to meet the political needs of the moment partly explained his extraordinary success. Boston's black community had rewarded him by providing the plurality for his close win, a lesson he would carry with him into subsequent campaigns.

CHAPTER 3

❧

Singing Dixie

Of all the obstacles standing in the way of racial reform, none was quite so implacable as the United States Senate, an antique institution with arcane procedures and time-honored rules of seniority that placed in the hands of southern lawmakers ideal weapons with which to guard the institutions of Jim Crow. Not since 1875 had a Civil Rights Act become law; subsequent bills that secured majorities in the House had either died in Senate committees or were filibustered to death on the Senate floor. In the twentieth century, reform-minded senators had not once managed to override a filibuster on civil rights. When Harry Truman, the first president since Reconstruction to push for new legislation, sent civil rights bills to Congress, in 1946, 1947, and 1948, a hardy group of southern Democratic lawmakers, working in concert with conservative Republicans, blocked each one. As members of the Southern Caucus well knew, a tightly organized minority could always thwart the will of the majority. Some-times the Senate was referred to as "the Old Southern Home," or, as veteran congressional correspondent William S. White put it, "the only place in the country where the South did not lose the civil war."[1]

At the time Kennedy was sworn in as senator on January 3, 1953, the twenty-two members of the Southern Caucus not only constituted the most cohesive voting bloc in the Senate but by far the most indomitable. Their strength stemmed from their dogged ability to hold onto their seats in election after election, which, in turn, brought them seniority and prestige and allowed them to control committee chairmanships, subcommittees, and powerful positions on Democratic steering committees. At the beginning of the 1950s, those positions were filled by white supremacists like James O. Eastland, a plantation owner from Sunflower County in the Mississippi Delta, who expressed his devoutly racist views with great force and monotonous frequency. "What the people of this country must realize," he barked during a wartime speech railing against the Fair Employment Practices Committee, "is that the white race is a superior race, and the Negro race is an inferior race." In 1955, he was joined by South Carolinian Strom Thurmond, the 1948 presidential candidate of the racist Dixiecrat Party, who had declared that "all the laws in Washington and all the bayonets of the army cannot force the Negro into our homes, our schools, our churches and our places of recreation and amusement." Other white supremacists spoke with softer voices but with no less determination—men like Harry F. Byrd of Virginia, an apple-orchard magnate, who, fittingly for such a dedicated segregationist, always wore spotless white suits; and Olin DeWitt Talmadge Johnston, a South Carolinian who had fended off a challenge from Thurmond during the 1950 midterm elections, by portraying him as a weak-kneed liberal.[2]

It was, however, Richard Brevard Russell of Georgia, a man of much greater intellect and courtliness, who became the untitled leader of the Southern Caucus and the region's most astute political strategist in the years following World War II. A chain-smoking bachelor over six feet tall, with a Roman nose and imperious bearing, Russell eschewed the inflammatory rhetoric favored by Eastland and Thurmond. Instead, he thwarted reformers with his encyclopedic knowledge of Senate procedures and the U.S. Constitution, his iron control of his caucus, and his sheer force of will. There was no more dedicated lawmaker on Capitol Hill—rumor had it he used to read the entire *Congressional Record,* the voluminous daily record of all proceedings of Congress, every day—and none more single-minded. At the age of just twenty-nine, he was elevated to the Speakership of the Georgia House, and four years later was sworn in as the state's youngest governor. At thirty-five, he became America's youngest senator, and had it not been for his inflexible views on race, few doubted he could have one day become president. During his nineteen years as senator, he fought on behalf of the South in some of the nation's bitterest and most protracted battles over civil rights legislation—from the thirty-day filibuster of the antilynching bill in 1935 to the nine-day campaign to prevent President Truman's 1950 fair employment practices bill from becoming law. He never once ended up on the losing side.[3]

A vocal group of liberal crusaders, determined to transform the Senate into a locus of reform, united in opposition to Russell and the Southern Caucus. They were led by Senator Paul Douglas of Illinois, a former economics professor, with a crook arm, two Purple Hearts, and a Bronze Star, whose trademark shock of unkempt hair had turned from brown to gray then white during his years trying to win enactment of a civil rights bill. At his side was Hubert Humphrey, the hero of the 1948 convention, who arrived in Washington determined to challenge the southern oligarchy. Within weeks of his swearing-in, Humphrey invoked their wrath by walking into the Senators' Dining Room accompanied by a black member of his staff, a breach of protocol that provoked audible sighs of disapproval from virtually every table. "Can you imagine the people of Minnesota sending that damn fool down here to represent them?" railed Russell one day in the Senate cloakroom, knowing Humphrey was within earshot.[4]

Though most Senate Republicans were racial conservatives, there was a small band of liberals, mainly from New England, steeped in the Lincolnian traditions of the GOP. This group included George D. Aiken from Vermont, Prescott Bush from Connecticut, Charles W. Tobey of New Hampshire, and Margaret Chase Smith from Maine. Like their liberal Democratic counterparts, however, they lacked the seniority and influence of members the Southern Caucus. "When the crunch came," Humphrey grumbled later, "Southerners with influence could often count on very liberal senators, and even more on moderates, to deliver a vote on some issue. It does not take long to discover that the best way to get along in the Senate is to get along with the committee chairman, subcommittee chairmen and the power structure." This was one of the first lessons Kennedy learned as a senator.[5]

Kennedy acknowledged the Senate's obstructionism when he addressed the NAACP at Howard University in January 1954, in his first appearance before the country's preeminent civil rights organization. "I must tell you in all frankness that the prospects of any suitable civil rights legislation being passed by this Congress are very dim indeed," he explained to his mainly black audience. "I know that this is a disappointment for all who believe in the cause of human and economic justice." But he did not isolate the Southern Caucus as the source of the problem and instead blamed the Republican-dominated Congress for this legislative inertia. He recognized the extraordinary power wielded by the Southern Caucus and was wary of criticizing them openly. Instead, he scolded the GOP. Republicans, he claimed, had proved "the empty meaninglessness of those forgotten campaign pledges."[6]

Kennedy made an uneventful start to his Senate career. Well aware that he was widely considered to be a playboy and a legislative lightweight, he angled to be taken more seriously in Washington. So the New England recession, not the most stirring of topics, became the subject of his maiden speech in May, the first in series of closely researched, but excruciatingly boring diatribes. As part of a numbing thirty-six-point program aimed at revitalizing the Massachusetts economy, he called again for measures to end racial discrimination in employment and government contracts, partly to protect New England textile mills against unfair southern competition, partly to improve America's image abroad. "Such discrimination," he told the Senate on May 20, "is one of the worst types of labor exploitation. . . . Such discrimination also has, of course, very serious adverse effects upon our international relations, our society and the individual." In no way noteworthy in themselves, these early speeches reflected the fresh influence of Kennedy's new aide, Theodore Sorensen, who helped draft them. Just twenty-four years old when he joined the senator's staff, the serious-minded

Nebraskan became Kennedy's most influential adviser and contributed more than any other aide in his campaign for intellectual heft.[7]

For Washington's gossip columnists, Kennedy's life beyond Capitol Hill provided a more colorful narrative than his work on it. On January 20, 1953, seventeen days after being sworn in as a Senator, he attended Eisenhower's inaugural ball in the company of a startlingly beautiful young photographer from the *Washington Times-Herald* named Jacqueline Lee Bouvier. After a swift romance, later that year they were married in Newport, Rhode Island, an event that attracted far greater press coverage than Kennedy's first eight months as a senator. Marriage helped counteract the commonly held view that Kennedy was an immature dilettante interested more in bedding beautiful women than in the affairs of state. While that remained true, of course, the remolding of his public image was going astoundingly well. Just thirty-six years old, Kennedy was already actively seeking a broader constituency beyond the boundaries of Massachusetts and sowing the seeds of a possible presidential campaign toward the end of the 1950s. His more immediate priority, however, was to position himself as a possible vice presidential nominee in the 1956 election. Over the next three years, this ambition would come to hinge upon his handling of postwar America's two most polarizing issues: McCarthyism and civil rights.

At the beginning of 1954, the Senate was heading for a showdown with Republican Joe McCarthy, the maverick "Red-Hunter" from Wisconsin, whose paranoiac rants were becoming increasingly demented. Four years earlier, McCarthy's startling claim that over 200 members of the Communist Party had infiltrated the State Department catapulted him to nationwide fame. But by the spring of 1954, his red-baiting heyday was passing, and even senior Republicans were tiring of his crackbrain tirades about how senior officers in the U.S. Army, most of them highly decorated World War II veterans, were shielding communist agitators. In late summer, a six-man committee recommended his formal censure for conduct contrary to Senate traditions.

For Kennedy, the censure of McCarthy presented both a personal and political dilemma. "Tail-gunner Joe" enjoyed a huge personal following in Massachusetts among fellow Catholics and also Eastern European immigrants who agreed with his anti-Soviet stance. The Wisconsin senator also happened to be a close friend of Joseph Kennedy, a one-time boyfriend of his daughter Eunice, and a regular visitor to the family's Hyannis Port compound. Robert Kennedy had even worked for five months on McCarthy's infamous subcommittee of the Government Operations Committee, though he had resigned in August 1953 in protest at the senator's guilt-by-association tactics.[8]

A fierce anticommunist himself, Kennedy supported the thrust of McCarthy's crusade, though, like his younger brother, he took issue with some of his outrageous tactics. But Kennedy would not be present for the Senate showdown over the issue. By the time the censure debate reached its climax in December, Kennedy had been forced into taking an extended leave from the Senate for life-threatening surgery on his wartime spinal injury—a procedure that according to physicians had only a fifty percent chance of success. Twice during the next four months, he was so close to death that a priest was rushed to his bedside to administer the last rites.[9]

By the time Kennedy was healthy enough to leave the hospital on December 21, the McCarthy era was over. Meeting in special session on December 2, the Senate had passed a censure motion by 67 votes to 22. On the final roll call, Kennedy was listed as "absent by leave of the Senate because of illness." But unusually for a senator forced to miss such an important vote, he had made no attempt to seek a "pair," a colleague on the opposing side willing to forgo his vote. Nor had his Senate office indicated how he planned to vote. He therefore occupied the ignominious position of being the only Democrat not to have voted for censure, which drew a howl of protest from civil libertarians and liberals.

Stung by the weight of criticism, Kennedy briefly considered issuing a statement from his hospital bed condemning McCarthy but decided that giving the ruined senator "an extra kick" would have looked "cheap." His failure to do so would remain a source of simmering resentment. For liberals, like Eleanor Roosevelt, Kennedy's silence over the censure proved that he was little more than a mouthpiece for his father's zealous anticommunism and social conservatism. As Joseph Rauh, a prominent figure in the liberal lobbying group the Americans for Democratic Action (ADA), put it much later during Kennedy's presidential bid: "A man who does not believe in the civil liberties of white citizens cannot be trusted to stand up for the civil rights of Negro citizens."[10]

∾

During the months of bedridden convalescence that followed his release from the hospital, Kennedy grew preoccupied by the notion of political courage—quite possibly because of the accusations of political cowardice swirling around him in the wake of the McCarthy censure. At first he considered writing a series of magazine articles exploring the subject in greater depth. Over time, however, the project became more ambitious, and he enlisted Sorensen to help him weave together his thoughts into a full-scale book. *Profiles in Courage* focused on the careers of eight lawmakers, "whose abiding loyalty to their nation triumphed over all personal and political considerations." Part popular history, part polemic, the book drew together an eclectic assortment of lawmakers around this unifying theme.[11]

Three of the eight essays focused on careers defined by the issue of slavery. Kennedy celebrated John Quincy Adams, America's sixth president and an impassioned opponent of slavery, whose setbacks were largely explained by his refusal to be swayed by political exigencies. He also reflected on the virtues of

Daniel Webster, who had, despite his own ideological opposition to slavery and criticism of his constituents, supported the Compromise of 1850 in an attempt to prevent the dissolution of the Union.

In one surprising chapter, Kennedy profiled Mississippi Congressman Lucius Quintus Cincinnatus Lamar, a lieutenant colonel in the Confederate Army who, by tempering his postbellum views on slavery, had helped engineer a rapprochement between North and South. For much of his career, Lamar was vilified by northern abolitionists as "one of the most rabid 'fire-eaters' ever to come out of the deep south," as Kennedy put it. But in later years he adopted a more conciliatory tone. The turning point came in 1874, nine years after Lee surrendered to Grant at Appomattox, when Lamar delivered an impassioned eulogy to Charles Sumner, the archabolitionist from Massachusetts and the scourge of the defeated South. Lamar issued a stirring appeal for national unity: "My countrymen, know one another and you will love one another." Met first with incredulous silence then with thunderous applause, Lamar's speech helped usher in a new phase in the fraught relationship between the North and South.[12]

For Kennedy, it offered as clear a profile of courage as any in his book. "As he passed through these troubled times," he wrote, admiringly, "Lamar came to understand that the sole hope for the South lay not in pursuing its ancient quarrels with the North but in promoting conciliation and in the development and restitution of normal Federal-state relations and the withdrawal of military rule." In his veneration of Lamar, a politician who tried to heal the country's sectional wounds, Kennedy was clearly working out his own ideas about the legacy of slavery. As the fifties progressed and the debate over civil rights became more rancorous, he would come to view himself in the same unifying role.[13]

In reflecting on Lamar, Kennedy also developed his ideas on the era of Reconstruction—a period in American history that, seventy-five years later, still infected the national debate about civil rights. In the years immediately following the Civil War, Republicans had taken advantage of their landslide majorities in the House and Senate to push through a series of landmark reforms, cementing the Union's victory over the Confederacy. The Fourteenth Amendment in 1868 gave all citizens equal protection under the law; the Fifteenth Amendment in 1870 guaranteed the right of all citizens to vote; and the Civil Rights Act of 1875 codified the equal protection provisions of the Fourteenth Amendment. To make sure these laws were enforced, the Republicans enacted the Reconstruction Act of 1867, which divided the eleven defeated states into five military districts, each one controlled by the army. The presence of federal troops on southern soil was anathema to the vast majority of white southerners, as was the arrival from the North of Reconstructionists, or carpetbaggers as they were labeled by the southerners. Some were unscrupulous opportunists hungry for money and power, whose corruption convinced southerners that they were being victimized yet again by vengeful northerners. Others were well-intentioned reformers looking to rebuild the South in the image of the North.

The humiliation of the defeated South did not last long. Within a few years, as northerners turned their attention elsewhere, state legislatures managed to roll back the reforms of the Reconstruction era. They blithely ignored the Fourteenth and Fifteenth Amendments and passed a string of notorious Black Codes, which subjected former slaves to brutal repression. But the ghosts of Reconstruction continued to haunt the South, and imprinted in the minds of segregationists a shared memory of vanquished degradation. Any subsequent encroachment by the federal government, especially in matters of race, would be viewed as a form of occupation—which partly explained its loathing of the civil rights movement. Its main thrust, after all, was to push the federal government into implementing the rights enshrined in the Fourteenth and Fifteenth Amendments—to bring about a Second Reconstruction.

In *Profiles in Courage*, Kennedy happily embraced this highly selective southern view of Reconstruction, describing it, rather clumsily, as "a black nightmare the South could never forget."[14] In Kennedy's judgment, "[n]o state suffered more from carpetbag rule" than Mississippi, which had been forced to endure the despotic leadership of Governor Adelbert Ames, a native of Maine hated throughout the South. "Vast areas of northern Mississippi lay in ruins," he continued. "Taxes increased to a level of fourteen times as high as normal in order to support the extravagances of the reconstruction government and heavy state and national war debts." And Kennedy reminded readers that Ames was the son-in-law of the Union General Benjamin Franklin Butler, who was viewed by white southerners as a brutal military dictator for his controversial tenure as commander of the Union forces in New Orleans in 1862. Using the epithet adopted by southerners, Kennedy called him the "butcher of New Orleans," even though Butler had been hailed by northern abolitionists for his staunch defense of freedmen's rights. Kennedy also lambasted Republican firebrand Thaddeus Stevens, the most incendiary lawmaker of his day, who recommended that the North treat the South "as we would any other provinces that we might conquer." Kennedy described Stevens as "the crippled, fanatical personification of the extremes of the Radical Republican movement . . . with a mouth like the thin edge of an ax."[15]

Kennedy's representation of Reconstruction was in keeping with the prevailing historiography. But Kennedy had clearly ignored a great deal of more recent work that cast the period in a different light (the bibliography accompanying the chapter on Lamar included just fifteen books). A new generation of historians, some of them black, were developing a more evenhanded assessment. Radical Republicans, they demonstrated, had helped establish the first public school systems and had brought about the rapid democratization of the South. Kennedy was not interested in, or quite probably not aware of, these nuances.

Instead, he portrayed Reconstruction as southerners did—an age of punishment and humiliation. Much later in his public career, when faced with the intransigence of white supremacists like Governor George Wallace of Alabama, he would come to reevaluate his view of the entire period. But for the time being, Thaddeus Stevens and the other Radical Republicans were quite simply the perpetrators of oppression of the South.[16]

Despite his admiration for Lamar, Kennedy does not emerge from *Profiles in Courage* as an apologist for slavery—after all, the chapter is dedicated to Lamar's courage in standing up to his Mississippi constituents. But the chapter does reveal a sympathy for a quintessentially southern view of history. In southern rage at the bureaucratic incursions of the Reconstruction era, Kennedy found a historical reflection of his own instinctive distrust of federal intervention. Although Kennedy claimed history as a guidepost, his portrait of Lamar revealed that he had only a fragmentary understanding of American history as regards the indignities of slavery and the brutal realities of its legacy throughout the South.[17]

∾

Kennedy's reflections on federal power were not merely theoretical. On May 17, 1954—just months before Kennedy began work on *Profiles in Courage*—the Supreme Court handed down the *Brown v. Board of Education of Topeka, Kansas* decision. The landmark ruling overturned the precedent of *Plessy v. Ferguson* along with the principle of "separate but equal." The Court did not, however, mandate the pace at which school integration should proceed, making *Brown* a statement of intent rather than a blueprint for action.[18]

On May 31, 1955—eight days after Kennedy ended his convalescence and resumed his Senate career—the Court returned to the issue. In a ruling dubbed *Brown II*, the Court called upon local school districts to proceed with desegregation with "all deliberate speed." Forced to compromise in the face of starkly competing interests, the Court's language was deliberately vague (NAACP lawyers had argued for "forthwith"). In the absence of any definitive deadline, recalcitrant school districts simply refused to desegregate their schools until compelled to do so by a federal court order.

In February 1956, in a speech before the New York Young Democratic Club, Kennedy responded publicly to *Brown* for the first time. Like other northern politicians, he came down in favor of the ruling and called upon Democratic leaders to endorse it at the upcoming party convention. In taking a forthright stand on *Brown*, he realized the party risked alienating southern voters and might even spark a Dixiecrat walkout at the upcoming convention. He maintained, however, that an important principle was at stake. The ruling was the "law of the land," he proclaimed to warm applause, and "it would cost us more [votes] elsewhere if we were to weasel on it." Kennedy conceded the platform drafting committee faced a "political quandary" and would probably arrive at some kind of compromise—supporting *Brown*, but only in "very general language." But he reiterated to his audience that his personal preference was for a clear-cut stance. The following morning, the *New York Times* ran a brief report on the speech under the headline: "Kennedy Presses Civil Rights Issue: Senator Calls on Democrats Not to 'Weasel.'" The *Times* made no mention of the fact that although he had supported *Brown* in principle, Kennedy had said nothing about how it should be practically enforced.[19]

One month later, segregationist lawmakers issued their own brittle response to the *Brown* rulings, which came to be known as the Southern Manifesto. Sounding the battle cry of states rights, it condemned the ruling as a "clear abuse of judicial power" in which the Warren court had "substituted their personal political and social ideas for the established law of the land." Signed by nineteen senators and seventy-seven representatives, the Southern Manifesto gave the appearance that the region's lawmakers were united in opposition to the Supreme Court's ruling. The reality was more complicated. Before it was published, disagreements over the final wording revealed subtle divisions between die-hard segregationists and a growing number of racial moderates. Senators J. William Fulbright of Arkansas, Spessard Holland of Florida, and Price Daniel of Texas questioned the wisdom of challenging the authority of the Supreme Court in such a brazen manner. Two reform-minded Tennesseans, Senators Estes Kefauver and Albert Gore, refused to sign on ideological grounds. For a short time, Russell even considered dropping the idea altogether, fearing that divisions within the Southern Caucus might burst into the open.[20]

Lyndon Johnson, the Democratic leader in the Senate and potential presidential candidate, chose not to sign the manifesto for very different reasons. Even though the Texan had voted against every civil rights measure to come before him, he knew that in the prevailing climate of national opinion an avowed segregationist could never hope to win the party's presidential nomination. He was nonetheless reluctant to alienate his southern backers. As Johnson told Bobby Baker, his congressional aide: "I'm damned if I do, I'm damned if I don't." Fortunately, Russell exerted no pressure on him to sign, largely because he was so eager to advance the Texan's ambitions in the hope that Johnson, a southerner, would become president and slow the implementation of *Brown*.[21]

The impending presidential election also hovered over the liberal reaction to *Brown*. For a time, liberal Democrats, led by Hubert Humphrey, Paul Douglas, and Wayne Morse, a former Republican from Oregon, considered publishing a counter-manifesto, setting out their case on behalf of the Court's ruling. Kennedy was instrumental in dissuading them, arguing that it was unwise to open up fissures within the Democratic Party on the eve of the election. But his argument was bred of self-interest. Like Johnson, he was reluctant to put his name to a document that would alienate a large, and still powerful, wing of the party. This in turn could scuttle his chances of becoming the vice presidential nominee at the convention, a position he coveted. Since Humphrey and Douglas quickly dropped their plan, Kennedy's behind-the-scenes lobbying campaign went largely unnoticed. Nonetheless, it marked a pivotal moment in his political career: the first time since entering Congress that he countenanced compromising on civil rights in order to curry favor with southern lawmakers. Thereafter, Kennedy rarely adopted a stance on civil rights without first considering its possible impact on his reputation in the South.[22]

In the months before the 1956 election, both Johnson and Kennedy were beginning to realign themselves politically. Both were staking early claims to being the kind of racial moderates around whom the whole party could unite. Slowly but discernibly, Johnson was moving to the left to avoid alienating northern voters, while Kennedy was leaning to the right so as not to inflame the southern bloc. As they plotted the trajectories of their careers, both knew they faced a precarious balancing act when it came to civil rights.

The difficulties of maintaining this balance became evident within weeks, when Texas Senator Daniel put forward a constitutional amendment to split Electoral College votes proportionately between the candidates. The move was intended to boost the influence of small, one-party states and curb the power of northern industrial states. Immediately realizing the implications of the proposed amendment, black leaders said they considered it a civil rights issue. And Kennedy agreed. On March 21, he argued on the Senate floor that this "revolutionary change in the federal system" would put "the balance of power quickly in the one-party Southern states." The following week, he wrote to every member of the Senate arguing that Daniel's reforms would give additional power to splinter parties (though he did not mention the Dixiecrats by name), increase the chances of deadlocked presidential elections being thrown into the House of Representatives—which had been the primary aim of Strom Thurmond's candidacy in 1948—and that it would discriminate against populous states. By spearheading the opposition to the reform of the Electoral College, Kennedy demonstrated he was capable still of taking a principled stand against the southern politicians.[23]

While politicians in Washington staked out their carefully worded positions on the *Brown* ruling, passions were flaring throughout the South. Senator Harry F. Byrd urged southerners to mount a campaign of "massive resistance," a destructive doctrine that, for segregationists, became the twisted metaphor of the age. State lawmakers in Alabama, Georgia, Mississippi, South Carolina, and Virginia, responded by enacting toughly worded new laws that set out to thwart *Brown* by imposing sanctions and penalties on white schools that admitted black students. In North Carolina, lawmakers responded to the threat of a string of desegregation lawsuits from the NAACP by dividing the state into 167 separate school boards, so that no single court ruling would be binding on the entire state.

By September 1956, only 723 out of the region's 10,000 school districts had been desegregated. In Alabama, Mississippi, Louisiana, Georgia, Florida, North Carolina, South Carolina, and Virginia not a single white school was integrated.[24]

Massive resistance also found violent expression. Out of a number of gruesome southern atrocities throughout the spring and summer of 1955, by far the most terrible was the murder in August of Emmett Till, a fourteen-year-old black boy from Chicago who was spending the summer in Money, Mississippi. Till made the prankish mistake of flirting with a white shop assistant, Carolyn Bryant, reportedly calling out "Bye baby" as he left her country store. Later on, the teenager was dragged from his grandfather's home by Bryant's husband, Roy, and brother-in-law, John Milam, who shot him in the back of the head with a Colt .45, and threw him in the Tallahatchie River, wiring a rusting gin fan to his neck so that his body would sink to the riverbed.

When the body was discovered, bloated and butchered, with an eyeball dangling from its socket, Till's mother insisted his mutilated remains be brought back to Chicago and put on public display in an open casket at a local funeral home. Before his funeral, 100,000 people saw Till's broken body, including scores of national journalists and photographers, whose descriptions and images of Till's suffering left an indelible mark on their readers and viewers. For once, the federal government felt compelled to act, and the White House exerted strong pressure on Mississippi authorities to arrest Bryant and Milam, whom everyone knew had carried out the killings. But when the case came to trial, an all-white, all-male jury took just sixty-seven minutes to acquit them. Both the murder and subsequent trial received prominent coverage in northern papers, some of which were now assigning their top reporters to the "civil rights beat." Their reportage meant the problem of southern racism was seeping more deeply into the nation's bloodstream.

Emboldened by the Supreme Court's ruling and enraged by the viciousness of segregationists, blacks were fighting back. Some unlikely foot soldiers appeared on the frontlines of the battle. None better personified the new spirit of militancy than Rosa Parks, a forty-two-year-old tailor's assistant from Montgomery, who sparked a citywide bus boycott by blacks in December 1955, when she refused to relinquish her seat to a white passenger. The ensuing protest lasted for over a year and ended only when the Supreme Court ruled that Montgomery's desegregation ordinances violated the constitution. The boycott highlighted the power of the "black dollar" in bringing about reform and also brought a twenty-six-year-old preacher in the city, Dr. Martin Luther King, Jr. to national prominence. "The South's terrible peace was rapidly undermined by the Negro's new and courageous thinking and his ever-increasing readiness to organize and to act," wrote King at the height of the campaign. "The extreme tension in race relations in the South today is explained in part by the revolutionary change of the Negro's evaluation of himself and of his destiny and by his determination to struggle for justice." Within two years of the *Brown* ruling, black Americans were in the throes of a revolution of rising expectations. The civil rights movement was coming of age.[25]

∾

For the Democratic Party, the newfound militancy of black Americans, both North and South, raised troubling political questions. How could the party of racist bitter-enders, like Eastland and Thurmond, continue to attract black support in bellwether states like Illinois, Michigan, New York, and Pennsylvania? By the same token, how could the party of liberal crusaders like Humphrey and Douglas sustain its traditional domination of the South? Could the party avoid a schism?

Those questions weighed heavily on the mind of Adlai Stevenson, the clear favorite to win the party's presidential nomination for a second time. Faced with the prospect of civil war within the party, he sought to ignore altogether the question of *Brown* and hoped the party's platform committee would come to his aid by fashioning some sort of artful compromise. He also needed to select a running mate who would be acceptable to both wings of the party. Segregationists were clamoring for a southerner, who could act as a moderating influence on Stevenson in the unlikely event he defeated President Eisenhower. Northerners wanted a liberal with a strong record on civil rights. Stevenson needed a politician who could straddle the divide.

The field quickly narrowed to two likely candidates: Kennedy, who made no secret of his desire to join the ticket, and Senator Estes Kefauver of Tennessee, whose strong showing in the Democratic primaries gave him by far the strongest claim. But in the eyes of southerners, Kefauver had committed apostasy by refusing to sign the Southern Manifesto, so Kennedy found himself in the anomalous position of being better placed to tap the support of southern Democrats than one of the region's native sons. Kennedy's fight for the vice presidential slot would prove to be one of the defining moments of his prepresidential career, for as the convention approached, he attempted to completely remold his political image. Throughout his nine years on Capitol Hill, he had been a staunch advocate of civil rights, with a blemish-free voting record. But in the space of just a few weeks he softened and reshaped his views, in a preconvention hasty attempt to make himself more palatable to the South.

Kennedy did not wish to alienate himself from northern Democrats. They remained essential to him politically, and ideologically he remained in step with his northern colleagues on a whole raft of issues, including civil rights. But he needed southern support to win the nomination. Faced with this dilemma, he attempted to devise a stance on *Brown,* along with a form of words to explain it, which would both satisfy northern supporters and offer succor to the South.

And so in the weeks leading up to the Chicago convention, he carved out a new stance on school desegregation. He publicly recast himself as a racial gradualist who supported black advancement in principle, but believed desegregation should be carried out over an extended period with the voluntary consent of southern communities. He arrived at much the same compromise as the Warren Court: He would continue to argue that segregation was unconstitutional but would stop short of prescribing just how quickly the *Brown* decision should be implemented.

On July 1, just four weeks before the start of the Chicago convention, Kennedy unveiled his revised position during an appearance on the new CBS political talk show *Face the Nation*. Joining him on the program was a panel of Washington journalists, who spent much of the interview interrogating Kennedy on the topic of civil rights. One panelist began by asking Kennedy for his opinion of the so-called Powell Amendment, an attempt by Harlem Congressman Adam Clayton Powell, Jr., to withhold federal funding from states refusing to integrate their schools. The Powell Amendment was toxic politically—southerners were of course adamantly opposed to it, and many liberal Democrats refused to support it because they feared it would scuttle the chances of a much-needed federal aid-to-education bill becoming law. Not surprisingly, Kennedy told the panel he was firmly opposed to the Powell Amendment. But without additional prompting, he went on to assert that Congress had *no* role to play in the implementation of *Brown*. "The question is being dealt with very satisfactorily by the Supreme Court," he stated, "and the federal courts are in control of the question of segregation." It was the first time that he had voiced this idea publicly.[26]

The panelists immediately picked up on Kennedy's bold statement and probed him further, asking him to be more explicit about the role that Congress should play in desegregating schools. "[W]e in the House and in the Senate have nothing to do with that decision," Kennedy reiterated, adding that federal judges should be left to determine the pace of integration.

The questions continued. "Was the Supreme Court moving too fast?" one journalist asked. Suddenly, Kennedy was at a loss for words. He was a northern Democrat, with a sizable black constituency, so it was impossible to say yes, but as a prospective vice-presidential nominee, eager to bolster his standing in the South, it was injudicious to say no. For a moment, his brain seemed to suffer political paralysis and produced spluttering fragments of a sentence rather than a coherent thought. "No, I don't think—they came to a decision in 1954, it was unanimous and it is the law. I don't think—I am not a lawyer—and I don't think any critique—if you are for the decision, you might say it is high time they did it, and if you are against it, you say they are intervening in political matters."[27]

The panelists were unrelenting. One asked him to define the phrase "with all deliberate speed." Kennedy regained his composure and stressed once more that the pace of integration should be decided by the lower federal courts rather than Congress or the Justice Department, since that would amount to an unreasonable encroachment of federal authority. The panel eventually moved on to other subjects, and it seemed Kennedy's interrogation on civil rights was over. But the most explosive question came toward the end of the interview: Should the Democratic platform endorse *Brown?* Having no doubt anticipated the question, Kennedy was ready with his response. And once more he leaned toward the South. "Now it may be politically desirable, some people may feel, to reemphasize it," he responded, regaining his fluency. "In my opinion it is unnecessary because I accept it." It was an artful way of saying "No."[28]

In less than five months, Kennedy had gone from warning Democrats against "weaseling" on *Brown* to doing just that before a national audience on *Face the Nation.* He was by no means alone in adopting this approach—even liberal luminaries like Eleanor Roosevelt were shying away from a fight over *Brown* in the hope of avoiding a Democratic Party rupture. Nonetheless, it was an unmistakable shift. Just two days before his television appearance, he had written to his father, who was vacationing on the French Riviera, describing how Florida Senator George Smathers was sounding out senior southerners about backing his vice presidential bid. By softening his views on *Brown,* Kennedy made Smathers's task a whole lot easier.[29]

When the convention opened in Chicago's International Amphitheatre on Monday, August 13, 1956, reporters believed still that Kefauver was the favorite to join the ticket. But once the convention cranked into action, events seemed to move in Kennedy's favor. On the opening night, his narration of *The Pursuit of Happiness,* a film produced by the Democratic National Committee (DNC), pitched him center stage. It allowed him to project the kind of glamour and charisma that Stevenson so conspicuously lacked. After the film finished, when he appeared for a brief moment on the rostrum, Kennedy brought the convention to life, with Massachusetts delegates jutting Kennedy signs into the air and snake-dancing through the aisles. "Senator Kennedy came before the convention tonight as a photogenic movie star," observed one reporter, who was also struck by his "considerable backing in the South."[30]

By the end of that first night, Stevenson's intentions were still shrouded in uncertainty. The ongoing debate within the platform committee over the wording of party's civil rights plank added an extra layer of confusion. Most commentators speculated that if the committee produced a strong civil rights plank endorsing *Brown,* Stevenson would select a southern conservative as a counterbalance. If, on the other hand, the committee put forward a compromise on *Brown,* he would enjoy more latitude in the selection of his running mate. In that event, Stevenson was now thought to favor Tennessee Senator Albert Gore, a racial moderate respected on both sides of the Mason-Dixon line, whose name had been leaked to reporters by Stevenson insiders.[31]

When the story appeared the second morning of the convention, it came as a crushing blow to Kennedy. When Stevenson asked Kennedy to deliver the main nominating speech, Kennedy assumed it was being offered as a consolation prize. Thinking his vice-presidential adventure was over, he instructed Bobby to rein in the lobbying campaign. He was determined nonetheless to take advantage of the opportunity to address the full convention, and stayed up with Sorensen until six in the morning working on the speech. It proved to be one of the most stirring addresses of the week, sparking colorful floor demonstrations that briefly revived his vice presidential hopes. Yet earlier that day the platform committee had produced precisely the kind of compromise on *Brown* that Stevenson had sought, increasing the likelihood of Gore's joining the ticket.

On Thursday night, Stevenson sprung the biggest surprise of convention week, when, fresh from his sweeping first-ballot victory, he announced a departure from "the precedents of the past" and asked the convention itself to select his running mate. "The choice will be yours," he declared in a rare moment of unscripted drama. "The profit will be the nation's."[32]

With little more than twelve hours to go before the vote, the Kennedy campaign swung into action. By midnight, almost the entire family had converged on the senator's suite at the Stockyards Inn, where Bobby paced the middle of the room, scribbling inexact delegate counts on a yellow legal notepad. According to his rough calculations, Kefauver was the favorite, but Gore remained a threat. Still, both provoked enmity from southern delegates, since they had refused to sign the Southern Manifesto, a weakness that Kennedy now seemed perfectly poised to exploit. For segregationists eager to register a protest vote against Kefauver or Gore, Kennedy was the ideal candidate.

As Bobby Kennedy walked nervously back and forth across the hotel suite barking out instructions, Jack seemed unusually introspective. Uncertain about his chances of victory, he was unsure even whether to place his name in nomination. Yet at that very moment, a delegate from Louisiana rushed into his hotel suite brimming with excitement. Following a midnight caucus, the Louisiana delegation had come down firmly in favor of Kennedy. "We went out on a limb for you," said the delegate, "and you can't leave us hanging there. You've got to run." It was precisely the spur Kennedy needed.[33]

Within minutes of the meeting breaking up, aides fanned out to the bars and hotel lobbies of Chicago, working through the night in a desperate, adrenaline-infused attempt to gather up delegate support. Somehow, in the midst of all the chaos, the campaign team managed to find a friendly printer who stayed up until dawn producing banners, buttons, leaflets, and placards, while Joe Kennedy pitched in from the Riviera, telephoning key party bosses. The competing campaigns pushed into high gear as well. On the neon-lit sidewalks of Chicago's "Golden Mile," late-night drinkers were bombarded with pamphlets and stick-pins from Humphrey supporters, while Kefauver convened a four

A.M. press conference, which attracted hundreds of high-spirited supporters and a scrum of bleary-eyed reporters.

At 1:05 the following afternoon, House Speaker Sam Rayburn brought down the gavel in a boisterous convention hall, its sharp crack barely audible over the chatter of political aides scrambling to line up delegates. When Rayburn managed finally to gain a semblance of order, the names of thirteen candidates were placed before the convention. Each one was accompanied by at least two nominating speeches. Determined to reflect his broad base of support within the party, Kennedy picked Connecticut Governor Abraham Ribicoff, a northeastern liberal, and Florida Senator George Smathers, whose performance was particularly memorable, since midway through he experienced sharp pains in his chest and thought he was having a heart attack. To deliver a third nominating speech, Kennedy then summoned his fellow New Englander House Majority Leader John McCormack, who despised the Kennedy family and almost had to be carried to the rostrum by Bobby Kennedy. Kennedy desperately needed his backing, not least because McCormack had been the chairman of the platform committee and the main architect of the compromise civil rights plank, which innocuously described *Brown* as the law of the land but said nothing specific about its implementation. To southerners in particular, he was a reassuring figure.

As the first ballot got underway, it quickly became clear that some of Kennedy's most vocal support was coming from the South. Bizarre though it was to see segregationists cheering on a Roman Catholic Harvard graduate, Mississippi's twenty delegates whooped rebel yells as they cast their votes for the New Englander, while Strom Thurmond's South Carolina delegation kept up a steady chant throughout of "We Want Kennedy, We Want Kennedy." There was support, too, from Alabama, Arkansas, Georgia, Louisiana, Virginia, and North Carolina, handing him 105.5 Dixie votes compared to Kefauver's measly 20.5. For all the support from the South, it was not enough to stop Kefauver opening up a first-ballot lead of 483.5 votes to Kennedy's 304, with Gore and Humphrey trailing far behind. Yet all was not lost, for Kennedy now had the look of a credible "unity candidate," with support from both wings of the party.[34]

When the second ballot started, Kennedy picked up much-needed delegate support from New York, New Jersey, and Pennsylvania. Then, with Texas delegates proudly waving Confederate flags behind him, Lyndon Johnson rose magisterially to his feet and announced that the Lone Star state would cast its vote "for the fighting sailor who wears the scars of battle." (Privately, though, he described his young colleague in less rapturous terms. "It was the goddamnedest thing," he reflected much later. "Here was a young whippersnapper, malaria-ridden and yellah, sickly, sickly. He never said a word of importance in the Senate and he never did a thing. But somehow with his books and Pulitzer Prizes he managed to create the image of himself as a shining intellectual, a youthful leader who could change the face of the country . . . his growing hold on the

American people was simply a mystery to me.") With Texas firmly in his column, the electronic tally boards flashed up a second ballot total of 618 votes for Kennedy compared with Kefauver's 551.5. This time, Kennedy had virtually swept the South, with Florida and Tennessee the only holdouts.[35]

The pause in voting after the second ballot gave delegations a narrow window to switch allegiances. Amid scenes of complete pandemonium, Kentucky jumped from Gore to Kennedy, its thirty votes bringing him within a hairbreadth of victory. Sorensen, who was watching the carnival alongside Kennedy at the Stockyards Inn, offered his hand in congratulation. But Kennedy refused to take it, knowing he had not yet won.

Back in the Amphitheatre, the atmosphere was growing ever more anarchic, and even Rayburn, a veteran of countless turbulent sessions in the House, struggled to maintain order. Amid the shouting, Gore somehow managed to catch Rayburn's eye and announced his withdrawal from the race. He then handed the Tennessee delegation over to Kefauver. Moments later, Oklahoma followed suit. Then, Humphrey announced Minnesota would back the Tennesseean. Now John McCormack spotted his chance to undermine Kennedy and clamored for the Speaker's attention. "Sam! Sam!" he shouted. "Missouri, Sam," he barked. "Missouri!" Rayburn motioned toward the Missouri chairman, whose delegation had originally backed Gore. Now it was switching to Kefauver. With spectacular suddenness, the momentum had swung behind the Tennessean. Over the next few minutes, in a rapid flurry of switches and turnarounds, Kefauver seized the nomination.

Less than an hour later, trying hard to affect cheerfulness, Kennedy appeared before the convention to thank supporters. He expressed his appreciation "to Democrats from all parts of the country, North and South, East and West, who have been so kind to nominate me this afternoon." Then, accepting defeat with his trademark grin, he called for Kefauver to be nominated by acclamation, a magnanimous gesture drawing raucous cheers from the floor.

Despite losing the nomination, Kennedy emerged from the convention as the party's brightest star. Even in the gloom of defeat, he could look ahead to a sparkling future. "In this moment of triumphant defeat his campaign for the presidency was born," reflected James MacGregor Burns, his first biographer. "[Y]ou clearly emerged as the man who gained most during the Convention," wrote Arthur Schlesinger, Jr., the historian of the presidencies of Andrew Jackson and Franklin Roosevelt and later of Kennedy himself. "You hit the bull's eye on every one of your appearances and your general demeanor and effectiveness made you in a single week a national political figure. You are bound to be in everyone's mind from now on in any future consideration of national candidates."[36]

The most enthusiastic praise, however, came from the South. "We were not *after* Kefauver," wrote Mississippi delegate Edgar Stephens, "we were *for you.* You have real friends in the South." Governor Marvin Griffin of Georgia, one of the party's most outspoken segregationists, told him, "While I regret that you lost, you won the respect from party leaders from all over the country and can look forward to greater things in the future." Mississippi Governor James P. Coleman was even more ebullient: "We are proud of having supported you, and would be happy to have the opportunity to do so much again." Kennedy graciously returned the compliments. A few weeks later, he replied to Coleman, assuring him that his previous comments in an article in *Atlantic Monthly* defending the New England textile industry against southern competition should in no way be interpreted as "anti-Southern." He even went as far as claiming something of a southern pedigree, noting, "I have lived a good share of my life in the South, where my parents have voted for 25 years; and own a house in Virginia at the present time." (He neglected to mention that his house was in McLean, more a Washington suburb than part of Dixie, and that by "the South" he meant his father's Palm Beach mansion.) In the words of the *New York Times,* the young New Englander had proved himself "as a personable, charming and spirited fighter in the best traditions of the Confederacy."[37]

Undoubtedly, Kennedy's celebrity and charisma played a large part in his success in 1956. But his decision to modify his views on *Brown* helped immeasurably. Kennedy had encouraged segregationists to believe they had less to fear from a New Englander on civil rights than from a Tennessean. As Harry F. Byrd, the architect of massive resistance, told Kennedy regretfully, his nomination would "have strengthened the ticket to a marked degree, while the nomination of Kefauver will have the opposite result." Bobby Troutman, an Atlanta attorney and close friend of Joe Kennedy, Jr., when they were at Harvard, best summed up the southern reaction. "You emerged as the brightest light of the Convention," he said, "and can be the leader of the party by 1960."[38]

At the end of his concession speech, Kennedy stepped down from the podium to the strains of "The Tennessee Waltz," the anthem of Kefauver's home state. But it was the air from another southern melody that just as easily could have danced in his mind. As he later confided to Arthur Krock: "I'll be singing Dixie for the rest of my life." Kennedy now knew that he was perfectly poised to mount a winning challenge for the Democratic presidential nomination four years hence. "With only four hours work, and a handful of supporters, I came within thirty-three-and-a-half votes of winning the Vice-presidential nomination," Kennedy told Dave Powers. "If I work hard for four years, I ought to be able to pick up all the marbles."[39]

CHAPTER 4

❧

Trial by Jury

After the election, John Kennedy's campaign to bolster his newfound support in the South produced a packed speaking schedule that placed him in front of audiences in an unlikely array of settings. It ranged from a keynote address at the Southeastern Peanut Association in Atlanta, where he delivered an unavoidably lifeless speech on farm price protection, to an appearance before the Arkansas Bar Association, where his speech was punctuated by two standing ovations. The June trip to Georgia proved a stunning success. He was invited to deliver the commencement address at the University of Georgia in Athens, where he highlighted the historical bonds between Georgia and Massachusetts—"a common history, a common citizenship and an inseparable destiny." He also made a joint television appearance with Senators Herman Talmadge and Richard Russell, the closest the state could come to political royalty. In Athens, Bobby Troutman, an increasingly influential figure in the Kennedy high command, invited 1,027 local political leaders to hear the senator, anticipating perhaps that 250 might attend. Almost 850 presented themselves.[1]

Throughout his tour of the South, Kennedy larded his speeches with reverential references to Lucius Lamar and deliberately avoided the question of civil rights, further burnishing his gradualist credentials. During a speech in Bristol, Virginia, in March 1958, he even praised Harry F. Byrd, the chief architect of the policy of massive resistance, as "one of most distinguished and courageous leaders." As segregationist columnist John Temple Graves pointed out, "He is too honest and New England-bred—and political—to take the Southern position on the race question, but he will never, never be a fanatic against us as [Walter] Reuther [the head of the United Auto Workers] and Nixon."[2]

While courting the South, Kennedy was simultaneously distancing himself from the progressive wing of the Democratic Party, which had reacted to Stevenson's resounding defeat by demanding the party take a more forthright stance on segregation. President Eisenhower won 39 percent of the black vote—the first time since the New Deal that blacks supported the GOP in such heavy numbers—and liberals believed that this was at least partly due to Stevenson's reluctance to outline his position on *Brown*. In the ritual of self-appraisal that followed, Kefauver predicted the party's future belonged to "true liberalism" rather than the watered-down version offered by his running mate. Humphrey argued that the Democrats needed to stem the loss of black voters in northern cities.[3]

In the New Year, Humphrey published the "Democratic Declaration of 1957," a sixteen-point plan that promised action on civil rights and a range of progressive causes. It was just as much an attack on the cautious leadership style of Lyndon Johnson and Sam Rayburn as on Eisenhower's conservatism. The declaration quickly drew support from Paul Douglas, Wayne Morse, and Michigan Senator Pat McNamara, all of whom were scornful of Johnson's appeasement policy toward the White House. Kennedy decided not to add his name to the list of six sponsors, considering it unwise to align himself with the liberal Democrats. Similarly, when liberals banded together in January to found the Democratic Advisory Committee (which was later renamed the Democratic Advisory Council [DAC]), a resolutely progressive policy forum, Kennedy steered clear. In February, when formally approached by DNC chairman Paul Butler, he politely demurred. "I must stand for re-election next year," he explained, "and the interests of my state do not always coincide with national party views." Kennedy's motives were clear. First and foremost, he was wary of upsetting Johnson, whom he had been courting for months in the hope of securing a seat on the Committee on Foreign Relations, a vacancy that should, by virtue of seniority, have been filled by Kefauver. Nor did he want to offend southerners following his success in Chicago.[4]

The growing polarization of the Democratic Party was making it harder for Kennedy to please his supporters nationwide. At its first meeting on January 4, the DAC called for curbs on the power of the filibuster and followed it up in February by demanding new civil rights legislation. On the question of filibuster reform, Kennedy came up with a compromise. He did not join fifteen liberal Democrats in co-sponsoring the necessary procedural motion but continued to pay lip service to the need for reform. He took a position, but not a stand.[5]

As the civil rights debate intensified further in the first half of 1957, so, too, did the conflicting political pressures upon Kennedy. They came to a head in March, when his manic speaking schedule placed him, in quick succession, before two of the Democratic Party's warring factions: educators in New Jersey and segregationists in Birmingham, Alabama.

Kennedy's speech before the American Association of School Administrators in Atlantic City was the kind of routine appearance that, at any other time, would have attracted little, if any, attention. But in post-*Brown* America, any speech touching on education was loaded with meaning. During his brief remarks, Kennedy argued that school policies should not be decided by Washington bureaucrats but rather left in the hands of local school boards. He later claimed he had been referring only to the choice of curricula, textbooks, and teaching methods. Yet any statement favoring "local control" over "federal intervention" was easily misconstrued—as Kennedy well knew—for in southern states the phrase "local control" was synonymous with "states rights." The *Chicago Defender,* one of the country's leading black newspapers, immediately seized on Kennedy's remarks. "This was a political speech intended primarily for Southern consumption," the paper's editors thundered. "We don't mind a donkey as a traditional emblem of the Democratic Party, but a jackass is out of the question."[6]

It was a chastening experience for Kennedy. After a decade of support, this was the first time he had provoked the wrath of a black newspaper. Sargent Shriver, the senator's brother-in-law who ran the family's business affairs in Chicago, read the editorial with mounting alarm and immediately contacted Sorensen. Kennedy could ill afford to alienate a paper as influential as the *Defender,* warned Shriver. Acting quickly to repair the damage, Kennedy approached John Sengstacke, the *Defender*'s editor, to clarify his position on *Brown.* He claimed that his comments in Atlantic City had nothing to do with race and were merely "a restatement of the principle that teaching practices, curricular, textbooks and other classroom policies would not be dictated from Washington" and were unconnected with race. But Kennedy had learned his lesson. After his run-in with the *Defender,* he paid much closer attention to black publishers and black reporters, handing them an open invitation to visit his Senate office whenever they were in Washington.[7]

His speaking engagement in Birmingham, America's most thoroughly segregated city, threatened to embroil Kennedy in even greater controversy. For that reason, Sorensen had drafted a bland speech studiously ignoring civil rights. But in a free-wheeling question-and-answer session afterwards, a member of the audience asked Kennedy how he would vote if the civil rights bill, currently bottled up in James Eastland's Judiciary Committee, came before the Senate. "That bill is still in committee," Kennedy answered, trying to dodge the issue entirely, "and for that reason I am not going to answer that question. After all," he added, with a coy smile, "I'm enjoying myself down here in Alabama. Let's keep it that way." There were knowing laughs from the audience. As a reporter from Alabama's *Montgomery Advertiser* wryly observed, "he did more political good in three hours than many a man could hope to do in a lifetime."[8]

But the coming months brought greater challenges for Kennedy. His words and actions would come under much more intense scrutiny during the congressional battle over the 1957 Civil Rights Act. Not since 1875 had Congress

passed a civil rights bill, primarily due to the strength and persistence of a conservative coalition between Republicans and southern Democrats. By the beginning of 1957, however, the coalition had splintered, and the chances of
passing a meaningful civil rights bill appeared better than at any point in the
past seventy years.

In early January, the Eisenhower administration had introduced a new bill,
calling for the creation of a bipartisan civil rights commission, a new Civil
Rights Division at the Justice Department, strong injunctive powers for the attorney general to protect the right to vote and other civil rights and to outlaw
discriminating practices committed by southern voting registrars. Attorney
General Herbert Brownell thought it was not only demonstrably necessary, but
politically felicitous, as the legislation would enfranchise thousands of southern
blacks who would end up supporting Republicans. In pressing for legislation,
Brownell could also rely on the loyal backing of Republican Senate Minority
Leader William Knowland, an ambitious Californian, who hoped the passage
of a civil rights bill would enhance his chances of winning the party's presidential nomination in 1960. Knowland therefore placed himself at the head of a
broad-based coalition of moderate Republicans and liberal Democrats determined to challenge the might of the Southern Caucus and to defeat its inevitable filibuster. At last, a breakthrough seemed possible.

Nobody better understood the mood of the upper chamber than Johnson,
who sat directly across the aisle from Knowland and harbored similar presidential ambitions. For the Texan to mount a realistic challenge for his party's nomination, he would have to attract northern support, an impossible task for a
politician identified so closely with the party's segregationist rump. As journalists Robert Novak and Rowland Evans pointed out, "Johnson had voted *no* on
civil rights 100 per cent of the time; *no* on an anti-lynching bill in 1940, *no* on
a Democratic leadership amendment in 1940 eliminating segregation in the
armed services; *no* on anti–poll-tax bills in 1942, 1943, 1945." In Johnson's
mind, the best way to remold his image was to become the main architect of a
new Civil Rights Act—to engineer a legislative breakthrough that would showcase his skill as a lawmaker and boost his standing as a national leader. The
question, of course, was how to do so without alienating southern supporters.[9]

For help he turned to Russell, his long-time friend and confidant, who had
sacrificed his own presidential ambitions to his unbending loyalty to the white
supremacist cause. "These Negroes, they're getting pretty uppity these days
and that's a problem for us since they've got something now they never had
before, the political pull to back up their uppityness," Johnson explained to
Russell. "Now we've got to do something about this, we've got to give them a
little something, just enough to quiet them down, not enough to make a difference. For if we don't move at all, then their allies will line up against us and
there'll be no way of stopping them, we'll lose the filibuster and there'll be no

way of putting a brake on all sorts of wild legislation. It'll be Reconstruction all over again."[10]

Johnson was offering Russell a deal: If southern Democrats agreed not to launch a filibuster, he would personally ensure that only a weak package of reforms won passage. Specifically, he promised to remove the bill's most controversial and far-reaching provision, a measure known as Part III, which granted the Justice Department wide-ranging injunctive powers that could be used to force local school boards to integrate their classrooms. Part III was the main legislative priority of NAACP. Because most southern blacks were either too poor or too scared to launch their own desegregation suits, the leaders of the NAACP knew that they could not achieve their goals through lawsuits alone. Federal enforcement was essential. In the hands of a liberal attorney general, like Brownell, Part III could ultimately lead to the complete and speedy desegregation of southern schools.[11]

Russell accepted the broad terms of the offer. With public opinion turning against the South, and with Republicans and senior Democrats ever more responsive to the demands of black voters, he realized the Southern Caucus was fighting a rearguard action. It was not even clear that Russell could muster enough senators to launch a round-the-clock filibuster. And if he did, the tactic could easily backfire, for it was certain to harden calls for a change in "Rule XXII"—the filibuster rule—a campaign that was gathering momentum. Russell realized that he could better protect his own interests, and those of his constituents, by accepting a weak bill and keeping the filibuster intact. Russell nonetheless hoped that he could head off the bill before it came to a vote, and plotted a wide range of tactics to impede the bill's progress. Here he was aided by Eastland, who, as chairman of the Judiciary Committee, had the authority to keep the administration's civil rights bill from reaching the floor.

In June, the House passed Eisenhower's civil rights bill by a majority of 286 votes to 126. For six months, Eastland's Judiciary Committee had bottled up the Senate version of the administration bill, but with its passage in the House Knowland was determined to avoid any further delay. Acting in tandem with his main Democratic ally, Senator Paul Douglas, he invoked a rarely used procedural motion that would enable the bill to bypass completely Eastland's committee. It was a highly controversial maneuver that contravened normal Senate procedures but only required the backing of a simple majority of senators. Knowland and Douglas believed that victory was easily within reach.

For once, Russell appeared to be stymied. Without allies from outside the South, he could never hope to defeat the "Knowland-Douglas axis." Even if he attracted support from conservative Republicans, who were indifferent toward civil rights and jealously protective of Senate procedures, it would be difficult to muster a majority. Refusing to admit defeat, however, Russell hatched a brilliant scheme. The plan centered upon a small group of reform-minded senators from

Idaho, Washington, Oregon, New Mexico, and Montana. They had been lobbying all year for the federally financed construction of the Hells Canyon project, a high dam on the Snake River between Idaho and Oregon, which would
bring much-needed power and jobs to the entire region. In secret negotiations,
Russell proposed a simple quid pro quo: If the westerners voted against Knowland and Douglas in the procedural motion, southern Democrats would support
the Hells Canyon project. Desperate for the dam to be built, the group reluctantly agreed. But even with their backing, Russell needed additional votes.

The Knowland/Douglas motion would prove to be an important political text
for Kennedy. By mid-June, as the vote edged closer, a rumor began to spread
through the corridors of the Senate: Kennedy was going to side with the segregationists. Douglas was among the first to harbor suspicions, since the New
Englander had been strangely reluctant to attend caucus meetings organized by
pro–civil rights senators. NAACP official Clarence Mitchell, one of Capitol
Hill's most astute and well-connected lobbyists, also picked up on the gossip and
took the precaution of firing off a brusque warning letter to Kennedy. Mitchell
cautioned that no friend of Eastland could possibly be a friend of the NAACP
and that a vote with the South would count against him in the future.[12]

Kennedy struggled to stake out some kind of middle ground between the
competing wings of his party. He knew he would be expected to side with the
North on the bill's substantive provisions, but procedural motions, such as
the move to bypass the Judiciary Committee, offered him more latitude. Here,
he could argue with a measure of plausibility that he was committed to adher-
ing to the long-established Senate custom that all bills should be first debated
in committee. In so doing, he could camouflage his true intentions: of casting
an early vote on the civil rights bill that would earn southern acclaim.

When the procedural motion was debated on June 20, Kennedy argued that
the civil rights bill should be sent to Eastland's Judiciary Committee, whatever
the consequences. "I think it would be disastrous for the Senate—liberals and
conservatives alike," he noted in a closely argued floor speech, "if we were to
give credence to an interpretation of the rules which would permit one Senator
to prevent important bills . . . from being referred to the respective committees."
Knowing full well that if the bill went back to Eastland's committee, it was unlikely to reemerge, Kennedy nonetheless downplayed the implications of his position. If the Judiciary Committee refused to release the legislation, he insisted,
there were other ways to bring it to the floor. Indeed, all that was required, he
claimed, were a couple of extra procedural votes, or "cloture votes," as they were
known. "I cannot see any justification," he argued, "for giving up one of our
maximum protections in order to save ourselves from the mechanics of an extra
cloture motion or two." Kennedy was being disingenuous—cloture votes were,
in fact, fiendishly difficult to secure. Since the adoption of Rule XXII in 1917,
just four had been successful—and none in the realm of civil rights. Kennedy

was attempting to pass off the motion as a minor parliamentary inconvenience, when, in reality, it was pivotal.[13]

When the procedural motion was finally put to a vote, Kennedy found himself on the losing side of the argument. Forty-five senators supported the move to bypass the Judiciary Committee and thirty-nine opposed it. While Knowland and Douglas celebrated an important victory, Russell plotted his next move. Despite the support of Kennedy and the Hells Canyon westerners, the segregationists had suffered an early setback: the fight to keep the civil rights bill from ever reaching the Senate floor.

Word that Kennedy had voted with the South swiftly reached Boston, and his black supporters reacted with anger and dismay. Some, like Herbert Tucker, felt personally betrayed. Writing to Kennedy the next morning, Tucker lamented that the Boston NAACP was "naturally quite disappointed that you chose this manner of expressing yourself, particularly since in the past we have known you to fight tooth and nail any subterfuge used within Congress to defeat the progress of human relations." Ruth Batson, the newly elected president of the New England Regional Conference of the NAACP and the only black on the Democratic State Committee, was typically plain-spoken. "I believe you to be a friend of civil rights," she wrote in a scathing letter, "and I would like to know, if you care to tell me, what your reasons were for voting as you did." The most acerbic criticism came from Long Island resident Robert S. Moore, who wrote contemptuously, "I am sure we Negroes are not going to let you forget about it as you forgot about us just when we needed you most."[14]

Jolted by their vehemence, Kennedy moved quickly to placate his critics. First, he sent a letter to Tucker arguing that his vote on the procedural motion had been wholly misinterpreted. In no way had it represented any weakening of his long-standing support for civil rights. On the contrary, he claimed, bypassing the Judiciary Committee would establish a dangerous legislative precedent, which opponents of civil rights could use to their advantage in the future.[15] With Batson, he took a different tack, explaining that his vote "was simply a question of [backing] the procedure which would best secure passage of this and other liberal legislation." Moore, his most vociferous critic, received a copy from Kennedy of a letter to the *Washington Post* written by Wayne Morse, highlighting the hazards of bypassing the committee. The following month, Kennedy also tried to mollify NAACP Executive Secretary Roy Wilkins, who had also been critical. "These are times when the friends of civil rights must be pulling together, not quarrelling amongst themselves," wrote Kennedy, "and the fact that Senators Morse, Anderson and other supporters of this bill, including myself, saw fit to secure its consideration and passage by another means does not, it seems to me, merit criticism from you at this time."[16]

Wounded by attacks on his civil rights record, and desperately seeking to control the damage to his support among blacks, Kennedy offered the *Chicago*

Defender an exclusive interview. It was published under the banner headline: "Kennedy Defends His Votes on Rights Bill in Senate." In an interview with reporter Ethel Payne, he denied having "sold out to the South" and continued to argue he had taken a principled position. "I realize that my action is difficult to explain," he acknowledged. "It would have been easy to just have gone along with those who voted to upset the usual order; but I felt there was a matter of principle involved. I have no apologies to make for my action."[17]

Had it not been for the unbending loyalty of the *Boston Chronicle* the backlash in Massachusetts would likely have been fiercer. In a remarkably generous editorial, the paper portrayed him as "a complex, not simple statesman, of such integrity that he does not please everybody all the time. . . . Many of our own people were displeased at his votes on the civil rights bill now before the Senate. From that vote some analysts have indeed drawn quite unwarrantable conclusions, owing to their failure to see that Senator Kennedy looks beyond the immediate to more distant and larger objectives. If he loses support in the process, that is the price which he is prepared to pay."[18]

Although Kennedy had temporarily alienated his black supporters, the response from southern Democrats could hardly have been more appreciative. Columnist John Temple Graves observed in the *Birmingham Post-Herald* that Kennedy's stance showed he was now capable of becoming the "living antithesis of Earl Warren," the liberal-minded Supreme Court chief justice, who had pressed for the *Brown* decision. Kennedy sent Graves a gracious letter of thanks, noting he was happy to have adopted a "moderate philosophy on behalf of the national interest" and to "feel a common bond with many southerners." Nor did he take exception at being labeled "the living antithesis of Earl Warren." Eastland, who had grown personally fond of his young colleague, also offered hearty congratulations, and went as far as to tell reporters he was prepared now to back Kennedy's bid for the presidency.[19]

∾

Even before Kennedy could finish thanking his southern supporters, the legislative battle entered a decisive new phase. Now the debate focused on Part III. In an earth-scorching speech, Eastland invoked the memory of Radical Reconstruction, warning that Part III would turn southern states once more into "conquered provinces" and was comparable with "the very worst form of Stalin tyranny." In a widely publicized Senate speech delivered on July 2, Russell complained that the measure was "as harsh as any proposed by the Radicals during Reconstruction" and would lead to "unspeakable confusion, bitterness and bloodshed in a great section of our common country." Vowing to fight "to the very death," he insisted that there would not be enough jail space to contain all the white southerners "who oppose the raw use of federal power to commingle white and Negro children in the same schools." But the very next day, Russell put aside his fiery rhetoric and brought the Southern Caucus together for a secret strategy meeting. A lengthy filibuster was out of the question, Russell explained. Instead, the Southern Caucus should rely on Johnson to strip Part III from the bill so long as they agreed not to paralyze the Senate.[20]

It was, however, Eisenhower rather than Johnson who ultimately played the decisive role in defeating Part III, by publicly expressing doubts about its constitutionality. On July 3, the president read, with mounting concern, a transcript of Russell's barnstorming Senate speech, which had raised the specter of federal troops enforcing the desegregation of southern schools. The prospect of his administration becoming enmeshed in a thicket of school desegregation cases terrified him. When asked by a White House reporter at the presidential press conference on July 17 whether Part III represented a wise extension of federal power, he replied, "Well no." It was a stunning turnaround, and one that torpedoed any hope of Part III's being enacted.[21]

Up in Boston, the NAACP refused to countenance defeat, and the following weekend took the unusual step of organizing an emergency statewide conference to lobby Massachusetts's two senators, Kennedy and Leverett Saltonstall. The conference brought together representatives of some 150 civil rights organizations from across the state, including liberal pressure groups like the American Civil Liberties Union (ACLU), the ADA, and the Jewish Community Council. Rather than appear in person, Kennedy dispatched Torbert "Torby" MacDonald, his most trusted friend at Harvard, who was now a popular Massachusetts congressman. Before flying to Boston, Kennedy aides warned MacDonald to expect a hostile reception from civil rights leaders, who were still smarting over Kennedy's vote on the procedural motion the previous week. MacDonald was nonetheless shocked by the degree of their animus. In the face of such open rancor, MacDonald mounted a spirited defense, citing Kennedy's long-standing support for civil rights. But his counterattack was blunted because he had arrived without any firm guarantee from Kennedy that he would support Part III. A telegram from the senator offered no illumination, for it simply noted, "I assure you an effective Civil Rights bill will be passed regardless of how long we have to stay in Washington."[22]

Eisenhower's withdrawal of support for Part III liberated Kennedy from what could have been an agonizing decision. Now that even moderate Republicans had turned against the measure, Part III was doomed, and Johnson and Russell no longer needed his support to defeat it. Since his vote was essentially irrelevant, Kennedy was free to come down in favor of civil rights without inflaming southern supporters. Two days before the issue came to a vote, he issued a press release declaring support for Part III. To strike the measure from the civil rights bill, he argued, would be akin to voting against the *Brown* decision. But since Part III was dead already, the drama had drained from the debate. Handed such an easy victory, Johnson could hardly conceal his delight, Knowland found it hard to hide his dismay, and Kennedy could hardly believe his luck.[23]

When the Senate debated the issue on July 23, Kennedy delivered a carefully nuanced speech, couching his support for Part III in terms that would least rankle southerners. Since there were ten "inherent safeguards" in the measure, he stressed, the region had little to fear. "Only if the President, the Congress, and the entire judicial system simultaneously fail their constitutional oaths and traditional reasonableness," he noted, "is there any danger of harsh and radical treatment under this bill." While speeches from other northern Democrats spoke of how Part III would transform the South by finally making good the promise of *Brown,* Kennedy devoted most of his speech to reassuring southerners that it would not lead to the dismantling of segregation. Kennedy advanced only one cautious endorsement of Part III, on the grounds it was being interpreted throughout America and "the watchful world" as a referendum on the Supreme Court's ruling. "My own endorsement of that decision," he said, "and its support in the State I have the honor, in part, to represent, has been too clear to permit me to cast a vote that will be interpreted as a repudiation of it."[24]

The following day the Senate voted by fifty-two votes to thirty-eight to strike the Part III from the bill. Kennedy had emerged unscathed—for while his vote was lauded by Massachusetts blacks, it caused little damage in the South. Even though the headline in the next day's *Boston Globe* read "Kennedy Risks the South's Ire in Stand on Civil Rights," his increasingly cozy relationship with the Southern Caucus remained intact, for the simple reason that Russell no longer needed his vote. Nonetheless, the *Boston Chronicle* described his speech as an act of great statesmanship. He had "emerged from that phase of the battle with glory and honor even though his side lost," it cooed, adding, "His national stature is further enhanced."[25]

With Part III defeated, the debate now moved on. The new question facing senators was how to deal with racist southern electoral officials who obstructed blacks from voting. In an effort to bar black applicants, registrars regularly asked poorly educated black sharecroppers to interpret complex passages of the state constitution knowing they would be unable to do so. Similarly, they scrutinized applications from black college professors looking for small errors of spelling or grammar as proof of "illiteracy." By contrast, uneducated whites were never disqualified, even though some could barely sign their names. Seeking to end this injustice, the civil rights bill called for recalcitrant voting registrars to be tried before a judge sitting alone in the absence of a jury, a measure favored by the Justice Department because of the difficulties in persuading all-white southern juries to convict errant officials. Predictably, Russell was implacably opposed, arguing that bench trials were not only unfair but unconstitutional. His argument was legally dubious, since bench trials were standard practice in civil contempt cases, the charge on which most racist voting officials would be indicted.

Senator Joseph C. O'Mahoney of Wyoming backed Russell and put forward an amendment to the bill, which became known as the "jury trial amendment." If adopted, it would ensure that voting officials stood trial before a jury. Like other southern Democrats, Johnson immediately threw his weight behind O'Mahoney's amendment, telling reporters, "The people will never accept a concept that a man can be publicly branded as a criminal without a jury trial." It was a clever distortion of the argument. As Johnson well knew, the debate turned on a much finer legal distinction, and one that Brownell believed would make the difference between a workable statute and a toothless act.[26]

This time Eisenhower understood the legal issues involved and was prepared to back his attorney general to the hilt. Like other leading Republicans, he also grasped the main political drawback of the amendment becoming law: Racist voting officials would still be in place before the congressional elections the following year and would bar tens of thousands of blacks from voting. Believing a new civil rights act would yield a rich harvest of newly enfranchised black voters, helping Republican candidates to make further inroads into the South, Eisenhower was unwilling to hand the southern Democrats an easy victory. He called a press conference on July 31 specifically to speak out against the amendment. Making a rare attempt to elucidate an issue, the president said it was not uncommon for contempt cases to be heard before a judge sitting alone, as defendants in such cases had no constitutional guarantee of a jury trial.[27]

Kennedy now faced the same political quandary. On this occasion, however, he assured black allies that he was unprepared to see the bill weakened further. In a telegram to Batson on July 10, he promised to support the civil rights bill "without crippling amendments." He offered NAACP official Alfred Lewis the same assurance. "On the jury issue," he wrote, "I assure you that I do not propose to support any amendment which would be contrary to long established judicial practice—in other words, I will not vote for any ruinous amendments with respect to the question of the right to vote or any other civil rights protected by the bill." When Clarence Mitchell arranged a meeting in Washington between Kennedy and a group of NAACP activists, the senator indicated once more that he would oppose the jury trial amendment. Asked toward the end of the meeting how he planned to vote, he stood up, gave a knowing nod and laughed. "You don't have to worry about me on that. I'm all right."[28]

Despite his repeated assurances, Kennedy hoped that Johnson would be able to negotiate some kind of compromise on the jury trial amendment that northern Democrats could agree to in good conscience and southerners would grudgingly accept. On this occasion, however, even Johnson seemed incapable of squaring the circle. With negotiations deadlocked, Sorensen warned Kennedy to be prepared for the worst. "If such [an agreement] is not forthcoming," he wrote in a secret memorandum, "you will have to play it by ear on each amendment, perhaps voting for some and against others." Kennedy would have to vote with the South on some amendments and with the North on others. The memo represented a turning point for Theodore Sorensen. A member of the ADA who had helped found a chapter of CORE in his home state of Nebraska, Sorensen had been an ardent supporter of civil rights. But now he was prepared to sacrifice principle for political gain. On civil rights, he was coming to share the cynicism of his boss. He ended his memorandum by reminding Kennedy, "Bobby Troutman wanted you to call him." Troutman was his most fervent southern backer.[29]

The politics of the jury trial amendment were complex. Kennedy found the legal arguments almost as fiendish. To help thrash them out, he turned for advice to three leading Harvard law professors—Arthur Sutherland, Mark De-Wolfe Howe, and Paul Freund. He asked all three the same question: Would the amendment weaken the bill? All three came back with the same answer: It unarguably would. "I am not impressed with the argument that wrong will be done to the defendants in contempt cases by denial of juries," Sutherland wrote. "Contempts have been tried without juries for many generations." In a second letter, sent three days later, Sutherland argued the amendment would cause "confusion and delay," making it harder to remove recalcitrant voting officials. For all that, Sutherland acknowledged that Kennedy would have to weigh political considerations against legal ones. If the choice was between an amended bill or no bill, he could be forgiven for voting with the South. "Your judgment of what is politically practicable is infinitely greater than that of anybody far from the scene of debate," he conceded. "If half a loaf is all that can be had, it is proverbially better than none."[30]

Like Sutherland, Paul Freund believed that the amendment was a blatant attempt to make the bill unworkable. The suggestion that all litigants had the right of a jury trial in contempt proceedings was "plainly unfounded." Writing on July 23, he made an impassioned plea for Kennedy to oppose the amendment. "I am afraid that many who have looked confidently to this Congress for the enactment of civil rights legislation will feel that the outcome has been 'to hold the word of promise to our ear. And break it to our hope.'" Like Sutherland, however, Freund penned a second letter, focusing on politics rather than legalities. While there was no question the amendment would lead to a "sacrifice of effectiveness," this had to be weighed against "the value of a more receptive statement on the part of the original opponents of the bill, a sentiment which presumably would filter down to the press and populace in the South." In the long run, that "state of mind," as he called it, "may be more important than the partial sacrifice of legal procedures involved in the compromise." Freund effectively presented Kennedy with the same advice as Sutherland: If the choice was between an amended bill or no bill at all, then voting for the amendment need not constitute a "betrayal of principle." Mark DeWolfe Howe, who was well-known at Harvard as a strong advocate of civil rights, arrived at the same conclusion as Freund and

Sutherland. If Kennedy thought the legislation was in jeopardy, he should support the amendment, since it need not involve "a surrender of principle to expediency." Speaking with Kennedy by phone on July 31, he suggested the legal arguments did not cut "too deeply," and that "a good deal is gained by the amendment" if it won southern acceptance of the civil rights bill as a whole.[31]

As the vote approached, Kennedy came under fierce political pressure from southern politicians, many of them militant segregationists. Foremost among them was Governor Marvin Griffin of Georgia, a foul-mouthed white supremacist, who once warned that blood would flow through the sewers of Atlanta before he allowed a single "nigger" to enter a white school. On July 26, Griffin wired Kennedy a telegram with a gentle reminder about his newfound popularity in the South. "Your many friends in Georgia are depending on you to aid us in guaranteeing trial by jury," he warned. Kennedy received similar thinly veiled threats from other southerners. Mississippi State Representative Thomas Upton Sisson hoped his decision would "not be such to make it difficult for those of us in the South who are genuinely for you to openly and ably support your nomination to high National Office at future conventions." North Carolina Governor Luther Hodges was more subtle, but the message was essentially the same. "Hope very much you will support jury trial amendment," he wrote Kennedy. "Still hearing good things about you and your future." Finally, Bobby Troutman chimed in. "Outside of Christianity," he suggested grandiloquently, "there is no greater safeguard for individual freedom than the jury trial—and every lover of freedom should strive to preserve it."[32]

As the vote approached, the pressures on Johnson were even more intense, since it appeared that Knowland had lined up enough support to defeat the amendment. For once the arithmetic favored the supporters of civil rights. With thirty-nine Republicans pledged to defeat O'Mahoney, along with ten Democrats, Knowland needed only one more vote for victory. In a desperate attempt to split the reformist camp, Johnson came up with an eleventh-hour ruse and planned to amend the amendment in the hope of making it more palatable to moderate Democrats, like Kennedy. The sweetener he had in mind was a "new civil right," as he beguilingly called it—a change to the federal code that would make it illegal to block blacks from jury duty, a widespread southern practice. Southern Democrats would get their beloved jury trials, while blacks, in theory at least, would be allowed to serve as jurors.

To introduce the revised version of the O'Mahoney amendment, Johnson needed a willing accomplice from the progressive wing of the Democratic wing. He chose Frank Church, an ambitious thirty-three-year-old freshman senator from Idaho, known as a supporter of civil rights. With O'Mahoney's prior knowledge, Johnson choreographed the entire scene. The "boy orator from Idaho" rose in the Senate that Wednesday night and called for the new amendment to be written into the bill. Then the theater played out. "O'Mahoney yielded, listened, then embraced Church's proposal as though he'd just heard it for the first time," wrote *Newsweek*. "It was a beautifully stage-managed performance." It also marked the turning point in the debate—the moment the tide shifted in Johnson's favor. More comfortable now with the wording of the new amendment, moderates like Warren Magnuson and Henry "Scoop" Jackson of Washington and Theodore Green and John Pastore of Rhode Island suddenly switched sides. Still, in order to secure a majority, Johnson needed the support of the junior senator from Massachusetts.[33]

Having secured the backing of Green, an eighty-nine-year-old liberal who was one of New England's most respected figures, Johnson hoped Kennedy would quickly fall into line. But as the vote approached, Kennedy continued to equivocate. With time quickly running out, Johnson tried to reach out to Kennedy through George Smathers. But the Smathers lobbying effort failed, and he suggested Johnson approach Kennedy directly. A meeting was quickly arranged, but even the Senate majority leader's famed powers of persuasion, "the Johnson Treatment," failed to have an immediate effect. At some point in the course of the next few hours, however, Kennedy changed his mind and decided to vote with the South. Precisely what provoked the sudden change of heart is impossible to say, but the meeting with Johnson may well have been critical. The support for the bill from his fellow New Englanders, Pastore and Green, probably also played a role, since it provided much-needed political cover at home. And he may have been influenced by the Harvard trio of law experts, who had all concluded that a weakened bill was better than no bill at all. (Just before he went in to vote, Kennedy told the ADA's Joseph Rauh that the advice from Harvard had been the main determinant.) The wording of Church's "amendment to the amendment" made the compromise palatable—it promised to mitigate the worst aspects of the jury trial amendment, and thereby enabled pro–civil rights moderates, like Kennedy, to vote for it in reasonably good conscience.[34]

Before announcing the decision publicly, Kennedy placed a phone call to Batson, realizing it would be better to convey the news in person rather than have her read it in the newspapers. "This made me feel terrible," Kennedy explained, but there was no other choice. If the amendment was defeated, he explained, southern Democrats would filibuster the entire bill to death. Batson was furious and ended the conversation feeling betrayed. She was convinced Kennedy had sold out to the South. She was unwilling this time to indulge him, and her personal relationship with him had never been at a lower ebb. His actions brought into question not just his judgment but his honesty.[35]

The night of the vote, the Senate chamber was packed, its galleries overflowing with journalists and curious onlookers. Word had spread through the capital's salons, clubs, and restaurants that the civil rights debate was about to reach its climax. Down below, the well of the chamber was a melee of clerks, ushers, and senators, but all eyes were on Johnson and Knowland. They wove through the arcs of desks, scribbling notes on heavily marked-up voting lists, looking more like bookies studying the form at the paddock of a racetrack. Knowland seemed the more anxious, knowing already that support for his position was draining away. That afternoon, in a last-ditch attempt to dredge up every single vote, he had dispatched an air force plane to Maine to fetch Senator Frederick Payne from the fishing lodge where he was recuperating from a heart attack. He had also recruited Missouri's Tom Hennings, who had been convalescing at his Washington home after surgery to remove gallstones. Hennings limped into the chamber with the help of aides.

Midway through the debate, Kennedy rose to his feet. Knowing that his support for the amendment would raise awkward new questions about his commitment to civil rights, he began with a stout defense of his voting record. He drew attention to his tireless support for civil rights legislation in the past, including Part III, and his efforts to revise Rule XXII. Yet the jury trial amendment posed a more delicate legal and philosophical dilemma: How could legislators protect the right to vote without sacrificing the rights of other citizens to enjoy full protection under the law? In searching for an answer, Kennedy stressed how he had sought advice from three distinguished Harvard professors, all of whom arrived at the same conclusion: that the amendment posed "no real obstacle" to the extension of civil rights. It was wrong to assume, he claimed, that southern juries were packed with racists, who would always side with recalcitrant voting officials. The people of the South were fair-minded and decent and, "ever mindful of the watching eyes of the Nation—and indeed the world—will convict those who dare to interfere with orderly legal processes." In any case, if ever the jury trial amendment was abused, Congress could change the law. Finally, Kennedy returned to the same argument he put to Batson the previous evening: that it was not worth jeopardizing the entire bill for the sake of the judge-only trials. "I consider it a mistake to insist dogmatically on the purity of the original act at peril to its large objectives," he said.[36]

Throughout the debate, Russell had sat with "his head back, his fingertips pressed together, sometimes closing his eyes when opponents' expressions oppressed him," according to one reporter. Nothing he heard from Kennedy would have made him flinch. The speech was less comforting for liberal opponents of the amendment, who believed Kennedy's arguments were overly legalistic and ignored the burning moral question. "There has been a great deal of talk in this chamber of the violators of injunctions, and we worry about the violators of the law," thundered Humphrey. "But what about the victims of discrimination? Where are the tears for them in this chamber?" After Kennedy had taken his seat, Leverett Saltonstall, his Republican Massachusetts colleague, also spoke out strongly against the amendment, arguing there was "no historic right or constitutional right to trial by jury in contempt cases," and that the jury trial amendment was designed to weaken the bill.[37]

Johnson finally brought the debate to an end. As he had throughout the controversy, he framed the whole question as a vote on whether the Senate should uphold the tradition of jury trials or overturn hundreds of years of English jurisprudence. "The tradition of trial by jury is deep within the heart of our liberty-loving people," he said. "Repeal that right, and our laws will become ineffective, except to incite disobedience."[38]

At midnight, after fourteen hours of debate, the clerk began to read out the names of the senators, a roll call received in almost perfect silence. Nineteen minutes later, with the votes tallied, the southern Democrats emerged victorious again. To the dismay of black supporters in Boston, Kennedy had cast his vote in favor of the amendment, helping it pass with a comfortable majority of fifty-one to forty-two. He had helped deliver Johnson's coup de grâce. Outside of the chamber, Richard Nixon angrily told reporters he had just witnessed "one of the saddest days in the history of the Senate, because it was a vote against the right to vote." Then, still bristling with anger, he marched up to Johnson and warned that the Republicans would soon press for tougher legislation. Knowland was inconsolable and was spotted crying in the Senate cloakroom. Kennedy, meanwhile, was seen congratulating Frank Church, whose last-minute amendment had turned the tide of the debate and allowed Kennedy to cast his vote with the South. Bumping into Church and his wife, Bethine, he was clearly in buoyant mood: "Frank did a great thing today," he said to the senator's wife. "He made it possible for me to vote for the jury trial amendment."[39]

Kennedy lost no time in trying to placate critics in Boston. He wrote a peace missive to Batson the very next day. Once more, he stressed that "the Southerners would have filibustered the civil rights bill if a jury trial amendment were not adopted and it would have been impossible to obtain cloture." He also drafted a letter to his old friend Herbert Tucker, assuring him his mind had been made up not by political considerations but legal arguments.[40]

Kennedy also reached out to Harvard professor Sam Beer, a prominent figure in the ADA. How could critics possibly question his commitment to civil rights, Kennedy asked indignantly, when he had cast a vote for Part III, a provision that "raised far greater issues of principle than did the long hassle over the jury trial?" Beer sympathized. "Naturally, I do not think that your vote was 'a betrayal of fundamental principles,'" he replied, although the jury trial amendment clearly opened up "vast opportunities" for evasion and delay. If there was a crumb of comfort, he concluded, it was that the amendment might create "some sentiment of acceptance" among white southerners.[41]

Later that week, Kennedy convened a meeting with Tucker, Edward L. Cooper, the executive secretary of the Boston NAACP, and Alfred Haughton, the editor of the *Boston Chronicle*, in a further effort to explain himself. The meeting had the desired effect—the paper decided not to editorialize against him in that week's edition. "The intrinsic nature of party politics caused Senators John F. Kennedy and Leverett Saltonstall of Massachusetts to stray from the narrow path of obligation to the paramount interests of the Bay State's Negro electorate," the ever-faithful *Chronicle* crowed, "but at the final tally both were found on the right side [when the civil rights bill finally was passed]." (Many of the *Chronicle's* readers reacted more angrily. Michael Allen, one of Kennedy's Massachusetts constituents, warned that Kennedy "will never be able to explain to the 'man in the street' the strange sight of his voting on the same side as Senators Eastland, Stennis and Talmadge."[42])

Apart from the *Chronicle,* the northern press was almost uniformly scathing in its indictment of Kennedy's vote. Columnist James Reston described his "eleventh-hour change of heart" as an attempt to impress southerners who "would not take kindly to any Presidential candidate who insisted on rejecting the jury trial principle." William S. White, the *New York Times* congressional correspondent, concurred. Whereas northern senators like Humphrey had been "hard civil rights men all the way," Kennedy had become a "stout bridge" to the southern and border states. The *New Republic,* the house organ of the liberal establishment, expressed deep discomfort "over Presidential aspirant John Kennedy's flirtation with Southern politicians."[43]

Not surprisingly, Kennedy's vote gained him almost universal acclaim in the South. Georgia publisher James Gray, the millionaire owner of the *Albany Herald* and a close political ally of Russell's, wrote to Kennedy to congratulate him on what "was not only the correct decision but one which will be extremely valuable to you in the future." Griffin Smith, a lawyer from Little Rock, was even more effusive. In breaking with his northern colleagues, Kennedy had "achieved an act of political courage comparable to those related in your book." Kennedy was delighted and basked in the goodwill. "In my judgment," he told Mississippi State Representative Thomas Upton Sisson, "this amendment improves the bill from both the Northern and Southern points of view." He was more direct about his motives in a letter to D. M. Nelson, the president of Mississippi College. "In my various votes, particularly that on the jury trial amendment," he told Nelson, "I attempted to understand the viewpoint of the South and to act accordingly." He even offered reassurance to segregationists. When a woman from Birmingham protested at his overall support for the bill in general, Kennedy wrote a conciliatory reply. "The present Civil Rights bill, is, I believe, a moderate one. In addition it would appear to me to be an error to overlook a significant factor: the Civil Rights legislation, if passed, will be effected by *SEVEN* Courts and juries considering Civil Rights cases will be *Southern* juries."[44]

Despite the hostile reaction from liberals and blacks, Kennedy remained staunch in his defense of his vote. Certainly, he did not consider them a betrayal of the black cause, telling black aide Harold Vaughan, "Harold, you're not in elected politics—you've got to understand the way the Congress works. Sometimes you've got to compromise." By telegram, he put the same argument to

Tucker. "My observation of the debate during the last several days led me to believe that the Southerners would have filibustered the Civil Rights Bill if a jury trial amendment were not adopted." He went on to argue that the compromise was also important in uniting North and South behind even an incremental advance of civil rights. "It seemed to me that this [the defeat of the jury trial amendment] would have placed all of us in an extremely difficult psychological position which was fraught with the most serious implications with respect to maintaining a broad base of support for a strong Civil Rights bill." This was his most explicit articulation up until this point of the logic underlying his increasingly gradualist approach. Progress was possible only with the backing, at best, or acquiescence, at worst, of southerners themselves—it could not be imposed from above.[45]

Days after the vote on the jury trial debate, Kennedy bumped into the NAACP's Roy Wilkins in the Senate restaurant, and the two men spent over an hour discussing his vote. As they talked, Wilkins sensed the senator "was coming to realize over the cold coffee and the numberous [sic] cigarettes that he probably had made a mistake as far as our side was concerned." But in fact Kennedy displayed little remorse. According to Wilkins, Kennedy did not consider "he had made a mistake in regard to his future ambitions" for "it was very important for him that Lyndon Johnson not be a foe." Kennedy was careful, however, not to alienate a black leader with so much influence, so in a letter to Wilkins the following day Kennedy said how much he had enjoyed their conversation and indicated that he looked forward to further opportunities to discuss civil rights over the coming months. "I regret that we have not established a closer working relationship in the past," he noted, "and hope that we may have the opportunity to do so in the near future."[46]

The civil rights bill came to a final vote on August 28, but with the jury trial amendment now appended, its passage into law became a mere formality. Only Strom Thurmond continued to sound the battle cry of massive resistance. On the evening of the vote he launched a marathon solo filibuster, sustaining himself through an all-night Senate session on malt tablets and party snacks. Thurmond rose to his feet at 8:57 P.M., and remained standing, with only a few brief interruptions, for twenty-four hours and nineteen minutes. It was the longest speech in Senate history. Russell looked on in dismay, worried that Thurmond's show of defiance would strengthen demands for a revision of the filibuster rule.

Thurmond eventually left the chamber, and two hours later the Senate passed the Civil Rights Act of 1957 by sixty votes to fifteen, a vote described by the *New York Times* as "incomparably, the most significant domestic action of any Congress in this century." With Part III eliminated, the bill was a fairly innocuous measure, and the jury trial amendment limited severely its application. For years to come, racist voting registrars would continue to bar blacks from participating in elections, knowing white jurors would never punish them.[47]

It was nonetheless an event of great historic importance, not least because it was the first time since 1875 that southern Democrats had failed to prevent a civil rights bill from becoming law. Moreover, its passage demonstrated the existence at last of a pro–civil rights bipartisan coalition, at a time when conservative forces had been dramatically weakened. Particularly noteworthy was the fact that no Republican voted against the bill. And voices of racial tolerance were emerging from the Old Confederacy. Both Estes Kefauver and Albert Gore voted for the final bill, as did Ralph Yarborough of Texas and George Smathers. So too did Lyndon Johnson, though for more self-serving reasons.

Throughout the two-month debate, Kennedy tried to straddle both sides. To appease northern supporters, he had supported Part III. To appeal to the South, he favored the jury trial amendment and opposed moves to bypass the Judiciary Committee. His positions were ideologically incoherent. He supported Part III, despite private misgivings about investing the attorney general with such strong injunctive powers. He opposed the jury trial amendment, despite his long-standing support for voting rights. What he tried to portray as reasoned judgments borne of reflection and belief were clearly little more than the result of careful political calculation.

For reasons of political geography, Kennedy's actions completely mirrored those of Johnson. Just as the Texan supported the civil rights bill to show northerners he had broken from the South, the New Englander voted for the jury trial amendment to reassure southerners he could disentangle himself from the North. But Johnson emerged from the civil rights debate with his reputation enhanced, while Kennedy came out looking opportunistic and unprincipled. He had made the twin mistakes of misjudging badly the mood of Senate liberals, who believed the only way to defeat the Southern Caucus was for northerners to band together; and of underestimating the growing militancy of black allies in Massachusetts, who viewed any form of compromise as a breach of faith. Singing "Dixie" might be pleasing to the South. But it sounded profoundly discordant in the North.

CHAPTER 5

❦

The Victory Room

Governor Orval Faubus of Arkansas, a soft-spoken lawyer from the Ozark Mountains, seemed a wholly unlikely figure to bring about the gravest crisis since Reconstruction between a state and the federal government. In the aftermath of *Brown,* Faubus had rejected the calls for "massive resistance" and even agreed to the gradual desegregation of classrooms in a handful of school districts as well as the integration of the state university. These decisions had brought a hail of criticism from die-hard segregationists. James Eastland called him "the most weak-kneed politician" in the South.[1]

Historically, Faubus had been impervious to such criticism. But he was facing a tough reelection battle in 1958, and so in the preceding fall he had decided to carve out for himself a new reputation as a hard-line white supremacist. Adopting vehemently racist rhetoric, Faubus challenged a federal court ordering the gradual integration of Little Rock's Central High School. Vowing never to allow a black child to walk through its gates, Faubus called out the Arkansas National Guard at the start of the new school year in September 1957, on the flimsy pretext that its presence outside the school gates would maintain order. But the guardsmen's true aim was to prevent the "Little Rock Nine," as the black schoolchildren seeking entry became popularly known, from entering.

On Wednesday, September 4, a day after the new school year was due to begin, a fifteen-year-old black schoolgirl named Elizabeth Eckford arrived at the gates wearing black sunglasses and a white-and-black-checked dress. A nervous-looking member of the Arkansas National Guard, barely old enough to be in uniform, blocked her way with an M-1 rifle. Unable to pass, Eckford turned and left. Her retreat drew mocking jeers from an angry crowd of parents who had lined the sidewalk from early that morning. Over the coming month, the Little Rock crisis came to symbolize the intransigence of the South, and Faubus became the living embodiment of massive resistance.[2]

Reluctant to intervene and aghast at the prospect of dispatching federal troops into the South to uphold the federal court order, President Eisenhower monitored events from his holiday cottage at the naval station in Newport, Rhode Island. But advisers told him he might soon have to take a stand. Secretary of State John Foster Dulles warned that global newspaper coverage of the crisis was "ruining our foreign policy" and "could be worse for us than Hungary was for the Russians." Attorney General Herbert Brownell believed that not only was the integrity of the courts at stake but so was the president's credibility. On September 14, Eisenhower summoned Faubus for talks in Rhode Island. During a twenty-minute discussion the president thought he had gained assurances from the governor that the court order would finally be obeyed. But when Faubus returned to Arkansas he immediately reneged on the agreement, an act of insubordination that led Eisenhower to take a much firmer line.[3]

On Monday, September 23, the Little Rock Nine tried once more to gain entry to the school, sparking scenes of gruesome violence. Mistakenly thinking a group of black journalists were the children themselves, some twenty local segregationists immediately gave chase. They kicked one of the reporters to the ground and struck him repeatedly in the face. Another black journalist was assaulted by a one-armed roughneck, whose dimpled stump flailed wildly from side to side. Somehow, in the maelstrom, the Little Rock Nine managed to slip unnoticed through a side door, and at 8:45 A.M., as the school buzzer sounded, the American flag was hoisted for the first time over an integrated Central High. Suddenly realizing the school had been breached by blacks, a white woman began to wail uncontrollably: "Oh God, the niggers are in the school. The niggers are in the school." Minutes later, two teams of neatly dressed schoolgirls trotted out onto the physical training ground to begin a game of softball, and the high school band could be heard rehearsing Felix Mendelssohn's "Spring Song." Yet for all the school administrators' attempts to project an air of normalcy, there was mayhem outside the gates. Panicked police commanders radioed City Hall with dire warnings that the mob was about to ransack the building. Fearing the black schoolchildren would be lynched, Woodrow Wilson Mann, Little Rock's reform-minded mayor, ordered their immediate removal. Central High's experiment in integrated education lasted precisely three hours and thirteen minutes.[4]

Eisenhower learned about the rioting as he drove toward the golf course. Only fourteen days before he had signed the 1957 Civil Rights Act into law. Now he made the momentous decision to dispatch troops into the South to enforce civil rights. Sherman Adams, Eisenhower's chief of staff, described it as his "most repugnant" act during eight years in office. But the violence, combined with Faubus's unreliability, forced his hand. First, he issued a public statement condemning the violence, and then, from the deck of his vacation home, signed a presidential proclamation ordering the mobilization of troops.

Brownell, alert to the political dangers of sending federal troops into the South, suggested they use federal marshals instead. But the former Supreme Allied Commander wanted the strongest possible show of power. Within hours, over forty C-130 and C-123 military transport planes headed from Tennessee toward Little Rock, carrying 1,000 paratroopers from the Army's 101st Airborne Division, an elite group known as the Screaming Eagles. It was the first time since Reconstruction that federal troops had been dispatched to the South and the first time in the twentieth century the government had used military force to compel equal treatment for blacks.[5]

Shortly before dusk on September 25, a convoy of twenty-six military vehicles rumbled through the streets of Little Rock to Central High, where paratroopers, dressed in full battle fatigues, assembled in formation on the lawns. Within hours, the school grounds were transformed into a makeshift military encampment, with tents thrown up on the tennis courts and emergency telephone lines threaded through the trees. By five the following morning, combat-ready paratroopers, with bayonets fixed, patrolled the main road leading to the school so that the Little Rock Nine could safely attend class. Later that morning, a U.S. army station wagon, protected in the front and rear by a convoy of jeeps, ferried the black schoolchildren to class.[6]

Appalled that a large section of Little Rock had effectively been placed under martial law, Faubus claimed the city was under military occupation. Herman Talmadge likened the paratroopers' arrival to the recent Soviet invasion of Hungary, while Richard Russell bemoaned the use of federal "storm troopers." Georgia Governor Marvin Griffin noted simply, "The Second Reconstruction of the south is underway."[7]

From the outset, Jack Kennedy tried to avoid being drawn into the crisis, fearing it would embroil him in further controversy. His only recorded comment came in early October in response to a question thrown to him by a reporter on Capitol Hill. "Neither mob violence nor the defiance of lawful court orders can ever be justified or condoned," he noted. "The Supreme Court's ruling on desegregation of schools is the law of the land—and though there may be disagreement over the President's leadership on this issue, there is no denying that he alone has the ultimate responsibility for deciding what steps are necessary to see that the law is faithfully executed." He was deliberately economical with his words—and deliberately evasive, as well. Though he agreed that the president had not overstepped his constitutional authority in dispatching troops to Little Rock, he did not address the question of whether he had been right to do so. Like the president, he framed the crisis as an issue of law and order, thereby avoiding the broader controversy: whether or not force should be used to execute school desegregation orders handed down by the federal courts. Unlike the president, who had referred to Faubus as a "demagogic extremist," he refrained from using such an accusatory tone. And other than his criticism of

mob violence—which even most southern lawmakers balked at—there was little, if anything, to anger his newfound southern allies.[8]

Despite its deliberately innocuous tone, the statement elicited an acerbic letter of complaint from Lloyd D. Bell, a South Carolina legislator. Bell vowed
thereafter to thwart Kennedy's presidential ambitions. "[W]e really hope you do
make an effort to obtain the nomination," he said, "so that we will have the
pleasure of voting and working for your defeat." Considering the criticism
wholly unfair, Kennedy wrote back noting how his votes during the 1957 civil
rights debate had drawn scorn from Adam Clayton Powell, Jr., and the black
press. "I tell you this not to seek your sympathy or support," he noted, "but to
illustrate the difficulties which face any man in public life who tries to follow his
conscience and considers each issue to the best of his ability on its own merits."
He then added, "No doubt you have encountered similar difficulties in your service in the Legislature."[9]

Commenting on how Kennedy's close ties with the South were now considered something of an embarrassment, *Newsweek* noted how "Democratic leaders"
thought his presidential chances were "seriously hurt by the Little Rock integration crisis." In the aftermath of the crisis, DNC Chairman Paul Butler had
made it clear that the party would not surrender to the South on civil rights,
and leading liberals like Chester Bowles of Connecticut and Governor W.
Averell Harriman of New York argued that the party would be much better off
without southern segregationists.[10]

Fearing further antagonism, and more unfavorable press coverage, Senate
staffers considered canceling an October visit to Mississippi, where Kennedy
was scheduled to speak before a dinner of the Young Democrats in Jackson. But
Kennedy was eager to make his first journey to Mississippi, and especially intent
on meeting its governor, James P. Coleman, whose delegation backed him during the second round of voting at the 1956 convention. Once they decided to
press ahead with the trip, aides hoped it would go unnoticed by the Washington press corps. As Ted Sorensen told Frank Smith, the Mississippi congressman who sponsored the visit, "our fingers are crossed on this whole event, and
we are particularly hopeful that there will be no out-of-state publicity before or
after Jack's arrival."[11]

Kennedy's hope of avoiding controversy was short-lived. As he flew into
Jackson on October 17 he immediately found himself under fire. Hours before
his arrival, in an attempt to sabotage the visit, Wirt Yerger Jr., the chairman of
the Mississippi GOP, highlighted the senator's recent support for Part III, and
then invited him to clarify his position on the Little Rock crisis.

Before the trip, Sorensen had drafted a speech for Kennedy that painstakingly avoided the question of civil rights. But Yerger's challenge was difficult to
brush aside, especially since a gang of northern reporters, who had learned
about the trip, already were en route to the dinner at the Heidelberg Hotel,

where 2,000 people were crammed into the Victory Room banqueting suite awaiting Kennedy's arrival.

As his limousine headed toward the hotel, Kennedy decided to respond directly to Yerger's challenge. Seated in the back of the car, he made some last-minute alterations to Sorensen's speech, frantically scrawling notes in the margins and crossing out large chunks of the prepared text. Eventually, he gave up on editing Sorensen's version and wrote out a completely new speech in childlike capital letters.[12]

By the time his audience had finished their $5-a-plate banquet of prime roast beef, the speech was ready. After a brief introduction from Congressman Smith, Kennedy rose to his feet looking rather "fidgety," according to one reporter. As so often during speeches in the South, he began by paying homage to Lucius Lamar, who had tried to soothe tensions in the aftermath of the Civil War. It was important to remember his legacy, particularly as the nation faced similarly testing times "of tension and bitterness"—his first, albeit oblique, reference to Little Rock. "I remind you tonight of his courageous call for unity because Democrats North and South, I believe, stand tonight in urgent need of Lucius Lamar's inspiration and message." Admittedly, it was easy at times such as these, he continued, "to put local popularity ahead of sectional prejudices and national responsibility. It is easy—too easy—to talk of third parties, of leaving the Democratic party . . . It is easy for some in the North to blame our troubles on our southern colleagues—it is easy for some in the South to blame your troubles upon Northerners." Even for those who had overindulged on cheap bourbon at the ninety-minute drinks reception, it was clear that Kennedy was about to pick up Yerger's gauntlet. Kennedy acknowledged he had never seen "eye-to-eye" with the South on every issue, and that segregation was one of them. Then, turning to his handwritten notes, he said, "I have no hesitancy in telling you the same thing I have said in my own city of Boston [the words "in every part of the country had been crossed out"]. That I have accepted the Supreme Court's decision on desegregation as the law of the land. I know that we do not agree on that issue—but I think most of us do agree on the necessity to uphold law and order in every part of the land." Initially his comments were met with an ominous silence. But the mood changed almost immediately, when Kennedy issued a challenge of his own. Where did Wirt Yerger stand on the question of troops? Did he agree with Eisenhower?[13]

The mood in the room immediately shifted. Kennedy had aroused his audience's partisan instincts, and the issue was no longer North versus South, but rather Democrat versus Republican. The audience offered Kennedy the most unexpected standing ovation of his eleven-year political career. "The crowd came to its feet, alive, roaring and stomping its approval," observed a reporter from *Time*. "Kennedy had won it by his own display of courage and by turning all good Democrats against odious Republicans." A local congressman was astonished by the reaction, commenting: "I never thought I'd see anybody in Central Mississippi speak up for integration and get a standing ovation." Even the *Clarion Ledger*, a staunchly segregationist newspaper, gave the performance a rave review. "His jokes were cleverly told," its reporter wrote, "his history was well-documented and presented, and his brief handling of the integration crisis was as masterfully done as it could have been in trying circumstances. On integration, he simply said that he accepted the law of the land, then tossed it, still scorching hot, on to the backs of absent and outnumbered Mississippi Republicans, to draw a laugh that he hoped, no doubt, helped his charitable audience forget."[14]

After the banquet, Kennedy stayed overnight at the governor's executive mansion and drank into the early hours with Eastland and his Mississippi senatorial colleague John Stennis. "Mississippi Democrats, who have expressed keen interest in the coming of Senator Kennedy, are now given new momentum for their political conversation," wrote the *Clarion Ledger*, which headlined the story: "Political Huddle Here Significant?" Indeed it was. Kennedy was forging alliances in advance of the 1960 campaign and had identified the South as one of his strongest areas of support. To cap his visit, Kennedy was allowed to spend the night in the magnificent, wood-carved bed used by two-time Governor Theodore Bilbo, the foul-mouthed prophet of southern racism. In Mississippi, it was an honor akin to sleeping in the Lincoln Bedroom in the White House.[15]

Flush with the success of his trip, Kennedy instructed aides to issue a press release trumpeting the speech as soon as he arrived back in Washington. They quickly produced a statement painstakingly crafted to appeal to both North and South. "Kennedy was applauded at the end of this statement and received a standing ovation at the close of his address," it noted, "although many Southerners were quick to express their disappointment."[16] Its dual message worked almost to perfection. Adam Clayton Powell, Jr., a strident critic during the civil rights debate, offered hearty congratulations, noting, "I think you did very well with a very difficult situation." And there was praise, too, from leading southerners. Governor Coleman saw the speech as further evidence of Kennedy's political promise. "I think he is our best Presidential prospect for 1960," he told *Time*, "and I am all for him." The columnist Arthur Krock, who toured the South shortly afterward, discovered that virtually every politician spoke favorably of the speech—valuable information that he quickly relayed back to the senator.[17]

For Kennedy, the speech was a turning point. In the wake of *Brown*, Kennedy had thought it wise to avoid altogether the issue of civil rights. His appearance in Mississippi demonstrated, however, that it could be turned to his advantage. If he chose his words carefully enough, he could position himself as a unity candidate acceptable to both segregationists and progressives.

Over the course of the next twelve months, Kennedy formulated his thoughts more fully on the Little Rock crisis and its implications in a series of letters to constituents. They showed he had emerged as a full-fledged gradualist on the question of school integration. At a time when many of his northern colleagues were pressing for the federal government to accelerate school desegregation— among them Joseph Clark, the newly elected senator from Pennsylvania who had arrived in Washington that year determined to organize a liberal rump capable of challenging the Southern Caucus—Kennedy advocated incremental reform, with the pace set not by Washington but local communities. Like the Warren Court, he favored deliberation over speed. "I wish to say emphatically that I am fully in accord with the decisions of the Supreme Court," he wrote Dr. Leroy Augenstine in early 1958, "and I believe that there is no course open to any citizen but to effectuate as rapidly as socially possible, the decisions of the courts." But he suggested the timetable "is purely one of local option," adding, "I think it would be inappropriate for the Federal Government to step in and tell local communities how they should proceed with the integration of their schools." Only a few months after endorsing Part III, Kennedy was already distancing himself from that position.[18]

Kennedy also weighed in on the separate but related question of whether Eisenhower had been justified in deploying troops. Kennedy held that the show of force had been disproportionate though lawful. "It is obviously debatable whether the President did the right thing psychologically or politically," he wrote Anthony Silveira in the summer of 1958. "But I do think what he did was constitutionally permissible." To Thomas Bennet, a constituent in Roxbury, he offered greater clarification: "I think there is a very real question whether timely action and assertion of presidential leadership could not have made unnecessary the action which the President at length did take in the sending of troops. Obviously, this is a very blunt and unpleasant solution which should be avoided, if at all possible."[19]

Kennedy believed that Washington should intervene only in exceptional circumstances, and that the military enforcement of civil rights was far from ideal. He failed to be persuaded by the argument that the smack of firm presidential leadership could have a strong deterrent on unruly segregationists: that a massive federal response might be the best way to confront massive resistance. Largely because Eisenhower had been so resolute in dealing with the crisis, there was not a comparable showdown between the federal and state authorities until the "Battle of Ole Miss" a full five years later. Eisenhower's decisive action also frightened Richard Russell, who feared now that segregation could no longer be preserved.[20]

∾

By the end of 1957, Kennedy had become one of Washington's most talked-about political celebrities. That year alone, he was awarded the Pulitzer Prize for *Profiles in Courage* and made his first appearance on the cover of *Time*.

When, after two unsuccessful pregnancies, Jackie Kennedy gave birth to a daughter, Caroline, on November 27, 1957, there was a welter of favorable press coverage, and soon Kennedy's younger brothers, Bobby and Ted, began attracting attention. That summer, *Look* magazine published an article entitled "The Rise of the Brothers Kennedy," including no less than sixteen photographs of Jack and Bobby. In early September the *Saturday Evening Post* headlined a story "The Amazing Kennedys." With astounding prescience, its author, Harold Martin, predicted Massachusetts's first family could look forward to the day when "Jack will be in the White House, Bobby will serve in the Cabinet as Attorney General, and Teddy will be the Senator from Massachusetts."[21]

Facing reelection the following year, Kennedy seemed invincible. It was hard to find a single Republican in Massachusetts who believed that he could be defeated. The only area of potential weakness was in Roxbury and Jamaica Plain, the black neighborhoods of Boston, where dissatisfaction about his 1957 votes threatened to spill over into the Kennedy campaign. While it was inconceivable that black resentment could prevent him from winning, Kennedy realized a poor showing would raise fresh doubts about the strength of his liberal credentials.

To complicate things further, in the spring of 1958 he came under hostile fire for his burgeoning relationship with southern politicians from a wholly unexpected source—Roy Wilkins, the executive secretary of the NAACP. Wilkins had built a national reputation on his talent as an administrator rather than as an orator. He lacked the showmanship of Adam Clayton Powell or the grandiloquence of Martin Luther King, Jr., and his lifeless speeches seldom generated much interest from reporters. At the beginning of 1958, however, Wilkins decided to adopt a more combative tone, partly to raise his public profile and partly to cement his leadership of the NAACP.

Wilkins used a visit to Pittsfield, Massachusetts, in April as an opportunity to deliver a speech excoriating Kennedy for his record on civil rights. The oration, before an audience of 500 at Pittsfield's Masonic Temple, was deliberately provocative. Wilkins organized his speech around the explosive image of a photo of a smiling Jack Kennedy with his arm draped casually over the shoulder of Marvin Griffin, one of the south's ugliest segregationists. To Wilkins, the image was not only repugnant but loaded with meaning—a graphic reminder of Kennedy's marriage of convenience with southern Democrats during the 1957 civil rights debate. "No pal of Griffin can possibly be a pal of mine," shouted Wilkins. "Griffin thinks I'm an animal. . . . You shouldn't find Negroes who vote for men who don't favor Negroes' rights." In fact, there was no photograph of Kennedy embracing Griffin. Eager to lend drama to his hard-hitting speech, he invented the entire story.[22]

Kennedy was stunned when he read about Wilkins's speech. He was aware the NAACP had been disappointed by his 1957 votes, but he thought he had repaired the damage during his chance meeting with Wilkins in the Senate restaurant shortly afterward. Only a few months later, Kennedy had been invited as special guest to an NAACP banquet, where he had impressed Wilkins with his easy charm. When a photographer tried to take a picture of Wilkins, his wife, Minnie, and the senator, Mrs. Wilkins instinctively stepped back so the two men could be photographed alone. But Kennedy would have none of it. "Oh, no, Mrs. Wilkins," he said, with a flirtatious smile. "You get in here with us, too." Kennedy was mystified by how their relationship could have soured so quickly.[23]

Kennedy was also truly furious that Wilkins had maligned him unfairly. To set the record straight, Kennedy fired off an angry letter to Wilkins. He pointed out he had met the governor on just two occasions—once during the 1956 convention and during a speaking engagement at the University of Georgia the year after—and that no photographer had been present at either meeting. It was unfair to conjure up a fictitious image, and then use it as a "political device." He challenged Wilkins on the subject of his civil rights record. "I ask you in all seriousness whether you believe my civil rights record over the past twelve years—or even the past year—rates such an attack in my home state." He went on: "I do not claim to have made no mistakes whatsoever in twelve years, nor do I assert that I have been able to participate as vigorously in this field as in others." He argued his support for Part III—"the really key vote," which was "vigorously criticized in the South"—demonstrated a deep-rooted commitment to the black cause.[24]

Wilkins waited three weeks before even replying to Kennedy's letter. When he did, he was unapologetic. "Since the Southern record on the denial of the vote was so flagrant, and so shameful, and of so long a duration," he wrote, referring to the jury trial amendment, we "should have had the non-quibbling support of non-Southern members." And while he admitted no photograph had ever been taken, it easily could have been. "Your friendly reception by Deep southerners easily conjures up in the minds of Negro citizens a picture of you arm in arm with them," he wrote. "It was this picture—figuratively—that I was calling up." Still angry, Kennedy shot back: "You state in your letter that I was hailed by the Dixiecrat leaders of South Carolina, Georgia and Mississippi. I have never appeared at a Democratic dinner in either South Carolina or Georgia—my only appearance in Mississippi was the speech in which I endorsed the Supreme Court desegregation decision and call for law and order in every part of the land—and I cannot name even a handful of leaders in these states who have 'hailed' me."[25]

Wounded by Wilkins's attack, Kennedy realized drastic action would be needed, since he was in real danger of being viewed as a southern apologist. But he was running short of black allies in Boston. He had alienated Ruth Batson, his close ally since 1952, with his wavering support on the civil rights bill and realized he could no longer rely on her support. Kennedy therefore decided to recruit a husband-and-wife team of Washington-based black attorneys to help repair his battered reputation.[26]

Belford and Marjorie McKenzie Lawson were a well-connected black power couple with a vacation home on Martha's Vineyard and a flourishing K Street law practice. Belford Lawson could also boast an admirable résumé: He had graduated from Howard Law School a year ahead of Thurgood Marshall, the preeminent black American lawyer of the time, who as a young attorney had argued a number of civil rights cases before the Supreme Court. Now he was the president of Alpha Phi Alpha, the country's preeminent black fraternity, which gave him a nexus of contacts in some 300 chapters, with an estimated membership of 35,000 men. Though nowhere near as famous or influential as Wilkins, Lawson was nonetheless prominent enough to act as a useful counterweight. Belford Lawson was so busy running his law practice, however, that he could not devote much time to Kennedy. But his wife, Marjorie, threw herself wholeheartedly into the project. Extraordinarily impressive in her own right, Marjorie held a law degree from Columbia and served as legal counsel for the National Council of Negro Women, which gave her an entree all over the country.

Reveling in her self-styled role as Kennedy's "black ambassador," Marge Lawson spent many weekends throughout 1958 traveling the country on Kennedy's behalf. She quickly realized the magnitude of her task. At the NAACP's annual convention in Cleveland, Ohio, in July, Wilkins delivered another withering attack. When Lawson informed Kennedy, he erupted in anger and fired off a strongly worded letter to the NAACP headquarters in which he complained that he was being victimized. "Certainly the evidence supports this," he moaned. "You came to Pittsfield in the middle of my campaign for reelection to say that my record (a solid civil rights record for twelve years, as contained in the memo I earlier sent you) did not deserve the support of Negro voters—while, according to the local press, treating comparatively lightly my Republican colleague who voted against Title III." It would be unfortunate, he said, "if an 'iron curtain' of misunderstanding were to be erected between our two offices," and suggested a meeting to clear the air.[27]

By accusing Wilkins of cozying up to Vice President Richard Nixon, the likely Republican candidate for president in 1960, Kennedy had made him only angrier still. With relations between the two men in deep-freeze, Lawson and Sorensen lobbied hard over the next three months in the hope of engineering at least a mild rapprochement before the November election. It became an urgent priority, as strong evidence emerged over the course of the summer that Wilkins's attacks were injuring Kennedy among black voters. Polls conducted in June by Louis Harris, Kennedy's official pollster, indicated a disturbing decline in the level of black support since the 1952 election, at a time when backing from other voting blocs, like the Italians and Jews, was holding firm. While Harris suggested 74 percent of Massachusetts blacks planned to vote for

Kennedy, 32 percent of black voters agreed with the statement "He has had a bad stand on desegregation." Harris suggested the criticism stemmed from two sources: first, "a fairly widespread belief that Kennedy has made a 'deal' with Southern Democrats for the Presidency, born, of course, of the Southern support he had in the 1956 national convention"; and second, his "hedging" during the 1957 civil rights debate. "Obviously, this weakness is not proving to be an over-all handicap, for he appears destined to win reelection by a record margin," noted Harris, who was worried more by the political embarrassment a drop of black support might cause. Kennedy's Republican opponent Vincent Celeste, from East Boston's waterfront district, was exacerbating the problem by making civil rights a central issue of his campaign, selling voters throughout Massachusetts on the idea that Kennedy was on the side of the Faubuses and Eastlands.[28]

Belford Lawson warned of "brewing trouble" if relations with Wilkins deteriorated further.[29] Lewis Weinstein, a lawyer from Boston with close ties with the NAACP, went further, telling the senator that the relationship had "reached a critical state." Knowing it was time to call a truce, Kennedy asked Weinstein to approach Kivie Kaplan, the Boston philanthropist and NAACP board member, who had been supportive in the past. "There appears to be a continuing personal and political vendetta directed at me by the national staff of that organization," Kennedy complained to Weinstein, "and it will be very helpful to have a real friend on the board." In June, the senator's office hastily arranged a tea reception for local black party activists at the Boston Professional and Businessmen's Club. It grandiosely billed the event as "[o]ne of the greatest tributes ever given to a Massachusetts legislator." After Vaughan and Belford Lawson had delivered fulsome tributes, Kennedy "reiterated his determination to see that all citizens of America enjoy full and equal rights," in the words of a press statement released afterwards.[30]

Ruth Batson did not join the tribute to Kennedy. She pressed Kennedy to strengthen his stance on civil rights and called for a crisis meeting with Sorensen. With the Massachusetts NAACP scheduled to meet in Boston in July, Batson suggested Kennedy send delegates a strongly worded personal message restating his commitment to civil rights. Without hesitation, Sorensen agreed, and Kennedy soon put his name to a telegram stressing his continued support for Part III and a change in the filibuster rule. Kennedy was still concerned that Batson was preparing to attack him publicly at the NAACP convention, so he invited her to his Bowdoin Street apartment, giving her the chance to unleash her anger in private instead. Batson did just that and made little attempt to conceal her contempt for Marge Lawson. She asked him to explain why he could not have found "a qualified black in Boston" to run his "black campaign."[31]

The Bowdoin Street meeting was a partial success. The NAACP delegates offered a reassuringly positive response to Kennedy's telegram, and Batson mounted no public attack on his record. Afterwards, Kennedy sent her a warm letter of appreciation, noting: "Again many thanks for your consistent friendship, Ruth, in what I know have sometimes been difficult times."[32]

Batson promised to vote for Kennedy in November, but she refused to campaign on his behalf. In an awkward meeting, she explained to Lawson that she had felt "personally violated" by the senator because he had "said one thing and done another" during the 1957 debate. Other local blacks, like Rheable Edwards, who had once tried to persuade Kennedy to join the NAACP, were "even more vocal," according to Lawson, who was able, however, to cajole Herbert Tucker into participating in the campaign. "Mr. Tucker's decision to join forces with us did not mean he brought along the rank and file of his [NAACP] membership," Lawson said later, "nor was it generally believed that he tried to change their attitudes except by his own example."[33]

In August, in a further attempt to set right his relationship with influential black opinion leaders, Kennedy tried to forge closer ties with the editors of all the main black newspapers and magazines in the country. He contacted the editors of the *Amsterdam News, Jet, Ebony, the Norfolk Journal and Guide*, the *Afro-American* group of papers, the *Pittsburgh Courier*, and the *Chicago Defender*. He asked to be put on their subscription lists and extended a fresh invitation to visit him when next they were in Washington.[34] The charm offensive worked. P. L. Prattis, the editor of the *Pittsburgh Courier*, wrote back to say that Wilkins's Pittsfield speech was grossly unfair. "I do not see how the points Mr. Wilkins tries to make can balance in any way your outstanding record on behalf of all Americans," wrote Prattis, who promised to commission a series of articles over the coming weeks setting the record straight. The *Philadelphia Afro-American* also offered valuable support, by accusing Wilkins of blundering with his reference to a fictitious photograph.[35]

∽

Escalating violence in the South in the wake of *Brown* gave Kennedy a fresh opportunity to reaffirm his civil rights credentials in the period leading up to the November election. In the year following the *Brown* decision, militant segregationists had tried to bomb the civil rights movement into submission by setting off a string of explosions intended to kill, maim, and intimidate individuals and organizations. Terror attacks, using crude, homemade explosive devices, had punctuated the Montgomery Bus Boycott. Martin Luther King, Jr., and other leaders of the campaign had been targeted in their homes. After the city's buses were integrated, the bombing campaign intensified, with fresh attacks on four of the city's Baptist churches, a local gasoline station, the homes of two local black ministers, and, for a second time, King himself. The violence spread beyond Montgomery. In Birmingham—or "Bombingham," as it quickly came to be known—there were a spate of racially motivated attacks, and the city's Fountain Heights section, which was the home to the city's most affluent black citizens, quickly became known as "Dynamite Hill." The campaign of terror even spread to other minority groups—Jews were targeted in Nashville, Tennessee, Jacksonville, Florida, and Charlotte and Gastonia, North Carolina, provoking additional demands for government protection.[36]

Blacks and other minorities feared for their lives, and liberals were outraged by the horrific violence. But segregationists were also deeply disturbed by the bombings, realizing that they would further mobilize national sentiment against segregation. Even Faubus indicated "unqualified disapproval" of the bombings. In the absence of a legislative response from the Eisenhower administration, Kennedy decided to take the initiative himself by introducing an anti-bombing bill that would make it a federal crime to import or transport between states any explosives that were to be used unlawfully. In a Senate speech on May 28, he argued that the recent spate of bombings had followed a clear pattern and was targeted deliberately against people or property associated with "the civil rights discussion," as he delicately put it. "Such blatant disregard of law and order, disrespect of properly constituted authorities and contempt for our democratic institutions must be stopped," he warned. If local law enforcement agencies were unable or unwilling to take effective action then the federal government had no choice but to intervene. Leading segregationists, like Sam Ervin of North Carolina, readily lent support, since the bombers were doing the South immeasurable damage.[37]

In the anti-bombing legislation, Kennedy had found a clever means of pursuing two seemingly contradictory ends: helping him repair relations with blacks, while strengthening his ties with leading southern figures. Kennedy found himself in the odd, but highly desirable, position of standing at the head of a coalition that included northern and southern Democrats. The bill also managed simultaneously to support civil rights and states rights: It restricted its reach to bombings carried out with explosives transported over state lines.

In response to a bomb attack in October on a synagogue in Atlanta, Kennedy strengthened his proposals. He amended his first anti-bombing bill to cover false bomb threats and the use of explosives in labor disputes. It included new provisions that would allow the police to arrest suspects who escaped into neighboring states. But the checks on federal power remained in place. Kennedy rebuffed demands from liberal Democrats to insert a provision making it a federal offense to use explosives to deny people their constitutional rights. In a telegram to Lyndon Johnson, which was leaked to reporters, Kennedy called for the bill's expeditious passage through the Senate, while at the same time he urged the FBI to pursue suspected bombers more aggressively.[38]

As Kennedy's reelection campaign reached its climax, the anti-bombing bill became the centerpiece of a three-point civil rights program designed to bolster black support. The program called for the bill's swift enactment and the revision of Rule XXII. Kennedy also restated his commitment to Part III. Despite his private reservations about investing the Justice Department with so much power, he had little choice but to publicly support the measure, since it was the chief legislative priority of the NAACP. It was also endorsed by groups such as the ADA, ACLU, the Anti-Defamation League (ADL), and the AFL-CIO, for whom it had become something of a liberal litmus test. Kennedy neatly set out his proposals in pamphlets mailed to black voters throughout Massachusetts.

Kennedy's civil rights program marked another turning point in his approach to civil rights. It was the first time he had ever called his proposals a "program," a subtle change, but one that Marge Lawson thought was important because it cast him as a serious-minded reformer. Just as deliberately, the Kennedy program mirrored the first three demands of a policy manifesto drawn up that year by the NAACP. Lawson promised the senator that the program would help bring NAACP activists, like Tucker and Batson, "back into the fold."[39]

The civil rights program, however, turned out not to be Kennedy's strongest selling point in the black community in Massachusetts. A year earlier, Kennedy had hired a black secretary, a move that enabled him to claim the distinction of becoming the first New England congressman to appoint a black member of staff. Kennedy had come up with the idea himself, in hopes that the appointment would help deflect criticism from his 1957 votes. Vaughan had tracked down a suitable candidate, a young Roxbury woman, Virginia Battle. After the senator's staff made sure her typing and secretarial skills were up to snuff, so as to avoid accusations of window dressing, Battle was installed in Kennedy's Boston office in December 1957. Though it had shades of tokenism, the tactic worked brilliantly, for it came at a time when black voters seemed as impressed by largely symbolic racial firsts, which brought recognition, as by more substantive reforms. Realizing Battle could be a tremendous asset to the campaign, in October Vaughan organized the distribution of thousands of pamphlets throughout black neighborhoods, featuring her smiling face on the cover.[40]

In ways small and large, the rehabilitation of Kennedy's public image was going well, but aides remained concerned over how the black press would interpret his 1957 votes. So they distributed a six-page dossier, rebutting the charge he had sold out to the South. To emphasize the point, the document quoted heavily from a blistering editorial in the *Shreveport Times* in Louisiana, which noted: "Kennedy's true political philosophies . . . were . . . quite unacceptable to the South on the issue of integration. . . . He is certainly far from being a conservative politically." The dossier also highlighted the Joseph P. Kennedy, Jr., Foundation's record in support of black causes. The foundation was a war chest that the senator frequently dipped into to win over various constituencies. The dossier noted, for instance, that Jacqueline Kennedy recently had presented a

YMCA in a predominantly black neighborhood of Washington with a "$1,000 birthday gift." The foundation had also given $450,000 for the establishment of the Joseph P. Kennedy, Jr., Memorial Community Center in Harlem and contributed $25,000 for the construction of a new gymnasium in Roxbury for the Massachusetts Boys Club ("Boston is justly proud of its first citizens," reported the *Pittsburgh Courier,* "they have magnanimous heart and have an indelible imprint wherever they go.") Reporters were also reminded that Kennedy had donated the $500 prize money from his Pulitzer Prize to the United Negro College Fund. Showing an acute appreciation for the benefits of political philanthropy, Kennedy bestowed the check in May during a small ceremony in his Beacon Hill apartment, staged primarily for the benefit of reporters from the *Boston Chronicle* and *Roxbury Citizen.*[41]

Vaughan wanted to do still more to erase the memory of 1957 and to ensure a substantial black turnout for Kennedy in the election. He planned a star-studded gala evening in Boston's opulent Statler Hilton, at which Illinois Senator Paul Douglas, one of the main architects of the 1957 Civil Rights Act, would present Kennedy with an award for his service to the cause. The only problem was that Douglas was unsure whether to pay tribute to his young colleague. "Douglas pondered what to do," according to his chief legislative assistant, Howard Shuman, since "he had qualms about it because of Kennedy's lack of vigor" during the 1957 civil rights fight. Eventually, though, he agreed to accept, and the black-tie event was scheduled for October 18, just over two weeks before Election Day. Six hundred invitations were sent out in the name of the Massachusetts Citizens Committee for Minority Rights, a phantom committee set up by Harold Vaughan and Herbert Tucker, which was a barely disguised front for the Kennedy campaign. Along with Douglas, Vaughan invited Nat King Cole, whose presence would lend the evening some show business glitter and guarantee prominent coverage in black newspapers.[42]

The evening was a surprising success. Douglas delivered a gracious speech, helpfully avoiding the controversy surrounding the jury trial amendment. Afterwards, Douglas went through with the presentation of the vanity award. More notable, however, was Tucker's reading of a letter from Roy Wilkins. Wilkins's criticisms had softened considerably over the previous three months, largely in response to the intensive lobbying campaign by Marge Lawson and Sorensen. They had targeted not only the civil rights leader himself but also members of the NAACP board (which, in Lawson's view, had "built up considerable pressure"). Wilkins had eventually succumbed partly because he did not want to be put in the position of having no influence with Kennedy if ever he became president. "It seems altogether fitting and proper that a committee of Boston citizens should pay tribute to Senator John F. Kennedy," Wilkins had written Tucker, "and although the NAACP as an organized body does not endorse candidates, we are happy that you, as an individual and as an officer of the

Boston branch, are participating in this affair. In response to your inquiry, we are pleased to report that, according to our records, Senator Kennedy has one of the best voting records on civil rights and related issues of any Senator in Congress." The letter was greeted with loud and sustained applause.[43]

As the clapping petered out, Kennedy launched into one of his most thoughtful speeches on civil rights to date. He outlined in detail each proposal of his three-point civil rights program. He called again for the enactment of Part III and implied that the violence in Little Rock could have been averted if the attorney general had been given the power to intervene earlier: "I believe that many of our current problems, in which our children may be the unwilling and unfortunate pawns of violent bigotry and lawlessness, could have been avoided if Title III had been enacted." Never before had Kennedy pushed so strongly for Part III, but coming less than two months after he had told Dr. Leroy Augenstine that "it would be inappropriate for the Federal Government to step in and tell local communities how they should proceed with the integration of their schools," it lacked the ring of authenticity.[44]

Coverage of the event was overwhelmingly positive. This came as no surprise—the campaign had invited two of the most influential black newspaper publishers, John Sengstacke, vice president of the *Chicago Defender*, and Carl Murphy, of the *Baltimore Afro-American*, to attend the event. The *Boston Chronicle* celebrated the evening with typical hyperbole, asserting that it cast Kennedy as one of Massachusetts's most promising ever lawmakers, with "greater potential than even Charles Sumner or Daniel Webster." Other black newspapers throughout Massachusetts published a syndicated account offering an equally extravagant commentary of the evening, written, anonymously, by Vaughan. Afterwards, Vaughan also had the letter from Wilkins reprinted on a poster, which was plastered on billboards all over Boston's black neighborhoods. The campaign for black votes had ended on a redemptive note: After the damaging prevarications of 1957, Kennedy had made peace with Wilkins and been publicly pardoned by Douglas.[45]

Kennedy went into Election Day with tremendous momentum in the black community. Much to the Republicans' disappointment, he actually improved upon his 1952 vote totals among blacks. In Ward 9, where the black vote was most heavily concentrated, he won 3,393 votes compared to Celeste's 560, a marked improvement on his 1952 showing. Four years earlier, he had taken a 72.8 percent share of the vote. Now, it was 85.6 percent. With similar gains from other voting blocs, Kennedy's margin of victory was a stunning 874,608 votes. It was the largest plurality ever recorded by any candidate seeking any office in Massachusetts history.[46]

Newspapers around the country were lavish in their admiration, nowhere more so than in the South where the coverage had almost a favorite-son feel. The stridently segregationist *Albany Herald* described it as a "staggering victory" and observed that "Kennedy's magnetism is widely felt throughout Dixie." Describing Kennedy in the most glowing terms as a presidential front-runner, the paper quoted Mississippi Governor James P. Coleman as saying the senator was "sober and temperate on civil rights. He's no hell raiser or Barnburner." Delighted by the upbeat coverage, Bobby Troutman, his long-time Georgian cheerleader, gleefully pointed out, "Your many friends in Georgia are greatly impressed with your splendid victory." Strom Thurmond even sent a letter of congratulations.[47]

Praise also poured in from blacks. A few weeks after the election, Wilkins sent a congratulatory letter, predicting that Kennedy would secure the presidential nomination and have little difficulty lining up black support. "[Your] civil rights record is one of the best in the Senate," he wrote, "with only our disagreement on the jury trial thing as a debit. . . . I am glad our evaluation of your civil rights record was useful."[48]

After a difficult twelve months, marked by almost continual anxiety about how to court the Democratic Party's divergent wings, Kennedy emerged from the 1958 election in a commanding position. He had repaired his relationship with Wilkins and cemented his support in the South with his adroit handling of the Little Rock riots and the anti-bombing legislation. And he had demonstrated to the Democratic Party leadership in the North that he was an astute politician and campaigner. Two years before the 1960 election, Kennedy was already the front-runner for the presidential nomination.

CHAPTER 6

❧

The Liberal Democrat

The 1958 elections transformed the character of Congress. Both the House and the Senate became much more progressive institutions. In the Senate, the influx of Democratic freshmen, the biggest since Franklin Roosevelt's 1936 landslide, meant the party now enjoyed a commanding majority of sixty-four seats to thirty-four over the Republicans, a net gain of fifteen seats. In the House, the Democrats achieved a net gain of over fifty seats, an electoral windfall that gave them a majority of 130. Within the Democratic Party itself, the winds were shifting: In the Senate, nine of the new arrivals were liberals, including Minnesotan Eugene McCarthy, one of the leading figures from the liberal bloc in the House, and Philip A. Hart of Michigan, a close political ally of G. Mennen Williams, the country's most liberal governor. Most had close ties with organized labor and had run on aggressively progressive platforms. Given the Democrats' dominance of the Senate, many quickly obtained more prestigious committee assignments than those to which they would normally have been entitled as freshmen.

Emboldened by such clear-cut evidence of a liberal revival, Democrats arrived in Washington complaining that the Democratic Policy Committee, a body chaired by Lyndon Johnson, did not reflect the mood either of the party or the nation, and that the Southern Caucus exerted far too much power. In the House, liberals formed the Democratic Study Group to rival, and ideally demolish, the conservative coalition. In the view of Pennsylvania Senator Joseph Clark, a long-time advocate of civil rights reform, the chamber was "a different place" following the 1958 elections. McCarthy claimed his fellow newcomers "changed the whole Senate."[1]

The face of the Republican Party was changing as well. The small band of Republicans who survived the Democratic landslide came mostly from the party's liberal wing, like Hugh Scott in Pennsylvania and Kenneth Keating in

New York. Boasting strong civil rights credentials, Nelson Rockefeller, the scion of New York's banking dynasty, beat Averell Harriman to become one of only fourteen GOP governors nationwide. In the California gubernatorial race, William Knowland, the former standard-bearer of conservative Republicans, was defeated by Edmund G. "Pat" Brown, one of the Democrats' most progressive young leaders.

Liberals were ascendant politically, and they were also dominating national debate. Civil rights issues were moving higher up the liberal agenda. Already in 1956, in a seminal article for the *Reporter*, Arthur M. Schlesinger, Jr. had called on progressive thinkers to shift their focus away from the "quantitative liberalism" of the New Deal/Fair Deal, which emphasized economic issues, and toward "qualitative liberalism," which would concentrate on "bettering the quality of people's lives and opportunities," by means including expanded civil rights. He elaborated on these ideas in his 1959 polemic *The Shape of National Politics to Come*. He argued that for all the economic and social changes of the fifties, the Eisenhower presidency had produced a "period of passivity and acquiescence in our national life." Segregation, he believed, was one of the primary sources of the national, post-Sputnik malaise. But he assured his readers that, given the cyclical nature of American history, it would naturally give way to an era of "affirmation, progressivism and forward movement." In *The Affluent Society*, his 1958 bestseller, John Kenneth Galbraith likewise urged Americans to renounce the self-serving materialism that had dominated American life in the 1950s and become more public-spirited and civic-minded. More accurately than any right-wing thinkers, Schlesinger and Galbraith were able to neatly articulate the national mood.[2]

For southern Democrats, now outnumbered in the Senate almost two to one by northerners and westerners, the midterm election results were a source of mounting concern. Southern moderates like Albert Gore, Estes Kefauver, Ralph Yarborough, and George Smathers were voting more regularly with their northern colleagues, and the once indomitable Southern Caucus was beginning to splinter. Russell, who had been described the previous year in the *New York Times* as the "leader of a lost cause," began to worry that there might be some truth to the characterization. He also doubted the loyalty of senators like Smathers, whom he derisively referred to as "Saturday night states righters." During a speech in February before the Georgia General Assembly, he conceded the southern voting bloc had "not only lost the support of many of those from other sections on whom we once relied, but the representatives from the states of the Old Confederacy no longer present a common front." In the midterm elections, just about the only solace for segregationists had come from Little Rock, where Congressman Brooks Hays, a racial moderate who had tried to mediate between Eisenhower and Faubus, was defeated by Dale Alford, a loud-mouthed segregationist. Given the liberal triumph elsewhere, it was a small consolation.[3]

In an increasingly divided Democratic Party, Kennedy's anti-bombing legislation was one issue around which the party could unite. Flush with his landslide victory in Massachusetts, Kennedy returned with renewed vigor to the bill, hoping it would bridge the chasm with his party and solidify his reputation as a unity candidate in advance of the 1960 presidential election. Needing a southerner to co-sponsor the bill, he turned to Sam Ervin, a genial former judge, who had signaled his support for the measure earlier in the fall. Like many southern Democrats, Ervin had come to believe that vigilantism was hardening northern opinion against the South and doing the region "an incalculable injury in the eyes of the nation which has demanded that the Congress take some action in this field," as he said in December. Anti-bombing legislation would create new laws "rightly belonging to the Federal government" and prove to a watchful nation "that the South does not believe in lawlessness or in a policy of pure negation."[4]

On December 14, Ervin agreed to issue a joint statement with Kennedy. The amended bill would mandate new penalties for the illegal use or transportation of explosives (a maximum fine of $1,000 and a maximum jail sentence of one year) and make the death sentence available in cases where victims were killed. They formally introduced the revised bill on January 13, 1959, after enlisting thirty-three co-sponsors. "Regardless of the divergent views many of us express upon civil rights," Kennedy noted in a press statement, "I know that all members of the Senate and all citizens condemn this use of force and the attempts at intimidation. . . . We must put a stop to it, and this bill should provide necessary machinery."[5]

From Kennedy's viewpoint, the relationship with Ervin was the most brilliant of pragmatic alliances, because it placed him at the head of a powerful coalition of northern liberals and southern conservatives. But Marge Lawson was aghast. "This is something that we should have talked about before the sponsorship was sought," she scolded Kennedy in a memorandum. "Maybe we could have devised something less potentially risky. . . . I am put in the ridiculous position of trying to sell Senator Ervin to the Negro press and I diminished my influence even when I succeed." Then she implored him to avoid any further southern alliances, warning that "seemingly inconsequential maneuvers can have troublesome consequences." The memorandum ended with the biting admonishment: "we cannot afford to express pragmatism as a doctrine."[6]

Kennedy dismissed Lawson's attack. Ervin's co-sponsorship would, he knew, make it easier to line up broad-based support for the bill. In the short term, his political instincts proved right, for the bill's list of backers soon came to include an eclectic crowd of northern liberals, like Paul Douglas, and pigheaded segregationists, like Herman Talmadge. By mid-January 13, 1959, thirty-nine senators had put their names to the bill. It was enough to force President Eisenhower to propose his own anti-bombing measures, which were eventually incorporated into the 1960 Civil Rights Act, passed the following May.[7]

Kennedy's easy embrace of Ervin was part of a broader strategy to court party bosses, labor leaders, fellow lawmakers, and state chairman from all over the country in his bid for the presidential nomination. But, as Lawson predicted, his desire to reach out to segregationists rendered him vulnerable to liberal attack. In January, the *Baltimore Afro-American* carried a scathing personal assault by the Reverend M. C. McKenny, which accused him (under the headline "Well Known Fact") of being "in cahoots with southern rebel Senators." "As you know," Kennedy wrote Herb Tucker on January 24, "this is sheer propaganda, has no basis whatsoever, and is completely irresponsible." Hoping he could "presume upon our friendship to ask you to undertake another chore," Kennedy requested that Tucker write a letter of rebuttal. Three weeks later, Tucker dutifully issued a corrective. "There is no more consistent supporter of civil rights legislation," Tucker wrote the *Baltimore Afro-American*. "Senator Kennedy has never compromised on any of these issues and has always been in the forefront of the battle for civil rights."[8]

Over the course of the spring, Kennedy continued to reach out to blacks in an effort to repair any lingering damage to his reputation. He accepted an invitation to address the United Negro College Fund in Indianapolis, where, in an elegantly worded speech, quoting Lincoln, Pericles, and Bismarck, Kennedy returned to a well-worn theme. He spoke of the "irrationality of racial discrimination" and once again linked it to the ongoing battle against communism. The eradication of prejudice, he said, was an "essential act of justice—in this world of crisis it is also an urgent requirement of national security." Young black students should "raise their sights beyond the difficulties of racial integration at home to see the challenges of our contrasting universe. . . . Here old prejudices are not entrenched—race is not important—talent is all that counts."[9]

When the speech ended, a line formed through the length of the hall. Members of the audience clamored for Kennedy's autograph. The scene fascinated James MacGregor Burns, a political scientist from Williams College, who was conducting research for his forthcoming biography of Kennedy. As he reflected later, "hardly anyone in the line talked about the speech, they seemed interested only in meeting the attractive young man who had delivered it. He had satisfied them intellectually and attracted them visually—but he had not aroused them spiritually." Perhaps it was his description of racism as irrational rather than immoral. Perhaps it was his failure to highlight the indignities facing southern blacks.[10]

April brought another, more significant, opportunity to woo skeptical blacks—the chance to chair the newly created Senate Foreign Relations Subcommittee on African Affairs. Kennedy was perennially interested in foreign affairs, but this committee in particular would also identify him more closely with the subject of African nationalism. The collapse of colonialism and the emergence of self-determined nation-states was a source of immense self-pride for black Americans—it was even thought to explain the precipitous drop in sales for skin whiteners and hair straighteners at the end of the 1950s. Kennedy, of course, viewed the subject of decolonization through the lens of his vehement anticommunism. With Africa becoming an increasingly important Cold War battlefield, Kennedy considered American support for the anticolonial movement as one of its key foreign policy priorities. He had outlined his stance in a blistering speech in July 1957, which assailed the Eisenhower administration for its failure to support Algeria's independence from France. Equating western imperialism with Soviet imperialism, he argued that "the single most important test of American foreign policy today is how we meet the challenge of imperialism, what we do to further man's desire to be free."[11]

For all these reasons, Kennedy was delighted to chair the subcommittee, and be so closely associated with an issue of such rising importance. And over the coming months, Kennedy referred to Africa in a number of set-piece speeches. During an address at New York's Waldorf-Astoria Hotel in June, he called on America to adopt a "strong Africa policy," by increasing economic aid, providing technical assistance, and helping produce an African regional economic plan. Otherwise, American would be outstripped by the Soviet Union, which already was carrying out "economic and educational activities." In a second speech devoted exclusively to African affairs, which he delivered in Lincoln, Nebraska, in October, he spoke of the "revolution" underway in Africa and America's need to respond to it in practical ways, out of geopolitical necessity. "Within ten years," he noted, "African nations alone may control 25 per cent of all UN votes." If Washington did not offer support, he argued, Moscow unquestionably would. With little risk of alienating key southern supporters, Kennedy hoped the speeches, along with his more frequent meetings with African diplomats, would boost his reputation among black skeptics. When Kennedy met with Ade Thanni, a government official from Western Nigeria, Senate aides made sure a photograph of the two men was sent to 159 black newspapers across the country.[12]

But once again Kennedy managed to squander whatever goodwill he had accumulated with his Indianapolis speech and his chairmanship of the Africa committee. Suspicions surfaced in the summer about his ties to the white supremacist John Patterson of Alabama, whom Kennedy invited to a secret breakfast meeting at his home in Georgetown in July. Patterson had first risen to prominence in the mid-1950s as the state's attorney general, when he had attempted to crush the Montgomery bus boycott through an endless stream of court injunctions. Having failed to defeat Martin Luther King's Montgomery Improvement Association, Patterson shifted the focus of his legal onslaught to the NAACP. He filed court suits to prevent the organization from raising money in Alabama or even recruiting new members. When he campaigned for the governorship of Alabama in 1958, Patterson then formed an informal pact with the Ku Klux Klan, which supplied hundreds of campaign workers and thousands of dollars in funding. He was soon installed in the governor's suite at the State Capitol Building, with an office overlooking King's Dexter Avenue Baptist Church.

Patterson was driven by two consuming desires: to demolish the civil rights movement and to wipe out the mobsters who had conspired in the 1954 murder of his father, a crusading state attorney general, who had tried to destroy a mob-run gambling operation in Phenix City, Alabama. It was the murder of his father that first brought Patterson into contact with Kennedy. In 1957, at the annual convention of the Alabama League of Municipalities, he listened with mounting approval as the senator delivered a hard-hitting speech against the mob. From that moment on, he decided to support the New Englander's campaign for the presidential nomination and by early 1959 claimed to have become a "fairly close personal friend."[13]

On trips to Washington, Patterson would regularly visit Kennedy's Capitol Hill office. But in July, Kennedy invited him for breakfast at his Georgetown townhouse, a far more intimate setting. Patterson arrived that morning accompanied by two of his closest aides, Sam Engelhardt, the head of the Alabama White Citizens' Council and one of the state's most outspoken segregationists, and Ed Reid, an influential party activist, whom Kennedy had asked to arrange some southern speaking engagements. The conversation over breakfast was fairly unexceptional, but before leaving Patterson pledged his support for Kennedy's candidacy. Realizing how inflammatory an actual endorsement would be for both of them, Patterson carefully refrained from using that word. He also suggested that they keep their meeting a secret.[14]

By the time the governor had flown back to Montgomery, however, rumors had spread that Patterson had become the first southern Governor to offer Kennedy his formal endorsement. The *Montgomery Advertiser,* Alabama's most conservative newspaper, struck a highly disapproving tone, and accused Patterson of betraying both his religion and region by coming out in favor of a northern Catholic. But the swirl of conjecture was far more damaging to Kennedy. His close personal relationship with a devout segregationist was incendiary enough. But the presence at the breakfast meeting of Engelhardt, Alabama's leading "country club Klansman," compounded Kennedy's problems. In his home town of Tuskegee, Engelhardt was behind a notorious local ordinance, which deprived virtually all local black citizens of voting rights in municipal elections.[15]

Northern reporters immediately posed the inevitable question: What had Kennedy promised in return for Patterson's endorsement? The answer seemed glaringly obvious to a group of leading civil rights campaigners in Alabama, who suspected Kennedy had agreed to "go slow" on school integration if ever he became president. Aubrey Williams, a white civil rights activist from Montgomery, described the meeting as "one of the most shameless pieces of cynicism in politics in recent years." In a letter to DNC chairman Paul Butler, which was quickly passed on to Kennedy, Williams asked what "price" had been paid for the deal. "[I]t must be assumed that it was considerable," he suggested, "for John Patterson is not looked upon, in Alabama, at least, as a generous man."[16]

Baseball legend Jackie Robinson, who had been disgruntled by Kennedy's votes during the 1957 civil rights debate, also expressed outrage. Only the previous month, Robinson had falsely accused Kennedy of attending the Southern Governors' Conference. Now he charged Kennedy with agreeing to downplay civil rights in return for Patterson's endorsement. Robinson signaled his displeasure by refusing to have his photograph taken with Kennedy at a New York dinner. Kennedy was particularly rattled by the snub from Robinson, inarguably the most famous black figure in America. As Belford Lawson recalled, "That occasion made a tremendous impression upon him. Kennedy was hurt by Robinson." Fearing a repeat of the Wilkins debacle, Kennedy therefore asked Chester Bowles, a Connecticut congressman, to make peace. A former advertising executive with close ties to the civil rights movement, Bowles was especially well qualified to serve as an emissary. He immediately sent a letter to Robinson offering firm assurances that Kennedy had no intention of foot-dragging on civil rights. Bowles claimed that in meetings with the senator, they had discussed civil rights on numerous occasions "and he has not only said the things I hoped he would say but he said them in a way that carried very great conviction." After reading the letter, Robinson complained that Bowles had failed to address the central question raised by the breakfast meeting: In the absence of a deal over school desegregation, why had Patterson described Kennedy as a "friend of the south"? Still, he conceded that Bowles's endorsement "changes my feelings considerably."[17]

Worried that Robinson's criticisms could easily undo all her good work over the past twelve months, Marge Lawson looked for other ways to mollify the baseball star. After learning that he was about to set up a scholarship enabling Kenyan students to attend American universities, she suggested the Kennedy Foundation establish a similar fund. Good philanthropy, she implied, would make good politics, and Kennedy could simultaneously demonstrate his "commitment to the international struggle." She then offered a more long-ranging and cynical reason to help: By supporting the Kenyan students, the Kennedy Foundation might soon come to rival the Rockefeller Foundation in the field of civil rights, she suggested, "thus depriving Mr. Rockefeller of an advantage should he become the Republican [presidential] candidate." Lawson was starting to think like a Kennedy.[18]

Lawson knew the Patterson meeting had caused lasting damage. That July, she traveled to the NAACP annual convention with a deep sense of foreboding, fully expecting a hostile reaction from the organization's rank and file. Still, she was taken aback at the level of rancor. Over the course of the week, Lawson hosted a series of informal parties in her hotel room for black delegates, but the charm offensive backfired, since the breakfast meeting dominated every discussion. NAACP activists were convinced Kennedy had agreed to a quid pro quo: to go soft on school integration in return for Patterson's endorsement.[19]

After she returned to Washington, Lawson presented Kennedy with the unvarnished truth: He was in serious trouble with blacks over his burgeoning relationship with Patterson. "What seems to bother them even more than the alliance itself is the nature of the agreement," Lawson warned. "What seems clear is that the critics cry louder" over the relationship between Kennedy and the South than anything else. "We would have been in very good shape," she said, "but for the Patterson endorsement." The only item of good news was that Wilkins did not seem overly concerned by the breakfast meeting and said Kennedy was just as liberal as Hubert Humphrey, one of his chief rivals for the presidential nomination.[20]

For Lawson, the NAACP convention was a jolting experience. It was the first occasion when she truly appreciated the full measure of Kennedy's "Negro problem," as she called it. From then on, she took it upon herself to help deepen his understanding of civil rights, convinced that he had only a fragmentary knowledge of the situation. She tried to impress on him most of all that blacks would no longer accept second-class citizenship; they had been infused with what King described as "the fierce urgency of now." "There is a very perceptible attitude among Negroes that the timetable on first-class citizenship must be advanced," Lawson typed, in a lengthy memorandum laying out her case. Black delegates in the key northern states, like Michigan, Pennsylvania, Illinois, and New York, would opt for a candidate who not only understood the new mood of blacks but was prepared to respond to it. Gradualism and tokenism would no longer suffice.[21]

Lawson wanted Kennedy to sever his ties with the South, and signal his intentions by delivering a widely publicized speech highlighting the need for Part III. "We know it won't pass," Lawson admitted, but it would help erase the memory of the Patterson meeting. "The idea is to go down fighting and thus convince the critics," she advised. "The importance of making this stand transcends a balancing of the relative importance of the southern vote and the Negro vote."[22]

Lawson's advice might well have gone unheeded had it not been echoed, less than a week later, by a more influential source—Ted Sorensen. In an attempt to bring sharper tactical focus to the campaign for the presidential nomination, Sorensen had come to believe Kennedy should position himself at the liberal edge of the party. It was a strategy borne of necessity, for it was now certain that southern delegations would line up behind Lyndon Johnson. On October 19,

Sam Rayburn announced the formation of an unofficial Johnson for President Committee and a campaign headquarters was established in Austin. Its mainly Texan staff members hoped to go "All the Way with LBJ."[23]

Evidence had also begun to emerge that Kennedy's Catholicism was beginning to harm him below the Mason-Dixon line. Religion was a complicating factor for Kennedy in the South, particularly because the region's Catholic clergy were among the strongest proponents of compliance with *Brown*. Faced with these new hurdles, Sorensen believed that Kennedy's best hope of winning the nomination lay in attracting support from the party's northern bosses— leaders of delegate-rich states where blacks were growing in influence. To continue singing "Dixie," Sorensen predicted, would do him more harm than good—especially since the party had tilted to the left after the 1958 elections.

In early August, Sorensen sent the senator a memorandum that posed a simple question: "Should there be a re-evaluation of how we are going to approach the South?" Sorensen was convinced he already knew the answer. He recommended a mass mailing to black activists across the country in which Kennedy could set out his record in full. Sorensen believed it was far stronger than the Senator was given credit for. In drafting it, Sorensen would make sure to portray him as a committed progressive rather than a gradualist.[24]

Though unwilling to sever completely his ties with segregationists, before Sorensen's push Kennedy had already begun to engineer a rapprochement with Democratic Party liberals, who disapproved of his record on McCarthyism and civil rights. In January, in a transparent attempt to identify himself with a cause dear to liberal hearts, he had co-sponsored legislation to repeal the loyalty oath, a measure inserted into the new National Defense Education Act that required schoolteachers to take an anticommunist pledge. He had also formed a brain trust to advise him on domestic issues, which met for the first time in December 1958. It was dominated by liberal intellectuals from Harvard and the Massachusetts Institute of Technology—Schlesinger and Galbraith foremost among them.[25]

In foreign affairs, too, Kennedy had begun to endorse the position papers of the liberal-dominated Democratic Advisory Council and asked Chester Bowles, one of its most influential members, to become an adviser. "I knew my primary importance to Kennedy was that I would associate him . . . with skeptical liberals," Bowles said later. A brand-name liberal with an impeccable record on civil rights—as the governor of Connecticut, he had established the country's first State Commission on Civil Rights and outlawed segregation in the Connecticut National Guard—Bowles could also help Kennedy reach out to black voters.[26]

In a further attempt to blunt liberal criticism, Kennedy staffers entered into a close collaboration with James MacGregor Burns, who had been commissioned by a New York publishing house to write a campaign biography. Burns, who had been offered a job in Kennedy's Senate office after running for Congress as a Democrat in the 1958 elections, had already assured Sorensen he planned to write a "pro-Kennedy" biography, which would "strengthen his standing with liberals and voters generally." Sorensen was most anxious about Burns's interpretation of the McCarthy censure motion, an episode that liberals had neither forgotten nor forgiven. But he was also concerned how the book would deal with the 1957 civil rights debate. He stressed to Burns that Kennedy had voted for the controversial jury trial amendment only after consulting with three Harvard constitutional law experts, all of whom were prominent liberals.[27]

Burns accepted this argument. "When it came to the substance of the bill," he eventually wrote, "Kennedy was all militancy." Assessing Kennedy's overall performance during the 1957 debate, Burns then asked whether he had shown a profile in cowardice? "His outspoken support of Section 3 [Part III] and his pledge to help vote the bill out of Eastland's embrace if necessary would indicate that the answer was no. Certainly, however, he showed a profile in caution and moderation." Sorensen was delighted with the final draft—even more so when Burns agreed to a number of late editorial changes that presented Kennedy even more favorably. Burns replaced the term "conservative" with "moderate," added a passage outlining Kennedy's opposition to the anticommunist loyalty oath and predicted leading liberals like Bowles and Adlai Stevenson would serve in Kennedy's administration, should he win the election. Such was their delight with the final product that when the book was published in January 1960, the Kennedy campaign purchased hundreds of copies and mailed them to liberal skeptics around the country. Eleanor Roosevelt, whose lingering hatred of Joe Kennedy, Sr., now extended to his eldest surviving son, was at the very top of the mailing list.[28]

At the beginning of 1960, Kennedy began to collect his foreign policy speeches for a book entitled *The Strategy of Peace*. The process brought him into even closer contact with leading liberal intellectuals and, in particular, a thirty-three-year-old academic named Harris L. Wofford, Jr., who had first started writing speeches for him in 1957. A law professor at the University of Notre Dame, Wofford had first gravitated toward Kennedy because of his interest in reshaping foreign policy toward Asia, Africa, and Latin America. But Wofford was also an expert in civil rights issues as well as foreign affairs. During a period living in India with his wife, Clare, he had become fascinated with Gandhi's philosophy of nonviolent protest, an interest he shared, on his return to America in 1950, with a little-known civil rights activist named Martin Luther King, Jr. Over the course of the decade, the two men forged a close friendship, and Wofford's interest in the civil rights movement began to deepen. While teaching at Notre Dame Law School, he became legal counsel to Father Theodore Hesburgh, a member of the newly formed United States Civil Rights Commission (CRC), and even edited the body's first report in 1959.[29]

Robert Kennedy approached Wofford as he was writing up the report and asked him to work more closely with the senator on civil rights. Initially Wofford demurred, largely because his workload that spring was too heavy already. But in September, Joe Kennedy contacted Father John Cavanaugh, president emeritus of Notre Dame, and asked him to intervene. It was the most powerful indication yet of the closer attention now being paid to civil rights by the Kennedy high command. Impressed by the senator and eager to work on a national campaign, Wofford quickly agreed. Over the next twelve months, his contacts within the civil rights movement proved invaluable, as did the trust that black leaders placed in him. The first white graduate of Howard University Law School, Wofford was viewed as "one of them."[30]

By the fall of 1959, Kennedy's strategy was falling into place, and he convened a meeting on October 28 which brought together fourteen of his top political strategists at Hyannis Port. The group was entirely male except for Marge Lawson. Her presence demonstrated once more the growing importance the campaign attached to attracting black delegates. Kennedy announced the plan for the campaign. The road to the White House, the senator announced, would pass through the North and West. He would cultivate the support of big state bosses like Mayors Richard Daley of Chicago and Robert Wagner of New York, and Governors Pat Brown of California, G. Mennen Williams of Michigan, Mike DiSalle of Ohio, and David Lawrence of Pennsylvania. There would be few detours into Dixie. With most southern leaders almost certain to line up behind Johnson, it was wise, he said, to distance himself from segregationists, since any premature support from the South could upset his North-centered campaign.[31]

Kennedy anticipated that his main difficulty in securing the nomination would be overcoming the long-held anti-Catholic bias within the Democratic Party, especially from Catholic co-religionists like Lawrence, who continued to believe that only a Protestant could win the presidency. It was therefore crucial to build momentum early in the campaign to demonstrate that he was a viable candidate, and so he planned to win the nomination by contesting the primaries. If he could win in heavily Protestant primary states, like Wisconsin and West Virginia, he would prove to his party that America was ready for a Catholic president.

The group discussed which of the sixteen scheduled primaries Kennedy should enter. New Hampshire, traditionally the first-in-the-nation, was a must. Maryland might be important, as well. At this point, Lawrence O'Brien reminded the group that Maryland's black vote, concentrated in the inner-city precincts of Baltimore, might well decide that state's primary. He suggested they set up a speaking engagement before a black audience in the city at the earliest opportunity. Lawson promised immediately to arrange a meeting with editors from the *Baltimore Afro-American,* Maryland's most widely read black newspaper. Kennedy then moved on, ticking off a list of other possible primaries he might enter—Wisconsin, West Virginia, Indiana, all of which were progressive states, with a distinctly New Dealish hue. A combination of political geography, a primary calendar front-loaded with progressive states, and the simple fact that his main challenge came from Johnson dictated that Kennedy should run as a liberal.[32]

Delighted by her elevated status, Marge Lawson left Hyannis Port with a fresh determination to exert more influence over the campaign. On her return to Washington she typed out a long position paper addressed to Robert Kennedy, the newly appointed campaign manager, calling for a bold approach to civil rights aimed at black party activists in California, Pennsylvania, Ohio, and Michigan. "If Negro leaders are for us," she argued, "this is a big moral advantage that Governors and state chairmen cannot escape." Lawson offered to work as an advance woman, traveling ahead of Kennedy to set up meetings with local black leaders. She suggested he nurture closer ties with the black press, especially the *Pittsburgh Courier*. He should also meet with Martin Luther King, Jr., while a high-profile trip to Africa in his capacity as chairman of the African Affairs Subcommittee would be hugely beneficial, especially if a group of prominent black Americans accompanied him.[33]

Robert Kennedy was deeply ambivalent about Lawson's advice. Even though the campaign had settled on a northern strategy, he considered it unwise to antagonize southern leaders, who controlled approximately a quarter of convention delegates. Even after the Hyannis Port meeting, he attempted to expand his brother's southern support, by secretly making overtures to Herman Talmadge, who was arguably even more extreme than Patterson. Robert Kennedy was intrigued, however, by the idea of a trip to Africa and seriously considered adding it to the candidate's schedule in December. Eventually, though, it was decided that the demanding speaking itinerary at home precluded any foreign travel.[34]

During his twelve-week, end-of-year swing across the country, Kennedy appeared in Ohio, Wisconsin, Indiana, West Virginia, New York, Nebraska, California, Oregon, Oklahoma, Kansas, Delaware, Colorado, Illinois, and Iowa. He visited only one southern state—Louisiana. Even then, advance men made sure it included a visit to Claver Hall, in the heart of New Orleans's black district, to shield Kennedy from criticisms that he was chasing segregationist support. As *Time* magazine noted, the visit demonstrated "his growing ability to do the right thing, pump the right hand, at just the right time."[35]

Yet even that brief foray was touched by controversy, when the *Washington Afro-American* seized upon the story of how a black woman, Dr. Katie E. Whickham, had been barred from a meeting where Kennedy spoke. Even though the story was wildly inaccurate—Dr. Whickham had been in Philadelphia at the time of the alleged incident—Kennedy still considered it necessary to invite the doctor to visit him on Capitol Hill. The goodwill visit received prominent coverage in the *Chicago Defender,* the *Pittsburgh Courier,* and a contrite *Washington Afro-American.* Before Whickham's visit to Washington, Kenneth O'Donnell and Lawrence O'Brien, two of Kennedy's top aides, had traveled to New Orleans for a meeting with black leaders to resolve any lingering confusion. It was an extraordinarily time-consuming mission for two such high-powered operatives and provided another indication of the importance now being attached to black delegates. They received a warm welcome in New Orleans, and O'Brien ultimately concluded that the "Dr. Whickham incident" had ended up being "an overall plus" for the campaign. Nonetheless, to avoid any further controversies—real or imagined—Lawson advised Kennedy to adopt a rigid policy of never addressing segregated audiences. "It is a good policy," she observed, "and will prevent future headaches." Thereafter, the senator's advance men ensured speaking venues were fully integrated.[36]

Even the wary Robert Kennedy now started to think his brother should loosen his ties with the South, if not sever them completely, and improve his standing with the party's liberal wing. It was for that reason that Kennedy finally announced plans to join the Democratic Advisory Council, the liberal-leaning policymaking group that he had shunned so determinedly since its formation in 1957. Still, Kennedy continued to turn down invitations to join the NAACP. When invited by NAACP official Kivie Kaplan to become a life member of the organization in August, Kennedy replied that he made it a policy not to join organizations of any kind while he was in the Senate.[37]

In November, Kennedy also wrote to Martin Luther King, Jr. for the first time, introducing himself and requesting a meeting. Ideally, Kennedy wanted his active support. More realistically, he needed to placate him, lest King's opposition undercut Kennedy's chances of lining up liberal support. But King considered Kennedy a political dilettante, with an unhealthy relationship with leading segregationists and a dismal voting record during the 1957 civil rights debate. He chose not to respond.[38]

As Christmas approached, a series of secret polls reinforced the view that Kennedy should seek the nomination as a liberal Democrat and distance himself from southern supporters. "It now seems as certain as any other fact that the South will likely band behind a sectional candidate both for bargaining purposes and for back-home consumption," wrote pollster Louis Harris. "Any premature support for Kennedy from this region can be a kiss of death" and "[a]dvancing liberal goals" should be the chief priority. But Harris also cautioned Kennedy against running too far to the left in the primaries, because it could scuttle his chances in the general election. "Ironically, it is certainly important for the standpoint of *election* insurance that the South be convinced that Kennedy can carry the region."[39]

By late December, plans were in place for the formal announcement of Kennedy's candidacy at the beginning of the New Year. The robo-type machine

in his Senate office began to churn out thousands of letters to mail to party activists. Most lawmakers had left Washington for the holidays, Congress was
virtually deserted, and a diligent young wire service reporter, walking through
the empty corridors of the Senate Office Building, heard the clatter emanating
from Kennedy's office. He picked up a letter from the machine, and within one
sentence he had his scoop. "I am announcing my candidacy for the Democratic presidential nomination," it read. Once the story got out, Pierre Salinger,
Kennedy's chief press man, offered reporters the implausible explanation that
Kennedy had not yet made a decision and that the unsigned draft was one of a
number of statements exploring his options. But no one was fooled. Kennedy
was running for president—and, in the words of the announcement, as a "liberal Democrat."[40]

CHAPTER 7

❧

Johnny Come Lately

Shortly after ten o'clock on Saturday, January 2, Kennedy bounded into his Senate office, glowing after a two-week vacation in Montego Bay, Jamaica. While his long-time barber began snipping away at his hair, Kennedy dictated a short statement to his secretary, Evelyn Lincoln. "I am announcing my candidacy for the Presidential nomination in 1960," he began. "I am convinced after touring every state in the last forty months, most of them several times, that I can win both the nomination and the election—and I do not intend to relax my efforts until both have been accomplished." Less than two hours later, with his wife, Jackie, at his side, he read from Mrs. Lincoln's faultlessly typed draft. "In the last twenty years I have traveled in nearly every continent and country," he declared. "From all of this, I have developed an image of America as fulfilling a noble and historic role as the defender of freedom in a time of maximum peril—and of the American people as confident, courageous and persevering. It is with this image that I begin this campaign."[1]

Over 140 reporters crowded into the Senate Caucus room to hear Kennedy deliver his announcement. Many had anointed him the early front-runner for the Democratic nomination, but most remained skeptical that a forty-two-year-old senator, with only a slim record of legislative accomplishment, could ultimately mount a successful presidential challenge. The problem of his Catholicism also loomed large—many party leaders, including several who were themselves Catholic, believed it disqualified him from serious consideration. As *Time* magazine reported, Kennedy's "shocked youthfulness, his wealth, and his Roman Catholic faith are mixed political blessings in a race where the Democratic bosses yearn for a candidate with no handicaps."[2]

Kennedy was the second Democrat to declare his candidacy. He had been preempted by Hubert Humphrey, who brought forward his announcement by three days to steal his thunder. Humphrey planned to fight a rags-versus-riches campaign, defined by the kind of Prairie populism that appealed to union members and blacks. Yet in the rush to outstrip his Senate colleague with an early announcement, aides forgot to invite black reporters to the news conference. It was a clumsy mistake that drew a sharp rebuke in the black press. By 1960, black reporters were determined to be treated with the same courtesies as their white colleagues.[3]

Like Kennedy, Humphrey planned to take the primary route to the nomination, hoping to demonstrate his popularity with a string of early victories. Other leading Democrats decided to bypass the primaries altogether, since the party's big state powerbrokers would ultimately choose the nominee. Lyndon Johnson, the first southerner with a realistic chance of winning the presidency in almost a century, was convinced that he would be anointed by his Senate peers. With almost twenty-three years in Congress, the last seven as Senate majority leader, he was confident the party would judge him the most qualified candidate. As early as January, Johnson claimed to be within a hairbreadth of victory, with pledges of support from almost 400 delegates in Texas and the South, 100 from the border states, and a further 100 or so from the Midwest and West. His strategy was to strong-arm delegations from the South, border states, and Southwest, to pick up a smattering of support from the western mountain states, and to browbeat leaders in some of the key, northern states into remaining neutral on the first ballot, in the hope of engineering a convincing second or third ballot victory. Johnson was confident he could transfer his legislative skills to the presidential arena. As the convention approached, he planned to call in a stack of political favors from Senate colleagues and entice state bosses with lavish servings of congressional pork. As yet, however, his candidacy remained undeclared.

There were two other viable candidates for the nomination, as well. Senator Stuart Symington of Missouri, a defense specialist known admiringly as "The Big Bomber Boy," was relatively unknown outside of Missouri. But he boasted his fellow Missourian, former President Harry Truman, as a patron and positioned himself as the unity candidate, popular in the event of a stalemated convention. Like Johnson, he had no intention of entering the primaries and delayed the announcement of his candidacy until the spring. Then there was Adlai Stevenson, lonely on his Libertyville farm and happy to secretly encourage the Draft Stevenson organizations springing up in California and on the East Coast. Inscrutable as ever, Stevenson refused to make any sort of formal announcement as to whether he would seek the nomination for a third consecutive time, but, like Symington, he secretly hoped for a deadlocked convention.

Kennedy was the only one of the five candidates to contest the traditional first-in-the-nation New Hampshire primary in early March. He easily overcame the challenge from a local ballpoint-pen manufacturer, who took just 10 percent of the vote. The Kennedy campaign then shifted its attention to Wisconsin, the second primary on the political calendar, where Humphrey enjoyed many of the same geographical advantages from which Kennedy had benefited in New Hampshire. The border between Wisconsin and Minnesota was just as blurred as the dividing line between Massachusetts and New Hampshire, and the demographic profile of the state's electorate—with its union members, farmers and polyglot ethnic mix of Scandinavians, Germans, Irish, Latvians, and Poles—mirrored that of Humphrey's home state. Such was Humphrey's popularity there, he was commonly referred to as "Wisconsin's third Senator." Traveling aboard his silver Scenicruiser campaign bus, with a sign reading "Over the Hump with Humphrey" on the windshield, Humphrey barnstormed through the state. He appeared on union picket lines, singing "Solidarity Forever" and donned a pharmacist's jacket to dispense medicine to remind voters of his humble roots. Humphrey's homespun appeal seemed to chime with voters, and in what commentators had already dubbed "the pivotal primary," he was considered the early favorite.

Even some of Kennedy's strongest supporters in Wisconsin were pessimistic about his chances against Humphrey. Madison Mayor Ivan Nestingen worried that his polished public image would be off-putting to many farmers, while state Democratic Party chairman Patrick Lucey, another admirer, thought his pro-southern stance during the 1957 civil rights debate remained a liability with Wisconsin's strongly liberal electorate. Moving quickly to allay Lucey's concerns, Sorensen assured him the jury trial vote was simply a "smoke scene"—a phrase he never explained—which had little practical effect on the bill's effectiveness. The overall aim, he said, was to secure passage for "a strong bill without completely shattering the Democratic Party, the Senate or the bill's chances for acceptability in the south."[4]

Recognizing his weakness in the state, and fearful that if he lost this early primary his presidential ambitions would be smashed, Kennedy moved quickly to silence detractors by demonstrating that he could appeal to blacks despite the flaws in his voting record. Even though blacks made up just one percent of the state's population, Kennedy devoted a disproportionately large amount of time to civil rights. Kennedy had laid the early groundwork in October of the previous year, when he delivered a speech before the Wisconsin NAACP, calling for the enactment of Part III, a revision to the filibuster rule, and the promotion of equal employment opportunities and equal housing opportunities. As so often, he connected the civil rights struggle to the broader battle of the Cold War. It was crucial to make "equality of opportunity a reality" for black Americans, in part because it would shield the United States from Soviet criticism. "The hard, tough question for the next decade," he stressed, was whether America "can meet the single-minded advance of the Communist system. For this we need the full participation of every American in our political and economic life." By the end of the 1950s, however, that kind of rhetoric was sounding rather outdated and inadequate. Inspired by leaders like King, the civil rights vocabulary now had a much more moralistic tone—a tongue that Kennedy had not yet mastered.[5]

Despite his October visit, there were disquieting signs that his support among black voters was slipping by the time he embarked on his primary campaign. Polls conducted in Wisconsin's black communities by Lou Harris in November 1959 had shown him in a surprisingly strong position, with 55 percent of the black vote. Yet by February, the figure had slumped to 45 percent. Black support was shifting perceptibly toward the Humphrey campaign. Harris was sufficiently concerned to recommend that Kennedy spend more time campaigning in black neighborhoods. "Perhaps a late campaign appearance on foot, hand-shaking in the Negro ward of Milwaukee—along the lines of the Boston campaign in 1958—would be in order here," he advised. Harris argued that his outreach would benefit Kennedy well beyond Wisconsin's small black community. By demonstrating his commitment to black causes, Kennedy would appeal to white voters as well. "On civil rights there is a strong strain among Wisconsins that civil rights should be granted to Negroes," Harris noted. "It is part of the abolitionist strain that runs fairly deep here. There is no reason that the Senator should not take a strong position here." Even before receiving Harris's memorandum, Kennedy knew that securing black support early in the race was vital in order to demonstrate his electability on the national stage. He was already confident of winning the black enclave of Milwaukee's Fifth Congressional District because of its large Catholic population, but he needed, at the very least, a respectable showing among blacks themselves. He had already asked Stephen Smith, his brother-in-law, to examine the issue. Kennedy asked Smith to determine "what they could do" with local black newspapers, and wanted to find out which "white" papers reached black voters.[6]

In March, Kennedy delivered two keynote speeches on civil rights in Milwaukee, where the black vote was most heavily concentrated. On Sunday, March 20, in "Protecting the Right to Vote," he focused on the civil rights bill currently before Congress. In February, the Eisenhower administration had put forward legislation that called for the appointment of voting referees by federal court judges in southern counties where there was evidence of local officials penalizing black applicants. Kennedy told his audience he favored even tougher proposals. The appointment of federal registrars should not be left to the federal courts, he argued, but be decided by the Civil Rights Commission, which was more likely to select reform-minded candidates. In addition, he called upon registrars to eliminate discrimination not just in federal elections but in state and local contests as well. Calling the 1957 Civil Rights Act "an eloquent but inadequate Act," he admitted it required strengthening, and said that no "interminable legal roadblocks" should be placed in the path of those seeking to vote, an oblique reference, perhaps, to the jury trial amendment. The speech put him fiercely at odds with southern Democrats, who were complaining that the appointment of federal registrars would be in flagrant breach of states' rights. Staking out his new, strenuously liberal stance, Kennedy argued that the direct intervention of Washington had now become unavoidable.[7]

The speech was well received, but Harris came back the very next day with disturbing new polling data showing Humphrey had extended his lead in black communities. He now enjoyed a commanding four-to-one advantage. Jackie Robinson, who had helped open a Humphrey for President office in Washington, was exacerbating the problem. First, he flew into Wisconsin to campaign on Humphrey's behalf. Then, soon after touching down in the state, he picked a public fight with Robert Kennedy, who had falsely suggested that Humphrey had financed the visit. "Whoever originated such a story," Robinson wrote in the *New York Post*, "is a liar."[8]

Senator Kennedy needed to redouble his efforts to woo black voters. On March 23, in a speech at the Jewish Reception Center in Milwaukee, he outlined an even stronger position on civil rights. He trumpeted a new, four-point plan that he described as "a minimum response to legislative obligation in this field." First, he stressed the right of every citizen to vote in all elections, whether federal or state; second, he called for the attorney general to be granted Part III powers to protect the right to vote; third, he called for the long-awaited enactment of his anti-bombing legislation; and fourth, he urged Congress to accelerate the process of school integration, through legislative and executive action. "All we ask now is that the Federal government demonstrate the leadership this issue so sorely needs," Kennedy concluded. "If the Congress fails its responsibility, no local community will meet its responsibility. But if Congress leads, others will follow."[9]

Kennedy's first three points closely mirrored the program he had advanced ahead of the 1958 election, but the fourth point was more far-reaching than anything he had proposed before. Not only did he call upon Congress to accelerate school integration, but he also suggested that as president he would be willing to use executive powers to circumvent obstructionist lawmakers. The idea had been proposed to him by Harris Wofford, his new civil rights adviser. Kennedy was certainly well aware that the proposal would be anathema to the South. But it served his immediate political interests in Wisconsin, where he now desperately needed to assert his progressive credentials. Kennedy was hastily casting off his gradualist clothing and redressing himself as a crusading liberal.[10]

As the primary campaign reached fever pitch in Wisconsin, a new battle for civil rights was spreading across the South. On February 1, four black freshmen from North Carolina A&T had tried to buy a cup of coffee at a whites-only lunch counter in Greensboro, North Carolina. They were refused service but remained at the counter—precipitating a sit-in movement that, within two months, had spread to over fifty cities and intensified the struggle between seg-regationists and civil rights activists.

On March 23, Kennedy traveled to Detroit for a speech before the Demo-cratic Midwest Conference, an event attended by delegates from Michigan, Illinois, and Ohio, many of whom were black. Here, Kennedy made his first comments on the sit-ins. Although the movement represented a potent threat to the southern way of life, Kennedy sided with the protesters. "We have not yet secured for every American, regardless of color, his right to equal opportu-nity," he told his Detroit audience, "and that includes equal opportunity at the polls, in the classroom, in the five-and-ten-cent stores and at the lunch counter." This was the strongest statement to date in support of the civil rights movement, and an explicit endorsement of the movement's strategy of nonvi-olent direct protest.[11]

Humphrey was furious at Kennedy's attempt to outflank him on the left. He complained to reporters that his rival's newfound ardor for progressive causes "can be credited less to a change in philosophy and more to the politics of a campaign to win the Democratic nomination." There was consternation within the Humphrey campaign on March 27, when one of the state's most popular black politicians, thirty-four-year-old Vel Phillips, publicly endorsed Kennedy. It was a coveted endorsement—Phillips was the first black female ever to win election to the DNC—and also, for Kennedy, a stunning personal triumph.[12]

Phillips had first become an admirer of Kennedy in 1956, when she admitted to a "small crush" after watching him on television at the Chicago convention. But her admiration soon turned sour less than twelve months later, after he sided with southerners during the civil rights debate. When the senator visited Wisconsin in 1958, Phillips pointedly refused an invitation to sit alongside him at a Milwaukee fund-raiser. Unable to look him in the eye, she only agreed to attend if seated at a different table.[13]

When Kennedy learned of Phillips's disapproval, he was determined to mollify her. After the dinner was over, he approached her table, politely intro-duced himself, and asked if they could talk. Phillips told him that although she had once been a devoted fan, she had been bitterly disappointed by his votes in 1957. Kennedy moved her to the edge of the room, and offered a ten-minute explanation. Kennedy confessed that he had relied too heavily on advice from a team of Harvard lawyers, who assured him the jury trial amendment would not weaken the legislation. In hindsight, he realized they were wrong. Phillips emerged from the conversation with her faith in Kennedy renewed. "I felt like I was walking on cloud nine," Phillips admitted later, though she re-alized Kennedy was trying to "butter her up." Phillips's later endorsement was distributed to the black press, and her picture featured prominently in cam-paign literature distributed in black neighborhoods. Because of her light com-plexion, Phillips wondered how much use the photograph would actually be.

But as arguably the state's most influential black activist, her name alone was good enough.[14]

As the Wisconsin campaign reached its climax in the first week of April, a swath of private polls suggested Kennedy was pulling ahead of Humphrey. With each new statistical sample, Harris grew more confident, and as primary day approached he predicted Kennedy could sweep all ten of the state's congressional districts. Expectations ran feverishly high. At the outset of the Wisconsin campaign, even a narrow victory would have been considered a stunning success. Now only a landslide would suffice.[15]

As the election returns began to dribble in on April 5, it became clear Kennedy's victory would not be as clear-cut as Harris had anticipated. When the final results were tallied, Kennedy had taken 56.5 percent of the vote compared to Humphrey's 43.5 percent. Under any other circumstances, it would have been considered a decisive victory. But Humphrey had won four of the states' ten congressional districts, trouncing Kennedy in Milwaukee's three black wards by a margin of two votes to one. Humphrey was quick to seize upon his success among black voters and boasted to reporters immediately after the election that "if you're talking about blocs, the Negro's a much bigger bloc nationally than labor." His message was emphatic: Kennedy's ties with the South made him unelectable in the North.[16]

∾

With barely a pause, the race shifted from the plains of Wisconsin to the mountains and hollows of West Virginia. The Kennedy campaign desperately needed to win a decisive victory in the state to keep the hope of winning the nomination alive. Robert Kennedy flew immediately to Charleston, where he convened a crisis meeting at the Kanawha Hotel, the campaign headquarters. Wanting to find out how the religious issue would play, Kennedy began the session by asking what would be his brother's main handicap. "There's only one problem," bellowed a local party worker. "He's a Catholic. That's our God-damned problem." In a state where 95 percent of the population was Protestant, the religious issue was bound to shape the entire race. Only four months earlier, a Harris poll predicted a Kennedy landslide over Humphrey of 70–30. But the results of his latest poll now showed the Minnesotan enjoyed a commanding lead of 60–40. The only difference, as far as Harris could discern, was that voters in the first poll were unaware of Kennedy's Catholicism. Now they spoke of little else.[17]

In addition to the religious problem, there was evidence emerging of a coordinated Stop Kennedy movement cranking into action, led by West Virginia's freshman Senator, Robert Byrd, who was a close Johnson ally. "If you are for Adlai Stevenson, Senator Stuart Symington, Senator Johnson, or John Doe," he declared, in his hill country drawl, "this primary may be your last chance to stop

Kennedy." Byrd threw his weight behind Humphrey but made no secret that his true affections lay with Johnson. Byrd's endorsement provided a much-needed early fillip within West Virginia, but it caused great consternation among out-of-state liberals due to the senator's past membership of the Ku Klux Klan. Arthur Schlesinger, Jr. strongly disapproved and stressed his disappointment in a letter to his old friend: "It deeply troubles me to see Hubert Humphrey accepting help from a former eagle of the Ku Klux Klan, from a man who remained on friendly terms with the Klan as late as 1946." If Kennedy had accepted his support, blasted Schlesinger, there would have been a liberal outcry.[18]

The controversy over the Byrd endorsement offered little comfort to the Kennedy campaign, which had known from the outset that the primary would be dominated by religion rather than race. Fearing defeat, Kennedy sharpened the tactical focus of his campaign by adopting a three-pronged strategy. The campaign set out to neutralize the religious issue, emphasize Kennedy's commitment to liberal causes, and use his father's million-dollar war chest to buy up as many votes as possible. To downplay his Catholicism, Kennedy returned once more to his saga of wartime bravery, appealing to the fair-mindedness and patriotism of West Virginians. "Nobody asked me if I was a Catholic when I joined the United States navy," he told a crowd in Morgantown, during one of his early speeches in the state, "and nobody asked my brother if he was a Catholic or Protestant before he climbed into an American bomber plane to fly his last mission." To emphasize his liberalism, Kennedy recast himself in the image of FDR and even recruited Franklin Delano Roosevelt, Jr., the late president's son. Willing to overlook their fathers' bitter rivalry, Roosevelt happily lent his support, drawing huge crowds in the failing mining communities, where the former president had achieved something close to sainthood. In stump appearances across the state, Roosevelt argued that Kennedy was the only Democrat capable of beating Nixon in the fall, and that he would tackle unemployment and poverty with the same determination as FDR had. Playing to this populist image, Kennedy made other, more cosmetic changes to his campaign. In order to downplay his family's affluence, which threatened to alienate poor voters, Kennedy ordered his glamorous sisters—an almost constant presence in previous campaigns—to stay home in Massachusetts.[19]

Civil rights gained hardly a mention in the West Virginia primary, even though blacks made up 5.7 percent of the state's population, a much bigger proportion than in Wisconsin. On rare occasions when the issue arose, Humphrey and Kennedy parroted the same lines. The only moment of potential drama came during a televised debate when they were asked to comment on Harry Truman's recent remarks that he would "chase out" sit-in protesters if he owned a southern lunch counter. Both distanced themselves from the cantankerous former president. Humphrey argued that the sit-in movement represented the application of a "higher moral law," which transcended the existing laws of segregation. Kennedy, in turn, expressed support for the students' right of protest. "I wouldn't [chase them out] providing the demonstrators are peaceful and respect the rights of others," he said. "It is in the great American tradition of peaceful protest, which goes back to the beginning of this country. I certainly wouldn't chase them out."[20]

As the primary entered into its final few days, polls conducted by Harris forecast a Humphrey win. Even the sober-minded *Wall Street Journal* predicted he would capture at least two-thirds of the statewide vote. Kennedy became increasingly agitated, complaining that Humphrey had become a "hatchet man" for Johnson and had used smear tactics to misrepresent him. "It's just one fucking lie after another," he moaned to campaign aide Richard Goodwin. Reports that Johnson associates had converged on Charleston, with black plastic bags stuffed with as much as $17,000, to pay off local politicians, fueled his anger, for it seemed as if the Stop Kennedy campaign might work.[21]

Ultimately, however, Joe Kennedy's two-million-dollar war chest proved to be far more effective than any campaign Humphrey or Johnson could wage in the state. For weeks, Lawrence O'Brien had crisscrossed West Virginia's fifty-five counties buying up support from sheriffs, union officials, county clerks, veterans' hall leaders, and even school board members. When voters arrived at polling stations on Election Day, the vast majority of slates carried Kennedy's name rather than Humphrey's. As a result, the Minnesotan was buried in an avalanche of purchased ballots, securing just 31 percent of the overall vote compared to his opponents' 61 percent.[22]

Kennedy left West Virginia basking in his victory. He had enjoyed the unexpected bonus of beating Humphrey in the black precincts of Charleston, Weirton, and Wheeling. Humphrey's ties with former Klansman Robert Byrd had certainly helped swing the black vote in his favor, as had the timely endorsement from Franklin Delano Roosevelt, Jr. "Negroes gave him their emphatic endorsement," reported *Time*, noting that Byrd's support for Humphrey had cost him dear. But the Kennedy millions were essential to counter the anti-Catholicism of black churchgoers, especially after Ambassador Kennedy secretly colluded with Boston's Cardinal Richard Cushing to flood black churches with generous donations. "We decided which church and preacher would get two hundred dollars or one hundred dollars or five hundred dollars," Cushing told Humphrey six years later. "What better way is there to spend campaign money than to help a preacher and his flock?" The most climactic battle of the 1960 primary season had been won by the richest candidate. Kennedy had spent millions of his father's personal fortune to keep his presidential ambitions alive. Humphrey was forced to withdraw from the race, effectively bringing the short primary season to a close after two head-to-head contests.[23]

∾

During Kennedy's months away from Capitol Hill, a new civil rights bill was making a troubled journey through Congress. Introduced in early February, the bill was part of a calculated effort by the Eisenhower administration to increase the number of black voters in time for November's elections. The move came in the wake of a CRC report published in December, 1959, which estimated that only a quarter of some five million eligible southern blacks were registered to vote. By appointing federal voting referees to certify qualified voters, Eisenhower's new attorney general, William Rogers, hoped to offer blacks a safe, intimidation-free way of registering. Civil rights advocates trumpeted the bill, of course, while southerners complained that it represented an unwarranted and unconstitutional encroachment of federal power. Kennedy was faced with a decision.

Even before the bill was put before Congress, Harris Wofford urged Kennedy not only to champion the legislation but to take a leading role in ensuring its passage. "As you know one thing holding you back among liberal Democrats and sensitive people of some influence, such as Mrs. Roosevelt, to name one of many, is the desire to see some sign of passionate courage on your part," wrote Wofford. "By your taking some issue in which there are political risks, something you believe in strongly, and speaking very strongly and warmly about it, despite the risks, might mean a lot to many people. Civil rights in the February debate might be one such issue." Wofford ended with an elegantly worded warning: "Your slow fire now needs a little brighter blaze."[24]

There was no way that Kennedy, distracted by the Wisconsin campaign and away from Washington more often than not, could have led a push on behalf of the civil rights bill early in the spring. He also considered it inadvisable politically with the convention approaching. There was no advantage to be gained by hurling himself into a potentially bloody floor fight that threatened to reopen old Democratic wounds. It was one thing to champion civil rights in the relative obscurity of a Jewish community center; it was a wholly different matter to confront southern Democrats on the floor of the Senate. Far better, thought Kennedy, to leave the problem in Johnson's hands. With typical bravado, Johnson had pledged to push through a new civil rights act before the 1960 election, partly to demonstrate his command over the party, partly to shake off his image as a racial conservative.

During the course of the civil rights debate, then, Kennedy made just one Senate speech in favor of the bill, a perfunctory five paragraphs delivered on March 10. He neither laid out the merits of the bill nor referred to the circumstances that made it necessary. He simply noted, "The Senate should now resolve the great and basic and ancient question of equality of rights and equality of opportunity." It was a scrawny speech, short on detail and devoid of passion, and contained nothing that would have rankled southerners in the chamber. Presumably, this was the intention. Over the course of the next two weeks, he would speak much more boldly about civil rights to audiences in Wisconsin. There he had a far more sympathetic, liberal audience. And his speeches were intended solely for local consumption. Kennedy and his campaign staff knew that even the most potent speeches would gain little or no national attention. Protected from the mistrustful gaze of the southern media, Kennedy could lay out a much different vision in Wisconsin than he could on the Senate floor.[25]

The 1960 Civil Rights Act was hopelessly watered down by the time it was passed in the Senate. It was extremely narrow in scope, and the administration's federal referee plan had been almost completely defanged. The bill made no mention of school segregation or black employment rights. Eisenhower dutifully signed the bill into law at a White House ceremony on May 6. But events far from home now dominated his mind. He was in the midst of the most serious foreign policy crisis of his presidency—a crisis that, through an unlikely sequence of events, would come to have a tremendous impact on Kennedy's handling of civil rights.

CHAPTER 8

❧

"Those Southern Bastards"

A plane was missing, its pilot suspected dead. According to State Department officials, it was a high-altitude weather aircraft operated by NASA, which had taken off from the Incirlik air base in Turkey on May 1 and been lost some 1,300 miles inside Soviet territory. The plane, officials explained, had been flying at 55,000 feet, close to the fringes of space, making meteorological observations over the Lake Van area of Turkey. It was said to be unarmed and had the letters N, A, S, A, emblazoned on its forty-foot fuselage in gold and black, along with the space agency's futuristic seal.[1]

Reporters dutifully recorded every detail, not realizing that they were being spun a CIA cover story. At the White House, military chiefs had already briefed the president that the aircraft was in fact a top-secret U-2 spy plane, and that its pilot had been conducting photo-reconnaissance flights of military installations across the Soviet Union. Initially, officials were reassured that the plane was equipped with self-destruct mechanisms, and that it would have been completely obliterated. It was near impossible for its pilot to have survived.

On May 5, however, Nikita Khrushchev sprung one of the most stunning propaganda coups of the entire Cold War. After waiting for the State Department to go public with their version of the story, he appeared before the Supreme Soviet in Moscow to announce that the plane had been shot down over Soviet airspace. Its pilot, a thirty-year-old air force officer named Francis Gary Powers, had not only survived but confessed to the true purpose of his mission.[2]

The incident dealt a major blow to U.S.-Soviet relations. Two weeks later, a long-scheduled Big Four summit in Paris between Eisenhower, Khrushchev, Harold Macmillan, and Charles de Gaulle, broke up after just one session in a mood of bitter acrimony, after the Soviet leader demanded an apology and Eisenhower refused to give it. Afterward, Khrushchev announced he would be unwilling to negotiate with America until after the November election.[3]

The U-2 incident transformed the presidential race. The escalation of the Cold War brought fresh scrutiny to Kennedy's youth and inexperience on the international stage. Stevenson, the elder statesman of the party and its most eloquent spokesman on foreign affairs, was the most obvious beneficiary. He started to position himself for a possible run. In a thinly disguised attempt to boost his undeclared candidacy, the former governor issued a blistering speech in Chicago on May 19 attacking Eisenhower for his failed diplomacy. He wrote the address with the help of a full-time speechwriter, part of an ever-expanding team of political hired guns. With Draft Stevenson committees sprouting up in forty-two states, his so far undeclared campaign had the feel of a nationwide movement.[4]

Lyndon Johnson was delighted that Kennedy's inexperience had finally become an issue in the campaign, and he welcomed Stevenson's newfound popularity, since it siphoned support from his young rival. In an effort to push Stevenson even further center stage, Johnson invited him to sign a protest telegram wired to the Kremlin by senior Democrats. He pointedly did not extend the offer to Kennedy. At the same time, the Senate leader conspired with Stevenson. "If I don't get it [the presidential nomination]," Johnson reportedly told him, "you will."[5]

Against the backdrop of U.S.-Russian turmoil, the LBJ bandwagon was "belatedly gathering momentum," according to *Time*. "Nikita Khrushchev had altered the whole tone and temper of the political campaign." Even Stuart Symington now had the look of a serious contender, for his long-standing criticisms of Eisenhower's defense policies now seemed startlingly prescient. Without question, the Kennedy campaign was beginning to falter. His political inexperience had replaced Catholicism as his primary liability.[6]

Kennedy was certain the party would never turn to a two-time loser like Stevenson. Still, he was sufficiently concerned that the former governor's shadow candidacy was drawing attention and support away from his own campaign that he flew to northern Illinois on May 21 to visit Stevenson at his Libertyville farm. He arrived for the forty-five-minute meeting in a combative mood and boasted that he was within 100 votes of the nomination. He predicted that delegates from California, Washington, Colorado, and Pennsylvania—all Stevenson strongholds—would soon fall in behind him. For two such seasoned politicians, Kennedy's message was clear: Stevenson would not only suffer a humiliating defeat if he announced his candidacy but destroy any chance of becoming Secretary of State if Kennedy were elected.[7]

Robert Kennedy was also galvanized by the threat of Stevenson's candidacy. He moved quickly to shore up his brother's support from liberals. And he seemed especially concerned about black delegates, who, though small in number were growing in influence, particularly in delegate-rich delegations like New York, Michigan, and California. Before the convention, Ted Sorensen warned that Kennedy faced a profound problem with the eighty-three black delegates heading to Los Angeles. "Negroes both leadership and rank and file have little feeling of identification with the Senator," he wrote. "Many are distrustful, some are suspicious, some are bitterly opposed, few are enthusiastic." Sorensen cited four reasons: a legislative record "with which the leadership is very familiar and can quote chapter and verse"; his support from the South in 1956; attacks from Jackie Robinson; and the "subtle and elusive reasons to which there is a very sensitive antenna . . . 'He doesn't go to Negro meetings!' 'When did he ever speak in Harlem?' 'I never see his picture in the paper.'"[8]

On May 10, just days after the U-2 incident first exploded onto the front pages, Robert Kennedy put through an urgent call to Harris Wofford and asked to meet him at the campaign headquarters at the foot of Capitol Hill. He admitted his brother was "in trouble" with black Democrats and instructed him to do "everything you need to" to line up their support. It was time to take an even bolder stance on civil rights. As Robert Kennedy later admitted, "We had to make more of an effort because [blacks] were not tied to John F. Kennedy as they would be ordinarily to a Democratic leader . . . they hadn't any strong feeling for John Kennedy."[9]

Three days after Robert Kennedy's meeting with Wofford, Senator Kennedy delivered a speech in Baltimore that included a ferocious, and highly personalized, attack on Eisenhower's civil rights policies. He lambasted the president for his refusal to tackle discrimination in publicly funded housing, despite calls from the CRC to make it an urgent national priority. He also criticized the president for his failure to exert firmer moral leadership on civil rights. In his most brazenly partisan comments to date, Kennedy insisted that unlike Eisenhower, he would place himself at the vanguard of the struggle for equality: "in 1961—with a Democratic President in the White House—we are going to begin a great march toward equal opportunity for all Americans—equal opportunity at the polls, in the schools, and at the lunch counter."[10]

Kennedy also raced to cultivate Stevenson's former black associates in an attempt to win them over before the former governor could line up their support. In May, he carved more than three hours out of his overcrowded schedule to meet with Harry Belafonte in his New York apartment. Kennedy knew that Belafonte, an unabashed admirer of Stevenson, was a lost cause, but he was nonetheless curious to know why so many blacks harbored such deep misgivings about his own candidacy. Belafonte explained that Kennedy's main problem was that he had no record of genuine accomplishment on civil rights and remained an unknown quantity to many blacks. Kennedy considered the criticisms unfair, but he let them go, and instead steered the conversation toward the presidential election in November. He asked for Belafonte's advice on how to counteract the influence of Jackie Robinson, who had campaigned for Humphrey in Wisconsin and was sure to endorse Nixon. Kennedy suggested Belafonte assemble a group of black celebrities who could travel the country up until Election Day. Though willing to help, Belafonte believed that Kennedy's preoccupation with Robinson betrayed a fundamental misunderstanding of the black struggle. While celebrity endorsements may well be valuable, blacks were turning for leadership to civil rights groups, like the Southern Christian Leadership Conference (SCLC) and the Student Nonviolent Coordinating Committee (SNCC), the driving force behind the sit-in movement. "Forget me," said Belafonte. "Forget Jackie Robinson and everybody else we've been talking about. If you can join the cause of King, and be counseled by him, then you'll have an alliance that will make the difference."[11]

As soon as the meeting finished, Belafonte telephoned King in Atlanta and suggested they should meet at the earliest opportunity. Soon after, Kennedy asked Wofford to approach King. This opened up a channel of communication that would remain in place almost until November.[12]

With the convention less than a month away, Kennedy's vulnerability with black voters was exacerbated by two high-profile attacks on his record. On May 29, in a speech before the American Jewish Congress, a body packed with Stevenson loyalists, Roy Wilkins noted "it is very difficult for thoughtful Negro voters to feel at ease [with Kennedy]" after the Patterson meeting. "Anything with an Alabama odor does not arouse enthusiasm among Negro citizens." Even though Wilkins had warmed up to the senator over the course of the previous year, publicly he had to adopt a more critical posture that reflected the politics of the NAACP membership and the demands of its board. As Marge Lawson told Kennedy afterward, Wilkins could "scarcely avoid his comment" because of "tremendous pressure" from within his organization.[13]

Only five days after Wilkins's speech, Robinson mounted his most withering attack to date. In his weekly column in the *New York Post*, he assailed Kennedy for his ties with Patterson and criticized his "carefully guarded token position on the sit-ins." Turning then to the 1957 civil rights debate, he asked why Kennedy had sought advice from three white Harvard law professors during the jury trial debate rather than Thurgood Marshall, who as chief counsel for the NAACP Legal Defense and Educational Fund had argued *Brown* and who had opposed the amendment. He also opened up a fresh line of attack, pointedly asking why Kennedy appeared so infrequently before black audiences, a wholly unfair criticism. Robinson concluded bluntly, "Senator Kennedy is not fit to be President of the United States."[14]

Kennedy aides read the column with mounting alarm. The most popular black American had just declared war on their candidate. The very next evening, at a Jefferson-Jackson Day dinner in Minneapolis, Kennedy offered his rebuttal. Addressing an audience comprised mainly of Humphrey loyalists, he delivered an unusually rousing speech. He claimed that victory in November would be "hollow" unless it was based on "great liberal principles" and that the party should unite around a "liberal candidate and a strong liberal program. . . . For only a liberal Democratic Party can win." On civil rights, Kennedy was cat- egorical: It was time for the party to come down unambiguously on the side of black Americans rather than hedge, as it had done in 1952 and 1956. "I say that if anyone expects the Democratic Party to betray that same cause—they can look elsewhere for a party." Kennedy promised that he would make the White House a place for "strong moral leadership" and that he would fight until every black citizen "has achieved equal access to all of American life."[15]

Despite the campaign's heightened attention toward civil rights, Marge Law- son worried in early June that Kennedy had done nowhere near enough to placate black critics. She identified five areas of weakness: his 1957 votes, the Patterson endorsement, the failure to campaign more in black areas in Wisconsin, reluc- tance to make a "strong civil rights statement from a national stage," and the "general hostility" toward the Democratic leadership, a holdover from the 1956 campaign and a byproduct of Johnson and Sam Rayburn's dominance on Capi- tol Hill. "Senator Kennedy represents some of the Stevenson qualities to Negro voters," she wrote. "He is an intellectual liberal, and being northern and eastern, is regarded as having little experience with Negroes—and hence no real under- standing of Negro problems and goals. Somehow, some warmth has to be added to this image of intellectual liberalism." Lawson made two recommendations: that Kennedy continue meeting with black opinion makers and that he work to "create a new image" by delivering a "national speech."[16]

On receiving Lawson's memorandum, Kennedy turned almost immediately to Harris Wofford. Kennedy asked him to prepare a wide-ranging briefing paper in an effort to help broaden his understanding of the intricacies of civil rights policy. Emboldened, Wofford produced a memorandum brimful of ideas in less than a week. "The task, in short, is to fill the gap between platitudes and bayonets," he wrote, in a sideswipe at Eisenhower. The new president should climb into the presidential "bully pulpit" and provide "direct" and "active" lead- ership. That leadership had to be both substantive and symbolic. "The President must by his own example—by meeting with Negro and white leaders, by the appointment of qualified Negroes to high office, and by more dramatic sym- bolic actions in moments of racial crisis—convey this sense of urgency and con- viction." As a first priority, Kennedy should assemble a civil rights task force, a kind of black brain trust, during his first weeks in office, drawing together gov- ernment experts, black leaders, and even white southerners. Its aim should be to produce clearly stated targets or national goals, such as the elimination of vot- ing discrimination by the hundredth anniversary of the Emancipation Procla- mation in 1963.[17]

The most pressing problem, however, was school desegregation. Wofford thought it was possible to fashion some kind of compromise between white southerners and blacks that would lead to the faster integration of classrooms, especially if it was modeled on a grade-by-grade scheme pioneered in Nashville, Tennessee. In other, less emotionally charged arenas—such as housing and employment—Kennedy could take a more direct approach. It was here that Wofford put forward his boldest and most innovative policy idea yet: that rather than promote reform through new legislation, Kennedy should do so by issuing a string of executive orders. With the mere stroke of a presidential pen, he could end discrimination in federally funded public housing and punish government contractors who discriminated against black employees. Bypassing Congress and the Southern Caucus, executive orders offered an unobstructed path toward reform.[18]

Wofford's ideas took hold almost immediately. Less than a week after he received Wofford's memorandum, in a speech delivered before a luncheon of the National Democratic Club in New York on June 17, Kennedy introduced the idea of using executive orders to enact reform. Kennedy called for presidential action not only in education, voting, and public accommodations but in federally funded housing as well.[19] But many in the audience were less interested in his innovative policy recommendations than in his relationship with Governor Patterson. On this occasion, Kennedy seemed happy to field questions on the subject, since it handed him an opportunity to distance himself from the South. "I don't think I have a delegate in Alabama," he said, disingenuously. "I know of no other candidate near the convention who ever had so little support in the South as I have." Then he added, "So far as civil rights is concerned, I want a clear, strong stand taken at the convention."[20]

Earlier that day, over breakfast with labor leaders at the Carlyle Hotel, Kennedy had gone even further in his effort to disentangle himself from the South. He boasted he was about to become the first Democrat to win the presidential nomination without the support of a single Dixie delegate. He also steered his breakfast guests toward a statement released that day by a group of liberals, which endorsed his candidacy. The statement, which was entitled "An Important Message of Interest to All Liberals," was signed by Arthur Schlesinger, John Kenneth Galbraith, and Joseph Rauh of the Americans for Democratic Action. As evidence of his commitment to the liberal cause, the message cited his support for a strong civil rights plank, including Part III. It also called attention to his new interest in executive orders by praising Kennedy's backing for "Congressional and Executive Action in support of the Supreme Court's desegregation and to whatever measures may prove necessary to make voting a reality for all citizens." Kennedy and Rauh, who had collaborated on the statement, had agreed that support for a civil rights program was "the most significant thing."[21]

Still, there were many liberals who remained deeply skeptical about Kennedy, and others were openly hostile. Among his fellow members of the ADA, Rauh predicted 50 percent favored Stevenson, 40 percent Humphrey, and just 10 percent Kennedy. Just as worrying, many black activists seemed particularly eager for Stevenson to enter the race. As *Jet* magazine's Simeon Booker observed in late June, the two-time candidate continued to have a "magical touch" with blacks and could boast the support of 52 percent of black delegates compared with Kennedy's rather lackluster 24 percent. Frustrating his supporters, however, Stevenson still refused to signal his intentions and indicate whether or not he planned to join the race.[22]

With each passing day, Kennedy ratcheted up his campaign for black support. Just three days after his speech at the National Democratic Club, he dispatched his private plane to fly a small but influential group of black delegates from Detroit to Washington for a visit, after learning from Herbert Tucker they were unhappy with his civil rights record and could possibly swing the Michigan delegation against him. Kennedy greeted them on the patio of his Georgetown home, where his guests mingled with Chester Bowles and Wofford, while waiters, both black and white, served glasses of cognac punch. But despite Kennedy's efforts to create a convivial mood, Damon Keith, the leader of delegation, was determined to press the candidate on the issues. He began by asking how Kennedy planned to tackle discrimination in the workplace and public housing, both burning issues for northern blacks. Kennedy, who had long supported the idea of a federal fair employment committee, promised that as president he would make it a top priority. Keith complained, however, that he was "compartmentalizing too much"—that the expansion of employment rights had to be viewed in the wider context of inadequate housing and poor schools. Kennedy was taken aback by Keith's combative tone, and, in the words of one observer, "was quite visibly affected by that response."[23]

Members of the delegation also raised the issue of Kennedy's controversial relationship with John Patterson and Sam Engelhardt, two previous house guests. Once more, he was forced onto the defensive. He stressed that he had not spoken to Patterson since the previous year and had not entered into any "deal" over school desegregation. If anything, he explained, the swirl of controversy surrounding the meeting had spurred him to reevaluate his relationship with southerners. Now he planned to win the nomination with northern and western support alone. Kennedy went on to reiterate his support for *Brown* and to endorse both the goals and tactics of the sit-in movement. He then launched into a list of provocative measures to combat segregation, including a new fair housing bill, tough measures protecting the right to vote, and a new "public accommodations" law outlawing Jim Crow ordinances at lunch counters and restaurants. Kennedy promised to include the policies in the Democratic Party's civil rights platform at the upcoming convention—while Bowles, who had recently been appointed chairman of the Democratic platform committee, listened in astonishment. Wofford was also stunned. He later recalled that Kennedy "went much farther than any of us, to that point, had heard him go." Afterwards, members of the Michigan delegation claimed they even heard Kennedy promise the complete desegregation of southern schools and other public facilities by the end of his presidency, an extraordinarily sweeping pledge he had never before hinted at.[24]

The Michigan delegation left N Street with most, if not all, of their concerns allayed. Speaking to reporters on the steps outside, one delegate rhapsodized not only about the senator's new proposals but the lavish hospitality he had offered the group: "There was chicken and some fancy kind of eggs, and there were whites and Negroes waiting on us. Afterward, that man must have given away $100 worth of cigars from some foreign country. Mrs. Kennedy was there, too and later they had the press conference for television and everything. We were all impressed."[25]

The meeting had jolted Kennedy. It was the first time he had been confronted directly by the new mood of militancy among the Democratic Party's black rank and file. It had transformed him, at least temporarily. Never before had he voiced such forthright support for such far-reaching policies. Gone was the incrementalism favored during the immediate post-*Brown* years. Instead, he had adopted the rhetoric of an ardent liberal.

When Johnson aides found out about the meeting, they, too, briefly considered bringing a meeting with the Michigan delegation. They believed that Kennedy's vulnerability with blacks could be turned to their advantage. As Johnson confidant George Reedy wrote the Senate majority leader, there were two main reasons why blacks harbored doubts:

1. Negroes considered Senator Kennedy's father an anti-Semite and they believe that anti-Semitism and racial bigotry against Negroes [are] connected.
2. They believe that Kennedy has made some deals with the "worst elements" in the South (specifically with Governor Patterson).

There was a delicious irony: Up until the 1957 Civil Rights Act, Johnson had consistently opposed every civil rights measure to come before him. Now, he intended to try and exploit his main opponent's vulnerability on civil rights.[26]

∾

In the weeks before the Democratic convention, Kennedy championed the cause of civil rights with ever increasing fervor. He also tried harder to distance himself from the South. In the spring, Kennedy had told Schlesinger that it would be "absolutely fatal" to have the support of segregationists. "I want to be nominated by the liberals," he proclaimed. "I don't want to go screwing around with all those Southern bastards." Kennedy's belligerent rhetoric was out of character; throughout his career, he had refrained from demonizing southern politicians, either privately or publicly, despite severe differences of opinion. In fact, he had saved his toughest language in recent times for Humphrey, who had colluded in the Stop Kennedy campaign, and Stevenson, for arrogantly believing he could get the nomination again. Kennedy's vitriol must have seemed somewhat contrived, inasmuch as he knew that his aides, including Bobby Troutman, were at the same time continuing in their efforts to discretely line up support from the Alabama and North Carolina delegations.[27]

Kennedy used an interview published on June 22 by the *Pittsburgh Courier* to move further away from the South. "Nearly all of the South appears to be supporting Lyndon Johnson," he told the paper's editorial board. "Out of the 352 delegates from the eleven southern states, I doubt if I will receive five per cent." He also argued that the unity of the Democratic Party must be built upon a program designed to bring about equal opportunity, adding, "If anyone expects the Democratic Administration to betray that same cause they can look elsewhere for a party."[28]

On June 23, the day after the *Pittsburgh Courier* published the interview, Kennedy met with Martin Luther King at Joe Kennedy's apartment in New York, amid fresh rumors the young civil rights leader was planning to endorse Nixon in the fall. It was their first face-to-face encounter, and King arrived with low expectations. He was surprised, then, when Kennedy dispensed with the normal pleasantries and launched immediately into a frank discussion of civil rights. Over the course of ninety minutes of a fairly one-sided conversation, Kennedy explained that it was only in recent months he had come to comprehend fully the true moral force of the civil rights struggle. If he won the presidential election, Kennedy promised to exert greater moral leadership.[29]

King emerged from the meeting with a totally altered impression of the senator. "I had very little enthusiasm for Mr. Kennedy when he first announced his candidacy," King told Bowles on his return to Atlanta, but their conversation had been "very fruitful and rewarding." King had been won over by Kennedy's conviction. "I was very impressed by the forthright and honest manner in which he discussed the civil rights question. I have no doubt that he would do the right thing on this issue if he were elected president." Bowles admitted that he, too, had underestimated Kennedy. "I have been increasingly confident of his conviction on the questions," Bowles assured King, "which most deeply concern all of you." Afterwards, King also contacted G. Mennen Williams of Michigan to report that he had been impressed by Kennedy's "sincerity and honesty." Williams sent word to Kennedy, saying the meeting had clearly been "helpful and rewarding."[30]

That same day, in a widely reported speech before the New York Liberal Party, Kennedy restated his plan to win the nomination without the support of a single southern delegate. To drive home the point, he devoted much of the speech to civil rights. Kennedy promised greater activism from the White House, pledging "to provide the effective, creative, persuasive leadership necessary if we are to fulfill our great Constitutional promise." He hinted at a much more aggressive role for the Justice Department in implementing *Brown* and promised to safeguard the right of peaceful protest. Federal law enforcement officials should step in to protect civil rights demonstrators where local sheriffs refused to do so, he pronounced. In the context of Kennedy's thinking, this represented a bold proposal for the extension of federal power.[31]

There was something more subtle at work as well—Kennedy was using a different rhetoric than he had in previous speeches. He stressed to his audience that, in addition to the practical issues of legal enforcement, he also understood the broader meaning of the black struggle. "It is not a matter of law and order," he said. "Above all, moral issues are involved. The high office of the presidency must be used to promote the effective, creative, persuasive leadership necessary if we are to fulfill our great Constitutional promise of equal protection to all Americans. Beginning in 1961, the Presidency will be a place of such strong moral leadership." Gone were the arguments of the Cold War hawk—Kennedy was beginning to learn the language of the civil rights movement.[32]

It was, however, Kennedy's forceful disavowal of southern delegates that generated the next morning's headlines. "Kennedy Assures Liberals He Seeks No Help in the South," noted the *New York Times*. It was enough to win him the endorsement of the New York Liberal Party, an organization packed with Stevenson sentimentalists. For Joseph Rauh, meanwhile, it provided further evidence of what he called the "no-compromise-with-southern-conservatism" strategy.[33]

On the same day that the headlines ran about his comments before the Liberal Party, Kennedy delivered another blistering speech at a lunch held in honor of the African Diplomatic Corps. He strenuously endorsed the sit-in protests, which, he said, were in keeping with the best traditions of American democracy: "Such action inevitably involves some unrest and turmoil and tension—[as] part of the price of change. But the fact that people are peacefully protesting the denial of their rights is not something to be lamented. It is a good sign—a sign of increased popular responsibility, of good citizenship, of the American spirit coming alive again. It is in the American tradition to stand up for one's rights—even if the new way to stand up for one's rights is to sit down." Journalist Anthony Lewis, who had followed the campaign closely, believed it was Kennedy's "most specific endorsement of the sit-in movement to date."[34]

Members of Kennedy's campaign staff began to fear that he had gone too far. Disturbed by the aggressive thrust of his speech before the Liberal Party, Robert Kennedy voiced the strongest concerns. "[T]his is going to look like a gratuitous insult to the Southern political leaders who have been interested in you over the last few months," he warned his brother. "You might not get votes from them but there is no sense in turning on them at this moment." Sorensen alerted the senator to the first signs of disaffection in the South. Mississippi delegate Frank Barber had transferred his support to Johnson in protest at Kennedy's speech before the New York Liberal Party, and Alabama delegates threatened to follow suit.[35]

Johnson, meanwhile, was delighted by the Kennedy campaign's tactical shift. On June 25, at a meeting of the National Governors' Conference in Glacier National Park, Montana, Johnson supporters had gleefully handed out copies of the previous day's front-page headline in the *New York Times:* "Kennedy Assures Liberals He Seeks No Help in the South." The Kennedy campaign tried to control the damage. Robert Kennedy instructed Governor Abraham Ribicoff of Connecticut, a close New England ally, to issue a statement saying the Kennedy campaign would be "happy and proud to receive support from delegates from any part of the United States." William C. Battle, one of Kennedy's closest southern associates, offered reassurance to high-ranking Democrats in Virginia, that, despite his fiery rhetoric, Kennedy would never ask Humphrey to be his running mate. The *New York Times* picked up on the inconsistent messages emanating from the Kennedy campaign. "Kennedy Appeals to the South to Support His Nomination" read the headline in the next morning's *Times.*[36]

Still, right up until the end, Kennedy continued to push hard for black delegate support. In early July he met with Jackie Robinson at Bowles's home. The meeting was a disaster. Robinson refused to accept Kennedy's explanation of his meeting with Patterson and complained that the senator was too cowardly even to look him in the eye. Kennedy was unused to being spurned and asked Robinson what he could do to gain his respect. Robinson took instant umbrage, assuming Kennedy was about to offer him a bribe. "I don't want any of your money," he retorted. "I'm just interested in helping the candidate who I think will be best for America." After the meeting fell apart, Robinson commented to journalists about Kennedy's shallow understanding of the race issue: "I was appalled that he could be so ignorant of our situation and be bidding for the highest office in the land."[37]

Kennedy was nonetheless unrelenting in his efforts to secure Robinson's support—or at least put an end to his outright condemnation. After the meeting, he sent Robinson a carefully worded letter in which he offered a more detailed explanation of the Patterson meeting. National politicians had to be prepared to meet governors from any state, wrote Kennedy. "That does not imply any agreement with them, or their agreement with me on particular issues." Although the letter may have been sincerely intended, it also represented a political opportunity. In order to salvage something from the disastrous summit, the campaign leaked it to *New York Times* reporter Anthony Lewis. The tactic worked—when Lewis read him the letter over the phone, Robinson agreed to soften his criticisms. In a story that ran in the *Times* on July 2, Robinson was quoted as saying that Kennedy "had come out openly against racist practices" and should be given the chance to demonstrate his sincerity in Los Angeles.[38]

Robinson did not even have to wait that long. Three days later, at a New York press conference, Kennedy reiterated his support for Part III and called for the adoption of a robust civil rights plank. "I think the times have changed since 1956," he said. "I think the language will be different. I think it will be clearer and more precise. I think it will affirm more clearly the right of every American to have an equal opportunity to develop his talents."[39]

The campaign was in overdrive in the days leading up to the convention. Robert Kennedy held a meeting with Ralph Bunche, the Nobel Peace Prize–winning diplomat and highest-ranking black American public official. Kennedy recognized that Bunche could lend substantial credibility to his brother's campaign, and pressed him to serve as a foreign policy adviser in the period before the convention. But Bunche declined, citing his heavy workload at the United Nations. In late June, the Kennedy high command also sent a team to the NAACP convention to lobby on the candidate's behalf. It included Wofford, Sargent Shriver, and a five-person group from Boston headed by Tucker.[40]

The candidate himself made a final effort to shore up black support. After the Fourth of July holiday, Kennedy interrupted a vacation in Cape Cod to fly to Harlem for a secret meeting with J. Raymond Jones, the so-called Harlem Fox. Jones's close ally, Congressman Adam Clayton Powell, Jr., had endorsed Johnson the previous week in exchange for Johnson's offer of the chairmanship of the House Education and Labor Committee. Jones was already working to line up black delegates behind Johnson when Kennedy swooped in with an extraordinary offer. He promised to assemble a committee of prominent blacks to advise him on racial affairs during the campaign and asked Jones to participate. Kennedy told Jones that the group would be spearheaded by King—although he had never raised the plan with the civil rights leader himself. Kennedy also repented his earlier sins against the cause—his meeting with Patterson, he lamented, was "the greatest cross I will ever have to bear."[41]

And yet, despite his new zeal for civil rights, Kennedy held back in certain areas. Kennedy demurred when Schlesinger and Galbraith suggested that, in the period before the convention, he should punctuate his civil rights position by demanding the removal of James Eastland as chairman of the Senate Judiciary Committee. "It wouldn't be in character for me to do that," Kennedy told Schlesinger. "After all, the Senate is a body where you have to get along with people regardless of how much you disagree. I've always got along pretty well with old Eastland." And when Marge Lawson implored him to deliver a national speech about civil rights on the eve of the convention, Kennedy again balked. Clearly, the "no-compromise-with-southern-conservatism" strategy had its limits.[42]

In the space of just two weeks, Kennedy had almost completely recast himself as a zealous reformer in the civil rights struggle. But how sincere was this conversion? In this short period, he had met personally with three of America's most influential blacks: King, the spiritual leader of the civil rights movement; Robinson, the country's most famous black celebrity; and Jones, arguably its most savvy black politician. It is possible that from these meetings he derived a richer understanding of the issues at stake. Certainly, his rhetoric had shifted— it was during this period that, for the first time, Kennedy emphasized the moral dimension of the black struggle, as opposed to its foreign policy implications.

The timing of Kennedy's conversion renders it suspect, however. Each modification of his stance on civil rights had coincided precisely with a twist in the fight for the nomination. When Johnson emerged late in 1959 as the candidate of the South, Kennedy and his campaign staff immediately reexamined his civil rights strategy and quickly carved out a higher profile on the issue. The process accelerated early in 1960 when Kennedy was up against Humphrey in liberal-leaning states. But it hit breakneck speed in the wake of the U-2 incident, as Kennedy embraced a whole raft of new civil rights policies in order to blunt the eleventh-hour challenge from Stevenson. At times, he almost literally ventriloquized his undeclared opponent. In his strongest support for the sit-in movement, in which he commended black Americans on standing up for their rights even if it meant sitting down for them, Kennedy echoed a line Stevenson had delivered only a few days earlier (in a speech at Northwestern University on May 13, Stevenson had said he did not want to lead a country where blacks were treated as human beings "so long as they stand up, but not when they sit down"). Whether or not Kennedy or his speechwriters purloined the phrase is unknown. But in this final phase, as Kennedy struggled frenetically to match his rival's liberal stance on civil rights, even his language sometimes seemed borrowed.[43]

CHAPTER 9

❧

Showdown in Los Angeles

K ennedy left Hyannis Port early on Friday, July 8, at the start of his three-thousand-mile journey to the Los Angeles convention, projecting the kind of glamour and celebrity that he hoped delegates would find irresistible. Irish maids from the homes of his wealthy neighbors lined the sidewalks to wave him away, while at New York's Idlewild Airport, television cameras captured his romantic farewell to his wife, who was now heavily pregnant with their second child. After an overnight stay in New York, he boarded an American Airlines jetliner, especially christened "Flagship West Virginia," for the flight. The welcome rally that greeted him at Los Angeles International Airport that Saturday afternoon had been intricately choreographed by Kennedy advance men. On the baking-hot tarmac, over 3,500 supporters snake-danced to the calypso beat of a steel band flown in especially from the Virgin Islands.[1]

The jubilant mood reflected Kennedy's front-runner status. "Can Anybody Stop Kennedy?" asked *Newsweek* magazine, which ran an article suggesting he could already boast 643 of the 761 votes needed for a first-ballot win, "to the political mathematician . . . only a hair-breadth" from victory. Other observers were less certain. Benjamin Bradlee, the magazine's Washington bureau chief, suspected his editors had erred. Even at this late stage, he believed Johnson was capable of pulling off a surprise victory. Since the U-2 incident, foreign affairs had topped the national agenda, a shift that favored Johnson, Symington, and Stevenson.[2]

Johnson had waited until July 5 to declare his candidacy officially. He arrived in Los Angeles three days later, appearing at the plane door wearing a wide-brimmed cowboy hat and spreading his arms in a victory salute. As he stepped onto the tarmac, a band thumped out his new campaign song, "Leadership," set to the tune of "Everything's Coming Up Roses." Volunteers, dressed from head to toe in "LBJ" paraphernalia, waved banners bearing the slogan "A Leader to

Lead the Nation." But despite the best efforts of his advance team, only a sparse crowd of about 500 supporters were on hand to greet him.[3]

The Kennedy high command knew the Senate majority leader still had enough delegate support to upset their plans. Kennedy remained 160 votes short of a decisive first-ballot victory, the point at which their support was likely to peak. In subsequent ballots, delegates would probably cast around for compromise candidates, and the nomination could easily slip away. To further complicate their calculations, the California delegation, led by the state's indecisive governor, Pat Brown, was now thought to be leaning toward Stevenson. Humphrey was steering the Minnesota delegation in the same direction. In New Jersey, Governor Robert Meyner, a popular figure among northern blacks, was determined still to put his name forward in the first ballot to gain national attention, an act of political vanity that greatly infuriated the Kennedy campaign and threatened to siphon off votes.

Adlai Stevenson remained a thorn in the side of the Kennedy campaign. He had been greeted on Saturday afternoon by some 5,000 banner-waving supporters and a battered old fire truck, which carried a troupe of showgirls dressed in spangled outfits and fishnet stockings. As he stepped from the plane, he played down his chances of a third consecutive nomination, telling reporters he had no intention of promoting his candidacy. If it were dangled before him, however, he would feel honor-bound to accept.[4]

The Stop Kennedy campaign seemed to be back in force. Eleanor Roosevelt, an enthusiastic Stevenson supporter, arrived in Los Angeles and immediately made needling comments to the press about Kennedy's commitment to liberal causes and the blemishes on his civil rights record. With carefully aimed condescension, she suggested that he be offered the vice presidential slot, which would hand him "the opportunity to grow and learn." Humphrey raised similar concerns, as did Adam Clayton Powell, Jr., who complained that Kennedy's ties with Patterson, "the South's number one segregationist," made him unelectable in New York. Johnson aides spread rumors about Kennedy's health, telling reporters he suffered from Addison's disease.[5]

∽

Of the 4,509 Democratic delegates in Los Angeles, only eighty-nine were black (a sharp improvement over the 1956 convention, which only forty-five black delegates attended). But however small their number, the black delegates wielded a disproportionate amount of influence, largely because they were concentrated in vitally important states such as Pennsylvania, Minnesota, New York, Michigan, Illinois, and New Jersey, all of which were crucial to Kennedy. In the crazed atmosphere of a close-fought convention, their opposition could

potentially sway big-state, liberal-leaning northern bosses, most of them machine politicians who relied heavily on black support. "It is not that Negro delegates can nominate a candidate," Lawson advised in June, "but they and the
Negro voters behind them have a veto power in their delegations."[6]

Even despite his frenzied efforts in the weeks leading up to the convention,
many black delegates remained suspicious of Kennedy. And some were openly
disdainful, because of his votes in 1957 and his cozy relationship with leading
segregationists. To overcome their doubts, Marge and Belford Lawson planned
to spend much of their time on the convention floor mingling with black delegates, and they opened a Kennedy hospitality suite to host a series of breakfast
meetings. "We can thus pull together the contacts we have," she told Kennedy,
"and consolidate the Stevenson, Humphrey and Symington stragglers for an
early Kennedy vote."[7]

Before the convention, Lawson had recommended that Kennedy be accompanied in Los Angeles by Ruth Batson and Herbert Tucker, since "Negro
support from Massachusetts should clearly be in evidence." Being seen in the
company of blacks would also highlight one of Kennedy's great political
strengths: his ease in their presence. "During the convention, or at least when
the nomination seems assured, or afterward, arrangements should be made to
have the TV cameras pick up pictures of Senator Kennedy talking to Negro delegates," she advised, especially Vel Phillips.[8]

On the eve of the convention, Kennedy had the opportunity to address black
delegates as a group at a NAACP rally at the Shrine Auditorium. He approached
this speaking engagement with greater seriousness than most. To prepare the
groundwork, Harris Wofford had contacted Roy Wilkins early in July, both to
sound him out about the preconvention mood of NAACP activists and to ask for
his help in subduing anti-Kennedy protesters at the Sunday afternoon rally. Much
to Wofford's relief, Wilkins offered reassurance. He even agreed to clear up any
lingering confusion over the infamous Patterson breakfast meeting by explaining
to NAACP associates that Kennedy had agreed to it only to stave off a possible
Dixiecrat bolt. Wofford reported back to Kennedy that Wilkins "wishes you well
and is in your corner" and that Minnie, his wife, was "an ardent fan."[9]

Kennedy nevertheless continued to fret over the speech. His anxiety grew
when he learned via radio phone on the way to the Shrine Auditorium that a
stand-in for Johnson had been roundly booed off the stage. "I'm still not sure
that it is wise to go," he told Vel Phillips, who had accompanied him in the car.
Knowing it was too late to back out, Phillips urged him to go ahead. "I'm not
sure," the senator replied. "But I'm going to chance it." His doubts resurfaced
when he saw the melee of black activists waiting outside the auditorium. "Vel,
it would be a very bad thing at this point if . . . they booed me right out,"
Kennedy said, anxiously.

"They wouldn't do that," said Phillips, who lost one of her shoes as she dashed for the door through the jostling crowd.[10]

They entered the auditorium accompanied by a phalanx of officers from the Los Angeles Police Department. Clarence Mitchell, the NAACP's chief lobbyist, struggled to maintain order. "For God's sake, let your manners rule," he shouted at the 6,700 members of the audience. But few took much notice. Kennedy was sandwiched between Phillips and G. Mennen Williams, and only two seats from King. "Vel, I'm afraid," he confided. "It's going to be fine, you see," said Phillips. "It's going to be alright."[11]

The announcement of Kennedy's name brought a smattering of boos, but he deflected them with a wry smile as he made his way to the podium. He took a small measure of comfort from the fact that the announcement of Johnson's retreat produced much louder catcalls. Wofford had helped Kennedy prepare his address and suggested he focus on the need for more vigorous presidential leadership. So when Kennedy launched into the speech, it was in a tone that one audience member described as "courteously aggressive." "The next President of the United States cannot stand above the battle engaging in vague little sermons on brotherhood," Kennedy proclaimed. "The immense moral authority of the White House must be used to offer leadership and inspiration to those of every race and section who recognize their responsibilities." (The words "immense moral authority" were underscored in his text.) He then moved on to policy, arguing that great advancements could be made by using the "immense legal authority of the White House." (The words "immense legal authority" were also underscored.) The audience was warming to him and cheered loudly when he endorsed the student sit-in movement. Gaining in confidence, he asserted that "more subtle" forms of discrimination would no longer be tolerated, a nod to northerners in the audience who often suffered discrimination in the workplace or in their search for decent housing. He turned then to the deliberations of the Democratic platform committee. Although he stopped short of offering specifics, he insisted that the party should "speak out with courage and candor on every issue—and that includes civil rights." Before retaking his seat, he made a final promise: that as president he would deliver "moral, political, legislative and, above all, executive leadership in civil rights." The statement drew sustained applause.[12]

"Senator Kennedy certainly knows how to steal a show and turn boos into cheers," wrote Robert Walsh of the *Washington Evening Star* the next day. Other observers read the mood differently; according to another reporter, the "audience applauded politely, though with no great enthusiasm." Kennedy himself was buoyed by the reaction. He returned to his suite at the Biltmore "feeling great," according to Dave Powers. But it was ultimately Humphrey who stole the show. A longtime darling of black delegates, he gave a rousing speech that brought the Shrine Auditorium to life. The NAACP activists and protesters who took part in the sit-in movement, he proclaimed, were "as patriotic as the men who fired the first shot at Lexington and Concord." Humphrey added that he would rather be right on civil rights than become president.[13]

The convention officially began on Monday, July 11. That morning, in the hours before the opening, Robert Kennedy seemed even more agitated than usual as he addressed the daily meeting of Kennedy "delegate shepherds" in his suite. Unsettled by both Stevenson's triumphant arrival and Eleanor Roosevelt's outspoken attack over the weekend, he seemed especially worried about wavering liberal and black delegates. Later that day, at the first meeting of the platform committee, Chester Bowles, its chairman, planned to introduce a strongly worded civil rights plank, drawn up with the help of Harris Wofford and Abram Chayes, of Harvard. Robert Kennedy wanted to use this as an opportunity to boost the campaign. "I want to say a few words about civil rights," he said. "We have the best civil rights plank the Democratic Party has ever had," he snapped. "I want you to make it clear to your delegations that the Kennedy forces are unequivocally in favor of this plank and that we want it passed in the convention. Those of you who are dealing with southern delegations make it absolutely clear how we stand on civil rights. Don't fuzz it up. Tell the southern states that we hope they will see other reasons why we are united as Democrats and why they should support Kennedy, but don't let there be doubt anywhere as to how the Kennedy people stand on this." (Earlier in the morning, when the candidate himself had bumped into Joseph Rauh in the hotel lobby, he had said the exact same thing: the Kennedy camp would go "all out" on civil rights, and was prepared to give the Platform Committee what he called a "blank check."[14])

Bowles and Wofford were dumbstruck by Robert Kennedy's vehemence. When they arrived in Los Angeles, they had just completed their sixth draft of the platform. It overflowed with far-reaching proposals that neither of them imagined would ever be adopted. They had included many for bargaining purposes alone, in anticipation that southerners on the platform committee would doubtless whittle them down. So with each successive draft, the platform became increasingly bold, as they added new recommendations. In draft two they strengthened the language on school desegregation, calling for every school board to submit integration plans by 1963. In draft three they called for the desegregation of all armed forces and the elimination of literacy tests in elections. Draft four included a passage endorsing the sit-in movement, much to the personal satisfaction of Bowles, whose children, Sally and Sam, had picketed the F. W. Woolworth five-and-dime in New Haven.[15]

Though Wofford and Bowles were delighted to hear Robert Kennedy endorse the strongest possible version of the platform—the "maximal draft"—they suspected his knowledge of its actual contents was entirely superficial. Prior to the convention he had demonstrated little interest in the drafting process. The same was true of Jack Kennedy, who had seen an early draft of the platform back in May, but given it only a "cursory glance." On the eve of the convention, when he was handed the maximum version, he studied it for fifteen minutes and made no comment. When probed by reporters about its contents, he said only that "Congressman Bowles is writing the platform [and] I'm confident that he and his committee will do the job." Aides went further. One told reporter Anthony Lewis that Kennedy was highly satisfied with Bowles's efforts, since a robust civil rights plank underscored his liberalism and was in line with his pre-convention strategy of distancing himself from the South. "We're not going out of our way to alienate anyone," the aide told Lewis, "but we certainly don't have to worry about accommodations with the South on civil rights."[16]

Like Wofford and Bowles, the Kennedy campaign almost certainly expected that the maximal plank would be watered down once it reached the drafting committee. They were in for a surprise. DNC chairman Paul Butler had packed the drafting committee with liberals; of its twenty members, only four were from the South, and none was prepared to launch a battle over civil rights. Johnson had specifically warned the southerners on the platform committee not to create a stir, since even mild resistance would harden northern delegations against him.[17]

When the drafting committee actually met, only two of the four southerners—Senator Sam Ervin of North Carolina and Congressman Oren Harris of Arkansas—bothered even to remain in the room while the civil rights plank was under discussion. Neither put up any resistance, which emboldened liberals on the committee to insert even stronger language on fair employment rights. When the plank was put before the full platform committee, southerners again shied away from a fight. Even Governor Ross Barnett of Mississippi, one of the region's most recalcitrant segregationists, passed up the opportunity to address the full committee. There was certainly no walkout or floor demonstration. "By 1960, the people of the South could see that segregation was doomed to pass away," Florida Governor LeRoy Collins, the chairman of the convention, reflected afterwards. "I felt that the vast majority of Southerners would not want to be associated with this kind of last-ditch or rear-guard action before the people of the nation."[18]

When the plank came before a vote of the full platform committee on Tuesday, it passed without amendment by sixty-six votes to twenty-four. It was a personal triumph for Bowles and Wofford. At the beginning of the week, they had assumed that their maximal draft would be ripped to shreds. Instead, it emerged even stronger. The approved version called for the elimination of the poll tax and literacy tests, Part III powers for the attorney general, the establishment of a Fair Employment Practices Committee, a permanent Civil Rights Commission, an executive order eliminating discrimination in federal housing programs, and, most controversially of all, a commitment to ensuring that every southern school district submit a plan "for at least first step compliance" by 1963. Without question, it was the most forward-thinking civil rights plank in party history.[19]

The Kennedy campaign had, however, continued to hedge on civil rights. At the same time as Kennedy and his brother were vociferously supporting the civil rights plank, the campaign's southern lieutenants—most notably Bobby Trout-man—were secretly reaching out to southern delegates. Troutman privately re-assured segregationists that they should not be overly concerned about Kennedy's newfound enthusiasm for civil rights. At heart, he was truly a grad-ualist, who would not as president feel bound by the platform's contents.[20]

Kennedy himself offered some succor to the South. He appeared on Monday before a secret caucus of the North Carolina delegation, where he criticized Eisenhower's handling of the Little Rock crisis. "I had never said I thought the use of paratroopers was necessary," he claimed. "I have never been convinced that the local police could not have handled the trouble." Kennedy surely as-sumed his comments would go unreported, but a correspondent from the *Washington Afro-American* soon caught wind of them. The flap further complicated Marge Lawson's efforts to line up black support.[21]

∽

Throughout the week, Stevenson's insurgent campaign gained momentum. On Monday, thousands of his supporters gathered outside the Los Angeles Sports Arena in a boisterous display of devotion. On Tuesday they invaded the con-vention hall itself, occupying many of its 22,400 seats and chanting his name so loudly that the steel girders of the newly built arena quivered. That afternoon, Stevenson decided to make an unscheduled appearance in the convention hall, hoping it would ignite the crowd. But even he was taken aback by the ensuing pandemonium. Later on, Stevenson provided even more unscripted drama by making a late-night appearance before a huge crowd of well-wishers gathered under his hotel window. He hinted strongly that he was intending to declare his candidacy. "The woods are lovely, dark and deep/But I have promises to keep," he said enigmatically, quoting Robert Frost. "And miles to go before I sleep/And miles to go before I sleep."[22]

Stevenson stood little chance of winning the nomination, especially after Illi-nois, his home state, announced its support for Kennedy. But his popularity increased the chances of a hung convention. That Monday, the all-important California delegation had decided to split its vote between Kennedy and Stevenson, and a rump of Kennedy supporters from New York started to waver. Lawrence O'Brien believed still that a Kennedy victory was close at hand, yet he knew they were twenty-five votes short of a first-ballot victory. So when Robert Kennedy delivered his final pep talk that Tuesday morning, there was a discernible note of frustration in his voice. "If we don't win tonight," said the fraught campaign manager, melodramatically, "we're dead."[23]

Given Stevenson's resurgence, the nomination speeches on Wednesday afternoon took on heightened significance. The Kennedy campaign needed to demonstrate the broadest possible support for his candidacy with their selection of speakers. Robert Kennedy chose Governor Orville Freeman of Minnesota, a Prairie Progressive in the Humphrey mold, and Terry Sanford, a determinedly moderate gubernatorial candidate from North Carolina. He also made sure that a black speaker was included in the roster of nominators and was allotted three minutes to speak, the exact same time as Sanford. Before the convention, Sorensen had vetted a possible shortlist of black speakers, which included Phillips, Frank Reeves, a Washington attorney and head of the District of Columbia chapter of the NAACP, and Jake Simmons, a lesser-known NAACP official from Oklahoma. The Symington campaign had already lined up Charles Diggs, one of only four black congressmen, to place his name in nomination, and Kennedy needed a figure of comparable stature. Reeves ultimately won out, partly because he had supported Humphrey in the primaries and partly because he had been the first black ever to have been elected to the Democratic National Committee. When he mounted the dais, Reeves told his fellow delegates Kennedy "will win in November." He added jokingly, "I know, I campaigned against him." Of Kennedy's nominating speakers, Reeves's was by far the most impassioned. "Boldness must be the course of America," he bellowed into the microphone. "And bold must be its leader."[24]

The convention reached fever pitch on Wednesday evening as the Draft Stevenson movement gathered force. Outside of the Sports Arena, so many of his supporters arrived that the Los Angeles Police Department had to bring in reinforcements, while inside the hall, Eugene McCarthy nominated the former governor with a spellbinding speech, even though Stevenson had not even declared his candidacy. "Do not reject this man who made us proud to be called Democrats," he shouted. "Do not reject this man who is not the favorite son of one state, but the favorite son of fifty states and of every country on earth." The convention exploded into life, and it was a full thirty minutes before the cheers subsided.[25]

Watching the Stevenson carnival on television, Jack Kennedy grew more anxious and called his brother. Robert Kennedy tried to calm his nerves, telling him once again that Stevenson's support had peaked the night before. Joe Kennedy, who was watching events unfold alongside Jack, then grabbed the telephone and demanded additional reassurance. Bobby told his father, "Stevenson has everything but delegates." Then the roll call began. Jack grabbed hold of a pencil and piece of cardboard so he could keep a running tally.[26]

Alabama was the first state to cast its votes. The Kennedy campaign faced an immediate problem: the possibility that Governor John Patterson would place his entire delegation in the New Englander's column, a move certain to infuriate liberals and blacks. Patterson had once been a valuable friend and ally, but as the Kennedy campaign veered left he had become an embarrassment. The issue, however, was far from being clear-cut. The campaign could not afford to discard much-needed votes at the start of the first ballot, just in case it fell short at the end. Just before the roll call started Stephen Smith, Kennedy's brother-in-law, approached Patterson to ask how many votes he planned to cast for the senator.

"I got fourteen," replied Patterson.

"Well, now we want you to vote six," demanded Smith.

Patterson complained that his delegates were enthusiastically behind Kennedy.

But Smith was immovable. "Do it," he said, firmly.

With that, the governor scurried off to a nearby stairwell, and instructed delegates to vote against Kennedy. A few minutes later, when the roll call started, Alabama cast 20 votes for Johnson, and just 3.5 for Kennedy.[27]

For the first few minutes the race between Johnson and Kennedy seemed close, since large blocs of southern delegates—Arkansas, Georgia, Florida— were near the top of the ballot sheet. But when northern states, like Illinois, Michigan, and Pennsylvania, threw their votes behind Kennedy his total climbed rapidly. Before the roll call, Bobby Kennedy had estimated that if his brother had passed the 700 mark by the time Washington cast its votes, then the nomination would be secure. After Washington, the tally board showed 710 delegates in his column. West Virginia, Wisconsin, and Wyoming clinched his victory. At the end of the first ballot, Kennedy had a final tally of 806, Johnson was second with 409, Stuart Symington third with 86 and Stevenson trailing in fourth with just 79.5. The presidential nomination was his.[28]

Black delegates made a small but significant contribution to his victory. Out of eighty-nine black delegates, Lawson estimated that forty-two or forty-three eventually cast their votes for Kennedy. Kennedy's tactical decision to abandon the South and fashion a bold stance on civil rights had worked. His resolute speech before the NAACP also helped drum up last-minute support. And Kennedy owed an enormous amount to his surrogates: Marge Lawson, who had toured the convention floor confronting disgruntled delegates; Ruth Batson and Herbert Tucker, who had defended Kennedy's record for several days on end at the Kennedy hospitality suite; and, more importantly, Chester Bowles and Harris Wofford, who had crafted a bold civil rights plank for Kennedy to endorse.[29]

೧

Kennedy's next move came as a shock to his party. Late on Thursday afternoon, Kennedy announced that he had chosen Johnson as a running mate. After lurching so far toward the progressive wing of the party in his quest for the nomination, Kennedy's choice of Johnson signaled a return toward the political center. Although the two men had vastly different pedigrees and personalities—producing the unlikely combination of an Ivy League, New England Catholic and an anti-intellectual "Rawhide" Texan—the ticket blended youth and experience and offered an almost perfect political and geographical balance. Whether Johnson was Kennedy's first choice is a matter still of historical conjecture—"a convoluted chronology of misreadings, miscommunications, and missed connections," in the view of one historian who has tried to patch together the bewildering tumble of events—but it produced a formidable ticket.[30]

According to Robert Kennedy, who despised Johnson for his double-barreled attack shortly after arriving in Los Angeles on Jack Kennedy's health and Joe Kennedy's appeasement toward Hitler, the decision emerged out of colossal misunderstanding. At ten A.M. on Thursday, July 13, the morning after the first-ballot victory, Robert Kennedy and Johnson held a private meeting in the Texan's hotel suite. Kennedy later claimed he meant only to sound out Johnson about joining the ticket. But Johnson interpreted it as a concrete offer and accepted on the spot. Realizing that the Kennedy camp would face a revolt from liberals, labor leaders, and blacks, shortly after one P.M. Robert Kennedy revisited Johnson's suite in an attempt to talk him off the ticket. But as the campaign manager scurried from suite to suite, the presidential nominee added to the confusion by personally telephoning the Texan at about 3:30 that afternoon with a much more clear-cut offer. The confusion did not end there. Half an hour later, Robert Kennedy reappeared in the Johnson suite. This time RFK tried to persuade Johnson to accept the chairmanship of the DNC rather than the second slot on the ticket.[31]

Johnson was bewildered by the vacillations in the Kennedy camp and was jumping up and down like a "Mexican bean," in the words of one eyewitness. Throughout the afternoon, Philip Graham, the publisher of the *Washington Post*, had been acting as an emissary between the Johnson and Kennedy camps, and Sam Rayburn shouted at him to telephone the candidate to bring an end to the chaos. Graham explained to Jack Kennedy that Bobby had just offered Johnson the chairmanship of the party, as a consolation for dropping him from the ticket. "Oh that's all right," Kennedy reportedly replied. "Bobby's been out of touch, and doesn't know what's happening." The matter finally settled in his own mind, Kennedy then offered Johnson the post again.[32]

Afterward, Kennedy never explained his decision to appoint Johnson, but a number of forces were clearly at work. Whatever their personal differences, Kennedy certainly understood that Johnson would be a tremendous asset to the ticket. Just that morning, he had met with southern governors J. Lindsey Almond of Virginia, Ernest Hollings of South Carolina, and J. Howard Edmondson of Oklahoma. All were in agreement: It would be impossible to carry the South without Johnson. Sorensen also thought a Johnson vice presidency might have its benefits. He "helps with farmers, Southerners and Texas" Sorensen had noted in the runup to the convention, and it would also be "easier to work with in this position than as majority leader." But liberals within the Kennedy camp were vehemently opposed. Before the convention, Wofford told Bowles, "Any southerner on the ticket would further alienate Negro and northern liberal votes. And Kennedy already faces serious trouble with the Negro vote." Schlesinger had cautioned, "A Johnson nomination for Vice-President would be a disaster in the North." Robert Kennedy, meanwhile, was almost inconsolable. That Thursday had been, he told the journalist Charles Bartlett, "the worst day of his life."[33]

Jack Kennedy knew that the decision would come as a blow to black delegates, so at around five o'clock that evening he summoned Reeves to his hotel suite. Standing in his boxer shorts, Kennedy informed Reeves of the decision. He knew Johnson's inclusion was bound to be unpopular among blacks, but politics had dictated his choice. Reeves warned that Johnson would be "difficult to sell." But Kennedy merely responded that everyone would simply have to "work a little harder."[34]

That Thursday evening, there was uproar in the Kennedy civil rights office when Wofford announced the news. Batson, for one, was "stunned" and received little comfort from Robert Kennedy when he visited the office later that evening. "Listen, you folks just have to be realistic," he stated, knowing he had to publicly back his brother's decision. "This campaign is going to be won on much more than civil rights. You've got to trust the Senator." When Herbert Tucker dashed upstairs to meet with the candidate and beseeched him to issue a bold and compensatory statement on civil rights, Robert Kennedy yelled at him. "What do you think we're running a campaign for?" shouted the young campaign manager. "Negroes alone?"[35]

The response outside the campaign was even more vitriolic. Joseph Rauh, who had been personally assured by Kennedy earlier in the week that Humphrey would be on the ticket, rushed to the convention hall and grabbed the first open microphone. "Wherever you are, John F. Kennedy," he shouted, "I beseech you to reconsider." At about the same time, Schlesinger came close to physically assaulting Philip Graham, whom he blamed for bringing the Kennedy and Johnson camps together. Had it not been for the timely intervention of Graham's wife, Katharine, Schlesinger might even have punched Phil Graham out. Walter Reuther, the head of the powerful United Auto Workers, led a delegation of labor officials to Kennedy's suite to warn him that black voters were now almost certain to back Nixon. Harried Kennedy aides reminded the group that Roosevelt had picked Texan conservative John Nance Garner as his running mate in 1932, and that Stevenson had selected Alabama Senator John Sparkman. But times had changed, the labor leaders argued. Given the concentration of black voters in key battleground states, and their heightened politicization, it was no longer possible to win a national election with a racial conservative on the ticket.[36]

Later that evening, Congressman William Dawson, the senior black lawmaker on Capitol Hill, placed Johnson's name in nomination. The Kennedy campaign had chosen Dawson for the job to placate liberals and blacks, and he performed ably. "[N]ever have I known him to do or say one thing based on questions of race, creed or sectionalism," insisted Dawson. But it was a Harlem congressman, the Reverend Adam Clayton Powell, Jr., who played the most pivotal role in quelling a black rebellion. Powell assembled all eighty-nine black delegates behind the curtain of the convention hall and pleaded with them to endorse the ticket. Powell argued Johnson was a far superior choice than either Sparkman in 1952 or Kefauver four years later and emphasized his role in the passage of the 1957 and 1960 Civil Rights Acts. Looking beyond the election, Powell forecast Johnson's place as a Senate majority leader would be taken by either Humphrey or Eugene McCarthy, another boon to liberals.[37]

Party chiefs had arranged for Johnson to be nominated by swift acclamation rather than a roll call, which threatened to draw out the process and expose the depths of the divisions within the party in the wake of Kennedy's choice. Nonetheless, there were scenes of anger and dismay on the convention floor. G. Mennen Williams bellowed "No, No," as the voice vote was taken, while his wife ripped off her Kennedy button in protest.[38]

For his part, Johnson felt unjustly maligned by the reaction among blacks, particularly since he had been the main architect of the 1957 Civil Rights Act. In the run-up to the convention, Johnson had been endorsed by a number of black newspapers, which recognized his central role during that legislative battle, and gained the sneaking admiration of Wilkins, who thought his "enormous knowledge of government" would be a huge asset in pushing civil rights. So when Kennedy aides came up with the idea of a joint appearance by the two nominees before a caucus of black delegates, the Texan enthusiastically agreed to participate. (He did, however, take Reeves's advice about leaving Lady Bird Johnson behind because the reception was likely to be so hostile.) Held at the Biltmore Hotel that Friday, the meeting was organized by Congressman Dawson.[39]

For Johnson, it was his first high-profile appearance as a national candidate rather than a son of the South, and he needed desperately to remold his public image. "I'll do more for you in four years in the field of civil rights than you've experienced in the last hundred years," Johnson pledged to his audience. "I won't let you down. . . . I assure you from the bottom of my heart that I have done my dead level best to make progress in the field of civil rights." He promised to campaign the length and breadth of the country and never compromise on the party's far-reaching platform. Then, with a theatrical flourish, he ended his speech with a quote from the old Baptist hymn, "where He leads, I will follow."[40]

Kennedy seemed just as startled as everyone else by Johnson's virtuoso performance and came no way near matching it when he took the microphone. But his message was essentially the same: The Democrats would not softpeddle civil rights. "I never thought a platform was a bunch of lumber that could be thrown aside after the election," he declared, to the applause of the black delegates.[41]

The Democratic convention reached its climax that Friday night in the openair setting of the mighty Los Angeles Coliseum. Kennedy delivered an impassioned acceptance speech and, for the first time, used the phrase "New Frontier"—a slogan intended to evoke memories of Roosevelt's New Deal. Key advisers, like Sorensen, O'Brien, and his brother, urged him to focus on the Democrats' main area of agreement: the communist challenge from the Soviet Union and China. And so Kennedy insisted the foremost question of the forthcoming campaign was whether the American system of freedom and democracy could endure. He made no mention of the battle for freedom at home. Even though the party had just adopted the most far-reaching civil rights plank in its history, it was as if Kennedy had already forgotten.

Kennedy was, in fact, already modifying his approach to the issue of civil rights. While he and his campaign were offering assurances that liberals and blacks has nothing to fear from Johnson, they were simultaneously trying to convince southerners they had little to fear from Kennedy's presidency. Governor J. Lindsey Almond of Virginia conducted private talks with Kennedy before leaving Los Angeles and publicly endorsed the campaign soon thereafter. "Kennedy stated his fundamental convictions and they are not any departure from principles Virginians stand for," he told reporters. "Kennedy is deeply concerned for our way of thinking: and the world knows just what the South's way of thinking is." Although no record survives of their private conservation, it is fair to assume that Kennedy stepped away from the Democratic platform—there could be no other explanation for Almond's fulsome endorsement. Soon thereafter, Kennedy began to offer other southern leaders similar assurances. Governor Ernest Vandiver of Georgia met Kennedy a few weeks later at Johnson's Senate office. In the privacy of the majority leader's bathroom, the candidate promised he would never send federal troops into Georgia to enforce school desegregation (although he refused to discount the possibility of U.S. marshals performing a similar role).[42]

Kennedy's shift did not go unnoticed. Commenting on Almond's endorsement, Gordon Hancock, a columnist for the *Afro-American* group of newspapers, noted, "We are beginning to wonder just what commitment Kennedy has made to make him so strong with the South. . . . Even the most gullible must suspect something irregular when Southerners do not fly in the face of anybody and anything that promises civil rights for citizens."[43]

                            ᘒ

With Congress due to reconvene for a special short session in August, there was a very real possibility that Democratic divisions could explode into the open. Liberal Democrats in the Senate were determined to introduce a new civil rights bill. Republicans recognized an opportunity to pry the party further apart. Everett Dirksen, the Republican Senate minority leader, planned to introduce his own bill, incorporating proposals from both the Democratic platform and Republican version, which was almost as bold. Senator Kenneth Keating of New York wanted to challenge Kennedy more directly on the issue by reading the entire Democratic platform on the floor of the Senate and then publicly inviting Kennedy to join him in co-sponsoring legislation minting it into law.[44]

Kennedy was worried about the effect of the Senate session on his presidential bid. "The general public is likely to be unaffected by all this or to see through it as merely a political play," wrote a Kennedy adviser at the end of July, "but Negro voters might be very seriously disaffected from the Democratic ticket unless effective counter measures are taken." Kennedy brought Johnson to Hyannis Port on July 30 in order to plot their counterattack. To cloak differences within the party, the Texan believed they should sideline civil rights and focus instead on economic issues like medical care for the elderly, a raise in the minimum wage, better public housing, and increased federal aid to education.[45]

Kennedy was torn. Like Johnson, he was worried about inflaming the South, but he was concerned, too, about ceding too much ground to the Republicans on civil rights. His liberal advisers pushed him on the point. Wofford advised that the "Republican thrust" should be met with "a hard-hitting offensive . . . otherwise, you and Senator Johnson will be isolated from those most identified with the struggle for civil rights legislation and you will be given the 'moderate' or 'gradualist' tag which proved so damaging to Stevenson with Negro voters in 1956." Schlesinger likewise warned that it would be foolish to allow the Republican initiative to go unanswered. He recommended that, at the very least, Kennedy should make a keynote speech at the beginning of the special session setting out his pro–civil rights philosophy. It would be "very important," he said, in bolstering the morale of liberal Democrats still unhappy with Johnson's inclusion on the ticket.[46]

Kennedy ultimately deferred to Johnson and decided to sideline civil rights during the special session. But to demonstrate his ideological commitment to the issue, he decided to launch a bold initiative aimed at black voters just days before Congress reconvened—the creation within the Democratic campaign of a new Civil Rights Section (CRS). The original idea had come from black delegates in Los Angeles. They felt, in the words of an internal memorandum to Robert Kennedy, "that a 'civil rights' section was a better approach than a 'Negro vote' or 'minorities' section," since "the latter have connotations of the very segregation which Negro voters want to end." The inclusion of blacks in "all parts of the campaign" had "never been done on a significant scale before," and it would clearly yield a political dividend. "Doing it should by itself have considerable impact on Negro voters," the memorandum noted. "It will be a sign that new opportunities will *in fact* open under the Kennedy Administration."[47]

On August 3, as senators made their way back to Washington, Kennedy invited reporters to Hyannis Port to announce the creation of a new Civil Rights Section. In the bright August sunshine, with a beaming Reeves at his side, the candidate promised that the CRS would be fully integrated, both racially and organizationally, "a departure from previous practice." Kennedy had learned from his early campaigns in Boston that by including blacks within his campaign he could demonstrate visibly his commitment to the cause of black equality. Now, he was convinced it could be a substitute for other, more substantive initiatives.[48]

When the special session opened at noon on Monday, August 7, it promptly deteriorated into a sorry spectacle of partisan bickering. Johnson launched into a blistering two-hour speech in which he railed against the Eisenhower administration's failure to raise the minimum wage, provide medical care for the aged, and pass a school construction bill. The following day, the Republicans countered with their civil rights bill. Speaking to reporters outside the chamber, Kennedy caustically dismissed the GOP bill as an example of "eleventh-hour politics" and pointed out that Dirksen had helped torpedo similar Democratic-sponsored proposals earlier in the year. Then Kennedy mounted a withering attack on Eisenhower for his failure to provide firm presidential leadership. "Eleven months ago the Civil Rights Commission unanimously proposed that the President issue an Executive order on equal opportunities in housing," he blasted. "The President has not acted during all this time. He could and should act now."[49]

To further blunt the Republican offensive, Johnson arranged for Pennsylvania's Joseph Clark, one of the chamber's great liberal statesmen, to introduce a motion tabling the administration-backed civil rights bill. "I believe I can recognize the hand of politics," shouted Clark, with marvelous theatricality. But Johnson, for all his great feeling for the drama of the Senate, was unable to choreograph the entire scene. To his chagrin, four leading liberals—Paul Douglas, Philip Hart, Wayne Morse, and Pat McNamara—could not bring themselves to kill any kind of civil rights bill. In their refusal to join in Clark's motion, they revealed the very divisions within the Democratic Party that the Republicans had hoped to expose. Before the August session, a Kennedy adviser had warned of the dangers of being "isolated from those identified with the struggle for civil rights legislation." That is precisely what had happened.[50]

Watching the debate unfold, Louis Martin, a black former journalist who had just joined the Kennedy staff, believed the Democrats were in danger of being outmaneuvered. "It seems obvious at this point that the GOP high command is determined to twist the arm of Democrats on civil rights on all fronts," he warned colleagues in the CRS. If the Republicans continued to make "grandstand plays" and "spotlight the soft spots in the Democratic front" then black support would hemorrhage. As Martin pointed out, Wilkins was already questioning the Democrats' credibility on civil rights, and even the normally pro-Kennedy *New York Post* had grown hostile. "Is Johnson the master in Kennedy's house?" the paper asked in a scathing editorial on August 10. If so, "the price of Southern comfort may prove to be prohibitive."[51]

Two days into the special session, Kennedy finally took center stage, thus becoming the first presidential nominee to address the Senate since Henry Clay in 1832. In a combative speech, Kennedy accused Dirksen of "political trickery" and of making a "mockery" out of "the greatest moral issue before this nation." Rather than play politics with civil rights, said Kennedy, the Democrats would come forward with their own civil rights bill as soon as Congress reconvened in January. He promised that it would be a far-reaching measure, incorporating fair employment measures, proposals to boost voting rights, and Part III powers for the attorney general aimed at accelerating southern school desegregation. In addition, he also pledged to bring about a change in Senate rules in order to weaken the power of the filibuster.[52]

There was a swift response from the South. That week, Mississippi Democrats announced they planned to put up two slates of electors in November, one supporting the Kennedy/Johnson ticket, the other unpledged electors dedicated to the segregationist cause. Citing the Democrats' "communistic" civil rights plank, which he described as "horrible," "repulsive," and "obnoxious," Mississippi Governor Ross Barnett announced his support for the unpledged electors and urged other southerners to follow his lead. By doing so, Barnett hoped both candidates would be deprived of an outright majority in the Electoral College, which would throw the election into the House of Representatives, where southern Democrats held more sway. Disgruntled Democrats in Louisiana and South Carolina tried, but failed narrowly, to follow suit.[53]

Faced with a nascent Dixie rebellion, Kennedy responded quickly. He convened a lunch that Saturday with southern senators and delivered an honest assessment of his electoral dilemma. According to Washington Senator Henry

"Scoop" Jackson, who was present at the meeting, he told senators that "we recognize their problems but we're not going to compromise" since the Democrats could not win without northern liberal and black support. Kennedy took a calculated risk in standing up to the southern senators. He placed enormous confidence in Johnson's ability to appease southern leaders and set great store in his own, longtime reputation as a racial gradualist.[54]

The August session, and the bitter squabbling it exposed within the Democratic Party, seemed a portent of things to come. The prospect weighed heavily on Kennedy's mind. One afternoon, midway through the August session, as he was driving toward the Senate in his open-top red convertible, he shared his frustrations with Harris Wofford, whom he had spotted hailing a cab on a sidewalk in Georgetown. Once Wofford was in the passenger seat, Kennedy gave him five minutes to "tick off the ten things a President ought to do to clean up this goddamn civil rights mess," as he put it. His left hand tapped incessantly on the window while he waited for Wofford to offer his advice.[55]

Crystallizing his many years of thinking on the subject, Wofford outlined how a steady stream of executive orders from the White House could obviate the need for congressional action. Kennedy could circumvent Congress and would thereby be able to eliminate discrimination in employment, federally assisted housing, and, even more controversially, southern schools. It was certainly not the first time Wofford had advocated the use of executive orders, and Kennedy had spoken already of their potential in a number of appearances in the run-up to Los Angeles. But in the midst of the August session, the notion seemed particularly attractive, for it offered an alternative to gridlock on Capitol Hill.[56]

Despite Kennedy's counterattack against the Republicans on the civil rights issue, liberals remained unimpressed. As Schlesinger pointed out in late August, Johnson's inclusion on the ticket had interrupted "the emotional momentum" of the campaign, which palpably lacked any "sense of crusading urgency." As a result, liberal activists, "the kind of people who have traditionally provided the spark in Democratic campaigns," were offering little in the way of practical support. "Once the issue-minded Democrats catch fire, then the campaign will gather steam," Schlesinger predicted. But that would happen only if Kennedy abandoned the evenhanded approach to civil rights that he had adopted since the convention. "Herbert Lehman and Tom Finletter [two leading liberals] will bring you many more votes than Harry Byrd and Howard Smith [two racist firebrands]," Schlesinger warned bluntly.[57]

Later that month, more unwelcome news arrived from the national meeting of the ADA. In protest at Johnson's inclusion, six chapters of the organization refused outright to endorse the Democratic ticket, while a further five expressed no preference. The New York chapter did so only after a tie-breaking vote by its chairman. Harvard academic Sam Beer, the president of the ADA and a close personal associate of Kennedy, was taken aback by the ferocity of liberal discontent and warned that it was "much wider and deeper than I expected. . . . There seems to be a hard core we can't do much about." Beer suggested a major civil rights speech, a tactic that Schlesinger had long advocated. Bowles proffered the same advice. "We would be wise, I believe, to go on the offensive as soon as possible," he told Kennedy, suggesting that a major civil rights speech might "help blunt the adverse reaction which will follow this session."[58]

But Kennedy still wanted to avoid taking a public stand on behalf of either wing of the party. He wanted to heal, or at least camouflage, divisions within the party—not make a fiery speech that could exacerbate them. And so, toward the end of the August session, he tried to persuade northern and southern Democrats to agree on a statement of general principle on civil rights, a "Unity Manifesto." While Democratic senators accepted the idea in principle, in practice it proved incredibly difficult to agree on actual wording—particularly since the task of drafting the manifesto had fallen to Harris Wofford and Senator Richard Russell, whose racial views were diametrically opposed. Russell rejected all of Wofford's draft statements and demanded watered-down rewrites. When finally they produced a delicately worded compromise, Kennedy vetoed it, out of fear liberals and blacks would reject such a weak statement. After tearing up more than half a dozen drafts, Wofford finally admitted defeat, believing it was impossible to reach agreement on a worthwhile statement of principle that southern lawmakers would sign.[59]

With compromise unattainable, Kennedy was forced to decide whether to abandon the whole idea of a unity statement or to issue a more liberal-leaning declaration that risked upsetting southerners. Eventually, he decided on the latter course, since his most urgent priorities by the end of August were to energize the party's northern liberal base and to satisfy black skeptics of his commitment to reform. Wofford drew up the statement, which included an excoriating attack both on Eisenhower, who was accused of failing to exert moral leadership, and the GOP Senate leadership, which was charged with playing politics with civil rights in an attempt to "conceal their own empty, negative record." There were harsh words, as well, for the Republican nominee, Vice President Richard Nixon, whose stewardship of the Government Contracts Committee, a body created to eliminate employment discrimination, had been a dreadful failure, according to the statement. During its seven-year existence, the committee had failed to punish any firms, aside from one or two threats in the District of Columbia, demonstrating that Nixon was interested more in pandering to the business lobby than in improving job opportunities for black Americans. The statement contained promises, as well, *"to obtain consideration of a civil rights bill by the Senate early next session that will implement the pledges of the Democratic platform,"* words italicized for emphasis. Twenty-three liberal Democrats signed the statement, with the one exception of Eugene McCarthy, who was still bitter over Stevenson's defeat in Los Angeles. Johnson also abstained. Since he was charged with winning back the southern states that had voted for Eisenhower in 1956, it was simply impossible for him to sign.[60]

Kennedy felt the need to go further still. Before leaving Washington for his opening campaign swing over the Labor Day weekend, he summoned reporters to the Senate Caucus room on September 1 for his first major press conference as the Democratic nominee. At his side were two of the party's most recognizably liberal figures, Congressman Emanuel Celler of New York, whose Brooklyn district included the largely black neighborhood of Bedford-Stuyvesant, and Senator Joseph Clark from Pennsylvania. Kennedy announced plans for a bold new civil rights bill, encompassing the proposals of the Democratic platform, early in the next congressional session. "This is a difficult fight," admitted the candidate, who had been chastened by the Democratic infighting of the past three weeks. "All I'm saying is that we are committing ourselves. I would not want our inability to do anything about civil rights in this session to mislead anybody to think we are not trying to do something about it."[61]

In holding the press conference, Kennedy had chosen to disregard warnings from Johnson aides that an appearance alongside two such militant liberals would anger southern voters. George Reedy, one of the Senate majority leader's top aides, expressed himself most vividly, telling Johnson that Clark and Celler had been chosen to "arouse the maximum amount of revolt in the South. The only name missing is Thaddeus Stevens." He also objected to the wording of the statement, since "it gives the impression that Senator Kennedy is going to hold a gun to the Senate's head and is delivering an ultimatum 'get out of town by sundown.'" Even Wofford was worried about the potential impact of so clear an alignment with northern liberals at this early stage of the campaign. In advance of Kennedy's appearance, he had suggested that rather than relying exclusively on Clark and Celler, Kennedy should appoint a commission made up of northern liberals and southern moderates. Despite these warnings, Kennedy pressed ahead—a measure both of the growing importance of the black electorate in big industrial states, and of the intensity of the liberal revolt he was facing in the wake of the convention. Though Kennedy did not intend to make civil rights central to his campaign, he desperately needed to repair the damage from the bobtail session.[62]

Less than a month after his triumph at the convention, Kennedy was mired once again in the ugly politics of the civil rights battle. The August session had been a disaster. It demonstrated his shortcomings as a congressional leader, reopened the fissures within the Democratic Party, and lodged lingering reservations in his mind about his ability to push meaningful civil rights legislation through an unruly Congress. For the remainder of the campaign, Kennedy carried on with the pretense that his administration would introduce bold legislation. But most of his speeches actually emphasized how the executive branch would shoulder the burden of reform rather than Congress. The intractability of the issue, as revealed by the August session, clearly made a deep impression on Kennedy. It may have even been the point at which he decided not to make a new civil rights bill one of his early priorities—although, of course, he did not announce the decision formally until after the election.

CHAPTER 10

❧

The Strategy of Association

A happy surprise awaited Richard Nixon when, two weeks after the end of the Republican convention, he made an early foray into the South. On August 17, while Kennedy was still trapped in Washington, he made his first stop in Greensboro, North Carolina, where his campaign had rented a local ice rink with a seating capacity of over 9,000 to host "An Evening of Skating and Coffee with Dick and Pat." The venue was too small to accommodate the unexpectedly large number of southerners eager to hear the vice president, and the 2,500 seats of an overflow auditorium next door quickly filled up as well, leaving more than 1,500 people stranded on the sidewalk. "That is the kind of crowd you get in the last weeks of a campaign," an excitable Nixon later told aides. "There is something happening down there. We are going to have to look at these southern states again."[1]

Nixon received an even more rapturous ticker-tape welcome the following week in Birmingham, as his blue convertible snaked through the city streets. "It is time for the Democratic candidate for the presidency to quit taking Alabama and the South for granted," he shouted, wiping confetti from his eyes. "And it is time for the Republican candidate for the Presidency to quit conceding Alabama and the South to the Democratic candidate." Later on that day in Atlanta, Ralph McGill, the publisher of the *Atlanta Constitution*, described his welcome as the "greatest thing . . . since the premiere of *Gone with the Wind*."[2]

Like Kennedy, Nixon was well aware of the tactical importance of the black vote in northern states. He was well placed to appeal to this constituency because the Republican Party had also embraced a strong civil rights plank—in fact, the strongest in the party's history after Governor Nelson Rockefeller of New York had pressed Nixon for changes on the eve of the convention, as part of their so-called Treaty of Fifth Avenue. In plotting his electoral strategy at the outset of the campaign, Nixon had been determined to emphasize civil rights.

But those early swings through the South altered his thinking. Perhaps the road to the White House passed through the states of the Old Confederacy.

Kennedy wanted it both ways—to earn support both in the North and South. With Johnson as a running mate, he was uniquely positioned to pull it off. Kennedy was determined to thwart the rise of southern "Presidential Republicanism," which meant he had to reclaim the traditionally Democratic states of Virginia, Florida, Louisiana, Tennessee, and Texas, which had voted for Eisenhower in 1956. But he could not afford to repeat Stevenson's mistake of neglecting blacks. The country's nine most populous states—New York, California, Michigan, Texas, Ohio, New Jersey, Pennsylvania, Illinois, and Massachusetts—together yielded 237 of the 269 Electoral College votes needed for victory. Each one had a sizable black electorate. "The significance of the Negro vote lies not in its numerical strength," Marge Lawson explained to Kennedy in June, "but in its strategic distribution." Kennedy subsequently told black journalist Carl Rowan, "I'd be a fool not to consider the Negro vote crucial. We've got to carry the key northern and western states or we're just not going to win." Even in the South, where only a quarter of eligible blacks were enfranchised, their votes were potentially decisive. In Texas, Tennessee, Louisiana, Virginia, and Florida, black voters could easily tilt the election in the Democrats' favor. In Texas alone, there were 226,495 registered black voters. In 1956, Eisenhower had won the state by 220,661 votes.[3]

To appeal to voters nationwide, Kennedy had to strike a delicate balance. Always the ablest thinker among Kennedy's group of advisers, Theodore Sorensen had spent much of the early summer trying to devise a strategy to appeal to black voters without alienating southern constituents. In a memo to Kennedy, Sorensen explained that racial politics were in a state of flux. The rise of an organized civil rights movement, the *Brown* decision, and the growing influence of northern black voters—all of these factors had transformed the struggle for equality. Blacks were now more politically astute, and they expected the federal government, as well as the federal courts, to take their grievances more seriously. Kennedy could not appeal to black voters solely by offering assurances of new civil rights legislation, because they had grown weary of seeing bills diluted or defeated by southern Democrats in Congress. Promises of more high-paying jobs and better housing had sufficed during the Roosevelt and Truman administrations, but this was no longer enough. Blacks wanted a candidate who offered a better standard of living but also first-class citizenship and meaningful racial change.[4]

To appeal to this transformed electorate, Sorensen proposed a two-pronged strategy, which he had outlined prior to the Los Angeles convention. The first requirement was a policy of "direct identification" with black demands for basic civil rights. This would involve a major speech on the subject and the enlistment of black experts to prepare "position papers on major problem areas," such as school integration and public accommodations. Sorensen described the second part of the policy as one of "indirect identification," which required "inclusiveness at both the substantive and organizational levels." In practical terms, this meant that the campaign should be racially integrated at every level. All staff should be made aware of the "problems, issues and sensitivities" of black voters. The idea of "indirect identification" was based on the idea that even small gestures and symbols, however seemingly superficial, could prove just as effective as promises of substantive reform. Even something as simple as renaming the "Minorities Section" the "Civil Rights Section" could potentially have a profound effect, since the former had long been regarded as a euphemism for a segregated campaign. Better still, these subtle differences would be almost imperceptible to white southerners. A strategy of association, based on a blend of symbolism and stealth, was taking shape.[5]

Kennedy pollster George Belknap had arrived at much the same conclusion. In a "Political Behavior Report" on the "Northern Negro Voter" back in May, Belknap observed that blacks had been loyal Democrats up until the early 1950s because the reforms of the New Deal/Fair Deal era raised their living standards. "Negroes, like low income people generally, saw the Democratic Party as the 'Party of the Working People,'" he wrote. But thousands had decamped to the Republican Party in 1952 and 1956 because of Stevenson's refusal to assert the moral case for racial justice. According to Belknap, economic issues had given way to emotive issues, "specifically racial dignity and prestige." "While the Democratic Party had an impressive record on economic matters," he argued, "it has not always succeeded in convincing the Northern Negro that it stands for his equality and dignity in such fields as education and recreation." Economic issues were no longer paramount. Instead, the "non-economic aspirations of the Negro must be recognized and met." The sit-in protests had highlighted the importance of nonquantifiable factors such as status and access. Belknap argued therefore that "[t]he Party's identification with Negro aspirations must be clear and pictorial."[6]

Marge Lawson had also been advocating this kind of approach since early in the summer. "The candidate who wins [black voters] will be the one who is most able to make them feel, not only that he understands, but that he cares about human dignity," Lawson told Kennedy in June. "Negro voters will not respond to a bread and butter campaign only." Now her advice began to take hold.[7]

Beginning in August, with the formation of the Civil Rights Section (CRS) at Hyannis Port, the Kennedy campaign began to introduce several symbolic changes. From the outset of the presidential campaign, the candidate himself decided to be accompanied at all times by a black aide. It provided precisely the kind of "indirect identification" with the black cause advocated by Sorensen. Herbert Tucker was first assigned to the role but was removed

when aides realized that his complexion was so light he was not instantly rec-
ognizable as black. Frank Reeves, a darker-skinned black, replaced him. Campaign staff nicknamed him "Exhibit One." (The pale complexions of some of
Kennedy's most prominent black supporters were a recurring problem. The
CRS needed three separate photo sessions to produce a leaflet featuring Vel
Phillips, since the transparencies from the first two had not made her look
dark enough.)[8]

As well as accompanying Kennedy, Reeves served as a black advance man. At
every campaign stop, he contacted local party officials before the candidate's arrival to ensure that blacks were included in welcoming lines at every stop. When
Kennedy officially launched his campaign on Labor Day, with the traditional
appearance before auto workers in Detroit's Cadillac Square, Reeves ensured
baseball star James "Mudcat" Grant, the Cleveland Indians' star black pitcher,
was photographed alongside the candidate.[9]

From the outset of the presidential race in September, Reeves made sure that
Kennedy's policy of never appearing in a segregated hall was rigidly enforced.
Johnson had to adhere to the same guidelines as he barnstormed through the
South. At times, when no desegregated venue was available, Johnson spoke
from the back of his campaign train. Segregated hotels were also off limits.
During a campaign stop in Paducah, Kentucky, Kennedy himself decided to re-
locate his entire entourage after a local hotel manager refused to accommodate
Simeon Booker of *Jet*. (Faced with a similar problem in 1956, Stevenson willfully refused to switch hotels.) In another important gesture, the Kennedy campaign invited black reporters to join their press pool on a fully integrated basis.
Andrew Hatcher, previously the managing editor of the *Sun Reporter,* a black
newspaper in San Francisco, became Salinger's deputy press officer. "Kennedy Is
the Hottest Campaigner for Negro Votes Since FDR," read a *Jet* headline in
October. The accompanying article cited as evidence that Kennedy's advance
staff guaranteed blacks were included among the VIPs and welcoming committees in every city.[10]

Throughout the campaign, Sorensen's call for a policy of "inclusiveness at
both the substantive and organizational levels" was treated with the same seriousness. The Kennedy high command instructed state chairmen of the Citizens
for Kennedy volunteers' organizations to appoint a black vice chairman and
recruit as many black volunteers as possible, in an attempt to integrate the campaign from top to bottom. Reeves wanted the campaign to appoint Harry Belafonte as vice chairman of the national Citizens for Kennedy campaign, but the
idea met fierce resistance from the organization's chairman, Byron "Whizzer"
White, a former all-American football star from Colorado who went on to become deputy attorney general and then Supreme Court Justice as Kennedy's
first nominee to the high court. White feared that the integration of the Citi-

zens for Kennedy campaign would undercut its efforts at building a volunteer organization in the South. "It may not be that Byron White fully comprehends the extent to which the effort for Negro votes might come to rest within his operation," warned Lawson.[11]

Although the CRS was housed in offices on K Street (along with the Businessmen for Kennedy and Farmers for Kennedy operation), rather than at the main headquarters on Connecticut Avenue, its members enjoyed unprecedented access to the candidate. They were included in most of the major strategy sessions, a notable shift from previous campaigns. Kennedy's brother-in-law Sargent Shriver served as the official liaison and shuttled between the two offices to ensure a smooth flow of information. Day-to-day control of the CRS rested in Wofford's hands, much to Lawson's annoyance. Lawson was placed in charge of buffering the impact of Kennedy's Catholicism among black churchgoers. This project involved cultivating black clergymen, foremost among them J. H. Jackson, the head of the National Baptist Convention. But DNC polling had concluded earlier in May that "Anti-Catholicism is less prevalent among Negroes than among northern urban Protestant whites," so it was considered only a marginal role.[12]

Eventually, the campaign chose Congressman William Dawson, the head of the Minorities Section in 1952 and 1956, as honorary chairman of CRS, a vanity title dangled in front of him after he refused initially to participate at all in the campaign. When he did join up, the seventy-four-year-old lawmaker almost immediately began to cause trouble. He took umbrage at Shriver's decision to construct an open-plan office space with no walls or partitions at the K Street headquarters. Horrified by the prospect of sharing office space with colleagues, Dawson demanded a separate room of his own. Since he personally controlled roughly thousands of black votes in Chicago's South Side, carpenters were summoned to erect a private "office" in the middle of the floor. It immediately became known as "Uncle Tom's Cabin," a snide reference to the Georgia-born lawmaker's overly warm relations with segregationists. After winning his battle for office space, Dawson then tried to get the CRS to revert to its original title of the Minorities Section. "Let's not use words that offend our good Southern friends, like 'civil rights,'" he told Wofford. But Dawson was unable to effect that change. Partly in protest, the congressman spent most of the campaign either closeted in his "cabin" or holed up in his much grander suite of offices on Capitol Hill. On the few occasions he attended high-level meetings, Robert Kennedy thought he was "senile."[13]

With Dawson reluctant to immerse himself in the campaign, Louis Martin became the most influential black member of the team. A former editor of the *Chicago Defender* and president of the Negro Newspaper Association, Martin had worked on previous presidential campaigns and possessed great savvy in public relations. The campaign first approached him right after the convention, when Shriver invited him to a day-long discussion with black activists in Washington to discuss how to contain the political fallout from Johnson's inclusion on the ticket. Martin immediately demonstrated his value. At the meeting he promised to ask colleagues in the black press "not [to] lynch him [Johnson] verbally in the newspapers until we could see what he was like." And he was effective—he managed to persuade a number of leading publications to exercise leniency.[14]

At the beginning of August, when Martin traveled to Hyannis Port for the launch of the CRS, he made an immediate impression on Robert Kennedy. Martin emphasized the importance of bringing Congressman Dawson back into the fold, since he was still cool toward Senator Kennedy and could not yet be relied upon to mobilize the South Side vote. To Robert Kennedy, Martin's judgment seemed remarkably astute, particularly at a time when he was growing increasingly frustrated with other members of the CRS. Lawson and Wofford seemed to spend much of their time on petty rivalries and were "idealistic and not very practical," in the words of one of his close aides, John Seigenthaler. Other CRC members appeared reluctant to leave Washington in order to build up contacts nationwide. So after a number of very unsatisfactory meetings with Wofford at the beginning of the campaign, Kennedy came to view Martin as his personal point man on civil rights, and the only member of the CRS who truly understood the requirements of a national campaign.[15]

Robert Kennedy put Martin in charge of negotiations aimed at securing the much-needed endorsement of Adam Clayton Powell, Jr., who had shocked party activists in 1956 by supporting Eisenhower. Corrupt to the core, Powell demanded $300,000 to return to the Democratic fold, an outrageous sum that he claimed would pay for a get-out-the-vote campaign in northern inner cities, but which everyone knew he himself would pocket. A tough negotiator, Martin was unwilling to pay anywhere near that amount, and instead offered Powell $50,000 to deliver ten set-piece speeches. Unhappy at such a paltry bribe, Powell telephoned the Kennedy campaign headquarters and threatened to embark on a speaking tour of the South. Bobby Kennedy refused to be intimidated and instructed an aide to phone the congressman's Harlem office to discuss a possible itinerary. Realizing his bluff had been called, Powell never returned the call. In late August, Powell finally agreed to Martin's offer. (It proved to be money well spent for the Kennedy camp. Without Powell's endorsement, Kennedy would have found it difficult to win the five black districts of Harlem, and thus the entire state.)[16]

Martin next focused on cultivating black reporters, a vital opinion-forming elite. "We need to have as much of the Negro press for us as possible," Lawson had cautioned earlier in the summer. "Its positive influence is mainly symbolic, but its opposition is highly damaging." At the beginning of the campaign, *Jet* and *Ebony,* the country's two biggest black magazines, were thought to be leaning toward Nixon. To win the backing of black publications, Martin started by reimbursing their publishers some $49,000 owed in outstanding advertising costs from the 1956 campaign, a popular move that built up a reservoir of goodwill. Then, he tried to "purchase" the popular "Ticker Tape" column in *Jet,* which he proposed would continue to appear under Simeon Booker's byline but be written by a Kennedy staffer. Bridling at such brazen "checkbook journalism," Booker and his publisher refused. Relations between the Kennedy campaign and the black press prospered nonetheless, aided by the appointment of Hatcher and Martin and also by the easy access that reporters were given to the candidate himself. Even Johnson appointed a black press aide, Alice Dunnigan, a veteran correspondent with the Associated Negro Press.[17]

From the start, the black press proved pivotal in the race, because it allowed the Kennedy campaign to tailor messages specifically for a black audience in publications such as *Jet, Ebony,* the *Pittsburgh Courier, Chicago Defender, Washington Afro-American,* and *Amsterdam News.* Since these publications were rarely read outside of the black community, Kennedy's campaign within their pages would go largely unnoticed in the mainstream media. Not insignificantly, Kennedy made some of his most forceful comments on civil rights in an interview with *Ebony.* "I don't know why people keep saddling me with that burden," he told Carl Rowan, speaking of his alleged ties to leading segregationists. "Where is all this Southern support they keep talking about? I didn't have fifteen Southern delegates for me at the national convention." In reference to the party platform, he commented, "Everybody agrees it's the strongest in the party's history. My people were the architects of that platform. Many of the sentences in that platform are taken almost verbatim from speeches I had delivered earlier."[18]

The Kennedy campaign also used advertising in the black print media to mold "blacks-only" messages to which white voters were completely oblivious. With Robert Kennedy's blessing, Martin invested heavily in fliers, handbills, posters, and newspaper ads targeted at blacks, a departure from past campaigns. Here, the strategy of association was emphatic. Virtually all of the advertisements linked Kennedy in some way with black heroes, past and present. One pamphlet, "A Time for Moral Leadership," featured a picture of Kenyan labor leader Tom Mboya, who had helped lead his country to independence from Britain. Other campaign leaflets linked Kennedy to prominent liberals such as Humphrey, Bowles, and G. Mennen Williams.

In plotting the advertising campaign, Martin was especially eager to establish a link with Franklin Delano Roosevelt. The campaign's most aggressively published advertisement in the black press was entitled "A Leader in the Tradition of Roosevelt." It featured an unexpectedly glowing endorsement of Kennedy from his widow, Eleanor, who, in the interests of party unity, had decided to back the ticket.[19]

The campaign spent thousands of dollars on free pullout sections inserted into black newspapers. They featured rows of photographs showing Kennedy alongside such blacks as Congressman Dawson, Ghana's Minister of Finance K. A. Gbedemah, and his own secretary Virginia Battle. One pullout featured a full-page photograph of Jackie Kennedy holding up a beautiful young black schoolgirl, who was handing the senator a white carnation. The CRS was especially proud of a flier entitled "Fair Employment Commission Ball Game," which contrasted Kennedy and Nixon's voting records on fair employment legislation. Kennedy, of course, scored six home runs, compared with Nixon's dismal performance of "No hits, No runs—all errors."[20]

The Republicans were less sophisticated in this arena; they ran the same advertisements in both the black and white press. Nixon had nothing equivalent to the CRS in his campaign. Having decided early on to target disgruntled whites, his efforts to win the black vote were an afterthought, at best. The campaign relied primarily on the support of Jackie Robinson, who toured the country speaking on the vice president's behalf. When campaign aides came up with innovative ideas to cause Kennedy embarrassment—one plan was to picket Joe Kennedy's famed Merchandise Mart during the week of the Republican convention to publicize its appalling record of employment discrimination—Nixon vetoed them. The Nixon campaign dedicated very limited resources to black outreach, and Nixon himself was rarely seen in the company of blacks. "No literature, no workers, no assistants," was the stinging critique from E. Frederic Morrow, Nixon's top black campaign official. "Unlike the Eisenhower campaigns of '52 and '56," he reflected later, "I was never seen with the Vice-President. I rode in caravans in a rear car and was never called into parleys or strategy meetings. . . . I never had a dime to spend for anything other than personal expenses."[21]

Sargent Shriver and the CRS delivered Kennedy a particularly stunning coup in August, which involved a group of 250 students from Kenya and other Eastern African British colonies planning to study at American universities. Earlier in the year, the African American Students Association (AASA) had approached the State Department with the hope of securing a $100,000 grant to help defray the costs of the scholarship program. The State Department rebuffed two overtures. In desperation, Frank Montero, the head of the AASA, decided to approach Nixon personally. He presumably thought that the vice president would recognize the political value of offering assistance to a group of African students in the run-up to the election. But Nixon's office carelessly forwarded Montero's application letter to Joseph C. Satterthwaite, a State Department functionary with slow political reflexes, who rejected the application a third time.[22]

When Shriver heard about the problem in July, he immediately spotted an opportunity to score an easy political victory. He hurriedly organized a meeting between Kennedy and Tom Mboya at Hyannis Port on July 26. By the time they met, Shriver, the managing director of the Joseph P. Kennedy, Jr. Foundation, had arranged to fund the lion's share of the $100,000 and promised to find the balance from other charitable institutions.

The Kennedy's political philanthropy immediately placed the GOP on the defensive. When Jackie Robinson learned of the Hyannis Port meeting he was aghast, and pressed the vice president to intervene. Reacting quickly, Nixon told his campaign research chief, James Shepley, to contact the State Department, which soon approached Montero with an offer of funding. Faced with this unexpected financial windfall, Montero decided to accept both the Kennedy and State Department money. Embarrassingly for Nixon, however, Montero announced on August 15 that the first wave of student visits would be funded with Kennedy family cash. Once again, Kennedy and the CRS had demonstrated not only their tactical nimbleness but also a keen understanding of the subtle nuances of the struggle for black equality—in this instance, an appreciation of black Americans' great enthusiasm for African decolonization.[23]

Kennedy had sprinkled references to Africa throughout a number of his speeches over the course of the year, and in the fall he dedicated an entire speech to the subject. Kennedy had for many years maintained a strong interest in Africa, particularly because he saw it as a major battleground in the Cold War. The subject was now vitally important to black Americans as well—twenty-five African states had achieved independence by 1960, and the press had dubbed it the "Year of Africa." Speaking before the National Council of Women in New York on October 12, Kennedy laid out a four-point action plan for the continent. It would boost educational links, "provide security against starvation," offer developmental capital, and make the United Nations "the central instrument of our effort in Africa." He also underscored the need to "wipe out" all traces of discrimination at home if America was to win "the respect and friendship" of the African people.[24]

Africa was a recurring campaign theme. During the course of the campaign, it was estimated that he mentioned the continent 500 times. "The best propaganda for the United States is to have a society which emphasizes opportunity for all our people," Kennedy noted during a speech in Buffalo on September 28, "which serves around the world as a beacon and advertisement for the cause of freedom." "Do you know the most important new area of the world today is Africa?" he asked during a speech at the beginning of November. "It controls one-fourth of all the votes in the General Assembly?"[25]

Throughout the campaign, Kennedy also lambasted the Eisenhower State Department for its dismal employment record, complaining it diluted American influence abroad and especially in Africa. "Do you know how many Negroes we have in our State Department Foreign Service out of 6,000?" he asked indignantly during a speech in California on November 1. "Twenty-six." The following day, during a speech in San Francisco, he highlighted the failure of the Eisenhower administration to appoint ambassadors in six new countries recently admitted to the United Nations. The issue of blacks in the Foreign Service was a perfect example of the strategy of association that Sorensen had endorsed over the summer. It was a topic important to black voters but irrelevant to most whites. The problem demanded no legislative action and posed no threat to the southern way of life.[26]

The strategy of association—as enacted in many forms ranging from advertising to hiring to the scholarships for Kenyan students—compensated for Kennedy's unwillingness to lend greater vocal support to the inflammatory Democratic civil rights plank. After the August session, Kennedy distanced himself from the contents of the civil rights plank, especially its demands for accelerated school integration. He was unforthcoming on the subject for the remainder of the campaign. Though in his stump speeches in the North he frequently mentioned the need to eradicate discrimination, it was always in the vaguest possible terms. At a steer roast in Cleveland on September 25, for example, he made the bold statement that "I would like it said that during these 4 years or 8 years we ended discrimination of all kinds in the United States, we finished it," but failed to indicate how or what forms of discrimination he intended to tackle first. Even when speaking before predominantly black audiences, Kennedy did not once refer to the complete set of proposals listed in the civil rights plank. Although he frequently highlighted the need for greater "moral leadership," he never explained what form it would take. More often, rather than delineating his own plans, Kennedy focused instead on the inadequacies of the Eisenhower administration and frequently cited Nixon's failed stewardship of the Government Contracts Committee. Attack was the best form of obfuscation.[27]

During the first five weeks of the campaign, his only major speech on the subject of civil rights came during an appearance at Howard University in Washington. Nixon had also been invited but turned down the invitation. Accompanied by his wife (a subtle but important gesture, since white women rarely appeared in front of black audiences), he called for the next president to set the correct "moral tone." He also called for the passage of Part III, but laid greater emphasis on employment as the primary means to achieve equality. And, as ever, he devoted a substantial portion of the speech to the foreign policy implications of segregation. He reminded his audience that the African nationalist movement was a "clear reminder that . . . those over the world who are colored are now reaching greater and greater power."[28]

When Kennedy did specifically address the issue of policy relating to civil rights, he generally stressed that executive action was far preferable to conventional legislative remedies. A presidential order could be used to eliminate discrimination in federally funded housing—an issue of particular concern to northern blacks. On the more contentious topic of school integration, apart from his speech at Howard University, he mentioned the possibility of federal action only once. His comments came during a question-and-answer session in Minnesota, with two leading liberals, Humphrey and McCarthy, in attendance. Kennedy called for the enactment of Part III and for the provision of technical assistance to school districts wishing to integrate. Even then, however, he stressed "there is a good deal that can be done by the executive branch without legislation."[29]

During the campaign, Kennedy was able to avoid a great deal of direct and substantive engagement with civil rights for a variety of reasons. Neither candidate had any interest in making it a central issue in the campaign. Nixon wanted the public to focus on Kennedy's inexperience. He constantly cited the number of presidential meetings he had attended, panels he had chaired, and official foreign visits he had completed. Largely out of necessity—Nixon was, after all, tied to Eisenhower's policies, whether he wanted to be or not—he made continuity the centerpiece of his campaign. It was hazardous to change course, he argued, especially if it meant turning to someone as unprepared as Kennedy. In response, Kennedy charged Nixon with being the candidate of the status quo. His inertia both at home and abroad threatened American prestige at a time when the Soviet threat had never been more real. In a campaign dominated by foreign affairs, Kennedy latched onto the perceived missile gap between the two nuclear rivals to hammer home his point.

Nor did the media press either candidate on issues of race and civil rights. Preoccupied with foreign affairs and daily shifts in the presidential horse race, the mainstream press displayed precious little interest in civil rights. This silence made the Kennedy campaign's strategy of association all the more effective. Much of the CRS's success in the early phase of the campaign stemmed from its ability to operate under the radar of the print and broadcast media. Its initiatives generally escaped the attention of "white" news desks but caught the eye of the editors of black publications.

But perhaps more importantly, Kennedy was largely able to evade the civil rights issue because he and Johnson had effectively divided their campaign along the Mason-Dixon line. Kennedy made only five trips to the South in the course of the campaign and avoided the Deep South states of Alabama, Mississippi, and Louisiana altogether. Instead, Johnson was left to deliver the South.

He toured the region in his thirteen-car LBJ Victory Special locomotive and addressed track-side audiences from the observation deck in the last carriage, wearing a wide-brimmed ten-gallon hat and a yellow ribbon in his lapel, with a smiling Lady Bird Johnson always at his side.

Harris's polling data indicated that the subject of civil rights was damaging Nixon in the South, and Democratic strategists were intent on keeping it that way. Because the *Brown* decision had been handed down on Eisenhower's watch, Nixon was considered by many to be guilty by association. "The Republicans are looked on as the party that presided over a vast inflammation of race relations," observed Harris in a secret report to Robert Kennedy, based on a sample of polls from Texas. "This issue can be counted on to work quietly and effectively for the Democratic ticket." On the rare occasions when Kennedy did visit the South, he studiously avoided the subject of civil rights. In late August, during a night-time open-air rally at the George Washington High School in Alexandria, Virginia, he remained silent on civil rights. In a swing through Georgia, he again dodged the issue, although, as Governor Vandiver observed during a motorcade, he did make "an extra effort to wave when they passed black schools." And on one or two occasions he stopped the car so he could shake hands with a black principal—a gesture of symbolic importance to blacks but one that generated little controversy among whites. During brief forays into North Carolina, Florida, and Virginia, Kennedy did not mention civil rights.[30]

Johnson did all the campaign's heavy lifting in the South and was an extraordinarily reassuring figure to voters and lawmakers who remained suspicious of Kennedy. While in the weeks leading up to the convention, Johnson had preferred the label "westerner," now he presented himself to southern voters as "the grandson of a Confederate soldier." Johnson tried to assuage concerns about Kennedy's Catholicism by constantly retelling the tragic wartime story of how Joe Kennedy, Jr. and his co-pilot, a lieutenant from Fort Worth, Texas, lost their lives over the English Channel. "When those boys went out to die so that you could live, nobody asked them what church they went to."[31]

Away from the crowds, in the privacy of his lounge car between stops along the line, Johnson smoothed relations with leading southern Democrats over the civil rights plank. He pledged that an incoming Kennedy administration would make no attempt to recast its recommendations into new legislation. He would be the eyes and ears of the South in Washington, he promised, and exercise a moderating influence on the new administration. It was crucial in placating southern opposition, and winning much-needed endorsements for the Democratic ticket. Johnson met with an estimated 1,247 local politicians over the course of the campaign. He played a crucial role in defusing southern opposition, and won a series of much-needed endorsements for the Democratic ticket. By the middle of September, Governors Farris Bryant of Florida and Orval Faubus of Arkansas had both pledged their support, although they openly rejected the Democratic platform. By late September Johnson had helped secure the backing of Richard Russell and Herman Talmadge, an even more important breakthrough. Talmadge appeared on the stump in mid-October in Macon, Georgia, and described Johnson as "the best of Georgia or the South." He had always come to the aid of the region when "extreme legislation" was being proposed, an unmistakable reference to civil rights.[32]

By October, even Richard Russell had agreed to campaign in Texas on Johnson's behalf—partly out of fondness for Lady Bird Johnson and partly because he feared Nixon was more likely to reform the filibuster rule than Kennedy. "I have never been disappointed in Lyndon Johnson," Russell proclaimed in Houston, with clear implications for segregationists. After the election, Russell told Johnson the South was depending on him and said the region expected him to shield it from the radicals in Congress, like Humphrey and Paul Douglas. And so as Kennedy pursued a strategy of association in the North, Johnson was working strenuously to disassociate their ticket from the Democratic plank in the South. As *Time* observed, they were trying to "project double images without being accused of being two-faced."[33]

In this context, the advent of the televised debates posed a peculiar problem. Up until this point, the campaign had aptly tailored messages for North and South, black and white. On national television, Kennedy would have to speak to everyone at once. As they prepared for the first encounter on September 26, Wofford and Martin realized that the gains of the CRS could easily evaporate if Kennedy downplayed civil rights, so they urged him to support reform, unequivocally. In a memorandum, Wofford argued that a bold statement on civil rights aligned with the campaign's broader theme of change: After eight years of failed leadership it was time to "get the country moving again." Wofford urged Kennedy to blast the administration for its "inaction and silence" on civil rights and to highlight its failure to issue a long-awaited executive housing order. Eisenhower should be singled out for criticism, for his failure to provide moral leadership and his refusal to reveal his personal position towards *Brown*. To draw a sharp line of distinction between the parties, Kennedy should endorse the sit-in movement and showcase the civil rights plank, "the Democrats' strongest asset."[34]

Wofford realized, of course, that Kennedy might be forced onto the defensive because of his votes during the 1957 civil rights debate and the Patterson breakfast meeting, which "still looms as a shadow over this part of the campaign." Wofford proposed a clever rebuttal: The breakfast demonstrated Kennedy's willingness to meet any political officeholder in the land, and that if Eisenhower had adopted the same approach with Orval Faubus, the Little Rock crisis could have been averted. Finally, he presented Kennedy with a barrage of statistics about the disadvantages a black baby faced in America. Wofford urged Kennedy to memorize them.[35]

Seventy million people watched the first debate on television. At the start, moderator Howard K. Smith asked both candidates to deliver an eight-minute opening statement. Preternaturally calm, Kennedy opened with a rehash of his stump speech, including the oft-repeated warning that America was in danger of losing the fight for global freedom if it did not meet the Soviet challenge and get "moving again." How could America possibly win the Cold War, he asked, when half of its steel mill capacity lay dormant, its universities turned out only half as many engineers and scientists as Russia's, and children in West Virginia were forced to set aside part of their school lunch so they could feed their hungry parents at night. Kennedy then turned to civil rights and immediately drew on the data in Wofford's memorandum. "When a Negro baby is born," he said, "he has about one-half as much chance to get through high school as a white baby. He has one-third as much chance to get through college as a white student. He has about one-third as much chance to be a professional man, about half as much chance to own a house. He has about four times as much chance that he'll be out of work in his life as the white baby. I think we can do better."[36]

Kennedy's comments were carefully nuanced and narrowly focused. In the most specific terms, he had identified with the unsettled grievances of black Americans but had avoided any proposal for redressing them. The opening statement was powerful rhetorically but vague politically—a perfect example of the strategy of association. Drenched in flopsweat, Nixon was not nearly so adept. He avoided any mention of civil rights, lest it displease his newfound southern friends.

Kennedy's performance made an immediate impact with black voters. Roy Wilkins found his comments about the disadvantages facing a black newborn "fresher and bolder" than anything Stevenson had said either in 1952 or 1956. And Minnie, his wife, was captivated. "This is what we have been looking for," she said, turning in wide-eyed amazement to her husband. Black newspapers agreed. "Mr. Kennedy, alone, referred to the problems of civil rights, pledged better things for colored people, Mexicans and Puerto Ricans," the *Washington Afro-American* editorialized—though it omitted to mention that Kennedy had stopped short of offering up concrete proposals. "Score the first [debate] for Kennedy."[37]

Kennedy's debate performance drew admiring reviews from the South as well. Some of the most enthusiastic praise came from the annual meeting of the Southern Governors Conference in Hot Springs, Arkansas. Of the eleven southern governors in attendance, ten signed a telegram congratulating Kennedy on a commanding display. Impressed by the strength of his overall performance, they were clearly not overly concerned about his opening remarks on race. The campaign was relieved; the telegram suggested that they were successfully stemming the tide of presidential Republicanism in the South. Had the candidate gone into any detail during the debate about how he planned to correct the injustice of racism, or made any reference to the Democrats' civil rights plank, the reaction would presumably have been much more severe.[38]

The day after the debate, while he was campaigning in northern Ohio, Kennedy found himself swamped by huge crowds of adoring supporters. The first Gallup poll taken after the debate suggested he had edged ahead, with 49 percent compared to Nixon's 46. With six weeks to go before Election Day, Kennedy had seemingly overcome his two biggest liabilities: his Catholicism and youth. Earlier that month he had started to neutralize the Catholic question with a high-profile speech in Houston, where he spoke of "an America that is officially neither Catholic, Protestant nor Jewish—where no public official either requests or accepts instructions on public policy from the Pope, the National Council of Churches or any other ecclesiastical source." And now, the television debate had apparently closed the so-called stature gap between the two candidates.[39]

Given his success in the first round, Kennedy was extremely confident going into the second televised debate on Friday, October 7—and arrived at the NBC studio in Washington in a flashy white Pontiac convertible. In keeping with the mood of his campaign, perhaps, Nixon pulled up in a somber black government limousine. The second encounter was intended to focus exclusively on foreign affairs, a subject with which Kennedy was extremely comfortable. But Alvin Spivak of the United Press International was determined to bring up civil rights, sensing an opportunity to create great mischief. "With both North and South listening and watching," announced Spivak, "would you sum up your own intentions in the field of civil rights."

Nixon delivered a stout reply. He promised new fair-employment legislation and greater federal assistance to schools wishing to integrate. He pledged that he would seek voluntary agreements between chain-store owners and student demonstrators to bring an end to the sit-in movement. With his partisan instincts aroused, Nixon momentarily discarded his southern strategy and mounted an excoriating attack on Kennedy for refusing to introduce civil rights legislation during the August congressional session. He also criticized Kennedy for ignoring civil rights during his campaign visits to the South. "Why do I talk, every time I am in the South, on civil rights?" asked Nixon, vaingloriously. "Not because I am preaching to the people of the South, because this isn't just a southern problem. . . . I do it because we have to solve this problem together."[40]

Rattled by Nixon's attack, Kennedy retaliated. He cited his opponent's poor performance as chairman of the Committee on Government Contracts and his unwillingness to advocate Part III powers for the attorney general. Then, he promised to eradicate discrimination in federal housing programs "by a stroke of the President's pen." He stressed that whoever emerged the victor needed to "establish a moral tone and moral leadership."[41]

Hal Levy of *Newsday* then followed up with a question on the Little Rock crisis. Kennedy modulated his response carefully. In his view, Eisenhower should have made it clearer from the outset that the integration of Central High was inevitable, since it was the law of the land. But when federal intervention became unavoidable, he should have deployed U.S. marshals not troops. Then, in keeping with Wofford's advice, he attacked Eisenhower for his failure to offer moral leadership, exemplified by his reticence on *Brown*. "We sit on a conspicuous stage," Kennedy stated. "We are a goldfish bowl before the world. We have to practice what we preach. We set a very high standard for ourselves. The Communists do not." He also asserted that the Eisenhower administration had failed to implement the 1957 Civil Rights Act aggressively enough, that the Justice Department had subsequently brought only six voting rights cases before the courts, and that Nixon's stewardship of the Government Contracts Division had been woefully inadequate. For only the second time during the campaign, he suggested the attorney general should be given Part III powers to initiate civil rights cases. But Kennedy stopped short of advocating the use of Part III to accelerate school integration. Quite deliberately, he spoke of the need to "protect constitutional rights" rather than to specifically advance school integration.

The campaign initially feared that Kennedy had been too strident on civil rights during the second televised debate. But new Harris polls quickly allayed their concerns. Kennedy's advocacy of civil rights had hurt him slightly in the South, but these losses were more than offset by his overall attractiveness as a candidate. "Unquestionably the Democratic platform on civil rights is a very bitter pill in Louisiana and throughout the Deep South," Harris wrote on October 20, almost two weeks after the second debate. "The important part is that Senator Kennedy seems likely to carry the state with the strongest civil rights program in the party platform ever written." The same was true of South Carolina, where there was a strong feeling Kennedy was too liberal and too "pro-Negro," according to Harris, "but this sentiment is more than offset by his commanding lead on the issues."[42]

Certainly, Johnson was invaluable in securing the support of the South. His presence on the ticket offered potent symbolic reassurance to southerners that, whatever Kennedy might say about civil rights, the ticket was essentially a moderate one. As a consequence, by October Nixon had gained little ground among southern voters, despite the fact that he had largely tailored his campaign to appeal to them.

Nixon's problems in the South were compounded in mid-October by a disastrous gaffe on the part of his running mate, Henry Cabot Lodge, Jr. In the early stages of the campaign, the former Massachusetts senator, who had served as U.S. Ambassador to the United Nations since his defeat in 1952, had maintained a low public profile. But speaking in East Harlem just five days after the second televised debate he generated one of the campaign's rare moments of real drama by promising, as part of an ambitious eight-point civil rights program, that Nixon would appoint the first ever black cabinet member.[43]

Three thousand miles away in California, Nixon was blindsided. His aides quickly issued a statement disowning Lodge's remarks. The repudiation was emphatic: Neither had Nixon been told in advance what Lodge planned to say nor would he ever have authorized such comments. Nixon "would not appoint a Negro just because he was a Negro," since that was racism in reverse.[44]

Lodge was scheduled to campaign in the South the next morning, and at the first stop in South Carolina he was forced into an embarrassing retraction. "I cannot pledge anything," he told reporters. Later on, in Norfolk, Virginia, he admitted the East Harlem speech had been drafted "hastily." For the next three days, the cabinet pledge fiasco dogged the Republican campaign. It drew fire not only from angry southerners, who bridled at the prospect of such a high-level black appointee, but liberals as well, who considered Lodge's East Harlem speech opportunistic and crass. "Mr. Lodge's Wednesday 'pledge' was all too apparently a bid for votes on a specious issue," thundered the *New York Times,* and when New York's most influential black newspaper, the *Amsterdam News,* endorsed the Democratic ticket two weeks later it cited the "cabinet pledge" as the main reason why: "Lodge's double talk about a Negro in the cabinet is enough for us to choose LBJ." Since the war, the politics of civil rights had been based on an elementary equation: Each action aimed at winning support from white southerners would spark an equal and opposite reaction from blacks. Nixon and Lodge had therefore achieved something of a first. Simultaneously, they had infuriated both.[45]

As the Republican campaign imploded, Kennedy handled the issue with considerable aplomb. Robert Kennedy had advised that it would be stupid to "out-promise Nixon," and his brother concurred. Kennedy referred to the controversy during an address on government ethics at Wittenberg University, in Springfield, Ohio on October 17. "I am not going to promise a Cabinet post or any post to any race or ethnic group," he told the 4,500 members of the audience. "That is racism at its worst. So I do not promise to consider race or religion in my appointments if I am successful. I promise only that I will not consider them." The speech also included a pledge that the Foreign Service would appoint a greater number of blacks, which had long been one of the candidate's personal concerns.[46]

Like Kennedy, the CRS took great delight in watching Lodge flounder and was determined to keep the story in the headlines. After scrutinizing the ambassador's employment record, they discovered he had played an indirect role in the removal of Assistant Secretary of Labor J. Ernest Wilkins, the Eisenhower administration's most senior black appointee. By extraordinary coincidence, Wilkins had been replaced by George Cabot Lodge, the ambassador's son. The CRS distributed the story, especially to black reporters.[47]

Partly due to the Lodge debacle and partly because of Kennedy's accomplished debate performances, Wofford was confident by mid-October that the black vote was safely in the Democratic column. He was nonetheless determined to press home the advantage. He recommended that the campaign should organize a conference in New York that would draw together senior Democrats and civil rights leaders—"a brand-name display," according to Wofford—to discuss how best to meld the party platform into government policy. Wofford envisioned the conference as the culmination of the black campaign. It would "generate steam" in the final weeks of the campaign, among blacks, Jews, and Puerto Ricans "and that overlapping minority group, the Stevensonians."[48]

Wofford originally wanted to call the two-day event a "Civil Rights Conference" and convene it at Philadelphia's Independence Hall. But he settled upon the less overtly symbolic venue of New York's Park-Sheraton Hotel since it was "understandable in the South." He also agreed to describe it as a "constitutional conference" because "[t]he 'Constitution' provides the frame least offensive in the South." Under pressure from Johnson aides, Wofford also agreed to delay the conference by a few weeks, since it risked undercutting ongoing efforts to shore up the support of key southern leaders. As James Rowe, one of Johnson's aides, pointed out, it would be unwise for Kennedy to deliver a strong speech at Democratic-sponsored civil rights conference while Johnson was walking his "Southern tightrope."[49]

Eventually, the constitutional conference took place in mid-October. Hubert Humphrey launched the event with an address stating that its primary goal was to provide "an action blueprint for the fulfillment of the civil rights commitments in the Democratic platform." "The plea of every witness was for a President who would speak on these issues and act on them ahead of time," he added, presciently, "before the crisis overtakes us—before violence erupts and the only question is maintaining order." With that, the conference divided into three working panels, each one charged with producing an interim plan setting out how best to implement the Democratic platform. Each group arrived at the same conclusion: Progress on civil rights was impossible unless Kennedy faced down the Southern Caucus. If elected, Kennedy needed to support moves to curb the power of the filibuster at the start of the new congressional session. Humphrey promised personally to lead the fight for the revision of rule XXII, and then read out a telegram from Wilkins saying it should become the new administration's "number one" priority.[50]

Johnson, of course, did not attend the conference. Instead, he sent delegates a 352-word message. "I want to say right now that the administration of Jack Kennedy and Lyndon Johnson will be an administration which will protect the constitutional rights of all Americans," it said. "We feel—as we have always felt—that before the law all Americans should stand equal." The language was calculated to offend no one.[51]

The two-day conference reached its climax with a visit from Kennedy, who delivered his longest civil rights speech of the campaign. In it, he pledged in vague terms to translate the Democratic platform "into legislative and executive action." But he avoided any explicit pledge to enact Part III, to create a fair employment practices committee, or to fight for rule revision in the Senate—although his audience had unanimously agreed that a change to Rule XXII was the essential precursor of meaningful reform. On school integration, he made no mention of the submission of desegregation plans by 1963 and spoke only of the need to "create the conditions in which compliance with the constitutional requirements of school desegregation takes place." "Moral and persuasive leadership" was the key, Kennedy insisted blandly.[52]

Kennedy devoted much of the speech to the potential of "executive leadership and executive action." He noted that "many things can be done by the stroke of a Presidential pen," and through more rigorous enforcement of existing legislation, most notably in the enforcement of voting rights ("the power already given by the Congress to protect the rights of voters"). He went on to comment: "I think the division of labor in this conference has been most significant. Two conferences on executive action and one on legislative action." Clearly, Kennedy was downplaying the need for fresh legislation, and dampening expectations of what a new Democratic administration could realistically achieve in the congressional realm. Chastened by his experience during the August session, worried about how the New York speech would be received in the South, and attracted, both intellectually and politically, to Wofford's ideas, he was clearly advocating a policy based on a maximum of executive action and a minimum of legislative action.[53]

After his speech, Kennedy addressed a boisterous open-air rally outside the Hotel Theresa on the corner of 125th Street and Seventh Avenue in Harlem. It was an especially symbolic setting, because only a few weeks earlier, during the U.N. General Assembly, it had been the site where Nikita Khrushchev had embraced Fidel Castro, and then lambasted America for its dismal racial record. In this context, the speech was, not surprisingly, rich in anti-Soviet rhetoric. Kennedy once again elided the struggles of black Americans with the issue of the nation's role in the world. "What has happened to America?" he asked, as Eleanor Roosevelt and Adam Clayton Powell, Jr., stood at his side. He deplored the fact that in a recent U.N. vote only two African nations, Liberia and South Africa, had sided with Washington over the question of whether to admit China. "We are the great revolutionary people. We believe in freedom. We believe in independence. The Communists do not." To the sustained applause of his Harlem audience, Kennedy expressed alarm that out of 6,000 U.S. Foreign Service officers only twenty-three were black. This was especially dire given that by 1962, a quarter of the votes at the General Assembly would be controlled by African nations. He spoke with an intensity and passion rare in routine stump speeches. But, then, Kennedy habitually delivered his strongest comments on civil rights when that issue was coupled with the question of the fight against communist tyranny.[54]

For the CRS, the Constitutional Conference marked the high point of the campaign. With three weeks to go before polling day Wofford and Martin were confident they would win the black vote by a landslide. Nixon's decision to chase white voters in the South seemed increasingly ill-judged, and polls suggested that Kennedy enjoyed a commanding lead in black communities. His comments on civil rights had not harmed him irreparably in the South—and his Catholicism remained his primary vulnerability. Johnson had served Kennedy masterfully throughout the fall by reassuring southern voters that whatever Kennedy might be saying in the North, he was sensitive to Southern concerns.

There was still time, however, for an October surprise.

CHAPTER 11

❦

Calling Coretta

I n an election in which black voters appeared likely to exert more influence than ever, Martin Luther King, Jr.—now widely considered the untitled leader of the civil rights movement—was determined to maintain a low profile and remain studiously neutral. It was an open secret, however, that he favored Nixon, who was an honorary member of the NAACP and a longtime supporter of the civil rights movement. Initially, King had dismissed him as a shameless self-promoter. Yet when they met for the first time in the spring of 1957 in the unlikely setting of Accra at celebrations marking Ghana's independence from Britain, King was more impressed than he expected to be. Over drinks at a glitzy cocktail party, Nixon seemed genuinely sympathetic to the cause of civil rights, explaining to King how America's "Negro problem" had undermined the country's prestige abroad. And he also displayed a keen understanding of the social and economic difficulties faced by black Americans. King was converted. "I should say that Nixon has a genius for convincing one that he is sincere," he wrote later. "And so I would conclude by saying that if Richard Nixon is not sincere, he is the most dangerous man in America." His admiration grew over the course of the year, as Nixon placed himself in the thick of the fight for the 1957 Civil Rights Act.[1]

As the 1960 election approached, close associates, like Ralph Abernathy, his SCLC deputy, suspected King would publicly endorse Nixon. His father, the Reverend Martin Luther King, Sr., the indomitable "Daddy King," had done so already, not out of admiration for the vice president but because he hated the idea of a Catholic president. Even so, the Kennedy team put a great deal of pressure on King to endorse their candidate. Harris Wofford, an old friend and confidant of King's, was particularly compelling. Chester Bowles likewise assured King that Kennedy had a genuine concern for black Americans. King ultimately decided that against formally endorsing either candidate, though he agreed to meet both and offer advice.[2]

Toward the end of September, King accepted an invitation to meet Kennedy at his Georgetown townhouse, their second encounter in less than two months. During their first meeting on the eve of the Los Angeles convention, Kennedy had seemed supremely confident of winning the black vote in the fall. But now he seemed chastened, King thought. More pessimistic about his chances, Kennedy indicated that he needed to do "something dramatic" to win black support and suggested they appear jointly at a SCLC dinner or even a civil rights rally. Quite why Kennedy was prepared to risk courting King so publicly was never explained. Perhaps Kennedy himself was worried still that King might endorse Nixon, or was simply eager to impress the young preacher. King laid out two stipulations: that the meeting take place in the South and Nixon must also be invited. But there was nothing to be gained by the meeting if his rival also attended, so Kennedy demurred.[3]

Over the coming weeks, however, Wofford was able to persuade King to drop his demand for Nixon to be invited. They tentatively agreed that the meeting would take place in Miami on October 18, where Kennedy was due to address the American Legion. But then King discovered that Nixon was also due to address the veterans' group, and the plan unraveled when he insisted that the vice president be invited, as well. "The hell with that," Kennedy shouted down the phone at Wofford, in a rare flash of anger. "Nixon might be smart enough to accept. If he does, I lose votes. I'm taking a much greater risk in the South than Nixon, but King wants to treat us as equals. Tell him it's off." The Kennedy campaign made no subsequent attempt to bring the two men together during the remainder of the campaign.[4]

Unwittingly, by abruptly canceling the Miami meeting, Kennedy precipitated a crisis that would have an even more dramatic impact on his campaign for the black vote. For King, the Florida meeting had held particular appeal because it would take him out of Atlanta on October 19, the launch date for a fresh round of sit-in demonstrations organized by the Student Nonviolent Coordinating Committee (SNCC). King had asked that the demonstrations be postponed until after the election, but the student leaders saw no reason to let up on their crusade. When it was clear that they were going to move forward with the sit-ins, and with no credible alibi after the cancellation of the Florida trip, King was forced either to join them or risk being upstaged by SNCC in his home city. And so at eleven o'clock on the morning of Wednesday, October 19, he strode into the Magnolia Room restaurant in Rich's department store, one of downtown Atlanta's most fashionable lunch spots. He was promptly arrested on anti-trespass charges and carted off to jail. He spent his first ever night behind bars.

King's imprisonment failed to generate much interest outside Atlanta. When his SCLC colleagues wired both presidential candidates asking them to intervene, neither responded. During the first twenty-four hours the only campaign official to establish contact was Frank Reeves, who had accompanied Kennedy to Florida. Acting on his own initiative, he flew from Miami to Atlanta, where he paid King a secret visit in jail. Their time together was brief, and, by all accounts, King did not ask for any assistance from the Kennedy campaign. Nor did Reeves offer any.[5]

Throughout that week, Wofford worried that news of King's imprisonment would taint the Kennedy campaign. By far his greatest fear was that black voters would blame the Democratic Party, since Georgia politics was dominated by three of the party's leading segregationists, Richard Russell, Herman Talmadge, and Ernest Vandiver, the state's forty-two-year-old governor. Without consulting the Kennedy high command, Wofford decided to intervene, hoping to secure King's release before the crisis escalated. That Saturday morning, from his home in Alexandria, Virginia, Wofford called attorney Morris Abram, a close friend of William B. Hartsfield, Atlanta's reform-minded mayor, who privately sympathized with the demonstrators. Fortunately, Abram was about to set off for a crisis meeting at City Hall, at which Hartsfield planned to discuss King's imprisonment with local black leaders.[6]

By the time Abram arrived, the mayor had already sketched out a plan to diffuse the crisis. He had personally guaranteed King's freedom if demonstrations were suspended immediately. Hartsfield's main challenge now was to sell the truce agreement to Atlanta's white community. When Abram informed him of the call from Wofford, Hartsfield spotted an opening. Rather than claim responsibility himself, he told reporters the deal had been brokered with the personal assistance of Kennedy.[7]

Wofford was horrified when he heard the news, and immediately called Kenneth O'Donnell, who was with the candidate in Kansas. "Hartsfield said what?" shouted O'Donnell. "You did what?" O'Donnell and Salinger felt the urgency of the situation, and hurriedly drafted a statement that downplayed the candidate's involvement. As it turned out, their concern was excessive—few reporters seemed particularly interested in events in Atlanta. The night before, Kennedy and Nixon had clashed over Cuba in their fourth televised debate. The story that day was Castro rather than King.[8]

But news was starting to spread throughout the South. Bobby Troutman heard a recording of Hartsfield's statement on the car radio and nearly veered off the road. For months, he had been reassuring southern leaders that Kennedy was a gradualist, unlikely to meddle in the ways in the South. Yet if the reports were true, he had just interceded on behalf of the man most closely associated with the civil rights struggle. Pulling to the side of the road, Troutman contacted Robert Kennedy in Washington, who assured him that the Hartsfield statement was false. On the strength of that denial, Georgia Democratic chairman Griffin Bell issued a strongly worded rebuttal: "We know that Senator Kennedy would never interfere in the affairs of a sovereign state."[9]

According to the Hartsfield plan, King was supposed to be released later that Saturday evening. But when his wife, Coretta, arrived for a celebratory meal at an Atlanta restaurant, she learned her husband had been kept in jail for violating parole. It turned out that, earlier in the year, King had been pulled over by a traffic cop in DeKalb County because a white woman, the writer Lillian Smith, was a passenger in the car. At the time, King had just returned to his home city from Montgomery and was therefore driving with an Alabama license, a minor violation punished at a court hearing a few days later with a $25 fine and six-month suspended jail sentence. But now that episode had taken on new significance, since technically his arrest at Rich's department store violated the terms of his probation. DeKalb County officials demanded to take him into custody, so instead of being released that Saturday evening he was transferred to a different jailhouse.

In court the following Monday morning, King came before Judge Oscar Mitchell, a curmudgeonly segregationist who had ruled on the original traffic offense. Mitchell was determined to make an example of King and issued the stiffest sentence possible, six months' hard labor in the state penitentiary at Reidsville. When news of the verdict reached Washington, Wofford was outraged. He urged Kennedy to condemn it unreservedly. Initially, Kennedy agreed, but later, unable to find wording that would not antagonize southern whites, he backed off.[10]

Instead, the candidate devised his own plan to diffuse the crisis. He opened a secret back channel communication with Governor Vandiver. At 6:30 that Wednesday morning, Kennedy awoke Vandiver with a phone call and asked if there was any way King could be sprung from jail. "It would be of tremendous benefit to me," Kennedy said. Vandiver was unsure how to help, but Kennedy was insistent: "Would you try and see what you can do and call me back?" Vandiver then apparently offered Kennedy a deal: If he promised to refrain from publicly criticizing Mitchell's ruling, he would endeavor to secure King's early release. Kennedy readily agreed.[11]

Shortly after, Vandiver contacted his brother-in-law, Bob Russell, a Democratic National Committeeman and nephew of Richard Russell. Bob Russell had close contacts in DeKalb County and reportedly contacted George B. Stewart, the secretary of the Georgia Democratic Party. Stewart was a close friend of Mitchell's and informed him that he would soon hear from the governor directly. Throughout the afternoon, Vandiver kept the Kennedy high command abreast of each new development and spoke on at least four separate occasions to Robert Kennedy, whose number had been given him by the candidate himself. No one said anything to Wofford about the secret negotiations, and when he learned about Vandiver's involvement late that afternoon, Robert Kennedy was decidedly sheepish. "What we want most is to get King out, isn't it?"[12]

That afternoon, Robert Kennedy made contact with Stewart, who instructed him to telephone Judge Mitchell's office at eight the next morning. Technically, the phone call was illegal—Kennedy, who had a law degree, could have been disbarred for contacting a judge with regard to a case pending before the court. The two nonetheless conducted a polite and businesslike conversation in which Kennedy urged Mitchell to release King at the earliest opportunity. Kennedy explained that the campaign needed to get King out of jail because otherwise, "We would lose the state of Massachusetts." (RFK later insisted—not altogether convincingly—that his phone call was borne of moral indignation. "The more I thought about the injustice of it," he told John Seigenthaler, his closest aide, "the more I thought what a son of a bitch that judge was."[13])

For the time being, the secret release plan was kept from Coretta King, who, heavily pregnant, spent the rest of the day at her home in Atlanta worrying about her husband's safety. Feeling anxious, she contacted Wofford, a longtime family friend. Her call placed Wofford in a difficult position. He was desperate to comfort her but could not disclose the details of the Vandiver plan. Instead, he offered vague assurances that Kennedy was doing "everything possible" to help.[14]

Later that night, over a beer with Louis Martin, Wofford expressed his frustration about Kennedy's refusal to condemn Mitchell. Then an idea came to him: The candidate should call Coretta King and convey his sympathy. Wofford rushed to contact Kennedy, who was still in Chicago but was unable to reach him. O'Donnell seemed reluctant to take Wofford's calls, since they always seemed to bring unwelcome news. Wofford then called Bowles, who immediately warmed to the idea and offered himself to call Coretta King. Without mentioning the Vandiver plan, Bowles assured her that everything was being done to guarantee her husband's release. He then offered the telephone to his dinner guest that night, Adlai Stevenson. To Bowles's surprise, Stevenson refused to take it, claiming it would be inappropriate for him to speak since he had never been introduced formally to Mrs. King.[15]

The situation in Georgia escalated overnight. At 8:30 the following morning, Coretta King awoke to the distressing news that her husband had been driven through the night in handcuffs and leg chains to Reidsville state penitentiary, a 300-mile journey into the backwoods of Georgia.[16] She feared her husband was about to be lynched. She again contacted Wofford, who had not yet heard of King's 4:30 A.M. transfer. He initially assumed Vandiver had reneged on the deal, but a few minutes later Abram called and assured him that King would be safer at Reidsville, a state facility run by a fair-minded warden. Growing increasingly frustrated with Kennedy's inaction, Wofford conferred with Sargent Shriver in Chicago. "The trouble with your beautiful, passionate Kennedys is that they never show their passion," he complained. "They don't understand symbolic action." He explained how Bowles had called Mrs. King the previous evening and suggested that Kennedy follow suit. "Give me her number," said Shriver, who had less than an hour to reach O'Hare Airport before the candidate's plane left, "and get me out of jail if I'm arrested for speeding." With that, he raced toward the airport, reaching Kennedy's hotel just as the candidate was concluding a breakfast meeting with a group of Illinois businessmen.[17]

Shriver found Kennedy in his suite surrounded by Ted Sorensen, Lawrence O'Brien, and Kenneth O'Donnell. Shriver knew all three would object to the idea of calling Mrs. King, so he waited until they had left the room. When Kennedy retired to the bedroom, complaining about feeling unwell, Shriver followed him. With only a few seconds to present his case, he blurted out a list of reasons why Kennedy should make the call. Black voters "want to know whether you care," he said, pleadingly. "If you telephone Mrs. King, they will know you understand and will help. You will reach their hearts." Perched on the bed, Kennedy nodded in agreement. "That's a good idea," he said. "Why not?"[18]

Shriver immediately put through the call to the King household in Atlanta and then handed the phone to his brother-in-law. "Good morning, Mrs. King. This is Senator Kennedy," said the candidate. "I want to express to you my concern about your husband. I know this must be very hard for you. I understand you are expecting a baby, and I just wanted you to know that I was thinking about you and Dr. King. If there is anything I can do to help, please feel free to call on me." Startled, Coretta King could not quite believe that Kennedy was on the line. "I certainly appreciate your concern," she said. "I would appreciate anything you could do to help." In all, the call lasted less than two minutes.[19]

Events were now moving at hurtling speed. Only a handful of people knew about the call—and, remarkably, the group included none of Kennedy's closest aides. As his plane flew from Chicago to Detroit, the candidate himself leaned over to Salinger and casually mentioned it. Salinger recognized the potentially explosive impact of Kennedy's call and immediately radioed Washington to warn Robert Kennedy. The young campaign manager flew into a blind rage. Suspecting Shriver was to blame, he contacted his brother-in-law in Chicago and delivered such a withering assault that for years it soured their relationship. After tearing into Shriver, he then summoned Wofford and Martin to his office. "Do you know that three Southern governors told us that if Jack supported Jimmy Hoffa, Nikita Khrushchev, or Martin Luther King, they would throw their states to Nixon?" he barked. "Do you know that this election may be razor close and you have probably lost it for us?"[20]

Robert Kennedy swore Martin and Wofford to secrecy; as a further safeguard, he prohibited the CRS from issuing any unauthorized press releases for the remainder of the campaign. But the *New York Times* was already onto the story—a reporter had spoken with Coretta King. The *New York Post* was not far behind. Later that evening, when Senator Kennedy touched down in New York, reporters at Idlewild Airport pressed him for his version of events. "She is a friend of mine," said the candidate in a deliberately vague response, as he hurried along on the tarmac, "and I was concerned about the situation." (By now, Kennedy had realized that he might have damaged his chances in the South, and as he walked away he muttered about having a "traitor in his camp" who had foolishly leaked the news.) With the confirmation it needed, the *New York Times* ran the story that night. But it ultimately allotted just two inches of copy to it and buried it on page twenty-two. The *Times* Washington bureau staff had filed a full-length story, but the news desk in New York decided it was of little significance.[21]

The Vandiver release plan took immediate effect that Friday morning, October 27. In a brief hearing, Mitchell released King on $2,000 bond. He noted that "a brother" of a presidential candidate had created "heavy pressure" to bring the case to a swift conclusion. After leaving prison, King spoke to reporters, and, though he stopped short of an outright endorsement, he expressed his gratitude openly: "I am deeply indebted to Senator Kennedy, who served as a great force in making my release possible."[22]

The CRS immediately spotted an opportunity. Martin contacted journalists from all the major black news organizations. Notably, he left white reporters off his call list, in the hope their papers would bury the story. The tactic worked. The *Pittsburgh Courier* reported that with the help of the Kennedy brothers King was now "the biggest Negro in the United States," while the *Washington Afro-American* placed the story on its front page under the headline: "King Freed After Senator Kennedy Intervenes." Major media outlets, however, downplayed the story or ignored it altogether. Although *US News and World Report* carried a report about King's imprisonment, it failed even to mention Kennedy's phone call to Coretta King. *Time* gave the story only a passing reference. On television, ABC News carried a brief report early on after Kennedy's comments at Idlewild, but CBS News waited two more days before running the story.[23]

Wofford and Martin were determined to use King's comments to the campaign's greatest possible advantage. They came up with the idea of distributing a pamphlet recounting the dramatic story. Both men, however, were mindful of Robert Kennedy's strict prohibition on any new initiative with the potential to stir controversy. To circumvent the campaign manager, they approached Shriver, who was still smarting from Bobby Kennedy's reprimand the previous week. He advised Wofford and Martin that if the pamphlet simply outlined the facts and did not commit the candidate to any new policy, there was no need for clearance from campaign headquarters. Within six hours, Martin and Wofford drafted a pamphlet with the working title, "'No Comment,' Nixon versus a Candidate with a Heart, Senator Kennedy: The Case of Martin Luther King." It contained adulatory quotes from Coretta King and her larger-than-life father-in-law,

"Daddy" King, who had decided now to endorse Kennedy. In all, the Kennedy campaign distributed tens of thousands of copies under the name of a phantom organization, "The Freedom Crusade Committee," lest southerners object. Soon it was dubbed the "blue bomb" after the color paper it was printed on and its near explosive effect in black communities.[24]

With the election now just nine days away, Wofford was eager to conclude one last piece of unfinished business: the release of the final report from the Constitutional Conference. For the past two weeks, Senator Joseph Clark and Congressman Emanuel Celler had been putting final touches on a "blueprint for presidential action," a proposal for a blend of new legislation and executive orders that would make the civil rights plank a reality. Robert Kennedy had already cleared the document, but Wofford needed the candidate himself to sign off on it. When Senator Kennedy briefly touched down in Washington on the penultimate Sunday of the campaign, Wofford met him off the plane at National Airport with a final draft. In a small holding area close to the runway, Kennedy, who had studied "speed reading," perused the proposals in what Wofford described later as a "quizzical, sympathetic but humorous way." After taking only a few minutes to read the entire document, Kennedy looked Wofford in the eye. "Tell me honestly," he said, "whether you think I need to sign and release this today in order to get elected a week from Tuesday. Or do you mainly want me to do it to go on the record?" The question placed Wofford in an awkward position. The Constitutional Conference had after all been his brainchild, and he thought that Kennedy should endorse Celler and Clark's proposals largely to dispel any lingering suspicions among blacks and liberals that he intended to soft-peddle civil rights as president. But he conceded that the black vote was safely in the Democratic column. "Then we can wait, and release when I'm elected," Kennedy breezily replied. "You can consider me on the record," he added. "With you."[25]

With just over a week to go before the election, the race was neck and neck, but Nixon appeared to be harnessing the all-important late momentum. In those final weeks, the vice president had stepped up his personal attacks on Kennedy, portraying him as a big-spending liberal whose fiscal profligacy would prolong the recession that had begun earlier in the year and driven up unemployment to seven percent. Realizing that the election had in many ways become a referendum on his own presidency, Eisenhower was determined to safeguard his legacy and thrust himself into the campaign at the last minute, making eleventh-hour appearances in Michigan, Illinois, and New York. For his part, Kennedy spent the final days of the campaign in New York and New England, finishing with a rally at Boston Garden. The following morning, he cast his vote in the basement of an old library close to the Massachusetts State House on Beacon Hill. A few hours later, on the other side of the continent, Nixon cast his vote in his hometown of Whittier, California, and then drove in an open-top convertible to Tijuana, Mexico, for lunch.

Blacks were heading to the polls in record numbers and voting overwhelming for Kennedy. IBM suggested Kennedy had achieved a 68 percent share of the black vote, while Gallup concluded it was 70 percent. *Frontier* magazine estimated the level of support to be even higher, at 81.7 percent. In 1956, Stevenson had won a rather dismal 61 percent. The gains were dramatic. In Philadelphia's ward 47, a black enclave, Stevenson had won a 74.3 percent share in 1956. Four years later, 84.3 percent voted for Kennedy. On the western fringe of the state, in Pittsburgh's Ward 5, blacks had voted two-to-one Democratic in 1956. In 1960, the proportion jumped to four-to-one. In the four "blackest" neighborhoods of New York City, the Democrats' share of the vote increased from 66.7 percent to 76.3 percent.[26]

This improved performance was not limited to the North. In Memphis's Ward 5, the Democratic vote rose from 36.2 percent to 67.7 percent; in eight precincts of Atlanta, it jumped from 14.8 percent to 41.9 percent. In Charles County, Virginia, a rural county with a black majority, the Democratic share climbed from 19 percent to 64.9 percent. In Tampa, Florida 1,011 voted for Stevenson in 1956, while 1,980 voted for Kennedy; in three black wards in Nashville, Tennessee, 3,258 voted for Stevenson in 1956 compared with 5,710 for Kennedy in 1960. In the states of the Old Confederacy, black votes helped stem the tide of "Presidential Republicanism," and although Nixon managed to carry Florida, Tennessee, Kentucky, and Virginia, as Eisenhower had done in 1956, black voters helped the Democrats regain Texas and Louisiana. In Houston's twenty-three predominantly black wards, 11,952 voters had supported Stevenson. More than 22,000 voted for Kennedy.[27]

In an election where Kennedy achieved victory with a plurality of just 114,673 votes, the black vote may well have determined the entire election. In battleground states in the North and Midwest, where the election was on knife-edge, blacks provided Kennedy with his margin of victory. In New Jersey, where 125,000 blacks voted for him, he had nudged out Nixon by a wafer-thin margin of just 30,000 votes. In South Carolina, as well, an increase in black support was thought to have kept the state's eight Electoral College votes in the Democratic column. Had it not been for black votes in South Carolina, and most likely North Carolina and Texas, Kennedy would have lost those critical states and with it the presidential election.[28]

Early the following morning of November 9, Nixon finally conceded defeat from California. Within the Republican Party, the postmortems began immediately, in a mood of bitter recrimination. Thruston Morton, the chairman of the Republican National Committee, blamed Nixon's defeat on his dismal performance among northern black voters. According to the GOP's own figures, he won just 10–12 percent of the black vote, compared with Eisenhower's 39 percent share four years earlier. Thruston decried the campaign's poor organization and inadequate financing, telling reporters that, as part of their drive for black votes, the "opposition spent five or six times as much and started spending it early." It was not until mid-October that the GOP's black campaign finally cranked into action, he complained, and by then it was too late. Eisenhower also pointed to Nixon's failure to attract black support as the single most important factor in the Republican loss. In the aftermath of the election, most commentators agreed the black vote had been unusually influential in determining the result. "If the Negro voters of America hadn't shifted last Tuesday to John Kennedy," judged the *New Republic*, "Vice-President Nixon would now be holding press conferences as President-elect." *Time* noted, "Kennedy's victory with the Negroes was nothing short of triumphant."[29]

In their rush to identify the single most important factor that had tipped the balance in Kennedy's favor, commentators, reporters, and politicians seized upon the significance of the King phone calls. Eisenhower, for one, considered them pivotal, blaming Nixon's defeat on a "number of calls." Ted Sorensen also included "the King calls" among his "seven decisive factors." Both Kennedys thought their support for King had contributed to victory, since the black vote had been especially important in Illinois and Michigan. As John Kennedy told John Kenneth Galbraith, "The finest strategies are usually the result of accidents."[30]

Yet the overall impact of the entire episode has probably been exaggerated; although it no doubt contributed to a boost in black turnout, Kennedy had established a commanding lead among black voters well before King's arrest. In Los Angeles, a private poll conducted in early October suggested 77 percent of the city's 200,000 blacks planned to vote for Kennedy, while party workers in Sacramento and Oakland put the figure at 80 percent. In Ohio, a poll conducted on October 19 showed Kennedy enjoying an 83 percent–17 percent lead among black voters. (A second poll taken in early November, just as the King calls were first being reported, revealed his support had increased to 88 percent.) Private polls from Pennsylvania showed that Kennedy's support in black communities rose steadily from the opening weeks of the campaign: A poll on September 9 gave him a 58 percent share, which had jumped to 66 percent by mid-October. A third poll, taken before the King call, suggested black support ran at 74 percent.[31]

Anecdotal reports from across the country supported the polling data. J. Raymond "The Harlem Fox" Jones described the election as a "symphony," with the King calls its "great last movement." Still, he thought the Constitutional Conference in New York was probably more significant. James L. Hicks, the executive editor of the *Amsterdam News*, thought Kennedy "had already shown enough interest in Negroes prior to King's imprisonment." Martin described the calls as "the icing on the cake. But the cake was already made." On Election Day itself, more blacks in Atlanta, the preacher's home town, actually voted for Nixon than Kennedy—across Georgia, Kennedy received only 49 percent of the black vote, his worst performance anywhere—another indication that the impact of the call was not as dramatic as has commonly been supposed.[32]

Kennedy's phone call to Coretta King did, nonetheless, represent the culmination—however unwitting—of a brilliant and groundbreaking campaign strategy. Sorensen, Wofford, and Martin had all recognized from the outset of the campaign that it was possible to make a vigorous play for northern black votes without alienating white southerners. Well-organized, well-financed, and well-connected, the CRS quickly overwhelmed the Republicans. Wofford and Martin, two of the most talented political strategists who had ever put their minds to winning the black vote, marketed Kennedy with flair and imagination. And, with few exceptions, they managed to comply with the constraints imposed on them by the Kennedy high command. Throughout the campaign, Wofford and Martin devised a series of initiatives that had impressed blacks but had gone almost unnoticed by whites. The call to Coretta King provided the campaign with the ultimate symbol of Kennedy's sympathy with the black struggle, and it came at no real political cost. However panicked Robert Kennedy may have been when he initially found out about the call, the fact remains that it caused no lasting damage in the South—in fact, it was barely noticed.

Martin and Wofford tried to portray the King phone call as a stirring profile in courage. Was it? There is ultimately no way to know; Kennedy never commented on his motives. Certainly, he could not have anticipated the impact of the call in advance. Presumably, he realized—or would have realized, if he had taken time to think it through—that his primary advisers would have cautioned against him making the call. One can only assume that the decision was impulsive, stemming perhaps from fatigue, gallantry, or genuine kind-heartedness. It was a rare and inexplicable moment in an otherwise highly coordinated—and frequently cynical—campaign.

King's imprisonment, taken as a whole, certainly revealed Kennedy's profound political limitations. Faced with the startling injustice of Judge Mitchell's ruling, Kennedy chose not to speak out but entered into a secret collaboration with Vandiver, a staunch segregationist who had vowed repeatedly never to allow a black child to study at an all-white school. That the Kennedy campaign was able to turn the entire episode into a political triumph reveals both the effectiveness of the strategy of association as well as its enduring ironies. Kennedy's success over the course of the campaign encouraged him to believe that, using symbolism rather than substance, he could continue to achieve the same level of black support as president.

Kennedy had aroused expectations among black citizens, despite his reticence throughout the fall on the subject of actual civil rights reforms. Herein lay one of the great paradoxes of the 1960 campaign. For blacks, the strategy of association had created the strong impression that Kennedy was a restless reformer who sympathized with their plight and was committed to dismantling segregation. For the president-elect, however, the success of the strategy had taught him that even a minimalist civil rights policy, if augmented by high-profile appointments and grand gestures, would be sufficient to secure his popularity. Kennedy would never fulfill the largely unspoken promise of his campaign.

CHAPTER 12

❧

Seventy-two Days

At lunchtime on November 9, a little more than an hour after the vice president's concession in California, Kennedy arrived at the Armory building in Hyannis Port, where some 400 excited reporters awaited him. At the dais, Kennedy was surrounded by every adult member of his family, including his seventy-one-year-old father, who stood imperiously at his side (it was the first time they had appeared together in public since the primaries). Kennedy made a brief victory statement, in which he pledged to advance the "long-range interests of the United States and the cause of freedom around the world." With that, he shot a playful smile at his pregnant wife and quickly brought the news conference to an end. "So now my wife and I prepare for a new Administration," he beamed at reporters, "and for a new baby." Kennedy had said nothing about the cause of freedom at home.[1]

Though determinedly upbeat in public, privately Kennedy was exasperated that he had not beaten Nixon more decisively. He had considered Nixon to be a woefully inferior candidate and had always set store in his tremendous ability to woo voters. Now his extraordinary self-confidence seemed to melt away. As Kennedy recovered from the campaign in Palm Beach in mid-November, he came to view his slim victory as a prescription for moderation. He soon abandoned plans to begin his administration with a quick flurry of legislation modeled on Roosevelt's 100 days. "The closeness of his election victory has wrought a change in Jack Kennedy," noted *Time*. *Newsweek* observed that "if the campaign battle cry had been 'this country has got to move ahead,' now the road sign seemed to read: 'Proceed with caution.'" Later in his presidency, Kennedy would echo the words of Thomas Jefferson: Great innovations should never be imposed upon slender majorities.[2]

Kennedy opted instead for a minimal legislative program. His administration would seek to raise the minimum wage, help promote economic development in depressed areas, grant federal aid to education, provide new housing, and offer medical care for the elderly. Civil rights was not on the list. When the president-elect announced the formation of a series of transition task forces to shape policy across a wide range of issues—including national security, the United States Information Agency, the Peace Corps, the reorganization of the Pentagon, Latin America, India, natural resources, depressed areas, housing and cities, health, social security, education, taxation, minimum wages, outer space, and even cultural exchanges—black advancement was not among them. Kennedy's Press Secretary Pierre Salinger told reporters that Senator Joseph Clark and Congressman Emanuel Celler would continue to work on the package of proposals Kennedy had requested in September. But it was an open secret that, although they had completed the project long before Election Day, the candidate had suppressed their report.

Kennedy's decision to back away from civil rights was uncomplicated, intellectually and emotionally. Certainly, he had grown skeptical about the prospects for legislative reform in the wake of the August Senate session. And despite his exhortations to black and liberal skeptics on the eve of the Los Angeles convention, Kennedy had never wanted to lead a vigorous assault on segregation. He felt in no way bound by the Democratic platform; he saw the platform as nothing more than the product of preconvention political maneuvering, not a statement of genuine intent. Temperamentally and ideologically, Kennedy was a gradualist. It is quite likely that even had he won the election by a broad margin, he would have proceeded with caution on the issue of civil rights. Kennedy's tiny margin of victory became a pretext for inaction, but his real instincts with regard to the politics of civil rights had already been in evidence for years. The narrowness of victory was important only in influencing the degree to which Kennedy recoiled.

And so on December 20, at a press conference held on the patio of his father's Palm Beach mansion, Kennedy confirmed that he had decided not to introduce a new civil rights bill. He offered reporters only vague assurances that the new administration "would do everything possible to provide for the protection of the constitutional rights of all American citizens" and "do whatever we feel could be helpful in accomplishing it." Kennedy's closest advisers supported his decision, claiming he had little choice given his lack of mandate and the strength of the southern bloc. "No amount of Presidential pressure could put through the Eighty-seventh Congress a meaningful legislative package on civil rights," Sorensen wrote afterwards. "Success required selectivity. . . . he would take on civil rights at the right time on the right issue." Lawrence O'Brien, who was placed in charge of the White House congressional liaison team, readily agreed. "Kennedy had no sweeping mandate from the voters, and he had few, if any, representatives or senators who owed their election to his political coattails," he argued. "The balance of power in the House of Representatives was held by southern Democrats."[3]

Indeed, Kennedy had grown even more fixated on the power of the Southern Caucus in the wake of the election. Pouring over the congressional results, Kennedy aides believed it was possible to identify a conservative coalition occupying 59 of the 100 seats in the Senate, and 285 of the 435 seats in the House. The seniority system placed southern Democrats at some of the most vital centers of power. Of the sixteen Senate committees, ten were controlled by segregationists, including many of the most important: Judiciary, Finance, Agriculture, Foreign Relations, Labor and Public Welfare, and Armed Services. In the House, the situation was much the same. Southerners held fourteen of the twenty chairmanships, including the Ways and Means Committee, which regulated the flow of legislation to the floor, and the Rules Committee, which posed a particularly serious obstacle to reform. It was controlled by Howard Smith, Virginia's elder statesman, who had accumulated so much power in his twenty-nine years on Capitol Hill that a House-passed bill could not be sent to conference without his consent.

The August session had reminded Kennedy of the ease with which a disciplined group of southern Democrats, acting in concert with conservative Republicans, could block the enactment of even a modest program of non–civil rights–related reforms. Kennedy now worried that any attempt to push Southern Democrats on civil rights was likely to produce a backlash. It could even drive away moderates like Senators John Sparkman and Lister Hill of Alabama. As he told Sorensen midway through the transition, "If we drive Sparkman and Hill and other moderate southerners to the wall with a lot of civil rights demands that can't pass anyway, then what happens to the Negro on minimum wages, housing and the rest?"[4]

Kennedy's fear of alienating the Southern Caucus was bred as much of personal insecurity as political arithmetic. As a senator, with only a slim record of legislative accomplishment, he had been overawed by southern grandees like Richard Russell and Sam Ervin. They were more skillful legislators and more imposing men. Now, as president-elect, Kennedy continued to view them in much the same way. They should be charmed and, on occasion, gently cajoled, but never confronted directly.

Kennedy was most intimidated by Russell. As well as leading the Southern Caucus, Russell boasted a daunting list of committee assignments including the chairmanship of the Armed Services Committee, the second-ranking Democratic seat on the Appropriations Committee, the chairmanship of its subcommittee on defense appropriations, and rare membership of both the Policy and Steering Committees. And he was an extraordinarily adept politician. "The really able Southerners that I've met in the Senate and in the Congress," Kennedy told Ralph McGill of the *Atlanta Constitution* in reference to the Georgian, "have been extraordinarily gifted men in parliamentary matters. The good ones seem to have a grasp of government and how to carry out the political maneuvers quite beyond that of the able men of other regions." When he arranged to meet with Russell in Washington on December 1, the president-elect made the extraordinarily submissive gesture of offering to present himself at the Georgian's office. Kennedy had asked all his other Senate colleagues to visit him in his private study. Even Russell himself considered the offer wholly inappropriate and refused to allow Kennedy to humble himself in that way. But Russell had achieved something of a psychological victory. After their meeting, a smiling Russell told reporters he hoped to preserve their "very cordial relationship." He did not seem overly concerned about Kennedy's stance on civil rights. Asked if the issue had figured in their discussion, he said simply, "We didn't wish to indulge in any futile discussions."[5] Just a few months earlier, Russell had confided to a constituent that it would be difficult to save "our Southland from the evil threat" of the Democratic platform, and that he could not see the "slightest ray of brightness" ahead. In Washington that day, after observing the acquiescent young president-elect up close, he must have thought the clouds were clearing.[6]

Kennedy frequently claimed that his backpedaling on civil rights was borne of political necessity, and a number of sympathetic biographers and historians have taken him at his word. But Kennedy's rationalizations were a product of his temperament and his long-standing aversion to even the slightest conflict with members of the southern bloc. The subsequent justifications put forward on Kennedy's behalf do not stand up in the face of historical evidence. Admittedly, the administration faced a congressional situation that was far from ideal. Yet it was by no means as dire as Kennedy imagined.

On Capitol Hill, die-hards in the Southern Caucus were becoming increasingly isolated. The caucus could no longer claim any members from Kentucky, Missouri, or Maryland. Senators Estes Kefauver and Albert Gore of Tennessee, George Smathers of Florida, and Ralph Yarborough of Texas rarely attended its meetings. And moderates, like John Sparkman and Lister Hill of Alabama, voted more regularly with northern colleagues. The once solid Democratic South was starting to splinter. As Russell conceded in his annual speech to the Georgia Assembly in February, 1959, the southern Democrats had "not only lost the support of many of those from other sections [of the party] on whom we once relied, but the representatives from the states of the old confederacy no longer present a common front." By the end of the 1950s, Russell realized he could only deploy the filibuster sparingly, since its overuse would stiffen demands for a change in Senate rules. The aging composition of the Southern Caucus presented another problem. Within two years time thirteen of its members would be over sixty, and four over seventy. Given the energy and stamina required to conduct a filibuster, it was not clear if they could muster the physical strength.[7]

In the weeks following the election, it was possible to detect a mood of cautious optimism not just among liberal activists but also among more sober-minded commentators. After studying the results of the congressional races, Russell Baker of the *New York Times* decided that the new Senate was "predominantly liberal in composition." Despite a net loss of two seats to the Republicans, there had been "no real erosion" of the liberal voting bloc from the high-water mark of 1958, and the notion that every GOP seat was occupied by a reactionary conservative was wholly misleading. The *New York Times* editorial board concurred. As far as the balance of Congress was concerned, "Nothing much has changed." *Newsweek* went further, predicting that Kennedy could look forward to a long and fruitful "honeymoon" with the new Democratic 87th Congress. If Kennedy "jumps right in with a broad new legislative program," its editors added, "he will find Congress so receptive that his record might well approach Franklin D. Roosevelt's famous 'One Hundred Days.'"[8]

In reality, the conservative coalition was neither as cohesive nor obstructionist as has generally been assumed. Of the thirty-six Senate Republicans who Kennedy identified as coalition members, as many as a dozen were reform-minded liberals from the party's pro–civil rights wing. Kenneth Keating and Jacob Javits, both of New York, were foremost among them. Then there was Hugh Scott of Pennsylvania, John Sherman Cooper of Kentucky, Clifford Case of New Jersey, Margaret Chase Smith of Maine, and Leverett Saltonstall of Massachusetts. During the transition, Senator Thomas Kuchel of California, the party's assistant Senate leader, counted as many as fifteen Republicans who would offer the administration support on certain issues, most notably civil rights. "Any so-called coalition simply to obstruct [the new administration] is unthinkable," said Kuchel. He was confident that the bipartisan cooperation on civil rights in evidence during the 1950s would endure into the 1960s. Liberal Republicans would support Kennedy's civil rights bills, just as liberal Democrats had backed Eisenhower's proposals.[9]

The face of the Republican Party was certainly changing. Largely owing to the dismal failure of Nixon's campaign to appeal to northern blacks, party chieftains, such as RNC Chairman Thruston Morton, called upon the party to adopt a more enlightened form of conservatism. Henceforth, the party would place greater emphasis on social justice and civil rights. Nixon's failures were particularly evident in urban centers—a detailed report carried out by the RNC and published in March revealed that out of forty cities with populations over 300,000 people, Kennedy had carried twenty-six compared to Nixon's fourteen. If the party was to reestablish a foothold in major cities, the report concluded, it would have to champion a raft of progressive issues, civil rights foremost among them. To support their argument, party strategists pointed out how liberal Republican Senate candidates, like Case, Cooper, Saltonstall, and Smith, had outperformed Nixon on the GOP ticket.[10]

There were certainly still a number of archconservatives within the Republican caucus, but figures such as Barry Goldwater of Arizona and Styles Bridges of New Hampshire seemed to represent the party's past. They were caricatured in the press as the Republican Old Guard. As the new session of Congress approached, Keating openly plotted a liberal coup to oust Bridges from the leadership of the GOP Policy Committee and planned to form a rival committee, modeled on the Democratic Advisory Council. Seven years after death of the conservative Ohio Senator Robert Taft, who was known as "Mr. Republican," much of the power within the GOP rested with politically moderate East Coast patricians, like Senator Prescott Bush of Connecticut, who proudly described himself as a progressive moderate, rather than Sunbelt radicals like Goldwater. The notion that Goldwater would become the party's next presidential nominee was almost laughable.

The Democratic Party was also growing more progressive. Its future seemed to belong to reformers like Eugene McCarthy, Edmund Muskie, Joseph Clark, Clair Engle, William Proxmire, and Hubert Humphrey. Over the previous four years, they had wrested control of the policymaking arm of the DNC and helped ensure that the party campaigned in 1960 on the most progressive platform in its history. Though they lacked positions of power on Capitol Hill, they believed fiercely in the strength of their arguments, and their ability to arouse public support. At the beginning of the new decade, they predicted that the Senate, for so long the bulwark against change, could finally become a locus of reform.

The results of the 1960 elections seemed to bear out their optimism. Paul Douglas was reelected in 1960 with an increased majority, as was Michigan Senator Pat McNamara, who believed black advancement should be the nation's top priority. In Oregon there was victory for widow Maurine Neuberger, an aggressive reformer who promised to follow the same ultra-liberal line as her late husband, Richard. The only Democratic incumbent who lost his seat was J. Allen Frear of Delaware. A crusty conservative who voted regularly with the southern Democrats, he was defeated by J. Caleb Boggs, a liberal Republican backed by labor unions and blacks.

Without question, the situation in the House of Representatives was bleaker. The Democrats had suffered a net loss of twenty-two seats. But the Republicans had gone into the election hoping to make much greater inroads, and Kennedy could still boast a working majority of almost ninety seats. Most of the Democrats who lost their seats in 1960 were freshmen who, in the 1958 Democratic landslide, had achieved unexpected victories in traditionally Republican districts. And as with the Senate, the conservative coalition was no longer monolithic. Even though Republican Congressman Charles Halleck, the House minority leader, threatened to join forces with southern Democrats to obstruct Kennedy's legislative program, it was by no means clear that he could bring his caucus with him. During the transition, in fact, a number of House Republicans signaled their willingness to break from Halleck and support the new administration on civil rights. "What Charlie doesn't realize," said an East

Coast GOP leader, "is that a lot of Republicans, if given the choice between Howard Smith and John Kennedy, are going to take Kennedy. Once the Republicans put on a McKinley starched collar and the string tie of a southern colonel, you might be sure we'll stay a minority party."[11]

While Kennedy exaggerated the looming threat on Capitol Hill, he underestimated the strength of his own support. His narrow margin of victory—at just 114,673 votes, the smallest since 1888—obscured the full measure of his achievement. Going into the campaign, Nixon had been expected to comfortably win the presidential election. Just three months later, Kennedy had pulled off an astounding upset. At a time of peace and relative prosperity, he had persuaded America to change its course. His campaign truly did represent a definitive break with the past. He was the first Catholic to win the presidency and would be the youngest president since Theodore Roosevelt. He was also the first member of the World War II generation to occupy the White House.

Kennedy's support in the election had been broad-based. He had performed strongly among blacks, Jews, and Catholics, of course, but also among "suburbanites"—an increasingly influential demographic group that had inclined toward Republicans in the previous two elections. He did particularly well in the suburbs around Chicago, New York, and Philadelphia, while in the fourteen top northeastern metropolitan areas he polled 49 percent of the vote. Four years before, Stevenson had gained just a 38 percent share. Suburbanites were expected to become the single most powerful voting bloc by the end of the decade; at its outset, they had responded with genuine enthusiasm to the restless young candidate and his message of change.[12]

Even in the South, Kennedy exceeded expectations. He won seven of the eleven states of the Old Confederacy with 50.47 percent of the vote (Stevenson had received 47.76 percent in 1956). It is not clear if Kennedy had managed to win an actual majority among white southerners—a number of polls indicated that he failed narrowly, while a survey from National Election Studies suggested a slim plurality among southern whites. Still, even winning close to 50 percent of the vote was a notable achievement. In a region where over 95 percent of voters were Protestant, even Kennedy's Catholicism had not proved to be an insuperable problem.[13]

The closeness of the election ultimately signified very little. Kennedy had won a 49.9 percent share of the popular vote; in the previous hundred years only Franklin Roosevelt had passed the 50 percent mark. Harry Truman had won in 1948 with 49.5 percent of the popular vote. Commenting on Kennedy's success, Truman himself argued that small margins of victory historically had little impact on presidential performance. He cited the examples of Lincoln and Wilson, who both lost the popular vote but served with great distinction in office. Kennedy could emulate their success, predicted Truman, if he brought to the White House "a new surge of dynamic, decisive and productive leadership."[14]

At the beginning of the 1960s, the South was also in the throes of a massive social and political upheaval—forces that were eroding the power base of southern Democrats on Capitol Hill. It was quickly becoming an industrialized, urban society with fast-rising living standards. By 1960, only ten percent of its population were engaged in agricultural labor. Hundreds of thousands of new workers were flooding into the South from northern and western states, and a large number were well-paid white-collar staff, who showed little interest in defending the outdated racial mores of their newly adopted home. When metropolitan Atlanta publicized its millionth citizen in October 1959, it was William Smith, a young, well-educated sales executive from Rochester, New York.[15]

The mind of the South was evolving along with its economy. Businessmen were, in the oft-heard mantra of the times, too busy to hate. "Happily, the chambers of commerce are increasingly aware that segregation is no longer economically practical," wrote Ralph McGill at the beginning of the decade. "Nothing better illustrates changes in the South than that the voice of the chamber of commerce is becoming more influential than that of the demagogues of politics and extremist organizations." In his landmark study, *The Emerging South,* published in 1962, Thomas Clark identified "new conditions in the South [which] make the old human image as out of date and antiquated as that the Yankee abolitionist and the slave baron."[16]

A more liberal southern media both reflected and shaped the shifting attitudes of southerners. Papers such as the *McComb Enterprise Journal,* the *Gainesville Daily Times,* the *Raleigh News and Observer,* the *Chattanooga Times,* Greenville's *Delta Democratic Times,* the *Memphis Commercial Appeal,* and the *Miami News* urged readers to support moves toward a more integrated society. The *Atlanta Constitution,* the New South's most influential newspaper, set the standard for racial moderation. Publisher Ralph McGill and editor Eugene Patterson both ardently believed the South had to embrace the future, both to escape the baneful legacy of slavery and to safeguard its economic future. In the final weeks of the 1960 election, Bowles had tried to alert the Kennedy high command to this changing tone. After a private meeting with Ralph McGill, John Popham of the *Chattanooga Times,* and Bill Baggs of the *Miami News,* three of the region's most forward-thinking publishers, Bowles told Robert Kennedy, "Strong liberal forces are beginning to develop all over the South, [and] within a few years these forces may be politically dominant."[17]

The emergence of television as a social force had made the South more finely tuned to its public image, as well. Whereas the gruesome murder of Emmett Till in 1955 had been a mainly print story, the Little Rock crisis, just two years later, marked a milestone in television newsgathering. Images of defiant mothers yelling rebel chants and vowing that "niggers" would never be allowed in their schools brought naked sectarianism to a new audience, shaping opinion in the North and embarrassing many in the South. Three years later, when the sit-in protests sprang up across the South, television cameras were on hand to capture the violence as hoodlums poured sugar and pots of syrup over the protesters' heads before punching and kicking them to the floor. Even segregationists were shocked. After watching the sit-in demonstrations on television, James J. Kilpatrick, the racist firebrand who edited the *Richmond News-Leader,* reevaluated his views. In sharp contrast to the young activists, who invariably were neatly turned-out and well-behaved, Kilpatrick described the southern segregationists as "a rag-tail rabble, slack-jawed, black-jacketed grinning fit to kill." Television had pricked the conscience of even one of Virginia's most doctrinaire racists.[18]

Segregationists were losing some ground in the battles over school segregation as well. By 1960, Alabama, Mississippi, and South Carolina had failed to integrate a single school, but elsewhere there were signs of slow progress. School districts in Texas, Tennessee, North Carolina, and Florida had started to comply with *Brown*. In Arkansas, where Orval Faubus had ordered the closing of Little Rock schools for the entire 1958–59 academic year, racial moderates seized control of the local school board in the spring of 1959 and quickly agreed to gradual desegregation.

Just a few weeks after the 1960 election, segregationists suffered a momentous setback in New Orleans. The Eisenhower Justice Department dispatched U.S. marshals to bring about the desegregation of two elementary schools, despite the vehement objections of Governor Jimmie Davis and his allies in the Louisiana state legislature. In Baton Rouge, over a hundred whites, most of them parents from New Orleans, staged a mock funeral. Women dressed in dark, gossamer veils and men wearing black suits lined up in neat formation behind a coffin bearing the burnt effigy of Judge Wright, the liberal-minded federal judge whose desegregation ruling triggered the dispute.[19]

When a group of Louisiana lawmakers flew to Palm Beach on November 20 hoping to discuss the situation with the president-elect, Kennedy refused to meet them. Clark Clifford, a key member of his transition team, explained that it would be "highly inappropriate" for the president-elect to comment on a case still pending before the federal courts. More likely, Kennedy did not want to become embroiled in a bitter dispute over the integration of southern schools on the eve of his presidency.[20]

A second blow fell in January. Integrationists achieved a major victory in Georgia, when black students were admitted to the University of Georgia for the first time in its 159-year history. This time, Ernest Vandiver had agreed reluctantly to integrate the state university in Athens rather than defy a federal court order calling for the admission of two young black students. For a brief period, Vandiver considered emulating Faubus's last-ditch stand in Little Rock. But he soon had a change of heart, since he knew the Eisenhower Justice Department was determined to enforce the desegregation order. Vandiver also realized that the state's reputation had been badly damaged when he refused to guarantee the students' safety on January 11, when they came under attack after attending their first classes. A white mob had rampaged through the campus following a nighttime basketball game, and even in Georgia, Vandiver was pilloried for his mishandling of the crisis. Two-thirds of the University of Georgia's 600-member faculty had put their names to a fiercely worded resolution deploring his arrogant defiance of federal law. Vandiver knew he would have to capitulate.[21]

Southern Democrats sensed they were engaged in a losing battle. "We knew, of course, the odds were against us," Vandiver later reflected. "We were realists as much as anything." In 1961, an opinion poll showed that seventy-six percent of southerners now thought desegregation was inevitable, compared to fifty-four percent in 1957. "I felt that the majority of Southerners would not want to be associated with this kind of last-ditch or rear-guard action before the people of the nation," said LeRoy Collins, Florida's former governor. Georgia Senator Herman Talmadge also admitted, "We knew that the old order of race relations would have to go. . . . We were simply asking to be allowed to settle our own problems in our own way and in our own time." Even Bill Hendrix, the Grand Dragon of the Ku Klux Klan, decided during the transition between the Eisenhower and Kennedy administrations that the end had come. "I see no way to stop racial integration," he told reporters, "and it looks to me like the best thing to do is to accept it."[22]

A new generation of southern public officeholders was on the rise. Many were self-styled racial moderates, who knew that the campaign of massive resistance was damaging their states' economies. "We need massive intelligence, not massive resistance," proclaimed Terry Sanford, who was elected governor of North Carolina in 1960, a business-oriented former state legislator who won election by championing a reformist agenda. Much of his financial backing came from bankers and industrialists, who knew the North Carolina economy was unlikely to attract northern investment with a hard-line governor. South Carolina Governor Ernest F. "Fritz" Hollings talked of state responsibilities rather than states rights. In Tennessee, Frank Clement, the state's dashing young governor, took a firm stance in 1956 against a group of militant segregationists protesting over the gradual integration of schools in the eastern town of Clinton. Clement even dispatched the Tennessee National Guard to ensure that black schoolchildren could attend class, another setback for massive resistance.[23]

Just as the South was going through a period of rapid change, so, too, was the country as a whole. America seemed ready to shake off the spirit of conformity that had dominated the 1950s. Elvis Presley, Miles Davis, Jack Kerouac, Allen Ginsberg—the spirit of the nation was rebellious. It was becoming unquestionably more reformist. George Belknap, who had been employed by the Kennedy campaign to conduct a series of secret opinion polls throughout election year, informed the candidate, "People are more liberal than you think."[24]

Belknap cited a "very New Dealish" mood among the public. Indeed, Americans were once again counting on government institutions to improve living standards and to remedy social and economic wrongs. Liberal policies, like publicly financed healthcare for the elderly—or Medicare, as it was soon dubbed—federal aid to ailing schools, and new civil rights reforms, were drawing much greater support than they had done four years earlier. Over two-thirds of the American people favored federal aid to education, even though it gave Washington a bigger say in how local schools were run. A similar number supported Medicare, despite the rise in the social security tax required to pay for the government-administered program.[25]

On civil rights, public opinion polls indicated that Americans were increasingly willing to embrace further reform. A series of public opinion surveys conducted between 1958 and 1960 by the University of Michigan's Survey Research Center found "strong support" for government action combatting discrimination in housing and employment. A "favorable majority" supported school desegregation. Congressional constituency polls carried out in northern states showed enthusiastic support for new civil rights legislation, suggesting eighty to ninety-five percent favored measures expanding voting rights and outlawing bomb attacks on schools and black churches. When pollsters asked during the transition what the top priorities of the new administration should be, respondents listed tackling inflation, granting medical aid to the elderly, and raising the minimum wage in the top three spots. But "doing more to end segregation" tied for fourth with reducing taxation. It ranked higher than unemployment, the reorganization of the armed services, federal aid to education, and even the Cold War.[26]

On school integration, a sizable majority supported reform. A poll taken in 1959 suggested ninety-two percent of people living outside the South had no objection to sending their children to an integrated school. Even in the South, Belknap produced a poll revealing that only nineteen percent of southerners opposed blacks being treated fairly in employment and housing. A Gallup survey in February 1961 revealed that three-quarters of white southerners thought the day would soon arrive when blacks attended the same schools as whites and ate at the same lunch counters. A poll in Texas showed that while almost a third of Texans remained implacably opposed to *Brown*, fifty-four percent favored integration.[27]

The fact that the Republicans and Democrats had both adopted such far-reaching civil rights planks reflected the new mood of voters throughout the country. "It is a mark of the advance already achieved in public thinking about this question," noted the *New York Times*, "that both parties have so seriously addressed themselves to it and have felt it necessary at the cost of much bitter internal disagreement to come up with unmistakable commitments to carry out the spirit of the Constitution." In the words of journalist Anthony Lewis, civil rights was no longer a "matter of tepid righteousness" but "a vital concern." The most striking aspect of the two parties' bold civil rights planks was their similarity. It hinted at an emerging national consensus on the need, at least, for racial reform, if not the policies required to engineer it.[28]

This reformist spirit came to be reflected in a landmark report from the President's Commission on National Goals, a blue-ribbon panel set up by Eisenhower after the Soviet's successful launch of Sputnik. It was tasked with recommending how America should contain the Soviet threat. Published less than two weeks after the election, the report called for massive increases in federal funding for education, improved teachers' salaries, and more generous grants for hospital construction, clinics, and nursing homes—policies of a decidedly liberal hue. In addressing the question of "equality," the commission recommended root-and-branch reform. The committee, a high-powered panel of industrialists, educators, diplomats, and labor leaders, argued that religious and racial discrimination were "economically wasteful and in many respects dangerous," and that equal opportunities and rights—"the core of our system"—required action at all levels. "Additional municipal, state and federal legislation is essential" to eliminate discrimination, the committee argued. It even suggested that state and civic leaders who failed to meet their responsibilities should be sanctioned with heavy financial punishments. Federal funding should be withdrawn from states that continued to discriminate on the basis of race, a radical idea that even few ultraliberals in Congress were bold enough to advocate publicly. The committee then laid out two ambitious goals: the complete abolition of discrimination in higher education by 1970 and "progress in good faith toward desegregation of publicly supported schools" in every state.[29]

More notable than the shift in white public opinion, however, was the transformation of black politics. The new spirit of activism had been most forcibly demonstrated by the sit-in movement earlier in the year. Over 70,000 activists had participated and 4,000 were arrested. As James Baldwin wrote that August, "They are not the first Negroes to face mobs, they are merely the first Negroes to frighten the mob more than the mob frightens them. . . . these young people are determined to make it happen and make it happen now." Earlier in the spring, King made much the same point in a brilliant essay in the *Progressive*. A "revolution is occurring in both the social order and the human mind," King asserted. But race relations would continue to disfigure the country until federal action put an end to segregation. Blacks had grown weary of "hollow legislative enactments," "empty electoral campaign oratory," the "red tape of litigation," token integration, and the persistent economic inequities of an "affluent society." All across the country, blacks were animated by the "fierce urgency of now."[30]

Kennedy was not unaware of the changing world around him, but he was politically myopic. So while he probably realized that the liberal Ralph McGill was fast emerging as the most prominent southern newspaperman, he continued to be fixated on Russell's dominance on Capitol Hill. While he may have been alert to the liberalization of the southern business community, the fact that Harry F. Byrd remained the chairman of the Senate Banking Committee mattered more. Kennedy may even have realized that social and demographic changes were slowly eroding the power of the southern oligarchs. But in his mind at least, even a weakened Southern Caucus posed a grave threat to his presidency.

Within weeks of the election, president-elect Kennedy faced his first challenge on the subject of civil rights. A battle over the revision of Rule XXII pitted reformers against reactionaries and presented Kennedy with a choice between the two. Liberals sensed that their best opportunity to engineer a change would come during the presidential transition, at the very start of the new session of Congress when the rules governing parliamentary procedures could be altered most easily. In a valedictory vice-presidential act, Nixon, who was still in place as president of the Senate when the new session opened in early January, had promised already to allow change to be brought about by a simple majority of senators. Nixon's controversial decision would bequeath the advocates of reform an enormous tactical advantage in their efforts to change the filibuster rule. When he replaced Nixon, by contrast, Vice President Johnson would almost certainly adjudicate that a two-thirds majority rather than a simple majority would be required to change Rule XXII.[31]

Liberal Democrats ideally wanted to change the filibuster rule so that the Senate could close off debate with "majority cloture." Under existing rules, sixty-six senators had to oppose a filibuster to put an end to it. Majority cloture would require just fifty-one votes to shut off debate. If this change was not possible, liberals were willing to accept the more realistic goal of a new rule requiring three-fifths of those "present and voting" to shut off debate. This change would still represent a crushing defeat for the Southern Caucus.

Unsurprisingly, Harris Wofford strenuously advocated reform. He advised the president-elect that rule revision was not only "the clearest commitment in the platform," but the "only thing that can bring major results or even major trends by 1963." Not only would the rule change pave the way for new civil rights legislation, he predicted, it could also lead eventually to a rapprochement between the warring factions of the Democratic Party. "There will never be real unity in the Party as long as the southerners can hold the filibuster pistol at the Party's head," he argued. Robbed of their traditional veto power over new civil rights legislation, "the talents and the experience of Southern leaders will be constructively utilized to resolve civil rights differences rather than to exacerbate them." And a victory in the rules fight would be an important symbolic gain, as well—it would demonstrate that Kennedy had the legislative muscle to "get the country moving again," as he had promised, and to force southern Democrats onto the defensive.[32]

Wofford predicted that Kennedy was more than capable of engineering the change. Forty-two senators "definitely" supported reform. A further six were "probables," and ten others were described as "waverers." With only fifty-one votes needed to bring about change, Kennedy required the support of just three "waverers" to achieve a definitive victory. Other advisers agreed. Schlesinger predicted a "hairline majority" favored "majority cloture," the more ambitious goal. "I know you have to choose your fights with care," Schlesinger told Kennedy midway through November, "but these figures suggest that the administration could probably win the rules fight if it chose to make it." A number of leading Republicans were coming out in support of the change. Senator Jacob Javits was already busy lining up GOP support for a rule change—partly to highlight the splits within the Democratic Party but largely to smooth the way for new civil rights legislation. When congressional correspondent Russell Baker conducted an early head count, he discovered the revisionists were within just two votes of victory. Clarence Mitchell, the NAACP's legislative director, predicted Kennedy needed just five more votes. Pennsylvania Senator Joseph Clark also smelled victory, telling Kennedy the "essential parts" of the new administration's legislative program would be doomed without filibuster reform and that a "lessening of the 2/3s requirement is clearly essential [for] passage of any meaningful civil rights bill called for by the Democratic platform."[33]

But Kennedy refused to intervene. He was fearful of antagonizing Russell and the rest of the Southern Caucus on the eve of his presidency. By this point, he had decided already not to prioritize civil rights issues in his legislative agenda and saw no point in aggravating southern lawmakers unnecessarily. Mike Mansfield, incoming Democratic Senate majority leader, announced the decision on December 11. Mansfield was a longtime supporter of rule revision but now argued that it would stymie Kennedy's legislative program. On December 20, at the Palm Beach news conference, Kennedy confirmed that he would not lobby for a rules change. He would prefer to see "a majority of members to work their will" but stressed it was for the Senate to decide. Standing at Kennedy's side, Mike Mansfield discounted the possibility of a rules fight at the opening of the new congressional session in January. A change in Rule XXII "should come at the right time, at the right place and in the right circumstances," said Mansfield.[34]

When the Senate convened in mid-January, liberal Democrats came forward with a motion amending Rule XXII, but Mansfield dismissed it as "a time-consuming, emotion-filled, dis-unifying, disrupting struggle" and refused to offer support. Mansfield instead referred the question to the Senate Rules Committee, which he himself chaired. It was a move calculated to bury rule reform for at least another two years, and, more likely, four. The Senate carried the motion by a margin of fifty to forty-six. The reformers had lost by a mere four votes. As Javits remarked, the Senate had just given up "the power to pass effective and meaningful civil rights legislation."[35]

Had Kennedy intervened in the fight and exerted more pressure on the "waverers" from the border and Rocky Mountain states, he would likely have won. "With only a very modest effort," wrote columnist Doris Fleeson, "the incoming President could have persuaded two Democrats to switch their vote against the filibuster curb." Instead, he handed the southern Democrats an effortless and much-needed victory. The ADA *Legislative Newsletter* accused Kennedy of "maintaining an attitude of inertia while his policies received a setback and his liberal supporters an almost humiliating defeat."[36]

Success within two weeks of the new administration taking office in its campaign to enlarge the House Rules Committee, an obstructionist body dominated by archsegregationist "Judge" Howard Smith, showed how the forces of reform could prevail over the forces of reaction on Capitol Hill. Knowing an unreformed House Rules Committee could prevent much of the New Frontier program from ever reaching the House floor, the incoming administration launched a full-scale lobbying effort before the vote on January 31. As congressmen prepared to vote, House Speaker Sam Rayburn delivered an impassioned floor speech that helped achieve a narrow but portentous victory of 217 to 212. Had Kennedy shown a similar determination to change the filibuster rule and mounted a correspondingly vigorous lobbying effort, the vote would no doubt have been just as tight. But victory had unquestionably been attainable.[37]

For Russell especially, the revisionists' defeat in the filibuster debate provided a much-needed morale boost. Over the past two years, Russell had watched as northern opinion hardened against the Southern Caucus, liberal Democrats had seized control of the DNC, and blacks, who now enjoyed greater political leverage than ever before, became more assertive in demanding first-class citizenship. The proposed rules change represented a genuine threat to the southern way of life he had defended for his entire legislative career. Kennedy had protected the Southern Caucus in its hour of maximum danger.

It was not only on the issue of civil rights that Kennedy had grown cautious. His early political appointments provided further evidence of the moderate tone his presidency would take. Despite having wrested control of the policy-making apparatus of the Democratic Party over the previous four years, liberals operated only on the fringes of the administration. Leading progressives, like Paul Butler, the former party chairman, were purged from the DNC. His successor, John Bailey, a close ally of Kennedy's, merged the national, senatorial, and congressional campaign committees, thus weakening the influence of progressive lawmakers, who had come to dominate them. Kennedy disbanded the Democratic

Advisory Council, the liberal-dominated policy forum, on March 11. And when Johnson vacated the position of Senate majority leader, Kennedy opposed the promotion of Humphrey to the role. Instead, he preferred Mansfield, a cautious and mild-mannered former history lecturer from Montana.[38]

The liberals who had played the most active roles in Kennedy's campaign found themselves almost completely marginalized at the outset of the new administration. Schlesinger became a historian-in-residence at the White House; while he lent considerable intellectual luster to the White House, he carried little political influence. John Kenneth Galbraith became the U.S. ambassador to India. With the single exception of Stevenson, who became U.S. ambassador to the United Nations, no cabinet posts were offered to "attitudinizing liberals," as Kennedy referred to them. Kennedy made Bowles the deputy secretary of state. Bowles fully expected that he would hold the top job, but southerners feared he was too liberal on the race question. The arch-progressive G. Mennen Williams, who had been considered a favorite to head the Department of Health, Education, and Welfare, was instead handed the much less prestigious post of assistant secretary of state for Africa. By the time of the inauguration, Harris Wofford, the staunchest liberal in the Kennedy campaign, had not yet been offered any post in the new administration.[39]

∽

On January 6, Kennedy held a thirty-five-minute meeting in New York with Roy Wilkins. In a speech at an ADA-sponsored conference in Washington on December 29, Wilkins had derided the "atmosphere of supercaution" since Election Day and opined, "we don't see why we should be Mickey Mouses or Minnie Mouses when it comes to civil rights." Despite Wilkins's objections, Kennedy confirmed he would not be seeking new civil rights legislation during the opening session of Congress. It was the first time he had conveyed the news directly to a senior black leader. He tried to appease Wilkins by enlisting his aid in the formulation of a nonlegislative strategy. "Why don't you call Ted Sorensen," Kennedy suggested. "Write him a memo. We'll see what comes of it." Wilkins was prepared to give Kennedy the benefit of the doubt, and he was open to the idea of a policy centered on executive action. But he nonetheless felt that the incoming president was "exceedingly naïve and mistaken" in retreating completely from a legislative fight.[40]

Kennedy's retreat was in fact a monumental tactical blunder. By publicly announcing his decision to back away from civil rights legislation he surrendered a crucial bargaining tool with southern Democrats. A more skillful politician certainly would not have withdrawn from the rules fight without at least extracting concessions from southerners for other elements of his legislative program in exchange. Instead, Kennedy would have to yield ever more over the course of the next twelve months to win from them even a modicum of support. Wofford had predicted this outcome. Prior to the rules vote, he had warned,

> For the incoming Administration to stand idly by while these pledges [the promise of majority rule] go down the drain is to evidence a weakness which will plague that Administration for years to come. Backing off from the first pledged civil rights effort—the rules change—will encourage those who oppose civil rights to maximize their nullifying abilities in every succeeding civil rights struggle and will even encourage harassment of necessary and significant executive action. There is only one course for an Administration that ran on civil rights and won on civil rights—and that is strength.[41]

Charismatic, tactically adroit, and seemingly tireless, Kennedy was at his best on the campaign trail. But over the course of the transition, his political limitations quickly surfaced. He was an unskilled negotiator; he had remained aloof during his years as a lawmaker and therefore lacked allies on Capitol Hill. He was preoccupied by short-term political goals but lacked dedication to any long-term policies or programs beyond the realm of foreign affairs. Though he came into office with strong ideas about foreign policy, he was virtually bereft of new thinking on domestic issues, having never attached himself to any great cause or movement. Kennedy had a clear vision of the style of presidential leadership he wanted to project, but he was far less interested in the mechanics of actual government. This was hardly surprising—since the early 1950s, Kennedy had been focused on the presidency, not on policy.

Kennedy's overly cautious decisions during the seventy-two-day transition bedeviled his thousand days in office. Southern Democrats had achieved an important psychological victory, and, newly emboldened, they started to exploit that tactical advantage to the full. Angry that the pendulum had swung away from them, civil rights leaders soon realized they would have to adopt more aggressive tactics to win the new president's attention. Right after the election, Kennedy had been handed an opportunity: The American public appeared favorably disposed toward reform, and many diehard segregationists seemed resigned to ultimate defeat. The possibility of progress was real. Compromise was inevitable, given the composition of Congress, but Kennedy had retreated too far.

CHAPTER 13

❧

Black Camelot

For many Americans, the era of Camelot was ushered in by the "Queen of Gospel," Mahalia Jackson. Standing center stage and illuminated by a single beam of light, she opened the pre-inaugural concert with a full-throated rendition of the national anthem. It was one of many stirring highpoints in a program of festivities that featured blacks almost as prominently as whites. Frank Sinatra had organized the Las Vegas-style gala, which was held on the eve of the inauguration at the D.C. Armory. By careful design, he had assembled a strong multiracial cast, which included Harry Belafonte, Ethel Merman, Ella Fitzgerald, Sir Laurence Olivier, Leonard Bernstein, Nat King Cole, and Sidney Poitier. The only notable absentee from the star-studded list of black performers was Sammy Davis, Jr. Although a long-time Kennedy supporter, Davis was considered too controversial by the new administration. Only a few weeks earlier, his marriage to a white woman, the Swedish actress Mai Britt, had provoked a scandal.[1]

Earlier that evening, Kennedy had attended a concert of classical music at Constitution Hall that featured the Howard University Male Chorus. The black ensemble performed on the very stage where Marian Anderson had so famously been barred from singing by the Daughters of the American Revolution in 1939. On the express orders of the president-elect, Anderson herself took a prominent role in the inauguration the following day, opening the national ceremony with "The Star Spangled Banner." Kennedy was not breaking new ground here; four years earlier Eisenhower had done the same.[2]

While blacks featured heavily in Kennedy's inaugural celebrations, they received very short shrift in his inaugural address. Drafted in close collaboration with Sorensen, its overarching theme was the containment of communism. Some passages sounded like a call to arms—a reminder to Americans of the sacrifices required to defend freedom in its hour of danger. Others were targeted directly at the Kremlin: "Let every nation know, whether it wishes us well or ill, that we shall pay any price, bear any burden, meet any hardship, support any friend, oppose any foe to assure the survival and the success of liberty." Kennedy celebrated the promise of global emancipation, in an oblique reference to Africa's newly decolonized nations. But as Kennedy and Sorensen prepared the final draft, there was still no explicit reference to the struggle for freedom within America.[3]

Harris Wofford and Louis Martin were both upset when they read a final draft of the speech on January 18, because it omitted any mention of civil rights. That day they drafted a memorandum to the president-elect that urged him to make a forthright commitment to the cause of racial equality. Ideally, they wanted Kennedy to insert two questions toward the end of the speech. They asked: "Can we forge against those enemies a grand and global alliance, North and South, East and West, that can assure a more fruitful life for all mankind? Will you join in that historic effort? Are you willing to demonstrate in your own life—in your attitude toward those of other races and those here from other shores—that you hold these eternal truths to be self-evident?" Wofford and Martin also suggested a less stirring alternative: that Kennedy add the words "at home and around the world" into a sentence nearer to the beginning of the speech on the subject of human rights.[4]

On the morning of January 19, as Kennedy sat in his study making last-minute amendments, he decided to change the draft. But the president-elect opted for the more moderate of the two alternatives that Wofford and Martin had presented. In the amended version, Kennedy promised that the new administration would be "unwilling to witness or permit the slow undoing of those human rights to which this nation has always been committed and to which we are committed today at home and around the world."

The following afternoon, on an imperious-looking stage, supported by eight fake Corinthian columns, Kennedy delivered his address. It was just fourteen minutes long—only George Washington's second inaugural speech had been shorter. But its impact was tremendous. It drew praise from across the political spectrum: Everett Dirksen, the Republican Senate minority leader, described it as "inspirational," Richard Russell commented on its "Churchillian touch," and *ADA World* praised its "deep ardor." Even though he had failed to mention civil rights in any explicit way, his message inspired many black listeners as well. "Words and phrases such as those used by President Kennedy in the inaugural address are the kind which sets men's hearts on fire," praised the *Pittsburgh Courier*. "These are the kind of words which in years passed have made men drop their hammers and leave their ploughs to tread the path of glory."[5]

Blacks took a full part in the exuberant celebrations that followed the inauguration. At five different inaugural balls, Kennedy danced happily with black women, something that would have been unimaginable to his predecessors. He applauded as Louis Martin was introduced as a member of his "political family." Andrew Hatcher also made his debut as a fully fledged White House press assistant, wearing white tie and tails and puffing on a fat cigar. It was "a symbol of success," according to one black reporter, "comparable to Jackie Robinson when he broke into baseball's big league." Hatcher's main task during the inaugural events was to corral the White House press pool—a group of twenty journalists and photographers who were shadowing the president throughout the revelry. For the first time, the pool included a black reporter and a black photographer, Simeon Booker and Ellsworth Davis of *Jet*.[6]

"The inaugural festivities were completely integrated," the *Pittsburgh Courier* reported with approval, from small cocktail parties to $100-a-plate galas. In all, an estimated 5,000 blacks participated in the five-day program. Five blacks chaired important inaugural committees, and 500 served as committee members. "Washington was a truly integrated capital," reported *Jet*, "as well-groomed visitors matched mink for mink, and suite for suite (at $65 a day) at swank receptions and parties in top hotels. . . . All official functions were heavily dotted with brown faces and many strictly private parties were not without color." *Ebony* simply noted, "Dark visitors flooded the city."[7]

The full participation of blacks in the inaugural ceremonies and celebrations represented a continuation of the strategy of association, which had served Kennedy so well throughout his campaign. It was a tactic he would rely on throughout his presidency—all too often in lieu of genuine policy initiatives. His grand gestures offered blacks what Simeon Booker called the "the façade of optimism." However unreal, on the first day of his presidency, it looked staggeringly beautiful.[8]

∾

Within hours of taking office, Kennedy signaled his dedication to integrating blacks into the government he now controlled. The problem of segregation literally marched in front of him during the inaugural parade, and Kennedy acted with impulsive anger. The procession was vast, an eight-mile pageant with forty-one floats, seventy-two marching bands, more than 32,000 marchers, and a thirty-two-ton replica of PT109, carrying members of its original crew. But amid all the revelry, Kennedy had been struck most by an honor guard from the United States Coast Guard Academy. Much to his surprise and annoyance, it did not include a single black cadet. As soon as the parade finished, the president raised the matter with Richard Goodwin, a campaign speechwriter, who was about to become a White House assistant special counsel. "Did you see the Coast Guard attachment?" asked the president. Goodwin was puzzled. "There wasn't a black face in the entire group," Kennedy said. "That's not acceptable. Something ought to be done about it."[9]

New to government, Goodwin struggled to recall which department held responsibility for the Coast Guard and soon discovered it was the Treasury

Department. Acting with New Frontiersman–like haste, he immediately contacted Treasury Secretary Douglas C. Dillon to relay the president's disapproval. "Tell him I'll get right on it," said Dillon sympathetically. True to his word, Dillon instructed Coast Guard officials to scrutinize the academy's recruitment policy to make sure it did not discriminate against blacks. But he demanded fairness rather than preferential treatment. When a rear admiral in the Treasury Department proposed the "direct appointment of members of minority groups," Dillon refused and stressed instead that entrance requirements should not be relaxed. A year later, in February 1962, Dillon's policy bore fruit when a young candidate named Merle J. Smith survived the rigorous vetting process and became the first black student in the Coast Guard Academy's eighty-six-year history.[10]

That Kennedy took such a strong personal interest in the recruitment policies of the Coast Guard on his first day in office demonstrated that on certain occasions, when he did not feel bound by political constraints, he could be extraordinarily sensitive to black aspirations. There was something visceral about his reaction when confronted directly—and especially visually—by segregation or discrimination. This impulse had been in evidence since his earliest days in Congress, when he was deeply troubled by the "whites only" signs in Washington, which he experienced firsthand, but less interested in the broader problem of Jim Crow further south, which lay beyond his gaze. The episode also reflected two of Kennedy's more ideologically grounded views. First, he had long believed that employment reform was among the best routes to black self-improvement. And he was constantly fearful that segregation threatened to undermine America's international reputation. The Coast Guard incident was not an isolated one. In March of that year, the president ordered an investigation after a presidential honor guard (the unit that protected the chief executive on state occasions) for the visit of Ghanaian President Kwame Nkrumah included only three black soldiers.[11]

Kennedy seemed particularly worried about the ceremonial face of the administration. He personally intervened to make sure the first black Secret Service agent was assigned to the presidential protection detail, Lieutenant James McCall became the first black officer to serve on the presidential honor guard, and a black sentry was assigned to guard the tomb of the Unknown Solider in Arlington National Cemetery. Kennedy showed heightened concern about the impressions of African diplomats. In the spring of 1961, Defense Secretary Robert McNamara ordered a review of black participation in ceremonial units and honor guard details. He asked his staff to pay "special attention" to ensure the "appropriate [participation] of black personnel in official visits by officials from emerging nations," in the words of one of his deputies.[12]

When his cabinet met for the first time on January 26, Kennedy placed employment reform high on the agenda. He urged officials to employ a greater number of blacks in more influential posts. Kennedy focused on the dismal employment record of the State Department, which was responsible for staffing

American embassies and consulates and therefore projected America's image abroad. In nonaligned countries, especially African states where the Soviet Union was determined to extend its influence, the absence of black officials had become a severe handicap for American diplomacy. Segregation in this area was not just a national disgrace but a threat to national security. During lunch with a journalist on the day before his inauguration, Kennedy had stressed his commitment to tackling the problem head on. Just six days after he took office, he fired off a memorandum to Bowles ordering a thorough investigation.[13]

As anticipated, the internal review offered incontrovertible proof of the department's appalling record. Out of 3,674 Foreign Service officers, only fifteen were blacks, and of the 1,166 staff on the Foreign Service Reserve, the number was just three. Of the 5,155 U.S.-based employees, 1,035 were black, but the vast majority were administrative personnel, secretaries, and chauffeurs.[14]

Appalled by the State Department survey, Kennedy returned to the question of black employment at a cabinet meeting on February 13. The topic monopolized virtually the entire meeting. Acting on advice from Fred Dutton, an energetic young Californian who became his cabinet secretary, he announced plans for the most comprehensive government-wide census ever undertaken. It would provide raw data not only on the number of blacks employed, but also the grades they occupied. The census was going to be an expensive undertaking. Kennedy warned cabinet officers they would have to finance it out of existing budgets, because Congress was unwilling to fund the project. The administration did not seek out publicity for the project, partly because Kennedy did not want black voters to find out about the federal government's dismal employment record until he could take remedial action. Southern Democrats might also exact revenge by disrupting the appropriations process.[15]

Published in the spring, the final report was dispiriting. Of over two million federal employees, about thirteen percent were black. But only a small handful occupied senior posts. Of the 6,900 employees in the upper reaches of the Agriculture Department, just fifteen were black. At the Pentagon the figure was only 444 of the 69,955 higher-grade staff. At the federal Civil Service only two blacks had reached the highest-ranking levels of GS 17 and GS 18.[16]

The president quickly instructed all government departments to prepare detailed reports setting out possible remedies. He stressed the need for immediate action. And he threw himself personally into the project, by lending his name to a presidential statement championing new employment opportunities for black employees. It was placed on prominent display in every federal building across the country.

Federal officials worked under strict directives in their efforts to hire blacks. Under no circumstances were they allowed to grant blacks preferential treatment. Although the term "affirmative action" had been absorbed into the bureaucratic lexicon, it did not imply any relaxation in entrance requirements. Federal officials stressed repeatedly that blacks would be employed only on merit and preferred the phrase "active recruitment." Department heads should encourage talented blacks to apply for jobs rather than passively waiting for their applications. In a letter to the deans of the country's law schools inviting black applicants for jobs at the Justice Department, Robert Kennedy emphasized only "qualified candidates" would be considered. "I have no desire to employ anyone on the basis of his race," he insisted. "Ability is the primary qualification."[17]

Strictly meritocratic, the government-wide policy was summarized in an internal memorandum. "Giving special appointments without requiring that existing standards be met," it made clear, "only aggravates the relationship between minority group employees and others in the Federal service." Even Harris Wofford stressed that "[n]o one should be employed just because he is a member of a minority group." When Lyndon Johnson explored the possibility of including blacks on the astronaut program, he made clear "that qualifications should not be modified to expedite attainment of this goal." Still, when John Glenn was launched into space on February 20, 1962, Johnson turned to Kennedy, and said, "If only Glenn were a Negro."[18]

Kennedy applied the same principle when the first vacancy arose on the Supreme Court in 1962. With an eye to the appointment's diplomatic benefits abroad, Robert Kennedy endorsed Judge William H. Hastie, a black Tennessean, who had graduated from Harvard Law School and advised President Roosevelt. JFK, however, vetoed the appointment, because he thought Hastie's rulings were rather prosaic and that there were better-qualified candidates.[19]

Among department heads, compliance with Kennedy's employment initiative was often admirably sincere. Dean Rusk even took the Foreign Service written exam to ensure it was not "culturally biased" against blacks. He then arranged for the Ford Foundation to provide grants for internal black candidates to have a special year of training. But progress was sometimes agonizingly slow. Partly due to inertia, partly due to fear that southern lawmakers would retaliate by starving them of appropriations money, federal officials were notoriously resistant to change. "I found out that the chairmen of congressional committees that control budgets had so intimidated the heads of the various agencies," Wofford commented, "that the personnel offices would employ Senator So and So's cousin and the same thing on the congressional side." Abraham Ribicoff, secretary of the Department of Health, Education and Welfare, grew so exasperated by his department's unwillingness to recruit more blacks that he talked openly of resigning. Part of the problem, as Louis Martin noted, was that "you could cut southern accents with a knife in any agency in the government and in those years the bureaucrats controlled everything." Even within the limited sphere of federal employment, integrating the workplace often meant standing up to the South.[20]

∾

At least since the late 1950s, when he had become the first New England law-maker to employ a black member on his staff, Kennedy had understood the symbolic value of black appointments. For political as well as altruistic reasons, he was determined to adopt the same approach as president. He entrusted the task to Wofford and Martin. Mindful of the need to find qualified candidates, Martin sought out "superblacks," as he called them and soon produced a list of black Ph.D.s including over 750 names. The black talent search was considered so important that he visited the White House every morning during the opening weeks of the administration to confer with Kenneth O'Donnell and Lawrence O'Brien, whose Little Blue Book listed 3,000 vacancies in the federal bureaucracy.[21]

Progress was instantaneous. Carl T. Rowan, a black newspaperman from Minneapolis, became deputy assistant secretary of state for public affairs, and thus the State Department's highest-ranking black; Clifton R. Wharton, a black Foreign Service officer, was appointed U.S. ambassador to Norway (an important development, since black diplomats normally were assigned to Liberia and the Canary Islands). Roger Wilkins, the nephew of Roy, was offered a post at Foggy Bottom. Cecil Poole became U.S. attorney for northern California, economist Dr. Samuel Z. Westerfield was made senior adviser in the Treasury Department's Office of International Finance, AFL-CIO official George Weaver became special assistant to the secretary of labor, and Franklin H. Whittaker became director of public information at the Commerce Department. (Kennedy offered Herb Tucker, Marge Lawson, and Vel Phillips ambassadorial posts, but all declined for personal reasons.) The sheer volume of appointments was astounding. By July, Martin calculated there were no less than forty-seven high-ranking black New Frontiersmen. The press took notice. The *Pittsburgh Courier* praised the "veritable landslide of new appointments."[22]

Kennedy was far more cautious when it came to his own cabinet. His was the youngest cabinet in U.S. history—with an average age of just forty-seven, it projected the dynamic image of the New Frontier. But most of its members shared the same pragmatic political instincts as the president. As Sorensen described it, the cabinet included "no crusaders, fanatics or extremists from any camp, all were nearer the center than either left or right." Treasury Secretary C. Douglas Dillon, a staunch Republican, had been in Eisenhower's State Department, while Defense Secretary Robert McNamara, the former president of the Ford Motor Company, had contributed financially to the Nixon campaign. Other cabinet appointees were chosen largely to appeal to specific voting blocs: Abraham Ribicoff, the former Connecticut governor, was Jewish; Labor Secretary Arthur Goldberg, also Jewish, hailed from the labor movement; Agriculture Secretary Orville Freeman, the former governor of Minnesota, represented the farm belt; liberal idol Adlai Stevenson became U.S. Ambassador to the United Nations; and Commerce Secretary Luther Hodges, a former governor of North Carolina came from the South. Still, there was no room in the cabinet for a black appointee.[23]

In an attempt to deflect potential criticism for this omission, Kennedy made a clumsy pretense of trying to hire a black cabinet official. The charade quickly became a public relations debacle. On December 15, Kennedy offered Congressman Dawson the post of Postmaster General, thus presenting him with the opportunity to become the first black American ever to join the cabinet. But Dawson expressed gratitude at being so honored and then turned the president down. No one was fooled. Within Washington, it was widely known that Dawson had no intention of leaving Capitol Hill and that the Kennedy transition team had already tapped J. Edward Day, an efficient young bureaucrat, for the job. Though Dawson had happily agreed to the deception, it drew a sharp rebuke from the press. Even Sorensen conceded it was "an unsubtle gesture." Recognizing that the Dawson fiasco had detracted from his sincere efforts to appoint high-caliber blacks, Kennedy was angry, too. It was one of the few occasions when the strategy of association had backfired.[24]

To compensate, the Kennedy transition team cast around for a prominent black to fill another high-profile post. They settled on Robert Weaver, an urbane, Harvard-trained economist, who had served in the Roosevelt administration and gone on to become the chairman of the NAACP national board. A nationally recognized authority on housing, he was appointed head of the Housing and Home Finance Agency. It was not technically a cabinet position, but it was likely to be elevated to one if Kennedy fulfilled his campaign promise to create a new Department of Urban Affairs.

When hardliners within the Southern Caucus got word of the appointment, they were outraged. They focused, however, on his leftist past rather than his color. Eastland complained about Weaver's "pro-communist background" and connections with "front groups" during the 1930s. Fellow southerners on the Senate Finance Committee, which had to confirm the appointment, called attention to a controversial article he had written, "No Race Problem in Russia." At one point during the February confirmation hearings, Senator A. Willis Robertson of Virginia even called a dramatic two-hour halt to proceedings and expressed his hope that Kennedy would reread Weaver's FBI file and reconsider the appointment. Ninety minutes later a letter of certification, signed by the president, arrived from the White House. The committee confirmed Weaver's appointment the following day.[25]

Even after his confirmation, Eastland continued to spout defiance, outrageously accusing Weaver of having encouraged blacks to urinate in the public spaces of New York's housing projects. And yet despite the vocal opprobrium of the South, Weaver's appointment received only a qualified welcome in the black press. "We're not quite sure whether his record justifies the word 'crusader,'" observed the *Chicago Daily Defender*, which suspected his appointment was "mere window dressing."[26]

The Southern Caucus complicated other appointments as well. The Kennedy administration wanted Frank Reeves to be the District of Columbia's first black commissioner. This would have been a particularly dramatic gesture, since even though fifty-four percent of Washington's population was black, the capital's three-man board of commissioners had always been entirely white. When word of the plan was leaked to the *Washington Evening Star,* southerners on the House District of Columbia Committee vowed to veto the appointment, citing Reeves's involvement in school desegregation suits launched by the NAACP in northern Virginia, as well as his close working relationship with Thurgood Marshall. Within hours of mounting their campaign, it quickly became clear that the nomination was doomed. Worried that Reeves's appointment risked alienating moderate southerners, whose support was needed the following day in a critical vote liberalizing the House Rules Committee, the White House quietly withdrew his name.[27]

Rumors swept round the capital that presidential aides had themselves torpedoed the appointment, since Reeves had been unwilling to publicly defend the new administration's cautious civil rights strategy or to help explain it to disgruntled black groups. By Reeves's own admission, his refusal to do so created "some friction" within the White House. By way of consolation, Reeves was sworn in a few days later as a special assistant to the president. Unusually, however, reporters were barred and no official photographer was present to record the brief ceremony. The aide Kennedy had called "Exhibit One" during the campaign was now a political embarrassment.[28]

Four months later, Reeves's name was linked once more with a vacancy on the Board of Commissioners. Yet this time, Reeves himself asked for it to be withdrawn in the wake of damaging press reports about his tax affairs. A few days later, following a meeting with Kennedy, Reeves announced his departure from the White House, after fresh allegations about disreputable business dealings made his position untenable. "If Reeves were white," complained Clarence Mitchell of the NAACP, "he would still be in a job." But few other blacks rallied in his support, thinking he had brought his problems on himself (rumor had it, however, that Reeves's financial problems stemmed from the inaugural celebrations, when he had personally picked up the tab for many of the parties held for black invitees). John B. Duncan was appointed to the Board of Commissioners soon after, thus becoming its first black member. There was little in Duncan's background to worry segregationists, however. A dutiful bureaucrat, who had served for nine years as the city's recorder of deeds, Duncan did not share Reeves's close links to the NAACP or anything like his crusading ardor.[29]

When Reeves departed, Kennedy decided not to replace him, despite Wofford's frequent exhortations about the need for a high-profile black in a high-profile White House job. "Since a sensitive Negro is still able to hear and sense the mood of his community better than a white man," he had urged the president during the transition, "it seems important to have some respected, intelligent and savvy Negro White House assistant serving this specialized function." Ideally, Wofford wanted Louis Martin to fill the position, since "you would have the Negro vote sewn up by 1964." Yet Kennedy feared that Martin was identified too closely with civil rights leaders and that his proximity to power would alarm southern Democrats. Instead, Kennedy offered Martin the deputy chairmanship of the DNC, which meant he was granted only limited access to the president.[30]

Just as Reeves was sacrificed, so, too, was Benjamin Mays, the president of Morehouse College and a close friend of Martin Luther King, Jr. Black reporters were told Mays would join the CRC or be made ambassador to Israel, but his appointment was vetoed by Senators Herman Talmadge and Richard Russell. Even though King warned Kennedy that black voters would be "gravely disappointed" if the Georgia senators held sway, Kennedy quickly backed down. Mays had been one of the few black southerners approached by the administration, whose talent search had been concentrated in the North. Other than Mays and Reeves, southern blacks, with a long history of antagonizing local white leaders, were generally overlooked.[31]

Though eager to adorn his administration with blacks, Kennedy also offered a number of positions to segregationists. His first choice for secretary of state was Senator J. William Fulbright of Arkansas, even though liberals, blacks, labor leaders, and even Robert Kennedy complained that the appointment of a segregationist would damage relations with newly independent nations. For black reporters, rumors of Fulbright's appointment were especially crushing, since they had been told during the campaign that the Nobel Peace Prize–winning black diplomat Ralph Bunche was earmarked for the job. Eventually, Fulbright settled the matter himself, by declining on the grounds that he was reluctant to relinquish the chairmanship of the Committee on Foreign Relations. In his place, Kennedy chose Dean Rusk, the head of the Ford Foundation.[32]

More controversial still was Kennedy's first choice as secretary of the army: Ernest Vandiver of Georgia. A much more outspoken segregationist than Fulbright, Vandiver had vowed during his 1960 state of the state address to defy *Brown* "again and again and again" and was on record as favoring the complete segregation of military personnel. His close ties with Russell and Vinson, however, made him immensely attractive to Kennedy (the governor's wife, Sybil, was Russell's niece). Wofford was stunned when he heard the rumors. He warned Kennedy that it "raises serious civil rights problems, aside from any concern about a militant segregationist being placed in a position where many new moves in military desegregation will be expected." If the governor were to be offered a job, it should first be dangled before him as an inducement to curb his racial intolerance. "If he gets Georgia through the token desegregation of Atlanta schools, without abandoning public education or racial violence," Wofford suggested, "he would deserve a top federal job." At the strong prodding of Bobby Troutman, however, Kennedy contacted Vandiver from Palm Beach on January 4 to sound him out about the post. At that very moment, the governor was fighting to block the integration of the University of Georgia, in defiance of a federal court order. Much to the president-elect's disappointment, the governor turned him down.[33]

Since neither Fulbright nor Vandiver ultimately accepted appointments, the most hotly disputed appointee became Charles Meriwether, Alabama's former state finance director, who joined the board of the Export-Import Bank. An avowed segregationist, Meriwether also had close ties with the Ku Klux Klan. A bipartisan group of liberals on the Senate Banking Committee urged the FBI to conduct a thorough investigation to determine the full extent of his links to the Klan. But with strong backing from the White House he was appointed nonetheless.[34]

The president's desire to boost black employment levels was laudable. But while the administration boasted an impressive number of black appointees, Kennedy rarely met or conferred with them. With Martin in semi-exile at the DNC and Reeves banished from view, Hatcher became the only high-ranking black official who regularly came in contact with the president, and then only to discuss press matters, not policy. Carl Rowan, who was used to convey messages from Dean Rusk before the president's televised news conferences, performed a similar role. Other black appointees hardly ever entered the president's orbit. State Department official Roger Wilkins met Kennedy just once in three years—a chance encounter in the underground garage of the State Department, when the president arrived for his press conference, which he held in the auditorium upstairs.

"You're Mr. Wilkins," said Kennedy.

"Yes, sir," he replied.

"I hear you're doing good work." With that, he was gone.[35]

As had been the case for the previous fourteen years, the black aide Kennedy spent most time with was George Thomas. His job each morning was to lay out the president's clothes.

∾

Kennedy continued to be preoccupied with the effects of racial segregation on America's image overseas, and early into his administration he focused on the mistreatment of African diplomats stationed in Washington. It was a problem that, he feared, the Soviets could easily exploit. He had first become aware of the issue as a congressman when aides sometimes found themselves helping visiting black diplomats to find overnight accommodation. In the more fashionable areas of the capital, Africans were prevented from leasing or buying even the most modest apartments and houses. For those who regularly made the journey from Washington to the United Nations in New York, there was the added humiliation of being denied service at the string of restaurants and motels lining Route 40, the main road linking the two cities. Wofford even told reporters that "there is no subject on which the President feels more deeply than this one," which, on the racial front at least, was most likely true.[36]

Kennedy decided to address the problem by setting up a Special Protocol Service Section at the State Department. It was headed by Pedro Sanjuan, a thirty-one-year-old Kennedy campaign worker with a reputation for being something of a maverick. He was ordered to bring about the complete desegregation of lunch counters and restaurants along Route 40. Armed with a strongly worded letter of recommendation from President Kennedy (which was actually written by Wofford), Sanjuan visited every restaurant, imploring owners to desegregate their facilities in the interests of national security. It proved to be only a partial success; within nine months only half of the seventy main roadside establishments on Route 40 complied.[37]

Soon it became apparent that African diplomats faced problems well beyond the Beltway and Route 40. In early March, William Fitzjohn from Sierra Leone was denied service at a Howard Johnson's restaurant in Hagerstown, Maryland. When the president was informed, he invited Fitzjohn to the White House, to apologize in person. The State Department also organized a dinner in Hagerstown, at which civic leaders presented Fitzjohn with a key to the city. To prevent other incidents of this sort, the State Department organized a conference in April for state officials, which was attended by seventeen of the twenty-three invited Governors. At a follow-up meeting a month later, Bowles encouraged state officials to establish hospitality committees geared specifically to black diplomats.[38]

Bowles also ordered a citywide investigation of over 200 rentable apartments. The survey revealed that just eight were available to blacks, a situation Bowles described as "unhappy, explosive [and] dangerous." And, as Kennedy feared, the Kremlin did exploit the problem; Soviet officials in New York offered to sign leases on behalf of at least three United Nations–based African diplomats who had been rebuffed by white landlords. Like Sanjuan, Bowles relied on persuasion, and convened a meeting of Washington realtors, whom he urged to eliminate restrictive covenants voluntarily.[39]

Even with strong presidential backing, it was hard to effect significant change. As a State Department report in June revealed, African diplomats still encountered hostility from Washington and New York landlords, and many of Route 40's restaurant and lunch-counter owners remained segregated. That very month, the problem was highlighted once more when Ambassador Adam Malik Sow of Chad, a recent arrival, was first denied service and then physically manhandled at a restaurant along Route 40. On hearing of the incident, the president was incensed and immediately contacted Angier Biddle Duke, the State Department's chief of protocol. "Can't you tell them not to do it?" he barked. Assuming the president was referring to the restaurateurs, Duke assured him slow progress was being made. "That's not what I'm calling about," snapped the president. "Can't you tell these African ambassadors not to drive on Route 40? It's a hell of a road—I used to drive it years ago, but why would anyone want to drive it today when you can fly? Tell these ambassadors I wouldn't think of driving from New

York to Washington. Tell them to fly!" Clearly, the problem for Kennedy was one of political embarrassment, not genuine moral outrage. "Are you sure the President is fully behind our efforts?" an exasperated Duke later asked Wofford.[40]

In the absence of legislative support, administration officials had only their powers of persuasion in dealing with landlords, restaurateurs, and hoteliers. The limited scope of their authority became apparent once again in late September when a Nigerian diplomat was turned away from a motel north of Baltimore. When Sanjuan asked the proprietor, a segregationist named Clarence Rosier, to desegregate his facilities, he was shown the door. "The hell with the United Nations and the hell with your colored diplomats," barked Rosier. "Go back to Washington and tell Kennedy he can feed 'em. I wouldn't have a customer left if I let them people in here." Sanjuan had no way to enforce his demands, since the administration was unwilling to enact new legislation ordering a blanket ban on segregated public accommodations. In 1961 Sanjuan found himself testifying instead on behalf of new legislation sponsored by the Maryland state legislature. And in the fall of 1961, Sanjuan encouraged CORE activists to picket segregated restaurants along Route 40, a campaign he believed would accelerate the desegregation process. But he was quickly upbraided by the White House, which feared it would draw unhelpful attention to the problem.[41]

The disproportionate attention paid to African diplomats soon became a source of bitter resentment in some quarters of the administration. "I do not believe that, in the Nation's Capital, a diplomatic passport should be required for the enjoyment of the normal rights of citizenship without discrimination," wrote Dean Rusk in a stinging letter to Robert Kennedy. By way of remedy, he suggested administration officials enter into discreet discussions with business associations and civic groups to bring about the desegregation of public accommodations throughout the country "without fanfare." When the president and attorney general failed to respond, a chastened Rusk took a small, but pointed, step of his own by refusing to sign a restrictive covenant on a $56,000 four-bedroom house in Spring Valley, Washington. Rusk became a devoted advocate of racial advance, and when he noticed that all the messengers outside his seventh-floor office at the State Department were black, he made sure to employ a white to demonstrate that jobs of that status were not solely for Negroes.[42]

By the end of the year, Sanjuan reported "some degree of success, but the problem is still grave." Of twenty-two requests from African diplomats for accommodation, twelve had been granted—although most with the help of the Sanjuan's Special Section. Only three diplomats found accommodations independently. African diplomats continued to be refused service in many of the city's barber shops and were even barred from using certain facilities at Union Station. Most African diplomats understood the White House had relatively little influence over local shopkeepers, and next to no legal power. As a result, reported Sanjuan, "their criticism of Federal government has virtually disappeared." Seemingly, they

had accepted the White House viewpoint: that the president was essentially pow-
erless to eradicate segregation. Most were not interested in the problems faced by
black Americans and, as Sanjuan put it, "behaved fairly abominably concerning
the civil rights movement in the United States."[43]

The administration response to the African diplomat problem revealed
Kennedy's strong preference for short-term fixes when faced by deep-rooted
racial problems. When the ambassador of Ghana demanded a room at the
Shamrock Hotel in Houston, Johnson personally intervened to make sure its facilities were temporarily integrated. Yet as soon as the ambassador left, blacks
once again were barred. When those strategies failed, Kennedy often used face-
to-face meetings to placate disgruntled diplomats. Notably, African diplomats
were granted access to the White House much more readily than civil rights
leaders, whose almost constant requests for meetings were denied repeatedly by
Kenneth O'Donnell, now the president's appointments secretary. This placed
Kennedy in the absurd position of receiving firsthand reports about racism not
from black Americans themselves but from foreigners.[44]

Kennedy found other, largely symbolic, ways of demonstrating his personal
commitment to black equality. From the very outset, he was insistent that blacks
should have access to the glamorous New Frontier, and his unannounced policy
took a variety of forms. At his first televised press conference, Andrew Hatcher
was carefully positioned to his side, one of only two White House officials given
that privilege (not that it impressed White House correspondents, who later
complained Hatcher was incapable of understanding complex international issues and had misspelled Tufts University in a press release). That afternoon, he
also made sure to call on two black reporters, Alice Dunnigan of the Associated
Negro Press and Ethel Payne of the *Chicago Defender*, a courtesy to black reporters that his predecessor had only rarely extended.[45]

Blacks were also invited to some of the most sumptuous White House dinners. At Kennedy's first state dinner, a white-tie banquet for the president of
Tunisia, State Department official Carl Rowan was included on the guest list.
For state dinners held in honor of African leaders, Kennedy always made sure
he accompanied their wives to their seats at the table. In April 1962, Ralph
Bunche and James Baldwin attended an event for Nobel Prize winners, which
set the standard for Kennedy chic, and by the end of that year it was difficult to
find a prominent black American, especially in the arts or sciences, who had not
been invited to the White House at least once. This honor was not, however,
extended to troublesome civil rights leaders like CORE's James Farmer and
Martin Luther King—although Roy Wilkins, the head of the less strident
NAACP, managed to avoid this blanket ban. Washington society columnists
took note of the aggressively integrated White House. They could not remember a single evening when Eisenhower had welcomed blacks in the same way,
save for the occasional foreign dignitary or possibly Bunche. Fittingly, images

from these events were captured on celluloid by members of the White House News Photographers Association, which was itself desegregated after the president threatened to boycott its annual dinner. Black photographers had been campaigning for admittance for three years.[46]

Now that Washington's most exclusive residence had been integrated, administration officials turned their attention to some of the city's most exclusive private clubs. In the spring, Secretary of Labor Arthur Goldberg targeted the Metropolitan Club, where the only blacks allowed into the dining room were stewards with napkins folded over their arms, and which had recently discontinued its policy of granting foreign ambassadors honorary membership following a recent influx of African diplomats. Soon other administration officials followed suit, with Robert Kennedy leading the boycott. In short order, the president withdrew his membership from the city's Cosmos Club because Carl Rowan, one of the administration's most high-profile appointees, was denied membership (in January 1962, the eighty-three-year-old club relaxed its rules). When Rowan issued a deftly worded statement, sardonically describing the Cosmos Club as "Washington's club of intellectuals," the president was delighted. "Your statement was perfect," said Kennedy, who hated the kind of pomposity perpetuated by the capital's elite institutions. "You couldn't have hurt the bastards more with a cannon." The New Frontiersmen had taken an impressive, and principled, stand. (Commonly overlooked, however, is the fact that the flurry of resignations started not with Goldberg but with Eisenhower appointee George Cabot Lodge, the son of Henry Cabot Lodge—a liberal Republican reprimanded for taking George Weaver, a black official at the Labor Department, for lunch at the Metropolitan Club.[47])

Kennedy's initiatives had an immediate impact on public opinion and particularly the opinion of black Americans. Even in 1962, *Newsweek* commentator Kenneth Crawford noted that "the Kennedy Administration has made an even deeper impression on Negro opinion by the resignation of some of its members from Washington clubs that draw a color line [and] the White House visit of Floyd Patterson, the heavyweight champion." Image was everything. Kennedy even ordered the "integration" of the White House kindergarten by inviting Hatcher's five-year-old son to join Caroline and John as a playmate. The first children were the subjects of some of the Kennedy era's most evocative snapshots.[48]

This kind of symbolism became a sustaining part of the president's appeal and reliably compensated for his refusal to push for civil rights in more overtly political ways. Sixty days into the new administration, Lou Harris conducted a secret poll that revealed "there are strong hints here that the public is judging the President for his style, manner and approach rather than on the specifics he is proposing or acting upon." This was especially true of blacks. "Despite his failure to urge civil rights legislation in Congress," wrote Simeon Booker in June, "Kennedy still is an overwhelming favorite of US Negroes, so popular that on the basis of his first months in office he could again win the colored vote." That same month a *Jet* readers' poll suggested eighty-seven percent of black respondents were satisfied with his overall civil rights record. Over eighty percent thought he had delivered on his campaign promises, while almost two-thirds reckoned the failure to seek the enactment of new legislation was "understandable."[49]

From federal employment for blacks to the desegregation of Washington's elite clubs, Kennedy personally supported several initiatives intended to make the White House and other Washington institutions more welcoming to blacks—and he demonstrated resolute commitment to ensure that his efforts were seen through to fruition. Many of the changes—such as inviting blacks to dinner at the White House—were largely symbolic, but they nonetheless sent an important message about the new administration.

His efforts to protect African diplomats from discrimination had nothing to do with Kennedy's concerns about segregation and everything to do with Cold War propaganda. But his commitment to fair employment within the federal government was sincere and exemplary. Kennedy had been an eager proponent of expanded black employment opportunities since first entering Congress—his dedication to the issue was long-standing. As a congressman, he had championed the creation of a statutory Fair Employment Practices Committee. He offered no such legislative response as president, however, even though liberals in Congress pressed hard for a fair employment bill.

Mandated fair hiring policies within the federal government were far easier to effect, both practically and politically. In pushing for this kind of reform, Kennedy did not have to grapple with southern officeholders or their allies on Capitol Hill. He simply had to convene the cabinet and order it to act. By and large, his vigorous appointments policy combined maximum impact with minimum controversy. The appointments sent a strong message to blacks without roiling southern conservatives, except in the most extreme cases where very high-level appointments were concerned. In these cases, Kennedy relented more often than not.

Kennedy's success with the strategy of association in the early months of his presidency soon created fissures within his administration and the country as a whole. A gap was emerging between black voters, who warmed to the style and èlan of the New Frontier, and black leaders, who had taken Kennedy's campaign promises more literally and were therefore severely disappointed by his political inaction. "The Kennedy administration has done with Negro citizens what it has done with a vast number of Americans," Wilkins wrote Wofford at the beginning of April; "it has charmed them. It has intrigued them. Every seventy-two hours it has delighted them. On the Negro question it has smoothed Unguentine on a stinging burn even though for a moment (or perhaps a year) it cannot do anything about a broken pelvis. It has patted a head even though it could not bind up a joint."[50]

CHAPTER 14

❧

Executive Inaction

Though bold in fashioning his administration to reflect the hopes and aspirations of black Americans, Kennedy was extraordinarily cautious in the early years of his presidency when it came to promoting substantive reforms. And though Harris Wofford had been able to cajole Kennedy into slightly altering his inaugural address, he was far less successful in persuading him to rethink the approach to civil rights decided upon during the transition. In late December, he tried to convince Kennedy of the need for swift reform, with a thousand-word memorandum advocating a strategy based on a "minimum of legislative action and a maximum of executive action."[1]

Looking ahead to the advent of the new administration, Wofford believed Kennedy could emulate Roosevelt's first 100 days by putting his signature immediately to a spate of executive orders. Wofford proposed orders that would end discrimination within the federal government, in publicly assisted housing programs, and at universities receiving federal grants. Wofford suggested that, after this initial flurry, the president should consider an executive order ending employment discrimination in government contracts. Then he could embark on an even more ambitious course: the complete desegregation of southern classrooms, an innovative policy that Wofford called "Part-III-by-executive-action." "[M]y strong recommendation is that instead of seeking legislation you should authorize the Attorney General to begin bringing some well-chosen suits and to intervene in many others," he wrote. "In drafting this part of the platform we carefully did not specify legislation because we had very much in mind such 'Part-III-by-executive-action.'" There would be no need for a substantive civil rights bill, argued Wofford, "if you go ahead with a substantial executive action program."[2]

While Wofford endorsed a policy comprised of a limited amount of legislative action and a maximum of executive action, Kennedy ultimately decided on a minimum of both. As a senator and as a candidate, much of his skill in handling civil rights derived from his ability to shape policies and postures at the very last minute in accordance with the politics of a particular moment. Determined to enjoy the same tactical flexibility as president, he preferred a pragmatic rather than programmatic approach.

Even before taking office, Kennedy quietly shelved plans to issue an executive order ending discrimination in federally assisted public housing schemes out of fear the initiative would wreck any chance of an administration-sponsored omnibus housing bill, which he planned to introduce at the beginning of his presidency, becoming law. The House and Senate housing committees were chaired by two Alabamans: Representative Albert Rains and Senator John Sparkman. Kennedy knew the housing order would inflame them. The housing order had been his most oft-made pledge during the 1960 campaign, and the decision to postpone it came as a particularly crushing blow to civil rights activists. Castigating him for promising repeatedly throughout the previous fall to eradicate housing discrimination through the "stroke of the presidential pen," they mailed tens of thousands of pens to the White House as part of the "Ink for Jack" protest campaign. For disgruntled black activists, the delayed housing order soon came to symbolize the stark difference between Kennedy's promise as a candidate and his performance as president.

The executive order to desegregate the National Guard, another platform commitment, was also postponed indefinitely. On this, the White House deferred uncomplainingly to the Pentagon, which had strenuously advised against it. The order threatened to disrupt military units that were currently on standby for possible deployment in Berlin, the latest flashpoint in East-West relations. When Father Theodore Hesburgh, president of Notre Dame University and the most liberal member of the CRC, criticized Kennedy for his failure to seek this executive order, the president was clearly exasperated. "Look, I have serious problems in West Berlin, and I do not think this is the proper time to start monkeying around with the army," he explained, when the two met in February, making little attempt to disguise his irritation. "I can't have them in the midst of a social revolution." But Kennedy also backed away from integrating the National Guard because it would have required him to confront Senator Russell and Representative Carl Vinson, the Georgians in charge of the Senate and House Armed Services Committees. As Assistant Secretary of Defense Carlisle Runge put it later in the year, "action of this type will place the Department in a difficult position with Congress. The chairman and ranking members of the Armed Services Committees in both houses are from Southern states, as are the key members of the Appropriations Committees." Given that Kennedy had set out to modernize the U.S. military, through a 15 percent increase in funding, he could not afford to alienate Russell and Vinson. Kennedy's aversion to confronting southern Democrats, combined with his long-standing reluctance to advocate punitive measures against the South, led him also to kill an executive order that would have cut off federal funds to universities and colleges that refused to desegregate their facilities.[3]

When Roy Wilkins met him during the transition, Kennedy had encouraged him to set out his ideas for nonlegislative action in greater detail. The NAACP leader came back a month later with a closely argued memorandum urging an executive order to block the use of federal money for southern National Guard units and public schools close to federal installations in so-called impacted areas. But nothing came of it. As Sorensen explained, it would cause "severe" political problems, and upset "customs which are very deeply rooted." Above all, Kennedy wanted to avoid imposing on the South an accelerated schedule for school desegregation. He discounted warnings from Fred Dutton that the administration risked losing black support if it continued to stand aside on the issue. "A Democratic administration can hardly long leave the initiative to the courts," wrote Dutton in early February, "if we are to affirm our general political philosophy and keep with us the minority population in the large northern cities." Still, Kennedy did nothing.[4]

At a press conference on February 1, a reporter asked Kennedy to clarify his plans for executive action. The president stonewalled: "We have been considering what steps could be taken in the field of expanding civil rights by Executive Action, and I'm hopeful that we will shortly conclude that analysis and have some statement to make on it. It's not completed as yet." Nobody even bothered asking about his legislative plans. Kennedy had already made himself clear on that point during the transition. When finally pressed on that issue at a news conference in early March, Kennedy noted legislative action would come only "[w]hen I feel that there is a necessity for a congressional action, with a chance of getting that congressional action." Kennedy tried to perpetuate the idea that while he and his administration were in favor of such reforms, their hands were tied by an unsupportive Congress.[5]

Kennedy did, however, recognize both the moral and political necessity of offering black voters some evidence of reform. Racial discrimination troubled him personally, and was a problem of strategic importance as well. He knew that the Soviets would continue to exploit America's race divide for their own propaganda, and that the problem was complicating his administration's relations with Africa's decolonized nations. But he wanted to offer far more incremental change that his aides, particularly Wofford, were advocating.

There was also an argument to be made that adopting a hands-off approach to civil rights in the South would help reformist officeholders in the region. Then they could go on bringing about piecemeal reforms, free from the potentially unwelcome interference of the federal government. Unquestionably, the go-slow approach enjoyed the quiet backing of a number of moderate southern governors, who in early 1961 warned Benjamin Muse of the Southern Regional

Council, a biracial pressure group, about the potential hazards of pressing too hard. "[E]ach emphasized the danger in 'stirring things up,'" wrote Muse in an internal SRC report, "told the importance of making 'quiet progress,' or 'unnoticed progress,' and keeping the thing out of politics and out of the papers as far as possible." But there is no record of Kennedy making this argument, publicly or privately. Instead, he focused on the risks of alienating southern hardliners on Capitol Hill, who chaired so many key committees, and southern moderates, whose legislative support was required for the New Frontier program. If that benefited moderate governors, like Ernest Hollings and Terry Sanford, then it was an unintended bonus, but never the primary motive.[6]

Rather than tackle school integration or the desegregation of public accommodations, which would require direct confrontation with the South, Kennedy decided his administration should focus on employment and voting reform. Here discrimination was more subtle and reforms were easier to engineer. Both were areas in which the Eisenhower administration had advanced moderate reforms, so the federal government had already crossed one important threshold. And southern Democrats would find it difficult to mount a sustained campaign of resistance on these issues, since even segregationists had acquiesced already in these limited kinds of reforms. After all, it was hard to argue, on intellectual or constitutional grounds, that blacks should be denied the vote or blocked from certain jobs. Segregationists, like Russell and Ervin, had tried to cloak their opposition to civil rights in the language of law and constitutional tradition. If they opposed voting and employment reform, they would be seen as crude racists and thereby undermine their cause.

For this reason, the one civil rights reform that Kennedy brought about through executive order focused on boosting employment opportunities for blacks. On March 7, he had created the President's Committee on Equal Employment Opportunity (PCEEO). At its opening meeting on April 11, Kennedy referred to the "high moral purpose" of its work and described equal opportunity as a "national goal," adding, "I don't think there's any more important domestic effort in which we could be engaged." Kennedy had created the PCEEO by amalgamating two existing bodies, the Committees on Nondiscrimination in Government Contracts and the Committee on Government Employment, set up by Eisenhower and chaired by Nixon. Its main aim was to stamp out employment discrimination among federal contractors. Kennedy charged Johnson with the chairmanship of the committee—a job Johnson resolutely did not want.[7]

Lyndon Johnson's vice presidency had been troubled from the outset. On Inauguration Day, he mangled his oath of office, accidentally dropping four words and adding one of his own. Two weeks earlier, on January 3, he had also made a brazenly unconstitutional attempt to maintain his influence on Capitol Hill, by asking to be appointed chairman of the Democratic Senate Caucus. Then he tried to vest the vice presidency with greater powers by urging the president to sign an executive order handing him effective control of the national security apparatus and space exploration—an impudent request that Robert Kennedy leaked to the press. Despite his parliamentary genius, Johnson was consulted only rarely by the new president. Nor were his famed negotiating skills brought to bear on recalcitrant southerners. Marginalized in Washington, Johnson tried to give his vice presidency some sort of meaning by making eleven separate foreign trips visiting thirty-three countries. He took great delight in handing out LBJ paraphernalia and pocket-sized copies of the U.S. Constitution to mystified locals.[8]

Kennedy had done Johnson no favor, when, during the transition, he asked him to chair the PCEEO. Johnson was reluctant to take the post, fearing it would undercut his chances of winning the presidential nomination in 1968. If the PCEEO succeeded, he would antagonize long-time southern allies. If it failed, he risked vilification by party liberals. As his adviser James Rowe pointed out, "You know perfectly it will be impossible to satisfy either group no matter what you do."[9]

Johnson reportedly said as much to Kennedy, during a tense discussion: "I don't have any budget, I don't have any power, I don't have anything." But Kennedy refused to back down: "You've got to do it, because Nixon had it before, even though he didn't do anything; you're from the South, and if you don't take it, you'll be deemed to have evaded your responsibility. And so you've got to do it."[10]

After the inauguration, Johnson redoubled his efforts to dodge the chairmanship, making one spurious argument after another. He had been asked to chair the Space Council and claimed it would be impossible for him to oversee both committees "without violating the Constitution." At one point he even asked aides to draft a letter to Kennedy questioning whether such a "large, costly, nationally-dispersed staff" would lead to a "perversion" of vice presidential power. When these attempts failed, Johnson aides searched for other constitutional or legal loopholes through which he could escape. They even questioned the very legitimacy of the executive order that had established the PCEEO. (Nicholas Katzenbach, the newly appointed head of the Justice Department's Office of Legal Counsel, assured Johnson that it was, in fact, well within the boundaries of presidential authority.)[11]

Johnson came under mounting pressure from Kennedy to accept the chairmanship. White House aide Richard Goodwin contacted Johnson to say the president was calling "just about every morning" to find out when the order would be released. Somewhat taken aback, the vice president said he could get it out "any time he wants." He then added, "I don't know why he doesn't ask me about these things. I saw him all Saturday morning, and he didn't mention it." Eventually, Johnson was forced to concede but insisted that the new body be called the "President's Committee"—both to give it the prestige of the White House and to shelter him from blame if it came under liberal attack. Once he had accepted the inevitable, however, Johnson threw himself wholeheartedly into the project and took over drafting responsibilities from the Justice Department to ensure the order had teeth. Johnson was fiercely competitive, and much of his newfound zeal stemmed from his determination to outstrip Nixon's record. Stronger still was his desire to prove liberal skeptics wrong.[12]

At the vice president's insistence, the revised executive order now allowed the federal government to cancel contracts, withhold new ones, and hold public hearings so disgruntled employees could air grievances. There were still weaknesses. The order did not allow the committee direct control over unions. Nor was the committee's staff of thirty sufficient to keep tabs on every federal contractor. With grating condescension, Justice Department officials also chided the vice president's office because the final draft included almost forty grammatical mistakes. Still, in virtually every detail, the new order was stronger than the old.[13]

The PCEEO was established by executive order on March 6, 1961. Kennedy promised "sanctions sweeping enough to ensure compliance," as he signed it into law. He reiterated his point about "powerful sanctions" when the committee convened for the first time on April 11. For all the talk of punitive action, however, Kennedy urged the committee to focus on voluntary compliance. "There is no intention to make this a harsh or unreasonable mandate for those sincerely and honestly seeking compliance," he said. Johnson also hoped that "sanctions and penalties will not be necessary" and that "voluntary compliance"—or "the jawbone approach," as he liked to call it—would produce results. Despite his essentially moderate approach, Johnson insisted on the fiercest possible rhetoric during the meeting. "Arbitrary and artificial restrictions upon individuals can no longer be tolerated, either morally or materially," he said, with the swagger of a Texan sheriff but with the voice of a northern liberal. "There should be no doubt about our purposes or program; we mean business."[14]

Kennedy set out his expectations for the PCEEO at its first meeting: The cancellation of federal contracts would be used only as a last resort in the most extreme circumstances. Johnson wholeheartedly concurred. "This is not a persecuting committee or prosecuting committee," the vice president became fond of saying. Here, he was no doubt mindful that his old friend Richard Russell had sponsored an amendment passed during the Truman administration limiting the amount of federal money allotted to contract compliance, a law that remained in place. As a result, the annual budget for the PCEEO was $425,000, a pittance given the scale of the problem. Later on, Jerry Holleman, the committee's executive vice chairman, claimed Johnson had assured Russell he would not seek additional funds. Nor did Johnson intend to hold on-site hearings in southern defense plants, a tactic used by Roosevelt's wartime FEPC. Johnson also assured southern lawmakers that blacks would not be given preferential treatment. "[The PCEEO] does not intend to state that certain types of people will be employed or that people will be placed in positions for which they are not qualified," he wrote Senator Russell Long of Louisiana. "In other words, the test will be merit."[15]

Under Nixon's chairmanship, the two committees that had come together under Kennedy to form the PCEEO had been wholly ineffective and failed to counter discriminatory employment practices, especially among southern-based defense contractors. With the limits Kennedy had imposed, nothing was likely to change under Johnson's stewardship. Indeed, one week after the creation of the PCEEO, the Pentagon awarded a $1 billion defense contract to Lockheed Aircraft Corporation in Marietta, Georgia. The company had close ties to Russell and ran a segregated plant—and did so on government-owned land.[16]

∾

During his first months in office, Kennedy's comments at the launch of the PCEEO had been one of the few occasions when he spoke out in favor of civil rights. At his first presidential press conference on January 25, carried live on national television from the State Department auditorium, Kennedy had referred to the topic just once. His comments came in response to the veteran black reporter Alice Dunnigan, who had bobbed up and down with her arm held aloft at countless press conferences during the previous administration, in mostly fruitless attempts to pose a question. Though somewhat startled that he had called upon her, Dunnigan asked Kennedy to comment on the plight of a group of black tenant farmers in Fayette and Haywood Counties, Tennessee, who had been evicted by white landlords in reprisal for voting in the presidential election.

In response to the question, Kennedy offered vague assurances about protecting the right to vote, stating that the administration would "pursue the problem of providing that protection with all vigor." But he clearly had only a sketchy understanding of the Tennessee situation. Afterwards, the administration soon intervened on behalf of the evicted farmers, by dispatching surplus food to Fayette and Haywood counties to alleviate the immediate distress for the 14,000 blacks living in conditions of extreme poverty. But Agriculture Secretary Orville Freeman was reluctant to take additional action, fearing southern Democrats on Capitol Hill would retaliate by trimming his department's budget. Moreover, the Justice Department refused to provide the "federal protection" to which Kennedy referred. White House officials had raised the possibility with black reporters of sending a top-ranking administration official to Fayette County, but that idea was also quietly shelved.[17]

Ten days after his inauguration, Kennedy reappeared on Capitol Hill to address a joint session of Congress. The speech was wide-ranging, a blend of foreign and domestic concerns, but he buried his only mention of the race question in a passage dealing with dwindling water supplies, juvenile crime, and corporate ethics. And, as ever, he focused on the issue as a concern in the Cold War: "The denial of constitutional rights to some of our fellow Americans on account of race—at the ballot box and elsewhere—disturbs the national conscience, and subjects us to the charge of world opinion that our democracy is not equal to the high promise of our heritage." By choosing to highlight the issue of voting rights, Kennedy was also making a cautious choice. It was a subject on which Congress had already twice acted over the past four years. The far more turbulent issue of that moment, as Kennedy well knew, was school integration. Kennedy chose to steer clear.[18]

Kennedy's reticence was nowhere more evident than in the ongoing school crisis in New Orleans, where angry white parents continued to boycott two recently desegregated elementary schools. At no time did Kennedy think to issue a statement condemning parents who picketed the schools, or even one upholding the right of black schoolchildren to attend them. A reporter picked up on this fact and pressed Kennedy for comment at the third press conference on February 8. The reporter framed the question as provocatively as possible. "During the campaign you spoke of using your moral authority as President in the civil rights field," he stated. "Can you tell us what you plan to say or do to help the New Orleans families who evidently want to obey the Constitution but are afraid to do so?" Kennedy's reply was stuttering and evasive: "I will—at such time as I think is most useful and most effective, I will attempt to use the moral authority or position of influence of the Presidency in New Orleans and in other places."

"But do you have anything to say specifically about New Orleans," a journalist shot back, citing the threats of violence against white parents with children at the integrated schools. Clearly rattled, Kennedy paused before delivering another guarded reply. "As far as New Orleans goes, it is my position that all students should be given the opportunity to attend public schools regardless of their race, and that is in accordance with the Constitution." Then he added, "On the general question, there is no doubt in my view: students should be permitted to attend schools in accordance with court decisions." Given the opportunity to condemn the campaign of racist intimidation, Kennedy had declined yet again.[19]

The media took note. The *Pittsburgh Courier* pointed out that these press conference remarks amounted to Kennedy's first substantive comments on civil rights since taking office, and its editors were distinctly unimpressed: "Such an answer might be satisfactory for those who can survive on the thin substance of words. It should provide little nourishment for Negroes." The *New York Times* was also critical. "Mr. Kennedy's position is now remarkably similar to the position of the former President Eisenhower's on the issue i.e. reiteration of the law, and, of what is right in principle, but extreme restraint in expressing moral judgment on the specific issue at hand." Others took greater solace in his remarks. The *Washington Afro-American* saw buried among his hesitant comments a lukewarm endorsement of *Brown*. While it hardly amounted to a ringing affirmation, Kennedy had indicated his personal support for the Supreme Court's ruling, something Eisenhower had repeatedly refused to do. "Kennedy Not Like Ike, Speaks Out on Schools," the paper applauded, congratulating Kennedy on the "history-making remarks" in which "Kennedy threw the power and prestige of the Presidency behind the 1954 school desegregation."[20]

Later that month, the president did lend his name to a much bolder statement in support of school desegregation. In a telegram wired to a CRC-sponsored conference on "Schools in Transition," Kennedy articulated an uncharacteristically strong opposition to school closures: "This is no time for schools to close for any reason, and certainly no time for schools to be closed in the name of racial discrimination." Alas, the president had not written the statement—Harris Wofford had. As with the civil rights plank, he suspected that the president might not have read it in any detail. [21]

The president's silence on civil rights was particularly deafening during his trips to the South. On three separate visits to the region during 1961—to North Carolina in October, an eight-minute airport appearance in Arkansas the same month, and Florida in December—he mentioned the issue just once. It came in a speech before the AFL-CIO convention in Miami, an audience comprised predominantly of labor officials rather than southerners, where he inserted a salutary paragraph on the need to improve black job opportunities. On more pressing issues, particularly school desegregation, he was mute.[22]

As the weeks and months passed, and Kennedy maintained his silence regarding civil rights, he came under stiff pressure from administration liberals. "Public apathy is always the bulwark of the *status quo*," warned Schlesinger in March. "Active government requires an active policy of presenting facts, alternatives and policies to the press and to the people." Bowles urged the president to conduct a "great national program of democratic self-examination," by means of a series of televised appeals and White House conferences. "Unless such grass-roots understanding and dedication to our national objectives can be mustered again," Bowles added, "an apathetic Congress reflecting a frustrated and confused electorate may refuse to free you and your administration to do what history requires of us."[23]

In March, Kennedy was forced to confront the issue of segregation head on. Controversy had arisen from a wholly unexpected place: Fort Sumter, the citadel on the shores of Charleston harbor in South Carolina, where, on April 12, 1861, the first shots of the American Civil War had rung out. With the hundredth anniversary of the battle approaching, the Civil War Centennial Commission, a body set up by Congress to organize the nationwide commemorations, planned an opening ceremony in the grounds of the fort. Guests would attend from all over the country. The problem was that Charleston's white hoteliers refused to accommodate a black delegate from New Jersey, an obdurate stance wholeheartedly supported by the chairman of Centennial Commission, Major General Ulysses S. Grant III. As his name suggested, Grant was a man of noble martial ancestry—his grandfather, General Ulysses S. Grant, had accepted the final surrender of the Confederate forces at Appomattox. In an almost comical historical inversion, Grant had decided states rights were more important than civil rights.

National news desks were already chasing the story, and Wofford knew that the White House would soon be drawn into the controversy. "In principle and on political grounds, I think you should take action," he told Kennedy, recommending that he personally contact Grant as quickly as possible. Kennedy acted on Wofford's advice and sent a letter to the general, reminding him that delegates of the Civil War Centennial Commission were government officials and deserved to be treated equally. Grant refused to cede ground, insisting that his chief responsibility was to commemorate the Civil War not to interfere in "racial matters." The general had forced a stalemate. With his credibility so visibly at stake, the president could not back down.[24]

Badgered for a comment at his news conference on March 23, Kennedy said it was his "strong belief that any program of this kind in which the United States is engaged should provide facilities and meeting places which may—do not discriminate on the grounds of race or color," a firm statement of principle. But it proved harder than the president had anticipated to find a workable solution to the standoff. Under existing federal law there was little the administration could do to compel Charleston hoteliers to integrate their facilities. So the White House exerted pressure on the members of the commission, by threatening to withdraw federal funding for the event if they refused to switch from the segregated hotels to Charleston Naval Station nearby.[25]

Grant eventually agreed to surrender. Yet as local segregationists gleefully informed reporters, blacks and whites were segregated on the naval base as well. Afterwards, the president was said by aides to be "very angry" over the whole affair, partly because of Grant's intransigence but largely because he had been drawn into the quarrel in the first place. He also worried that his press conference remarks could easily have been interpreted as a rebuke to South Carolina's governor, Ernest Hollings, its state's congressional delegation, and white citizens.[26]

The Charleston episode was revealing inasmuch as it demonstrated Kennedy's predilection for remedial solutions. Much as he hoped black diplomats would choose to fly rather than subject themselves to the segregated restaurants of Route 40, in this case he recommended a change of venue to circumvent stubborn hotelkeepers. Not until 1963 did he raise the possibility of a legislative solution to the problem of segregated public accommodations.

Soon Kennedy had another problem on his hands—this time from a more predictable source. In January, Adam Clayton Powell, Jr., had been elevated to the chairmanship of the House Labor and Education Committee and was now in a much stronger position to press for the so-called Powell amendment, a measure that would cut off federal funding to school districts that refused to integrate their classrooms. A natural showman who reveled in the balm of press attention, he was also now better placed to embarrass the president. The rancorous debate that would inevitably ensue if the Powell amendment were introduced could easily jeopardize other important pieces of legislation, most notably Kennedy's cherished federal aid-to-education bill.

When the president-elect met with the congressman at Kennedy's Georgetown home during the transition, Powell seemed willing not to push his controversial amendment through committee. But Powell soon came under intense pressure from the NAACP, which hoped he would prod the incoming administration into acting more aggressively. Powell refused therefore to discount the possibility of introducing his eponymous amendment on the House floor. But Powell was eminently bribable. Charges of tax evasion had been hanging over him since the 1950s, and it is possible that officials offered to halt the Justice Department investigation in exchange for the congressman's promise not to introduce the bill. There is no irrefutable evidence of a deal, but the circumstantial evidence strongly suggests one existed. On April 14, Powell formally announced that he would not add his amendment to the administration's federal aid-to-education bill. The same day, a U.S. attorney in New York informed a federal judge that the Justice Department was dropping its case. "We certainly weren't claiming and could not prove a deal," commented a disgruntled NAACP official. "But, knowing Powell as we did, well—it was not a good day for civil rights."[27]

Dealing with Powell was relatively easy, given his susceptibility to bribery. But shortly thereafter, the president had to contend with the more vexing dilemma of how to handle Joseph Clark and Emanuel Celler, two unimpeachable lawmakers who were much more principled in their support of civil rights. During the campaign, Kennedy had asked them to draft a far-reaching civil rights bill that he could introduce early in the new congressional session. Although Kennedy had withdrawn his support for the bill, Clark and Celler were determined to press ahead. The administration feared that their proposals could easily become a rallying point for disgruntled liberals and black leaders. From the beginning of February, the president himself harbored deep concerns, and instructed White House counsel Myer Feldman to speak directly with Clark and Celler. "What I am concerned about now," wrote Kennedy, "is that we maintain close liaison with them." He also raised the possibility of some kind of face-saving deal: that if Clark and Celler backed down, he might agree to congressional hearings on civil rights later in 1961 "and then have the fight next year." Kennedy did not want to be forced into a public disavowal of his pledges on civil rights: "I don't want statements to be issued that we have withdrawn our support of this matter."[28]

When it became clear that Clark and Celler planned to forge ahead regardless, White House aides focused on limiting the political fallout. In a secret White House memorandum, they assessed a range of possible responses: Should the president consider making a brief statement at the time the bill was introduced? Should he announce that he consented to the bill's introduction? Should he invite Celler and Clark to the White House to "permit them to 're-port' that their assignment is completed," without necessarily introducing the bill? How should he respond at the next press conference when asked if he backed the measure or not? Perhaps there should be a presidential statement promising legislation in the future but arguing that "the timetable which I have laid out calls for prior action by the Executive branch."[29]

Wofford had, of course, wanted Kennedy to support the bill, but having failed once again to persuade him he urged him instead to voice his "agreement on goals." As he advised the president, "This course permits Clark and Celler to complete their assignment, it promises *some* civil rights action . . . and leaves open the question of action on the substantive bills." This, in turn would hand the president "maximum bargaining power" in Congress and put a "shadow over the heads of anti–civil rights Democrats," who might then cooperate on other aspects of the program.[30]

Once again, Kennedy rejected Wofford's advice. He decided instead to appeal to the goodwill of Clark and Celler in the hope they would quietly drop the measure. The White House therefore approached Hubert Humphrey, who agreed to serve as an emissary. Although he failed to persuade Celler and Clark to back down, he convinced them not to lead a full-blown liberal revolt. As Mike Manatos, a senior member of the White House congressional liaison staff, reported to O'Brien, "Senator Humphrey tells me that Senator Clark is somewhat pacified with regard to his Civil Rights bill."[31]

On Monday, May 8, Clark and Celler introduced their long-awaited bill. They did so with little fanfare, and when questioned about the president's failure to offer support, Clark said the administration already had taken "a number of far-reaching steps." Even though Humphrey had implored Kennedy to mark the occasion with a presidential statement, he refused. Officials cited "political" reasons. The White House immediately disassociated itself from the bill. Salinger told reporters that while the administration continued to support civil rights, "[t]he President has made it clear that he does not think it necessary at this time to enact civil rights legislation." Salinger went on to suggest that there had in fact been "very little pressure" for civil rights legislation, an assertion that Wofford considered a painfully "low blow." As Salinger well knew, there had been relatively little pressure because the White House had persuaded liberal Democrats, like Humphrey, and civil rights groups, like the NAACP, to explore nonlegislative alternatives. Salinger's use of the word "necessary" was clumsy as well. Civil rights legislation might not be "practicable" or "possible," as the *New York Times* pointed out, but few aside from southern segregationists would deny it was "necessary."[32]

Liberal Republicans immediately seized upon Kennedy's refusal to offer any statement of support for the measure. New York Senator Kenneth Keating complained that the administration was "still somewhat timid and reluctant to put its full weight behind civil rights legislation. I hope I am wrong about this, because without persistent White House backing there is little likelihood that the majority party in Congress will move forward." There were harsher words from Roy Wilkins, who lambasted the administration for a "mistaken and regrettable decision." Coming as it did so close to the seventh anniversary of the *Brown* ruling, he protested that it "constitutes an offering of a cactus bouquet to Negro parents and their children." He also questioned the strategy behind the White House decision. While Kennedy might have alienated southern politicians by supporting the bill, it could hardly have mattered given their committed obstructionism. "As for practical politics," Wilkins explained, "the record is conclusive that whether a President sponsors civil rights legislation or not, his general legislative program is subject to hatchet treatment by Southerners and their allies."[33]

Like Wilkins, Louis Martin took the president's withdrawal of support as a betrayal. The promise to introduce a new civil rights bill had been the clearest commitment of the Democratic platform, he wrote in a stinging memorandum to Sorensen. By abandoning Clark and Celler, Kennedy risked a rash of unfavorable headlines. The decision would be particularly hard to explain to black constituents. Democrats faced tough election races in New Jersey and New York, and black support was vital. "It may be difficult to explain to the unsophisticated that Northern Democrats have concluded that the 'time is not ripe' for civil rights fights," he noted, caustically. "Most Negroes would know that the time has never been ripe."[34]

∾

By the spring, Harris Wofford was miffed. It had become abundantly clear that the president's civil rights policy would be wholly comprised of piecemeal reforms, such as the creation of the PCEEO, and a series of largely token gestures. After the election, he expected a position in the intellectual forefront of the incoming administration. Instead, he operated only on the fringes of power.

He found himself in the ignominious position of preparing a maximum of briefing papers and memoranda, a minimum of which were acted upon.

Wofford had been appointed as White House civil rights adviser on February 7, more by accident than design. That day, Kennedy had endured a fractious meeting with John Hannah and Theodore Hesburgh of the CRC, who both complained that, since the resignation of Eisenhower aide Rocco Siciliano in 1958, the White House lacked a point man on civil rights who could shape policy, coordinate the work of different departments, and communicate with the CRC. For a brief moment, the president seemed perplexed. "I already have a special assistant who is working full-time on that," he told them. "Harris Wofford."

On hearing the news, Hannah and Hesburgh were puzzled. They had met Wofford earlier that day, and he had explained, rather forlornly, that he would probably end up working at the Peace Corps since he had been snubbed by the president.

"That's only temporary," said Kennedy, without skipping a beat.[35]

An hour later, Kennedy summoned Wofford to the White House. Soon, a solemn-looking man carrying a Bible arrived to swear Wofford in. The impromptu ceremony complete, Kennedy beckoned him into the Oval Office. "I need you here to get this civil rights works on the tracks at the White House," said Kennedy, who had retrieved a copy of Wofford's December memorandum. "We've got to do these things we promised we were going to do. You ought to have the best office that's left. I'll back you up." Wofford should start by coordinating with officials at the Justice Department and with Sorensen, the main architect of domestic policy. "You're the expert," said Kennedy. "Get going."[36]

Despite the president's bustling enthusiasm at that initial meeting, however, Wofford quickly discovered that the policy of inaction was firmly entrenched. Sorensen was committed to the idea that it was impossible to get even a mild civil rights bill through Congress and that executive actions would also complicate relations with southern Democrats. Robert Kennedy, who had long been wary of Wofford, totally agreed.

Lacking a clear mandate, Wofford's job was often stultifyingly dull. One of his assignments was to serve as a one-man early warning system and to raise the alarm if a civil rights–related problem was about to land on the president's desk. And so with the help of Martin, Wofford kept a close eye on the activities of civil rights leaders, like King, in order to predict where trouble might next spring from. He also maintained close ties with members of the black press, like Simeon Booker, whose intelligence was always up-to-the-minute.

Long stretches of time were devoted to fielding complaints from liberals and civil rights activists about the president's excessive caution. And Wofford's cramped office soon started to fill up with thousands of pens from the "Ink for Jack" campaign. Ostracized and ridiculed, Wofford grew increasingly disillusioned with the president he had helped elevate to power. There were times when he seemed to wish that Johnson—whose vice-presidential candidacy he had considered a disaster only a few months before—had become president. "Your leadership in this field," he wrote the vice president in April, "is the best news of the year."[37]

Desperately in need of allies, Wofford turned to Louis Martin, now installed at the DNC, and Fred Dutton. They quickly banded together in an effort to overcome the defeatism that had infected so many administration officials. They created a kind of rearguard action by forming a subcabinet committee of high-ranking federal officials. The goal was to use the instruments of government already at their disposal to promote quiet but meaningful reform.

Dutton had first come up with the idea of a Sub-Cabinet Group on Civil Rights, as he called it. He suggested in a memorandum to the president that it should meet on a monthly basis to work out problems that were "economic and social in nature rather than legalistic" and "anticipatory rather than only after-the-fact." If nothing else, he argued, the group could be "an additional string in our civil rights harp." Its activities, at least initially, should be shielded from the press, so there would be no embarrassment if the group failed. Like Dutton, Wofford believed the group should function quietly until it had established its worth. "The theme is the application of maximum intelligence and the most effective, and wherever possible, quiet use of the Federal power to solve civil rights problems that are within our power to solve," he told Salinger, adding there would be no publicity until "it had some results to show." Thinking the initiative could do little harm, the president granted his blessing.[38]

At its inaugural meeting on April 14, Dutton delivered a brief pep talk in which he stressed that the committee's primary function was "to assist and reinforce these existing civil rights agencies, particularly on matters calling for interdepartmental cooperation." In keeping with aims set out by the president, its first priority would be to increase government employment opportunities, although Dutton emphasized that "[n]o one should be employed just because he is a member of a minority group." He also ordered each member of the group to scrutinize his department's programs and expenditures to ensure that "federal money should not be spent in a way which encourages discrimination." Dutton stressed that any leaks to the press should be passed on to black rather than white reporters. That way, the activities of the group would remain beyond the gaze of southern lawmakers and administration conservatives like Kenneth O'Donnell and Lawrence O'Brien. The Sub-Cabinet Group would therefore operate much as the Civil Rights Section had during the presidential campaign: surreptitiously and under the radar of the white press. The aim, as Wofford put it, was to "do anything we could get away with without causing [the President] undue political trouble."[39]

Some of the new administration's most enthusiastic supporters of civil rights were seated around the table that day, and many were disappointed with the president's timorous approach. Hyman Bookbinder at the Commerce Department, Jack Conway at the Housing and Home Finance Agency, James Quigley and Lisle Carter at HEW, and especially Adam Yarmolinsky at Defense (who was hired by Sargent Shriver and had worked alongside Wofford in the Civil Rights Section) were not only efficient administrators but imaginative policymakers, who believed they were acting in the spirit of the New Frontier, even if they did not always have the president's official sanction.

The group quickly went to work within their respective spheres of influence. On Yarmolinsky's recommendation, Robert McNamara had by June quietly disallowed a long-standing policy by which military policemen would escort black servicemen out of segregated restaurants if white owners ordered their removal. Thereafter, military policemen were forbidden "to support enforcement of racial segregation or other forms of racial discrimination," in the words of an internal memorandum. With the goal of desegregating northern National Guard units, Pentagon officials conducted behind-the-scenes negotiations with state governors and adjutant generals. Their efforts yielded impressive results. By the fall of 1961, Connecticut, New Jersey, Indiana, New York, California, Hawaii, and Maryland agreed to fully integrate their National Guard units, and they had made progress as well in Massachusetts and Ohio. Southern units remained untouched.[40]

Hyman Bookbinder at the Commerce Department came up with the idea of banning so-called hate signs—the racist slogans usually erected by the Ku Klux Klan or White Citizens' groups—from the shoulders of any highway constructed with federal funds. The Interior Department ordered the desegregation of the country's national park system, while Interior Secretary Stewart Udall forced the Washington Redskins to end its ban on black players by threatening to bar it from playing at D.C. Stadium, its federally financed home. He also suggested that Kennedy should boycott Redskins games until the changes came into effect. The very next season, the Redskins hired three black players.[41]

Many of the changes seemed trivial, but in aggregate they marked an unmistakable break with the past. In early April, the postmaster general ordered that any newly constructed postal facilities should be completely desegregated, a policy also applied to all new leased premises. The U.S. Employment Service and Bureau of Apprenticeship and Training issued anti-discrimination directives prohibiting labor exchanges from posting "whites only" job advertisements. Secretary of Health, Education, and Welfare Abraham Ribicoff ordered universities with language counseling institutes set up under the National Defense Education Act to run them on a nondiscriminatory basis.[42] At the Department of Agriculture, Orville Freeman canceled the annual meetings in Washington of the segregated 4-H club and ordered black youngsters to be included in the official encampment of all U.S. farm groups rather than carrying on the tradition of holding a separate meeting on the campus of Howard University.[43]

Far beyond Washington, this quiet revolution was taking effect. At the Sub-Cabinet Group's prompting, lunchrooms, toilets, and other public accommodations in federal government buildings across the South were desegregated. Federal officials were instructed that racial discrimination, in any form, would no longer be tolerated. There were small victories, as well; for instance, when it emerged that black servicemen attending the annual Army-Navy game were offered inferior seats behind the goal posts, Wofford brought an end to the practice. When Dutton discovered that bleachers at an army base in Virginia were segregated, they were integrated immediately. McNamara even prevented Pentagon bowling teams from competing at segregated bowling alleys.[44]

When planning speaking engagements in the South, federal officials were instructed not to accept invitations that would require any member of the cabinet to address a segregated audience. Soon after, Secretary of State Rusk refused to attend the Atlanta Bar Association's annual dinner unless black attorneys were invited as well. His firm stand brought about the first fully integrated gathering in Atlanta Bar Association history. Secretary of Agriculture Freeman canceled a speaking trip to Delta State University in Cleveland, Mississippi, so that he would not have to appear before an all-white group on an all-white campus.[45]

The first cabinet official to break the unwritten rule was Commerce Secretary Luther Hodges. His presence at a Democratic Party banquet at an all-white hotel in Columbia, South Carolina, drew pickets from local black party members who had been excluded from the dinner. Afterwards, Hodges issued an embarrassing apology, in which he claimed the unfortunate episode had been an honest mistake—he insisted that South Carolina's governor, Ernest Hollings, had given personal assurances beforehand that nobody had been excluded.[46]

The only other cabinet official to break the unwritten rule was McNamara. In November he attended a dinner honoring Senator Richard Russell and Representative Carl Vinson. After the event was picketed by forty black protesters, contrite administration officials claimed McNamara merely wanted to pay tribute to the seventy-five years of combined public service that Russell and Vinson had given the nation. In fact, McNamara felt he could not turn down the invitation, since the Georgia lawmakers wielded such enormous power as the chairmen of the Senate and House Armed Services Committees. As he himself had put it at the dinner, he was the "newest pupil in the Russell-Vinson school for Secretaries of Defense."[47]

Kennedy was supportive though largely unaware of the full scope of the Sub-Cabinet Group's activities. Wofford wanted to build momentum behind the reforms before informing the president, so they would be harder to interrupt or block. Eventually by June, when the Sub-Cabinet Group had built up an impressive record of accomplishment, Wofford suggested that Kennedy, Johnson, and Robert Kennedy attend one of its meetings to demonstrate its seriousness and to strengthen the hand of members whose cabinet chiefs remained skeptical about its work. Kennedy attended the inaugural meeting of the group but did not address it thereafter.[48]

The Sub-Cabinet Group met with great success. It made extraordinary advances in changing the culture of the federal government with regard to race—not just in Washington but throughout the country. Many racist practices that had long been routine were now outlawed, and there was a new awareness emerging throughout the federal government of the sensibilities of black employees. To a great extent, this new consciousness had been raised through the work of the Sub-Cabinet Group, whose reforms were enacted by liberal-minded officials disappointed by the performance of an irresolute president.

CHAPTER 15

❧

The Sheriff of the New Frontier

The chief architect of his brother's campaign victory, Robert Kennedy had intended to assume a much lower profile in the new administration. He fully expected to take a position at the Pentagon, where he planned to serve a rarefied kind of government apprenticeship before entering the cabinet at a later stage. But in mid-December, Abraham Ribicoff, the top candidate for the position of attorney general, turned down the post, and the president-elect insisted that his brother take it. John Kennedy recognized that the enforcement of *Brown* was likely to become one of the thorniest issues faced by his incoming administration. He needed an attorney general "who's going to tell me the unvarnished truth, no matter what," as he put it, and whose loyalty was complete.[1]

Bobby was loath to accept such a contentious post. Ribicoff had declined because he believed that a northeastern Jew would have trouble pressing school integration on the South. RFK himself was mindful of the experience of William Rogers, the present attorney general, who was forced to hide in the plane when Nixon made a campaign stop in South Carolina. But family loyalty eventually prevailed. The decision was announced publicly on Friday, December 16. Jack Kennedy had to plead with his disheveled-looking younger brother to at least drag a comb through his hair before stepping before the cameras camped out on the doorstep of his Georgetown home. He knew that he had left himself open to charges of nepotism—after all, his brother was still only thirty-five years old and had never argued a case in court.[2]

Robert Kennedy's nomination met with a variety of responses from liberals and blacks. The *New Republic* was scathing, arguing that Kennedy was too young and raw and would provide southern Democrats with "that vulnerable target they seek." Joseph Rauh, a lawyer himself, complained that the new attorney general possessed neither the political judgment nor legal expertise to handle such a demanding brief. Roy Wilkins welcomed the appointment, however.

He remembered Bobby Kennedy's call to Judge Mitchell on behalf of Martin Luther King during the campaign and viewed his impetuousness and his access to the president as definite advantages.[3]

The reaction from southern Democrats was also mixed. Russell was "absolutely shittin' a squealin' worm," according to Lyndon Johnson. "He thinks it's a disgrace for a kid who's never practiced law to be appointed." The vice president, who despised Bobby Kennedy for humiliating him in Los Angeles, agreed. He consoled himself with the thought that the new attorney general would have little influence, telling Bobby Baker, his former Senate aide, "I don't think Jack Kennedy's gonna let a little fart like Bobby lead him around by the nose." Even so, Johnson agreed to help pacify angry southerners, largely to demonstrate his value to the president. "I want you to lead all our Southern friends in here by their ying-yangs and let me work on them," he told Baker.[4]

Most southerners, however, acquiesced in the appointment, partly because they feared that someone more daunting might be named. James Eastland promised a painless confirmation, as did Sam Ervin. Ervin reckoned Kennedy, having studied law at the University of Virginia, would at least understand the racial mores of the South. "[H]e will view these problems [the question of race relations] with a sympathetic attitude," Ervin wrote a constituent, "something which could not have been said of the last two Attorney Generals."[5]

Unbeknownst to Ervin, Robert Kennedy's experience in Virginia had not inclined him toward sympathy with segregationists—quite the opposite, in fact. In the spring of 1951, as a twenty-five-year-old law student, he had demonstrated a fierce crusading streak by inviting Ralph Bunche to speak in segregated Charlottesville. Bunche agreed to accept the invitation only if the audience was integrated, a stipulation the university's governing body rejected outright. With fellow students reluctant to protest the decision, Kennedy, the head of the Student Legal Forum, erupted in a blind fury, shouting at them, "You're all gutless!" Then he took his fight to the university administration. He sent an angry letter to the university president, Colgate W. Darden, complaining that the policy was "legally indefensible, morally wrong and fraught with consequences calculated to do great harm to the University." Kennedy ultimately prevailed, and Bunche delivered his lecture before an integrated audience.[6]

Robert Kennedy had a fiery core that his brother lacked. After the death of JFK, Robert Kennedy downplayed his early commitment to civil rights: "I won't say I stayed awake nights worrying about civil rights before I became attorney general." But the Charlottesville incident suggested that he had been engaged with the issue, however sporadically, from an early age. That said, he was also, like his brother, an adept politician. It was Robert who had been most dubious about his brother's outreach to black voters at the start of the campaign and who had been most fearful of alienating the South. The moral fervor that had propelled him at the University of Virginia in the early 1950s had been subsumed by 1960 by the demands of politics. As incoming attorney general, he understood his brother's decision to back away from the civil rights battle, and supported his approach.[7]

Robert Kennedy's political prudence was fully in evidence during his confirmation hearings before the Senate Judiciary Committee. Kennedy "looked suitably pale and tense, rather like a schoolboy about to undergo his orals," according to one observer. On civil rights, his comments were purposely inoffensive. He promised to enforce existing laws and said nothing about enacting new ones. Pressed on the issue of school integration, he promised merely to uphold the law, whatever Congress decided it should be. He accepted that the country had to "move more strongly and vigorously in the field of civil rights," but cautioned, "I do not think this is a subject or matter that can be solved overnight." Probed about implementing the Democratic platform, Kennedy said he would await instructions from the president.[8]

Beforehand, most commentators had predicted that the most hostile questioning would come from southern Democrats. Russell and Talmadge had made it known they wanted RFK "roughed up," so as to place him on the defensive. Yet Eastland, who was personally fond of the former campaign manager, decided strong-arm tactics were unnecessary. Bobby would take orders from the president, reasoned Eastland—and the president had signaled already that civil rights was a low priority for the administration. Eastland said nothing during the hearings and left Ervin, another close acquaintance of the Kennedy brothers, to speak for the South. Ervin could hardly have been more courteous, describing Kennedy as a man of "profound personal and political courage." As James Reston observed, Robert Kennedy had arrived "expecting to do battle with Jack Dempsey and instead found himself confronted, most agreeably, by Shirley Temple."[9] Kennedy received the committee's unanimous backing and later reflected: "The strongest support I ever received as Attorney General came from Southerners." Still, Russell shouted "nay" as a voice vote was taken on the floor of the Senate confirming his appointment.[10]

Cautious during his confirmation hearing, Kennedy was more expansive during an interview published in *Look* magazine in March. He admitted that he did not have "a great deal of experience" and conceded that civil rights was going to be the Justice Department's "most difficult problem . . . because of the emotional factors involved." Asked about the sit-in movement, he answered that "my sympathy is with them morally," adding, "Logically it follows that integration should take place today everywhere." But then he tempered his remarks. "[T]hose of us who believe this must realize that, rightly or wrongly, other people have grown up with totally different backgrounds and mores, which we can't change overnight." On the explosive question of school desegregation, he signaled a gradualist approach. "I think the Supreme Court recognized this when it ordered integration 'with all deliberate speed' instead of immediately. I will take this order seriously. This doesn't mean we are going to stand for mob defiance of court orders. Nor does it mean that there will be sweeping transformations without adequate groundwork." Asked for his likely response to "another Little Rock," again he leaned toward the South: "I don't think we would ever come to the point of sending troops to any part of the country on a matter like that."[11]

Even before his confirmation, the new attorney general began to staff the Justice Department with Kennedy loyalists. Many had Ivy League backgrounds, all were highly competent, and most were politically cautious. Byron "Whizzer" White, who became Kennedy's deputy, was the model appointee. A former Colorado football star, graduate of Yale Law School, and Rhodes Scholar, he was urbane, unemotional, and pragmatic—everything a New Frontiersman should be. He also had scant interest in promoting civil rights. This indifference first became evident during the campaign, when he repeatedly turned down requests from Wofford to appoint a greater number of blacks in the Citizens for Kennedy volunteer organizations.

Soon after taking up his post, White was entrusted with finding an assistant attorney general to head up the Civil Rights Division. It was an enormously influential position. Liberal Democrats wanted the vacancy filled by Wofford, and he himself coveted the post. But Robert Kennedy considered him a "slight madman," whose provocative policy ideas were certain to embroil the administration in an endless stream of controversy. White concurred and proposed Burke Marshall. Marshall, a thirty-eight-year-old corporate lawyer at the Washington law firm of Covington and Burling and a graduate of Yale Law School, had spent his entire career in private practice. He was little known in political circles and had no connections with the civil rights movement. Temperamentally, he was bland and imperturbable, the antithesis of Wofford. Though he possessed a formidable intellect, he was excruciatingly shy.[12]

On White's strong recommendation, Robert Kennedy summoned Marshall for a meeting in his office at the Justice Department. The encounter started disastrously and then got worse. Since neither man was particularly skilled at small talk, it was several minutes before the attorney general finally broke the silence. Even then, the conversation was stilted. Marshall left convinced he was no longer in the running. Despite this setback, White continued to argue that Marshall's unassuming style made him the perfect candidate, and eventually Kennedy agreed.[13]

To ensure a smooth confirmation process, Robert Kennedy now had to convince Eastland of Marshall's suitability. Ahead of the hearings, Kennedy took Marshall to meet Eastland in his office on Capitol Hill, announcing his arrival with typical irreverence: "I have Mr. Marshall outside who is going to be head of our Civil Rights Division. I thought you'd like to meet him. He's going to put the Negroes in your white schools in Mississippi." Eastland failed to appreciate the joke and shot back, with typical ill humor, that he had no wish to meet Marshall. Soon, though, he relented, and their brief meeting persuaded Eastland that the South had little to fear from such a diffident corporate lawyer.[14]

Marshall's appearance before the Senate Judiciary Committee on March 2 was therefore largely uneventful. Asked about his experience of civil rights, Marshall replied he had "virtually none" (even though he had proffered informal advice during the drafting of the 1960 Civil Rights Act). He revealed "no specific plans" with regard to policy. Pressed by Eastland on whether he supported Part III powers for the attorney general, Marshall merely replied that the federal government had a duty to uphold existing law, an intentionally inoffensive reply. His only mildly provocative comments concerned voting rights. Marshall pledged to investigate registration figures that revealed a "heavy imbalance" against blacks. Although his comments reflected only an interest in upholding the terms of the 1957 and 1960 Civil Rights Acts, they nevertheless delayed his appointment for two weeks.[15]

Southerners eventually came to realize that Marshall's views on the constraints on federal power comported closely with their own. Above all, he was a constitutional originalist. He rejected the contextualism of legal scholars such as Wofford, who believed laws were subject to the shifting standards of politics and public opinion. He believed that the Constitution prescribed clear and definite boundaries for the authority of the federal government. During his early tenure at the Justice Department, the mantra "no-basis-for-federal-action" was his reflexive response whenever civil rights activists tried to persuade or force the government to intervene. He always opted for patient negotiation geared toward measured progress over litigation aimed at more immediate results.

When lobbied to enact universal Part III powers, which would enable the Justice Department to bring any kind of civil rights suit, Marshall argued it would "destroy the federal system." Marshall would eventually codify his views about the juridical restraints on federal authority in his legal treatise, *Federalism and Civil Rights*, published in 1964. His central argument was that "no matter how far-reaching the equitable decrees of the federal courts may be, the states and local political institutions are going to retain operating control over all of the institutions involved in the granting or denial of equal rights." His views on the hotly disputed question of federal protection for black activists neatly encapsulated his philosophy. "Problems of protection [were] the responsibility of local law enforcement agencies," he said in 1964, adding that if southern law enforcement temporarily broke down in the midst of black demonstrations, "we ought to live through it."[16]

Marshall seemed content to work within the legal and institutional constraints imposed upon him. He did not seek the expansion of the Civil Rights Division, which had forty attorneys (compared with 300 at the Antitrust Division). Nor did he wish to augment the small band of U.S. marshals who had been deployed by the Eisenhower Justice Department in New Orleans to enforce school integration and were likely to be called upon in other racial hot spots in the South. He also categorically rejected the creation of a national police force, with the power to protect civil rights protesters. It would violate the Constitution, he believed, and create the misleading impression that civil rights crusaders could look to Washington for protection.

On March 6, Robert Kennedy first brought his civil rights team together for a brainstorming session. He announced that Justice Department efforts would be concentrated on expanding voting rights and improving employment opportunities. "Top priority to voting," wrote Edwin Guthman, the attorney general's press adviser, whose scrawled bullet points on a reporters' notepad provide the only record of the meeting. In particular, Kennedy wanted to "explore [the] adequacy of referee provisions," an early acknowledgment that the 1957 and 1960 Civil Rights Acts were inadequate in boosting black enfranchisement. But since his brother had ruled out the possibility of new legislation, the discussion centered on how blacks could empower themselves. To counter what was deemed widespread "apathy" among southern blacks, the group considered sponsoring a voter registration campaign, a scheme that became increasingly attractive as the year progressed.[17]

The civil rights group also discussed how "leadership by [the] President" could change the "climate of opinion" and provide "leadership beyond [the] lowest common denominator of [the] population." To boost employment opportunities, they considered compiling a list of federal contractors to "get more jobs for Negroes." But the federal government should put its own house in order, as well, especially in the South. "[G]ovt. can't overestimate effort of cleaning up own operations in the South," wrote Guthman, with "*hiring*" and "through integration of its own operations."[18]

There was discussion, though no agreement, on whether to test the Hill-Burton Act, which allocated federal money for the construction of segregated hospitals. They also failed to reach any conclusions on desegregating National Guard units or on appointing a "roving" district attorney in the South to focus on civil rights–related problems. But on school integration there was greater clarity: They planned little action. In Alabama, for instance, Guthman noted, "don't rock boat on school seg[regation] until a negro student gets in U of A [University of Alabama]," a breakthrough still more than two years off. Among the sixteen bullet points that Guthman scribbled down, this was the only one that mentioned school desegregation.[19]

At this stage, Robert Kennedy was content to follow his brother's mandate in seeking to enforce only those voting statutes already enshrined in the 1957 and 1960 Civil Rights Acts. The issue of voting rights was far less incendiary than other topics on the civil rights agenda—as the attorney general himself explained: "How could anybody, really, get very mad because you're making an effort to make sure that everybody votes?" It would be no great challenge for him to outstrip the Eisenhower Justice Department, whose enforcement record on voting rights was feeble. But broader enfranchisement might also bring about further reforms: If blacks voted in greater numbers, Kennedy predicted, office-holders would be forced through political necessity to adopt more conciliatory policies. Robert Kennedy had no grand strategy for desegregating the South at this early stage, but over the course of the administration he saw ever greater potential in boosting black enfranchisement. In a challenge to the nonlegislative policy, Robert Kennedy eventually became an advocate for additional voting rights legislation—a view considered almost heretical by the White House tri-umvirate of O'Brien, Sorensen, and O'Donnell, who over the coming years reg-ularly stood as a bulwark against change.[20]

Shortly after arriving at the Justice Department, Marshall placed a map on the wall of the Civil Rights Division, dotted with multicolored pins, to indicate the location and progress of voting suits brought by his staff. But rather than taking court action against recalcitrant voting officials, Marshall hoped he could persuade them to comply with the law voluntarily. He assembled a small task force to hold informal talks with southern officials. Marshall and his assistant, John Doar took the lead in these negotiations. But they were both northerners (Marshall was from New Jersey and Doar from Wisconsin) so they brought in two Justice Department officials who hailed from the South—John Seigen-thaler, a Tennessean, and Jerry Heilbron, a lawyer from Arkansas hired by Marshall on the recommendation of southern lawmakers. "I'd go in, my south-ern accent dripping sorghum and molasses, and warm them up," Seigenthaler said later. "Burke would tell them what the law was." The aim was to avoid the kind of Yankee haughtiness that aroused such deep resentment in the South. In some instances, their solicitousness proved effective. But it quickly became ap-parent that extralegal persuasion alone would not suffice, even if Marshall's team of lawyers presented their case in fluent Dixie.[21]

Though he preferred it, Marshall did not confine himself to the tactic of per-suasion. During his first ten months, his office launched fourteen voting rights suits—a noteworthy improvement over the Eisenhower Justice Department, which had brought just six cases in the previous three years. Marshall also decided to mount a number of suits in the Deep South. He launched four separate cases in Mississippi alone, a first for federal officials (curiously, Eastland did not seem overly concerned, for he thought William Rogers, Robert Kennedy's predecessor, had been derelict in his duty by not mounting more suits under the terms of the 1957 and 1960 Civil Rights Acts). In all, the Justice Department launched inves-tigations into voting rights abuses in sixty-one southern counties.[22]

Progress was painfully slow, however, since the process was incredibly labor in-tensive. In Hinds County, Mississippi, for instance, federal officials had to sift through over 14,000 voter application forms and interview hundreds of witnesses in order to establish a pattern of discrimination. It required thousands of hours of manpower to process a single case. This should have come as no surprise. By 1959, lawyers at the CRC had concluded that patchwork, case-by-case litigation was impracticable, given the workload and the limited size of the staff.

Between 1961 and 1963, a total of 37,146 blacks were enfranchised as a result of the Justice Department's forty-six suits. In those counties, 548,358 black adults should have been eligible to vote. This sluggish pace of reform revealed the essential weakness of the administration's policy. Prior to becoming president, Kennedy had supported legislative proposals in 1960 that would have accelerated the process through the appointment of federal voting referees in communities where there was a clear pattern of discrimination against black applicants. But having settled on its nonlegislative strategy, the White House refused to countenance a new voting rights bill.[23]

School integration was even more problematic. Passions were more easily aroused, the views of southern Democrats were much more entrenched, and the statutory authority of the federal government was much less clear. But school desegregation was the top priority of the NAACP. Southern blacks had made only limited progress after *Brown;* at the time Kennedy took office, less than one percent of black children attended integrated schools. Civil rights leaders demanded Part III powers for the Justice Department so that it could initiate lawsuits to accelerate the process.

Robert Kennedy was happy not to have Part III powers available to him, because he had no intention of hastening the pace of school integration. He was, however, expected to enforce school desegregation orders handed down by federal judges, just as his predecessors, Herbert Brownell and William Rogers, had done in Little Rock and New Orleans. Here, as with voting suits, the Justice Department intended to rely primarily on a policy of voluntarism—compliance without confrontation. At his inaugural press conference in early April, Robert Kennedy made clear that if local officials took voluntary action to comply with the law "then it is no longer necessary for the Department of Justice to take action. If they do not then we will move in."[24]

Robert Kennedy could not, however, avoid legal action altogether—the Civil Rights Division had inherited a number of high-profile cases from the Eisenhower administration, and the Justice Department was forced to intervene. Its first test came in New Orleans, where three months after the beginning of court-decreed integration, angry parents continued to mount daily demonstrations aimed at disrupting the desegregation of two local schools. At William Frantz School, only seven white students attended class with a six-year-old black child, largely because parents who considered breaking the boycott were threatened with violence. The boycott was also nearly complete at McDonogh 19.

Segregationists across the South looked to see how the young attorney general would respond. Harris Wofford hoped the new administration would intervene forcefully. He believed that if the administration engineered a decisive victory in such a highly charged setting then New Orleans might come to be regarded as the segregationists' last stand. Wofford wanted the administration to take a "great symbolic action" and urged the president to host a White House reception for the black and white children attending the city's desegregated schools. "Some special recognition of the courage and Americanism of these people might help now," Wofford told the president in late December 1960. The president declined.[25]

Robert Kennedy was determined to avoid a headline-grabbing showdown similar to the clash between Eisenhower and Faubus. The Justice Department should adopt a neutral stance, he believed, and carry out its responsibility to enforce the desegregation order without taking sides. When officials at the Department of Agriculture proposed punitive action, offering to block some $2,224,607 from Louisiana's school lunch program on the grounds that the state refused to fund the school dinners of black pupils, the attorney general flatly rejected the idea. To endorse the highly controversial notion of withdrawing federal funds from states maintaining segregated schools could only aggravate the situation and provoke fierce protests from the Southern Caucus. Kennedy also dismissed Wofford's suggestion that he dramatize the dispute by taking legal action against Louisiana Governor Jimmie Davis, who was orchestrating the campaign of massive resistance.[26]

Instead, Robert Kennedy hoped that Burke Marshall could negotiate a voluntary settlement. Faced with the first crisis of his new job, Marshall attempted to cultivate racial moderates in Louisiana, in hopes that they could resolve the dispute. Marshall pinned his hopes on deLesseps S. Morrison, New Orleans's reform-minded mayor, who was desperate for a speedy end to the standoff. But there were limits to what Morrison could achieve. Even though the mayor enjoyed the support of many leading New Orleans businessmen, who also wanted an end to the boycott, he was unable to control the mob of enraged parents who were picketing daily outside the two elementary schools.

Burke Marshall soon realized that the Justice Department would have to target the state officials who were leading the campaign of massive resistance, and he reluctantly conceded that litigation might be necessary. Rather than take action against Davis directly, however, Marshall focused on Shelby Jackson, the state superintendent of education and a close political ally of the Louisiana governor. Jackson was withholding some $350,000 of federal funding to prevent the two schools in New Orleans from functioning properly. At first, Marshall hoped he would bow under the threat of litigation. But Jackson refused to surrender, despite a personal call from Robert Kennedy.

Only after its attempts at negotiations had failed did the Justice Department decide to pursue charges of contempt against Jackson. The Justice Department "couldn't back down," Robert Kennedy explained later, if it was to preserve its credibility. Without consulting the White House, Kennedy instructed Marshall to do "whatever is necessary," short of the deployment of federal troops or drawing his brother into the crisis. By keeping the White House out of the process, Robert Kennedy intended to underscore to reporters that civil rights was primarily the domain of the attorney general, not the president.[27]

On February 16, the contempt trial came before Judge J. Skelly Wright, an Eisenhower appointee who had first ordered the desegregation of New Orleans's schools. Jackson quickly capitulated and released the urgently needed federal funds. For the Justice Department, it was an important victory. It had succeeded in breaking the back of the New Orleans anti-integration movement, and within four weeks of taking office triumphed over the forces of segregation. But rather than advertise his success, Robert Kennedy described the legal success in the most judicious terms possible. In his public statements, he emphasized that the Justice Department had merely upheld the law. Robert Kennedy even backed away from his initial plan to reward Judge Wright, the true hero of the standoff, by nominating him to the U.S. Court of Appeals for the Fifth Circuit, through fear of angering Louisiana Senator Russell Long. Instead, Johnson was made a judge in Washington, and the southern vacancy went to Frank Ellis, an avowed segregationist. Ellis soon started overruling some of Wright's pro–civil rights rulings.[28]

The New Orleans confrontation was a formative experience for Robert Kennedy. At points during the crisis, he was genuinely appalled by die-hard segregationists like Davis and Jackson and found it hard to comprehend how the desegregation of two elementary schools could stir such violent emotions. "He was really mad," Marshall reflected later. "It was the first time that either one of us had been involved [directly] . . . with the way that the segregation system worked in practice, and how difficult it was going to be. And they were so irrational about it down there." But Robert Kennedy nonetheless stuck to the official administration line: The Justice Department had taken action to maintain the integrity of the courts, not to strike a blow for racial justice.[29]

Robert Kennedy was far more candid during an interview with a local television station in New Orleans two months later. Speaking with much more passion, he described the schools crisis as "a deplorable situation" and argued that opposition to token integration was "just inexplicable." During the interview, he also spoke in more detail about his personal feelings. "I feel that as a Christian nation, a nation that believes in Christianity and believes in the equality of man, that we are going to have to continue to make progress . . . we are committing a major moral error if we don't at least take steps forward and keep fighting for the proposition that all men are created equal." But he knew when to rein himself in. Kennedy tempered his more aggressive comments by remarking that, particularly when it came to compliance with *Brown*, states should be given time "to work it out themselves," so that the federal government had a "smaller and smaller role in it."[30]

Kennedy's television interview met with a surprisingly positive reaction in New Orleans itself. "My own belief is that Mr. Kennedy managed to convince a good many people that he and the administration are sincere about what they are doing and have good reasons for it aside from the basic matter of enforcing the law," noted Bill Monroe, the reporter who conducted the interview, "and he apparently managed to do this without stirring up a violent reaction." Perhaps the administration was excessively cautious; perhaps senior officials *could* speak out in favor of civil rights in the South without invoking the wrath of southern voters. But this was a proposition the president was unwilling to test.[31]

If the New Orleans standoff angered the attorney general, the situation in Prince Edward County, Virginia, was even more deplorable—"a tremendous blight on our country," he told Peter Maas of *Look*. In response to the *Brown* decision, many school districts in the state had decided to shut their schools rather than see them integrated. In January 1959, however, a three-judge federal panel ruled that the policy of school closures violated the Fourteenth Amendment, but the school board in Prince Edward County defied the panel's ruling. Rather than shut its schools, which would have been illegal, the board decided to dismantle the public education system altogether. They replaced it with a newly constructed private institution, the grandly named Prince Edward Academy, where 1,500 white schoolchildren received an education financed by subsidies from the state and county authorities. Meanwhile, the county's 1,700 black children received no education at all.[32]

Determined once again to avoid litigation, the Justice Department began by exploring grounds for a voluntary settlement. The Civil Rights Division discreetly opened up a dialogue with local school board officials to identify areas of compromise. At the same time, Robert Kennedy approached Virginia politician William Battle, an old friend and ally, to assess whether local political pressure could be brought to bear.

Only when negotiations failed did Kennedy decide to mount legal action. The Justice Department entered the case on May 8—not as a "friend of court" but as an active party in a suit aimed at reopening the public school system. It was a fine but crucial legal distinction. In Little Rock and New Orleans, the Eisenhower Justice Department had filed amicus briefs. In Prince Edward County, for the first time the federal government took on the role of plaintiff in a segregation suit. As part of its motion, the Justice Department asked for six injunctions, which included halting tuition grants to children attending Prince Edward Academy and also a far more controversial penalty that would withdraw federal funding for all Virginia's schools until the situation was satisfactorily resolved.[33]

The Justice Department was taking a bold action in Prince Edward County. But Robert Kennedy was determined to downplay its significance. In talking to reporters, he emphasized the Justice Department's initial efforts at mediation.

In talking about the case itself, Kennedy framed it primarily as a question of law and order. "We have tried to work this out to permit Negro children to go to school," he told reporters. "They are unable to. Court orders are being circumvented and nullified. Therefore, we have brought this action to protect the integrity of the judicial process."[34]

Kennedy's comments were somewhat disingenuous. As he well knew, litigation would not permit black children to return to school any time soon, since the legal process was tortuously slow. (It was not until February 1963, that the Justice Department tried to provide alternative schools for the black students.) And Kennedy must also have been fully aware of the symbolic magnitude of entering the case as a plaintiff. The disconnect between Kennedy's strident legal approach and his cautious remarks is revealing. As evidenced in his interview broadcast in New Orleans, two aspects of his character—the fiery crusader of his early years at the University of Virginia and the pragmatic politician he had since become—seemed to be at war with each other. But at this stage, the politician was winning.

Angry that the Justice Department had intervened at all in Prince Edward County, Virginia lawmakers cried foul. Congressman Watkins M. Abbitt described the court action as "an attempt by totalitarian executive action and judicial usurpation of power to make hollow shells of our state and local government and assure dictatorial controls over a purely local function." Senator Harry F. Byrd complained that if the courts backed the Justice Department "such a decree would be unprecedented in American history."[35]

Worried about Byrd's intemperate tone, the White House went to extraordinary lengths to placate him. The president even paid a hastily arranged visit to Byrd's country estate in Berryville that very weekend. Flying in by helicopter, with only a few minutes' notice, Kennedy touched down in the middle of the senator's birthday party. His appearance smacked of political pandering. The vociferous reaction from southern lawmakers might explain the Justice Department's eventual reluctance to pursue the case with greater vigor. As the case crawled through the courts, the federal government showed little interest in taking remedial action to ensure in the meantime that black schoolchildren received an adequate education. Local blacks complained about the half-hearted intervention. Some worried that the Justice Department had inadvertently aided segregationists by reinforcing their contention that the schools should remain closed while legal action was pending.[36]

Both the New Orleans and Prince Edward County cases were holdovers from the Eisenhower administration. Under Kennedy, the Justice Department showed no enthusiasm for taking new action. Indeed, of the three school desegregation cases in which the Civil Rights Division intervened in 1961, only one was initiated after Kennedy took office. Even then it involved a school district in the North: New Rochelle, New York, the first desegregation case to go before the Supreme Court since *Brown*. Action here seemed a somewhat disingenuous attempt to suggest that the problem of school segregation was just as pronounced above the Mason-Dixon Line.

Robert Kennedy's cautious approach was vindicated, at least in the eyes of the Kennedy administration, in September 1961, when a new academic year opened peacefully in Atlanta with the token integration of four previously all-white schools. Justice Department officials had been negotiating quietly with local officials throughout the summer months. The president was so delighted by their success in bringing about integration without legal action that he began his weekly press conference with a statement on civil rights. It was the first time he had done so. He congratulated Governor Vandiver and Mayor William Hartsfield, along with the city's school superintendent and parents for carrying out the operation in an "orderly manner . . . with dignity and without incident." Other communities, he said, should follow suit. That month, Memphis voluntarily admitted thirteen black schoolchildren to first-grade classes in four of its schools. The new academic year began without incident in New Orleans as well as Dallas, the country's largest segregated school district, where eight schools adopted a grade-a-year integration plan. In all, thirty-one school districts in seventeen southern and border states "token-integrated" their schools, in the language of the time, ten through court orders, twenty-one through voluntary action. Most noteworthy of all, though, was the complete integration that fall of high schools in Little Rock, a city forever associated with defiance against *Brown*. Most remarkable of all, the desegregation plans were endorsed by Governor Orval Faubus.[37]

The Justice Department played a limited role in most of these victories. In Little Rock, as in other southern cities, the peaceful transition owed more to local business and civic leaders, who understood that protracted racial disputes harmed the economy and damaged their prestige. Atlanta had a progressive mayor, William Hartsfield, a sensible police chief, Herbert Turner Jenkins, a president of the Chamber of Commerce, Ivan Allen, who believed racial harmony was the key to economic development, and two antisegregation newspapers, which helped mobilize public support. In Texas, where the greatest numerical gains were recorded, change came about as a result of a liberal-minded state attorney general who overturned a 1957 law requiring local referendums on integration. In Arkansas, Faubus reversed himself after the election of a new school board president; Everett Tucker, a director of the Chamber of Commerce, insisted that racial harmony would bring economic expansion. In early September, Marshall acknowledged as much, when he suggested that Robert Kennedy make a series of congratulatory telephone calls to an eclectic assortment of civic and business leaders. They included the chief of police in Dallas, the president of the city's main power company, the president of the Little Rock school board, and the city's mayor, Warner Knoop.[38]

Civil rights activists were concerned about the president's overly enthusiastic response to what were, in the broader context, very nominal gains. These small but symbolic—and much publicized—victories seemed to validate the administration's noninterventionist approach both in Kennedy's own mind and to the public. In Memphis, local schools accommodated just thirteen black pupils—an important step, certainly, but a tiny fraction of the black students in the city. Thurgood Marshall of the NAACP Legal Defense and Educational Fund claimed massive resistance had simply been replaced by token compliance. By integrating a small number of classrooms in a small number of schools, he complained, state authorities had carried the principle of gradualism to its absurd conclusion—and done so with the support of the federal government.[39]

Like the president, Robert Kennedy disregarded voices within the administration advocating a more vigorous approach. When Fred Dutton called for a federal task force to tour southern cities where local schools had successfully segregated, his idea was dismissed by the attorney general. He feared an interdepartmental task force would be difficult to coordinate and staffed by officials from the Housing and Home Finance Agency (HHFA) and the Department of Health, Education, and Welfare (HEW) who were "too ideological in their approach." Besides, highlighting success stories in racially moderate cities would only fuel demands for the task force to attack more formidable "hard core areas," as Marshall described them. Kennedy likewise rejected Dutton's proposal of using federal contracts to leverage compliance with *Brown*. And he also dismissed Wofford's pressure for "Part III by executive action," even though leading constitutional lawyers, like Paul Freund and Mark DeWolfe Howe, believed it represented a wise and lawful extension of federal power (as did legal teams at Covington and Burling and at Arnold, Fortas, and Porter, two patrician Washington law firms known for their vigilance). Even in his efforts to secure voluntary compliance, Kennedy could have been more proactive—after the *Brown* ruling was handed down, Attorney General Herbert Brownell had convened a meeting of the state attorneys general to personally lobby for its speedy implementation.[40]

The greatest strides toward implanting *Brown* came only after the passage of the 1964 Civil Rights Act, which finally enabled the attorney general to initiate desegregation cases and allowed HEW to withdraw federal funds from offending school districts (in 1964, just 1.18 percent of black children attended integrated schools, while by 1969, it was almost a third). In 1961, they were twin powers that neither the president nor his attorney general either sought or wanted.[41]

In the spring of 1961, Robert Kennedy faced the political and personal dilemma of deciding whether to accept a speaking invitation at the University of Georgia. The setting could hardly have been more highly charged. The Athens campus was still recovering from the violence surrounding the admission in January of Charlayne Hunter and Hamilton Holmes, the first black students in the university's 175-year history. The most sensible option would have been to decline. But the invitation had come from an enterprising young student named Jay Cox, the president of the Student Advisory Council, who had traveled from Athens to deliver it personally. Granted a meeting with the attorney general, Cox explained that a visit from Robert Kennedy would help ease tensions on campus. Kennedy was impressed by Cox's bold idealism, perhaps seeing something of himself in the audacious young student.[42]

Alert to the political risks, Kennedy nonetheless decided to accept the invitation. He spent the next five weeks agonizing over his speech. For guidance, he assembled a "southern Brain Trust," which included John Seigenthaler; Louis Oberdorfer, a recent appointee to the Tax Division (and a member of one of Alabama's most prominent Jewish families); Sylvan Meyer, the editor of the liberal-leaning Gainesville *Times;* the *Atlanta Constitution*'s Ralph McGill; James Landis, a New Deal stalwart and close associate of his father; and John Barlow Martin, a campaign speech writer. Marshall, whose almost umbilical relationship with Robert Kennedy had begun to mirror Sorensen's close bond with the president, also contributed. In their quest to find areas of common ground between the Justice Department and the South, the group decided that the overarching theme of the speech should be the majesty of the law and integrity of the courts. By May 6, after going through at least seven drafts, the speech was ready.

That Saturday morning, the attorney general flew south on board the *Caroline,* his brother's twin-engined plane, and was greeted at Atlanta airport by Jay Cox. The night before, five people had been arrested for painting "Yankee Go Home" on the sidewalks, and Cox predicted a hostile reception. But the only protesters to show up were a group of fundamentalist preachers who were vehemently opposed to a Catholic having become president. Vandiver protested with his absence, by leaving Georgia to attend the Kentucky Derby in Louisville, Kentucky. Other state officeholders boycotted the event after hearing rumors that Kennedy was about to drop a "civil rights bombshell."[43]

Ushered into the university's auditorium, Kennedy received a polite welcome from over 1,650 faculty staff, alumni, and students. It was a virtually all-white crowd. The lone black faces belonged to Hamilton Holmes and Charlayne Hunter (who, she later said, "was applauding wildly"). After a brief ceremony honoring the top students at the university's law school, it was soon time for the attorney general to deliver his speech to a nervous and expectant audience. Speaking from behind an ornate wooden lectern, which almost dwarfed him, Kennedy tried to lighten the atmosphere with a joke about how he, too, had received an award as a law student at the University of Virginia—"for having the fifth best sense of humor." Then, in another attempt at levity, he feigned disappointment about his inability to claim a familial connection with Georgia. "I have no relatives here and no direct ties to Georgia, except one," he said. "This state gave my brother the biggest percentage majority of any state in the Union, and in this last election that was even better than kinfolk."[44]

Kennedy then embarked on the primary theme of his address: the need to uphold the law. Disobedience, he warned, was a challenge to liberty itself, for "we know that if one man's rights are denied the rights of all are endangered." While he made no explicit mention of civil rights at this point, or the desegregation crisis in Athens, the allusion was clear to everyone. After briefly outlining how the Justice Department planned to confront organized crime and price fixing, he turned to by far the most eagerly awaited passage of the speech—the section concerning civil rights. RFK addressed the crisis at the University of Georgia, stating clearly from the outset that he supported the right of entry for Charlayne Hunter and Hamilton Holmes, deliberately mentioning both by name. Then he turned to the topic of school desegregation and the Justice Department's recent action in Prince Edward County. He stressed that litigation had been necessary to uphold the integrity of the law. "We are maintaining the orders of the courts," he noted. "We are doing nothing more nor less." The federal government had no intention of seizing control of local schools or overstepping its constitutional bounds. But it was compelled by law to ensure that federal court orders were acted upon. "Our position is quite clear—if the orders of the court are circumvented, the Department of Justice will act," he said. "We will not stand by or be aloof."

Next Kennedy turned to "the 1954 decision," as he gingerly referred to *Brown,* and told his audience that it was his personal belief that the Supreme Court had been entirely correct to call for gradual school desegregation. "But my belief does not matter," he went on. "It is the law. Some of you may believe the decision was wrong. That does not matter. It is the law." Then he promised that the Justice Department would strive for "amicable, voluntary solutions and to get voluntary compliance," and that the federal government would adopt more forceful tactics only if negotiation failed. Both sides should do everything they could to avoid situations like the Little Rock crisis, a confrontation, he claimed, which eroded American prestige abroad. But it was entirely "understandable," he recognized, that such a "delicate and complex" problem should stoke such passion.

In a further attempt to find common ground with his audience, he then claimed to have some understanding of the South because of his time at the University of Virginia. But he added that "my knowledge is nothing to yours." Above all, he said, racial discrimination was a national problem requiring national solutions, and it was hypocritical for officials at the Justice Department, where only ten of the 950 lawyers were black, to lecture the South. The same charge of hypocrisy could be leveled at northeastern business executives, who complained about discrimination in the southern factories but belonged to whites-only gentlemen's clubs. Kennedy ended as he began, with a heartfelt plea to uphold the sanctity of the legal system.

At first, his speech was greeted with ten to fifteen seconds of silence. But then applause spread throughout the hall and lasted for over a minute. A number of students and faculty staff even gave him a standing ovation. According to a reporter for the *Washington Post,* the reception marked an "appreciation for his frankness." Beforehand, the Kennedy entourage feared the speech would be interspersed with heckles and jeers. The response had been surprisingly cordial. A local reporter claimed that the applause "was as loud and long as they gave the football team for winning the Tech game last fall."[45]

In the midst of a crowded reception afterwards at the Georgia Center for Continuing Education, Kennedy had a brief exchange with Charlayne Hunter. It was her first contact with any official from either the Eisenhower or Kennedy administrations. "He did not say 'hang in there' or anything like that," she reflected later, but he was "polite, relaxed" and "pretty pleased to meet" her. Already, he had paid her the "highest compliment," she recalled, "just by mentioning our names."[46]

Plaudits soon rained in. Father Theodore Hesburgh of the CRC, who deeply mistrusted the Kennedy brothers, commended Robert for his "great courage." Ralph McGill was even more effusive. "Never before," he wrote, "has the South heard so honest and understandable a speech from any Cabinet member." After printing the speech in its entirety, the *Pittsburgh Courier* deemed it "courageous, rank and all-embracing . . . one of the most forthright statements ever uttered on the status of contemporary race relations in the United States of America by a high-ranking federal official." Even Jackie Robinson described it as "most encouraging." Louis Martin found it hard to contain his delight. "Your speech in Georgia was a peach," he told the attorney general. "Congratulations are pouring in from brothers everywhere. I am honored to call you 'honorary brother.'"[47]

Kennedy had not, in fact, dropped any "civil rights bombshell" on school desegregation. (The rumors had most probably been fanned by Justice Department officials, who recognized that, in the context of such expectations, anything short of a bombshell would seem positively temperate.) Kennedy had essentially reiterated the administration's policy on civil rights compliance. But many were simply impressed that the attorney general had delivered such an honest and forceful speech in the heart of the South. "Although there were no new programs or statements," observed James Clayton in the *Washington Post,* "it was notable on two counts. The first is that the President's brother explained his intention to enforce civil rights laws in firm, tough language. The second is that he chose the Deep South, an area from which most national leaders shied away from when they began to talk civil rights."[48]

Robert Kennedy had made a bold decision and then mitigated its impact with gentle words. He reserved his strongest rhetoric for discriminatory practices in the North (as columnist Ralph McGill remarked, "If any region was excoriated, it was the north"). Although he firmly stated that the Justice Department would enforce existing laws, Kennedy's posture was one of moral neutrality—a fact reflected in the *Washington Post* headline: "Robert Kennedy's Aim in the South: To Uphold Law but Take No Sides." Kennedy had ultimately done little more than set out—and justify—the administration's minimalist doctrine.[49]

Kennedy had made a brave choice in delivering a civil rights speech before a southern audience so early in his tenure. His rhetoric was vigorous, and his voice was resolute. But the new attorney general had chosen a bold setting for what was, in many respects, a cautious speech. As in the wake of the Prince Edward County case, there was a clear dissonance between Kennedy's words and his actions—evidence, perhaps, of a restless moral spirit at war with a more circumspect political mind.

CHAPTER 16

❦

Project Freedom Ride, 1961

Civil rights leaders had looked forward optimistically to the advent of Kennedy's presidency, but by the spring the slow pace of reform had begun to trouble them. In early February, Roy Wilkins warned Ted Sorensen that young firebrands in the civil rights movement were growing increasingly frustrated with the administration's nonlegislative strategy. "Already there are grumblings at the delay in indicating more than run-of-the-mill action in this area," he complained, adding it was "surely too late for the Kennedy administration to offer warmed-over, slightly revised, or piecemeal civil rights proposals which might have been daring in 1948 or 1953, but are mild as milk and toast today." Two months later, after the White House had repeatedly turned down his requests for a meeting with the president, Wilkins wrote Harris Wofford an even angrier letter. He complained that Kennedy had failed to ease the passage of other "black-friendly" bills, which had been the original justification for the nonlegislative strategy. Southern Democrats had been handed an easy victory over Senate reform, and they had also gutted the minimum wage bill. Wilkins was particularly enraged because when he had met with Kennedy in January, he received "definitive assurances" that rule revision was a high priority.[1]

Martin Luther King also wanted to meet the president, but on March 25 Kenneth O'Donnell told him that the "present international situation"—by which he meant the Berlin crisis—made it impossible. Louis Martin felt that it was essential that King be allowed to meet with the new administration, so he lobbied for an off-the-record meeting with high-ranking administration officials. Robert Kennedy agreed to the idea but insisted that the meeting be secret so southern Democrats would not suspect the administration of colluding with the country's most controversial black leader. The group met on April 22 in a private dining room at the Mayflower Hotel, with waiters barred so they could not tip off reporters. As a further precaution, King was allowed to bring just one aide, and the size of the administration team was also limited—to Wofford, O'Donnell, Martin, RFK, John Seigenthaler, and Burke Marshall.[2]

The normally taciturn Marshall dominated the discussion and repeatedly emphasized the constitutional restrictions upon the federal government. In what seemed like a premeditated attempt to steer King's focus onto voter registration campaigns, Marshall stressed that Justice Department lawyers had limited authority to intervene in school desegregation or police brutality cases. Voting rights offered wider scope. The administration officials considered the meeting only a partial success. King did promise to step up the SCLC's registration work, but he had refused to rule out other forms of direct action.[3]

After the meeting, Wofford walked King over to the White House for a more informal talk, breaking the unspoken rule that had kept him and other civil rights leaders out of federal buildings for months. Still, when the president learned that King was in the building, he decided to drop in at Wofford's office to pay his respects. "It's good to see you," said Kennedy, who was meeting King for the first time since September. After exchanging pleasantries, Kennedy said he had been keeping up with King's activities through the attorney general and promised that the administration would support any southern voter registration drive. But the president was clearly distracted—preoccupied, presumably, by the Bay of Pigs fiasco, the U.S. government's attempt to overthrow Castro on March 22. At one point, King asked how the president enjoyed White House life. In a moment of candor, Kennedy admitted it had become much more difficult since the Cuba disaster. The conversation lasted roughly five minutes and hardly touched on civil rights. Their brief encounter was kept from reporters. The only mention of it came a few weeks later when *Jet* reported that King had "quietly met" with the president and attorney general in "unpublicized sessions."[4]

Like Wilkins and King, James Farmer, the newly appointed national director of CORE, was unimpressed by Kennedy's first months in office. He was determined to jolt him into more forthright action. Farmer planned to revive the so-called Journey of Reconciliation, a campaign in the late 1940s aimed at desegregating interstate buses. "Project Freedom Ride, 1961" would test compliance throughout the South with the Supreme Court's recent ruling in *Boynton v. Virginia*, which had outlawed segregation at interstate bus terminals. But the true aim of the campaign was to provoke a Dixie backlash that would shame the administration into action—"to create a crisis," as Farmer put it, "so that the federal government would be compelled to act." After setting off from Washington, the riders planned to travel through Virginia, the Carolinas, Georgia, and then on to Alabama, Mississippi, and Louisiana. Farmer and John Lewis, a young divinity student and SNCC activist who was among the first group of riders, were confident the riders would encounter violent resistance. The "Freedom Rides" would culminate in New Orleans on May 17, the seventh anniversary of the *Brown* decision. Farmer informed Marshall of his plans for the protest and itinerary. He also sent identical letters to the FBI, the White House, and the chairmen of Greyhound and Trailways. None elicited a response.[5]

Simeon Booker, who planned to report on the Freedom Rides for *Jet*, also warned Robert Kennedy about the protest during a meeting in April. Booker predicted the protesters could easily fall prey to the Klan. Kennedy indicated that, if they did, he should immediately notify the Justice Department. As the reporter rose from his chair, Kennedy wished him well. He seemed moved by the courage of the young civil rights activists, telling Booker, "I wish I could go with you."[6]

The freedom riders left Washington on Thursday, May 4, in two buses, one Greyhound, one Trailways. The thirteen demonstrators—seven black, six white—traveled without incident through Virginia. But trouble soon flared in Rock Hill, South Carolina, the so-called door to the Deep South. Police stood by as a band of segregationists attacked John Lewis and some of his fellow riders. Worse violence lay in store outside Anniston, Alabama, on May 14. A mob surrounded the Greyhound bus, barricaded the front door, and hurled a Molotov cocktail through one of the broken windows. As dense black smoke billowed into the air, the freedom riders stumbled off the bus, coughing and vomiting phlegm. The white mob then attacked them with clubs and iron bars.[7]

An hour later, the Trailways bus pulled into Anniston terminal carrying the second group of freedom riders. They also came under attack. James Peck, a slightly built man who had taken part in the 1947 Journey of Reconciliation, was hauled over two seats and pummeled until he fell to the floor. The mob then turned on Walter Bergman, a retired professor. They dragged him from his seat and beat him unconscious. As the violence went unchecked, Bergman's wife watched in horror, convinced her husband was about to be killed.

Eventually, the Trailways bus left Anniston. But further on at Birmingham's Magic City terminal, some forty heavy-set men had gathered in the loading bay, awaiting the arrival of the freedom riders. As the Trailways bus slowed to a halt, Peck disembarked and walked slowly toward the main waiting room. His face was spattered with congealed blood. He was attacked yet again, this time with such violence that he would require fifty stitches to stem the flow of blood from a deep head wound.

Even though their headquarters was just two blocks away, police did not appear at the Magic City terminal until ten minutes after the attack had begun. When reporters sought an explanation for their delay, they were told by the local public safety commissioner, a former radio announcer named Theophilus Eugene "Bull" Connor, that most of his men were on leave because it was Mother's Day. In fact, Connor had helped to orchestrate the beatings. He had promised his friends in the Klan that they would have at least ten minutes to wreak havoc before his officers would intervene. Unbeknownst to reporters, a team of FBI agents had witnessed the entire attack. They had been tipped off in advance by Gary Thomas Rowe, Jr., one of their KKK informants. One agent even managed to capture photos of the attacks. But none of the agents did anything to restrain the troublemakers or apprehend them afterwards.[8]

When Marshall informed Robert Kennedy that Sunday evening, he was furious—not because the freedom riders had been assaulted so viciously, but because the Justice Department had been caught so completely unaware. Why had he not been informed about the freedom riders before? he asked, having apparently forgotten his meeting with Booker. The timing of the Freedom Rides campaign could hardly have been worse. The attacks threatened to plunge the administration into another crisis less than month after the Bay of Pigs debacle, and only a few weeks before the president's first meeting with Soviet Premier Nikita Khrushchev. The Soviet leader rarely missed an opportunity to point out America's racial injustice, and now he would have an opportunity to humiliate the president on the world stage.[9]

The next morning, over breakfast at the White House, President Kennedy read a front-page account of the Birmingham beatings in the *New York Times*, and his thoughts turned immediately to his forthcoming European trip. Even though civil rights leaders had called already for a forceful administration response—just hours before, Wilkins had wired Robert Kennedy complaining that the "Alabama dictatorship seems to be as great a menace to America as any foreign threat"—the president had no intention of intervening. Nor did he even consider issuing a statement condemning the violence. Instead, his first instinct was to bring the crisis to a swift end, by pressuring the freedom riders into canceling their protest. Kennedy contacted Wofford. "Tell them to call it off!" barked the president. "Stop them. Get your friends off those buses!" Shortly after, the president left for a planned visit to Canada, his first foreign trip since taking office. According to Nicholas Katzenbach, he considered the protesters "a pain in the ass." Robert Kennedy was left to handle the crisis on his own.[10]

At the Justice Department, Robert Kennedy moved with great caution. He did not issue any statement denouncing the mob violence. Nor did he order Justice Department lawyers to take legal action on the freedom riders' behalf. Though segregationists were openly flouting the *Boynton* ruling, Kennedy agreed with Marshall's assessment that no federal laws had been broken. The violence infringed local laws instead. He thought that the protection of the protesters was a matter best left to the local police, even though there was compelling evidence already that Connor had in fact facilitated the Birmingham violence. By providing federal protection, the administration would encourage the Freedom Rides to continue, which was exactly what it did not want to happen. Ideally, the freedom riders would call off the protest out of fear for their safety. At the very least, they should be encouraged to leave Birmingham.[11]

In Birmingham, Connor was coming under greater pressure to put an end to the crisis—not from the Justice Department but from local business leaders.

They issued a strongly worded statement condemning his handling of the situation. In response, Connor sent word to the attorney general that he would guarantee the safety of the freedom riders as far as the Birmingham city line if they agreed to leave immediately. Robert Kennedy seized upon the offer and immediately contacted Booker, hoping he would urge the freedom riders to accept its terms. But Booker explained that the protesters felt trapped and wanted federal protection.[12]

Kennedy refused to offer federal protection and decided instead to try to convince state officials to provide security. This required him to deal once more with Governor John Patterson, the archsegregationist whose early support for his brother had provoked such a liberal outcry. Patterson remained an ardent admirer of the president—the two had lunched together in Washington on May 8—and his first inclination was to help. He therefore agreed to provide an escort of Alabama state troopers to the Mississippi border. By the afternoon, however, Patterson reneged on the deal, telling reporters "the citizens of the state are so enraged that I cannot guarantee protection for this bunch of rabble-rousers." By now, the battered freedom riders were en route to the Magic City bus terminal to catch the three o'clock Greyhound service to Montgomery. When they arrived at the terminal, they learned that Patterson had withdrawn the offer of state protection, but the riders were determined to go ahead regardless. The problem now was finding a Greyhound driver prepared to take the wheel.[13]

In Washington, Robert Kennedy erupted with fury at suffering his second major setback in as many hours. He vented his anger at a Greyhound supervisor in Birmingham. "I think you should—better be getting in touch with Mr. Greyhound or whoever Mr. Greyhound is and somebody better give us an answer to this question. I am—the Government—is going to be very much upset if this group does not get to continue their trip." Kennedy then briefly considered dispatching a government plane from Washington to airlift the protesters out of Birmingham but quickly rejected the idea for fear it would draw the administration deeper into the crisis.[14]

As RFK contemplated his next move, the freedom riders decided that it would be suicidal to journey on in the absence of a police escort. Their protest over, they unloaded their luggage from the bus and booked plane tickets to New Orleans. At the Justice Department, the news was greeted with enormous relief but little celebration. The attorney general was genuinely shaken by the events of the past thirty-six hours, and believed they were a portent of even worse racial crises to come. Wilkins, who had met with Kennedy that afternoon, recalled that he seemed particularly shocked by the bare-knuckle brutality of the Alabama mob. Yet much to Wilkins's dismay, RFK indicated far greater concern about the repercussions on the president's upcoming trip to Europe. He believed the freedom riders' protest had handed the Soviets a crushing propaganda coup. Wilkins argued that a pledge of federal protection would prevent a recurrence of such violent episodes. But Kennedy balked at the idea. His only concession was to promise Wilkins an FBI investigation into the Anniston violence.[15]

That evening, Kennedy's most immediate concern was to ensure the freedom riders' swift departure from Birmingham. He dispatched John Seigenthaler to Alabama to oversee their evacuation. When Seigenthaler asked what federal protection he could offer, Kennedy told him none. "I think they primarily need somebody along just to hold their hand," he said, "and let them know that we care."[16]

Later that night, when Seigenthaler arrived in Birmingham, he found the freedom riders cowering, bloodied and bandaged, in the departure lounge of the airport. Just before eleven that night, after repeated bomb threats had delayed their departure, the plane finally taxied away from the terminal, with Seigenthaler and the freedom riders safely on board. As the lights of Birmingham disappeared below them, it appeared the crisis was over. As soon as they arrived in New Orleans, Seigenthaler retired to his hotel room believing his mission was complete.

Seigenthaler was jolted awake at three in the morning by a telephone call from Burke Marshall. A fresh group of SNCC protesters were intent on reviving the freedom rides campaign. Sure enough, the following morning—Wednesday, May 17, the seventh anniversary of the *Brown* decision—ten young protesters set off for Birmingham, led by the indomitable John Lewis (Lewis had left the original group of freedom riders before reaching Alabama to attend a job interview in Philadelphia). On arrival at Magic City terminal, Lewis told the policemen that the freedom riders should be allowed to use the facilities before carrying on their journey. But the words had hardly escaped his lips before he felt the sharp crack of a police billy club in his stomach. For the next three hours the protesters remained on the bus. When they were finally allowed to disembark they were greeted by Connor, who announced that the group was being taken into custody for its own protection.[17]

The arrests triggered no response from the Kennedy administration. The only civil rights–related statement that emanated from the Justice Department that day concerned Robert Kennedy's threat to resign from the Metropolitan Club. But concerns were mounting at the White House, prompting the president to take a more central role in determining the administration's response. After returning from his two-day visit to Canada, he summoned his brother, Byron White, and Burke Marshall for a breakfast meeting in his private quarters. It was Marshall's first meeting with the president, and he was struck by his informality. Kennedy was still dressed in pajamas and balanced a tray of eggs and toast precariously on his knees, as he listened to a brief situation report. "As you know, the situation is getting worse in Alabama," said the attorney general. Even worse, Patterson had stopped cooperating and refused to take the attorney general's calls. In the face of such intransigence, he warned that the Justice Department might be forced to intervene more aggressively.[18]

How could they guarantee the riders' protection without inserting federal troops? After the Bay of Pigs debacle, and on the eve of his Khrushchev summit meeting, the administration could hardly risk another military misadventure that would draw renewed attention to the young president's uncertain leadership. Robert Kennedy proposed a new plan, whereby hundreds of U.S. marshals would be dispatched to Alabama rather than thousands of troops. With precisely this kind of crisis in mind, former Attorney General William Rogers had started training U.S. marshals in riot control. As White explained, this ad hoc force of 100 men could be augmented by federal officials from the Bureau of Alcohol, Tobacco and Firearms, the Immigration Service, and the Bureau of Prisons. Most important of all, it would relegate the role of the U.S. Army to providing logistical support alone—trucks and planes at the very most. And as Marshall pointed out, this plan had a significant political advantage: To dispatch troops, Kennedy would have to issue a presidential proclamation publicly announcing that the state of Alabama faced a breakdown in order requiring federal intervention. To order the marshals into action, Kennedy needed only to send a private letter to the attorney general.

As the breakfast meeting drew to a close, Kennedy asked when he had to make a final decision. Nobody knew. Ideally, Patterson would cooperate and agree to offer protection so that the jailed freedom riders could leave the city. But Patterson's behavior had become increasingly erratic. Kennedy then tried to contact the governor personally, but Patterson's receptionist misleadingly told him that he was unavailable—on a fishing expedition in the Gulf of Mexico. No one was fooled. Patterson had snubbed the president.[19]

That Thursday night, the freedom riders prayed and sang as they prepared for their second night in the Birmingham jail. But as midnight approached, their choruses were interrupted by the unexpected arrival of Connor, who had concocted a new plan to get the young protesters off his hands. He had decided to drive them personally to the Tennessee line. Connor had already divulged the scheme to Kennedy and Marshall, who were initially afraid he was setting a trap for the protesters. Connor therefore promised that two reporters could accompany the group and explained that they needed to leave in the dead of night to avoid a Klan ambush rather than invite one. After a pause, the attorney general decided that Connor's offer to bring an immediate end to the crisis was simply too attractive to turn down. In his desperation, he was prepared to place the safety of the protesters in the hands of the very man who had helped orchestrate the violence against them only a few days before.[20]

Connor drove the riders to the state border, but the crisis continued to escalate. That night, another group of freedom riders set off by train for Birmingham. In Washington, officials were dismayed. The president tried again to contact Patterson, to no avail. Justice Department officials then threatened the governor's aides with the use of federal force if they refused to negotiate.

That threat brought Patterson to the phone, but he was in no mood to compromise with the attorney general. On taking office, he had pledged to maintain strict racial separation, he reminded the attorney general, not "guarantee the safety of fools."

"You're making political speeches at me, John," Kennedy shot back. "You don't have to make political speeches." Eventually, Patterson consented to a meeting with Seigenthaler in Montgomery later that day. After their conversation, he grudgingly agreed to offer protection in exchange for a promise that the federal government would refrain from intervening.[21]

Shortly after six the following morning—Saturday, May 20—the freedom riders reassembled at the Birmingham bus terminal. They were confident that they could now complete the two-hour journey to Montgomery. Again, there was no driver willing to take them on their journey. A man named Joe Caverno had been slated to take the wheel, but then backed out, telling reporters, "I only have one life to give and I'm not going to give it to CORE or the NAACP." Robert Kennedy was furious and contacted senior Greyhound executives to pour out his anger. A short while later, under fierce pressure from his bosses, Caverno relented. At 8:30 A.M. the bus drove away, escorted out of the city by a convoy of Connor's police cruisers. At the city limit, control passed to the Alabama highway patrolmen, and then the sixteen-vehicle convoy hurtled down the highway until it reached the outskirts of Montgomery, where city police were expected to take charge.[22]

But as the state patrol cars peeled off and a lookout plane banked away toward the horizon, no Montgomery officers appeared to escort the freedom riders on the final leg to the downtown terminal. The bus proceeded on unescorted, and pulled into the empty Montgomery terminal at 10:23 A.M. An unsettling silence hung over the entire area. In a flash, local whites appeared from every direction, carrying baseball bats, iron pipes, chains, bottles, and bricks. "Get them Niggers," they cried. "Get them Niggers."

From the U.S. attorney's office overlooking the bus terminal, John Doar observed the frenzy of violence. He had spent the week in Alabama preparing a series of voting rights cases. Now all he could do was telephone Washington to provide a running commentary. "Oh, there are fists, punching," he winced. "A bunch of men led by a guy with a bleeding face are beating them. There are no cops. It's terrible. It's terrible. There are no cops in sight. People are yelling 'Get 'em, get 'em.' It's awful."[23]

Seigenthaler arrived late on the scene after the violence had erupted. As his car swung round the corner he saw a young black girl being beaten up by a group of men. As he tried to intervene, Seigenthaler was smashed over the head with a lead pipe, knocking him unconscious. Seigenthaler lay prostrate on the sidewalk for twenty-five minutes, before being taken off to hospital in a police squad car. When he finally regained consciousness, a doctor was on the telephone explaining to White that Seigenthaler had suffered a possible fractured skull. As in Birmingham, FBI agents witnessed the entire beating but did nothing to intervene.[24]

Robert Kennedy heard the news while he was watching an FBI baseball game and raced back to the Justice Department. By the time he reached his office, Marshall, White, and Edwin Guthman had already assembled for a crisis meeting. Provided with more details about Seigenthaler's beating, the attorney general "was possessed by an enormous anger," according to Peter Maas of *Look*, who was allowed to sit in on the meeting, and "looked like he'd just been poleaxed himself. He took it as if he had been down in Montgomery himself and been hit." Kennedy's first reaction was to call Patterson and demand an explanation, but when he did he was told the governor had left town.[25]

The caution that had marked Robert Kennedy's first three months in office now gave way to blind fury. Kennedy decided the federal government now had no other choice but to intervene forcefully. He ordered White to assemble his force of 400 U.S. marshals and federal agents and told him to prepare immediately to leave for Montgomery. Then Kennedy spoke by phone to Seigenthaler, who was dazed but conscious. "You did what was right," Kennedy told his thirty-one-year-old aide.

"Let me give you some advice," Seigenthaler responded, dryly. "Never run for the Governor of Alabama. You couldn't get elected."[26]

Seigenthaler's beating had a transformative effect on Robert Kennedy. It brought home, in the starkest personal terms, the brutality of southern racism. The school crises in New Orleans and Prince Edward County had rattled his conscience. But now one of his closest friends had almost been killed by a segregationist mob. He continued to weigh the political ramifications of various strategies, but now he took a far more uncompromising stance. After ordering up the marshals, Kennedy also initiated legal proceedings that would prevent the KKK and other hate groups from interfering with the freedom riders' right to peaceful interstate travel. Burke Marshall opposed the idea, on the grounds it would "create a very bad precedent legally" that would force the Justice Department to intervene in every crisis where civil rights protesters were attacked. But Kennedy felt that a clear-cut legal basis for action would help justify the decision to dispatch marshals. "I would feel much more comfortable if we were enforcing some sort of court order," he told aides.[27]

Despite his rage, Robert Kennedy's public response to the Montgomery riot was measured. He refused still to publicly condemn the violence or issue any press statements on the crisis. He had apparently cut a private deal with segregationists on Capitol Hill to prevent the rhetoric from reaching a boiling point. As *Business Week* reported later, he had contacted southern lawmakers and urged them to maintain a moderate tone; in exchange, Kennedy promised he would not lend any sign of support for the freedom riders apart from offering them "the protection of the law." Even the announcement that U.S. marshals were about to be dispatched came not in a press statement but in a telegram to Alabama officials. The decision had been made, the telegram read, because it was "necessary to guarantee safe passage in interstate commerce." In private briefings to reporters, Justice Department officials emphasized it was marshals being dispatched not federal troops. Any comparisons with Little Rock, they said, were ludicrous.[28]

At the Montgomery bus terminal that afternoon, the violence continued in waves. In a street near the bus terminal, a group of white teenagers attacked four young blacks unconnected with the freedom rides. One of the attackers poured gasoline on one of the blacks and set his clothes on fire. Inside the terminal itself, fifteen whites pummeled a black man with such fury that he nearly died. Order was only restored when eleven sheriffs mounted on horseback intervened in the riot.[29]

But the calm was fleeting. News arrived at the Justice Department that Martin Luther King now planned to visit Montgomery. He told reporters that he would arrive by air as an "inter-state traveler," thus entitling him, in theory at least, to federal protection. Administration officials tried to persuade King to stay away and at one stage even considered asking Seigenthaler to appeal to the civil rights leader from his hospital bed. But King steadfastly refused.[30]

President Kennedy spent the weekend at his private retreat in Middleburg, Virginia. On Saturday, May 20, he issued his first public statement on the crisis. Rather than appear before the cameras, however, he put his name to a perfunctory written statement. The situation was "a source of deepest concern to me as it must be to the vast majority of the citizens of Alabama and other Americans," the president noted, adding the Justice Department had been instructed to take "all necessary steps." Primary responsibility for protecting the riders, he stressed, lay with the state authorities. Then, in a sentence that implied that the freedom riders bore as much responsibility for the crisis as the violent mobs who attacked them, he urged restraint: "I would also hope that any persons, whether a citizen of Alabama or a visitor there, would refrain from any action which would in any way tend to provoke further outbreaks." The statement ended with a veiled threat to Patterson: "I hope the state and local officials in Alabama will meet their responsibilities. The United States Government intends to meet its." Once the statement was released, the president's press secretary, Pierre Salinger, instructed reporters to direct their questions to Guthman, the attorney general's spokesman. The president, he signaled, was no longer involved.[31]

That Saturday evening, the Justice Department was alive with activity. While White finalized plans for the mobilization of marshals, Kennedy contacted Patterson. When they spoke at 7:30 P.M., Patterson promised that the situation in Montgomery was under control and asked Kennedy to dispatch an administration official with whom he could communicate. Kennedy sarcastically pointed out that Seigenthaler had traveled to Montgomery to do just that.[32]

White arrived in Alabama late that night. He stressed to local reporters that his team of marshals would remain "for a limited period of time." That same night, in a further attempt to prevent the situation from escalating, John Doar tried to obtain the legal injunction banning the KKK from interfering with the freedom riders. With midnight approaching, Doar went to extraordinary lengths to locate Frank M. Johnson, the judge whose rulings during the Montgomery bus boycott had led to the desegregation of the city's services. Doar eventually tracked him down at a lakeside cottage where he had spent the weekend fishing, and Johnson signed the temporary restraining order. From a strict legal standpoint, marshals could now offer federal protection to civil rights activists—a bold departure in policy for the Kennedy administration that had come largely in response to Seigenthaler's savage beating.[33]

By dawn, 400 federal officials assembled at the Maxwell Air Force base on the outskirts of Montgomery, with 250 men on stand-by at Fort Benning in neighboring Georgia. A thousand federal officials were held in reserve. When King landed in Montgomery, he was driven in a high-speed convoy through the streets of the city accompanied by some fifty marshals, a spectacle that made Patterson bristle with anger. He fired off a telegram to the White House to complain that King was being treated "just like he was the President of the United States."[34]

By mid-afternoon, the unfolding drama centered on the First Baptist Church nearby, a fortress-like building with sturdy red-brick walls, where dozens of local blacks were already gathering to hear King speak. In the park opposite, meanwhile, a menacing crowd of whites had assembled, whooping rebel yells and waving Confederate flags. White commanded the U.S. marshals to head toward the church in a fleet of U.S. postal vehicles that had been especially commandeered so as to avoid using military equipment. Acting on Byron White's orders, Chief U.S. Marshal James McShane shouted to the trucks to leave the gates of the Maxwell Air Base immediately, not realizing no marshals were on board. "Oh God," said Justice Department official Louis Oberdorfer. "It's going to be another Bay of Pigs."[35]

Soon some 100 federal marshals managed to form a cordon of protection outside the church, carrying nightsticks, teargas, and sidearms. They watched, with mounting concern, as the mood became more menacing. By sunset, some 3,000 whites had gathered, yelling "Nigger King" and hurling the occasional missile toward the church. From his makeshift command post at Maxwell Air Force base, White opened a line of communication with the Justice Department, where the attorney general's office, strewn with maps and charts, looked like a military command center. It would be a long night.[36]

After dark, the mob grew more restless. They threw a volley of bricks, Molotov cocktails, and rocks at the church's stained-glass windows and set fire to a car parked nearby. Then the mob surged forward, forcing the marshals to fire teargas into the air. From inside the church, King called Robert Kennedy to plead for increased federal protection. The mood in the sanctuary was becoming more strained, since the mob was now close enough to the church to thump on its doors and walls. Some male members of the congregation took up positions at the back of the church, openly brandishing knives and guns, ready to fire on the mob if it breached the marshals' lines.

Finally, White gave the order for the insertion of more marshals, whose arrival was heralded by a volley of teargas, which shrouded the church in a dense, foggy mist. There was a brief lull in the violence, but then the mob converged on the church once again. They managed to break open one of its heavy wooden doors, spreading panic through the congregation. In an instant, a line of marshals, who had entered the church through the basement, burst past the packed pews, and somehow managed to repel the rioters. Moments later, a brick crashed through the window, striking an elderly man on the head and littering the sanctuary with shards of broken glass. Pungent clouds of teargas drifted in through the broken window, and children were rushed downstairs to the crypt, while those left in the sanctuary covered their faces with handkerchiefs.

With the marshals' supplies of teargas almost exhausted, Robert Kennedy started laying the groundwork for the insertion of federal troops, though he hoped fervently they would not be needed. First, he contacted the Pentagon, where Army Secretary Cyrus Vance agreed to place a contingent of troops on stand-by at Fort Benning, Georgia, ready to be flown to Alabama. Then he tried to reach Patterson, who refused to take his calls. Fearing a massacre, Kennedy contacted his brother in Middleburg to ask permission to mobilize troops. President Kennedy withheld the authorization. He was worried about escalating the conflict still further, and he claimed that the procedural course of action was by no means clear. Was it unconstitutional to move troops before he had signed a presidential proclamation? If so, the military operation would have to be delayed for well over an hour, while a helicopter flew the requisite paperwork to Middleburg. Marshall immediately went to work on the legal questions, while JFK considered one of the most arduous decisions of his fledgling presidency. Even as the mob was on the verge of overrunning the church, with almost certain loss of life, Kennedy remained disinclined to authorize the use of federal force.[37]

Before reaching a final determination, Kennedy was rescued by news from Montgomery. Patterson had just declared martial law at nine P.M. Forty minutes later, the first group of Alabama National Guardsmen arrived at the church, marching in double time with bayonets fixed. White immediately ordered McShane to place the marshals under National Guard control, at which point the local commander ordered them to evacuate the scene. As the federal marshals started to leave, many of the rioters began to drift away. The "Battle of First Baptist" was seemingly at an end.

Shortly after ten o'clock, the mass meeting finally began, culminating in an emotionally charged sermon by King. It included severe words for the Kennedy White House. "Unless the Federal government acts forthrightly in the South to assure every citizen his constitutional rights," he warned, "we will be plunged into a dark abyss of chaos. The federal government must not stand by while bloodthirsty mobs beat non-violent students with impunity." With cries of "Amen" and "Praise God," the congregation roared in approval.[38]

When members of the congregation attempted to leave the church, however, they were blocked by Alabama National Guardsmen. Moments later, Adjutant General Henry Graham, the officer in command, strode to the front of the sanctuary and announced that the congregation would probably be held inside until the morning, since it was too dangerous to exit. The marshals had left; the Alabama National Guard was in control. Outraged at the withdrawal of marshals, King complained to Robert Kennedy. "My people are concerned for their safety," he explained. "Patterson's National Guard won't protect us." Kennedy harbored misgivings about Patterson, but he trusted General Graham. And he seemed irritated that King had such little faith in his judgment.

"Now, Reverend, don't tell me that," he replied, curtly. "You know just as well as I do that if it hadn't have been for the United States marshals you'd be as dead as Kelsey's nuts right now." King grudgingly accepted the attorney general's assurances.[39]

A few minutes later, Patterson finally contacted the attorney general, breaking their forty-eight-hour silence. "You got yourself a fight," shouted Patterson. "You got yourself what you wanted. And you've got the National Guard called out, and martial law. And that's what you wanted." Unwilling to listen to Patterson's tirade, Kennedy interrupted. He tried to focus the conversation on the more urgent question of precisely when the congregation could leave. Patterson refused to say, nor would he guarantee King's safety.

Kennedy exploded. "Now John. You can say that on television. You can tell that to the people of Alabama, John, but don't tell me that. Don't tell me that, John. I don't believe that, John. Have General Graham call me. I want him to say it to me. I want to hear a general of the United States army say he can't protect Martin Luther King."

"You're destroying us politically," countered Patterson. But Kennedy was unsympathetic: "John, it's more important that these people in the church survive physically than for us to survive politically."[40]

Throughout the evening, the president remained in Middleburg, relieved that he had not had to authorize the use of federal troops. But he had since heard from William Orrick, a Justice Department official in Montgomery, that local FBI agents had witnessed the attacks and done nothing to stop them. He was so angry at the news that shortly after midnight he contacted FBI Director J. Edgar Hoover to complain. The very next morning, under orders from Hoover, four men were arrested in connection with the Anniston firebombing. Many Justice Department officials urged that the suspects be charged under U.S. Criminal Code 242 for willfully depriving the protesters of their civil rights. But they were charged with the lesser offense of damaging vehicles used in interstate commerce. Had the Justice Department prosecuted the alleged firebombers under the U.S. Criminal Code 242 it would have set the Justice Department on a bold new path, since logically it would have extended federal protection to every civil rights protester. The Justice Department was reluctant to set that precedent.[41]

In Washington that Monday morning, the president assembled his Justice Department team for a forty-five-minute meeting. The goal was to bring the crisis to a swift conclusion. Though there was widespread support in Congress for the deployment of U.S. marshals, the president wanted to extricate them as quickly as possible, even if, as seemed likely, the Freedom Rides continued. Robert Kennedy was in total agreement and ruled out the possibility of marshals escorting the protesters as far as New Orleans. Even if they were arrested by local police officers, he recommended against government intervention. Later, when asked what would happen if the freedom riders were arrested by local authorities, he flippantly replied, "That would be a matter between the freedom riders and local officials. I'm sure they would be represented by competent counsel."[42]

The administration was desperate to contain the political fallout from the weekend's events. To that end, Robert Kennedy wrote to every member of Alabama's congressional delegation, assuring them that marshals had been introduced only as "a last resort" and with "great reluctance." Furthermore, the administration had "no intention of permitting the Marshals to remain . . . a minute longer than is necessary." Offering further succor, he emphasized the close cooperation between federal and state authorities and indicated, disingenuously, that the administration had never considered the possibility of inserting federal troops. As part of its political strategy, the administration deliberately deflected attention away from the president and onto the Justice Department. As one columnist noted, it was an "equivocal line of conduct [to] those with a literal memory of Mr. Kennedy's campaign statements." Liberal Republicans, led by Senator Kenneth Keating of New York, called for a "strong statement" from the president about the Freedom Rides. There was no response from the White House, and his aides canceled a presummit press conference to shield Kennedy from potentially hostile questioning. To project an air of normalcy, the president pushed ahead with a full schedule of events.[43]

By coincidence that Monday, Kennedy was scheduled to meet with the Peace Corps's National Advisory Council, a liberal-minded group including Harry Belafonte, Eugene Rostow, the dean of Yale Law School, and Benjamin Mays, president of Morehouse College. All were dismayed by Kennedy's refusal to speak out about the violence in the South. "Mr. President, I know how much you're doing in civil rights," ventured Belafonte. "I deeply respect your leadership in civil rights. I trust you in civil rights. And I know all these other things are going on. But perhaps you could say something a little more about the Freedom Riders." Rostow was bolder and called upon Kennedy to issue an emphatic statement demanding the desegregation of all public accommodations. Taken aback by the force of criticism, Kennedy asked if they had read his comments on the crisis in the morning paper (the innocuous statement released by Salinger over the weekend). The president promised it would alleviate their concerns.[44]

As Wofford ushered the group out, a Secret Service agent rushed up behind and summoned him to the Oval Office. "Who the hell was that man with Harry Belafonte?" Kennedy shouted. Wofford explained that Eugene Rostow was the brother of Walt Rostow, one of his chief foreign policy advisers. "Well, what in the world does he think I should do?" he asked indignantly. "Doesn't he know I've done more for civil rights than any President in American history? How could any man have done more than I've done?"[45]

On Tuesday morning, the freedom riders decided to resume their protest. King, however, turned down an invitation to join them on the bus leaving Montgomery. "I think I should choose the time and place of my Golgotha," he said, haltingly, a statement that drew scorn from SNCC activists, who thought it betrayed cowardice. Meanwhile, Robert Kennedy threw his energies into fashioning an agreement with state officials in Alabama and Mississippi to provide local protection. First off, Burke Marshall contacted state officials in Jackson, but when that failed the attorney general approached Eastland. Eager to avoid a recurrence of the Alabama violence, which he feared had brought only shame on the South, Eastland was open to a deal. Over the course of some twenty phone calls he and Kennedy agreed to the broad outline of a plan. It was a simple quid pro quo: Eastland would guarantee the protection of the riders along the 258-mile route between Montgomery and Jackson, but only on condition that the Justice Department allowed local police to arrest the protesters on arrival. Though uncomfortable with the idea that the protesters would be arrested, Kennedy's desire to end the crisis was paramount. He therefore accepted Eastland's terms. So, too, did Mississippi Governor Ross Barnett. Patterson eventually signed on as well.[46]

By dawn that Wednesday morning, some 300 Alabama National Guardsmen had surrounded the Trailways bus terminal. The freedom riders arrived at seven A.M., their faces marked with cuts and bruises. After buying their tickets, they wandered through to the waiting room, with King at their side, where they successfully ordered coffee and breakfast, thus becoming the first blacks ever to be served, according to the snack bar's manager. Then the riders boarded the bus, which pulled out of the terminal escorted by over forty vehicles, with two helicopters and three U.S. Border Patrol aircraft circling overhead. At Scratch Hill, a town straddling the state border, the escort duty passed from the Alabama troopers to a Mississippi contingent, which accompanied them on the ninety-mile journey to Jackson.[47]

On arrival in Jackson, the riders were arrested. Under state laws passed in response to the sit-ins, blacks could be arrested for "refusing to disperse and move on when ordered to do so by any law enforcement official." So when the protesters refused to move along, they were bundled into paddy wagons and driven off to jail. Barnett was jubilant. "I feel wonderful," he told reporters. "The nation had its eyes on Mississippi today, and I think we showed them that we could handle our own affairs in an orderly manner." Patterson was delighted, too, and announced to reporters that, despite their disagreements over the past twenty-four hours, he still considered the president a personal friend. As Barnett and Patterson recognized, the arrests marked a pivotal moment. Washington had signaled that segregation could remain intact, free from federal interference, if public order was maintained. Barnett took note. Fifteen months later, over the desegregation of the University of Mississippi, he famously defied the Kennedy brothers, confidently believing they lacked the determination or courage to enforce federal court orders. Nor did it go unnoticed in Albany, Georgia, soon the focus for a fresh round of protests, where city officials planned to emulate Barnett's tactic of mass arrests. Marshall admitted later the arrests "were unconstitutional . . . without any question," since they violated the Fourteenth Amendment. But they served the immediate needs of the Justice Department, which simply wanted to put an end to the protests without further federal involvement.[48]

The welcome news of a smooth handover at the Alabama/Mississippi border prompted Robert Kennedy to issue his first official public statement of the entire crisis. In it, he praised state authorities for protecting the riders and indicated that the federal government's short-lived role in the crisis was about to end: "The evidence at this time is that these officials fully intend to see that law and order is maintained and that any new outbreaks of mob violence will be controlled by local law enforcement officials." Then he offered an explanation for federal intervention. "The Federal government's responsibility is quite clear in this situation," he noted. "Our obligation is to protect interstate travelers and maintain law and order only when local authorities are unable and unwilling to do so." The attorney general appealed to the patriotism of the riders and the rioters. "I think we should all bear in mind that the President is about to embark on a mission of great importance," he added. "Whatever we do in the United States at this time, which brings or causes discredit on our country, can be harmful to his mission." As his brother had in his statement from Middleburg the previous weekend, Robert Kennedy seemed to imply that the freedom rides and their assailants bore equal responsibility for the crisis.[49]

Once the freedom riders had left Alabama, the attorney general decided to move against law enforcement officials in Montgomery and Birmingham. He did not want them to go unpunished for their complicity in the attacks. He instructed Justice Department officials to file suit against them in the U.S. District Court in Montgomery, citing their failure and refusal to provide adequate police protection "for persons traveling in interstate commerce through their cities." The most noteworthy name on the list was Bull Connor. It also included Montgomery Public Safety Commissioner Lester Sullivan. Kennedy was clearly taking a risk that his actions might inflame tensions further, and it is hard to disentangle the attorney general's motives in prosecuting those officials so aggressively. Kennedy was not going beyond mainstream opinion, however—even leading southern Democrats thought Connor should face censure, with Ervin agreeing they should receive "adequate public attention." In June 1961, the NAACP Legal Defense and Educational Fund sought to enjoin the Jackson prosecutions, a move that the Justice Department supported with an amicus brief. But supporting the action placed the attorney general in a strangely anomalous position, since he had sanctioned the arrests in the first place. And, in any case, in December the NAACP's motion to "stay"—or delay—the prosecutions was ultimately denied.[50]

The Justice Department hoped the Jackson arrests would bring the immediate crisis to an end. But midway through the morning, news came from Montgomery that a second group of freedom riders was determined to board the Trailways service to Jackson. For the past forty-eight hours, Robert Kennedy's calculations had been based on only one group of protesters making the journey. The prospect of a second wave threatened to derail the whole plan. Fortunately, the Montgomery authorities had anticipated the move and had left the security cordon in place at the bus terminal. So when the second bus pulled out it was escorted by virtually the same number of squad cars and jeeps as the first.

In Washington, officials were only just learning the identity of the new freedom riders, which included John Lewis and William Sloane Coffin, Jr., the thirty-six-year-old chaplain of Yale University. His presence was certain to generate more headlines. Robert Kennedy tempered his anger with humor, telling aides, "Those people at Yale are sore at Harvard for taking over the country, and now they're trying to get back at us." But as the day went on, his frustrations grew to the point where he decided to issue a second written statement to reporters, blasting Coffin and his colleagues. "A very difficult condition exists now in the States of Mississippi and Alabama," it began. "Besides the groups of Freedom Riders traveling through these states, there are curiosity seekers, publicity seekers and others who are seeking to serve their own causes." The statement also commended law enforcement officials in Alabama and Mississippi, who were "meeting the test today, but [whose] job is becoming increasingly difficult." Then the attorney general called for a "cooling off period," an immediate postponement of any further rides.[51]

Thrilled by its southern-friendly tone, Patterson wholeheartedly endorsed the statement, telling reporters it was "the first time the federal government has displayed any common sense in some days." W. J. Simmons of the Mississippi White Citizens' Council echoed his comments and commended Kennedy on "a display of common sense." "With your continued help in keeping the agitators away," he wired the attorney general, "Mississippi will continue to enjoy peaceful race relations." In other words, segregation would remain in place.[52]

James Farmer, meanwhile, was livid. "We had been cooling off for 100 years," he complained. "If we got any cooler we'd be in a deep freeze." So, too, were the arrested freedom riders held at Jackson jailhouse, who responded by refusing bail and threatening hunger strikes. When Robert Kennedy telephoned King to find out how long they planned to remain in jail, he was told they would hold out until their aims were met. "That is not going to have the slightest effect on what the government is going to do in this field or any other," snapped Kennedy, adopting a tougher line with King than with Barnett. "The fact that they stay in jail is not going to have the slightest effect on me."

"Perhaps it would help if students came down here by the hundreds—by the hundreds of thousands," threatened King.

"Don't make statements that sound like a threat," Kennedy responded icily. "That's not the way to deal with us."

Astonished by the attorney general's dismissive remarks, King considered it necessary to explain the fundamentals of their crusade. "Ours is a way out," he said. "Creative, moral and non-violent. It is not tied to black supremacy or Communism but to the plight of the oppressed. It can save the soul of America." It was impossible to make gains, he said, without applying pressure, but his tactics would always be "moral, legal and peaceful." Kennedy relented slightly and acknowledged that the problems facing black Americans went far beyond the protest in Jackson. He admitted, too, they could only be resolved "by strong federal action."[53]

At that point, King expressed appreciation for the administration's actions to date but intimated they were wholly inadequate. While older activists, like his father, had been content with gradualism, younger protesters, himself included, "feel the need of being free now!"[54]

The conversation lasted an hour, and by its end Kennedy was exasperated. Afterwards, he called Wofford to vent. "This is too much," he complained. "I wonder whether they have the best interest of their country at heart. Do they know that one of them is against the atomic bomb—yes, he even picketed against it in jail! The President is going abroad and this is all embarrassing him." Speaking to a *Washington Post* reporter later on, he betrayed the same bitterness. "It took a lot of guts for the first group to go," he complained. "But not much for the others." They were just about the "safest people in America" and merely providing "good propaganda for America's enemies." In pique, Kennedy withdrew some 500 marshals from Montgomery, an eighty-five-percent reduction in manpower, thereby sending an unmistakable signal that protesters could no longer rely on federal protection.[55]

It had been a long day for the attorney general—arguably his most traumatic since taking office—and he ended it in his Justice Department office in bare feet, wearing only shorts and a dressing gown. He had never finished dressing for a dinner earlier in the evening. Around midnight, he sat with two aides, drinking whiskey. "These situations are something we are going to have to live with," Kennedy lamented. "This is going on and on."[56]

At the White House that Wednesday night, the president celebrated his forty-fourth birthday, but much of the evening was spent finishing a "second state of the union." Grandly entitled a "Special Message on Urgent National Needs," it was organized around four broad themes: economic growth, national defense, increased foreign aid, and the bold galactic adventure of landing a man on the moon and returning him safely to earth within the next ten years. At the heart of his speech lay what he called his "Freedom Doctrine," an ambitious scheme to halt the spread of communism and strengthen democracies around the globe. Despite the tumultuous events of the past ten days in Alabama and Mississippi, Kennedy had no intention of mentioning civil rights. Wofford and Marshall were particularly disappointed by this omission. Both believed the president should condemn the Alabama mob, or, at the very least, offer vocal support for the freedom riders. But the president was unyielding.[57]

Listening to the speech the next day, Theodore Hesburgh was dumbfounded. "Personally, I don't care if the United States gets the first man on the moon," he told Wofford, "if . . . we dawdle along here on our corner of the earth, nursing our prejudices, flouting our magnificent Constitution, ignoring the central moral problem of our times, and appearing hypocrites to the world." Wofford agreed and decided to redouble his efforts to persuade the president to issue some kind of statement before leaving for Europe. "The only effective time for such moral leadership is during an occasion of moral crisis," he said. "This is a time when your words would mean the most." But the president left for his Vienna Summit meeting with Khrushchev without commenting any further on the crisis.[58]

On the president's return from Europe, Wofford pressed once more for a "few stout words" about civil rights as part of a television address that JFK planned to deliver on June 6. He suggested that it "would fit the theme of strength and unity required to meet the world crisis." Marshall also agreed that a presidential statement would be "very useful." Once again, however, Kennedy refused. His address focused exclusively on the perilous state of East-West relations. Kennedy's only public remarks on the Freedom Rides crisis came at a press conference in July, long after the immediate crisis was over. Even then his comments were willfully dispassionate: "I think the Attorney General has made it clear, that we believe that everyone who travels, for whatever reason they travel, should enjoy the full constitutional protection given to them by the law and by the Constitution. They should be able to move freely in interstate commerce."[59]

By the end of May, public attention had shifted from Mississippi and Alabama, even though many freedom riders remained in jail. In calling on protesters to observe a cooling-off period, RFK had helped cultivate a climate of opinion in which protesters rather than segregationists were branded the main troublemakers. The press began to question the tactics of the freedom riders and accused them of cynically fomenting trouble. In June, a Gallup poll suggested sixty-four percent of the American people disapproved of the Freedom Rides, a poll often cited as evidence that the civil rights movement lacked widespread public support. But in fact the evidence is more ambiguous. Nationally, seventy percent of poll respondents indicated their support for the president's decision to use marshals in Montgomery. In the South, the figure was fifty percent— only twenty-nine percent were against the president's action. No doubt some southerners were pleased that marshals rather than troops had been inserted, and viewed the tactic as an admirable display of restraint on Kennedy's part. Still, the national figure indicated that an overwhelming majority of Americans were prepared to back federal action to ensure the safety of black protesters.[60]

In Congress, too, there was strong bipartisan support for the federal protection of the riders. According to Joseph Clark, eighty senators were prepared to sign a Republican-sponsored resolution congratulating the president on the decision to insert marshals, indicating strong bipartisan support for a muscular approach (southerners ultimately blocked the resolution from coming to a vote). Wofford hoped the president would seize the opportunity to mobilize public support for an aggressive assault on segregation. But the administration recoiled.

Robert Kennedy was, however, sufficiently troubled by the conflagration that he moved to address directly the segregation of interstate bus terminals in the South. According to an FBI study, a third of southern terminals continued to display "Whites Only" signs, which was in clear contravention of the Supreme Court's December ruling in *Boynton*. After consulting Nicholas Katzenbach at the Office of Legal Counsel, Kennedy decided that the Justice Department should lean on the Interstate Commerce Commission (ICC) to issue a clearly worded ruling calling for the integration of bus terminals. Even though the ICC was a notoriously torpid and conservative bureaucracy, which often took years to issue important directives, Kennedy and Marshall undertook an intense, behind-the-scenes lobbying campaign, and the order was issued less than three months later. Put into action on September 22, 1961, it outlawed segregation in bus terminals used by travelers passing between states and ruled that seating in interstate buses should also be integrated.[61]

The ICC ruling represented a significant gain for the civil rights movement, but even though the measure had been initiated by Robert Kennedy, the ad-

The "Kennedy teas" proved dramatically successful in attracting the support of white housewives during Massachusetts Senate races. So the same technique was eventually used with blacks. Herbert Tucker (far right), one of Kennedy's early black advisers, looks on admiringly, at this event in 1958. (Hotel Photo Service/John F. Kennedy Presidential Library and Museum, Boston)

Vel Phillips was the first black female ever to win election to the DNC and a civil rights activist in the crucial primary state of Wisconsin. Kennedy tried for two years to win her endorsement and had a difficult time persuading Phillips that he had not sold out to the south during the 1957 civil rights debate. (Bettmann/Corbis)

An influential adviser during the 1960 campaign, Harris Wofford eventually became Kennedy's "point man" on civil rights. But after a year at the White House, he became increasingly dispirited by the president's policies and asked to be transferred to the Peace Corps. (Condé Nest Archive/Corbis)

Kennedy standing alongside black adviser, Frank Reeves at the launch of the Civil Rights Section in August 1960. Reeves traveled with the candidate throughout the presidential campaign and soon became known as "Exhibit One." Despite his prominence during the campaign, Reeves was quickly sidelined after the election. (Bettmann/Corbis)

Former newspaperman Louis Martin (right) became the Kennedy campaign's most influential black adviser during the 1960 presidential race. But after the election, he was given a post at the Democratic National Committee rather than a position at the White House and was rarely granted access to the president. This Oval Office meeting took place in August 1962, shortly before Augustus Hawkins (center) won election to the House of Representatives, thus becoming the fifth black Democratic lawmaker in Congress. (Robert Knudsen/John F. Kennedy Presidential Library and Museum, Boston)

Kennedy invited a string of black celebrities to the White House, from the boxing heavyweight champion Floyd Patterson to Marian Anderson, the world famous contralto. He also made sure Anderson sang at his inauguration, so that a black took a prominent part. These kinds of gestures burnished his reputation among black voters, but failed to impress civil rights leaders. (Abbie Rowe/John F. Kennedy Presidential Library and Museum, Boston)

Harlem's preacher politician Congressman Adam Clayton Powell, Jr., had to be bribed during the 1960 campaign to support the Democratic ticket. In early 1961, he then had to be strong-armed by administration officials into dropping his eponymous "Powell Amendment," a measure that would have blocked federal funding from segregationist states. (Bettmann/Corbis)

Housing expert Robert Weaver was the most senior of Kennedy's black appointees. After hearings before the Senate, he was confirmed as the head of the Housing and Home Finance Agency. But Kennedy's attempt to elevate him to the cabinet, as head of a new Department of Urban Affairs, ended in failure early in 1962. (Bettmann/Corbis)

Kennedy only rarely agreed to meet the commissioners of the United States Commission on Civil Rights (CRC), a body created by the 1957 Civil Rights Act to study the problem of racial discrimination. The President repeatedly clashed with the CRC and derided their reports, which were often critical of administration policy. (Abbie Rowe/John F. Kennedy Presidential Library and Museum, Boston)

Mindful that the newly decolonized African continent was fast becoming an important Cold War battlefield, Kennedy was much more welcoming to visiting African leaders on their visits to Washington than leaders of the American civil rights movement. On March 20, 1962, he laid on a carefully integrated presidential honor guard for the arrival of Sylvanus Olympio, the President of the Togolese Republic. (Abbie Rowe/John F. Kennedy Presidential Library and Museum, Boston)

Kennedy was reluctant to become personally involved in the celebrations marking the 100th anniversary of the Emancipation Proclamation in January 1963. But he finally agreed to hold a White House reception on February 12, Lincoln's birthday. The aim was to host more blacks at the White House on a single evening than in its entire history. (Robert Knudsen/John F. Kennedy Presidential Library and Museum, Boston)

This Associated Press photograph was taken in Birmingham, Alabama, on May 3, 1963. It provided the Reverend Dr. Martin Luther King, Jr. with a graphic snapshot of the brute force of southern racism. The following morning, when the image appeared on the front pages of newspapers, Kennedy called it a "terrible picture" but did not think it would make it any easier to persuade Congress to enact civil rights legislation. (Associated Press)

After the Birmingham crisis in the spring of 1963, Attorney General Robert Kennedy and Burke Marshall, the head of the Justice Department Civil Rights Division, both realized the administration would have to introduce far-reaching legislation. Marshall warned the President that in previous racial crises, "we had a white mob against a Negro. Here we have a Negro mob against whites." (Bettmann/Corbis)

In his televised address on June 11, Kennedy described civil rights as a moral issue that was "as old as the scriptures" and "as clear as the American Constitution." It was by far his strongest civil rights speech, which he delivered with Andrew Hatcher, his deputy press secretary, at his side (though not in view of the camera). (Abbie Rowe/John F. Kennedy Presidential Library and Museum, Boston)

Kennedy chose not to attend the funeral of the murdered civil rights activist Medgar Evers, but invited his family to the White House after the ceremony at Arlington National Cemetery had finished. Myrlie Evers was accompanied by her two eldest children and her brother-in-law Charles Evers. It was the first time Kennedy had invited victims of segregationist violence to the White House. (Cecil Stoughton/John F. Kennedy Presidential Library and Museum, Boston)

During the summer of 1963, Kennedy hosted eleven separate White House meetings where he addressed over 1,600 business, political, and community leaders. The central aim was to persuade participants to form biracial committees in their local communities that would help repair frayed social ties between blacks and whites. (Abbie Rowe/John F. Kennedy Presidential Library and Museum, Boston)

SNCC leader John Lewis planned to deliver an incendiary speech at the March on Washington, but it was heavily edited after complaints from fellow black leaders, churchmen, and Kennedy administration officials. He omitted the line: "I want to know: which side is the federal government on?" (Bettmann/Corbis)

The Kennedy administration ordered the biggest peacetime military buildup in American history, because of fears that the March on Washington could turn violent. The President was also concerned that unruly protesters might "shit" on the Washington Monument. (Bettmann/Corbis)

Kennedy welcomed leaders of the March on Washington to the White House, after the demonstration had passed peacefully. He greeted them with a cheery "I Have a Dream," the captivating refrain used by King at the climax of his speech. (Abbie Rowe/John F. Kennedy Presidential Library and Museum, Boston)

Kennedy's coffin lies in the Capitol Rotunda, watched over by an integrated honor guard. But the Kennedy family failed to invite leading civil rights leaders to the late President's funeral, and Martin Luther King watched from the sidewalk. (Wally McNamee/Corbis)

ministration was determined to downplay it. Before the ruling, Wofford tried to prod the president into making a presidential statement welcoming the new regulations, but he refused. The administration also rebuffed the original free-dom riders when they asked for a presidential meeting. And the administration's enforcement of the order was ultimately half-hearted. As soon as the freedom riders crossed from Alabama into Mississippi, segregation returned immediately to the transportation facilities in Birmingham and Montgomery.[62]

In McComb, Mississippi, where the ICC ruling was blatantly ignored, pro-testers launched fresh demonstrations at the Greyhound terminal in August, but the Justice Department refused to offer protection when they came under assault from local segregationists. Over the weekend of August 26 and 27, when rioting erupted after a mob of white segregationists, bearing banners reading "Open Season on Coons," attacked a group of freedom riders in Monroe, North Carolina, policing was left to the local authorities, even though the situation was clearly beyond their control. From Montgomery, Patterson wired the attor-ney general urging him not to send in U.S. marshals, "but to leave North Car-olina alone and let them handle their own domestic matters." Robert Kennedy and Burke Marshall agreed. In the absence of federal protection, local blacks, led by the militant firebrand Robert F. Williams, armed themselves with pistols, a shotgun, and a military semiautomatic carbine.[63]

Much later in the year, the administration was equally craven in its handling of demonstrations in Albany, Georgia. On November 1, SNCC activists tar-geted the local bus terminal, where waiting rooms remained segregated even after the ICC ruling came into effect. But the great misfortune of the Albany Movement, as the loose coalition of SNCC, CORE, and SCLC activists came to be known, was to come up against Laurie Pritchett, the city's chief of police. Pritchett had studied the Gandhian philosophy of nonviolence, and he realized after revisiting the events of the spring in Alabama and Mississippi that the administration would only retaliate in the case of extreme violence. Just as Pritchett predicted, even though hundreds of protesters were jailed between late November and the end of December, King most prominent among them, Robert Kennedy announced a "hands off policy" from the Justice Department. The demonstrations had not spilled over into rioting. Although Robert Kennedy worked frantically behind the scenes to secure King's release, fearing the political consequences of his continued incarceration over the Christmas holidays, he failed to exert any equivalent effort to settle the protesters' griev-ances. Once King was free, Robert Kennedy even sent a telegram to Albany's mayor, Asa Kelley, congratulating him on his handling of the crisis—despite the fact that the city's transportation facilities remained segregated, in defiance of the ICC ruling. In ebullient mood, Kelley and Pritchett invited reporters for a celebratory meal at a segregated country club. Brandishing his telegram from Washington, Kelley rejoiced in the failures of the Albany Movement.[64]

After their successes in Alabama, Mississippi, and Georgia, segregationist hard-liners seemed even more determined to uphold the southern way of life. "I'm a segregationist," crowed Governor Patterson. "And I tell you 98% of the people down here feel the way I do. There shouldn't be any battles over rights. There shouldn't even be court fights." Likewise in Mississippi, segregation laws were also as strictly enforced as ever. After seeing off the freedom riders, Barnett called a celebratory press conference on May 25 at which he gleefully informed reporters that state authorities planned to "enforce all the laws of the state when efforts are made to violate them," adding that the segregationist code would remain "paramount." Right after the election, even die-hard segregationists had anticipated their ultimate defeat. Nine months later, the inaction of the Kennedy brothers had fueled a culture of impunity among southern officeholders like Barnett and Patterson. The administration's diffident response to the Freedom Rides had taught them that so long as they maintained public order, they could rely on the federal government to stand aside, even as they denied blacks their most basic civil rights. In August, Patterson expressed his gratitude in a telegram to the attorney general: "I wish to commend you for your strong stand for good law enforcement and the position that you have taken against the so-called freedom riders, who are nothing more than outside racial agitators and law violators."[65]

Throughout the crisis, Robert Kennedy's actions spoke of an almost bewildering ambivalence. He had sought to punish Bull Connor and had pushed for the ICC ruling. But he had also cut a flagrantly illegal deal with Eastland and had temporized throughout the crisis in his public statements—most notably in calling for a cooling-off period rather than asking for a straightforward cessation of violence on the part of segregationists. After his brother's assassination, he reflected on his thinking at the time: "Now maybe [desegregation is] going to take a decade and maybe a lot of people are going to be killed in the meantime; and I think that's unfortunate. But in the long run I think it's best for the health of the country and the stability of this system; and it's the best way to proceed."[66]

What the president was thinking is even less clear. Throughout the crisis, he had remained almost entirely silent.

CHAPTER 17

❧

The One-sided Bargain

While John Kennedy believed that his moderate approach would enable peaceful, if slow, reform, it in fact had the unintended consequence of radicalizing black activists. Younger blacks in particular were growing tired not only with the administration but with moderate civil rights groups, like the NAACP, that abetted its gradualism. Thurgood Marshall noticed the shifting mood when he remarked in June 1961, "The kids are serving notice on us that we're moving too slow. They're not content with all this talking." Writing in April, the black journalist Julian Mayfield observed an angrier energy in the movement: "It can be heard in the conversations of black intellectuals and students from the south who regard the efforts of the NAACP, the Urban League, and most religious and civic leaders with either disdain or despair, in the belief they are doing too little, too timidly, too late." Between May 1961 and December 1962, membership of CORE, a far more radical organization than the NAACP, doubled from 26,000 to 52,000, and the organization intensified its campaign by sending field secretaries into the Deep South cities of Jackson, New Orleans, and Montgomery. Many activists openly questioned the tactic of nonviolent protest, and three of CORE's chapters—Hartford, New Orleans, and Baltimore—established close ties with the Nation of Islam. Their members sympathized strongly with its separatist message. Even the NAACP, a civil rights organization dominated by middle-class blacks, became more combative. It placed heightened emphasis on boycotts and direct action. That summer it announced a statewide campaign in Florida to test compliance with the *Boynton* ruling, an important tactical shift for an organization that had long preferred court action over street-based protests.[1]

The radicalization of young protesters became a pressing concern for members of the Sub-Cabinet Group on Civil Rights. When the group met on June 16, its first meeting since the Alabama violence, Jack Conway, an official at the

Housing and Home Finance Agency (HHFA), warned that the battle against segregation had "caught fire" on student campuses. Richard Murphy, the assistant postmaster general, feared that there would be no more "cooling off"—unless the federal government deployed its full power to promote equal rights, he warned, young black activists would become even more restless. Burke Marshall worried that black activists wildly overestimated the capacity of the federal government to settle their grievances: "The effect of that lack of understanding on their part, and a corresponding lack of ability to act effectively and immediately on our part is going to create a series of problems over a long period of time until the segregation is eliminated."[2]

Faced with the threat of rising militancy, Marshall proposed at the June meeting that the administration should channel civil rights activists away from street protests and toward litigation-based reform. He suggested a government-sponsored voter registration campaign. Marshall had already raised the possibility of a registration drive with CORE, the SCLC, and SNCC earlier that month. Like Robert Kennedy, Marshall believed that if blacks registered in sufficient numbers, southern politicians would be forced to take more moderate positions on racial issues. To Marshall's surprise, the young activists had responded favorably to his proposal. Many had taken Marshall's advocacy as an indication that the Justice Department was offering federal protection for voting rights workers. Delighted by this apparent turnaround in administration policy, Wiley Branton of the Southern Regional Council believed "the Justice Department would take all necessary steps to protect federal or constitutional rights."[3]

Justice Department officials arranged a secret meeting on June 16 between Robert Kennedy and the members of the Freedom Riders Coordinating Committee. Kennedy offered them a deal: If protesters focused on voting rights, the administration would offer support and protection. If, on the other hand, they persisted with street-based protests, they would not enjoy equivalent backing. SNCC activist Charles Sherrod sensed immediately that the administration was attempting to steer the civil rights movement in a more moderate direction. "You are a public official, sir," he said, approaching the attorney general with such menace that Wyatt Tee Walker of the SCLC feared he might actually punch him. "It's not your responsibility before God or under the law to tell us how to honor our constitutional rights. It's your job to protect us when we do." Undeterred, Kennedy restated his case: that the registration campaign would not have the eye-catching impact of the Freedom Rides, but it would ultimately accomplish more. In subsequent meetings, Wofford came up with a pithier formulation: Southern jails could be filled either with freedom riders or noncompliant voting officials.[4]

The Voter Education Project—or VEP, as it came to be known—was fast taking shape. The Justice Department spent much of the early summer providing the project with a solid financial footing. To that end, Kennedy explored the possibility of gaining tax-exempt status for the project from the Internal Revenue Service and sought funding from three philanthropic organizations. By the end of July, Marshall and Wofford felt confident enough to put the plan before the leaders of the major civil rights organizations.

At an all-day meeting in New York on July 28, Justice Department officials pitched their proposal to the leaders of the main civil rights groups. Wilkins expressed concerns that voter registration might distract from school desegregation, which had been the focus of the NAACP campaign for over a decade. James Farmer feared CORE might lose momentum just as it was beginning to rival the NAACP. But over the course of the late summer Wilkins's concerns abated, especially after pledges of additional financial support came through. By late August, even SNCC decided to participate—though not for the reasons Marshall and Kennedy laid out. James Forman, the organization's first executive director, thought that the voter registration campaign would raise black political consciousness even further and precipitate precisely the kind of racial confrontations the Justice Department hoped to avert. Farmer ultimately agreed for much the same reason—rather than killing the movement, the administration might inadvertently be fomenting the very kind of explosive standoff that would force it to accelerate the pace of reform.[5]

The Voter Education Project was officially launched in January 1962. It enjoyed the active support of all five major civil rights organizations—the NAACP, CORE, SNCC, the SCLC, and the National Urban League. It was the first time they had collaborated in such an extended campaign. While there was never any suggestion that Justice Department officials would actively participate in the VEP, in its early stages there was a surprisingly close degree of cooperation. At one point, John Doar invited SNCC representatives to his office, where he showed them a map of southern counties studded with pins to indicate where the Justice Department thought the VEP should first concentrate. Doar and Marshall even handed out their office and home phone numbers to black registration workers (a gesture they quickly came to regret, because activists interpreted it as an unmistakable sign the federal government was offering round-the-clock protection).[6]

But the Justice Department could not control the activists. Almost from the outset, the more radical elements within the various civil right organizations sought to steer the VEP in the boldest possible direction. Forman targeted rural counties in the Deep South, where he hoped to precipitate Klan attacks, which would force the federal government to intervene. Over the next eighteen months, SNCC placed 180 full-time field secretaries in southwest Georgia and Mississippi, two of the South's fiercest pockets of resistance. Between 1961 and 1963, SNCC recorded sixty-two registration-related incidents in Mississippi alone. But participants quickly discovered that their collect calls to Marshall's office were being politely refused. Seeking an explanation, Lonnie King of SNCC discovered that southern Democrats had learned of Marshall's promise of assistance and "raised hell." As the Justice Department retreated from its assurances of federal protection, activists became even more inflamed.[7]

∽

At the very moment the Kennedy administration tried to persuade young civil rights activists that they could use existing federal laws to engineer major racial change, it promoted a slew of die-hard segregationists to the federal bench in the South who placed additional legal obstacles in their path. As judicial vacancies had arisen throughout the 1950s, Eisenhower had selected unusually enlightened southern candidates, including Frank M. Johnson, J. Skelly Wright, and Elbert Tuttle—all Republicans, who went on to author a series of pro–civil rights rulings in Montgomery and New Orleans. But on May 19 Kennedy signed a new Omnibus Judgeship Bill into law, which created 130 judicial vacancies, many of which were filled with friends and associates of leading segregationists.[8]

As a reward for steering the Omnibus Judgeship Bill through committee, Eastland demanded that the first appointee come from Mississippi. His choice was William Harold Cox, a friend from the University of Mississippi. In 1955, the Eisenhower Justice Department had blocked Cox from becoming a judge because of his strident white supremacist views—William Rogers, the then Deputy attorney general, dissolved into laughter when Cox's name was first suggested. Robert Kennedy moved forward with the nomination nonetheless. When the Judicial Selection Review Committee of the American Bar Association (ABA) raised concerns, Cox was invited for an interview at the Justice Department. In conversation with Robert Kennedy, Cox pledged to enforce the law. But Kennedy was concerned sufficiently by Cox's responses that he dispatched Byron White to meet with Eastland to see if Cox might accept a seat instead on the U.S. Court of Appeals for the Fifth Circuit, an appellate court made up of a panel of judges where he could wreak less damage. But Cox wanted to remain a trial judge in Mississippi, so Eastland refused to budge. The president quickly capitulated.[9]

Black leaders were incensed when the Cox nomination was announced. Clarence Mitchell complained that the White House was beginning to take on the appearance of a "dude ranch," with Eastland as general manager. Wilkins fired off a fiercely worded telegram to the president arguing that for 986,000 black Mississippians Cox would become "another strand in their barbed wire fence, another cross over their weary shoulders and another rock in the road up which their young people must struggle." Their fears were soon borne out: In one of his first rulings, in July 1961, Cox blocked a Justice Department request to inspect electoral records in Clarke County, Mississippi, where blacks had been disqualified from voting for thirty years. It was as if the 1957 and 1960 Civil Rights Acts had been erased from the statute book. Cox became one of the most virulent proponents of segregation on the federal bench. (He reached a nadir in 1964, when he described a group of black plaintiffs in a voting rights case as a "bunch of niggers . . . acting like a bunch of chimpanzees.") [10]

Other segregationists quickly followed Cox onto the federal bench. The most notorious was Judge E. Gordon West, whom Kennedy appointed in September 1961, at the behest of West's former law partner, Senator Russell Long. From his perch on the federal bench he later described the *Brown* ruling as "one of the truly regrettable decisions of all time." On one occasion, he refused to order a voting registrar in East Feliciana Parish to unlock the doors of his office, where local blacks had spent over six months attempting to register. In January 1962 Kennedy appointed J. Robert Elliott from Georgia, who had been a prime architect of the 1948 Dixiecrat revolt and was a well-known white supremacist. Elliott would play an instrumental role in crushing the Albany Movement, and over the course of his career on the bench ninety percent of his civil rights–related rulings were overturned by the appellate court. [11]

Kennedy did not just nominate segregationists for positions on the federal bench. On at least one occasion the Justice Department even lobbied the ABA to revise its original assessment of a racist judicial candidate so that he could be deemed more acceptable during the confirmation process. Judge Clarence Allgood of Alabama, a bankruptcy referee with scant legal experience, had been deemed wholly unqualified by the ABA—partly on grounds of competency, partly because of his racial views. But Alabama Senators John Sparkman and Lister Hill demanded his appointment, and the administration capitulated. Assistant Attorney General Louis Oberdorfer persuaded local ABA officials to adjust their rating from "unqualified" to "qualified." Allgood was a close friend of Oberdorfer's father, and Oberdorfer himself thought "he would uphold the law." It proved a bad misjudgment. Allgood persistently tried to thwart the civil rights movement and delivered a string of hostile rulings during the Birmingham demonstrations in 1963. [12]

The Justice Department rejected racist nominees in only a handful of cases. In Georgia, the Justice Department bypassed a segregationist candidate recommended by Russell in favor of Lewis Morgan, a racial moderate. All too often, however, the administration willfully disregarded the views of judicial nominees on the question of race, and for the most part overlooked more highly qualified southern moderates who were prepared to uphold the Constitution. For the civil rights movement, the damage was incalculable, since the segregationist judges held lifetime appointments, and their influence extended well into the 1970s. Blacks living in southern Mississippi and southern Georgia, where Cox and Elliott sought to nullify the voter registration campaigns, were hardest hit.

During the rest of the decade, they became two of the fiercest battlefields of the civil rights struggle.[13]

While Eisenhower's appointments had encouraged blacks to believe the federal courts were firmly on their side, Kennedy's candidates had the opposite effect. Throughout the fifties, most blacks believed they could settle their grievances through the courts. By the mid-sixties, the streets replaced the courts.

The appointment of Thurgood Marshall to the federal bench in New York was one of the few bright spots for black activists. The great-grandson of a Congolese native who had been wrenched from his homeland into slavery, Marshall had fought over 500 civil rights cases, more than thirty before the Supreme Court. Marshall's crowning achievement was the *Brown* decision, and no black American was more closely identified with the campaign to end school segregation. At first, Robert Kennedy opposed the nomination, since he feared an angry response from southerners during Senate confirmation hearings. Finally, however, he relented after an intense, ten-day lobbying campaign from Louis Martin. Martin told him it would be "a tremendous stroke" to get "Mr. Civil Rights" onto the federal judiciary.[14]

Marshall was ultimately confirmed as the result of a gratuitous quid pro quo proffered by James Eastland. When Robert Kennedy approached him in early 1961 to broach the subject of Marshall's nomination, Eastland reportedly offered him a deal: "Tell your brother that if you give me Harold Cox I will give him the nigger." The protests of southern Democrats were therefore muted when Marshall's name was put forward on September 23 for a vacancy on the Second Circuit Court of Appeals. And even though Eastland held up Marshall's confirmation until September 1962, a full year after his nomination, he was appointed nonetheless. Inarguably, Marshall's appointment ranked as the bravest of Kennedy's presidency. It elicited an immensely appreciative response from black voters. As the *Washington Afro-American* observed, it "would do more for the Democrats than their previous ten appointments." Even James Farmer, one of the administration's most strident critics, heralded the nomination of "one of the nation's strongest voices for racial equality." Nonetheless, the appointment hardly compensated for the president's legacy of racist judges. In New York, Marshall rarely dealt with civil rights litigation, unlike Kennedy' appointments in the South. And it was hardly an equal exchange—if Eastland truly did offer Marshall in return for Cox, he received the added windfall of Elliott, Allgood, and West.[15]

⁓

By fall, it was clear that the administration was failing in its approach to civil rights. In a series of damning progress reports published beginning in September, the Civil Rights Commission provided irrefutable evidence that the country was making little progress toward black equality. The reports made uncomfortable reading for the Kennedy brothers. The first, a two-year study on voting rights, revealed that in some 100 counties across eight separate states, there was "reason to believe that Negro citizens are prevented, by outright discrimination or by fear of physical violence or economic reprisal, from exercising the right to vote." In twenty-four "Black Belt" counties, including thirteen where blacks outnumbered whites, no blacks at all were registered. Across the South, the CRC calculated only fifty-three percent of eligible blacks could vote. Rejecting the Justice Department's policy of county-by-country litigation, four of the six CRC commissioners implored the administration to enact more stringent federal voting laws. The Justice Department had launched just fourteen voting suits, the commissioners pointed out, a tiny fraction of the 100 counties experiencing chronic problems.[16]

The CRC report on school desegregation, published in October, contained a familiar litany of complaints against the administration. It cited an excessive reliance on voluntarism and failure to seek new legislation. Highlighting the fact that 2,062 southern school districts had not even embarked on the preliminary stages of compliance, the CRC demanded legislative action, which would give school districts a six-month deadline to file desegregation plans and also grant the attorney general additional injunctive powers. In the meantime, the CRC suggested the federal government should protect school board members, parents, and children who were victims of segregationist harassment. It should also create a government agency charged with providing information and advice to school districts preparing integration plans, the very idea Fred Dutton had proposed unsuccessfully earlier in the year.[17]

The CRC report on police brutality, published in the fall, was particularly harsh. Police brutality was "a serious problem throughout the U.S," the CRC concluded, but blacks in the Deep South were by far the hardest hit. Too many "lived in fear," the report noted, "partly because they do not know if local policemen will help them or the mob when violence strikes." As Theodore Hesburgh wrote in a personal addendum that police brutality "just made my blood run cold. . . . With those horrible things going on all over, somehow I felt a cry of anguish, or a real blast from my mortal soul." Again, the CRC demanded changes in federal law and called on the FBI to investigate more fully allegations of brutality.[18]

Unused to public criticism, FBI Director J. Edgar Hoover was particularly enraged by the report. "I strongly resent any implication that there is any reluctance or lack of enthusiasm in fulfilling our investigative responsibilities in this most important area," he complained to CRC chairman John Hannah. Fearing their dispute might burst into the open, Burke Marshall asked Hannah to let the matter drop. Marshall advised Berl Bernhard, the CRC's staff director, that "poison pen correspondence never leads to satisfactory results." Marshall also thought the CRC "overstated the police brutality picture" and argued that the report contained numerous unsubstantiated allegations. Prior to publication, Marshall dispatched Seigenthaler to the offices of the CRC, to persuade the report's authors to withdraw some of the most inflammatory accusations and to soften the tone.[19]

Even before the publication of its fault-finding reports, the relationship between the Kennedy administration and the CRC had grown increasingly antagonistic. Kennedy derided CRC commissioners as histrionic moralists, who failed to understand the reality of politics, and was particularly critical of Chairman Hannah and Father Hesburgh, its most outspoken member. Robert Kennedy had clashed with the commission over its plans to hold public hearings on housing discrimination in Washington, D.C., early in 1961, fearing it would highlight the need for the housing executive order to be issued. They quarreled again in the aftermath of the New Orleans school crisis, when the CRC wanted to investigate the extent of racial discrimination across Louisiana. The administration signaled its disapproval of the CRC by refusing repeatedly to introduce legislation extending its life. With the body's statutory authority set to expire in September, Hannah warned in the spring that the CRC would be forced to start firing its seven-strong investigative staff unless Congress acted soon. But the White House did not take action until late August, by pressing the Senate for a two-year extension of the body (Senate liberals wanted to make the commission permanent). By then, many staff members, faced with the termination of their contracts, had found other jobs, leaving the CRC with only a skeletal workforce. The White House did not seem overly concerned. If anything, the president was happy to see the increasingly intrusive body weakened.[20]

And so despite the highly critical assessment of the CRC, Robert Kennedy's annual Civil Rights Report, delivered to the president on December 29, overflowed with enthusiasm for the administration's progress. Much of it read like a manifesto on behalf of the policy of voluntarism. "We know that you feel strongly that these matters should be resolved at the local and state level and the Federal Government should intervene only if all other efforts have failed," it noted. "This has been done quietly and without publicity." The attorney general congratulated himself and his department on their impressive record of accomplishment. On the railways, eighteen companies operating in the South had agreed to desegregate their passenger compartments following negotiations with the Justice Department, while airport terminals in Columbus, Georgia and Raleigh-Durham, North Carolina, voluntarily desegregated their facilities. By focusing on voluntary compliance—what Robert Kennedy termed an "affirmative anticipatory action"—the Justice Department had improved on the policy of "abstention," which had defined the previous administration. The comparison with the Eisenhower Justice Department was especially telling, for the Kennedy brothers continually used the record of the previous administration as their yardstick. By that standard, they considered themselves to be making exceptional gains, especially in voting and employment rights. (Both tended to overlook the fact that Eisenhower had signed two Civil Rights Acts and dealt a major blow to massive resistance in Little Rock.) [21]

The president also took enormous pride in his administration's record, convinced it already surpassed that of his predecessors. "We have, I think, made substantial progress in the field of civil rights," he noted at a press conference on November 8. "There have been more suits filed to provide for voting and . . . [w]e have put some people to work under, under our Vice-President's Committee . . . than was ever done in the previous eight years." When White House aides compiled a list in September of "Major Foreign Policy Measures Taken by the Kennedy Administration," they included "the orderly evolution of desegregation in the United States," adding that progress in civil rights and education had been "noteworthy."[22]

Privately, the president derived greatest satisfaction, perhaps, from nearly fifty high-profile black appointments. For the first time on the continental United States, blacks were made U.S. attorneys (Cecil F. Poole of California and Merle M. McCurdy of Ohio), and there were district judgeships for Wade McCree of Michigan and James Parsons of Illinois, another first. Then there was the nomination of Thurgood Marshall. In Washington, most government departments endeavored to improve their employment record, with measurable success. By the end of 1961, the number of blacks in senior grade 12 posts at the Labor Department had risen from twenty-four to forty-one, and from fifteen to forty-six at Agriculture. While the Justice Department started the year with only ten black lawyers, now there were fifty.[23]

President Kennedy was sincerely proud of his administration's progress in the area of civil rights. And he was extremely defensive when challenged on the subject. When a delegation from the Americans for Democratic Action visited the White House in February, Joseph Rauh asked the president if he sympathized with liberal demands for more vigorous policies. "Absolutely not," Kennedy shot back. "It's a totally different thing. Your criticism on civil rights is quite wrong." As Rauh reflected: "I've never seen a man's expression turn so fast." When Sam Beer of the ADA urged him to issue the housing order, Kennedy told his old Harvard friend to "lay off." Similarly, during an Oval Office meeting with Lyndon Johnson and the vice president's confidant Abe Fortas after the signing ceremony for the PCEEO in March, Kennedy said he failed to comprehend why black activists were pressing for further reforms, given the administration's admirable appointments record. When Fortas suggested blacks were in the throes of a "social revolution" and implied that appointments alone would not suffice, the president looked "startled."[24]

Robert Kennedy reacted to criticism of his department's civil rights record in much the same way. Confronted about the administration's failure to introduce civil rights legislation on *Meet the Press* on September 24, Robert Kennedy argued that they had taken "a great of action . . . which in my estimation accomplished more than ever could have been accomplished by any possible legislation, or any legislation that might have been possible to get passed in Congress." Asked why three million black schoolchildren were attending segregated schools, he snapped: "I don't know whether all of those three million want to be integrated." Challenged during an early meeting with the CRC on the failure to support voting rights legislation, his response was even more ill-tempered. "You're second guessers," Robert Kennedy told them. "I am the one who has to get the job done. . . . I can do it, and will do it, in my way, and you're making it more difficult."[25]

At a Thanksgiving weekend meeting in Hyannis Port, Robert Kennedy called merely for a small refinement in policy: the introduction of voting rights measures that would ban literacy tests and the poll tax. Even the attorney general did not believe the White House should fight hard for the bill's passage, but he thought it would be shrewd to put the administration firmly on record in favor of new voting rights measures, if only to show participants in the VEP that it was acting with serious intent. The president himself accepted the idea but thought it would be all but impossible to pass legislation of any significance in the current Congress and feared the bill would prove to be a waste of time. He deferred any decision on new legislation until after Christmas. He also rejected demands for the long-awaited executive order on housing, even though the 1961 Housing Act had been passed into law, the original reason cited for its delay. Now he feared it would complicate plans to elevate Robert Weaver to the cabinet as head of a new department of urban affairs in the New Year—even though it was pointed out to him that Weaver himself considered the order more important than his promotion. Instead, the foremost question in the president's mind was who persuaded him to promise its issuance in the first place. "It wasn't me," said Sorensen, defensively.

"Oh, I guess nobody wrote it," the president shot back. For his part, Robert Kennedy spent most of the meeting outside in the rain playing touch football. Occasionally, the president would shout, "Hey Bobby," and he would venture inside to offer his opinions. But by the end of the meeting, the president decided to leave his civil rights policy unchanged.[26]

Kennedy had good reason to be complacent about his civil rights record. For despite everything—the CRC reports, the rising militancy of young black activists, the frustration of senior black leaders, and even dissent within his own administration—Kennedy remained immensely popular with black Americans. The very gestures that black leaders and liberals derided as token were, in fact, highly effective in terms of sustaining widespread black support. The gap was widening between mainstream black politics and the advocacy of civil rights leaders. Although activists were increasingly dismayed by Kennedy's inertia, most black voters judged the new president by a different set of standards. So while Wilkins bemoaned the inadequacy of Kennedy's appointments blitz, blacks outside of the civil rights movement seemed delighted. Whereas Farmer attacked the administration for its failure to intervene more aggressively in Alabama and Mississippi, the simple fact that U.S. marshals were dispatched to protect King satisfied many blacks. Polling data on the freedom riders were particularly informative. Asked whether they approved of the way Robert Kennedy handled the racial disturbances in Alabama, more than seventy-four percent of black respondents said yes. On the question of whether he had moved quickly enough to protect the freedom riders, almost sixty percent replied in the affirmative. "For the first time in years, praise from Negroes far exceeds the criticism of the nation's chief executive," Simeon Booker concluded in June. In the New Jersey gubernatorial race, returns from three predominantly black wards in Trenton, Newark, and Camden suggested that the Democratic vote was not only holding firm but growing in size.[27]

Thurgood Marshall's nomination also made a deep impression on blacks, as did the other high-profile appointments, which were given prominent coverage in the black press. Commenting on what it called a "bright interlude of accelerated progress," *Ebony* cited the "unprecedented flurry of appointments" as "the biggest breakthrough made by Negroes in 1961." Equally important were symbolic gestures, such as Robert Kennedy's resignation from the Metropolitan Club and the well-publicized invitation of high-profile blacks into the White House. Although they marked no genuine political advance, this kind of symbolic action tapped into black aspirations for access and status.[28]

At times, Kennedy was even able to charm his most strident black critics. On July 12, 1961, Kennedy hosted a sixty-strong NAACP delegation at the White House—a meeting offered as a way of apologizing for his refusal to address the organization's fifty-second annual convention in Philadelphia. In rebellious mood, Bishop Stephen Gill Spottswood, the new NAACP chairman, opened with a toughly worded statement, thanking the president for setting a "new moral tone" but deriding him for his failure to push legislation. "The absence of a clear call by you for enactment of civil rights legislation has become a source of dismay to the forces working for civil rights," complained Spottswood, adding "there is grave concern over the prospect that without support from the White House, there might be no congressional action on the various, urgently needed bills now in various stages of unpreparedness." Angry that his motives and methods had been questioned, Kennedy went on the defensive: "We remain convinced that legislation is not the way," he told the group. "At least, it is not advisable at this time." NAACP officials tried once more to press home their argument, pointing out that there was little to show for the nonlegislative strategy. Yet when they called for a civil rights bill in 1962, Kennedy gave them a one-word response: an unequivocal "No."[29]

Despite the fractious tone of the meeting, perhaps its most noteworthy aspect was the convivial mood of the NAACP activists at its end. They seemed completely spellbound by the president's hospitality. At the start, Kennedy provided chairs for the women, and afterwards he offered some of the delegates a tour of the executive mansion. At one point, Jackie Kennedy had even dropped by and delivered a brief talk on the history of the Lincoln china. Disarmed completely, many delegates returned to the NAACP convention in Philadelphia in a buoyant mood.[30] As he had throughout so much of his career, Kennedy had been able to deflect a tremendous amount of criticism by sheer force of his celebrity, charm, and hospitality. "There was more rush to run up the White House steps," went the joke among black reporters, "than run down to Mississippi."[31]

Kennedy deployed similar tactics on King, whom he finally invited to the White House in October 1961. Rather than conduct their meeting in the more official setting of the Oval Office or Cabinet Room, the president invited him for lunch in the Executive Mansion—apparently the first time such a courtesy had been extended to a black leader. Jackie Kennedy joined them, which meant there was little chance for a frank discussion on the country's race problem. Kennedy treated King instead to a tour of the couple's family quarters. Pausing for a moment in the Lincoln Bedroom, where a framed copy of the Emancipation Proclamation hung above the mantelpiece, King spotted his chance. "Mr. President, I'd like to see you stand in this room and sign a Second Emancipation outlawing segregation, one hundred years after Lincoln's. You could base it on the Fourteenth Amendment." Kennedy politely suggested that King should help draft a new proclamation, but nothing came of it.[32]

The president was noticeably less welcoming toward the leaders of SNCC, whom he refused to invite to the White House, and James Farmer of CORE, whom he grudgingly agreed to meet in the Oval Office in the late fall of 1961. Still angry with Farmer over his refusal to cancel the freedom riders before the Vienna Summit, the president arrived at the meeting late, with a sheaf of papers under his arm, which he then proceeded to read for the next forty-five minutes as Farmer spoke. Soon realizing that he did not have the president's attention, Farmer offered to reschedule the meeting. Kennedy said that would not be necessary. After forty-five minutes, Farmer said he would not impose any further on the president's time. Kennedy got up, shook his hand, and then returned to reading his briefing papers. As Farmer later reflected: "He was telling me: 'I don't like you.'"[33]

With black approval ratings so high, there was little incentive for the administration to reconsider its policies or alter its tactics. The president believed that if the poll numbers were high, his strategy must be right, a simplistic but dangerous conflation. Southern lawmakers were well aware that Kennedy, confident in the support of black voters, had little reason to press forward on civil rights issues. As a consequence, Kennedy had no real leverage with the Southern Caucus. The nonlegislative strategy, which he had engineered in order to secure southern support for the New Frontier program, in fact accomplished nothing of the sort.[34]

By October, as the first session of 87th Congress wound up business, much of the administration's legislative program had been defeated, delayed, or watered down, largely through southern obstructionism. The Area Redevelopment Act, one of the first administration bills to go before the Senate, set the pattern, for it was passed only after leading southerners, like J. William Fulbright, had been offered substantial financial incentives in the form of large federal grants. In a further concession, Luther Hodges, the administration's North Carolinian commerce secretary, was placed in charge of allocating federal funds. Even then, half of the Southern Caucus opposed the measure. Likewise, the Fair Labor Standards Bill, a measure raising the minimum wage from $1 to $1.25 an hour, was passed only after major inducements to the South—namely the exclusion of the region's large laundry operators, with its predominantly black workforce.[35]

The expansion of social security, which Kennedy touted as one of his administration's boldest successes, was again the product of tremendous compromise with southern lawmakers. So, too, was the passage of a $4.8 billion Omnibus Housing bill. Despite having already delayed the long-awaited executive housing order, the White House was forced into further concessions, an increase of $450 million in federal loans targeted specifically at rural and small communities. Aid to education, the centerpiece of the administration's legislative program, was defeated in the House Rules Committee, even though the administration had presented a scaled-down version of the bill and offered southerners specific assurances that grant funds would not be withheld from segregated schools. Similarly, the new administration's plans for medical care for the elderly, or Medicare, remained bottled up in the House Ways and Means Committee, chaired by Wilbur Mills of Arkansas. Increased price supports for major southern crops, like cotton, peanuts, and rice, along with a steady stream of federal contracts, public works programs, and redevelopment subsidies did little to help. By the end of 1961, just 48.4 percent of the president's proposals had been passed into law by Congress. In 1962 that figure dropped to 44.6 percent.[36]

What *Congressional Quarterly* identified as the forty-six most critical amendment and final passage votes in 1961 demonstrated the administration's limited returns from courting the southern grandees. James Eastland voted with the administration just eight percent of the time, Olin Johnston eight percent, A. Willis Robertson of Virginia eight percent, Richard Russell seven percent, Harry F. Byrd six percent, and Strom Thurmond four percent. In October, the ADA pointed out that Russell, Eastland, Thurmond, and Robertson all had a "0 percent" record on ten crucial pro-administration votes. "The South couldn't be wrangled into the slightest crumb," complained Roy Wilkins, "if Kennedy said from the start that [civil rights] legislation was out." Even southern Democrats were surprised at Kennedy's inept handling of Congress. Senator Allen

Ellender of Louisiana described him as "a poor bargainer" and "not as aggressive as he could have been." Wilbur Mills was shocked by his "timid approach."[37]

Kennedy's deference toward the Southern Caucus is all the more inexplicable given that the group had suffered even further setbacks since Kennedy took office. Texas Senator Ralph Yarborough no longer attended its meetings, and Lyndon Johnson had been replaced by Republican John Tower. The caucus could no longer boast a Texan member. And yet Kennedy continued to treat its surviving members, particularly Russell, with reverence. Kennedy even asked Russell to represent him during the Memorial Day wreath-laying ceremony at the Tomb of the Unknown Soldier. "I hope your Confederate grandfathers do not learn of you joining forces with the G.A.R. [Grand Army of the Republic]," the president wrote. What Kennedy failed to understand was that Russell's own generation of Confederate soldiers had long been reconciled to ultimate defeat.[38]

Kennedy's first year in the White House had been a baptism of fire. Over the course of the year, he had mishandled the Bay of Pigs crisis, performed poorly at his meeting in Vienna with Khrushchev, and lost tremendous international credibility with the erection of the Berlin Wall. When, at the end of 1961, Sorensen informed him that a number of reporters were planning books on his first year in office, Kennedy was despairing. "Who would want to read a book on disasters?" he asked. Having manifestly failed to demonstrate authority in his handling of foreign affairs, which he had always considered his greatest area of strength, Kennedy looked to his accomplishments in civil rights as one of the few bright spots in his record. With his black approval ratings high and a largely appreciative black media behind him, Kennedy sincerely believed that his efforts on behalf of black Americans had been genuinely admirable.[39]

CHAPTER 18

❦

The Presidential Literacy Test

With its eyes focused on the midterm elections in November, the Kennedy administration began 1962 on a campaign footing. Partisan politics, never far from Kennedy's mind, would come to define much of the year. In 1961, foreign affairs had dominated the presidential agenda. In 1962, Kennedy planned to pay equivalent attention to the domestic economy. In an effort to shore up his Democratic base, Kennedy focused on winning congressional approval for tariff reduction, to counter the rising economic threat from the European Common Market, and also for tax-revision measures, aimed at modernizing American industry through a tax credit for new investment. He also intended to redouble his efforts to enact a federal aid-to-education bill, which was presently stalled in the House, and to broaden access to public health care, another of the previous year's legislative failures.

Kennedy was certain he could not make advances in Congress on the civil rights front, but he was ambivalent as to whether he should nonetheless support legislation in this area in order to assist Democratic candidates in the fall. In mid-November 1961, Lee White, who by the end of 1961 had slowly started to take over from Wofford as the White House point man on civil rights, outlined the political dangers of inaction in a memorandum to the president. White identified two areas of particular vulnerability for Kennedy: the long-delayed housing order and the administration's refusal to commit to new legislation. On the housing order, White called for speedy action, since black voters expected the measure and "failure to issue it could generate bitter disappointment and criticism." On the legislative front, he called upon the administration to sponsor a bill before the November elections, since Democrats could easily be outstripped by the GOP. New York Senator Jacob Javits was calling for Part III "at every turn," warned White, while northern Democrats feared an electoral backlash if they failed to record a vote in favor of new legislation. White was well aware that any civil rights measure was certain to endure "very rough going" from southern Democrats, but he nonetheless recommended a bold civil rights bill, including Part III powers and the creation of a statutory fair employment practices committee. "Any package of relatively easy items (e.g. anti-poll tax and literacy legislation) would not satisfy the civil rights groups," cautioned White, who was sensitive to the mounting demands of civil rights activists, "and would still make the opponents unhappy—thus it should be a strong package or none at all."[1]

At the Justice Department, both Robert Kennedy and Burke Marshall also wanted to see the president go on record in favor of new legislation—if only to demonstrate the administration's commitment to voting rights, the issue toward which they wanted to steer civil rights groups. They advocated far weaker proposals than White put forward, however, in order to stay clear of the incendiary topic of school integration. Instead, they favored the abolition of the literacy tests and the poll tax, two devices used by southern voting officials to bar blacks from voting. But Lawrence O'Brien, the administration's archpragmatist, reminded John Kennedy that he needed to secure support from southern lawmakers to ensure the passage of his tariff-reduction and tax-revision measures. With such a busy legislative calendar ahead, he therefore counseled Kennedy not to alienate key southern committee chairmen by introducing or supporting any civil rights initiative. Sorensen concurred.[2]

And so, once again, Kennedy tried to have it both ways. He decided after Christmas that he would not send up a new civil rights bill from the White House. He would, however, allow the Justice Department to draft a voting rights bill to which he would lend his support. The bill, according to Kennedy's plan, would eventually be sponsored by Senate Majority Leader Mike Mansfield. The difference was subtle but important: The administration would back new legislation, but it would not introduce it.

In his State of the Union address on January 11, 1962, Kennedy laid out his position before a national audience, beginning a three-paragraph section on civil rights with a strong statement of intent: "America stands for progress in human rights as well as economic affairs, and a strong America requires the assurance of full and equal rights to all its citizens, of any race or color." He went on to mount a robust defense of his administration's record but conceded that there was "much to be done—by the Executive, by the courts and by Congress." Then, he indicated "full support" for the voting rights proposals, noting: "The right to vote should no longer be denied through such arbitrary devices on a local level, sometimes abused, such as literacy tests and poll taxes." Evoking Lincoln, he ended with a flourish: "As we approach the 100th anniversary, next January, of the Emancipation Proclamation, let the acts of every branch of Government—and every citizen—portray that 'righteousness does exalt a nation.'"[3]

They were stirring words, but vacated of true intent. As soon as the president concluded his address, White House officials reminded reporters off the record that the president had made "no urgent request" for new legislation. Nor had he instructed congressional leaders to place any civil rights bill on the calendar. As the *New York Times* neatly summarized Kennedy's stance in a headline after the speech: "Kennedy Asks New Rights Laws But Is Unlikely to Push Adoption."[4]

Black leaders were unimpressed. Martin Luther King conceded that it was "very encouraging" to hear Kennedy demand additional legislation but stressed that the speech had "failed to state anything original and forthright on this issue." He reemphasized his view that school desegregation should take precedence over voting rights. The black media responded in much the same way. "The President gave a disappointing 'pat on the back' to his limited progress to date," noted the *Washington Afro-American*, "and made no vigorous effort to push for additional critical legislation." The omission of any mention of the housing order fueled suspicions of further delay.[5]

Those fears were borne out at the first presidential press conference after the State of the Union address, when Kennedy confessed that he had no intention of signing the executive housing order until he "considered it to be in the public interest, and when I considered it to make an important contribution to advancing the rights of our citizens." Then, almost parenthetically, Kennedy added that he was "proceeding ahead in a way which will maintain consensus, and which will advance the cause," implying his cautious approach accurately reflected the public mood. Liberal Republicans immediately challenged Kennedy on this issue and assailed him for his failure to mobilize public support for new reforms. "Where is his courage?" asked Representative Steven Derounian of New York. "Where is his leadership?"[6]

Kennedy's determination to solidify his party's electoral base in advance of the midterm elections was nowhere more clear—or more disastrous—than in the case of Robert Weaver. Weaver had been Kennedy's most prominent success in his frenzy of black appointments at the beginning of the previous year. Weaver had taken on the position of head of the Housing and Home Finance Agency, with the expectation of being upgraded to a full cabinet position at the beginning of 1962, as soon as Congress passed legislation creating a new Department of Urban Affairs.

Southern Democrats were determined to block Weaver from becoming America's first black cabinet secretary and therefore rejected the creation of the new department. Republican leaders also resisted, not because of Weaver's race, but because of the party's long-standing opposition to big government. In the House Rules Committee, five Republicans had already vowed to defeat the measure by preventing it from reaching the floor. So, too, had two moderate southern Democrats on the committee, James Trimble of Arkansas and Carl Elliott of Alabama, who on occasion voted with the administration. Elliott faced a statewide at-large primary in the spring and was afraid of a backlash from voters. Trimble was known to be wavering, though he had signaled that he could be persuaded to support the measure if his vote became pivotal.

The administration faced a tactical decision: It could mount a lobbying campaign aimed at Trimble and Elliott, in an effort to push the measure through committee. Or it could allow the bill to die and then blame its demise on the GOP. With its attention focused on the upcoming elections, Kennedy opted for partisanship. If the Republicans blocked Weaver's elevation to the cabinet it would benefit northern Democrats in November.[7]

Kennedy put his plan into almost immediate effect on January 24, just hours after the House Rules Committee had defeated the measure by a nine-to-six margin. Speaking to reporters at his weekly news conference, he placed the blame for defeat squarely on Republicans. "I am somewhat astonished at the Republican leadership which opposed this bill," he said, in a deliberate over-simplification of the vote. "Obviously if the [bill] had been passed, Mr. Weaver would have been appointed. It was well known on the Hill. The American people might as well know it." Kennedy pledged to retaliate. He announced that he would resubmit the measure as part of a government reorganization plan. He had thrown down a gauntlet—the GOP could either support his reorganization plan, or the party would be tainted with charges of racism in the upcoming elections.[8]

Kennedy won his short-term strategic victory. In a report headlined, "JFK Comes Out Swinging on Civil Rights," the *Washington Afro-American* noted how the president had "come out of his corner like a heavyweight champ" and dealt Republicans a "knock-out blow." Martin Luther King told *Newsweek:* "Negroes may use their political power at the polls this fall to defeat congress-men who allowed the race question to sabotage their most cherished dreams." But the *New York Times* columnist James Reston was warier and derided Kennedy's ostensibly bold challenge as opportunistic and crass. It marked, in Reston's words, "the start of the political campaign of 1962." Roy Wilkins complained that Weaver's proposed elevation to the cabinet would not make up for the repeated failure to issue the executive housing order: "We submit that it is in no sense the equivalent of putting a stop to the disgraceful financing of racial discrimination with Federal tax dollars." Charles Abrams, the chairman of the National Committee Against Discrimination in Housing, concurred. "Everyone . . . including Southern elements" expected Kennedy to sign the order, he told Burke Marshall. He feared that Kennedy's equivocal message would offer "encouragement to irresponsible elements in the South as well as in the North who are being given hope that they can win the battle that had already been lost." Louis Martin wrote a one-line memo to Robert Kennedy in April: "How about the housing order?"[9]

The rhetoric grew more heated in subsequent weeks. Republican leaders expressed their outrage at how the president had contaminated the issue with race.

Justifiably, both Everett Dirksen, the Senate minority leader, and Representative Charlie Halleck, the House Republican leader, correctly stated that their opposition to the new department had predated any suggestion that a black would become its first secretary. Rather than creating a new cabinet position, they promised to support Weaver's appointment as head of the Department of Health, Education, and Welfare (HEW) when Abraham Ribicoff stepped down later in the year in order to run for the Senate seat in Connecticut.[10]

Weaver's appointment had become a full-blown partisan dispute. Largely because the issue had become so politicized, the White House and Democratic leadership soon began to make clumsy tactical errors. Determined to race ahead with an early Senate vote, so Republican senators would be blamed for defeating the reorganization plan before southern congressmen killed it in the House, Senate Majority Leader Mike Mansfield used strong-arm tactics to bring the measure to the floor as speedily as possible. Casting aside Senate protocol, he therefore rushed ahead on February 20 with a highly controversial motion to immediately discharge the reorganization plan from committee before members could debate it adequately. The strategy backfired. Enraged by Mansfield's disregard for Senate traditions, eight pro–civil rights Democrats sided with the Southern Caucus. Mansfield's discharge motion was defeated fifty-eight to forty-two. As expected, the House crushed the reorganization plan the very next day 264 to 150. The prospect of a Department of Urban Affairs was now dead; the idea was not resurrected until 1966, when President Lyndon Johnson created the Department of Housing and Urban Development (HUD) and named Weaver its head.[11]

It was a humiliating defeat for the White House. Republicans emerged from the battle uncompromised, and Kennedy lost his gamble, despite Democratic majorities in both the House and Senate. The *Washington Evening Star* assailed Kennedy and Mansfield for "crude political pressure tactics" and a "contrived effort to inject racism" into the debate. It was a shabby strategy and, to their credit, Republicans had refused to be intimidated.[12]

Rather than making a serious attempt to elevate Weaver to the cabinet, by building public support or mounting an intense lobbying campaign, Kennedy transformed the issue into a political stunt. In the first year of his presidency, he had used black appointments to boost his standing among black voters. Now, with the midterm elections looming, he had tried unsuccessfully to use a non-appointment to achieve the same end. While the tactic seemed ingenious to the administration in January, it was ultimately incredibly damaging to the cause of civil rights. By willfully confusing the issue with the politics of party, Kennedy made it much harder for his administration to overcome the resistance of southern Democrats to civil rights reform. After all, legislative progress in the 1950s was possible only through bipartisanship. The debacle also brought into question yet again the president's true purpose on the subject of civil rights. When he spoke with such obvious insincerity of his determination to see Weaver in his cabinet, southern lawmakers quickly realized that he was merely laying a political trap for the Republicans. Kennedy had renounced whatever lingering credibility he had with southern Democrats on the question of civil rights.

∽

Mike Mansfield and the Kennedy administration had no more success piloting the voting rights bill through Congress than in elevating Weaver to the cabinet. Drafted by Justice Department officials, the bill sought to put an to end to the use of the arbitrary and invidious literacy tests that southern voting officials used to disenfranchise even the most highly educated blacks. The Justice Department wanted to impose a meritocratic and uniform standard nationwide: The completion of the sixth grade. Though a modest proposal, applicable only in federal elections, it promised nonetheless to put an end to the obstructionist tactics of racist voting registrars. The literacy test bill was introduced in the Senate on January 25 by Mansfield, who had asked the Justice Department to give him a draft of the proposals "immediately," in the words of a White House official writing on January 19, because he was worried the Republicans would "steal our play." Five days later, however, it was referred to Eastland's Judiciary Committee, where it languished for a further three months.[13]

From the very beginning, the White House believed that there was little chance of defeating a southern filibuster and therefore showed little enthusiasm for the measure. The president was altogether dismissive. In early April, while the measure remained stalled in Eastland's committee, Kennedy jokingly asked Burke Marshall, "What's this bill of yours and Bobby's?" The Justice Department also had trouble rounding up support from a number of leading liberal Democrats, for whom school desegregation, rather than voting reform, remained a much higher priority. Senators Hubert Humphrey, Paul Douglas, and Joseph Clark all made it clear that they wanted the measure to apply to state as well as federal elections but promised not to openly criticize the administration's timidity on this matter. For the same reason, there was no groundswell of support from the civil rights movement. Knowing a sure loser when he saw one, Roy Wilkins scathingly described the bill as a "token offering on the full civil rights program pledged by the administration's party platform of 1960." The ADA and the AFL-CIO also favored a broader measure and suspected the administration was again playing politics, coming up with another preelection ploy to embarrass the GOP.[14]

Faced with such a feeble and disorganized opposition, the Southern Caucus saw the opportunity to score yet another victory. Not since the mid-fifties had its leaders succeeded in defeating an administration-backed civil rights bill. Now they spotted their chance. In March, Russell and his cohorts had already demonstrated their renewed strength by delaying the passage of a constitutional amendment abolishing the poll tax. Levied in just five states, the poll tax had become virtually obsolete by the end of the 1950s, and in 1960 the Senate had already voted to scrap it by a lopsided majority of seventy-two to sixteen. The latest move to amend the Constitution in the Senate, which had the strong backing of the administration, should also have been a mere formality. But the Southern Caucus decided to mount a ten-day filibuster, partly to needle Mansfield and partly to discourage the White House from pushing civil rights legislation in the current session.[15]

It was a highly symbolic gesture of defiance. At the end of the 1950s, segregationist lawmakers in the House and Senate were increasingly reluctant to deploy the filibuster, for fear it would harden northern opinion against them. Fifteen months into the Kennedy administration, with a string of victories behind them, they were no longer so apprehensive. Eventually on March 27, after almost a two-week delay, the poll-tax amendment was passed by seventy-seven votes to sixteen. But Russell had made his point.[16]

If his intention during the poll-tax debate had been to merely delay its passage, Russell approached the literacy test battle determined to defeat it outright. Once more, Russell was prepared to use the filibuster if necessary, but began his campaign against the bill by challenging the legal basis of the new proposals. Russell and Ervin spearheaded the strategy. If they could destroy the bill on constitutional grounds, they rightly believed that they could set back the cause of civil rights for years. Ervin—an assiduous lawmaker who maintained at his office a four-room library crammed with books on the Constitution—took the lead. He contended that states retained the prerogative to decide who voted in elections, a principle affirmed in Article 1 Section 2 of the Constitution, which maintained that "electors in each state shall have the qualifications requisite for electors of the most numerous branch of the state legislature." The 17th Amendment had confirmed this principle.

In an effort to galvanize academic support for his argument, Ervin fired off letters to the deans of 150 law schools enumerating the bill's constitutional flaws. He sent a similar letter to all the state attorneys general. Upon learning of Ervin's preemptive strike, Emanuel Celler warned the White House about the dangers of being underprepared, and urged the attorney general, or ideally the president, to publicly elucidate the constitutional basis of the bill.[17] An unnamed White House official also warned of a bruising battle: "the proper groundwork has not been laid for legislation in Congress . . . If legislation is submitted to Congress before the moral issue is clearly drawn, the result will be disaster. The country will be exposed to several weeks of divisive and inflammatory debate. The debate is likely to come to no conclusion—thus disillusioning the Negroes and strengthening the bigots in their conclusion the country 'is really with' them." The White House ignored both warnings.[18]

Justice Department officials had developed an argument for the constitutionality of the measure. They invoked Article 1 Section 4 of the Constitution,
which enabled the federal government to end abuses in federal elections, and
the Fourteenth and Fifteenth amendments, which made it illegal for any state
to "abridge the privileges or immunities of citizens of the United States," or
deny or abridge the right of any citizen to vote on account of "race, color, or previous condition of servitude." Burke Marshall told Harvard law professor Paul
Freund in mid-March that "the bill, if enacted, would withstand constitutional
attack without much doubt." The constitutional arguments put forward by the
Justice Department were just as persuasive as those advanced by Ervin. But
there was a crucial difference: Administration officials were not prepared to
argue on behalf of them with anywhere near the same vigor as southern lawmakers. It did not help that they had taken just two days to draft the bill.[19]

From mid-March through to early April, both the House and Senate held
hearings on the literacy test bill. The hearings demonstrated that southerners
were far more determined to defeat the measure than liberals were prepared to
fight for it. On March 15, Republican Congressman William McCulloch, a
longtime ally of the civil rights movement who could normally be relied upon
to support any civil rights bill, criticized the administration for its "half-way
measures" and argued in favor of a much broader bill. Michael Padnos of the
ADA complained that school desegregation and the creation of a statutory
FEPC should take precedence over abolishing the literacy test. On March 29,
Andrew J. Biemiller, the legislative director of the AFL-CIO, called for an omnibus civil rights bill, rather than one that was limited to voting rights alone.[20]

On April 10, Robert Kennedy appeared before the Senate Constitutional
Rights Subcommittee to rally much-needed support for the measure. He referred to a case where a black applicant had been denied the vote after failing to
correctly interpret a provision of the state constitution dealing with debt liqui-
dation. But Sam Ervin, who chaired the subcommittee, tried to bring him back
to the constitutionality of the measure rather than dwell on its emotional appeal. "I love the Constitution too much," said Ervin, to allow the abolition of
the literacy test to reach the statute book.

"I love it, too, Mr. Chairman," the attorney general shot back.[21]

It was a rare moment of drama during hearings that had failed to generate
any enthusiasm for the bill. After they were over, Ervin immediately went on
the offensive. He issued a press release on April 13 claiming that not once during the testimony of twenty separate witnesses had anyone proved that Congress had the constitutional power to abolish the literacy test.[22]

In late April, in advance of the measure reaching the Senate floor, Russell
brought together his filibuster teams to plot their line of attack. He issued strict
instructions that they should stick to constitutional arguments and avoid the
kind of meaningless diatribes, quoting recipe books and obscure Biblical pas-

sages, that were the staple fare of Dixie talkathons. The goal was not merely to prolong the debate, but to win it—just as Ervin claimed he had done during the Senate hearings.

On April 25, Mansfield and Dirksen agreed to bring the literacy test bill before the Senate by attaching it as an amendment to a private bill—a clever parliamentary maneuver that meant Eastland could no longer keep it bottled up in committee. Almost immediately, the Southern Caucus launched a filibuster, which, as Russell intended, focused only on the constitutional merits of the bill. With the administration offering little in the way of counterarguments, the Southern Caucus achieved its breakthrough on May 8 when Senator John Sherman Cooper of Kentucky, a liberal Republican who was ordinarily a supporter of civil rights proposals, confessed to serious misgivings over the bill's constitutionality. Heavily influenced by Ervin's arguments, he agreed that any attempt by Congress to impose a national standard represented an unlawful extension of federal authority. Cooper held tremendous sway over GOP moderates, and by withdrawing his support he consigned the measure to almost certain defeat.[23]

The following afternoon, at his weekly press conference, the president argued strongly in favor of new legislation: "I've seen these cases of [holders of] college degrees who were denied being put on the register because they supposedly can't pass the literacy test. It doesn't make any sense." But he did not defend the constitutionality of the proposals, the main point of contention.[24]

The administration's failure to design a thought-out legislative strategy had also multiplied its problems. In the absence of strong White House backing, Mansfield was left to navigate the bill through Congress, but he, like the president, had no appetite for a protracted fight. Even worse, Mansfield mistakenly admitted so publicly by revealing his unwillingness to force the Senate into round-the-clock sessions, the tactic successfully used by his predecessor, Lyndon Johnson, during the 1960 civil rights debate to break the southern filibuster. By doing so, he hoisted a white flag even before the first shots were fired. The Southern Caucus was allowed to conduct its filibuster through normal Senate hours, which meant holding the floor from noon until 6:30 P.M. at the latest. Mansfield did not even call for Saturday sessions.

Further tactical blunders followed. Two weeks into the debate, Mansfield announced prematurely that if a cloture vote shutting down the filibuster failed to muster enough votes, he would afterwards introduce a tabling motion—or killing motion—to assess the general level of Senate support for civil rights. It was an astonishing act of political charity to his Republican opponents. Moderate Republicans from northern states, who cherished the Senate tradition of unlimited debate but were worried about hemorrhaging black support in the upcoming midterm elections, could now vote against cloture with impunity. Mansfield's tabling motion enabled them to register a vote in favor of the literacy test bill immediately afterwards. Predictably enough, when Mansfield moved to shut off debate on May 9, he suffered a dreadful rebuff. Only thirteen Republicans and thirty Democrats voted to end the southern filibuster. Yet when he offered his tabling motion immediately afterwards, it was defeated by sixty-four to thirty-three. As expected, moderate Republicans had switched sides to register a pro–civil rights vote. As reporters pointed out, "the tabling motion was something of a political free ride enabling Senators to claim a 'vote for civil rights' which in the procedural situation was meaningless." On May 14, Mansfield tried once more to shut down the southern filibuster, but he was defeated once more—this time by fifty-two votes to forty-two. The White House had not made any concerted effort to change a single vote, and no senators revised their position.[25]

In the aftermath, much of the blame for this legislative rebuff was rightly leveled at the hapless Mansfield. Liberal Republican Clifford Case accused him of having "no intention of giving serious consideration to getting the job done." The same criticism could have been leveled at the president. Kennedy had refused to lend the bill his active public support during the battle. Nor had he instructed his congressional liaison team to mount a behind-the-scenes lobbying effort, as he had done during the federal aid-to-education or Medicare battles the year before. Senator Joseph Clark lamented that the measure had died due to the "lack of any deep conviction" on the part of the administration. *Time* observed that the literacy test debate "had all the conviction of a professional wrestling match: everybody played his role for the crowds, but nobody got hurt. . . . Almost as if they whole thing were merely to make propaganda in the North, Kennedy aides made no real effort to push the bill." Speaking in New York on May 17, King criticized Kennedy's failure to fight for the literacy bill: "I do not feel the President has given the leadership that the enormity of the problem demands." As Burke Marshall later admitted: "We didn't handle it properly. We were very casual and could have been much more orderly."[26]

The Southern Caucus reveled in their victory. Russell praised his Senate colleagues for acting "as a bulwark against precipitate action inspired by the unthinking passions of a great mob." And the means of their victory made it still more gratifying. They had not been forced to rely solely on the filibuster, which could have rendered them vulnerable to a liberal backlash. Instead, they had triumphed by exposing the bill's constitutional weaknesses. For Ervin, especially, it was a stunning feat. Russell learned from the experience that his small band of bitter-enders could continue to defend Jim Crow for a good many years to come—a total reversal from his despondency on the eve of Kennedy's inauguration. The president and the Senate majority leader had handed the Southern Caucus yet another legislative—and psychological—victory.[27]

Kennedy drew another lesson from the debacle: that he had been correct to believe that it was impossible to make any headway on civil rights in Congress. It had reinforced his nonlegislative strategy, and strengthened the position of advisers, like Lawrence O'Brien and Kenneth O'Donnell, who had always wanted him to soft-pedal civil rights. As O'Brien wrote in a memo to the president in July, there was "no possibility" of enacting a civil rights bill during the present Congress.[28]

❧

In mid-June, the effectiveness of the president's executive action in the field of civil rights also came under fresh scrutiny. And once again, the administration was found wanting. This time attention focused on the failures of the President's Committee on Equal Employment Opportunity (PCEEO) to secure meaningful gains in black employment through voluntary measures. Bobby Troutman was at the center of the crisis. A cheerfully anti-intellectual lawyer, with a degree from Harvard Law School and a flourishing law practice in Atlanta, Bobby Troutman was one of the president's favorite southerners. Always a welcome visitor at the Oval Office, Troutman delighted the president with his bawdy anecdotes and folksy aphorisms. He was also Kennedy's most trusted southern political "fixer." Before the Los Angeles convention, he had helped line up support in the region, and during and after it, he had taken a leading role in quelling a possible Dixiecrat rebellion.

Shortly after the inauguration, Troutman had continued to demonstrate his value to the president by helping to mediate a potentially embarrassing dispute between the NAACP and the Lockheed Aircraft Corporation in Marietta, Georgia. Right after the formation of the PCEEO, the Pentagon had awarded a $1 billion defense contract to the plant, a move that provoked outrage from local NAACP activists, who had long complained about Lockheed's discriminatory labor practices. Troutman helped persuade the company to remove all the White and Colored signs from the plant's washrooms, to desegregate its cafeteria, and to replace its Jim Crow water fountains with paper cups. Since ninety percent of its orders came from the air force, Lockheed soon backed down. Convinced that the discreet negotiations that produced the Marietta deal could serve as a model for disputes elsewhere, Troutman lobbied Kennedy to replicate the approach with other defense contractors. Always in favor of voluntary rather than punitive action, the president had happily agreed. He gave the go-ahead for the so-called Plans for Progress to be launched in May 1961.[29]

Soon after, Troutman became the chairman of the Plans for Progress, which operated as a special subcommittee of the PCEEO. He set out its mission in an August memorandum. The Plans for Progress would be centered on "surveys the companies made themselves without any compulsion whatever." The subcommittee would not "create a vast Federal bureaucracy." Nor would it become "an employment agency or a policeman with nightstick chasing down alleged malefactors." The participating firms themselves would "open the doors of job opportunities." The memorandum read like a manifesto for voluntarism.[30]

By the summer, some of America's largest manufacturers, including Boeing, North American Aviation, United Aircraft Corporation, General Electric Company, and Douglas Aircraft Company had signed up for the plans, and more than 800,000 jobs were covered by voluntary agreements. Glitzy signing ceremonies took place at the White House, which themselves became an important inducement for other companies to sign up, largely because business leaders wanted to gain access to the president. As Lyndon Johnson was fond of telling his staff, "Let's make it *fashionable* to end discrimination."[31]

The White House signing ceremonies were indeed fashionable, but participating companies quickly learned that they could flout the agreements without fear of reprisal. By the beginning of 1962, it was an open secret that participating firms operated under a much more lax compliance regime than other federal contractors regulated by the PCEEO. Blacks started to complain. In April, Herbert Hill, an NAACP labor specialist, criticized the program for generating "more publicity than progress." The administration, he claimed, had failed to press for more concrete results out "of fear of conservative forces in Congress." At the same time, "Chuck" Stone, the influential publisher of the *Washington Afro-American,* wrote a letter to Johnson in which he complained that the plans were little more than a "publicity sham." Troutman, who had long been viewed by many black activists as a southern apologist, personally bore the brunt of much of the criticism, and the attacks increased after he attended a dinner held at a segregated hotel honoring Congressman Carl Vinson.[32]

By May, the PCEEO threatened to become a major political embarrassment. Robert Kennedy voiced loud concerns about its mismanagement and blamed Johnson for most of its failings. Johnson defended himself with a report highlighting the committee's successes, but it failed to impress the attorney general. "It certainly shows that some progress has been made," he responded sarcastically.[33]

In June, the internal rivalries between PCEEO "hawks," who favored strict enforcement, and "doves," who preferred voluntary compliance, burst into the open. Drawing heavily upon leaks from John Feild, the committee's liberal-minded executive director, the *New York Times* published a damning report that dismissed the Plans for Progress as little more than a political stunt. Liberal Republicans seized upon the report to mount their own attack, not on Johnson but on the president himself, for adopting such a weak stance on civil rights. In particular, New York Senator Jacob Javits demanded that Kennedy "clarify the role of his 'alleged good friend,' Bobby Troutman."[34]

Troutman realized that he had become an embarrassment to the president and decided to step down in late June. In a resignation letter larded with self-pity, Troutman explained how he had devoted "long, arduous" months to the Plans for Progress, at the personal expense of some $50,000. He was hurt by the lack of recognition from black leaders at the "amazing results" he had achieved. "While the venture became immediately impressive to those (the nation's key employers) who could help achieve great nationwide success," Troutman wrote, "it became equally unimpressive to those who speak for the people whom Plans for Progress sought to aid (the nation's large Negro population). Incredible but true!" The president sympathized and told Johnson shortly after Troutman's departure that "a great deal of criticism directed at the Plans for Progress resulted from completely irrelevant factors quite unrelated to the merits of the program."[35]

Kennedy was chiefly concerned, however, that the negative publicity surrounding the PCEEO would prompt leading corporations to withdraw from the Plans for Progress. Such a defection could supply the GOP even more explosive political ordnance. He ordered Johnson to find a replacement for Troutman as quickly as possible. The Plans for Progress had to continue. Kennedy refused to accept the criticism that the plans were "phonies"—as the NAACP had complained—and that the compliance regime was too weak. As he pointed out in a memorandum to Lyndon Johnson, the advances made by the Plans for Progress were "most impressive" and "we might well be embarrassed if the companies that have already participated pull out."[36]

With the PCEEO seemingly in a perpetual state of crisis, earlier in the spring Johnson had in fact already asked Theodore Kheel, a New York labor lawyer and former president of the National Urban League, to prepare an independent report on its work. Published in mid-August, the Kheel report called for the Plans for Progress to continue, just as Johnson had hoped, but suggested they come under much tighter control from the central committee. Johnson initiated a few minor reforms as a result, the most notable of which was the elevation of the vice president's closest black associate, Hobart Taylor, from his position as special counsel of the PCEEO to the newly created post of executive vice chairman, with special responsibility for the plans. But the Plans for Progress remained in place, as did the flashy White House signing ceremonies that promoted them. Voluntarism remained the watchword. In time for November's elections, the PCEEO had undergone a superficial makeover rather than a much-needed root-and-branch reform.

The administration did take a few small steps toward civil rights reform in the first half 1962, but they tended to be made by the attorney general and other liberal-minded cabinet officials rather than the White House. In early May, on the very day that hopes of securing the passage of the literacy test bill finally evaporated, Robert Kennedy moved to outlaw racial segregation in any hospital that had been built with the assistance of the federal government. Justice Department officials intervened in a lawsuit brought by a group of black physicians in Greensboro, who had challenged the 1946 Hill-Burton Act, which included a "separate but equal" provision allowing federal money to finance segregated hospitals. Since the act became law, Hill-Burton aid had contributed to the construction of more than 2,000 southern hospitals, many of which placed black patients in segregated wards and refused to employ black doctors. Justice Department officials viewed Hill-Burton as unconstitutional and wanted to overturn the act. Robert Kennedy, however, stressed publicly that their initiative did not imply the administration's support for the withdrawal of federal funds from existing segregated hospitals. That, he felt, would set a dangerous precedent, because the same principle could be applied to southern schools.[37]

In a separate but related attempt to reduce the federal financing of segregated facilities, HEW threatened to set up schools for children living on southern military bases if local public school boards refused to adopt integration plans. The scale of the problem was enormous, since more than 200 federal installations were served by school districts with segregated schools. The administration was threatening to withdraw federal funding from recalcitrant school districts, the kind of forceful action for which civil rights leaders were clamoring. But John Kennedy's lack of credibility with regard to civil rights led many to suspect that the administration was merely posturing for political reasons. The *New York Times* dismissed the move as a feeble attempt to neutralize criticisms levied by liberal Republican lawmakers and black activists "who had demanded more Administration action." HEW Secretary Abraham Ribicoff fueled these suspicions with his assertion before stepping down that the "major responsibility for taking affirmative action rests with Congress" rather than the executive branch.[38]

In June, Kennedy appointed a President's Committee on Equal Opportunity in the Armed Forces, under the chairmanship of Washington attorney Gerhard A. Gesell. Ostensibly, the committee was formed to accelerate the integration of the armed services and to look into off-base discrimination. But in fact the committee was only mandated to study the problem. It had no enforcement function and did not even have a dedicated staff (Gesell had to persuade staffers at the Civil Rights Commission to help). Still, the inclusion on the committee of Whitney Young, the head of the National Urban League, and John Sengstacke, one of the country's most prominent black publishers, gave the body a measure of credibility among black activists disappointed by the Weaver fiasco and the defeat of the literacy test bill.[39]

Kennedy did little to advertise the committee's work. Its creation was announced not in a ceremony at the White House—as had been the case with the PCEEO and Plans for Progress—but in a letter to Gesell. To have made a great show would have angered Russell and Vinson, the chairmen of the Senate and House Armed Services Committees. Unhappy at the committee's limited sphere of activity, Young soon warned Gesell, "we must in no way give the impression that we have white-washed the situation."[40]

Black activists became ever more vocal over the course of the spring about Kennedy's shortcomings. "Despite all his promises, fireworks and impressive-looking appointments," vented Jackie Robinson in the spring, "we feel the President has not made one genuine move on behalf of the whole colored constituency of the United States." Even the normally pro-Kennedy *Jet* magazine observed in April that "JFK's reputation is pockmocked [sic] with attacks from Negroes—the hardest pounding he's taken from us."[41]

Kennedy's partisan strategy in the months before the midterm elections cost him a great deal of credibility with both black activists and civil rights proponents on Capitol Hill. Kennedy had revealed himself as a cynical political operator, and his consequent loss of credibility on the subject did lasting damage to the cause of civil rights. Focused on obtaining short-term electoral gains for his party, Kennedy had poisoned his relationships with key Republican moderates and thus greatly diminished the prospects of compromise. In the meantime, he had allowed a resurgent Southern Caucus to remain above the partisan fray and take advantage of the opportunity to defeat the literacy test and block Weaver's appointment—momentous victories that convinced them they could maintain the status quo indefinitely.

CHAPTER 19

❧

Albany Revisited

Early in 1962, Harris Wofford decided that there was no point in continuing to fight on behalf of civil rights in the torpid climate of the Kennedy White House. Frustrated with his diminished access to the president, Wofford had already come close to resigning at the end of 1961. Kennedy's condescension had also started to grate. "Are your constituents happy?" Kennedy would ask as he rushed past Wofford in the corridor, but he rarely waited for a reply. As the sacks of "Ink for Jack" pens cluttering his office amply demonstrated, clearly they were not. Kenneth O'Donnell made Wofford's job even harder by repeatedly turning down requests for presidential meetings from civil rights leaders. In October 1961, Wofford had written defiantly to O'Donnell, "I will keep bothering you, so why don't you try to set them [the meetings] now so that we can both move on to greater things."[1]

But in January 1962, Wofford finally burned out. He had taken a six-week trip to Africa toward the end of 1961 and felt galvanized upon his return to Washington. On January 20, Wofford issued his first memorandum of the New Year, which called on the administration to move "[f]ull speed ahead in ending discrimination at home." But three days later he decided to leave, in the wake of a disappointing meeting with the president in which he had pleaded for the issuance of the housing order. When Kennedy stonewalled him yet again, Wofford requested a transfer to the Peace Corps. On January 23, Wofford outlined the reasons underpinning his decision to leave in a memorandum to Kennedy. "The Big Integration of us less-colored Westerners in a largely colored world is the question that interests me the most," he wrote. He hoped that Kennedy would continue to work on behalf of civil rights. Louis Martin, he suggested, should oversee initiatives in this area once Wofford left. "You need someone like Louis here," he warned, "for we are heading into stormier weather with [the] Negro leadership in view of rising disappointment over our current slower strategy."[2]

313

Kennedy did not respond to the memo, and, in March, Wofford tendered his formal resignation. "I believe that the creative work I can do for you on civil rights is for the most part done," he told Kennedy. "You know the big steps which I believe you should take." For the last time, he enumerated the areas of primary concern to civil rights activists: the housing order, the integration of the National Guard, and the withdrawal of federal funds from segregated universities.[3]

Wofford's future was finally settled at a meeting in April, at which Kennedy tried to persuade him to take up an African ambassadorship rather than a post at the Peace Corps. That way his departure could be presented as a well-earned promotion rather than an embarrassing retreat from the battle for civil rights. But Wofford was determined to join the Peace Corps. The tone of the meeting was otherwise wistful. As the president read through Wofford's valedictory memorandum, he circled various recommendations with his pen. Perhaps Kennedy felt guilty about all of the promises he had left unfulfilled since the 1960 platform, or perhaps he simply wanted to end their formal relationship on an uplifting note. For whatever reason, he made a vow to Wofford: "It will take some time, but I want you to know that we are going to do all these things. You will see, with time I'm going to do them all."[4]

When it came to replacing Wofford as a senior White House adviser, however, Kennedy did not follow Wofford's suggestion of appointing Martin. The president decided to allocate this responsibility to Sorensen, his most trusted—and more moderate—aide. When Wofford's resignation came into effect in July, he left an enormous vacuum at the White House. The administration could no longer boast of a senior official with longstanding ties to the civil rights movement, or even one with a thoroughgoing grasp of the issues. The Sub-Cabinet Group, which had done so much to stamp out discrimination within the federal government, was now rudderless. After his departure, Wofford had no further impact on administration policy. He stayed up to date with major civil rights developments through the press clippings that Sargent Shriver, his new boss, sent him in Ethiopia. His departure was brutally symbolic to civil rights leaders. "No doubt Mr. Wofford got tired of butting his head against a brick wall," wrote Jackie Robinson, on learning that Wofford was on his way out, "and decided it would be more fulfilling to work with the Peace Corps."[5]

⌒

Seven months after Martin Luther King's campaign to desegregate the city had ended in such ignominious failure, Albany, Georgia, remained what one reporter called "a monument to white supremacy." In January 1962, new city commissioners had taken office who were even more conservative than their predecessors; and the city's mayor, Asa Kelley, who was considered a moderate by Albany standards, became an increasingly isolated figure. In March, a campaign to bring about the integration of the city buses resulted in a suspension of services, after the city bus company suffered huge financial losses and the City Commission refused, by a vote of six to one, to countenance a desegregation pact. In April, the City Commission decided to end all negotiations with the Albany Movement and rebuffed protesters' renewed efforts to desegregate the main library in the city and other municipal facilities. Chief Laurie Pritchett also made sure that the rail and bus terminals remained segregated, in clear violation of the ICC ruling, by ordering his men to prevent blacks from using them.[6]

When members of the Albany Movement visited Washington in June to complain to the Justice Department, they were told by John Doar that the federal government had no authority to intervene. Pritchett had arrested blacks trying to use the terminal facilities on public order charges, he claimed, which meant no federal laws had been broken (even though Section 242 of the U.S. Criminal Code made it a crime for any local law enforcement official to subject "any inhabitant of any State . . . to the deprivation of any rights, privileges or immunities"). The Albany Movement, meanwhile, continued to be beset by bitter internal rivalries. Veteran NAACP activists in the city continued to resent the arrival of SNCC firebrands, who themselves deeply distrusted King. There was little agreement over how to take the movement forward.[7]

King had last visited the city in February 1962, when he and his associate Ralph Abernathy stood trial for leading a protest march to City Hall on December 16. After less than a day of hearing evidence, during which Chief Pritchett was the sole prosecution witness, Judge A. N. Durden, Sr. announced he would deliver his verdict in sixty days. During that period, King monitored events in the city from his headquarters in Atlanta. Rather than participate in direct-action campaigns, in Albany or elsewhere, he spent the early part of the year building up the SCLC across the South and intensifying his attacks on the Kennedy administration. In a scathing article published in March entitled "Fumbling on the New Frontier," King criticized the administration's "cautious and defensive" strategy: "Its efforts have been directed toward limited accomplishments in a number of areas, affecting few individuals and altering old patterns only superficially. . . . It is a melancholy fact that the Administration is aggressively driving only toward the limited goal of token integration." On Monday, April 9, King reiterated the same point in separate meetings with Robert Kennedy and Lyndon Johnson. At a time when forthright leadership was required, he complained, the president refused to provide it. He also wanted the Justice Department to offer voting-rights workers greater federal protection, which was fast becoming one of the key demands of the civil rights movement.[8]

When King returned to Albany in mid-July to be sentenced, he viewed it as an opportunity to build upon his work of the past six months. A period behind bars would enable King to rebut the oft-heard criticism from SNCC activists that he was notoriously unwilling to put himself on the line physically. His imprisonment would also ratchet up pressure on the administration to intervene more forcefully in Albany.

On Tuesday, July 10, Judge Durden handed down severe sentences of forty-five days in jail or a $178 fine to both King and Ralph Abernathy. Since paying the fine meant acceding to the injustice, King and Abernathy opted for jail. The imprisonments had the electrifying effect that King intended. Newspapermen descended upon the city, fully expecting to cover their first major civil rights crisis of the year. Local blacks flocked to two mass meetings that Wednesday evening, which were full to overflowing.[9]

The timing of King's imprisonment could not have been worse for the Kennedys. The Georgia Democratic gubernatorial primary was less than two months away, and the administration hoped that Carl Sanders, a racial moderate, would prevail. Officials feared that any inflammation of racial tensions would benefit his opponent, archsegregationist Marvin Griffin. To compound their worries, Washington reporters were demanding a presidential response to the sentencing and drawing parallels to King's imprisonment during the 1960 campaign. Kennedy was under great pressure to make a comment. On July 11, in response to a deluge of questions from journalists, Salinger issued a perfunctory holding statement, in which he indicated that the attorney general was preparing a situation report.[10]

In fact, JFK had taken an unusually keen interest in the crisis. Perhaps he had taken Wofford's resignation, and their final conversation, to heart—or maybe he was more concerned about the upcoming primary in Georgia, and the midterm elections more generally. For whatever reason, on July 11 he had several telephone conversations with Burke Marshall, who was on a fishing vacation in the Pocono Mountains of Pennsylvania. The president instructed Marshall to contact to King's wife, Coretta, in Atlanta, to assure her of the administration's interest in the case, and to open a dialogue with Albany officials. Kennedy was perplexed when Marshall explained that from a legal standpoint there was very little the administration could do.[11]

In Albany, King's unexpected imprisonment frightened Mayor Asa Kelley, who feared his city might again be engulfed by mass protests. Determined to bring about King's speedy release, on July 11 he approached James Gray, the Massachusetts-born local newspaper publisher who had known the Kennedys in his youth, to explore the possibility of making some sort of deal with Washington. With Kelley beside him, Gray immediately telephoned the Oval Office with the vague outline of a plan. "Jack, we've got Martin Luther King in jail," he told the president. "The damn media is having a field day. . . . It would be very nice if you sent someone down here to pick him up." Kennedy knew it would be politically hazardous to dispatch a presidential emissary to spring

King from jail, and he was reluctant to commit himself to any other bold course of action that would commit the administration to public involvement. Instead, the president suggested that Kelley send a representative to Washington for private discussions with the attorney general.[12]

Within a matter of hours, B. C. Gardner, a senior partner in Kelley's law firm, set off on a flight to Washington, where he met with Robert Kennedy. Both agreed that King's continued incarceration did not serve the administration's interest or those of Albany politicians. But how to secure his release? As Gardner flew back to Georgia, a plan took shape in his mind. Secretly, the Albany City Commission could pay King and Abernathy's fines and then spread a cover story about how a mysterious donor had proffered the funds. When Gardner presented the plan, Kelley initially balked fearing that if reporters uncovered the commission's complicity, his political career would be over.[13]

That Wednesday evening, however, after trouble flared between police and local blacks close to Shiloh Church, the main venue for mass meetings in the city, Kelley reconsidered. Dreading further disturbances, he decided to take the risk. Before sunrise on Thursday morning, Gardner handed over $356 in fines to a sergeant on the duty desk at the Albany jailhouse, and a short while later King and Abernathy were told to leave. When Police Chief Pritchett refused to reveal the donor's identity, King protested—putting himself in the peculiar position of arguing for his right to remain in jail. But since the fine had been paid, Albany officials could no longer detain him.[14]

When he heard the news of King's release later that morning, Robert Kennedy was delighted and quickly issued an upbeat statement: "Dr. King's release should make it possible for the citizens of Albany to resolve their differences in this situation in a less tense atmosphere." (His comments were so sanguine, in fact, that they fueled rumors that the "anonymous donor" was a Justice Department official—an allegation Edwin Guthman, RFK's spokesman, vigorously denied.[15])

But King did not retreat from Albany. Upon leaving jail, King vowed to remain in the city until the main demand of the Albany Movement, for face-to-face discussions with the Albany City Commission, had been met. He broke his vow only once: in order to fulfill a longstanding commitment to address the National Press Club in Washington on Thursday, July 19. It was an important occasion—King was the first black to appear before that organization, and he used the opportunity to deliver a warning to journalists and lawmakers: Blacks were no longer prepared to wait complacently for an end to southern segregation. Now there was a "new Negro on the scene with a new sense of dignity and destiny." While King praised the Justice Department for its efforts on behalf of voter registration, he insisted that the "majesty of federal law must assert its supremacy over the reign of evil and illegality dominating defiant southern communities."[16]

King returned to Albany the next day. With the Albany City Commission refusing to negotiate, he planned to lead a fresh round of street protests, with the
expectation that he would be arrested and thrown once more in jail. He would
thereby ratchet up further pressure on the Albany Commission, and, by extension, the White House. But officials in Albany had anticipated his strategy.
While King was in Washington, Kelley had met secretly with Governor Vandiver and vowed to halt the Albany Movement in its tracks. There was no question of giving in to any of the Albany Movement's demands, but the city could
not continue to arrest hundreds of demonstrators indefinitely. Instead, Vandiver
and Kelley decided to seek a federal court order banning protesters from
mounting further demonstrations. The proposal was in clear violation of the
constitutional right to free assembly, but Vandiver knew exactly who he could
turn to for support: J. Robert Elliott, the white supremacist whom Kennedy had
appointed to the federal bench early in 1962.[17]

Indeed, Elliott was happy to sign a temporary injunction barring King, Abernathy, and the Albany Movement from participating in further protests. In one
of the more perverse judicial decisions of the entire civil rights era, early on Saturday, July 21, Elliott ruled that protest marches infringed the civil rights of
Albany's white community. Forced to withdraw policemen from affluent neighborhoods to patrol protest routes, the city was denying white residents their
right to equal protection.[18]

In Washington, Justice Department officials responded with dismay. Elliott's
ruling highlighted the president's misjudgment in appointing him and simultaneously threatened to drag the administration deeper into the crisis. If King and
his fellow protesters mounted fresh protests, the federal government could ultimately find itself responsible for enforcing Elliott's temporary injunction. That
in turn raised the unsavory prospect of U.S. marshals arresting black demonstrators for simply venturing onto the streets. Already that Saturday morning,
federal marshals had suffered the ignominy of conducting a citywide search for
King to serve him with Elliott's court order.

King confronted what was arguably his most agonizing decision since founding the SCLC: whether or not to obey the injunction. Since the ruling was so
manifestly unjust, he was naturally inclined to defy it by proceeding with the
march. But the issue was far more complicated. King was well aware that the civil
rights movement had derived much of its progress from rulings from the federal
bench. Faced with white supremacists who violated those rulings, King had argued consistently that the federal government was morally and legally beholden
to enforce federal court orders. How could he himself now stand in defiance of
this principle?

King suspected, however, that the Justice Department had given its secret
blessing to Elliott's ruling, and he feared that if he obeyed it he would play directly into Washington's hands. In fact, the Justice Department had done no

such thing. When Robert Kennedy learned from FBI wiretaps that King was planning to defy the ruling, he contacted him directly by telephone. If he violated the court order, the attorney general argued King would give segregationist governors an argument for rejecting school integration orders. Though partially in agreement, King indicated that there was also a higher moral law at stake. Kennedy was incensed by King's intransigence and insisted that no individual was above the law. [19]

King finally snapped. If the president had not appointed Elliott in the first place, he blasted, the problem would never have arisen. Kennedy realized he was losing the argument and quickly handed the telephone to Marshall, who spent the next two hours trying to persuade King to back down. Eventually, the two men reached a compromise. King would encourage a group of demonstrators whose names had not been included in the injunction to march on City Hall, but would not participate himself. That Saturday night, after a boisterous mass meeting at Shiloh Church, over a hundred protesters, led by a local minister who had not been named in Elliott's order, marched on downtown. Close to City Hall, they were blocked by Chief Pritchett and his men, who bundled them off to jail amid a chorus of boos and chants from black observers gathered on the sidewalks.[20]

Any hopes in Washington that King's decision against marching would ease tensions were dashed quickly. The following Monday afternoon, news reached Albany from the nearby town of Camilla that the wife of Slater King, the Albany Movement's most prominent lawyer, had been viciously attacked by local police. With her three young children in tow, Marion King had gone to the Mitchell County jail to show her support for the many protesters who were being detained there. A large group of sympathizers had already assembled. King was six months pregnant, and when the police started to break up the crowd she could not move quickly enough to get out of their way. Police officers kicked and hit her twice on the side of the head. She was knocked unconsciousness (she later miscarried because of her injuries).

When they learned of the attack later on that Monday, protesters immediately mounted a prayer vigil on the steps outside Albany City Hall, and Martin Luther King contacted Marshall to demand a robust federal response. Later on, the FBI sent an agent to Marion King's home to take a statement, but Marshall insisted that the Justice Department could not pursue the matter further. In a telegram to Martin Luther King later that week, Marshall stressed that the Justice Department had no jurisdiction over the administration of a state penal institution, unless it violated a federal law.[21]

On Tuesday, July 24, the U.S. Court of Appeals for the Fifth Circuit in Atlanta ruled that Judge Elliott's ban on demonstrations was unconstitutional, which paved the way for further protests. That evening, in an ebullient mood, King addressed a mass meeting at Shiloh, after which a group of about forty protesters marched toward downtown Albany. When they reached the intersection of Jackson and Oglethorpe, Albany's racial interface, police immediately arrested them. The city remained on edge in the wake of Marion King's assault, and the new arrests provoked a violent reaction. A group of black onlookers hurled rocks and bottles at the police. Within hours, Pritchett's men were faced with a crowd of some 2,000 angry blacks. One of the missiles struck a state trooper in the face, and another hit a policeman in the jaw and knocked out two of his teeth. Pritchett saw his chance to turn the tide of public opinion against the Albany Movement. "Did you see those non-violent rocks?" Pritchett remarked caustically to a nearby reporter.[22]

The next morning King read national newspaper reports placing the blame for Tuesday night's violence squarely on the shoulders of black protesters. King immediately called for a "day of penance"—a twenty-four-hour moratorium on further demonstrations. Then he set off on a tour of the town's pool halls and taverns, where he cautioned young blacks not to participate in any further violence. But many were growing impatient with King's message of peace. One reporter who accompanied him on the tour observed that "[h]e preached a theme that Albany's restless Negroes were finding harder and harder to accept: nonviolence in their drive to desegregate the town."[23]

Throughout the week, King repeatedly demanded a meeting with the city's white leaders, the main goal of the Albany Movement, but to no avail. Exasperated, he presented himself at City Hall in person early that Friday afternoon to demand a face-to-face meeting with Mayor Kelley. Instead, he was confronted by Pritchett, who threatened to arrest him unless he left within three minutes. King responded by kneeling in prayer, and, three minutes later, was taken into custody by officers on the scene. It was his third imprisonment in Albany in eight months.

By returning to jail, King hoped to galvanize the Albany Movement, restore unity in its bitterly divided ranks, and spark new protests. Yet with local SNCC leaders now openly working against him, King found it increasingly difficult to recruit new volunteers. Many believed that King had spent too much time in the national spotlight, diluting his message and his influence with the civil rights movement. When Andrew Young and Charles Sherrod called for fresh protesters to come forward at a mass meeting that evening just fifteen of the 500 people present volunteered.[24]

The reaction to King's imprisonment was much stronger outside of Albany. Black leaders put intense pressure on the White House to intervene on King's behalf. Appearing as a substitute for King that weekend on *Meet the Press*, William G. Anderson of the Albany Movement called on the president to facilitate talks between Albany's white leadership and demonstrators, and to order an FBI investigation into allegations of police brutality and illegal arrest. At a bare minimum, the president should lend moral support and reaffirm publicly the right of peaceful assembly.[25]

Pierre Salinger, however, stonewalled reporters when they asked for Kennedy's response to the crisis in Albany. The president was spending the weekend in Hyannis Port, he said, and was unavailable for comment as he and his family were celebrating Jacqueline Kennedy's birthday. Civil rights leaders continued to demand a statement from Kennedy. On Monday, July 30, both Roy Wilkins of the NAACP and James Farmer of CORE called on the president to make a strong public comment on King's arrest and the breakdown of law in Albany. Walter Reuther of the United Auto Workers urged Kennedy to deploy the "full moral persuasive and executive powers invested by your high office." That Tuesday, Illinois Democratic Senator Paul Douglas contacted Marshall on behalf of a bipartisan group of senators to demand that all possible steps be taken to help the arrested demonstrators.[26]

Nelson Rockefeller, an early contender for the 1964 Republican presidential nomination, also tried to impose himself. A liberal Republican with considerable black support, Rockefeller recognized Kennedy's vulnerability on civil rights and intended to exploit it. He wired Robert Kennedy on the night of the arrest to demand that King be guaranteed adequate protection in jail. He also called for an investigation into the arrest policy of the Albany police to determine if they had violated the protesters' constitutional right to peaceable assembly. With the congressional midterm elections just over three months away, King's imprisonment threatened to become enmeshed in partisan politics, with echoes of the 1960 presidential campaign.[27]

The president expressed his deep concern over the turn of events in Albany. He had grown increasingly frustrated at the Justice Department's failure to resolve the crisis, and increasingly exasperated over the Albany City Commission's refusal to hold talks with representatives of the Albany Movement. Over the weekend, he had inundated Marshall with calls asking why they weren't doing more. Marshall later reflected that Kennedy had "found it difficult to believe that there wasn't something the Justice Department should do about Albany."[28]

The president had also read a series of front-page reports published in the *New York Times* over the course of the week, which graphically highlighted the brutish realities faced by disenfranchised blacks in rural Georgia. The first, published on Friday, July 27, provided an extraordinary account of the voter rights campaign in nearby Terrell County—or "Terrible Terrell" as it was more commonly known—a small community close to Albany. Two nights before, reporter Claude Sitton had traveled with Charles Sherrod, a founder of the Albany Movement, to a voter registration meeting in Terrell County, where out of an 8,209-strong population, just fifty-one blacks could vote. Sitton described a chilling scene that had taken place at Mount Olive Baptist Church. The setting was bucolic: a rustic wooden church with farmers, old ladies in straw hats, and little girls in pigtails. A large portrait of President Kennedy hung to the left of the pulpit. But midway through the registration meeting, just as Sherrod was reading from the Scriptures, thirteen flashlight-wielding policemen clattered into the sanctuary, as if they were about to attack. Sherrod responded by launching into a prayer. Then he invited the congregation to sing "We Are Climbing Jacob's Ladder," an anthem of the movement. Halfway through the hymn, the local sheriff, seventy-year-old Z. T. Mathews, swaggered through the door, walked to the front of the sanctuary, and addressed the meeting. "I have the greatest respect for any religious organization," he said, "but my people is getting disturbed about these secret meetings. I don't think there is any colored people down here who are afraid. After last night the people are disturbed. They had a lot of violence in Albany last night."

Then he addressed the local black congregants. "Are any of you disturbed?" he asked.

"Yes," came the muffled reply.

"Can you vote if you are qualified?"

"No," they said.

"Haven't you been getting on well for a hundred years?"

"No," came the reply once more.

Then his nephew and chief deputy, M. E. Mathews, chimed in. "Negras down here have been happy for a hundred years, and now this has started," he said. "We want our colored people to live like they've been living. There was never any trouble before all this started. It's caused great dislike between colored and white."

Mathews's deputies then walked through the pews and wrote down the names of the "outsiders" who led the registration campaign. As Mathews left the sanctuary, the group hummed "We Shall Overcome." When the meeting drew to a close, shortly after ten o'clock, the congregation filed out to find themselves confronted once again by the police and local troublemakers. "I know you," an officer snarled at one member of the congregation, his voiced spiked with hatred. "We're going to get some of you." (In early September, the church was burned to the ground.)[29]

Claude Sitton followed up with a second report, published on Sunday, July 29. He described an incident in which a black attorney, C. B. King, Jr., had visited the Dougherty County sheriff's office to check on the condition of a white SNCC field worker, who had been beaten unconscious by a prison trustee. Before King was even able to reach the prison, he was assaulted by the seventy-six-year-old local sheriff, "Cull" Campbell. On the street outside, in plain view of passersby, Campbell attacked C. B. King with a walking stick. He beat him repeatedly over the head until King's hair was matted with blood and the cane had broken in two. "Yeh, I knocked hell out of him, and I'll do it again," Campbell had boasted to Sitton. "I let him know I'm a white man and he's a damned nigger."[30]

Like the president, Robert Kennedy read Sitton's stories with horror. On July 26, he had delivered a self-congratulatory speech before a black insurance convention in Los Angeles, in which he boasted that black employment opportunities had improved dramatically under the Kennedy administration. Sitton's articles reminded him of the many problems still unsolved. The attorney general quickly instructed John Doar to investigate. When Doar seemed to hesitate, Kennedy barked at him: "Move." According to a progress report submitted by Marshall at the end of August, the Justice Department filed a civil rights complaint against Sheriff Mathews within two weeks of the publication of Sitton's account.[31]

Up until that point, neither of the Kennedy brothers had publicly vented their frustrations. But that was about to change. At his weekly press conference on Wednesday, August 1, the president broke his silence. "I find it wholly inexplicable why the city council of Albany will not sit down with the citizens of Albany, who may be Negroes, and attempt to secure them, in a peaceful way, their rights," he said. "The U.S. Government is involved in sitting down at Geneva with the Soviet Union. I can't understand why the government of Albany, the city council of Albany, cannot do the same for American citizens. We are going to attempt, as we have in the past, to try to provide a satisfactory solution and protection of the constitutional rights of the people of Albany, and will continue to do so. And the situation today is completely unsatisfactory from that point of view." It was the first time during his nineteen months in office that Kennedy had sided publicly with civil rights demonstrators, or reproached segregationists so openly.[32]

The following day, King wired a message to the president from jail: "Gratified by directness of your statement to Albany crisis. I earnestly hope you will continue to use the great moral influence of your office to help this crucial situation. There is no need for another Little Rock here." King also spoke to reporters that day and expressed gratitude for Kennedy's forthright statement of support. Wilkins sent a telegram to Kennedy to express his appreciation, as did veteran civil rights leader A. Philip Randolph, who welcomed the president's "forthright and constructive" statement. Howard Zinn of the Southern Regional Council was more circumspect and later noted that Kennedy "carefully skirted the moral issue of racial equality and stuck to procedural questions: the law, negotiation."[33]

Segregationists, meanwhile, were furious at Kennedy. Richard Russell was particularly hostile. "This stamp of approval upon the constant violations of the city laws from the highest source in our land," he complained, "is certain to encourage the importation of other professionals and notoriety seekers and worsen an already bad situation." Kelley deemed the president's comments as "inappropriate" and restated the City Commission's position that Albany would never negotiate with "outside agitators." But the strongest denunciation came from James Gray, who wrote in the *Albany Herald* that his old friends, the Kennedy brothers, had seemingly gone mad. He ridiculed them as "two ambitious Bostonians, who have been as practically connected with the American Negro in their lifetimes as Eskimos are to the Congo Democrats."[34]

Southern fears that the Kennedy administration was taking the side of the Albany Movement intensified the following evening when Robert Kennedy discussed the crisis with a seven-strong delegation of black leaders, which included Wilkins and Clarence Mitchell of the NAACP, Richard Haley of CORE, and Walter Fauntroy, the SCLC's Washington representative. Emboldened by the president's remarks, the group challenged the administration to support two civil lawsuits filed by the Albany Movement aimed at dismantling segregated facilities. Mitchell even suggested the administration could threaten the closure of military installations in the area. The Justice Department should at least arrest one of the police officers or sheriffs involved in the beating of Marion King and bar Pritchett from arresting demonstrators exercising their constitutional rights.[35]

Kennedy listened patiently but considered their proposals naïve. "You know as well as I do, Clarence, that we have done what we can do under existing law," he said, derisively. "We could do a great deal more if our hands weren't tied." Though the attorney general did not foreclose the possibility that the department could take legal action at some point, he stressed that the administration's immediate priority was to encourage the start of negotiations between the Albany Movement and the City Commissioners. All the time, King remained in jail.[36]

On Wednesday, August 8, the Justice Department finally intervened on the side of the Albany Movement, by filing an amicus brief opposing the permanent injunction sought by the Albany City Commission banning further protests. Jerry Heilbron, a Justice Department official from Arkansas, presented the Justice Department's position in court. Mayor Kelley and his fellow commissioners did not have "clean hands," he insisted, because they had defied past federal court orders and subverted others with the use of police power.[37]

Why did the Justice Department file the brief, when less than a week earlier Robert Kennedy had openly stated that the administration did not intend to insert itself into the crisis? Certainly, the Kennedy brothers wanted to avoid a situation in which U.S. marshals, or even troops, were forced to uphold a permanent injunction that prevented blacks from exercising their right of protest. But they also knew that such a patently illegitimate court order was sure to be overturned on appeal, just as Elliott's temporary injunction had been. The administration clearly wanted to put itself on legal record in support of the civil rights demonstrators. The amicus brief sent a clear signal to the City Commissioners in Albany—and, implicitly, to other southern segregationists—that they could no longer treat blacks unlawfully. Along with the president's remarks at the press conference, the brief signaled that the administration was moving away from its policy of studied neutrality. A Justice Department statement released on the day it filed its brief indicated that the administration wished to offer "formal assurance to Negroes of the federal government's continuing interest." As the *New York Times* headlined its coverage the following day: "U.S. Intervenes on Negroes' Side."[38]

King recognized this important shift and issued a statement welcoming the Kennedy administration's "legal and moral support." Segregationists also understood the broader implications of the brief. Mayor Kelley described it as "an affront to those of us in the South who are prepared to stand fast for law and order."[39]

Apart from its symbolic support of the Albany Movement, however, the administration strenuously sought to avoid anything that could be perceived as a close collaboration with civil rights activists. When a group of 103 black ministers had arrived in Washington on August 6 demanding a meeting with the president, Kenneth O'Donnell refused to let them into the White House. Salinger briefed reporters that the president was simply too busy to see them (in fact, Kennedy had time that day to attend a concert on the South Lawn performed by young musicians from the National Music Camp and to meet with the Yugoslav ambassador, who turned up over thirty minutes late). Kennedy also turned down a request from the CRC to demonstrate his support for the protesters by dispatching a presidential emissary to Albany. CRC staffers William Taylor and Berl Bernhard claimed that the arrival of a presidential emissary would be "an action dramatic enough to nullify the carping of the critics and to provide tangible evidence of support for civil rights."[40]

By mid-August, the crisis in Albany was abating and compromise was in the air. On August 10, two days after the Justice Department filed its amicus brief, Martin Luther King was given a suspended sentence and released from jail. He immediately announced to the packed courtroom that he was prepared to leave town and call a temporary halt to the demonstrations if Albany's white leadership agreed to hold talks. On Wednesday, August 15, those discussions finally took place. But the city commissioners refused to back down. In fact, they pledged to enforce even more vigorously the city's segregation laws and ordinances. To demonstrate their seriousness, the previous weekend they had ordered the immediate closure of the city library when a black tried to borrow a book and shut down "whites only" parks when a biracial group arrived to play an integrated tennis match.[41]

Before leaving Albany, King had threatened renewed protests if talks failed to yield progress. But by mid-August, the Albany Movement had lost much of its momentum. Largely because of the fierce rivalries within the movement, it had become harder to mount protests and recruit new volunteers, and Anderson announced on August 16 that its energies would henceforth be channeled into a voter registration campaign rather than street protests. Partly out of desperation, partly out of anger, King wired a telegram to the White House on August

31 in hopes that Kennedy could combat the intransigence of Albany officials. He implored Kennedy to deliver a nationwide address and to convene a meeting of the Albany City Commission and Albany Movement at the White House. But with the intensity of the crisis already subsiding, the White House failed even to acknowledge King's request. Albany was finally quiet—the aim of administration policy from the outset.[42]

The Justice Department also backed off. A group of seven liberal senators held a meeting with Burke Marshall in the last week of August and called for a more forceful response from the administration. But Marshall reminded them there were limits to what the Justice Department could do, not least because the segregation of the city's parks, libraries, and swimming pools violated no federal laws. With the Albany Movement slipping off the front pages, Marshall had no intention of disturbing the city's fractious peace. Even when two black churches in "Terrible Terrell," including Mount Olive Baptist Church, were firebombed by local segregationists on September 9, the Justice Department did little and left the FBI to mount an investigation. King called for a thoroughgoing federal investigation and complained that the FBI showed little interest in solving the crime. James Farmer and Charles McDew of SNCC demanded that the Kennedy administration end "the Nazi-like reign of terror in Southwest Georgia."[43]

By September, King had left Albany for Atlanta. He had been humiliated by the collapse of the Albany Movement and felt badly let down by the Kennedy administration, which, he believed, should have exerted greater pressure on the City Commission to grant more concessions. Over the coming weeks, he became more openly critical of the president and strengthened his ties with Rockefeller. In a joint appearance at a New York fund-raiser in mid-September, Rockefeller pledged $5,000 to the SCLC and $10,000 toward the costs of rebuilding the churches burned down in Terrell County. King used the opportunity to issue a scathing attack on Kennedy's leadership. In reference to Kennedy's submissive relationship with the Southern Caucus, he pronounced that "No President can be great if he attempts to accommodate to injustice to maintain his political balance."[44]

But the standoff in Albany had unquestionably pricked the president's conscience, even if his interest in the immediate crisis had quickly waned. During a press conference on September 13, a journalist asked him to comment on a recent spate of violence against black voter registration workers, which included a gun attack on Charles Sherrod on September 4 and the arson attacks in Terrell County four days later. Kennedy responded in a tone of genuine moral indignation: "I don't know any more outrageous action which I have seen occur in this country for a good many months or years than the burning of a church—two churches—because of the effort made by Negroes to be registered to vote. To shoot, as we saw in the case of Mississippi, two young people who were involved in an effort to register people, to burn churches as a reprisal. . . . I consider both cowardly as well as outrageous." He was determined to punish those responsible and promised that "as soon as we are able to find out who did it, we'll arrest them and we'll bring them before a jury, and I'm sure that they'll be appropriately dealt with." He went further still when he hinted that the Justice Department would take a greater role in protecting voter registration workers. "They deserve the protection of the United States government, the protection of the state, the protection of the local communities, and we shall do everything we possibly can to make sure that the protection is assured and if it requires extra legislation and extra force, we shall do that." Never before had he raised the possibility of introducing new civil rights legislation in response to attacks on black demonstrators, a potential sea-change in policy, which there is no record of him having discussed with advisers. But despite his fiery rhetoric, Kennedy did not follow up in the course of the fall with any new legislation. He also continued to procrastinate over the issuance of the housing order.[45]

The Justice Department did adopt a somewhat more aggressive approach to school integration. In September, it filed its first school desegregation suit in a so-called impacted area, Prince George County, Virginia, where local schools received federal funding because many pupils were the children of military personnel stationed nearby. By the end of January 1963, it had launched four additional suits in Louisiana, Alabama, and Mississippi. Certainly, the administration could have taken a sterner position. Robert Kennedy might have threatened the complete withdrawal of federal funds from segregated schools. Case-by-case court proceedings remained the gradualist alternative. (By early 1963, in the face of southern opposition to even these limited measures, the administration opted for a long-discredited "salt and pepper" desegregation plan, whereby one school was provided for whites, and one for blacks. It was, in effect, merely prolonging the "separate but equal" principle deemed unconstitutional by *Brown*. As an administration official privately conceded, "You could hardly call it a blow for freedom."[46])

Albany was little changed by the protests that had defined it over the course of eight months. At the end of 1962, it remained one of the South's most thoroughly segregated cities. But the Albany Movement—often cited as a low point of the civil rights era—did subtly transform the president's thinking about America's racial crisis. He had never before used words like "outrageous" or "cowardly" in public to describe attacks on blacks—nor, for that matter, is there any record of him using them privately. His outraged public comments suggest that he had come to empathize much more deeply with southern blacks and that he was developing a richer understanding of their grievances. The cool detachment with which he had responded to the Freedom Rides crisis seemed to be giving way to a more heartfelt involvement.

There was another crucial advance in his thinking. During 1961, Kennedy had viewed civil rights primarily through the prism of foreign affairs. He intervened on behalf of African diplomats through fear that the Soviet Union would exploit the situation. Equally, his chief concern during the Freedom Rides crisis was its possible impact on the Vienna Summit. Albany marked a shift. Though the president had drawn contrasts during his press conference between the refusal of the city commissioners to negotiate with local blacks and his own administration's willingness to enter into discussions with the Soviet Union, he considered Albany a mainly domestic crisis. It exposed the country's internal problems rather than damaged its external relations.

Kennedy had crossed an important psychological threshold over the course of the summer of 1962. A rapid succession of blows—Wofford's resignation, Sitton's articles in the *New York Times,* the intransigence of the Albany City Commission—had galvanized him to speak out against segregation in America in more forceful terms than he ever had before. Even so, his comments hardly amounted to a full-blown conversion to the black cause. Kennedy had used his strongest language to describe arson attacks on black churches—heinous acts of segregationist violence that had provoked almost universal condemnation. And his heightened concern did not translate into an immediate reappraisal of administration policy.

For Martin Luther King, it was too little, too late. The failure of the Albany Movement had humiliated him and revealed deep fissures in the civil rights movement. King soon decided to emulate SNCC and CORE and adopt more belligerent tactics. They would be unveiled in Birmingham the following May.[47]

CHAPTER 20

❧

"Go Mississippi"

Throughout the year, White House officials had been grappling with how best to commemorate September 22, 1962, the hundredth anniversary of the first printed edition of the Emancipation Proclamation. In May, Kennedy told CRC chairman John Hannah that "the Federal government has a grave responsibility to bring home to the nation the full meaning of the Emancipation Proclamation," and indicated his intention of taking a leading role. In turn, both Lee White and Theodore Sorensen relayed Kennedy's enthusiasm to the head of the organizing committee, Republican Congressman Fred Schwengel. In May, black reporters had even been tipped off that Kennedy planned to use the occasion to deliver his first major civil rights speech since becoming president.[1]

When Schwengel tried to firm up plans for the commemoration with the White House in early August, Kenneth O'Donnell, the president's appointments secretary, claimed to have no knowledge of the event and explained disdainfully that the president would be unable to attend. Sorensen also contacted one of the congressman's aides and told him there had been a mix-up in scheduling. Taken aback by this presidential rebuff, Schwengel complained that the full impact of the ceremony would be lost if Kennedy was absent and even offered to bring it forward to ease the scheduling problem. But O'Donnell refused to budge and explained that the president had an important "out-of-town" commitment. Angry at O'Donnell's sneering tone, Schwengel sent him a curt letter two days later setting out a full record of his correspondence, and in which he claimed to have been duped. Fearing Schwengel might leak the letter to reporters, Lee White warned that it "may even become the basis of a public blast of some sort," which could be particularly damaging in the congressional midterm election campaigns. White feared the president's absence could become a major political embarrassment, especially since the "out-of-town" commitment was the America's Cup yachting races off Newport.[2]

The debate within the White House over the president's participation revealed the growing schism between liberals, like Lee White and Arthur Schlesinger, who had always pushed for a vigorous civil rights policy, and hard-nosed political operators like O'Donnell and O'Brien, who had no great interest in promoting equality and were much more concerned about safeguarding the president's relationship with the Southern Caucus. On this occasion, they reached a compromise. In lieu of Kennedy's personal appearance, the White House arranged for him to record a taped message, which could be broadcast over the public address system during the centenary celebrations. Six paragraphs long, the statement was vague and numbingly banal. The Emancipation Proclamation represented not an end but a beginning, he declared. The last century "has seen the struggle to convert freedom from rhetoric to reality." Kennedy gave no indication of how he intended to advance that process.[3]

There is no record of the president's private thoughts on whether or not he should participate. After his comments during the Albany crisis, both castigating the City Commission for its refusal to negotiate with black protesters and attacking the segregationist arsonists who torched the two churches, he might have viewed the event as a particularly timely opportunity to address the nation on the subject of civil rights. But he might also have been apprehensive about turning up at the Lincoln Memorial armed with such a threadbare speech, which omitted any mention of any new policy initiatives. As it was, on the morning of the commemoration, White House aides had to quash rumors circulating on Capitol Hill that he might well use the address to finally announce the issuance of the housing order. Perhaps there was a simpler explanation: He preferred to watch the sailing rather than remain in Washington.[4]

Kennedy's only other contribution to the event was to recommend that Mahalia Jackson perform. It was the kind of symbolic gesture that had worked well at his inaugural celebrations, but this time the symbolism worked against him. Noting the president's absence, the *New York Times* published a front-page picture of Mahalia Jackson seated alongside Thurgood Marshall and Nelson Rockefeller. Vying for the affections of black voters, Rockefeller had arrived at the ceremony brandishing the original copy of the Emancipation Proclamation, which his family owned. Robert Kennedy was annoyed at what he regarded as "blatant politicking" and believed the governor had hijacked the event to boost his 1964 presidential bid (soon after, perhaps to counteract the impact of Rockefeller's appearance, White House officials told black reporters that the president planned to take a more prominent role in the centennial celebrations, by appearing in a telecast marking the 100th anniversary of the issuance of the Proclamation on January 1). Robert Kennedy's characteristically ambiguous participation in the event hinted at his continuing personal struggle over the administration's handling of civil rights. Though happy to attend, he was reluctant to speak on behalf of the administration. Instead, that responsibility fell to U.N.

Ambassador Adlai Stevenson, who had no involvement in the conduct of the administration's civil rights policy.[5]

∾

Kennedy's failure to attend the ceremony took on particular significance because the administration was on the brink of a battle with Governor Ross Barnett over the admission of James Meredith at the University of Mississippi. Meredith, a twenty-nine-year-old former air force man, had embarked a year earlier on an arduous legal campaign to become the first black student to enroll at Ole Miss in its 114-year history. The grandson of a slave, Meredith had wanted for many years to launch a crusade against segregation in his home state. The final impetus came when he listened to Kennedy's inaugural address. Furious that the new president failed to mention civil rights, Meredith immediately sent off for an application form to the university with the hope, as he later explained, that it would "put pressure on John Kennedy and the Kennedy administration to live up to the civil rights plank in the Democratic platform."[6]

Meredith was willfully challenging one of the most intractable institutions in one of America's most segregated states. Writing in 1963, James Silver, a liberal academic from the University of Mississippi, described it as a "closed society," which had "been on the defensive against inexorable change for more than a century."[7] It was also one of the few states where the plight of black Americans had, if anything, grown worse in the early years of the civil rights era. In 1952, 22,000 blacks were registered to vote, but by December 1955, the number had slipped to 12,000—just five percent of the black population. Eight years after *Brown*, every school district remained segregated.[8]

"Ole Miss," the state's most esteemed university, was determined never to enroll a black student (although they admitted other applicants of color). When a black minister named Clennon King tried to enroll in 1958, he was thrown off campus by state highway patrolmen. When he vowed to return, the then Mississippi governor, James P. Coleman, ordered that he should be locked up in a mental institution for twelve days. Any black crazy enough to apply to Ole Miss, went the joke, must be insane.[9]

In September 1962, eleven months after Meredith launched proceedings against the university, the legal battle reached its climax. Through July and August, Judge Ben F. Cameron, a member of the Fifth Circuit Court of Appeals, had repeatedly delayed the injunction ordering the desegregation of Ole Miss by issuing four separate "stays." To overcome Cameron's stubbornness, Meredith's lawyers appealed to the country's highest federal court. On September 10, Supreme Court Justice Hugo Black, a native of Alabama, delivered his ruling, after discussing the case by telephone with his fellow justices. Black ordered Meredith's admission in the upcoming fall semester.[10]

The ruling was supported by the Justice Department, which had joined the case as a friend of court on August 31, primarily so it could serve as an interlocutor between the courts and state authorities and exercise a measure of control over unfolding events. With the Kennedy administration ultimately responsible for enforcing the Supreme Court's ruling, reporters already predicted that the battle to secure Meredith's entry could easily spark a federal/state showdown comparable to the Little Rock crisis in 1957. By the middle of September, the impending crisis already dominated the news. Reveling in the publicity, Meredith announced that he planned to drive to the Ole Miss campus in a gold Thunderbird.[11]

The Kennedy brothers were determined to prevent the crisis from escalating into another Little Rock and were desperate to avoid the insertion of federal troops. As Robert Kennedy later reflected, "What I was trying to avoid basically was having to send troops and trying to avoid having a federal presence in Mississippi." A full-blown conflagration would damage relations with the Southern Caucus. With the midterm elections looming in November, an increase in racial tensions also threatened to damage the electoral chances of southern moderates, like Carl Sanders in Georgia. Robert Kennedy understood his responsibilities as attorney general and also personally sympathized with Meredith's legal campaign. But he had no intention of picking a fight with Ross Barnett, a politician whom he believed was "genuinely loony." The assessment was not wholly unfounded—the governor still bore the scars from an accident four years earlier, when the propeller of a light aircraft sliced through his left side and severed five ribs. Robert Kennedy suspected the propeller might also have struck him on the head, causing him to become mentally unhinged.[12]

Like his brother, the president was determined to avoid a showdown with such a volatile figure. He intended to remain in the background and leave the Justice Department to manage the problem. Despite his criticisms of the Albany City Commission just a few weeks earlier, Kennedy had no intention of building public support behind Meredith's right of admission and had no appetite for a head-to-head fight with Barnett. Criticizing a City Commission was one thing. Risking an all-out confrontation with a headstrong southern governor was quite a different matter. There were also political considerations to weigh. Barnett was believed to be plotting a 1964 primary challenge against Senator John Stennis, one of the Southern Caucus's more temperate members, and the president did not want to help his cause. Then Kennedy had his own electoral prospects to consider. Eisenhower had been vilified in the South for sending troops into Little Rock in 1957. Kennedy did not want to undercut his own popularity in the region by pursuing a similar course. Kennedy "felt it was extremely important not to have a big fight about this," reflected Norbert Schlei, a Justice Department aide intimately involved in handling the crisis.[13]

On September 13, three days after the Supreme Court had handed down its ruling, U.S. District Court Judge Sidney Mize issued the necessary court order to bring about the integration of University of Mississippi. In a statewide television address that evening, Barnett vowed to fight the order and issued his own declaration of war against the federal government. Evoking South Carolina's attempt in 1832 to nullify federal law, Barnett called upon his fellow Mississippians to resist the ruling from Washington. "There is no case in history where the Caucasian race has survived social integration," he declared. "We will not drink from the cup of genocide."[14]

When Edwin Guthman and Arthur Schlesinger drafted a strongly worded response to Barnett's television address, Robert Kennedy refused to issue it. Rather than intensify the crisis with inflammatory rhetoric, he hoped to enforce the court order through personal diplomacy and a minimum of fuss. To that end, RFK contacted the governor by phone on Saturday, September 15 (at this point, he had no way of knowing that this would be the first of twenty-two telephone conversations over the next thirteen days). In their first conversation, Kennedy hoped to establish a good rapport and politely laid out "some of the details of how to work this thing out with his fellow," as he referred to Meredith. Kennedy told Barnett that Meredith would attempt to be registered in five days' time, on September 20.[15]

Despite the cordial tone of that first phone conversation, Barnett refused to back down. The governor's interposition speech had made him the pride of Mississippi, and he basked in the adulation. ("Place Assured in History for Fearless Barnett" ran the headline in the *Clarion Ledger* on the morning of his first phone exchange with the attorney general.) Over the next four days, Barnett's stance toughened; and on September 19, in a tense meeting with the university's board of trustees, he vowed to block Meredith's entry, even if it meant being in contempt of the federal court.[16]

The next morning, Thursday, September 20, James Meredith prepared to make his first attempt at registering as a student at the Ole Miss campus in Oxford. He had been billeted overnight in Memphis and would be escorted onto campus by a team of U.S. marshals, led by the U.S. chief marshal, James McShane, a veteran of the freedom riders riots. Later that morning, however, Mississippi state legislators sought to deny his admission by rushing through emergency legislation, which came to be known as the "Meredith Law." It made anyone found guilty of a criminal offense ineligible to attend Ole Miss. Within hours, Mississippi law enforcement officials brought trumped-up charges against Meredith accusing him of false voter registration, a wholly specious allegation. But after a ten-minute trial held just a few hours later, the black veteran was found guilty in absentia on the bogus charges and sentenced to a year in jail.[17]

Shortly afterwards, Barnett contacted Robert Kennedy and told him Meredith would be arrested if he appeared on campus. The attorney general responded by ordering Justice Department officials to seek a federal court injunction preventing any arrest. As soon as the injunction was issued, Barnett agreed reluctantly to rescind the arrest warrant and informed Kennedy that no attempt would be made to apprehend Meredith. The way was now clear for his registration later that afternoon.

When Meredith's convoy arrived on campus at 4:30 P.M. (CST), it was met by a crowd of some 2,000 segregationists shouting "Go Home Nigger." Inside one of the university buildings, Barnett waited along with a small group of state officials. Coming face-to-face with the governor for the first time, Meredith announced in a loud, confident voice, "I want to register at the University." Barnett countered by reading from a gold-sealed proclamation. "Using my police powers as the Governor of the Sovereign State of Mississippi," he announced. "I do hereby deny you, James Meredith, admittance to this University." Dumfounded, Meredith stood motionless, until John Doar and James McShane seized his arms and forced their way through the hostile crowd. As Meredith's government sedan sped away toward Memphis, it was chased down the road by 500 protesters.

Three hours later, the Justice Department mounted its counterattack, by charging three university officials—the chancellor, the dean, and the registrar—with contempt for failing to obey the federal court order. But Robert Kennedy chose not to bring charges against Barnett, because he did not want to confront him directly. To avoid exacerbating the situation, Kennedy also shied away from publicly condemning Barnett's obstructionism and even barred other administration officials from doing so. Even a "blandly general statement" about the need to obey the court order was removed from a speech prepared by Solicitor General Archibald Cox. As an anonymous Justice Department official told the *Wall Street Journal,* "We are not going to let this become a personal fight between Bobby and Barnett." But the crisis clearly was escalating. Claude Sitton of the *New York Times* said it "threatened to bring on the most serious Federal-state controversy since the Civil War."[18]

At the contempt hearing in New Orleans on Monday, September 24, the three university officials capitulated immediately and agreed to Meredith's registration the very next afternoon. Robert Kennedy was delighted by what seemed to be an easy victory and put through a call to the governor in the hope that his resistance would now fold. "I think there's a great problem here," said Kennedy. "If we don't follow the order of the federal court, we don't have anything in the United States. I understand how you feel and the feeling of the people down there," he went on. "You are citizens of the State of Mississippi but you are also citizens of the United States."

"Kennedy, you ought to rescind this order," Barnett shot back. "Really and truly, you ought to do something about this thing, General. I am frank."

Kennedy tried to project firmness. "The federal courts have now issued a ruling and to prolong this further any further, we are all on the brink of a very dangerous situation." The conversation accomplished nothing.[19]

After lunch, Kennedy and Barnett resumed their talks. Barnett threatened once more to disobey the federal courts.

"Governor, you are part of the United States," said the attorney general.

"We have been part of the United States," replied Barnett, "but I don't know whether we are or not."

"Are you getting out of the Union?" responded Kennedy.

"Looks like we're being kicked around," Barnett said, "like we don't belong to it. General, this thing is serious."[20]

Worried that Barnett could prolong the standoff indefinitely, Robert Kennedy offered him a crucial concession: that Meredith could be admitted at the Woolfolk State Office Building in Jackson, where university trustees maintained a suite of offices, rather than Oxford, a far more emotionally charged setting. Kennedy also assured Barnett that he had no intention of deploying troops to enforce the court order. "We are hearing you have ordered an Army here," said Barnett during one of the key exchanges of the entire crisis. "Oh, no, Governor," replied Kennedy. "I wouldn't do that."[21]

In discounting the possibility of using troops, Robert Kennedy had made a grave tactical error. Going into the crisis, Barnett already had sufficient reason to doubt the administration's resolve given the president's vacillations on civil rights over the course of his presidency and particularly in light of the Freedom Rides crisis the year before when the Justice Department had refused to press Mississippi state officials over the integration of Jackson's bus terminal. By promising not to use troops to enforce the order, the attorney general had relinquished whatever leverage the administration might have had. So when the *New York Times* reported on September 26 that the Kennedy administration was about to toughen its stance—"US Is Prepared to Send Troops As Mississippi Governor Defies Court and Bars Negro Student," read the headline—Barnett had every reason to believe that the administration was bluffing. Robert Kennedy had thought that by agreeing to register Meredith in Jackson he had won the governor's compliance. Barnett, however, had decided to continue his fight.[22]

On the afternoon of Tuesday, September 25, Meredith boarded a government plane for the flight to Jackson, fully expecting to gain admission. Robert Kennedy had asked Barnett to avoid a "big circus" and thought he had received assurances that would be the case. But when Meredith arrived at the Woolfolk Building, an unruly crowd of some 2,000 was there to greet him. Barnett himself stood in the doorway of the university's offices, with fifty state legislators lined up behind him. Chief Marshal McShane tried to hand Barnett an injunction summoning him to appear before the Fifth Circuit Court of Appeals on contempt charges. But the governor brushed it aside and read instead from another embossed proclamation, blocking Meredith's admission.[23]

Minutes later, Meredith left the building to cries of "Goddam dirty nigger bastard." He had been forced to endure a degrading spectacle. With television pictures of the confrontation soon broadcast around the country, Barnett had humiliated both him and the federal government. Robert Kennedy was furious when he heard the news. He immediately contacted Barnett and told him that Meredith would show up for classes at Ole Miss Oxford campus the following day. But Barnett remained defiant. "If you knew the feeling of about 99.5% of the people in this thing you would have this boy withdraw and go somewhere else," he said.

"Let's try it for six months," said the attorney general, rather feebly, "and see how it goes."

"It's best for him not to go to Ole Miss," replied Barnett, sternly.

"But he likes Ole Miss," countered the attorney general.[24]

Later on that evening, Robert Kennedy spoke for the first time with James Meredith himself. "It's going to be a long, hard and difficult struggle," the attorney general told him, "but in the end we're going to be successful."

"I hope so," said Meredith, disconsolately. Thereafter, Meredith did not speak to either of the Kennedy brothers for the duration of the crisis.[25]

The next morning, Meredith made a third attempt at registration, with McShane once more at his side. This time he was blocked on the edge of the Ole Miss campus by Lieutenant Governor Paul Johnson. Confronted by a phalanx of Mississippi state troopers, who had set up roadblocks to bar Meredith's entry, McShane tried initially to push Johnson out of the away, having been mistakenly advised beforehand that Barnett would stand aside after "the mildest kind of force." With television news cameras capturing every moment, McShane tried to use his large stomach to push Johnson out of the way. But after a few moments of slapstick pushing and shoving, it soon became clear that Johnson had no intention of ceding ground. McShane retreated and returned to his car with Meredith as the sheriffs at Johnson's side applauded sarcastically. For the third time, the federal government's attempt at registering Meredith had failed. In a further act of defiance, that afternoon Mississippi state officials blocked a U.S. marshal from serving the governor with a contempt citation handed down by the Court of Appeals for the Fifth Circuit, which called for his appearance in New Orleans that Friday.[26]

Despite the series of embarrassing setbacks, Robert Kennedy was prepared still to negotiate. On Thursday, September 26, he opened a new round of talks with Barnett, who, worried about the prospect of imprisonment, appeared prepared finally to back down. In talks with Kennedy, the governor agreed to enroll Meredith with one crucial stipulation: that when the Justice Department next tried to secure Meredith's entry, it would lay on a massive show of force. This display would allow Barnett to retreat with his political credibility intact.

Desperate to avoid a further escalation of the crisis, the attorney general was prepared to indulge Barnett with his sham confrontation, and receptive even to the idea of federal officials openly brandishing weapons—though with reservations. "I hate to have them all draw their guns," Kennedy explained to the governor when their deliberations resumed at 2:50 that Thursday afternoon, "as I think it could create harsh feelings. Isn't it sufficient if I have one man draw his gun and the others keep their hands on their holsters?" But Barnett wanted to orchestrate the most dramatic photo opportunity. Emboldened by Robert Kennedy's willingness to negotiate on this point, Barnett pushed even further. He asked for a U.S. marshal not only to pull a revolver but aim it directly at his head. On this point, Kennedy objected. But a final deal seemed within reach.[27]

Meredith, in the meantime, had grown even more adamant. He was angry at the Justice Department for its repeated failure to get him registered, and he doubted the attorney general's resolve. He now refused to return to Oxford unless the federal government backed him with overwhelming force. On the same day that Kennedy and Barnett worked feverishly to formulate a plan that would allow Meredith to enroll at Ole Miss without humiliating the governor, Justice Department officials made a series of frantic telephone calls, in which they implored Meredith to make another attempt at entering.

He finally relented and took his place alongside McShane and Doar in a motorcade that had now expanded to include over a dozen U.S. Border Patrol vehicles. A Border Patrol plane with a radio link to Robert Kennedy's office in Washington circled overhead. Even as the convoy thundered toward Oxford, the attorney general was locked in negotiations with Barnett, trying to finesse the precise sequencing of the showdown. "I am taking a helluva chance," said Robert Kennedy during their third conservation that afternoon. "I am relying on you." But the governor was becoming increasingly panicky, largely because of fears his deal with the Justice Department would leak to the press.

"You understand we have had no agreement," said Barnett.

"That's correct," replied Kennedy, promising secrecy.

"I am just telling you—everybody thinks we're compromising," said Barnett.[28]

As they awaited Meredith's convoy, Barnett and Lieutenant Governor Johnson became increasingly edgy. A crowd of 2,500 had converged on the campus, its ranks swelled by well-known Klansmen. Violence seemed inevitable. "General, I'm worried," Barnett blurted out in a telephone call with the attorney general at 6:35 P.M., their fifth since noon. "I'm nervous, I tell you. You don't realize what's going on. There are several thousand people in here in cars, trucks. . . . We don't know these people."

Fearing a bloodbath, Kennedy capitulated immediately. "I had better send them back," he said, disconsolately. Contacted via radio phone, the federal convoy came to a halt just forty miles outside Oxford. Then it turned around and returned to Memphis.[29]

The next day, the focus of the drama shifted back to the federal courtroom in New Orleans. The Court of Appeals tried Barnett in absentia on contempt charges

and gave him until eleven A.M. on Tuesday, October 2, to complete Meredith's registration. Barnett would be fined $10,000 for every day he remained in defiance.
Now that federal courts had spoken so unambiguously, and set a deadline for compliance, Robert Kennedy had a clear duty to uphold the integrity of the courts.
From a political viewpoint, this clear-cut federal court order was of enormous value
to the administration. It meant southern senators would find it much harder to
criticize the Kennedy administration for using military force.[30]

That day, Robert Kennedy traveled to the War Room at the Pentagon, where
he met General Maxwell Taylor, the chairman of the Joint Chiefs of Staff, and
Army Secretary Cyrus Vance to plan for the insertion of troops. Still, he dearly
hoped marshals would suffice and latched onto the idea, modeled on the Montgomery deployment the previous spring, of dispatching an initial force of just
110 army engineers to provide them with logistical support, but nothing more.[31]

By that stage in the crisis, there is no record that Robert Kennedy had discussed the crisis in any great detail with the president. As aides explained to reporters, Kennedy was content to support the Justice Department's strategy of
patient legal maneuverings and gentle persuasion and wanted to give Barnett
every opportunity to voluntarily back down. But Judge Elbert P. Tuttle told
Marshall that further delay risked making a mockery of the courts, and the crisis was clearly coming to a head. This raised fears among Kennedy's close circle
of White House advisers that he would soon have to become involved. On September 28, the day after Barnett was charged with contempt, Ted Sorensen
wrote from his sickbed, where he was recovering from stress-induced stomach
ulcers. First of all, he urged the president to refrain from public comment and
avoid questions from reporters. "There are too many questions you should neither evade nor answer directly," he warned. For the time being, the present policy
of quiet negotiations offered the best course, he advised, and the administration
should avoid a repeat of Little Rock. "In contrast to your predecessor," said
Sorensen, "you are demonstrating how many graduated steps there are between
inaction and troops." If the president was forced into publicly remarking on the
crisis, Sorensen suggested that he frame Meredith's admission as a straightforward matter of law and order and avoid a head-to-head confrontation with Barnett. "Defiance should be against the majesty of the United States," Sorensen
noted, "and not John F. Kennedy." If all else failed and the mobilization of federal troops became unavoidable, Kennedy should be prepared to speak to the
nation. "Such an address could well be an historic document in the annals of the
American presidency," he suggested, "as well as having a beneficial effect in
Mississippi and on the country as a whole."[32]

By the end of the week, there was broad bipartisan support for taking a firm
line with Barnett, which gave the president more political latitude as the crisis
came to a head. Even though the congressional midterm elections were less
than five weeks away, liberal Republicans declared a partisan ceasefire and de-

cided against goading the administration for its failure so far to secure Meredith's entry. Senator Jacob Javits of New York, a strident critic of Kennedy's civil rights policies, announced on September 26 that the president was entitled to the full support of the country "in his effort to preserve the authority of the Federal Government." On September 27, New York Republican Kenneth Keating sponsored a joint resolution with Illinois Democratic Senator Paul Douglas expressing full support for the president in bringing about Meredith's admission. That same day, former President Dwight D. Eisenhower described Barnett's actions as "absolutely unconscionable and undefensible" and called for the court orders to be enforced.[33]

Calls for the president to adopt an uncompromising stance had also come from two wholly unexpected sources—two former governors from the Deep South, who had known and dealt with Barnett for many years. On September 19, former Alabama Governor James "Big Jim" Folsom had come up with the innovative idea of federalizing both the Mississippi and Alabama Guard. "Tell them [the Mississippi Guard] to stay at home," he wired the president, "then get the Alabama Guard to go and get Meredith in." The plan offered an alternative to the deployment of federal troops and meant that Kennedy would never have to test the loyalty of Mississippi guardsmen, who would no doubt be reluctant to help facilitate Meredith's entry. Folsom realized his scheme was unconventional, but he claimed it could win public backing from southern moderates and bring a quick end to the crisis. "With this even Governor Barnett will be happy," wrote Folsom, adding as a sign-off: "You are in good shape here in Alabama. . . . Your friend for law and order, James E. Folsom." Former Mississippi Governor James Coleman, an ally since the 1950s, also advocated an uncompromising stance. In particular, the president should threaten the immediate suspension of all federal aid to Mississippi, including help for the elderly. Yet there is no evidence that the White House sought the help of either former governor or seriously considered their proposals.[34]

The administration continued to pursue its own conciliatory approach instead. That week, cabinet secretaries were told to contact members of the university's board of trustees and to urge compliance with the court orders. The Justice Department also asked the *Wall Street Journal* to conduct a survey of businessmen in Mississippi, to show how the crisis was damaging the local economy (the survey revealed that many businessmen wanted Barnett to comply with the court order but feared a boycott from segregationists if they said so publicly). The strategy was designed to undercut Barnett, in the hope that he would finally capitulate. But the governor continued to believe that Mississippians were firmly on his side. On September 26, James Eastland had described the Justice Department's legal moves as "judicial tyranny." Senator John Stennis, who was normally more circumspect, congratulated Barnett for his stout defense of the Constitution. There was support, too, from Governor John Patterson of Alabama. The use of troops or marshals in Mississippi would be "catastrophic," Patterson wired the president: "it will mark the end of our existence as a democratic Republic. . . . are you prepared to invade Alabama as well?"[35]

On Friday, Robert Kennedy arrived at the White House, accompanied by Cyrus Vance, to give his brother a full briefing on the Pentagon's contingency plans. The attorney general still clung to the hope that marshals alone would suffice. To that end, he bolstered the force protecting Meredith at the Millington Naval Air Station near Memphis, with reinforcements brought in from as far away as California and the Texas-Mexico border. But the attorney general also accepted what seemed now to be almost inevitable: Troops might soon be necessary. Later that afternoon, Arthur Schlesinger was summoned to the Justice Department, where he was instructed to draft a presidential statement explaining why federal intervention had become necessary.[36]

Throughout the week, the mood in Oxford had become increasingly volatile, and now it threatened to boil over. On Saturday morning, segregationists and Klansmen descended from all over the state, among them former Major General Edwin A. Walker. Walker had previously commanded the 101st Airborne Division—the famed Screaming Eagles—in Little Rock, but he had resigned his commission in 1961 to protest what he called the Kennedy administration's "collusion with the international Communist conspiracy." Secret FBI field reports suggested he might even be planning to assemble a militia to rebuff the federal government.[37]

Fearing widespread violence, Robert Kennedy decided to accelerate plans for the insertion of troops. "We'd better get going with the military," Robert Kennedy told Edwin Guthman, his press chief, that Saturday morning. "Maybe we waited too long."

"No," said Guthman. "The result would have been the same, and the record is clear that we've done everything to avoid this step." At that, Kennedy nodded.[38]

That afternoon, sixteen heavy army helicopters landed at Millington Naval Air Base carrying an estimated 250 soldiers from the 503rd Military Police Battalion, to augment the 400 soldiers flown in earlier. The Justice Department downplayed the deployment and claimed the troops were on hand only to provide marshals with logistical support. They also tried to conceal another, more explosive fact. The 503rd MP battalion was one of the most successfully integrated units in the entire U.S. military, with black platoon sergeants placed in charge of southern whites. When General Creighton W. Abrams, the army's director of military operations, informed Robert Kennedy that "Negro personnel would be withheld from committed units," the attorney general seemed content with that edict. But officers on the ground ignored the order. They feared the withdrawal of black personnel would hamper their operational ability. On eight separate occasions, the Pentagon ordered the black troops to be held back. Eight times the order was ignored.[39]

With troops on the verge of deployment, the president decided finally to take a more active role. Over the weekend, the crisis looked set to come to a head, and he had no other choice but to assert his leadership. He interrupted his weekend to convene an Oval Office meeting attended by his brother, Burke Marshall, O'Donnell, and Schlesinger, the first time he had brought together such a high-level team of advisers to discuss the Mississippi situation. At 1:30 P.M. (EST), Robert Kennedy had made another attempt to persuade Barnett to accept the ruling of the court. But once again Barnett refused to back down. Now the burden fell on the president to decide what course to take.

Over the course of the next hour, the president decided to take Sorensen's advice and to deliver a nationwide televised address on the crisis. There is no record of the reasons underpinning Kennedy's decision. But the president must certainly have been mindful that Eisenhower had addressed the nation in September 1957, after making the momentous decision to dispatch federal troops into the South for the first time since Reconstruction. Given the magnitude of the Ole Miss crisis and the legal and political issues it raised, a speech was almost unavoidable.

During the Oval Office meeting, the president also decided that he should lobby the governor directly, since his brother had failed to achieve a breakthrough. At 2:30 P.M. (EST), the White House switchboard patched through the call to Mississippi. As Kennedy waited to be connected, Robert Kennedy started to egg him on: "Go get him Johnny boy."

The president joined in the lampoon. "Governor, this is the President of the United States. Not Bobby, not Teddy, not Princess Radziwill," he said, lapsing into locker room comedy. Moments later, with the president trying hard to suppress his laughter, Barnett came on the line.[40]

"Well now here's my problem, Governor," said Kennedy, adopting a friendly tone. "I don't know Mr. Meredith and I didn't put him in the University, but on the other hand, under the Constitution, I have to carry out the order and I don't want to do it in any way that causes difficulty to you or to anyone else. But I've got to do it. Now, I'd like to get your help in doing it."

Barnett soon came to the point. "You know what I am up against," he said. "I took an oath, you know, to abide by the laws of this state, and our Constitution here, and the Constitution of the United States. I'm on the spot here, you know. I've taken an oath."

"The problem is, Governor," the president came back, "I got my responsibility, just like you have yours."

Kennedy indicated he wanted to resolve the crisis in "an amicable way" and said he did not "want a lot of people down there getting hurt." He suggested they devise a new plan with the attorney general.

Relieved that the administration had softened its stance, Barnett promised to do just that. As the conversation drew to a close, Barnett thanked the president for his help on "the poultry program." Barnett's sycophancy brought great merriment to the Oval Office. As he replaced the receiver, the president turned to his brother: "You've been fighting a sofa pillow all week."

"What a rogue," replied the attorney general.[41]

Shortly afterwards, Robert Kennedy called Barnett, who had a new plan. On Monday, Meredith could register in Jackson. Barnett would remain in Oxford and pretend that he had been duped by the administration. But this time Kennedy refused to play along with the governor's trickery and demanded instead that Meredith be registered in Oxford. Barnett would not back down, so within the hour the president was forced to telephone him again. It turned out to be the defining conversation of the entire crisis.

The governor remained defiant: "I've taken an oath to abide by the laws of this state and our state constitution and the Constitution of the United States." He pressed upon the president to authorize the Jackson admission plan, which the attorney general had categorically rejected. At this most critical juncture, and in flat contradiction of his brother, the president suddenly embraced the Jackson admission plan, thereby indicating that the nonnegotiable had suddenly become negotiable. "What we really want to have from you," said the president, "is some understanding about whether the state police will maintain law and order."

Handed an unexpected opening, Barnett seized it immediately. "Oh, we'll do that," he responded eagerly, promising the university offices in Jackson would be guarded by 220 highway patrolmen.

"This is not my order, I have to carry it out," admitted Kennedy. "So I want to get together and try to do it with you in a way which is the most satisfactory and causes the least chance of damage to people in Mississippi. That is my interest." During the conversation, the president even appeared open to the idea of postponing Meredith's registration for a further two weeks.[42]

In the space of just a few hours, the Kennedy brothers had executed a complete turnaround. No wonder Barnett questioned the federal government's resolve: In what should have been the decisive conversation of the entire crisis, the administration spoke with two distinct voices, and with endless flexibility. Had the president stuck to a firmer and more disciplined line, it is possible Barnett might have capitulated there and then. Instead, by seven o'clock that evening, the administration had colluded with Barnett to finalize the broad outline of the decoy plan. Meredith would be registered in Jackson, while Barnett would remain in Oxford, feigning ignorance.

But the deal quickly fell apart. Saturday night, Barnett attended a football game between the Ole Miss Rebels and the Kentucky Wildcats at Jackson's Memorial Stadium. Some 41,000 fans jammed the whites-only stadium, singing rebel songs and waving dime-store Confederate flags. At halftime, with Ole Miss enjoying a seven-point lead, a gigantic Confederate flag was unfurled on the field. The sight ignited the crowd. "We Want Ross!" they shouted in unison.

"We Want Ross!" To deafening screams, Barnett marched onto the field. He strode purposely toward a microphone placed at the fifty-yard line. He stood there for a moment to soak up the applause and then jutted a clenched fist defiantly into the air. He barked out an impassioned, fifteen-word speech. "I love Mississippi. I love her people. Our customs. I love and respect our heritage."[43]

The crowd went wild. The university band, dressed in gray Confederate uniforms, struck up "Go Mississippi." Energized by the frenzied reaction, Barnett left the stadium and immediately called Robert Kennedy. The decoy plan was off. When the attorney general contacted his brother, the president was livid. "Why that god-damn son-of-a-bitch," he exclaimed, his face turning red. Robert Weaver, who happened to be with him at the time, had never seen the president so visibly angry.[44]

Burke Marshall sensed immediately that the deployment of federal troops had become inevitable. He contacted his Justice Department colleague Norbert Schlei and told him to prepare the requisite presidential proclamations. By midnight, Schlei was at the White House. He carried with him an unsigned proclamation ordering persons obstructing justice in Mississippi to desist and disperse and also an executive order that would bring the Mississippi National Guard under the president's command. When the president saw the documents, he quickly recognized their historic import. Kennedy took Schlei into the Indian Treaty Room to study them more closely. "Is this pretty much what Ike signed in 1957 with the Little Rock thing?" he asked. There had been certain refinements, replied Schlei, but essentially the papers were the same. Sitting at a desk that once belonged to Ulysses S. Grant, Kennedy added his signature. "You know that's General Grant's table," sighed the president, ironically. But as Schlei headed downstairs to brief reporters, Kennedy rushed to the balustrade. "Wait!" he shouted down to him. "Don't tell them about General Grant's table," fearing it would revive memories of the Civil War and Reconstruction.[45]

At five minutes before midnight, Andrew Hatcher announced to reporters that Kennedy had federalized the Mississippi National Guard. Even at this point, however, the Kennedy administration still hoped to fashion an eleventh-hour deal. So on Sunday morning, Robert Kennedy entered into a new round of negotiations with Barnett, despite the fact that the governor had proven himself to be wholly untrustworthy. Overnight, the governor had designed a new plan—an extravagant masquerade in which he planned to stand at the head of 300 Mississippi lawmen and rifle-wielding members of the Mississippi National Guard. The governor promised to stand aside only if the Kennedy administration agreed to lay on an equivalent show of force. But Robert Kennedy did not want the federal government to be cast in the role of aggressor. "I think it is silly going through this whole facade of your standing there; our people drawing guns; your stepping aside," said Kennedy. "To me it is dangerous and it has gone beyond the stage of politics."

"I can't just walk back," Barnett countered. "I have to be confronted with your troops."

The discussions continued, until Kennedy finally snapped. He threatened that the president would announce the secret decoy plan on nationwide television if Barnett refused to yield.

Blackmail proved devastatingly effective. "That won't do at all," gasped Barnett. "You broke your word to him," replied Kennedy.

"You don't mean the President is going to say that tonight? . . . Don't say that," he pleaded. "Please don't mention it."

"We have it all down," replied the attorney general, knowing a secret taperecording system installed by his brother had recorded every word for posterity.

Barnett imploded, and he became increasingly incoherent. If the sham registration plan were leaked to the press, his political career would be over. If the president revealed it on television, he might even be lynched. Robert Kennedy had Barnett cornered. He surely realized that Barnett would agree to anything to avoid such public humiliation. But rather than press home his advantage, he allowed Barnett to set out the way in which Meredith would be admitted. In accordance with Barnett's wishes, Meredith would be flown to Oxford that night, sleep in a dormitory on campus, and be registered at Ole Miss the following day.

"Please let us treat what we say as confidential?" asked Barnett. "I am sorry about the misunderstanding last night. I am extremely hurt over it really. I didn't know I was violating my agreement."

Robert Kennedy told Barnett he had until 7:30 P.M. (EST) to put the plan into effect—thirty minutes before the White House had requested television time for a nationwide presidential address. This would allow Barnett to announce to the people of Mississippi that Meredith would be registered either on Monday or Tuesday and then express mock indignation when it proceeded ahead of schedule. "If I am surprised, you won't mind if I raise Cain about it?" he asked sheepishly.

"I don't mind that," replied attorney general, indulging him again. "Just say law and order will be maintained."[46]

That Sunday afternoon, Justice Department officials scrambled to assemble the same kind of ad hoc force dispatched to Alabama. So quick was the mobilization that many of the Border Patrolmen left their gas masks behind, and nobody thought to bring enough teargas. For his part, Deputy Attorney General Katzenbach, who was placed in charge, arrived without any military plan in place. He had no reconnaissance information on the topography of the campus and limited intelligence reports on the opposition his small band of ill-trained marshals would encounter. He also lacked adequate communications equipment and was forced to use a local payphone to speak with the attorney general. The deployment was a fiasco.[47]

Shortly before four o'clock (CST) the first marshals arrived on campus. They encircled the Lyceum Building, which contained the registration office. News of the marshals' arrival spread quickly through campus, prompting hundreds of students to converge on the Circle, the oak-studded patch of land directly in front of the Lyceum. By late afternoon, about 400 people filled the park, some dressed in Confederate-style marching band uniforms, throwing eggs and small stones at the marshals and chanting: "2-4-1-3, we hate Kennedy." When a local pastor pleaded for calm, he was beaten up.[48]

Shortly after six P.M. (CST), Meredith was met at Oxford airport by Katzenbach and driven in convoy through a back entrance onto campus. He was billeted at Baxter Hall, a dormitory building fifty yards from the Lyceum building, where he was protected by two dozen U.S. marshals under orders to shoot anyone trying to break into his room. Nearby in the Circle, the mood was becoming increasingly agitated, with the crowd hurling a steady volley of stones and eggs at the marshals. At the steps of a gray limestone Confederate monument, General Walker stood with a crazed look in his eyes, exhorting the crowd to fight. "Protest! Protest!" he shouted. "Keep it up."

By then, the president was huddled in the Cabinet Room with Robert Kennedy, Burke Marshall, O'Donnell, and O'Brien. Sorensen had discharged himself from the hospital earlier that day to join them. The president was also feeling unwell: Earlier that day he had flown in Dr. Max ("Dr. Feelgood") Jacobson from New York to administer cortisone injections to relieve his back pain. (The president had told Jacobson that the Mississippi crisis was a real "ball-breaker.") Originally, Kennedy had planned to address the nation at 7:30 P.M. (EST) but decided to wait until Barnett delivered his statewide address. Justifiably mistrustful, he wanted to make certain the governor kept his word. "We can't take a chance with Meredith's life," said the president, "or let that bastard make the Federal government look foolish."[49]

At 7:25 P.M. (EST), about five minutes before the governor was scheduled to go before the cameras, FBI agents monitoring radio transmissions from the Mississippi Highway Patrolmen reported that an order had gone out from Barnett to withdraw state troopers from the campus. The U.S. marshals would be left isolated. Moments later, Barnett's personal representative on the scene, Mississippi State Senator George Yarbrough, conveyed the same message to Katzenbach. "You have occupied this University and now you can have it," shouted Yarbrough. "What happens from now on is the responsibility of the Federal Government."

"That would be a horrible mistake," countered Katzenbach, but to no avail. Yarbrough refused to budge.[50]

A few minutes later, Barnett delivered his most impassioned speech yet, in which he announced to the people of Mississippi that Meredith had arrived on the campus of Ole Miss. He admitted defeat but sounded defiant: "My heart

still says 'never,' but my calm judgment abhors the bloodshed that would follow." Then he spewed venom at the Kennedy brothers: "Gentleman, you are
trampling on the sovereignty of this great state and depriving it of every vestige of honor and respect as a member of the United States." Minutes after,
Barnett received a telephone call from Robert Kennedy. The attorney general
was less concerned by Barnett's speech than by the withdrawal of the Mississippi Highway Patrolmen. Once again, he threatened to reveal the decoy plan.
After putting down the phone on the attorney general, Barnett told Yarbrough
to leave the patrolmen in place. Just moments later, a Molotov cocktail exploded at the feet of his marshals. McShane was forced to respond. "Load your
guns," he barked. "Gas guns ready." With that, a volley of teargas exploded into
the night sky.[51]

Poised to address the nation, the president was relying on regular progress reports from Katzenbach. "What are they chanting?" he asked.

"Go to Hell, JFK," shouted his deputy attorney general.

In the brief time it took the president to walk from the Cabinet Room to the
cable-strewn Oval Office, the situation in Oxford had deteriorated further. With
just five minutes to go before airtime, Marshall relayed the news that a full-blown
riot was underway. As technicians made final lighting adjustments, Kennedy
waited nervously for the final draft of the speech. In the thirty minutes since Barnett's televised address, Sorensen, Marshall, and Bobby Kennedy had completely
rewritten it, largely to rebut the charges leveled by Barnett. The president wanted
to dispel any notion that the federal government was acting as the "oppressor."
Meredith's admission was a straightforward matter of law and order. But Kennedy
did not want to aggravate the situation further. He wanted to make a conciliatory
speech and to "heal wounds," as Marshall put it. With that in mind, Jack Rosenthal from the Justice Department press office had provided Marshall with a briefing paper on Mississippians or Mississippi units with outstanding military
achievements. Kennedy wanted to refer to them in his speech.[52]

Just a few minutes before he was due to go on air, the final text was placed in
his hands. It was his first major presidential address on the subject of civil
rights, and it had been cobbled together in less than an hour. The overarching
theme of the speech was that the federal government bore the responsibility of
upholding the sanctity of the courts. Kennedy claimed it had done so with admirable restraint. "This has been accomplished thus far without the use of the
National Guard or other troops," he noted. "And it is hoped that the law enforcement officers of the State of Mississippi and the Federal marshals will continue to be sufficient in the future. . . . ""This is how it should be," he continued,
"for our Nation is founded on the principle that observance of the law is the
eternal safeguard of liberty. . . . Americans are free to disagree with the law, but
not to disobey it." Then he explained the legal background to the case, under-
scoring the court action precipitating the crisis had been instigated by a private

citizen—"Mr. Meredith"—not the Justice Department. The case had been up-held by the Fifth Court of Appeals in New Orleans, which was, Kennedy noted, made up entirely of southerners—one Alabaman, two Georgians, a Floridian, a Louisianan, and two Texans. "Even though this Government had not originally been a party to the case, my responsibility as President was there-fore inescapable. I accept it. . . . I deeply regret the fact that any action by the executive branch [of the federal government] was necessary in this case," he went on, with the air of a reluctant sheriff, "but all other avenues and alterna-tives, including persuasion and conciliation, had been tried and exhausted."

Throughout the speech, Kennedy had attempted to find areas of common agreement with southerners. Toward the end, he addressed them directly. "Nei-ther Mississippi nor any other southern State deserves to be charged with all the accumulated wrongs of the past 100 years of race relations," he said. "To the extent that there has been failure, the responsibility for that failure must be shared by us all, by every State, by every citizen." Kennedy then reached back into Mississippi's vaunted past. Not only was Mississippi the state of Lucius Lamar, he said, but of four Medal of Honor winners in the Korean War alone: "You have a great tradition to uphold . . . [and] have a new opportunity to show that you are men of patriotism and integrity."

The speech notably lacked the element of compassion he had shown during his early September press conference when he addressed the situation in Al-bany. Kennedy made no mention of Meredith's bravery nor of the humiliations he had endured over the previous weeks. He also offered no explicit criticism of segregation. Rather than asking southerners to examine their consciences, he had merely implored them to abide by the law.[53]

The president's appeal to the fair-mindedness of Mississippians, which crackled through the air from transistor and car radios on the campus of Ole Miss, fell on deaf ears. Some rioters had filled their Molotov cocktails with acid stolen from the university's chemistry laboratories and hurled them at the mar-shals. Gunmen lurked in the darkness. The marshals were running out of tear-gas, and, recognizing their vulnerability, some Mississippi highway patrolmen even considered turning their guns against them.

Injured marshals were strewn along the wall of the Lyceum, their wounds dressed with makeshift bandages. There were no ambulances available to ferry them to the hospital or even rudimentary first-aid equipment immediately at hand. With every passing minute, there were new reports of gunfire. And then a border patrolman took a bullet in the leg. It was clear that the gunmen were shooting to kill. The riot at Ole Miss now had the feel of an armed insurrection.

At the White House, administration officials struggled to separate fact from conjecture, as Katzenbach fed them sketchy reports from his position at the Lyceum. At one point, late in the evening, they received word that Meredith's dormitory building had been ransacked. O'Donnell worried out loud that the riot could easily turn into a lynching. Robert Kennedy realized that the marshals might have no other choice but to pull their guns. "I think they have to protect Meredith now," he said. "They better fire, I suppose. They gotta protect Meredith." The president toyed with the idea of flying in a government helicopter to airlift Meredith to safety. But given the chaos on campus, it was hard to imagine where it might land. Robert Kennedy showed more determined resolve, writing in firm handwriting on a yellow legal pad at one point in the evening: "It should be clearly understood that Meredith is going to remain at the University as a student. Not just go in."[54]

Events were now running beyond the president's control. With the U.S. marshals so heavily outnumbered and the president still opposed to sending in troops, state law enforcement officials offered the only hope. At ten P.M. (EST) he decided to personally contact Barnett to plead with him to maintain order. By now, the governor was unable to control a violent shaking in his hands, and his daughter had to physically hand him the phone.[55]

When Barnett came on the line, Kennedy blundered almost immediately. He revealed that he was now considering the idea of removing Meredith from campus. Barnett understandably misinterpreted the president's remarks as an indication the federal government was no longer prepared to enforce the federal court order. It took a few more minutes before the president realized they were talking at cross-purposes. "How can I remove him, Governor," Kennedy shouted, "when there's a riot in the street, and he may step out of that building and something happen to him?" "All right," said Barnett, bringing the conversation to a close.[56]

A short while later, Barnett came back on the line, hoping to persuade the president to remove Meredith from the campus. Kennedy indicated it was safer to leave Meredith at Baxter Hall: "Yeah, well our people say that it's still a very strange situation," he said. "They wouldn't feel that they could take a chance on taking him outside the building." Of most concern to Kennedy were the snipers targeting the Lyceum Building, whom he wanted Barnett's Mississippi highway patrolmen to weed out of the bushes. "We got to get this situation under control," the president said. "That's much more important than anything else." Barnett still hoped that Kennedy would agree to remove Meredith, which he could portray as a victory to the people of Mississippi. "Mr. President, people are wiring me and saying, 'Well, you've given up.' I had to say, 'No, I'm not giving up, not giving up any fight. I never give up.'"

"I understand," replied the president, reassuringly. "But I don't think anybody, either in Mississippi or any place else, wants a lot of people killed." Kennedy implored Barnett to call in as many state police as possible in order to quell the rioters. He stopped short of threatening the insertion of troops.[57]

As he returned to the Cabinet Room, Kennedy leaned toward spiriting Meredith off campus, even though it would represent a humiliating retreat. But marshals on the ground in Oxford were pressing heavily for the insertion of troops. Robert Kennedy still desperately hoped to avoid that and was also anxious that Katzenbach and his men should use live ammunition only as a last resort. "Can you hold out if you have gas?" the attorney general asked of his deputy. "Is there any way you could figure a way to scare them off?" Yet many of the marshals desperately wanted to draw their revolvers to at least fire warning shots into the air.[58]

News filtered through of further bloodshed. Paul Guihard, a thirty-year-old French journalist, had been found dead near the Lyceum Building. He had a bullet in his back, indicating an execution-style killing. (In his last dispatch, filed earlier that afternoon, he had written "the Civil War has never ended."[59])

Katzenbach now demanded that the president send in troops. Robert Kennedy seemed most concerned by the likely global reaction to Guihard's death. Summoning Guthman to the phone, he noted, "We're gonna have a hell of problem about why we didn't handle the situation better." At that moment, Kennedy rose from his chair in the Cabinet Room and walked across the green carpet of his secretary Evelyn Lincoln's office to the Oval Office. He sat down behind his desk, picked up the phone, and asked to be put through to Army Secretary Cyrus Vance. To prevent further bloodshed, he had reluctantly decided to send in troops. The president issued orders for regular army units to leave their base in Memphis and travel to Oxford by air. In the meantime, the local Mississippi National Guard unit based at the armory in Oxford should take up positions on campus.[60]

Chaos erupted at the Pentagon. Vance had only just discovered that troops on stand-by in Memphis were nowhere near ready to move. Told to return to barracks by their commanding officers after listening to the president's address, they were armed only with nightsticks. The long wait for rifles and ammunition delayed their departure by hours.

In the meantime, the violence continued in waves on the Oxford campus. Shortly after eleven P.M. (CST), there was a second fatality. The victim was Ray Gunter, a white twenty-three-year-old jukebox repairman who had been drawn to the campus that evening out of curiosity rather than malice. Gunter was discovered, slumped on the ground, with a bullet wound in his forehead. Like the killing of Guihard, the circumstances surrounding Gunter's death remain a mystery.

At the White House, the president and his advisers became increasingly edgy. "Where's the Army?" the president screamed down the phone at Vance at one point. "Where are they? Why aren't they moving?" But the information from Vance was garbled and contradictory. One minute, he assured the president the troops had taken off. The next, he conceded they were still on the ground. After initially promising the army would arrive on campus in two hours, it took five hours before the full deployment was complete.

"Damn Army!" shouted the attorney general. "They can't even tell if in fact the MPs have left yet."

"They always give you their bullshit about their instant reaction and their split-second timing," said the president, "but it never works out. No wonder it's so hard to win a war." Fast losing patience with his army secretary, Kennedy now insisted on speaking directly to General Creighton Abrams, the head of military operations. In a further embarrassment for the Pentagon, the communication system failed to function. Robert Kennedy later recalled those conversations between the president and Vance as "the worse and harshest" of his brother's presidency.[61]

Finally at 12:30 A.M. (CST), the first helicopter touched down at Oxford airport, carrying combat-fatigue-clad members of the 503rd Military Police Battalion. There was a further delay, while the 117 members of the advance party assembled on the tarmac and boarded a convoy of waiting buses. Sixty-five minutes after the first helicopter had landed, they finally arrived on the edge of the campus. Katzenbach was on the phone to the president when they came into view. "They're here, Mr. President," he said, with palpable relief. As the MPs arrived, they took up positions on the steps of the Lyceum Building, reinforcing the lines of beleaguered marshals. Soon they were joined by the units from the Mississippi National Guard, whose commanders had reluctantly obeyed the presidential order. At 5:30 (EST) in the morning, knowing that Meredith's life was now safe and that the marshals were well protected, the president finally retired to bed. "I want to be called if anything happens," he told aides.[62]

At 7:55 A.M. (CST), Meredith was driven to the Lyceum Building. He was accompanied by Doar and McShane, who was still wearing his white helmet with the words "US Marshal" stenciled in black letters. With a university official standing over him, Meredith completed the necessary paperwork and was officially registered as a transfer student at Ole Miss. On the Circle outside, crowds of students gathered once again to protest his presence on campus, breathing in bittersweet mouthfuls of teargas still hanging in the air. Held at bay by a small army of combat troops, all they could do was shout "Black bastard! Black nigger!" as Meredith was led away for his first class, a lecture in colonial American history.

President Kennedy spent part of the morning locked in discussions with Barnett, who seem terrified by the prospect that their secret negotiations might be leaked. But with sporadic fighting continuing on campus, the president's primary concern was still security. He feared that another pitched battle could erupt—not just on campus but throughout the entire town. "Now, I want your help in getting these state police to continue to help during the day," he insisted, "because they're their own people." But with the governor continuing to equivocate, Kennedy knew he could only rely on federal troops to maintain order. To that end, he placed a call to Vance, who promised that there would be 20,000 troops in Oxford by midnight. Still worried that a greater show of firepower might be needed, Kennedy raised the possibility of airlifting in 40,000 marines. By the end of the week, 23,759 troops were stationed in Oxford. According to one reporter, the campus looked "like a cross between a bivouac and a prisoner-of-war camp."[63]

In Washington, however, the White House tried hard to project a false air of normalcy. Kennedy did not issue any statement heralding Meredith's registration as an important milestone in American race relations. Neither did he castigate Barnett, either in private or public, for allowing a situation to escalate to the point where two people were murdered. The morning after the Ole Miss riot, when the governor still refused to maintain order, Kennedy had briefly discussed with Solicitor General Archibald Cox the possibility of arresting Barnett. But thereafter he took a much softer line. Indeed, afterwards he issued strict orders to the Justice Department that Barnett should not be prosecuted on criminal charges, for fear that it would offend southern voters and lawmakers. "He was in a good deal of trouble politically in the south anyway," Marshall reflected later.[64]

Although the Justice Department could certainly have brought criminal contempt charges against Barnett, Robert Kennedy preferred the lesser charge of civil contempt, punishable by a $100,000 fine rather than a prison sentence. But the Fifth Circuit Court of Appeals found the charges inadequate and ordered in November that the Justice Department bring criminal, not civil, charges against both Barnett and Lieutenant Governor Johnson. At the beginning of January, Burke Marshall urged the attorney general to give serious consideration to his possible testimony in the case. He should be particularly mindful "about how to deal with the President's conversations with the Governor," which were the most politically sensitive of all. Marshall appeared concerned that the Kennedy brothers' vacillations before the Battle of Ole Miss would anger not only civil rights activists but segregationists as well. (The case was still moving slowly through the courts when President Kennedy was assassinated the following year.)[65]

Rioters, many of them murderous, also received great leniency from the administration. Two men had been killed, and over 200 marshals and troops injured. Three hundred people were subsequently apprehended by troops and U.S. marshals, but only twelve were eventually charged under federal law. Numerous witnesses came forward to support the prosecution, including Professor James Silver, with eyewitness evidence that at least one of the accused had gone around the Circle handing out weapons. But none of the defendants was ever successfully prosecuted. Other than retired Major General Edwin A. Walker, whom the Justice Department committed to a U.S. medical center claiming he was deranged, no one was ever punished.[66]

The reaction from diehard segregationists to Meredith's registration was swift. In Jackson, Barnett ordered the state flag to fly at half-mast over public buildings to mourn the desegregation of Ole Miss. Strom Thurmond called the introduction of troops "a terrible blot on the administration which could never be erased," while Mississippi Congressmen John Bell Williams asked, "How long will our people be subjected to this kind of Hitlerian oppression?" Richard Russell was incensed by Kennedy's flagrant subversion of states' rights. "I shall continue to protest this attack on the states and the death of our dual federal system," he wrote a constituent, "but I know of no way that we can throw back the military might subject to the order of the Commander-in-Chief."[67]

Other southern politicians, however, expressed their support for Kennedy's decision. At the Southern Governors Conference meeting in Hollywood, Florida, in October, two moderates, Terry Sanford of North Carolina and Farris Bryant of Florida, contrasted Barnett's recklessness with the president's good sense. Ernest Vandiver openly criticized his southern colleague, noting, "I hope this tragic chapter in the nation's history is over and the exercise in futility is done with." Of the sixteen governors gathered in Florida, only two supported Barnett: Orval Faubus and John Patterson.[68]

On Capitol Hill, the Southern Caucus was also split. Senator Allen Ellender of Louisiana argued the administration had been right to uphold the rule of law, and even Eastland privately informed Robert Kennedy that Barnett had overstepped the mark. Ervin thought the White House a little hasty in introducing federal troops but conceded it had little choice: "I must confess," he wrote in a letter to a constituent, "that the President was presented with a terrific responsibility by the actions of the courts." In a letter to another constituent, Ervin described Barnett's actions as "foolish." An Alabama congressman, who wished to guard his anonymity, told the *Wall Street Journal* that "most of us know the Southern cause is doomed and it's ridiculous to keep spouting defiance."[69]

White southern voters were somewhat less understanding. From early September to late October, the president saw his approval rating in the region drop from sixty-five percent to fifty-one percent. But it was only a temporary setback—by November, it had rebounded to sixty-five percent and remained steady until the spring. Even at the height of the crisis, his popularity rating never dipped below fifty percent, another sign perhaps of a newfound tolerance in certain southern quarters. In the North, Louis Harris reported major gains in the wake of the Ole Miss crisis. Kennedy's approval had skyrocketed as a result of what he characterized as the president's "firm and resolute" leadership. "I am frank to say that I have never seen the temper and mood change so drastically as this election outlook," he wrote in early October. "In key Northern industrial states, sentiment is behind you 2-1/2 to 3-1 on Mississippi."[70]

The response from black voters was particularly enthusiastic. In New York State, Kennedy's approval ratings jumped from sixty-five percent before the Ole Miss crisis to eighty-four percent afterwards. The black media was also broadly supportive of Kennedy's handling of the crisis. The editorial page of the *Am-*

sterdam News praised Kennedy in the most effusive terms: "Mr. President, your courageous and forthright actions Sunday night have placed you with the greatest Presidents of the United States."[71]

Civil rights leaders, however, were far less sanguine. Although A. Philip Randolph commended Kennedy for his "great statesmanship," the younger generation of black activists was far less impressed. Though reluctant to say so publicly, King was especially disappointed that the president had skirted the issue of civil rights in his handling of the crisis and emphasized the integrity of federal law in such a way as to avoid altogether the issue of race. He was angered also by the protracted negotiations between the administration and Barnett, since it "made Negroes feel like pawns in a white man's political game." James Farmer spoke out directly and criticized the president for failing to draw attention to Meredith's quiet courage. Charles McDew, the chairman of SNCC, blasted him for allowing the federal government to be forced into a compromising position by Barnett. McDew attacked the president for his "wishy-washy speech" and his failure to "display the moral initiative."[72]

A week after the Oxford riot, Robert Kennedy tried to undo some of the damage during a little-publicized speech in Milwaukee, in which he stressed the centrality of the young air force veteran, noting, "there is so much that a single person can do with faith and courage. . . . James Meredith brought to a head and lent his name to another chapter in the mightiest internal struggle of our time." Robert Kennedy had chosen to characterize the Ole Miss crisis in starkly different terms than his brother. The president had delivered a dry and legalistic speech that stayed within clearly delineated political and constitutional boundaries. Robert Kennedy had been much more expansive, impassioned, and personalized. For him, upholding the integrity of the courts was only secondary. Laws were less important than the ideals that James Meredith had sought to uphold.[73]

Overall, the Kennedy brothers showed little interest in reflecting on their own failures. Once the immediate crisis passed, they focused on more tactical concerns. The federal government had to protect Meredith's safety on campus. But as the threat to Meredith's life diminished in the weeks after the riot, so, too, did the scale of the military operation. Under strict orders from the White House, Defense Secretary Robert McNamara produced a plan that would keep troop numbers to a minimum. By late October, there were just 1,200 troops on campus. By the following April, there were just 297 military personnel in Oxford, and never more than thirty-six on campus at one time. By June there had been another reduction, from 297 to 150. As Vance stressed in a memorandum to McNamara, the mission had been carried out "with the minimum number of troops possible"—the policy the administration had insisted on from the outset.[74]

In an effort to minimize white resentment in Oxford, black soldiers were withdrawn from campus at the beginning of October. When Meredith complained, the Justice Department asked him not to release a statement to reporters. Louis Martin quickly weighed in with heavy criticism of the measure, and on October 5, Robert Kennedy instructed McNamara to redeploy black soldiers. But the administration continued to make every effort to mollify Barnett. In January 1963, under intense pressure from Barnett, Robert Kennedy insisted that troops vacate their temporary headquarters at the Oxford Armory and at the local airport. The army set up a new command post one mile from campus, on land that had to be especially procured by the U.S. Forestry Service. Pentagon spokesmen ensured that local reporters were informed of the redeployment, part of the administration's public relations strategy to restore good relations with angry southerners.[75]

The White House also spent a great deal of energy in the final months of 1962 investigating the atrocious mishandling of the crisis by the Pentagon. At a time of heightened Cold War tensions, the president was more concerned about the military failures than by any other aspect of the crisis. "The evening would have been quite different if the troops had gotten there at the time they were supposed to have gotten there," Robert Kennedy reflected afterwards. Even at a time of such violent domestic crisis, civil rights played a subordinate role in JFK's thinking to the implications on his foreign and defense policies.[76]

Embarrassed by his department's dismal performance, McNamara oversaw an urgent postmortem into the Pentagon's handling of the crisis and ordered Vance to investigate the delayed deployment of troops on the night of the riot. At the Justice Department, Katzenbach conducted his own informal inquiry, which relied heavily upon the testimony of Dean Markham, a member of the White House Special Projects staff deployed as a U.S. marshal in Oxford. Markham catalogued a series of hapless errors: of how the convoy that picked up Meredith from Oxford airport had gotten lost; how desperately needed supplies of teargas had to be flown in from Pittsburgh, Pennsylvania; how there had been no walkie-talkie at Baxter Hall, the dormitory where Meredith was being protected. "Future: check tires, gas, battery—Medic," wrote Dean Markham, who suggested that marshals should refrain from giving press interviews lest they reveal the grave lack of planning. Robert Kennedy's scrappy notes from the night of the Ole Miss spoke of the chaos. Seated in the Oval Office, the vital hub of one of the country's most sophisticated communications networks, he was forced at the height of the crisis to scribble down the telephone number of John Doar, one of his most trusted aides: the pay phone at the dispensary of the University Hospital. To get a sense of the geography of the area, he relied on a Shell gas station folding roadmap.[77]

As ever, the administration made every effort to limit the political fallout in the South and normalize relations with the region's lawmakers. The task was fairly uncomplicated, largely because many southern politicians privately agreed that it was Barnett who was mainly culpable. Even so, Robert Kennedy sought a rapprochement with southern lawmakers unhappy with the administration's tactics. "What we did at the University of Mississippi had nothing to do with integration or segregation," he wrote in a letter to the wife of Mississippi Senator John Stennis, the wording of which he had discussed at length with Burke Marshall. "If we accept the proposition here in the United States that a state official or a local citizen can determine what laws they are going to follow and which ones they are going to disobey or reject, we are going to have anarchy or insurrection. We acted in Mississippi to prevent that." The president continued to frame the question as a straightforward matter of law and order. During an hour-long television special in December, Kennedy once again reiterated his duty to uphold the law: "I don't know what other role they would expect the President of the United States to play." But at no stage of the interview did he commend Meredith or lend support to the general principle of integrated education.[78]

The Kennedy brothers had mishandled the crisis from the outset. The riots at Ole Miss were by no means inevitable. But due to erratic handling by both the president and the attorney general, the situation escalated to the point where two people were murdered, and Meredith was nearly lynched. Had the federal government shown firm resolve when Meredith first tried to gain entry, Barnett might well have shied away from an all-out confrontation. The governor was clearly unstable, and his resolve was weak. He caved easily when confronted with the threat of being exposed as a fraud. Faced, however, with the Kennedy brothers' haphazard and endlessly accommodating approach to negotiation, it is hardly surprising that Barnett refused to back down.

The administration's paralysis in confronting the crisis at Ole Miss was due, to a large extent, to the president's almost paranoid fear of using the army to enforce federal law in the South. Even after Meredith had been blocked from registering by the governor on two separate occasions, he was accompanied by only two federal officials when he tried to make a third unsuccessful attempt. Kennedy's anxiety about creating a public standoff akin to Little Rock led him to a greater failure—as *Time* pointed out the following week: "President Kennedy could have learned from Eisenhower's performance in the Little Rock crisis, if forced to intervene, then intervene with sufficient force. That's what Ike did, and there was no death toll in Little Rock, nor any serious casualties."[79]

Nor did the administration use the aftermath of the riots to push forward on the issues of civil rights. Instead, both brothers focused on quelling the rage of segregationists in the South. Although the president emerged from the confrontation with Barnett with broad support from most members of the Southern Caucus, he seemed to become ever more fearful of antagonizing their constituencies. Had Robert Kennedy sought a tougher punishment for Barnett in the fall, the administration would have sent an unmistakable signal to diehard segregationists like Bull Connor and George Wallace, who was by this point a race-baiting candidate in the Alabama gubernatorial race.

If anything, the Oxford riots set the administration back in its handling of the civil rights agenda. Louis Martin had pressed for a National Conference on Civil Rights in the days leading up to the crisis. It would be an opportunity to discuss the broader implications of the crisis and provide a setting in which the president could signal a new direction in policy. The White House and Justice Department immediately raised objections. "I think a conference might sometime be of some use," conceded Marshall, "but not now." In the aftermath of the riots, the White House also rejected the idea of inviting Billy Graham to speak at the Ole Miss campus, so he could set out the moral case for reform.[80]

For the Kennedy brothers, this had been one of the most traumatic episodes of their spell in office. And it highlighted growing differences in their approaches to civil rights. Throughout the crisis, they had been totally allied in their desire to avoid the use of troops, partly because they had long-held qualms about the military enforcement of civil rights and partly because both had been so very critical of Eisenhower for allowing the Little Rock to escalate to the point where troops became necessary. But at key moments, differences emerged. On the eve of the Battle of Ole Miss, when both men implored Barnett to back down, the attorney general adopted a much firmer negotiating stance than the president. In the week before the riot, Robert Kennedy spoke to Meredith directly; at no point during or after the riot did the president contact him. In the week after the riot, Robert Kennedy publicly commended Meredith. Again, the president remained silent. RFK was too loyal to his brother to be critical of him, publicly or even privately. He was also an extremely disciplined politician. But as the struggle for black equality intensified, he was less and less able to suppress his impatience with the retrograde forces of segregation.

There was, perhaps, one moment of quiet revelation for the president. On the night of the Battle of Ole Miss itself, Kennedy asked his brother if there would be "any more like this one coming up soon." The attorney general explained that court action was underway aimed at integrating the University of Alabama, which would probably come to a head in the spring. The president simply told him: "Let's be ready."[81]

CHAPTER 21

⚬᷎ᴑ

In Lincoln's Shadow

Only three weeks after the riots at Ole Miss, the mounting tensions be-
tween the Soviet Union and the United States came to a head. On Octo-
ber 16, Kennedy was shown aerial reconnaissance photographs proving that
Khrushchev had been secretly building military installations in Cuba. (When
Kennedy saw the images of ballistic missiles capable of striking the White
House, he jokingly inquired if they could be used to obliterate Oxford).[1]

With the Pentagon's incompetent handling of Ole Miss fresh in his mind,
Kennedy had little faith left in the U.S. military. When the Joint Chiefs pressed
for a full-scale military campaign against Cuba, with immediate air strikes followed by an invasion, Kennedy doubted their ability to carry it out. Instead, he
decided to implement a naval quarantine around the island, to prevent the arrival of additional weapons. His cautious strategy worked. At the end of thirteen
perilous days—in the course of which Defense Secretary Robert McNamara
and others predicted an impending nuclear Armageddon—Kennedy found a
diplomatic solution. The Kremlin would dismantle its missiles, and in return
the United States would sign a nonaggression pact against Cuba and remove its
Jupiter missiles from Turkey.

Kennedy's deft handling of the crisis marked the high point of his presidency.
His personal approval ratings soared—rising to seventy-three percent in January, and never dropping below sixty-one percent up to his death. Ever optimistic, the administration's few surviving liberals hoped Kennedy would exploit
his popularity to issue the long-awaited housing order. Martin presented the
case to the president most forcefully, arguing that the order would not only
blunt criticisms from civil rights leaders but help Democratic candidates in November. Before the Cuban missile crisis, Martin had already told Robert
Kennedy, "The issuance of the order would have a terrific impact upon all civil
rights critics who will be stumping the country."[2]

As ever, Lawrence O'Brien opposed Martin's recommendation on the grounds that the housing order would lose Democratic candidates more votes than it would gain. According to O'Brien, Michigan Congresswoman Martha Griffiths had contacted his office "absolutely screaming" that the order would alienate Roman Catholic and middle-class constituents alarmed by the prospect of blacks invading their suburbs. O'Brien reported that similar fears were echoed by James O'Hara of Michigan, Byron Rogers, of Colorado, and Leonor Sullivan of Missouri. Michigan Senator Pat McNamara had told him that if the order was intended to boost black support it was unnecessary; the state's blacks were solidly behind Kennedy. O'Brien also worried the housing order would undercut moderate southerners, namely Alabama Congressmen Albert Rains, the chairman of the Housing Committee, who faced a tough challenge from a vehement segregationist. Ted Sorensen also discouraged Kennedy from signing the order in October and argued it would be politically superfluous. Sorensen admitted that the literacy test debacle, combined with the administration's cautious approach to civil rights, had caused "rumbling" among black leaders, though the president's standing remained high among black voters.

The president therefore decided to delay issuing the order until after the congressional midterm elections.[3]

∾

The Democratic Party fared well in the November elections. In the Senate, the Democrats picked up four additional seats. In the House, they suffered a net loss of only four seats—a fraction of the off-year losses traditionally suffered by incumbents. In bullish mood, staffers predicted the freshman congressmen might supply as many as twelve extra votes for the administration's legislative program. As added bonuses, Ted Kennedy swept to victory in the Massachusetts Senate race, while Richard Nixon suffered a humiliating defeat in the gubernatorial race in his native California. In an effort to explain their defeat, Republicans complained that they had been "Cubanized"—overcome by the wave of patriotism that engulfed the country after the missile crisis.

Blacks remained particularly loyal. After examining the results, Louis Harris reported to the president that the black vote "held rather well on the whole"— it had dropped by just 0.4 percent since 1960. (By contrast, the Democrats' support among Jewish voters had slipped 3.1 percent, 4 percent among Catholics, 4.5 percent among the Irish, and 5.6 percent among Italians.) The Democrats were especially pleased at the loyalty of black voters in Michigan, New Jersey, and especially New York, where Nelson Rockefeller had tried hard to woo black voters in Harlem but been outperformed by his Democratic rival, Robert M. Morgenthau. There were also noteworthy victories for black Democratic candidates. Augustus F. Hawkins, a native of Louisiana who had moved to California, became the fifth black lawmaker in Congress and the first from west of the Mississippi. In Georgia, LeRoy A. Johnson became the first black elected to the state legislature in ninety-two years.[4]

Below the Mason-Dixon Line, the elections provided evidence of two starkly different trends—both the growing popularity of racial moderates generally but also the resurgence of massive resistance in the Deep South states of Mississippi and Alabama, which had become the primary battlegrounds of the civil rights struggle. In Mississippi, Frank Smith, a racial moderate favored by the Kennedy brothers, was defeated in a June primary runoff by Jamie Whitten, an ardent segregationist who claimed his opponent had "crawled into bed with the Kennedys." Even though the administration tried privately to help Smith (the president had personally donated $2,000 to his campaign, and Robert Kennedy had delayed a much-needed inspection of voting records in his home county until after the primary), Whitten won easily.[5]

In Alabama, the results were jarring. Incumbent Senator Lister Hill won his campaign by only a tiny margin of 6,000 votes. He had run against James Martin, one of a new breed of race-baiting southern Republicans, who branded Hill as a "liberal" and "Kennedy man." It was the closest the Deep South had come to electing a Republican since Reconstruction. George Wallace, an ardent white supremacist, beat two racial moderates—former Governor James "Big Jim" Folsom and State Senator Ryan deGraffenreid—in the gubernatorial race. Wallace had crafted his entire campaign around the issue of racial segregation. He had promised to "stand in the schoolhouse door" if the federal government threatened to integrate Alabama's classrooms. When he took the oath of office in January, Wallace vowed to maintain the strict separation of the races. "I draw the line in the dust and toss the gauntlet before the feet of tyranny," he declared, in comments aimed directly at the Kennedy brothers. "Segregation now . . . segregation tomorrow . . . segregation forever." A beaming Ross Barnett applauded at his side.[6]

Elsewhere across the South, however, there was cause for optimism. In the Georgia gubernatorial race, former State Senator Carl Sanders, a thirty-seven-year-old moderate, supported by both the business community and the Kennedy brothers, defeated former Governor Marvin Griffin, an archsegregationist. Though Sanders promised to maintain Georgia's "traditional separation," as he delicately put it, he stressed throughout his campaign that school integration should no longer be the state's defining political issue. Donald S. Russell, a racial moderate, won the governor's seat in South Carolina and pledged during his inaugural address in January to "give *all* our people the opportunity they truly deserve."[7]

Louis Harris saw in Sanders's and Russell's victories the dawning of a new political era, and he advised the president that "the entire Democratic Party of the South is changing rapidly into a far more moderate and liberal party." Harris recognized that the staunchly segregationist Democratic South was now in terminal decline and predicted that the Republican Party would seek to move into the political void by fielding more conservative candidates. With great prescience, Harris also forecast that Senator Barry Goldwater of Arizona would become the Republican Party's presidential nominee in 1964.[8]

The president was also heartened by the election results. Now in a stronger position politically, Kennedy finally decided to issue the housing order. Kennedy gave the go-ahead at a meeting on November 13, but there was still one crucial issue to be resolved: the question of scope. For months, administration officials had debated whether or not to draft a maximal order, which extended coverage to federally assisted loans from savings and loans institutions and private lending banks, which provided funding for most new housing construction. Beforehand, Norbert Schlei had distilled the issue into a two-page briefing paper, but Kennedy had not even bothered reading it, so the meeting quickly degenerated into fifteen minutes of "completely disorganized comment," according to Schlei. Robert Weaver argued for an expansive order but was fiercely opposed by Treasury Secretary Douglas Dillon. Dillon argued that the housing industry was already in the doldrums and had shown a worrying decline in new start-ups over the course of the year. On November 9, Kennedy had already been warned by Leonard Frank, the head of the National Association of Home Builders, that a drop in new construction could have a $6 billion impact on gross domestic product. Fearing that the housing order would act as a further break, Kennedy sided with Dillon and Frank. He therefore opted for a minimal order, which limited its coverage to housing built or bought with federal aid or financed by private mortgages guaranteed or insured by the Federal Housing Authority (FHA), the Veterans Administration (VA), and the Farmers' Home Agency. Weaver continued to argue that the order would be essentially meaningless if it did not include banks and savings and loans institutions. But the president overruled him, on economic grounds.[9]

As well as limiting its reach, Kennedy also decided against making the order retroactive. This was a key demand not just of civil rights activists but of an already disgruntled Weaver. Such a move would have greatly extended the order's reach, but Justice Department officials questioned its legality. Fearing he might resign in protest, Robert Kennedy and Marshall were dispatched to deliver the news in person, a courtesy that kept him in line.[10]

On Tuesday, November 20, the president announced the new housing order during a press conference. But by putting forward the order with minimum fanfare on the eve of the Thanksgiving holiday, Kennedy ensured that it would receive limited coverage. He sandwiched his remarks on the housing order between comments on the withdrawal of Soviet IL-28 bombers from Cuba and the Indian-Chinese border dispute. The press conference was thus dominated by the subject of Cuba rather than civil rights—of the seventeen questions asked by reporters only one touched upon the housing order. After twenty-two months of delay, the president might have expected a tougher line of questioning, especially since in detail and scope Executive Order #11063 was far from the robust measure civil rights activists had championed.[11]

Relieved the president had finally acted, civil rights leaders responded enthusiastically to the order. Both Roy Wilkins and A. Philip Randolph fired off congratulatory telegrams to the White House, while Martin Luther King commended Kennedy on his "political courage." King quickly became more circumspect, however, and wrote in the *Amsterdam News* on December 13 that although the measure was a "good faith step in the right direction," it fell significantly short of expectations. He noted the glaring absence of a retroactive clause and also highlighted concerns about the compliance regime under which contractors would be regulated. The *Pittsburgh Courier* struck the same pessimistic note: "Negroes are getting very weary of tokenism hailed as victories."[12]

Black appointees within the administration also voiced criticisms. Roger Wilkins at the State Department, who was the nephew of Roy Wilkins, was the most vocal. The day before Kennedy announced the order, Wilkins had written a scathing memo to White House aide Ralph Dungan, who quickly forwarded it to the president and attorney general. "It is my judgment," Wilkins wrote, "that the record the administration has written in civil rights is unimpressive, shows no commitment to firm and steady progress and fails to live up to the excellent statements made by the President during the 1960 campaign." Wilkins demanded a complete policy reappraisal—he called for new legislation aimed at accelerating school desegregation, as well as more appointments and greater moral leadership from the White House.[13]

The administration did little to assuage critics of the order in January when it appointed David L. Lawrence as head of the newly created President's Committee on Equal Opportunity in Housing. Lawrence, a former governor of Pennsylvania and old-style Democratic boss, held a condescending view of blacks. The seventy-three-year-old Lawrence showed little enthusiasm for his new role of enforcing the housing order, and it took him months to fill the eight seats of his committee (the long delay prompted CORE activists to picket the Housing and Home Finance Agency). Even when the committee was fully staffed, it did little more than "paper shuffling," in the damning words of Oliver Hill, a black official at the FHA. One of the few times the president talked to Lawrence on the subject of fair housing, the former governor shared a crude joke about blacks moving into white neighborhoods: "Knock, Knock!" . . . "Izya" . . . Izya who? . . . Izya new neighbor."[14]

❦

Since the beginning of 1961, civil rights leaders had been calling for a summit at the White House. Now that the midterm elections were safely out of the way, and Kennedy had boosted his standing among moderate black leaders by issuing the housing order, he decided to hold one. It would be the most high-powered gathering of black leaders to assemble before a president. The White House sent invitations to the heads of four of the Big Six civil rights groups—Roy Wilkins of the NAACP, Martin Luther King of the SCLC, Whitney Young of the National Urban League, and James Farmer of CORE—as well as Dorothy Height of the National Council of Negro Women. SNCC was purposely excluded. Administration officials had grown increasingly worried and irritated by the group's radicalism.

The meeting, on Monday, December 17, was a debacle. In the wake of the Cuban missile crisis, it is perhaps not surprising that Kennedy focused almost completely on the plight of black Africans fighting colonial rule, rather than the condition of black Americans struggling still for equality. Throughout his administration, Kennedy displayed much of the same hard-nosed pragmatism with regard to Africa that he had in his handling of domestic civil rights policies. A strong opponent of colonialism from his earliest days in Congress, he had made strenuous efforts to cultivate ambassadors from newly decolonized African nations, in the hope they would align with the United States rather than the Soviet Union. But the geopolitics of the Cold War also made Kennedy much more hesitant in his approach toward two of the continent's problem nations: South Africa, which had adopted a much stricter form of racial apartheid after seceding from the British Commonwealth in May 1961; and Angola, where an armed rebellion against Portuguese rule had begun in February 1961. The Kennedy administration was critical of South Africa's apartheid policies but was reluctant to impose sanctions against such a staunchly anticommunist government that also controlled a rich variety of strategically important minerals. Equally, the administration was reluctant to criticize Portugal, a key NATO ally, because it wanted access to its mid-Atlantic airbase on the Azores.[15]

Civil rights leaders had long called for the administration to take a more principled stance toward the Portuguese and South African governments. They saw troubling parallels between Kennedy's accommodationist stance toward Prime Minister Hendrik Verwoerd in South Africa and Portugal's dictator Antonio Salazar, and his reluctance to confront southern segregationists. They also wanted Kennedy to adopt a Marshall Plan for Africa, to boost the development of the newly decolonized nations.

At the December meeting, Kennedy indicated he was open to the idea of a Marshall Plan for Africa. But he was firmly opposed to imposing sanctions against South Africa and reluctant to exert too much pressure on Portugal. As Kennedy explained to his assembled audience, America's obligations to NATO made it impossible to stem the flow of arms to Portugal—he did not want to jeopardize that alliance and therefore opposed a U.N. resolution that would reproach Portugal's leaders for suppression of rebel groups in its African colonies.

At a time of such heightened Cold War tensions, Kennedy considered the unity of NATO much more important than castigating Portugal.[16]

Kennedy dedicated very little time to the subject of domestic civil rights issues. He did acknowledge that the State Department could improve on its dismal employment record and told the group that he shared their frustration about the paucity of black ambassadors. But he remained unyielding with regard to demands for a new civil rights bill. Kennedy stressed that he had no intention of abandoning his nonlegislative strategy.[17]

Afterwards, King held a brief private session with the president, to discuss the bombing of a black church in Birmingham on December 14, and to press for new legislation. But the president claimed the situation on Capitol Hill was hopeless, and that there was no point in pressing for new legislation.[18]

Although Kennedy had devoted three hours to the meetings—an unprecedented demonstration of interest—the civil rights leaders left without any concrete commitments to show their members. They were also deeply resentful that the discussion has been dominated so completely by Africa. They immediately poured out their frustrations to Simeon Booker, the dean of the black press corps, who spent much of the evening filling his notebook with spiteful quotations. "Negroes want their freedom now in America," seethed one unnamed participant. "Here we have met longer with the President of the United States than any other Negro group and we're asking help for Africans, who've fought for and won their freedom." "We're not going about it right," complained another. "We've got to stop begging the Kennedys for this and that. We've got to start demanding our rights." An aide to one of the Big Six leaders wondered aloud what he would tell his friends in SNCC. "How the hell can we tell these sit-in demonstrators we came to Washington, met the President and didn't demand help?" A few days later, King went on the record, telling a reporter, "[We] still have not had a strong voice from the White House dealing with the moral issues" of civil rights.[19]

When he later reflected on the meeting, Booker considered it pivotal. "No single meeting so undercut the influence of Negro leadership," he wrote. Estranged from the president, the civil rights leaders decided they must go over his head to secure genuine reform. "To hell with the Kennedys," said one participant. "They can't direct our campaign. We must break all contact. We must give up this protocol life." Another signaled a radical shift in tactics. "We're headed for a revolution. We're losing our mass support. Unless we go back to them and lead them forward, we're sunk. And to do this will mean some active demonstrations which would touch off coast-to-coast violence. But it must be done."[20]

∾

The president had seen in the results of the midterm elections the success of his existing civil rights policies. Robert Kennedy took the results as a sign of support for further reform and a prescription for renewed action. He wrote to the president in January 1963, describing an "emerging spirit of the South" defined not by the violence of Mississippi, but Carl Sanders's election in Georgia. The Justice Department could now accelerate its progress on civil rights, in part because the new breed of governors would offer less resistance. He agreed with Marshall's request to launch a fresh batch of voting suits in Louisiana, Mississippi, Alabama, and Georgia, provided that the Justice Department was not "overtaken by other events which require the time of too many lawyers."[21]

Robert Kennedy even gave the go-ahead to launch a voting rights suit in Sunflower County, Mississippi, the home and political fiefdom of James Eastland. Civil rights activists called Sunflower County "the worst county in the worst state," since only 114 out of 13,524 local blacks had been registered to vote. The Justice Department's decision to target the county gave the clearest indication of its aggressive new approach. When Justice Department officials launched the suit on January 12, Eastland responded with the briefest of press statements: "There is no foundation in fact for the allegations in the bill of complaint."[22]

Robert Kennedy was also more determined to make a second attempt at passing voting rights legislation, which would help expedite the Justice Department's work. He was frustrated by the slow progress of the Justice Department and worried about the impact it was having on the mood of young civil rights activists, particularly in SNCC. For him, black militancy was no longer just a disturbing undercurrent; it had risen to the surface. In late 1962, he instructed aides to draft a voting rights bill, which he encouraged his brother to introduce during the new congressional session. His request led to another of the administration's intermittent debates over whether to introduce its own legislative proposals.[23]

Widening the growing rift between the Justice Department and White House, O'Brien and O'Donnell were implacably opposed to the measure. The president also remained unconvinced that the bill was necessary given the Democratic Party's impressive performance in the midterm elections. 1963 also promised to be a busy legislative year, with the president seeking the enactment of huge $13.6 billion tax cuts, which would require the support of moderate southern Democrats, who traditionally favored balanced budgets over tax cuts. The measures would also require hearings before the Senate Finance Committee, which was chaired by Senator Harry F. Byrd. In early December, the president therefore informed Sorensen there would be no new civil rights bill in the upcoming session, other than a routine measure extending the life of the CRC, whose two-year jurisdiction was up for renewal. Kennedy clearly continued to believe that the promotion of civil rights would hamper his wider legislative program. In an end-of-year television interview recorded on December 16, he claimed that the bitterness caused by the Ole Miss crisis was a major reason why Congress had not passed a federal aid-to-education bill.[24]

In the final weeks of 1962, the president also came under fierce pressure to take a major role in the celebrations marking the hundredth anniversary of the official signing of the Emancipation Proclamation. For almost a decade, the NAACP slogan had been "Free by 63." The date had almost arrived and "Freedom Now" became the new mantra. To celebrate the centennial of the abolition of slavery, civil rights leaders had been preparing for months to usher in the New Year with great fanfare and had lobbied the president since the summer to appear in person. CRC staff director Berl Bernhard was determined to launch the celebrations on December 31 with a television spectacular, in which the president would play a starring role. With echoes of the presidential inauguration, it would include poems especially commissioned for the occasion from Carl Sandburg and Robert Frost. White House aides had assured black reporters after the Lincoln Memorial ceremony in September that the president would take a full and active part.[25]

Louis Martin also urged Kennedy to demonstrate his commitment to racial equality by participating in a gala event at Constitution Hall on January 1. Martin and Bernhard had also lobbied the administration to host a series of events at the White House during the first week of January to kick off the celebrations, which would be modeled on the famed Pablo Casals recital and Nobel laureates' dinner. (Martin and Bernhard had deliberately suggested swank events in hopes that the plans would appeal to the gala-loving president.) "The President must be the focal point," Martin and Bernard told Sorensen, "and set the tone for the entire commemorative year."[26]

But as he had shown with the Lincoln Memorial event in September, Kennedy was unwilling to take a leading role. At a time when he needed to attract southern Democratic support for his massive tax cuts, he was perhaps reluctant to associate himself too closely with Lincoln's contested legacy in the South. And by making himself a figurehead of the commemorative celebrations he would send out a misleading message: that he viewed the anniversary as an opportunity for national introspection, and a chance to rally public support for a fresh assault on segregation. Kennedy turned down the request to take part in the televised extravaganza and rejected plans for a series of White House events. He planned to remain in Palm Beach for the New Year rather than marking the anniversary in Washington.

Even until as late as December 26, Lee White continued to hope that Kennedy would at least issue a presidential proclamation. White drafted his proposed statement and forwarded it to Salinger, who was with the president in Palm Beach. "The advice of our Civil Rights Commission people," warned White, "is that not to issue some statement would be regarded as a minor disaster." Unworried about courting controversy, the president decided against issuing it. Given the Democrats' strong showing among black voters in the congressional midterm elections, he still believed that the Southern Caucus posed much more of a threat to his presidency than black discontent.[27]

The first statement to emerge from the "Winter White House" in January 1963 was a New Year greeting to the leaders of the Soviet Union. The administration left it to Lyndon Johnson to speak on behalf of civil rights. "To strike the chains of a slave is noble," said Johnson, during a speech in Detroit on January 7. "To leave him the captive of the color of his skin is hypocrisy. While we in America have freed the slave of his chains, we have not freed his heirs of their color."[28]

Liberal Democrats were angry that Kennedy had failed to mark the centenary of the Emancipation Proclamation by advancing fresh proposals. On January 8, a group of liberal grandees including Paul Douglas, Joseph Clark, and Hubert Humphrey sent the president a joint letter urging "forthright action in the legislative field." The inclusion of Humphrey's name was particularly disquieting to the administration. He had served as an invaluable intermediary between the White House and disgruntled liberals over the course of Kennedy's presidency but was no longer willing to play that role.[29]

Humphrey was also annoyed that Kennedy had not come to the aid of liberal Democrats in their ongoing efforts to revise the filibuster rule. When the new Congress convened early January, Senate liberals tried once more to change Rule XXII, to make it easier to break southern filibusters. But in the absence of White House backing and without the support of Senate Majority Leader Mike Mansfield, they failed in early February to overcome a coalition of southern Democrats and conservative Republicans by nine votes.

Humphrey's defection was a source of serious concern to O'Brien and Sorensen, who advised the president to woo him back into the fold with a personal meeting. Even more troubling, liberal Republicans planned to introduce an omnibus civil rights bill of their own, and liberal Democrats intended to support it. Their political rebellion was certain to embarrass the White House. But liberal Democrats felt it was the only way to galvanize the president to action.

At the start of the New Year, the attorney general redoubled his efforts to persuade his brother to support new legislative proposals. In January, he even enlisted Martin Luther King to help make the case. During a meeting with King at the Justice Department ahead of the president's State of the Union address, the attorney general took the extraordinary step of inviting the civil rights leader to use his telephone to call the president in order to emphasize the benefits of a new voting rights act. But Kennedy refused to budge. He told King that civil rights legislation would "arouse the anger of the South" and "block his whole legislative program." Refusing to let the matter rest, Robert Kennedy finally extracted a grudging concession from his brother that he would keep open the possibility of introducing a new voting rights bill later in the year.[30]

The president alluded to this pledge in the vaguest possible terms during his State of the Union address on January 14. "I wish that all qualified Americans permitted to vote were willing to vote," said the president, "but surely in this centennial year of Emancipation all those who are willing to vote should always be permitted." But the president's proposed tax cuts grabbed the headlines in the newspapers the following morning, and his mention of civil rights was treated merely as an aside. Commentators remarked afterwards on the president's self-assurance in delivering his third State of the Union, as compared with his first two—James Reston noticed "confidence and optimism" in his 1963 address, whereas his 1961 speech had been "almost funereal." But the president was unwilling to expend any of his newfound political capital from the midterm elections and Cuban missile crisis in championing civil rights.[31]

After the State of the Union, the attorney general redoubled his efforts to get the president to make a firmer commitment. "Additional legislation is required to ensure prompt relief," he wrote the president on January 24, "where the facts indicate that substantial numbers of Negroes are being deprived of the right to register and vote because of race."[32]

Only the week before, Robert Kennedy had made a highly personalized attempt to bring about a much-needed overhaul of southern democratic institutions. He did so by launching a fresh assault on malapportionment, the problem of the over-representation of rural counties in primary elections and state legislatures, which was particularly pronounced in the South. Malapportionment often meant state governments neglected the urban poor, a large percentage of whom were black. It was also a key pillar of the region's white power structure, because support for hard-line segregationists was often strongest in the very rural counties that were over-represented. On January 17, 1963, in the only case he ever argued personally before the Supreme Court, Robert Kennedy took aim at the county-unit system in Georgia. The ideal, he noted, was "to have one's vote . . . given equal weight with the votes of other citizens," which was especially important in Georgia, a state that was becomingly increasingly urban and suburban. The move invoked the wrath of Richard Russell, a long-time beneficiary of malapportionment in Georgia, who claimed its abolition would trample over the Constitution. But Kennedy was adamant: Southern democracy must move into the twentieth century.[33]

Liberal Democrats also ratcheted up the pressure on the president to do more for black Americans. Paul Douglas wrote to the president on January 26, and noted: "there is general agreement, as well as puzzlement, about the inadequacy of our effort." Then, on January 31, liberal Republicans launched an attack, by criticizing the Kennedy administration for its failure to promote new civil rights legislation. Led by Congressman William McCulloch, one of the most respected lawmakers on Capitol Hill, six Republican members of the House Judiciary Committee announced they would soon introduce legislative proposals of their own.[34]

Louis Martin predicted that the president could easily find himself overtaken by events if he did not come out quickly and firmly on behalf of civil rights.

"American Negroes through sit-ins, kneel-ins, wade-ins, etc., will continue to create situations which involve police powers of the local, state and Federal government," he warned Ted Sorensen on January 30. But Martin was unable to engineer a concrete shift in policy. Until the end of January, civil rights were still low on Kennedy's list of priorities. On January 28 and 31, when Kennedy privately listed twenty-seven questions to be settled in the "coming months," Charles de Gaulle received three mentions, but racial equality did not even merit one.[35]

Martin made one last attempt to persuade Kennedy to mark the anniversary of the Emancipation Proclamation and tried to push the idea of a White House reception for leading black Americans. Martin told Kenneth O'Donnell it would make a huge splash in the black press but go largely unnoticed in the South. Eventually, after an intense lobbying campaign, he secured the president's blessing.

Martin planned the event for February 12, Lincoln's birthday, and drew up a guest list a thousand names long. The plan was to entertain a greater number of blacks on a single night at the White House than in its entire 170-year history. Several crucial civil rights leaders decided to boycott, however, which diluted the event's political impact. A. Philip Randolph and Clarence Mitchell shunned the president in protest at his refusal to promise new legislation in the upcoming session of Congress. King, who also declined, was on a family vacation in Jamaica.

The gala event—dubbed "Cullud Folks Night at the White House" by some of the invited guests—was nonetheless a tremendous success. Over 800 black VIPs, ranging from judges to jazz musicians, packed into four White House state rooms, where they were served curried chicken and shrimp Creole. The president and first lady mingled happily in their company.[36]

The only moment of potential controversy came when the president caught sight of Sammy Davis, Jr., whose interracial marriage had made him a target of particular vitriol for white supremacists. Though Kennedy and Davis had socialized on numerous occasions at West Coast parties, they had never been seen or photographed together in public. If a snapshot emerged with the two of them together, it could be used as a powerful weapon of propaganda in the presidential election of 1964. So when Kennedy caught sight of Davis at the gala, he was "absolutely feathered," according to Lee White. Panicking, he quickly drew together his team of advisers and demanded an explanation as to how Davis's name had been included on the guest list. (Martin was the guilty party. He had mischievously added Davis's name to the list every time it was removed.) In more than a hundred photographs taken that night by White House photographers, Davis did not appear in a single frame.[37]

The evening was a "milestone," in the words of one *Newsweek* correspondent. It would have been unimaginable under Eisenhower, Truman, or Roosevelt.

With Judge Thurgood Marshall and Robert Weaver, Kennedy's most high-profile black appointees, on prominent display, the event's symbolic value was incalculable. As one reporter for the *Washington Post* put it, "Now the Republicans can no longer claim Lincoln's birthday as their traditional day for political rallying and oratory."[38]

The White House had, however, done everything in its power to minimize the political impact of the extravaganza. In an attempt to shape newspaper coverage, Pierre Salinger had spoken to white reporters in advance of the dinner and dismissed it as little more than a minor social event tacked onto the end of the president's busy day. The tactic worked to perfection. The next morning the *Washington Post* featured a photograph of Kennedy posing with eleven leading blacks in its "For and About Women" section rather than in the news pages. The *Chicago Daily Tribune* reported that Kennedy had held a dinner in honor of Lincoln but failed to mention that the majority of guests were black. Salinger had also directed the White House press corps toward the grandly titled "Lincoln Centennial Report," a 246-page document prepared by the CRC and presented to Kennedy before the dinner. In particular, Salinger urged them to focus on the passages dealing with the denial of civil rights in the North, and especially the section on overcrowding in black schools. On the basis of those briefings, the *New York Times* declared in its headline, "Civil Rights Fight Shifting to the North." It mentioned the White House gala only in passing.[39]

Black leaders were not impressed by Kennedy's grand gesture. Their relationship to the federal government was growing even more adversarial. Meeting that week at Detroit's Wayne State University, they discussed new tactics to increase pressure on the administration. Whitney Young of the National Urban League called for "crash programs" to improve black hiring and raised the specter of militant organizations, such as the Black Muslims, vying for the loyalties of disaffected black youths. James Farmer spoke more plainly. "If we have to wait another 100 years there will be violence," he said. "Frankly, we can't even wait another 25 years—or even fifteen years—in our Northern cities without violence. And in the South many of the homes—if not most—are armed. . . . Unless the process can be speeded up, the non-violent forces will fight a losing battle."[40]

The Lincoln event also failed to silence Kennedy's liberal critics. Chester Bowles was most outspoken in his criticism of the administration. Bowles, who had once served as deputy secretary of state, had been sidelined by Kennedy during the so-called Thanksgiving Day massacre, the bloody reorganization of the State Department in 1961. Since that time he had grown increasingly disappointed at Kennedy's failure to deliver on the promises of the Democratic platform, which he himself had written. On February 15, 1963, in a speech at Lincoln University in Oxford, Pennsylvania, he delivered a stinging critique of the administration's record. He lambasted the White House for failing to implement the 1960 civil rights plank and derided the administration for its tokenistic approach to school desegregation.[41]

Bowles also spoke of his alarm at the rising anger of blacks. He cited *The Fire Next Time,* an incendiary new book by James Baldwin. The book began with a dedicatory letter entitled "My Dungeon Shook: Letter to my Nephew on the One Hundredth Anniversary of the Emancipation Proclamation." In startling prose, Baldwin went on to explain the appeal of militancy for an angry generation of young blacks and warned that they were poised to embark on a violent new course. Though Baldwin exhorted young blacks to seek a peaceful path toward racial reconciliation, many whites—including Bowles—responded with horror to Baldwin's description of deep alienation of black Americans, and his explicit warning about the dangers it could pose: "[I]t is possible that the new dynamism we are witnessing among today's Negro students and leaders may in fact be turned towards negative and destructive channels." Soon after Bowles delivered his speech, a copy landed on the desk of Robert Kennedy.[42]

From the governor's mansion in Albany, New York, Nelson Rockefeller, an early front-runner for the Republican presidential nomination, hoped to turn the rising tide of resentment to his political advantage. Rockefeller had first been elected in 1958 and had since built up strong civil rights credentials by passing stiff antidiscriminatory housing regulations and promoting progressive employment practices. Before the Republican's 1960 convention, he had pressured Nixon into adopting an unusually strong civil rights plank. And over the course of the Albany crisis, he had strengthened links with civil rights groups by calling repeatedly on the Justice Department to guarantee the safety of Martin Luther King and other jailed activists and had made hefty personal donations to help defray their bail costs. And he had financed the reconstruction of black churches in Georgia in September 1962, which had been burned to the ground by the Klan.

Rockefeller's efforts had paid off. In the spring of 1962, he was the subject of a flattering profile in *Jet* magazine. He also came to enjoy the backing of Jackie Robinson, who in turn tried to enlist the help of King. "I cannot help but wonder in what way we can help Rockefeller get a bigger plurality," he told King in October. "If he does, I believe that we will see changes made in the Kennedy administration."[43]

Over the course of 1962, Rockefeller also cultivated Wilkins, who used a speech in New York at the beginning of 1963 to indicate that the black vote was up for grabs in the next presidential election. Wilkins showered praise on Rockefeller's efforts to strengthen New York's antidiscriminatory housing regulations, which, as he pointedly noted, were stronger than the administration's lackluster housing order. In almost the same breath, he attacked the Kennedy administration for its tokenistic approach toward school integration. Later that spring, Wilkins told *US News and World Report* that the New York governor would be a popular candidate among blacks.[44]

Rockefeller stepped up his assault on the administration in early 1963. On January 1, when he was sworn in for a second term as governor, he began his speech by paying homage to Abraham Lincoln: "This is an historic anniversary. Just 100 years ago, on January 1, 1863, the Emancipation Proclamation became law." The night of the Lincoln gala at the White House, the GOP held a rival dinner. Rockefeller used the opportunity to launch his most excoriating attack to date. Claiming to be the true heir of the Great Emancipator, he declared the president had "abdicated virtually all leadership toward achieving necessary civil rights legislation." The criticisms clearly rankled Kennedy. "Rockefeller gets away with murder," he commented to the journalist Theodore White over dinner at the White House on February 13, the night after the governor's Lincoln dinner attack. "What's he done for Negroes in New York?"[45]

Faced with a legitimate—and increasingly vocal—rival for his office in 1964, and by a cadre of rebellious liberal Democrats on Capitol Hill, by late February Kennedy decided to give more serious thought to the question of new legislation. Acting on orders from the president, Lee White joined with Justice Department officials in drafting an omnibus bill. It included new voting rights measures, the promised extension for the CRC, a plan for providing technical assistance to school boards that would allow them to accelerate desegregation, and reforms aimed at tackling discrimination within labor unions. White insisted that it would be essential to offer a large bundle of measures, since "Civil Rights groups have been lukewarm on voting legislation: not so much because they believe it would not be helpful but because they want the emphasis placed on school legislation."[46]

White presented his proposals to the president at a meeting on February 25. Kennedy thought the package was a good one, partly because its proposals were fairly narrow in scope. He seemed to be on the verge of giving it his approval. Before he made a final decision, however, Lawrence O'Brien urged him to at least test moderate southern opinion by talking to Florida Senator George Smathers and Louisiana Congressman Hale Boggs. While the president understood O'Brien's concern, he leaned toward pressing ahead regardless and "tentatively scheduled" White's proposals for introduction the following Thursday. Two days later, on February 27, after bringing his advisers together again, Kennedy reached a final decision. He resolved to send a special message to Congress the very next day, in which he would announce his legislative intentions and offer a broad summary of the bill. White worked through the night to have it finished on time.[47]

On February 28, in the form of a written statement, Kennedy sent his special message to Congress. Given his tight deadline, White produced an astonishingly eloquent message. He opened it by quoting Justice John Marshall Harlan, the former slave owner from Kentucky and the sole Supreme Court judge to vote against *Plessy v. Ferguson*. In his dissenting opinion, Harlan had written that the "Constitution is color blind, and neither knows nor tolerates classes among citizens." Then, echoing language from the first televised debate, the special message highlighted the disadvantages that blacks faced from the moment they were born: only half the chance of finishing high school as a white baby born at the same time, and destined to die seven years earlier. Racial discrimination had also hampered economic growth and undermined America's global authority. And, most importantly, discrimination was morally wrong. "Let it be clear, in our own hearts and minds," the statement noted, "that it is not merely because of the Cold War, and not merely because of the economic waste of discrimination, that we are committed to achieving true equality of opportunity. The basic reason is because it is right."[48]

The administration offered a variety of remedies. To boost black enfranchisement, it called for the appointment of federal referees and the abolition of the literacy test in federal elections. A single national standard—the achievement of a sixth-grade education—would be the sole qualification for voter registration. The CRC's mandate would be extended another four years.[49]

With regard to education, the special message conceded that compliance with *Brown* had been "too slow, often painfully so." It was the first time that the Kennedy administration had ever made such a stark admission, or even hinted at it. New legislation would correct these failures by establishing an "advice shop" at the Office of Education that would offer technical and financial assistance to school districts wishing to desegregate their classrooms. However, the message stopped well short of calling for Part III, which would have given the attorney general strong injunctive powers with which to push school integration.[50]

The message culminated with an inspiring promise: "The centennial of the issuance of Emancipation Proclamation is an occasion for celebration, for a sober assessment of our failures, and for rededication to the goals of freedom. Surely there could be no more meaningful observance of the centennial than the enactment of effective civil rights legislation and the continuation of effective executive action."[51]

The language of the message implied deep commitment on the part of the administration to racial reform. But in fact Kennedy had made no attempt to build public support for the measures ahead of time. Nor had he sounded out congressional leaders about placing the measure on the calendar. Kennedy would need the support of Republican leaders to overcome southern resistance, but he never followed up on the advice of Mike Manatos, an aide in the congressional liaison office, who indicated that it would be vital to meet with liberal Republicans like Leverett Saltonstall, Clifford Case, and Thomas Kuchel.[52]

For many in the civil rights movement—and for administration officials like White and Martin—the passage on the Emancipation Proclamation had come eight weeks too late. It was the kind of statement they had wanted to hear on January 1. After years of deflecting demands for a new civil rights bill, Kennedy's haste in rushing out legislation in February seemed deeply cynical. In an article published in the March edition of *The Nation*, Martin Luther King accused the administration of tokenism: "The Administration sought to demonstrate to Negroes that it has concern for them, while at the same time it has striven to avoid inflaming the opposition. The most cynical view holds that it wants the votes of both and is paralyzed by the conflicting needs of each." He expressed contempt for the "white moderate . . . who paternalistically believes that he can set the timetable for another man's freedom"—a statement that read like a direct condemnation of the president. The danger of such wavering, warned King, was that it would unleash "the militant spirit which alone drives us forward to real change."[53]

Rockefeller also continued to needle Kennedy on civil rights, despite the president's February message to Congress. On March 5, Rockefeller opened up a new line of attack, by lambasting the president for appointing numerous hard-line segregationist judges onto the federal bench. Eager to play up the rivalry between Kennedy and Rockefeller, reporters seized upon the speech and asked the president to respond at his news conference the following day. Forced onto the defensive, Kennedy conceded that not all his judicial appointees had ruled as he would have done. He stressed, however, that in aggregate his judicial appointees were "extraordinary and very credible." The following morning, the *New York Times* printed the president's comments alongside some of his appointees' more asinine statements and rulings. Kennedy read the article over breakfast and was sufficiently concerned to telephone Katzenbach. Kennedy probed him on the subject of his judicial appointments and asked Katzenbach specifically about "the one from Mississippi" (he was apparently unable to remember the name of Judge William Harold Cox, Eastland's old friend). Hesitant to present the president with the unvarnished truth, Katzenbach admitted that Cox had "not been good" but reassured him that other appointees were far better. Kennedy nonetheless sensed that he might be vulnerable on this issue and asked Katzenbach to prepare a memorandum on Eisenhower appointees with dubious records. (On April 23, the Justice Department sent the White House a robust defense of the judicial nominees: "All of the Kennedy appointees with the possible exception of Cox have meticulously followed the decisions of the higher courts when given specific direction."[54])

In early March, Republican senators spotted their own opportunity to attack the president over civil rights. During his February message, Kennedy had gone on the record as a proponent of civil rights reform. But the administration had not yet put forward legislative proposals to back up its noble promises. Liberal Republicans decided to fill this legislative void. Eight of them, led by Jacob Javits of New York, started to draft legislative proposals, which went beyond those outlined in his February message. To accelerate compliance with *Brown*, the proposals called on all southern school districts to file desegregation plans within 180 days. The attorney general would receive Part III powers to initiate school desegregation suits. They planned to introduce the measure later in the month.[55]

At the same time, a new racial crisis was coming to a head in Greenwood, Mississippi, a cotton hub on the eastern edge of the Mississippi Delta and the home of the state headquarters of the White Citizens' Council. In early 1963, it had become the locus of a new civil rights battle between voting rights activists and segregationists—precisely the kind of dispute that Robert Kennedy hoped the passage of new legislation would prevent.

Even though two-thirds of Greenwood's citizens were black, only a small handful were allowed to vote. The town had been targeted for a SNCC voter registration drive in the summer of 1962. Two activists in their mid-twenties, Bob Moses and Sam Block, headed the drive. But on February 20, a group of local hoodlums set fire to four black businesses close to SNCC headquarters in an attempt to drive them out of town. Moses was undeterred. Eight days later he was targeted for assassination. Moses survived the drive-by shooting, but James Travis, a twenty-year-old civil rights worker, was shot and wounded in the neck. (Governor Ross Barnett suggested four days later that Travis had shot himself as a publicity stunt.[56])

The shootings had a radicalizing effect on even moderate black leaders. On March 7, Wilkins demanded that the president withdraw federal funds from Mississippi. A. Philip Randolph urged the president to declare an immediate "state of emergency," and insert federal marshals. James Forman of SNCC demanded troops to protect the young civil rights workers.[57]

On March 27, SNCC launched its first street marches in Greenwood. Local police officers immediately arrested eight of the movement's leaders and set their snarling police dogs on the protesters. When the president read reports of these aggressive tactics, he asked Marshall what steps could be taken to keep the police dogs in their kennels. Marshall first tried to broker a local truce between the protesters and Greenwood officials. But on March 30, the Justice Department sought a federal court order that would force the local police to respect the constitutional right of protesters and ban interference with black voter registrations. Yet the judge slated to deal with the request, Claude F. Clayton, Jr., was a well-known segregationist and refused the federal request for a temporary injunction. The prisoners therefore remained in jail. Civil rights activists descended on Greenwood from all over the country, among them the black comedian Dick Gregory. Gregory himself was manhandled by police on Tuesday April 2, and the ensuing publicity ensured that the demonstrations would remain on the front page.[58]

As Robert Kennedy struggled to contain the Greenwood situation, the president revisited the politically sensitive question of when to introduce the administration's civil rights bill. On March 25, Kennedy came under heavy pressure from Lawrence O'Brien to delay the announcement until the end of a newspaper strike in New York. That way, O'Brien pledged, the bill "would receive full coverage" and therefore have the maximum impact on black voters in key northern states. On March 28, Senate Republicans came forward with bolder proposals, including the tough measures aimed at accelerating school integration. "If the President will not assume the leadership in getting through Congress urgently needed civil rights measures," announced the group of eight Republican senators who had drafted the bill, "we in Congress must take the initiative." The following morning, March 29, the front page of the *New York Times* featured a group photograph of Republican senators brandishing their omnibus civil rights bill. The *Times* also ran a front-page picture of Greenwood police officers chasing their dogs into the crowd. The two images provided a particularly awkward juxtaposition for an administration under fire from black leaders for not doing more to protect SNCC protesters and under attack from liberal Republicans.[59]

On April 2, the administration finally introduced its own civil rights bill. Robert Kennedy held a press conference at the Justice Department to explain its provisions and to call for its enactment. But the president made no statement at all on behalf of the bill—a silence that once again raised doubts among black activists about the strength of his resolve.[60]

The introduction of its civil rights bill offered no respite for the administration. By now the White House had come under mounting pressure to intervene more forcefully in Greenwood, and to protect the civil rights workers being harassed by local police. On March 28, King wrote to the president asking him to take "whatever steps that are necessary to safeguard the lives and property of voter registration workers and those who apply." On April 1, labor leader Walter Reuther told the president: "Federal protection is essential for these people."[61]

On Wednesday, April 3, Robert Kennedy responded by intervening on behalf of the eight imprisoned leaders of the Greenwood movement. John Doar visited the eight activists in jail and informed them that the Justice Department would seek an injunction against Greenwood officials to make sure that the police stopped harassing them. Later that afternoon, the president was asked at his weekly press conference if the Justice Department could do more. Kennedy sided with the protesters by revealing that he hoped the federal court in Mississippi would agree their rights had been infringed, "which seems to me evident." Then he brought up the administration's civil rights package. Its enactment, he claimed, would help alleviate the problem.[62]

The following morning, Thursday April 4, the Greenwood authorities succumbed to administration pressure and agreed to release the prisoners. In return, the Justice Department agreed to drop its injunction. For a time thereafter, Greenwood authorities allowed local blacks to take registration tests unencumbered.

But voting registrars continued to discriminate against black applicants. Of 1,500 blacks who attempted to register between April and October, only fifty were successful. By the end of November only six percent of black citizens were allowed to vote.[63]

The Justice Department had won the freedom of the imprisoned protesters but done little to advance the rights of Greenwood blacks themselves. As had been the case in Albany in 1962, the administration grasped at a deal with the authorities that took the heat out of the crisis. The grievances that gave rise to the demonstrations remained wholly unresolved. SNCC leaders responded to this retreat by announcing plans to enlarge its operations in southwest Georgia, Mississippi, South Carolina, and Alabama over the course of the summer when young black students would be out of college. At SNCC workshops, young recruits were told they must be prepared to die for their cause and that they should not expect much help from the federal government.[64]

By mid-April, the president had done little to advance the civil rights bill introduced at the start of the month, which once again raised the perennial question about his dedication to civil rights. Liberals within the administration were dismayed by his manifest lack of support for the measure. Lee White shared his concerns with O'Brien directly in a memo in mid-April: "One of the criticisms that the Administration received last year when the literacy test effort fizzled out was that the President and Administration really did not seem interested in making an all out fight." White called upon Kennedy to convene a high-level meeting that would include Vice President Lyndon Johnson, the attorney general, and members of the CRC "to ensure coordinated efforts by all to secure civil rights legislation." He even proposed that the administration set up a kind of War Room in order to strategize in advance of their impending showdown with the Southern Caucus. The president refused to take such an aggressive approach to securing passage of the bill. Without his backing, the legislation quickly floundered. King told an aide the February message and the vacillations after it over when to come forward with new legislation offered proof of the administration's "schizophrenic tendency."[65]

∽

In April, shortly after the Greenwood crisis had dissipated, Kennedy was forced once more to confront directly the problem of segregation in the Deep South— and the responsibilities of the federal government to mitigate it. Two reports— one written by the CRC, the other by the Mississippi state legislature—were published in the wake of the battle at Ole Miss. Both reports lambasted the Kennedy administration. Not surprisingly, one assailed the president for doing too little to protect civil rights protesters, while the other claimed he had breached the constitution by doing too much.

Kennedy had little respect for either the CRC or the Mississippi state legislature. From the beginning of 1961, the CRC had been "a thorn in the side," as White bluntly put it. The situation deteriorated rapidly in the early months of 1963. The commissioners had clashed with administration officials over the centenary celebrations, and became embroiled in a venomous dispute over whether to conduct its first ever hearings in Mississippi. In December 1962, Hannah had announced his intentions in a typically caustic letter to O'Donnell, in which he argued that the CRC would be derelict in its duty if it failed to hold hearings in the country's most segregated state. He also used the opportunity to complain that CRC commissioners had not been granted a meeting with the president for over a year.[66]

Robert Kennedy had clashed with Hannah on numerous occasions before: most notably, over the CRC's plans to hold hearings in Louisiana in the aftermath of the New Orleans schools crisis in 1961, and its desire to hold hearings that year in Washington, D.C. He now bridled at the prospect of Mississippi hearings, fearing they would prejudice its contempt proceedings against Ross Barnett. They might also have an adverse effect on a case being brought by Mississippi authorities against U.S. Chief Marshal James McShane (a grand jury in the state had indicted McShane with inciting the riot). The attorney general was immovable. Even though Berl Bernhard warned Marshall that four leading members of the CRC would resign in protest, he refused to back down. On December 15, RFK wrote to Hannah, "It is my judgment that the work of the Department of Justice might be severely hampered by hearings."[67]

At their meeting with Kennedy before the Lincoln dinner on February 12, Hannah protested that the CRC should be allowed to conduct hearings in Mississippi. Hannah nonetheless agreed to put the plans for the hearings on temporary hold and to explore other means of publicizing Mississippi's racial troubles. But as the Greenwood crisis escalated from late February into March, Hannah and his fellow commissioners became increasingly exasperated.[68]

At a meeting of the CRC on March 29, Hannah decided to publish a preliminary report on the Mississippi situation. It described the shooting of James Travis in Greenwood, of how a minister had been bitten by a police dog during street demonstrations in the city, and the bombing of the home of a local civil rights worker. The report also pointed out that the federal government allotted $380 million more to Mississippi than it received back in tax revenues.[69]

In early April, Hannah sent an advance copy of the report to the Justice Department. Marshall believed it was one-sided and inaccurate and rebutted many of its allegations in a detailed memorandum to the president on April 8. In the report, the CRC claimed black voter registration workers in Greenwood had been set upon by vicious police dogs. In his rebuttal, Marshall noted that just one preacher had the misfortune to be bitten, and added, "The use of police dogs is not a prohibited activity." Nor had Marshall heard of any protesters who had been "beaten and otherwise terrorized because they sought to vote," as the report claimed. While he conceded that one black registration worker had been pistol-whipped by the registrar of Walthall County, he pointed out that the Justice Department had "brought a successful case in that instance" (in reality, it had merely stopped Mississippi authorities from prosecuting John Hardy, the victim of the attack, on the preposterous charge that his cries of pain had disturbed the peace). White was equally biting and criticized the CRC report for its factual inaccuracies as well as bias. "Implicit is the suggestion that the President and the Administration have not done all that could be done for the Mississippi situation," he wrote the president. "This, of course, is manifestly wrong."[70]

When the president himself read the as yet unpublished report, he was most troubled by the CRC's most contentious recommendation: that the federal government withdraw funding from any state refusing to abide by the U.S. Constitution. Judging the report short-sighted and naïve, Kennedy complained to Bernhard that it was sure to "poison an atmosphere that is already pretty bad." He seemed particularly aggrieved that Erwin Griswold, the dean of the Harvard Law School, was such a strong advocate of cutting off aid to Mississippi. "Who the hell appointed Griswold [to the CRC]?" he barked.

"You did," replied Bernhard.

"Probably on the recommendation of Harris Wofford," hissed the president.[71]

When the preliminary report was released on April 16, the media focused on the CRC's most radical proposal, the withdrawal of federal funding, rather than the many passages in which the commission described the rampant harassment and intimidation of blacks in Mississippi. The *Washington Post* referred to the recommendation as a "drastic" and "dangerous remedy," injurious to blacks. It was the very line that the White House hoped reporters would follow. The *New York Times* noted, "We can think of no suggestion less calculated to promote civilized race relations or to cool the inflamed passions that erupted in the Civil War." Even the *Pittsburgh Courier* thought the withdrawal of funds would be counterproductive, because it would injure blacks.[72]

With editorial opinion firmly behind him, Kennedy wrote to Hannah on April 19 and rejected the report's main conclusions. In his view, the Justice Department's record in Mississippi was "outstanding." He also claimed that "[w]ith regard to the incidents referred to in the Commission's report, I am advised that every case, but one, has been successfully resolved." On the withdrawal of federal funding, the president noted how thousands of black Mississippians received Social Security, veterans' welfare, school lunches, and other benefits from federal programs, adding, "In many instances the withholding of funds would serve to further disadvantage those that I know the Commission would want to aid." Privately, in a background briefing with reporters, he went further. The withdrawal of federal funding "doesn't do any good," he said, in comments quoted in newspapers the next morning as coming from a high administration official. "It just makes people mad."[73]

In focusing on the issue of federal funds, both the Kennedy administration and the journalists who covered it overlooked one of the preliminary report's most important sections. It was written by Commissioner Robert S. Rankin, a southern moderate at Duke University, and published as a personal addendum. (Rankin said he had written the passage "with the hope of avoiding insurrection and armed conflict within the state of Mississippi.") Mississippi faced a grave crisis, he warned, and there was a genuine possibility of open racial conflict. This time, however, the violence would come not from white segregationists but angry blacks.[74]

The CRC report briefly irritated Kennedy, but a scathing report on the Oxford riots from the Mississippi state legislature had a much more profound and lasting impact on his thinking. The report, released in late April, took a ludicrously one-sided view of the Ole Miss crisis. The report blamed the "tragic chain of events and errors" on Kennedy's decision to take control "illegally" of the Mississippi National Guard. Kennedy's marshals, the report claimed, had beaten and tortured prisoners. The Mississippi legislature accused federal officials of "[d]eliberate and repeated brutalities," specifically targeted at the most vulnerable victims—young boys between twelve and fifteen years of age and disabled veterans of World War II. The second part of the report published in early May stated that if the president had exercised more caution, "the tragic events would not have occurred." The state legislature blasted his decision to introduce federal troops as an act of calculated aggression, which had directly challenged the sovereignty of Mississippi and the very principles of federalism.[75]

The report was so histrionic that it was impossible to take seriously. The Justice Department dismissed the first part of the report as "so far from the truth that it hardly merits an answer," and the second part as "characterized by bias, factual errors and misstatement." But Kennedy did dwell on the reports, because he found the tone and accusations eerily similar to southern accounts of the period of Radical Reconstruction. He began to wonder if perhaps southerners had unfairly vilified their northern conquerors. In *Profiles in Courage*, Kennedy had himself portrayed Republican leader Thaddeus Stevens as "the crippled, fanatical personification of the extremes of the Radical Reconstruction movement." Would his actions one day be cast in similar terms? Kennedy questioned whether he could fully trust southern accounts of their own history. In a rare moment of introspection, Kennedy revealed himself to his brother. "They must have been doing the same thing a hundred years ago." As Robert Kennedy later recalled, Kennedy said that he "would never believe a book on the Reconstruction again."[76]

This moment represented an important intellectual step for President Kennedy. In February 1962, Robert Kennedy had organized an after-dinner discussion on Reconstruction at the White House. David Herbert Donald, the Pulitzer Prize–winning historian who led the seminar, later said that he was decidedly unimpressed by the president's grasp of American history. The president's view of Reconstruction, he recalled, reflected "a sort of general textbook knowledge of about twenty-five years ago and not much familiarity with recent literature or findings."[77]

Yet the Battle of Ole Miss, and its controversial aftermath, seemed to fuel his desire to learn more about southern history. He familiarized himself with the work of C. Vann Woodward, a liberal-minded southern historian, whose work focused on the humiliations suffered by freedmen. The contemporary parallels were unmistakable and must have been particularly disquieting for a president who tended to understand civil rights in the context of the past.[78]

At the beginning of 1963, Kennedy had done everything he could to avoid being identified with the legacy of Abraham Lincoln—Kennedy had never set out to become the Second Emancipator President. It was only when Rockefeller tried to seize Lincoln's mantle for himself, and claim it as the Republican Party's rightful inheritance, that Kennedy realized how vulnerable he was on the subject of civil rights. Black voters might look elsewhere in 1964 if his administration did not do more to make good Lincoln's promise of truly first-class citizenship.

With the publication of the reports from Mississippi state legislatures, Lincoln's shadow loomed large once again. Kennedy had made little attempt to dismantle southern segregation. He had been respectful of the Southern Caucus and solicitous of southern voters, but he now faced the same kind of criticisms that Lincoln and his successors had endured.

But there was little time to reflect on the historiography of the Reconstruction era and its implications for present policy. By early May, when the Mississippi state legislature published its report, the Kennedy administration was on the verge of one of the most climactic battles of the entire civil rights era—a fight that ushered in an era of racial reform that would come to be known as the Second Reconstruction.

≪≫

CHAPTER 22

"Let the Whole
Fucking City Burn"

Diminished and frustrated by his failure in Albany, Martin Luther King had come to believe that only through inciting segregationist violence could he secure the Kennedy administration's close attention. King was also worried about his own status within the civil rights movement. At the start of 1962, the SCLC was stalled. King faced criticisms that he merely hijacked demonstrations launched by CORE and SNCC, such as the Freedom Rides and Albany, rather than initiating them himself. At an SCLC strategy meeting held January 11–12, King decided to target Birmingham, Alabama, famously described by reporter Harrison Salisbury as "the Johannesburg of America." King was influenced by the Reverend Fred Shuttlesworth, the black founder of the Alabama Christian Movement for Human Rights, Birmingham's local civil rights organization. Shuttlesworth, who was also a co-founder of the SCLC, knew that in Bull Connor, the city's hot-headed public safety commissioner, King had the ideal adversary. Connor had come to personify police brutality in the South. In 1962, he had boasted that Birmingham's racial problems could easily be solved with "two policemen and a dog."[1]

King knew what was at stake. After the bombing of a black church in Birmingham on December 14, he had wired the president to complain about the city police force's "Gestapo like methods" and noted that Birmingham was "by far the worst big city in the United States." The protests were all but guaranteed to provoke violence. "In my judgment," King observed at the SCLC strategy meeting in January, "some of the people sitting here today will not come back alive from this campaign."[2]

The ostensible aim of the planned sit-in protests was to bring about the desegregation of lunch counters in downtown stores. But that seemed almost secondary. King wanted to pressure the administration to take further action on civil rights reforms and to reinstate himself as the acknowledged leader of the civil rights movement.[3]

King's plans were complicated, however, by a major overhaul of Birmingham's form of civic government—reforms that had been sponsored by moderates in the city in the hope of ousting Connor. In November, the city had abolished its Board of Commissioners and replaced it with the position of mayor. In the municipal election that ensued on March 5, Connor came second behind Albert Boutwell, the candidate of reformists. With the field whittled down to two candidates, Boutwell and Connor prepared for a runoff election in early April.

The Kennedy administration had been alerted to King's plans on January 19, a week after the SCLC strategy meeting, when white moderates in Birmingham caught wind of the impending protests. The Justice Department took its cues from David Vann, a local attorney instrumental in the campaign to oust Connor. "We are trying to create a political miracle," Vann told Burke Marshall in January, and anything that might "grate on the emotions" would be deeply unhelpful. The strong feeling within the Justice Department was that Connor would be the only beneficiary of street protests.[4]

Black leaders in Birmingham put the same argument to King, who had originally planned to launch Project X, as he had come to call it, on March 14—nine days after the mayoral election. But with the runoff looming, King agreed to a postponement. Now he intended to launch his campaign on April 3.

In a runoff election held on April 2, Boutwell triumphed again. But Connor was unwilling to recognize the result and retained his job as the city's public safety commissioner. He eyed the upcoming protests as a last-ditch opportunity to cling to power. By driving King from the city, he could burnish his racist credentials with segregationists and mobilize public support behind his legal challenge before the Alabama Supreme Court.

On Wednesday, April 3, the very morning the *Birmingham News* celebrated Boutwell's victory election with the headline, "New Day Dawns for Birmingham," King decided to proceed with Project X. Encouraged by Boutwell's victory, he now anticipated a less aggressive campaign than the climactic showdown that he had described at the SCLC strategy meeting January. Nonetheless, King promised a "full-scale assault" on segregation and predicted on April 3, "They may set the mad dogs on us."[5]

At ten in the morning, Marshall tried to reach King directly at the SCLC campaign headquarters at the Gaston Motel in order to urge him to postpone the demonstrations once more. King's associate Wyatt Tee Walker took the call, and Marshall explained that Boutwell should be given an opportunity to bring about peaceful reform in Birmingham. Marshall suspected afterwards that Walker never passed on his message.[6]

Shortly after ten that morning, the first groups of protesters entered the "whites only" lunch counters of five downtown stores. But the opening skirmishes were decidedly unpromising. Four of the lunch counters simply stopped serving food. At the fifth, thirteen demonstrators were arrested without trouble. After six days of further protests only 150 demonstrators were imprisoned, less than the number arrested on the opening day in Albany. At a mass meeting on Saturday, April 6, King tried to rally the movement by vowing to go to jail: "The white power may think that things will blow over, but we are just getting started."[7]

On Wednesday, April 10, a state district court judge granted Connor's request for an injunction forbidding King from leading further marches. King described it as "an injunction from heaven." Two days later, on Good Friday, April 12, he set out from the Zion Hill Church at the head of two columns of fifty protesters. He was certain that he would be arrested and imprisoned. Less than five blocks from the church, on the edge of downtown, Connor's men obliged. Told to halt by a motorcycle policeman, King and Ralph Abernathy dropped to their knees in prayer. Then they were bundled away in a paddy wagon. King was taken to Birmingham jail and placed in solitary confinement. Connor had handed King the martyrdom he craved.[8]

King's imprisonment generated a great deal of publicity, but little sympathy. The morning after his arrest, the *New York Times* carried on its front page a picture of King and Abernathy being hauled off to jail. Four days later, however, the *Times* criticized the civil rights leader on its editorial page. Without mentioning King specifically, it noted that everyone in Birmingham should be promoting racial peace in order to give the new City Council a chance. Most journalists simply thought that King had been trying to foment trouble. *Time* called the protests "poorly timed." Even the *World*, Birmingham's black weekly, questioned King's timing and tactics.[9]

That Saturday morning, the president called Marshall from the Kennedy family's Palm Beach mansion, where he had gone to visit his sick father. Kennedy asked what could be done on King's behalf. Marshall told Kennedy what he repeated to reporters later on: that there was no basis for federal intervention. But Marshall also interpreted the president's weekend phone call as a sign that he should take a more active role in adjudicating the standoff between King and Connor. He contacted Arthur Shores, a moderate lawyer in the city, to check on King's condition. That weekend, Marshall also came under pressure from Robert Kennedy, whose displeasure at the SCLC's decision to launch demonstrations vied with his hatred of Connor. When Kennedy asked him to explain why the Justice Department could not intervene in the dispute, Marshall had to tell him that no federal laws had been broken. "Well, who do you want to lead the army—me or you?" said Marshall. "One step leads to another, and if you don't understand where you're going you've got to resist starting."[10]

The attorney general displayed less sympathy for King's plight when he took a call that Monday from Harry Belafonte, who complained about the dreadful jail conditions King was being forced to endure. "I'm not sure we can get into prison reform at this moment," Kennedy sarcastically replied.[11]

Early the next week, however, both Kennedy brothers bore out the truth of King's remark earlier in the year about the administration's "schizophrenic tendency" on the subject of civil rights. On Monday, April 15, Coretta King, now pregnant with their fourth child, personally contacted the White House asking for help. Shortly afterwards, she received a call from Robert Kennedy. "I am returning your call to my brother," he gently explained. "The President wasn't able to talk to you because he's with my father, who is quite ill. He wanted me to call you to find out what we can do for you." Then he added, "We have a difficult problem with the local officials. . . . Bull Connor is very hard to deal with. . . . But I promise you I will look into the situation." Later that night, FBI agents visited King in jail to check on his condition.[12]

The next day, the president contacted Coretta King directly. Kennedy apologized for not calling before but explained he was unable to leave his father's side. The president said FBI agents in Birmingham had checked on her husband and found he was "all right." "I want you to know we are doing everything we can," he added. "I have just talked to Birmingham and your husband will be calling you shortly. If you have any further worries about your husband or about Birmingham in the next few days, I want you to feel free to call me." Fifteen minutes later, her husband telephoned her and learned for the first time about the president's intervention. "So that's why everybody is suddenly being so polite," said King, who had now been provided with a mattress and pillow. "This is good to know."[13]

Though somewhat heartened by the president's expression of sympathy, King nonetheless spent his eight days in solitary confinement in a state of despair. He was deeply wounded by the criticisms of eight liberal-leaning white Alabaman clergymen, who had responded to King's arrest by proclaiming his protests unwise and untimely. On scraps of toilet paper and in the margins of newspapers, King composed his rebuttal. "For years now I have heard the word 'Wait!'" he wrote. "It rings in the ear of every Negro with piercing familiarity. This 'Wait' has almost always meant 'Never.'" His most caustic remarks were targeted at the "white moderate . . . who is more devoted to 'order' than justice; who prefers a negative peace which is the absence of tension rather than a positive peace which is the presence of justice." His "Letter from Birmingham Jail" soon came to be viewed as one of the most eloquent descriptions of black subjugation ever penned. But it remained a secret for a month. Had it been released sooner, King might possibly have generated a groundswell of sympathy, both in the eyes of black moderates as well as the mainstream media. As it was, his release from jail on Saturday, April 20, attracted little nationwide interest.[14]

Given King's loss of stature within the civil rights movement, as well as the lack of public outcry in the wake of his arrest, the Kennedy brothers could easily have ignored the situation altogether. That the president contacted Marshall early on, and that both brothers reached out to Coretta King, suggests both a growing attentiveness and mounting concern on behalf of the administration. The Kennedy brothers were clearly impatient to see Boutwell installed as mayor and increasingly frustrated by mulish segregationists, such as Connor. But their efforts also reveal a more sympathetic attitude toward King. Still, they stopped short either of publicly backing King or publicly scolding Connor. Official statements from the Justice Department restated the familiar position: that there was nothing the administration could legally do.

The murder of a white postman by segregationists also gave Kennedy reason to pause. On April 17, William Moore had arrived at the gates of the White House with a handwritten letter addressed to the president detailing plans for a ten-day "freedom walk" from Chattanooga, Tennessee to Jackson, Mississippi. Three days later, ten miles outside Gadsden, Alabama, Moore was found dead on the side of Highway 11. He was still wearing a two-sided sandwich board that read "Equal Rights for All (Mississippi or Bust)" and "Eat at Joe's—Both Black and White," and had with him a copy of his letter to the president. Moore had been shot in the neck and the head in an execution-style murder.

On hearing of the killing, Lee White retrieved Moore's original letter from the White House mailroom and made sure the president was fully briefed before his press conference that afternoon. When the Washington press corps failed to mention Moore's murder, Kennedy decided to refer to it himself: "We had an outrageous crime, from all accounts, in the State of Alabama in the shooting of the postman who was attempting, in a very traditional way, to dramatize the plight of some of our citizens, being assassinated on the road." Kennedy offered FBI assistance but stressed that there was little more the federal government could do in relation to the killing: "We do not have direct jurisdiction, but we are working with every legislative, legal tool at our command to insure protection for the rights of our citizens, and we shall continue to do so." Once more, Kennedy had been uncharacteristically demonstrative. And once more, he had empathized with an individual, rather than the broader political constituency of which that individual was a part. In these instances, Kennedy was capable of genuine sympathy. But he became incredibly defensive when civil rights group latched onto episodes like Moore's murder to apply greater political pressure on the administration. At his press conference Kennedy downplayed expectations of what the federal government could achieve in relation to this case, perhaps anticipating that civil rights protesters would soon converge on Gadsden to take up Moore's one-man crusade.[15]

On April 20, the day that Moore was murdered, King was finally released from jail. He immediately began to lay the groundwork for a fresh round of protests. Faced with the collapse of the Birmingham campaign, he desperately needed to galvanize the movement. As aides pointed out at a strategy meeting on April 29, Birmingham had not appeared on the front page of the *New York Times* for two weeks. Now Project X was renamed Project C. The "C" stood for confrontation. He decided to embark on a hazardous new strategy: a "children's crusade" involving over a thousand school pupils, some as young as six.[16]

On Thursday, May 2, in an operation dubbed D-Day, several hundred children filed out of the Sixteenth Street Baptist Church to confront Connor's policemen, who were waiting in the Kelly Ingram Park on the opposite side of the street. At first, Connor did not know how to respond. But soon he ordered his officers to start arresting the young protesters for parading without a permit. By four o'clock that afternoon, 959 demonstrators had been carted off to jail, only a handful of them adults. King was elated. If Thursday had been D-Day, he proclaimed triumphantly to his congregation at a packed mass meeting that evening, Friday would be Double-D Day.[17]

Connor was much better prepared for the next round. He planned to deploy the Birmingham Fire Department, confident its high-pressure hoses could disperse even the most antagonistic crowd. If that failed, K9 units were in reserve. At lunchtime on Friday, when the first group of some sixty children marched out of the Sixteenth Street Baptist Church they were confronted by one of Connor's most trusted deputies, Captain Glenn V. Evans. Evans gave them the option either of retreating or getting wet. The protesters stood their ground, and the firemen unleashed their hoses. One-hundred-pound jets of water knocked the children off their feet and ripped the shirts from their backs. When a group of ten protesters refused to retreat, the firemen screwed on a specially designed attachment, which allowed a single hose to harness the power of two. Mounted on a tripod, it had enough force to rip bark off a tree from thirty yards.[18]

Alarmed by the ferocious tactics, a crowd of blacks gathered on the sidewalks hurled bricks and missiles at the firemen. At that moment, Connor unleashed the dog units. As five snarling German shepherds leaped from the police cars and sent the crowd scurrying, Connor looked on smugly. "Look at those niggers run," he commented.

A few brave protesters stood their ground. The dogs attacked, ripping their clothes and snapping at their flesh. Standing in the melee, an Associated Press photographer captured a terrifying image as one of the dogs lunged ferociously at the stomach of a young black protester. The photograph perfectly crystallized the ferocity of die-hard segregationists. Soon after, King called a halt. He had already achieved his aim: an extraordinarily vivid illustration of the grotesque violence at the heart of the segregationist cause.

In Washington, Robert Kennedy rushed out a statement in response to the violence. It was critical both of King and Connor. "These demonstrations are the understandable expressions of resentment and hurt," he noted. But he added that they had been poorly timed given that Boutwell had not been allowed the chance to enact reform. He was scathing about King's decision to thrust children into the frontline of the protest: "Schoolchildren participating in street demonstrations is a dangerous business. An injured, maimed or dead child is a price that none of us can afford to pay."[19]

The Associated Press photograph quickly flashed around the world and appeared on the front page of the next morning's newspapers. The *New York Times* printed the picture under the headline: "Violence Explodes at Racial Protests in Alabama." The following day, in an editorial entitled "Outrage in Alabama," the paper noted, "The use of police dogs and high pressure hoses is a national disgrace." The *Times* had accurately captured the national mood. Before Connor unleashed his dogs, just four percent of Americans thought that civil rights was the country's most pressing issue. Afterwards, that figure leaped to fifty-two percent.[20]

That morning—Saturday, May 4—the image dominated a meeting between the president and a twenty-strong delegation from the liberal lobbying group Americans for Democratic Action. It turned out to be one of the most revealing meetings of his entire presidency. The ADA had long been pressing for bold new legislation, and Kennedy now found himself on the defensive from the outset. "There is no federal law we could pass," the president stuttered. "I mean what law can you pass to do anything about police power in the community of Birmingham? There is nothing we can do. . . . The fact of the matter is that Birmingham is in worse shape than any other city in the United States, and it's been that way for a year and a half." The president defended his decision not to endorse King publicly: "If I was in charge down there I'd wait for the new mayor. That's the only hope."[21]

Then, almost parenthetically, he added, "I think it's a terrible picture in the paper. The fact of the matter: that's just want Connor wants. . . . Birmingham is the worst city in the south. It's done nothing for the Negroes. It's an intolerable situation." Clearly, the image had affected him, for at this point the president launched into a fifteen-minute soliloquy on the subject of race in America.

Kennedy began with a defense of his administration's policies but then quickly conceded that more could have been achieved. "We worked as hard as we possibly could given the laws we had." Then he added, "We have not done enough for a situation so desperate. We have shoved and pushed and . . . there is nothing that my brother's given more time to. . . . I quite agree if I was a Negro I'd be sore."

Then Kennedy focused on the subject of new civil rights legislation. He continued to pin his hopes on the passage of his administration's voting rights proposals introduced in April and predicted they would win enactment by the end of the year. "If we get enough Negroes registered," he said, "then you are going to begin to have a situation like you are beginning to get in Georgia," where the moderate Governor Carl Sanders had only recently won election. Still, he admitted, "I don't think the voting thing is the whole answer."

Kennedy was speaking at a frenetic pace, bouncing from one subject to the next. There was no clear logic to his positions, and at times he flatly contradicted himself. Within minutes of telling the ADA delegation that the administration's voting rights proposals would win enactment, he delivered a much bleaker assessment. The legislative situation was hopeless, he claimed, and he did not think the events in Birmingham would influence the voting intentions of a single lawmaker. "The reactionary forces are extremely powerful," he noted. Then he explained how all of his boldest proposals, from Medicare to federal aid to education, had been whittled down or defeated by a conservative coalition of southerners and Republicans. They would do the same with civil rights.

Kennedy was characteristically defensive on the subject of the liberal newspaper columnists who assailed his policies. They were guilty, he complained, of gross hypocrisy. "I had some newspaperman in here the other day talking about Birmingham and I said why are you eating over at the Metropolitan Club, they won't even let a Negro ambassador in. . . . [M]ost of your columnists that you read, they are all over at the Metropolitan Club."

Bringing the thirty-minute meeting to a close, Kennedy finally considered the wider implications of Birmingham. "I think we have worked hard on civil rights, I think it's a national crisis, and the Negro leadership is divided and I think very dangerous. . . . The most important problem is to try to prevent this economy from going down again, and that's what we're trying to do in a major way. The other problem is the problem of civil rights, I couldn't agree with you more. . . . That's a disastrous picture this morning." Once again, the president's comments were disjointed. It was not clear whether he thought that a strong economy would alleviate the racial crisis, or whether he was simply calling for the ADA to support his tax proposals, the administration's number-one priority.

Earlier in the conversation, Kennedy had commented on the propaganda value to the Soviet Union of the Associated Press picture. "What a disaster that picture is. That picture is not only in America but all around the world." But while Kennedy recognized the potent symbolic value of the image, he was unwilling to counteract it with a symbolic gesture of his own. A member of the ADA delegation had suggested that the president could use the widespread disgust the photo had generated to mobilize public support for his civil rights legislation. He could speak to the nation directly on television and conduct a series of fireside chats. But Kennedy dismissed the idea in a flash. "I don't have Franklin Roosevelt's voice," he replied, adding, "I've always thought that a half hour speech on television is pretty disastrous."

Arthur Schlesinger, who attended the meeting, later claimed that Kennedy told the ADA delegation that the photograph made him "sick." In fact, the president said nothing of the sort. The most striking aspect of the recording of the meeting is that Kennedy offered up no new concrete policy measures in response to the extraordinary violence in Birmingham. The AP photograph had clearly unsettled him, but his immediate response reflected deep confusion rather than enhanced resolve.[22]

The Birmingham protests—and the photograph that encapsulated them—were not a watershed moment in Kennedy's presidency. Kennedy did not take an aggressive stance with regard to new legislation or make a public address. As Andrew Hatcher told reporters after the May 4 meeting finished, the president "continues to hope that the situation can be resolved by the people of Birmingham themselves."[23]

The administration did, however, subtly shift its tactics and moved from conflict management into conflict resolution. In Albany, Kennedy had sought to encourage a dialogue between black demonstrators and white civic leaders. Now, in Birmingham, he worked actively to bring dialogue about. Later that Saturday, the Kennedy brothers dispatched Burke Marshall to Birmingham. His mission was to fashion an agreement between two groups of moderate business leaders, one white, one black, both of which wanted an end to the demonstrations. But the protests continued unabated. On Monday afternoon, a thousand more black schoolchildren were arrested—many of them carrying toothbrushes and prepared for a night in jail.

Theodore Sorensen, normally a voice of caution, thought Kennedy might soon have to become more personally involved. On Monday, May 6, he drafted a memorandum in which he set out a number of possible presidential responses. Kennedy should consider addressing, via loudspeaker telephone, a meeting of the Senior Citizens Committee, the seventy-member group of Birmingham business leaders presently engaged in talks with Marshall. Another option involved dispatching Commerce Secretary Luther Hodges, a former governor of North Carolina, or a specially appointed board of mediators. Perhaps the president himself should spearhead the effort, suggested Sorensen, by inviting representatives of both sides to the White House.

Looking beyond the immediate crisis in Birmingham, Sorensen proposed that Kennedy should host a Washington conference involving business, labor, and racial leaders from across the country. Most important, Sorensen suggested an out-and-out reconsideration of the administration's legislative strategy. He called for far-reaching legislation, which would outlaw segregation in public accommodations engaged in interstate commerce and vest the Attorney General with broad injunctive powers, the famed Part III. It was the first time such a high-ranking administration official had envisioned such sweeping proposals.[24]

The president, however, continued to center his hopes on a locally negotiated settlement that would bring the demonstrations to an end. To that end, Kennedy encouraged cabinet members to contact influential Birmingham businessmen and press them into backing a deal. His refusal to countenance new legislation showed that the appearance of Connor's German shepherds had only a very limited impact on his thinking. The Birmingham protests had been a watershed moment for the country, but not for the president. As Kennedy stated at the outset of his meeting with the ADA, "[T]here is no federal law we could pass. . . . I mean what law can you pass to do anything about police power in the community of Birmingham?" No comment more neatly encapsulated his narrow view of one of the most extraordinary episodes of the entire civil rights era.[25]

On Tuesday, May 7, there were further clashes in Birmingham between police and protesters, and some of the worst violence. Trapped in the middle, Fred Shuttlesworth found himself pinned against a wall by the full force of the fire hoses as he tried to lead of group of schoolchildren out of the Sixteenth Street Baptist Church. Eventually, Shuttlesworth collapsed under the pressure and was taken away to a hospital. Connor could hardly contain his delight. "I wish they had carried him away in a hearse," he told reporters. Reports of Shuttlesworth's hospitalization rushed through the city, further heightening tensions.[26]

That Tuesday night, the Kennedy brothers dined together at the White House. Their meal was constantly interrupted by situation reports from Marshall. At eight o'clock, for the first time in forty-eight hours, Marshall conveyed encouraging news. Under intense pressure from Marshall, the Senior Citizens Committee had finally agreed to negotiate with the city's black leadership. By the following afternoon, the broad outline of a deal was in place. Business leaders promised to immediately desegregate the dressing rooms at downtown stores and to integrate lunch counters within sixty days. The deal was conditional on a suspension of protests.

The president was delighted. At four P.M. on Wednesday, May 8, Kennedy announced the ceasefire at the beginning of his weekly news conference. "While much remains to be settled before the situation can be termed satisfactory," he said in his introductory remarks, "we can hope that tensions will ease and that this case history which has so far only narrowly avoided widespread violence and fatalities will remind every State, every community, and every citizen how urgent it is that all bars to equal opportunity and treatment be removed as promptly as possible." Asked about the possibility of a fireside chat on the Birmingham situation, he said he might consider if it would serve a "constructive purpose." But he added that his speech on the night of the Battle of Ole Miss was of limited use.[27]

Just as the news conference drew to a close, events in Birmingham took another unexpected turn. King and Abernathy were informed that a local judge had increased the value of the release bonds from their arrest three weeks before to the legal maximum of $2,500 each. In a brief court appearance later that afternoon, both men said they would be unable to pay such an exorbitant amount.

As King and Abernathy were carted off to jail, Shuttlesworth gleefully announced a resumption of protests.

King's imprisonment shattered the city's fragile truce. Justice Department officials worked frantically to resurrect the deal by getting King out of jail. Robert Kennedy took the lead by trying to raise $5,000 in bond money from Harry Belafonte and A. G. Gaston, Birmingham's richest black businessman. Knowing an end to the crisis was impossible while King remained imprisoned, Gaston happily handed over the money. King was released later that evening. But in a late-night news conference, King threatened the biggest demonstrations of the entire campaign unless business leaders agreed to desegregate downtown lunch counters, promote black sales clerks, establish a biracial commission, and release children still held in prison from the D-Day and Double-D Day protests.

As King issued his ultimatum late that night, negotiations between the Senior Citizens Committee and black leaders continued apace. But there was a sticking point: City authorities were demanding $250,000 in bond money in exchange for the release of over 500 imprisoned children. Burke Marshall urged King to relax his position. But King was adamant: The demonstrations would continue if the children remained behind bars.[28]

Once again, Robert Kennedy threw himself energetically into the task of raising the necessary funds. Labor leader Walter Reuther soon agreed to transfer $160,000. AFL-CIO president George Meany promised a further $80,000. Acting independently, Nelson Rockefeller also proffered help and issued orders for an aide to hand over a suitcase full of cash, a secret transaction which took place in the vault of the Chase Manhattan Bank in New York. The fund-raising target met, King agreed to halt the demonstrations, which removed the last obstacle to an agreement. White business leaders now agreed to the desegregation of downtown stores and better employment opportunities for black workers and to continue the interracial dialogue.

A truce was announced on Friday, May 10. "Birmingham may well offer twentieth century America an example of progressive racial relations," King announced to reporters, "and for all mankind a dawn of a new day." Then King indicated he would soon leave Birmingham for Atlanta.[29]

Late that Saturday night, however, Birmingham's delicate truce was brutally shattered. Three bombs detonated in quick succession, in what was a clear attempt to intimidate King and his family. The first two bombs went off at 10:45 outside the home of A. D. King, his brother. It blew a hole more than eight feet high in the front of the house and almost killed A. D. King's wife, Naomi, and five young children. As a vengeful crowd of black youths gathered outside, there was a third explosion. This time the target was the Gaston Motel, where a bomb destroyed a small room on the second floor. Throughout the Birmingham campaign King and Abernathy had shared the room. That afternoon, just before King left for Atlanta, he had convened a strategy meeting there. Had the meeting lasted thirty minutes longer, King would almost certainly have been killed.[30]

News of the bombings immediately spread through the city and brought a 2,500-strong crowd of angry young blacks out onto the streets. Wyatt Tee Walker, one of the main strategists behind "Project C," emerged from the bombed-out Gaston Motel to appeal for calm: "Please do not throw any bricks anymore." But he was forced to retreat after being struck on the ankle by a missile. As Walker limped away, blacks shouted, "They started it! They started it!"[31]

For the next five hours, blacks rampaged through a twenty-eight-block area, wrecking scores of police cars and private vehicles, razing six stores to the ground, and setting fire to a two-story apartment house. "Let the whole fucking city burn," one rioter shouted. "This'll show those white mother-fuckers." Firemen who had turned their hoses on young black protesters, now fought to control the blaze.[32]

Shortly before 12:45 A.M., Sunday, May 12, the Birmingham police brought in a six-wheeled armored car to contain the violence, which raced through the streets with its siren blaring. Soon it was followed by the first wave of state highway patrol cruisers. The squad cars contained three police dogs, which enraged the mob even further. "You better get those dogs out of here," a black rioter yelled. As the rioters swept through the city streets, whites stayed away. As Claude Sitton of the *New York Times* observed, "Aside from the authorities, only a relative handful of whites became involved."[33]

By the early hours of Sunday morning, a force of 250 state troopers had arrived to restore order. Many had Confederate flags bolted to the fenders of their patrol cars. They quickly came under assault in a hail of rocks. Blacks screamed "Kill 'em. Kill 'em." It was not until 4:30 A.M. that Birmingham police and state troopers managed to regain control. More than seventy people had been hospitalized in the course of the night. The injured included a policeman, who had been stabbed twice in the back. It was the first urban riot of the 1960s.

At six o'clock the next evening, Monday, May 13, after returning by helicopter from Camp David, the president convened an Oval Office crisis meeting. It was attended not only by top Justice Department officials but also by Defense Secretary Robert McNamara, Secretary of the Army Cyrus Vance, and General Earle Wheeler, the army chief of staff. Such was the scale and ferocity of the previous night's violence, that the president needed to discuss the administration's military options. Marshall began with a brief overview. He described the situation as "almost out of hand," on the brink of descending into "complete chaos."[34]

Robert Kennedy agreed with Marshall's bleak assessment. He had seen a situation report from a local sheriff, and it frightened him. It had shown that young blacks had instigated the street violence. "The Negroes are mean and tough," he said, "and have guns and have been worked up about this. . . . If you have another incident . . . another bombing, for instance, or fire, or something like that and it attracted a large number of Negroes, then the situation might very well get out off hand." The attorney general stressed that it was no longer the white segregationists who were inciting the riots—the tables had turned since the Battle of Ole Miss. "The group that's gotten out of hand has not been the white people; it's been the Negroes, by and large."

Robert Kennedy feared that the violence in Birmingham could easily spark trouble elsewhere. "The feelings of the Negroes generally and reports that we get from other cities—not just in the South—is that this could trigger off a good deal of violence around the country now with Negroes saying they've been abused for all these years and they're going to start following the ideas of the Black Muslims." For this reason, Robert Kennedy believed that it was essential for the administration to take a stronger stance: "If they feel, on the other hand, that the federal government is intervening for them, is going to work for them, that's the strongest argument for doing something."

The president shared his brother's unease but focused on restoring the original truce rather than proposing new legislation. "We can't just have the Negroes running around the city and then have this agreement blow up," said Kennedy. Legislation was the fallback option. "If the agreement blows up, the other remedy we have under that condition is to send legislation up to Congress this week as our response to that action . . . as a means of getting relief we have to provide legislation. We may have to do that anyway."

Marshall cut in. "If the agreement blows up, the Negroes . . . "

But before he could finish his sentence, the president interjected, "Uncontrollable."

"And I think not only in Birmingham," replied Marshall, who quickly distilled the crisis into a tidy formulation. In previous crises, "we had a white mob against a Negro," he explained. "Here we have a Negro mob against whites."

It was the black-on-white violence of May 11—not the publication of the startling photograph a week earlier—that represented the real watershed moment in Kennedy's thinking, and the turning point in administration policy. Kennedy had grown used to segregationist attacks against civil rights protesters. But he—along with his brother and other administration officials—was far more troubled by black mobs running amok. Based on his fraught exchanges with his brother and Marshall that afternoon, it is clear that it was this fear that prompted him to reconsider his civil rights proposals, and to push soon afterwards for far stronger measures.

The meeting was unlike any previous discussion among high-level administration officials on the subject of civil rights. At no point did anyone broach the subject of political pressures from liberal Democrats or the GOP. Nor was there any mention of the foreign policy implications of ongoing racial hostility. And no one said anything about the shift in public opinion caused by the Birmingham demonstrations. The subject was black violence; controlling it was now the administration's primary focus.

At the end of the meeting, the president issued instructions for the immediate movement of some 3,000 troops. The troops would not be deployed immediately on the streets of Birmingham but would remain in bases within easy reach of the city. (Kennedy remained skeptical about the Pentagon's ability to execute a successful deployment: "When they say the flying time's an hour, the mistake you always make is that's what you think—that they'll be there in an hour.")

While General Wheeler shuffled off to make the military arrangements, the others adjourned to the Cabinet Room to draft a nationwide television address announcing the troop deployment. Marshall, Salinger, RFK, and Katzenbach drafted a forceful statement, which would lend the full moral prestige of the presidency to the peaceful demonstrators. Their draft marked a sharp change in tone and language from the Ole Miss speech, which had merely called for the maintenance of law and order. This time the group aimed to make a far broader statement about segregation. "One of the great moral issues of our time is the achievement of equal opportunity for all citizens," their draft noted. "Too long have Negroes been denied fair treatment and equal opportunity in all parts of our land. . . . There are problems which must concern all of us and to which all of us have a moral obligation to put right."[35]

Once again, Kennedy balked. Upon reading the draft, he insisted that the speech should justify the insertion of troops on legal rather than moral grounds. He also feared the final draft placed the administration too heavily on the side of the demonstrators. With only minutes to go before the speech, Sorensen made the necessary changes.[36]

At 8:48 P.M., all three television networks ran Kennedy's address live from the White House. In contrast to the great drama of the previous night's events, the president's statement was sparse. Kennedy portrayed the federal government as a neutral arbiter in what was essentially a local dispute. "This Government will do whatever must be done to preserve order, to protect the lives of its citizens, and to uphold the law of the land," he said, using language borrowed from the Ole Miss speech. Then he announced that Marshall would return to Birmingham in an attempt to salvage the truce agreement; that troops trained in riot control were on their way to military bases near to Birmingham; and that preliminary steps were being taken to federalize the Alabama National Guard. He hoped, however, that the people of Birmingham would act in a manner that would render any "outside intervention unnecessary."[37]

Over the next twenty-four hours, tensions eased in Birmingham itself. Alarmed by the violence, King returned to the city and toured pool halls and bars urging young blacks to remain calm. The presence of boxing champion Floyd Patterson and Jackie Robinson at a mass meeting later that night also helped lighten the mood. On Wednesday, May 15, Marshall persuaded the Senior Citizens Committee and black leadership to reaffirm the truce agreement. "The situation in Birmingham appears to be improving," noted a secret military report that landed on the president's desk that day. "Incidents reported during this period are significant only when considered in light of developments in that area during the past three days." Kennedy was never forced to deploy the troops waiting outside Birmingham.[38]

For the rest of the week, the administration's efforts remained focused on safeguarding the truce agreement and maintaining order. The president himself took a leading role in persuading civil rights activists against descending on Birmingham. At one stage he even personally contacted black comedian Dick Gregory, who refused at first to even take the call and only did so after being upbraided by his wife. "Please don't go down to Birmingham," Kennedy pleaded. "We've got it all solved. Dr. King is wrong, what he's doing." But Gregory was adamant. "Man, I will be there in the morning," he said, defiantly.[39]

Robert Kennedy took a different tack when he spoke to a group of twenty-six newspaper editors from Alabama at the White House on Tuesday, May 14. The attorney general alerted them that if southern leaders refused to negotiate with King, radical forces would soon supplant him. "Remember it was King who went around the pool halls and door to door collecting knives, telling people to go home and to stay off the streets and to be nonviolent," he warned ominously. "If King loses, worse leaders are going to take his place."[40]

CHAPTER 23

✧

Repairing the Breach

The racial crisis had quickly spread well beyond Birmingham and burst all regional borders. On May 14, there were violent clashes in Harlem, when a group of Black Muslims disrupted a 3,000-strong protest rally outside the Hotel Theresa with cries of "We want Malcolm. We want Malcolm." Two days later, on May 16, Malcolm X delivered his own withering verdict on the Kennedy administration's response to Birmingham: "President Kennedy did not send troops to Alabama when dogs were biting black babies. He waited three weeks until the situation exploded. He then sent troops after Negroes had demonstrated their ability to defend themselves." The Black Muslims were thought to have only 5,500 to 6,000 signed-up members. But in the new atmosphere of militancy, his message had much greater resonance for disaffected black youths, especially in northern inner cities. Black Congressman Charles Diggs warned the White House, "Malcolm X represented a potential threat, not only because of his potential ability to become a spokesman for a large mass of Washington negroes" but because "he was not a person with whom one could deal on a rational basis."[1]

That week alone there were demonstrations in Jackson, Mississippi, Cambridge, Maryland, and Raleigh, North Carolina, that targeted segregated lunch counters, hotels, and restaurants. More frightening still, the protests spread to the North, with large-scale demonstrations in New Rochelle and Syracuse, New York, Philadelphia, and Chicago. In another bold departure, the NAACP announced plans for a twenty-five-state direct-action campaign aimed at ending de facto segregation in northern schools. Unless there was speedy action, warned Robert Carter, the NAACP's general counsel, "major explosions" would accompany the start of the new school year.[2]

That Saturday, May 18, the president flew south to meet a long-standing commitment to attend the ninetieth-anniversary celebrations of Vanderbilt University in Nashville, Tennessee. The city had long been associated with racial progress—a model for other cities in the South. But throughout the preceding week, gangs of white and black youths had exchanged volleys of rocks and glass on downtown streets in ugly racial clashes. There were even worries that black protesters might create disturbances along the president's motorcade route.

This was Kennedy's first opportunity to address southerners directly since the Birmingham riot. His speech was for the most part unsurprising—replete with lofty references to Bismarck, Aristotle, and Goethe—but it included a carefully written portion on the racial crisis. "This nation is now engaged in a continuing debate about the rights of a portion of its citizens," Kennedy stated. He went on in vague and unremarkable terms. "That will go on, and those rights will expand until the standard first forged by the Nation's founders has been reached, and all Americans enjoy equal opportunity and liberty under law." But then the president went further and commended King and his fellow protesters. "No one can deny the complexity of the problems involved in assuring to all our citizens their full rights as Americans. But no one can gainsay the fact that the determination to secure these rights is in the highest traditions of American freedom."[3]

The speech represented a departure for Kennedy. In previous civil rights statements during his time in office, Kennedy focused on the administration's impartiality and stressed that enforcing civil rights primarily meant implementing neutral laws. In Nashville, Kennedy committed himself to upholding moral principles as well. It was arguably the strongest statement in support of basic civil rights that any sitting president had ever delivered below the Mason-Dixon Line.[4]

Kennedy received a warm reception from the 30,000 students and faculty members who had crowded into the Vanderbilt stadium to hear his speech. A huge crowd of 150,000 well-wishers lined the eight-mile motorcade route and gave the president a "warm southern welcome," in the words of one correspondent. Robert Kennedy had demonstrated with his speech at the University of Georgia in May 1961 that it was possible to speak forcefully on civil rights without inflaming moderate southerners. His brother was just learning that now.[5]

After leaving Nashville, Kennedy headed straight to Muscle Shoals, where he was due to attend another ceremony, this time commemorating the thirtieth anniversary of the Tennessee Valley Authority in Alabama. Coming at such a volatile time, there were obvious dangers in pressing ahead with the visit. White House officials feared that Alabama state officials might even attempt to serve Kennedy with a suit or summons protesting the presence of federal troops around Birmingham. Anticipating such an ambush, Justice Department official Norbert Schlei suggested that a Secret Service agent should intercept the official: "If this for some reason was awkward, the President should not try to avoid being given the suit but he should dismiss it in a humorous vein." Then there was the thorny question of how to handle his appearance at Muscle Shoals alongside Governor George Wallace. Wallace was at odds with the administration over Birmingham and had also vowed to defy the court-ordered desegregation of the University of Alabama scheduled for early June. Given the governor's flair for the theatrical, the one-hour trip could easily degenerate into farce. That week, Wallace had described the president as a "military dictator."[6]

But the Muscle Shoals visit passed without incident. When Kennedy and Wallace shared the same platform there, the latter behaved impeccably, even when Kennedy strayed onto the hotly disputed subject of federal-state relations. Kennedy observed how the TVA had proved its early critics wrong by showing that the federal and state governments could cooperate for the common good. Then he referred obliquely to the present racial crisis: "From time to time statements are made labeling the Federal Government an outsider, an intruder, an adversary. But the people of this area know that United States Government is not a stranger or not an enemy." The subtext was unmistakable. Nonetheless, the crowd of some 10,000 gave the speech another enthusiastic reception. Afterwards, Kennedy spent a good ten minutes glad-handing admiring supporters.[7]

From Muscle Shoals, Kennedy set off for his next speaking engagement in Huntsville. He asked Wallace, Senator Lister Hill, and Congressman Bob Jones to accompany him onboard his helicopter so they could discuss the Birmingham crisis. Kennedy pressed for an agreement between business leaders in the city and representatives of the black community over the hiring of black sales clerks in Birmingham's department stores. He was at a loss to understand why white businessmen found it so difficult to make concessions. Why did store owners bar black sales clerks, he asked rhetorically, when they employed black servants at home?

"I have no objection to the businessmen hiring who they want," Wallace shot back. "What I do object to is the government telling a businessman what he should or should not do." On the question of the demonstrations, Wallace conceded the vast majority of blacks had been well-behaved. He blamed the violence squarely on outside agitators, particularly that "faker" King, whom he claimed was in competition with Fred Shuttlesworth to see "who could go to bed with the most nigger women, and white and red women, too." Trying to steer the conversation back, Kennedy said there would be no need for federal intervention if local business leaders remained true to the truce agreement. Their fifty-minute discussion ended on a note of unexpected sycophancy. Wallace expressed pride at having campaigned for the Democratic ticket in 1960.[8]

With demonstrations flaring up around the country, Kennedy found most of his time upon returning to Washington consumed by the crisis in race relations. His civil rights team started to perform a similar role to the famed ExComm, the informal group of advisers that had proved so useful during the Cuban missile crisis the previous October. The dangers were quite different, but the same sense of urgency prevailed.

At an Oval Office meeting on May 20, Robert Kennedy spoke of his rising panic. Citing a conversation with Dick Gregory, he warned, "These Negroes are all mad and they're all over the country" saying "we've got them scared now. Let's make them run." Having conferred with northern lawmakers, Lawrence O'Brien found himself in the unusual position of agreeing wholeheartedly with the attorney general. "I'm not going to watch the parade pass me by, I'm gonna lead it," Adam Clayton Powell, Jr., had warned O'Brien, when they discussed the growing militancy of one-time moderates. Robert Kennedy added that even Robert Weaver, once the administration's "proudest symbol," had become a target of scorn.

The normally imperturbable Burke Marshall joined the discussion. "There's going to be an awful lot of trouble," he said.

"This summer?" grunted the president.

"Yes sir," replied Marshall.

"Why this summer? People will get out of school?"

"People will get out of school," said Marshall, nodding his head.

"If you look around the country right now," Bobby Kennedy chipped in, "there must be a dozen places that are having major problems today." For a brief moment, he paused. "You're going to have an eruption. . . . It's because the Negroes are now just antagonistic and mad and they're going to be mad at everything. . . . My friends all say the Negro maids and servants are getting antagonistic. She said you don't know how they're sassing me back in my house." It was a curious observation, which spoke of the rarefied atmosphere in which the Kennedy brothers had grown up and their consequent isolation from black Americans. Perhaps RFK was trying to speak to his brother in terms he thought the president would understand: warning him that even domestic servants, the only blacks with whom Kennedy came into daily contact, were rebelling.

The president initially seemed overwhelmed, as he had been at the ADA meeting during the Birmingham riots. At one point he proposed that the administration could put forward a bill that would limit the protesters' right to demonstrate—an outlandish proposal that spoke both of his sheer desperation and muddled thinking.

It drew a polite but stiff rebuke from Marshall. "I think that legislation . . . would get us in more trouble," he said firmly.

Realizing his error, Kennedy added, "I don't think we ought to touch that one."

Kennedy also realized that tokenism would no longer suffice and that even his most senior black appointees had lost the confidence of sections of the black community. "Of course they say Weaver's sold out," said the president, flying off on a new tangent. "Any Negro who does well has sold out . . . the trouble is the Negroes are going to push this thing too far."

With that, the group turned to the idea of bolstering the administration-backed civil rights bill introduced in April. Here, Marshall took the lead. He suggested that some kind of Part III injunctive powers were essential since "it would have a personal impact on their daily lives." He lobbied, too, for a ban on segregation in public accommodations, since it was the "one thing that makes all Negroes, regardless of age, maddest." (Robert Kennedy initially disagreed and argued that blacks "can stand at the lunch counters. They don't have to eat there. They can pee before they come to the store or supermarket." Robert Kennedy had become much more attuned to the grievances of southern blacks during his two years at the Justice Department. But his comments here revealed the limitations of his thinking.)

As ever, O'Brien was wary of new proposals. And even Sorensen, an earlier proponent of new legislation, now harbored doubts. Sorensen feared a new civil rights bill could possibly exacerbate the situation. In a joint memorandum a week earlier, together they had posed the question "Does public and Congressional opinion outside the South make it desirable to submit new legislation which could give the federal government additional authority to act?" Clearly, both thought the answer was no. Now Sorensen reiterated the point, warning how new legislation would create "enforcement problems," which would spark repeated federal/state confrontations. O'Brien put it more starkly: "We are going to run smack into a straight-out brawl that will position the extremes on both sides and probably create an impasse in Congress."[9]

The president, however, had come to realize that the nation was embroiled in a genuine racial crisis. "Real progress" required the passage of bold legislation, he said, including a public accommodations title—which seemed to him "the big story." Blacks needed a "remedy in law," as he put it, which would persuade them to pursue court- rather than street-based campaigns. Robert Kennedy argued that new legislation would be "damn helpful. Good for the Negroes. Relax this thing. And everybody thinks we've been doing something." It would give the administration "weapons we don't have at the present time." While the legislation was pending, he suggested they convene a meeting of black leaders, explore the possibility of setting up biracial commissions in racial trouble spots and hold a White House conference of corporate executives, in the hope of persuading them to voluntarily desegregate their shops and restaurants.

The president agreed with the overall approach but was concerned about the timetable for the meetings. "I think we ought to have some of these other meetings before we have in the King group; otherwise the meetings will look like they got me to do it." He was also wary of meeting King individually. "The trouble with King," he said, "is everybody thinks he's our boy anyway. So everything he does, everybody thinks we stuck him in there. So we ought to have him well surrounded. . . . King is so hot these days that it's like Marx coming to the White House. I'd like to have some southern governors, or mayors, or businessmen first. And my program should have gone up to the Hill first."[10]

This had been by far the most intense Oval Office meeting since the Cuban missile crisis, and the differences were revealing. In October, Kennedy had maintained great poise under enormous pressure and had spoken much more lucidly and creatively about the policy options under consideration. He also had the self-confidence on foreign affairs to reject advice from domineering figures like former Secretary of State Dean Acheson and the Joint Chiefs of Staff. Now, faced with a racial crisis, Kennedy demonstrated much less control. His response bordered on the incoherent, and he relied much more heavily on Robert Kennedy and Marshall. For his first two years in office, the president had worked within clearly delineated political boundaries. His narrow view of federalism circumscribed the range of policy options he was willing to consider. But now the lines had been erased by the rapid escalation of violence across the country, and the threat of black militancy. Kennedy was clearly disoriented and was unable to think creatively about how to address the crisis. He ricocheted from one policy idea to another—from a prohibition on demonstrations to a tough new public accommodations law. Faced with a crisis to which he had given only limited thought for decades, Kennedy's legendary grace under pressure gave way to near panic. By the end of the meeting, Kennedy started to reassert himself, and started to understand more clearly that new legislation was most probably the only option. But as Marshall later reflected, the "conclusive voice within the government at that time" belonged to Robert Kennedy.[11]

In this frenzied climate of the meeting on May 20, President Kennedy and his advisers had made no final decision as to whether or not the administration would introduce a new civil rights bill. On Wednesday, May 22, he nonetheless hinted for the first time in public that new legislation might be on the way. In the course of his first press conference since the rioting in Birmingham, he alluded to "additional proposals" under consideration that would offer demonstrators a "legal outlet" and "legal remedy." However, no definitive decision on whether to introduce a new civil rights bill had yet been made.[12]

If Kennedy had intended to calm the mood of black protesters with his remarks, he demonstrably failed—and his brother realized this firsthand only two days later during a meeting with eminent black intellectuals in New York City. The supposedly secret meeting organized with the help of James Baldwin was held in the Kennedy family apartment on Central Park South. The eclectic group included the psychologist Dr. Kenneth Clark, singers Harry Belafonte and Lena Horne, the playwright Lorraine Hansberry, and Clarence B. Jones, a close associate of Dr. King's. But it was Jerome Smith, a young veteran of the Freedom Rides campaign, who dominated the discussion. When Robert

Kennedy began the meeting by enumerating the administration's achievements in the area of civil rights, Smith went on the attack: "You don't have no idea what the trouble is," said the young activist. "I'm close to the moment where I'm ready to take up a gun." Smith, who stammered when he was annoyed, was having difficulty enunciating his words, but nobody doubted their meaning. "I've seen what government can do to crush the spirit and lives of people in the South," describing a spell in a Mississippi jailhouse during which the Justice Department refused assistance. As Smith drew breath, Baldwin asked if he would fight for his country. "Never, Never, Never," he shouted.

"How can you say that?" asked Kennedy, incredulously.

But Smith was unrepentant. "I want to vomit being in the same room as you," he went on. Shocked, Kennedy surveyed the room, fully expecting one of the other participants to upbraid the young activist. Instead, they nodded in agreement.

"You've got a great many accomplished people in this room, Mr. Attorney General," observed Lorraine Hansberry. "But the only man you should be listening to is that man over there."[13]

Kennedy left the meeting "shocked, disappointed and hurt," according to Louis Oberdorfer, who had accompanied him on the New York visit. The attorney general could not believe that the young activists were not more appreciative of his department's efforts. Robert Kennedy later reflected that there was "obviously a revolution within a revolution in the Negro leadership. We could see the direction going away from Martin Luther King to some of these younger people, who had no belief or confidence in the system of government."[14]

That week there was no letup in the racial disturbances. On Tuesday, May 28, black students in Jackson, Mississippi, mounted a sit-in protest at Woolworth's, where they came under attack from a gang of segregationists. The mob began by hurling insults, then picked up ketchup bottles and mustard and sugar dispensers and poured the contents over the protesters' heads. The demonstrators were unflappable, which only fueled the segregationists' fury. Suddenly, a burly ex-cop dragged Memphis Norman, a twenty-year-old demonstrator, from his stool. He threw Norman to the ground and kicked him in the head, over and over, until his face was beaten raw. Then, with great relish, he poured salt on Norman's bleeding flesh. Local policemen finally intervened only after the savagery subsided. As Norman lay semiconscious in a pool of his own salt-laced blood, the police arrested him for breaching the peace.[15]

Local NAACP leaders responded by threatening a "massive offensive." Jackson Mayor Allen Thompson promised a "massive response" and ordered the construction of a hog-wire enclosure at the state fairground capable of holding 10,000 prisoners. That Friday morning, May 31, an army of protesters, including over 600 schoolchildren, swarmed onto the streets. They were met by a phalanx of police officers armed with repeater shotguns. The police made 500 arrests, herding protesters into municipal garbage trucks for the journey to jail. On June 1, another 100 demonstrators were arrested, foremost among them Roy Wilkins—the first time during his thirty-year career he had gone to jail.[16]

King also planned to ratchet up the pressure on the administration. Acting on information gleaned from FBI wiretaps on Stanley Levison, a King aide suspected of being a communist spy, FBI Director J. Edgar Hoover warned Kenneth O'Donnell and Robert Kennedy that the SCLC was also laying plans for a new wave of protests: King "would like to see so much pressure on the President that he will have to sign an Executive Order making segregation unconstitutional." On June 1, wiretaps also picked up a phone conversation, in which King told Levison, "We are on the threshold of a significant breakthrough, and the greatest weapon is mass demonstration." As ever, King had twin motivations: He wanted to maintain pressure on the administration, and he wanted to cement his leadership of the civil rights movement. He warmed to the idea of a mass protest in Washington. It would provide a platform for his leadership, and, as he told Levison, "the threat itself may so frighten the President that he would have to do something."[17]

∿

After the Birmingham demonstrations, Lyndon Johnson had been quick to grasp how the tenor of the black freedom struggle had changed. He believed that the situation required a more forceful response from the administration. Johnson's own record on civil rights could, at best, be described as mixed. The President's Committee on Equal Employment Opportunity (PCEEO), which he headed, was widely deemed to be a failure by civil rights groups, and in January 1963, Johnson had angered liberal Democrats by hampering their efforts to reform the filibuster rule at the opening of the new congressional session. But Johnson was also capable of surprises. On January 7, he had delivered a strong speech marking the centenary of Lincoln's Emancipation Proclamation, in which he noted, "While we in America have freed the slave of his chains, we have not freed his heirs of their color."[18] Later that month, during a speech before a mainly black audience in Cleveland, he called for federal action to finally make good the promise of the Emancipation Proclamation.[19]

On May 18, Johnson delivered another stout civil rights speech. During an appearance before the Capital Press Club in Washington, the largest organization for black newspapermen, Johnson sided with the Birmingham protesters and called publicly for a more aggressive federal response. He argued there was no "moral justification" to asking blacks to be more patient. "It seems to me," he said, "that in the field of human rights, we are all well past the stage where half a loaf will do. . . . Progress must come faster . . . morally and economically . . . otherwise the tragic headlines which speak of the breakdown of law and order will increase rather than diminish."[20]

The Birmingham situation came to dominate what turned out to be a venomous meeting of the PCEEO on May 29, which was chaired by the vice president. Robert Kennedy burst into the meeting midway through, with Marshall trailing hurriedly behind. The attorney general unleashed a barrage of barbed questions about the committee's performance. One of the reasons that Birmingham business leaders had been resistant to employing a greater number of blacks, Kennedy claimed, was because the federal government's own employment record was so dismal. "Why should we hire Negroes? You don't hire Negroes," civic leaders had moaned, since out of 2,000 federal employees in Birmingham, just fifteen were black. RFK demanded answers.[21]

Stunned and angry, Johnson invited NASA Director James Webb to outline the space agency's efforts. But even though Webb, the vice president's personal friend, spoke optimistically about impressive recent gains, Kennedy was enraged. He asked why an agency that dispensed $3.5 billion in federal funds had assigned just two staff members to boost black employment. A fumbling Webb could not provide an answer. Then Kennedy turned on Hobart Taylor, the body's executive vice chairman and another Johnson associate, whom he pressed on the PCEEO's much-criticized compliance regime. When Taylor replied that a tough new compliance form was being drawn up, Kennedy "read the riot act," according to the CRC's staff director Berl Bernhard, who watched in bewilderment as the diatribe continued.[22]

Finally, a shell-shocked Johnson hit back. He launched a thinly veiled attack on the Justice Department and claimed that Birmingham's employment problems stemmed from the slow pace of school integration. Johnson described how 2,000 blacks in the city had recently taken the civil service examination, as part of an effort by the Civil Service Commission to boost black employment levels. But only eighty had passed. "It may be, Mr. Attorney General," Johnson said accusingly, "that deliberate speed is not enough." Not long after, Kennedy stormed out.[23]

Johnson had long been sensitive to criticisms about his civil rights record. And he took particular exception to being lectured by Robert Kennedy, whose nickname in the press—"the Assistant President"—had always intensely annoyed him. On May 18, before his speech at the Capitol Press Club, black journalists had presented the vice president with a distinguished service award in recognition of his work in improving race relations—an honor that Johnson appeared to think was thoroughly deserved. Within the civil rights community, Johnson had other notable admirers. Prior to leaving the administration, Harris Wofford had come to view Johnson as an important ally and later reflected that "civil rights was burning pretty strongly" in him by the middle of 1961. James

Farmer, who met with the vice president early on in the administration, had also been won over: "He was very sincere, he was very interested, almost a passionate concern came through."[24]

So on Thursday, May 30, the day after being so thoroughly humiliated at the PCEEO meeting, Johnson delivered what could easily have been interpreted as his response to the attorney general's tirade: a resounding civil rights speech delivered in the emotionally charged setting of the Memorial Day commemorations at Gettysburg. Standing in for the president, Johnson went into the event armed with an unusually elegant speech, which rivaled even Sorensen's best efforts. The speech bore the heavy fingerprints of his close adviser George Reedy, who had argued since late May that a senior administration official—the president, ideally—needed to spell out the moral case for reform. "This country is going through one of its most serious internal clashes since the Civil War itself," wrote Reedy on May 24. "The backbone of white resistance is not going to be broken, until the segregationists realize that the total moral force of the United States is arrayed against them."[25]

Johnson's speech went some way towards answering that call. "One-hundred years ago, the slave was freed," he stated. "One hundred years later, the Negro remains in bondage to the color of his skin. The Negro today asks for justice. We do not answer him—we do not answer those who lie beneath this soil—when we reply to the Negro by asking 'Patience.'" Then, in what could easily have been interpreted as a nuanced attack on the gradualism favored by the Kennedy brothers, he called for immediate change. "It is empty to plead that the solution to the dilemmas of the present rests on the hands of a clock," he said. "The solution is in our own hands." Johnson was more impassioned and expansive on the subject of civil rights than the president ever had been. "Our nation found its soul in honor on these fields of Gettysburg one hundred years ago," he declared, ending with a rallying cry. "We must not lose that soul in dishonor now on the fields of hate."[26]

It was precisely the sort of speech civil rights leaders had wanted the president to make. But it was Johnson who offered genuine moral leadership—and in the most symbolic setting possible.[27] The *New York Times* commended Johnson for his political bravery and noted that many of his fellow southerners regarded him as a "traitor to the cause." The speech was all the more impressive, wrote Cabell Phillips, because Johnson's "forebears were on the losing side of the Civil War."[28]

Flushed with editorial praise for the speech, Johnson quickly found himself taken more seriously within the administration. On June 1, he received a rare invitation to attend an Oval Office meeting. Kennedy had convened the meeting to reach a final decision on the introduction of new legislation. "What's going to be the result if we don't have any further legislation?" he asked Marshall. "Will we just have these riots and everyone will say—"

Marshall cut the president off, with a curt "I don't think [we] really have an alternative. You couldn't go on and not have legislation. . . . You'd have a major fight in Congress, you'd have a lot of Republicans and a lot of Democrats putting legislation in. Everybody would be saying 'where is your legislation?' I couldn't possibly defend that position. I think it's absolutely essential that you have legislation."

The president was eager to hear the thoughts of Lyndon Johnson, the chief architect of the 1957 and 1960 Civil Rights Acts and one of the few postwar politicians with enough legislative guile to outwit Richard Russell. But in the presence of the Kennedy brothers, Johnson reverted to his typically sullen demeanor. Asked by the president for his thoughts on the civil rights bill, he replied guardedly, "I haven't seen it." Later, when Kennedy probed him again, Johnson responded with almost childlike timidity, saying he was "not competent to counsel you." His most useful contribution came still later, when he said that if the administration proposed a new civil rights bill it should fight for it unrelentingly. "And if we do that, then we got to go through with it and pass it," said Johnson, "gotta bear down . . . got to do that, or else yours will be just another gesture."[29]

By the end of the meeting, Kennedy had crossed the Rubicon. He knew that further equivocation could engender further violence. Kennedy finally committed himself to a bold civil rights bill that he truly wanted—and needed—to enact. His exchange with Marshall had settled the issue. The only outstanding questions related to the scope, timing, and tactics of the proposals.

After the meeting, Ted Sorensen was placed in overall charge of drafting the administration's proposals. The task required all his prodigious skills, for the package needed to satisfy two seemingly contradictory aims: to be bold enough to mollify angry protesters but also palatable enough for moderate Republicans. Without bipartisan support, the bill stood little hope of success. To break a filibuster in the Senate and to win a simple majority in the House, the administration required solid Republican support—about twenty-two senators and sixty-five members of the House. As Sorensen himself put it, the measure had to be "the minimum we can ask for and maximum we can stand behind."[30]

To line up Republican votes, and to give his policies a truly bipartisan gloss, Kennedy approached Dwight D. Eisenhower on June 10 and asked him to publicly endorse the measures. But the former president demurred, citing his familiar, vaporous homily that legislation could never change the minds of men. So Kennedy focused instead on Senate Minority Leader Everett Dirksen, a fair-minded man likely to put country before party. "I think it's possible that as the mood of the country gets uglier and uglier, the Republicans are going to say we can't play the Southern Democratic game anymore," Kennedy had said at the May 20 meeting, where the legislative option had first been discussed. "They'll join in cloture and something will get by."[31]

To guarantee Dirksen's support, the White House offered assurances that the civil rights bill would be a genuinely bipartisan endeavor, with politics put to one side. To help depoliticize the issue, Robert Kennedy held an unprecedented meeting with the Republican Senate Caucus on June 10. The very next day, the president convened a follow-up meeting with the party's congressional leadership at which he promised to share credit for the bill's passage. Before those meetings, Dirksen had informed Sorensen and Norbert Schlei that bold civil rights reforms were "an idea whose time has come." On June 13, Dirksen gave Senate Majority Leader Mike Mansfield a formal assurance of Republican support.[32]

Now that the GOP leadership was on board, Kennedy secretly hoped a southern Democrat could be persuaded to become a modern-day Arthur Vandenberg, the Michigan Republican who in the 1940s had spurned the isolationism of his party and region and thrown his support the Democrats' interventionist foreign policies. Perhaps Senators Lister Hill or J. William Fulbright might fill the role, he wondered—although he did nothing to line up their support.[33]

Lyndon Johnson would have been an ideal candidate for the role. But after his stuttering performance at the June 1 meeting, he was sidelined once again. After the Oval Office meeting, Johnson had requested a fifteen-minute private meeting with the president, but O'Donnell turned him down. Johnson's humiliation became complete later that week when Lee White finished the final draft of an additional executive order extending the PCEEO's writ to include federal apprenticeship and construction programs. The changes were announced on June 4, but White forgot to inform the vice president. "I've never seen a more surprised, disappointed and annoyed guy than Lyndon Johnson when the President of the United States issued [the] executive order changing the jurisdiction of his committee," White remembered, adding that he took the news "about as good as a guy when he gets a mackerel in the face!"[34]

On June 4, the very day that the changes to the PCEEO were publicly announced, Johnson approached Schlei, an assistant attorney general, and vented his frustration. On the question of the civil rights bill, Johnson thought its timing was questionable, since it would be "disastrous for the President's program." It should therefore be introduced only after the administration's controversial tax proposals had passed both houses of Congress. More importantly, Johnson urged the president to deliver a major civil rights speech in the South. Johnson wanted the president to speak at the NASA installation in Mississippi, where he could stress the chief purpose of the space race was to ensure that *all* Americans could live on earth in freedom and at peace. Southerners would respond favorably if the president couched the case for civil rights in patriotic terms, he said. At one point, Johnson even grasped the American flag behind his desk to illustrate a point. How could the president order a black citizen to die in a foxhole in some foreign jungle, he asked melo-dramatically, when a black man was unable to buy a cup of coffee at a Missis-sippi lunch counter?[35]

When Sorensen learned of the meeting between Johnson and Schlei, he im-mediately contacted the vice president by phone. Sorensen was fearful that if differences between the president and vice president burst into the open it would damage the administration in the South. Sorensen listened in deferen-tial silence as Johnson unleashed a torrent of concerns, most of which flowed from the same point: that legislation alone would never assuage black demon-strators. The nation needed moral leadership from the president. "As it is now, the President's message doesn't get over," said Johnson, who suggested Kennedy deliver a major southern speech, ideally in San Antonio. "Now the President has to go in there without cussing anybody or fussing at anybody with a bunch of congressmen sitting there listening to him, and be the leader of the nation and make a moral commitment to them. . . . Negroes . . . want a moral commitment and that will do more to satisfy them than your bill will." Of course there would be political dangers in making such a speech—"it may cost us the South," he blithely noted, "but those sorts of states may be lost any-way." If nothing else, southerners would "at least respect his courage." Johnson also suggested many white southerners were amenable to reform, having rec-ognized they were on the losing side of history. Still, his prime concern was the violent mood of blacks. "The Negroes feel and they're suspicious that we're just doing what we got to do. Until that's laid to rest I don't think you're going to have much of a solution."[36]

Time and again, Johnson hammered home his main point that legislation of-fered an incomplete solution: "What Negroes are really seeking is moral force . . . until they receive that assurance, unless it's stated dramatically and convinc-ingly." Southern lawmakers should be invited to join him on the platform and forced to listen to an address that echoed the same themes as Lincoln's "Get-tysburg speech." The idea would be "to make a bigot out of nearly anybody that's against him." Then the vice president expressed anger, as he had done previously, at being excluded from so many White House discussions. "Hell, if the Vice-President doesn't know what's in it, how do you expect the others to know what's in it? I got it from the *New York Times* and from that message of yours this morning." Now, Johnson demanded the lead role in negotiations with southern grandees, his area of unrivaled expertise. "I would make them show every card they got," boasted Johnson, suggesting the threat of canceled defense contracts would bring them to heel. "We got a little pop gun, and I want to pull out the cannon. The President is the cannon. . . . You let him be on all the TV networks, just speaking from his conscience, not at a rally in Harlem, but at a place in Mississippi or Texas or Louisiana, and just have the honor guard there with a few Negroes in it. Then let him reach over and point and say, 'I have to order these boys into battle, in the foxholes carrying the flag. I don't ask them what their name is, whether it's Gomez or Smith, or what color they got, what religion. If I can order them into battle I've got to make it possible for them to eat and sleep in this country.'" Finally, the stream of advice ran dry. Sorensen, who had listened in stunned silence, courteously thanked the vice president for his time and replaced the receiver. Then he contacted the president and relayed the conversation in full.[37]

Throughout the racial crisis, Kennedy had been reluctant to exert himself publicly in the way that Johnson had suggested. He had shied away from a forceful presidential statement in response to the Birmingham riot and discounted the value of a fireside chat or nationwide speech. While his Nashville address signaled his administration's closer identification with civil rights groups, it hardly amounted to the ringing endorsement that the black leaders craved. During his meeting with the Americans for Democratic Action, Kennedy had insisted that presidential speeches were of limited value, a comment he reiterated at a press conference the following week when he said that his Ole Miss speech had not had much impact. These comments suggested that he wholly failed to appreciate the incalculable power of presidential persuasion, especially in the television age. It was tantamount to saying that the president could not make a moral difference.

In the first week of June, however, Kennedy left Washington for a five-day tour of the West. Perhaps the vice president had jolted him into action: Kennedy decided finally to deliver a major civil rights speech. Kennedy had headed west to visit military installations in Colorado, New Mexico, and California. But he made a last-minute change to his itinerary, over the objections of Kenneth O'Donnell and Lawrence O'Brien, and decided to end his western swing with a stop in Honolulu. The trip to Hawaii enabled Kennedy to address the U.S. Conference of Mayors annual meeting, which opened a day early to accommodate the president.[38]

Kennedy began his June 9 speech with a message of alarm: that the racial crisis was set to intensify. Already that week, there had been demonstrations as far afield as Oakland, Sacramento, and San Jose in California; Daytona Beach, Gainesville, Tallahassee, Winter Haven and Miami, Florida; Savannah, Georgia; Baton Rouge, Louisiana; Cambridge, Maryland; Greensboro, North Carolina; Lexington, Kentucky; Oklahoma City, Oklahoma; Chattanooga and Nashville, Tennessee; Jackson, Mississippi; Danville, Virginia; and St. Johns, Michigan. "Students will be out of college and out of high school," he said. "Large numbers of Negroes will be out of work. The events in Birmingham have stepped up the tempo of the nationwide drive for full equality—and rising summer temperatures are often accompanied by rising human emotions." New legislation would help move the disputes off the streets into the courts, but action was required locally, especially in persuading restaurateurs and hoteliers to desegregate their facilities. "The problem is growing. The challenge is there. The cause is just. The question is whether you and I will do nothing, thereby inviting pressure and increasing tension, and inviting possible violence, or whether you will anticipate these problems and move to fulfill the rights of your Negro citizens in a peaceful and constructive manner." The time for "token moves" had passed.[39]

Had he given the speech six months previously, civil rights leaders might have welcomed Kennedy's comments with great enthusiasm. But the overriding message of the speech was that it was expedient to promote reform rather than right to do so. Compared to the high emotion of Johnson's Gettysburg speech, Kennedy's address rang hollow. Black leaders were distinctly unimpressed. That very day, King delivered a trenchant attack on the president. King argued during a television interview that the Kennedy administration had merely substituted "an inadequate approach for a miserable one." King added that although Kennedy may have done "a little more" than Eisenhower, it was not enough. Even the slavishly loyal *Boston Chronicle,* Kennedy's hometown black newspaper, was critical. On June 10, the paper's editors called upon the president to assert moral leadership, "to call out the best in this nation, among the broad-based majority of his fellow countrymen."[40]

∾

Even before his trip to Hawaii, the president had realized that new legislation alone offered only a partial solution to the crisis that had overwhelmed his presidency. And the civil rights bill would also take months, possibly even a year, to enact. In the meantime, the situation required a raft of remedial measures to temper the mood of protesters—or "safety valves," as administration officials sometimes described them in background briefings to reporters. Across Washington, there was a clamor for immediate action. Justice Department lawyers mounted their biggest voting suits since the passage of the 1957 Civil Rights Act, symbolically targeting Jefferson County, Alabama, which included the city of Birmingham.

The Justice Department also tried to settle the long-running school dispute in Prince Edward County, Virginia, which it had first tackled in 1961. On August 14, after months of behind-the-scenes negotiations orchestrated by Justice Department official William J. vanden Heuvel, Governor Albertis S. Harrison of Virginia announced the formation of the Prince Edward Free School Association to provide schooling for the 1,700 black pupils denied an education since June 1959.[41]

On June 22, following the publication of a report from the President's Committee on Equal Opportunity in the Armed Forces, Kennedy described discriminatory practices within the military as "morally wrong." He added that the military community "take a leadership role" in stamping out segregation.[42] Acting on the president's orders, Defense Secretary Robert McNamara authorized military commanders stationed in the South to designate as off-limits any area in the vicinity of military bases that practiced "relentless discrimination." It was an important advance. Up to that point, commanders had been tasked merely with eliminating on-base discrimination. Now they were being handed the responsibility of tackling discriminatory practices in host communities.

In late June, the Pentagon eliminated segregation in the Armed Forces Reserves. It was the hurried culmination of a tortuously slow fifteen-year process. At the same time, Defense Department officials conducted negotiations aimed at integrating southern National Guard units, a reform that Kennedy had shied away from during the first two years of his presidency through fear of upsetting Senator Richard Russell and Representative Carl Vinson. (Still, the Pentagon backed off when southerners complained that a group of Air Force personnel had participated in civil rights demonstrations in South Dakota. McNamara responded by curtailing the right of military personnel to demonstrate, which he considered "highly inappropriate and unnecessary" with new legislation was pending. At the same time, Lee White, the administration official who initially gave the go-ahead, received the "worst beating" he ever took from the president. When Kennedy called to upbraid him, he asked simply, "Why didn't you ask me?")[43]

Boosting black employment took on a new urgency. On June 3, Kennedy ordered a comprehensive review of all federal construction programs to eliminate discriminatory hiring practices. At the same time Kennedy ordered Labor Secretary Willard Wirtz to issue a directive stating that all young workers serving federal apprenticeships would be admitted on a nondiscriminatory basis. Administration officials privately conceded that the change in policy stemmed in part from a spate of ugly violence in Philadelphia in May, when blacks had protested their exclusion from a school construction project. In late July, when a vacancy arose on the National Labor Relations Board, the president also ensured it was filled by a black appointee, Howard Jenkins, Jr., a move intended to underscore his plea for equal opportunities in government and private industry.[44]

At a cabinet meeting on May 23, the president pressed officials to do more to combat racism within their own departments. As Robert Kennedy emphasized, the Justice Department found it difficult to press Birmingham businessmen into recruiting more blacks when the federal government maintained a largely segregated workforce in the city. Immediately, John Macy, the chairman of the Civil Service Commission, ordered a task force into Birmingham to boost black employment in the Post Office and Veterans Administration, where they held just one percent of the jobs (in a city where they were thirty-seven percent of the population). In a stroke of good fortune, its task was made much easier by the opening of a new Social Security payment center, creating 120 vacancies. Between May 15 and June 19, forty-eight blacks were appointed after being allowed to take special sittings of the Federal Service Entrance Examination. By July 16, the figure stood at sixty-four. (Crucially, however, no applicants were offered preferential treatment. As Macy stressed to the president in a meeting on June 13, the commission strictly followed two key guiding principles: that jobs would never be opened up specifically for blacks, and that entrance standards would never waver.) After their success in Birmingham, Civil Service Commission task forces descended on the racial hot spots of Montgomery, Savannah, Greensboro, and Jacksonville. On June 26, Johnson also delivered another toughly worded speech, in which he claimed that tokenism would no longer suffice. "Placing a few Negroes in prominent jobs is not enough to satisfy the dictates of conscience." Like his comments on school integration in Birmingham, the speech could have been construed as an attack on the president.[45]

As well as this crash employment program, the administration considered longer-term economic remedies. The president and his brother saw a direct correlation between racial tension and black unemployment, especially in the North. The American economy had been growing steadily over the past two years, and at the beginning of the year Kennedy had claimed that the recession of 1960–1961 had passed. But in inner-city ghettoes, the black unemployment rate stood at twenty percent, compared with a national average of five percent. In response, the Departments of Labor, Commerce, and Health, Education, and Welfare began to target employment relief programs on areas of deep black unemployment. The Manpower Development and Training Program received additional funds. The president also lobbied hard for the passage of the Youth Employment bill, which was designed to channel the energies of unemployed youths into a constructive outlet, to strengthen the pending vocational education amendments and expand work relief and training programs. But Kennedy received a depressing assessment on the effect of these changes from Wirtz: ". . . in the present state of the economy it would be a mistake to hold out the hope that setting up a 'crash' program for Negroes would mean them being employed. It isn't true with whites, and it would be less true with respect to non-whites."[46]

Eager to stimulate the overall economy, the president also pressed ahead with plans for massive, Keynesian tax cuts. "The most important problem," Kennedy had told the ADA leaders in May, "is to try to prevent this economy from going down again, and that's what we're trying to do in a major way." Afterwards, when Kennedy spoke repeatedly, and with rare passion, of the need for tax cuts, black leaders misinterpreted it as a sign he considered the civil rights bill a much lower priority. The reality was that he viewed both as inextricably linked.[47]

As well as unemployment, the president redoubled his administration's efforts to tackle poverty. Kennedy had started taking a much keener interest in the issue towards the end of 1962, following the publication of Michael Harrington's landmark work, *The Other America*, which revealed that at least a fifth of the population had an unacceptably poor standard of living. As a result of the racial crisis in June, Kennedy implored Walter Heller at the Council of Economic Advisers to look much more closely at the problem, with the aim of introducing a major antipoverty bill at the beginning of 1964. In September, after Heller had made little progress, Sorensen formed a poverty task force and challenged it to formulate an antipoverty program. It would eventually form the basis of Lyndon Johnson's War on Poverty.[48]

Robert Kennedy, who had become the chairman of the President's Committee on Juvenile Delinquency when it was established in May 1961, had thought much more trenchantly than his brother about the problem of poverty. Juvenile delinquency fueled the racial crisis, especially in northern slums, "where," he told the president, "the basic problems of jobs, training, and housing may take more than a generation to resolve." RFK called for the administration to promote summer job programs, to rehabilitate recreation centers and playgrounds, and to encourage black celebrities and sports stars to visit black communities to bring attention to the problem. The measures were designed, said Robert Kennedy, "to show the children and juveniles that their government cared about their problems." Black youths needed to have their faith restored in government. Fearing further outbreaks of violence, the attorney general also called for black communities to be better policed, advocating a federal grant-in-aid program for additional training, equipment, and men. The administration would be tough on black crime but also address its root causes.[49]

Black crime was also a symptom of a much larger crisis: the breakdown of social interchange between black and white Americans. On this subject, the president had been attracted to an idea from Berl Bernhard of the CRC, who suggested a series of White House meetings and conferences aimed at tackling the growing "polarization of Negro and white, the rupture of already strained channels of communication." By bringing together business leaders, clergy, governors, mayors, and eventually black leaders, the administration could mobilize support behind the new legislation and simultaneously remind local civic leaders of their responsibility to nurture ties within their communities. "This is a long range approach," said Bernhard. "It strikes me as constructive, not punitive; cooperative, not dictatorial. An obvious by-product would be that of overcoming the isolation from the Administration many Negro leaders feel and express." The idea was put into immediate effect, with the president himself sounding the call for civic leadership at eleven separate meetings at which he met over 1,600 business, political, and community leaders.[50]

In his first meeting on May 29, with the governors of Illinois, Delaware, Indiana, Massachusetts, Minnesota, New Hampshire, New Jersey, Tennessee, and Vermont, Kennedy underscored the need to establish better communications between the races through the creation of biracial committees at the local level. He also urged the governors to combat the school dropout problem and boost state training and educational programs to tackle black unemployment. He mentioned the need for new federal legislation and asked that the states themselves enact new public accommodations laws. But the president's main focus was community relations and the economic sources of discontent.[51]

Kennedy echoed the same themes at a meeting of labor leaders in early June. He told the group that the best way to limit interracial violence would be to reduce black unemployment and discrimination in the workplace. He asked the labor leaders to study discrimination in their own organizations, and to sponsor job referral programs and apprenticeship schemes. They should take a leading role in the creation of local biracial committees. Kennedy asked them to support his civil rights bill but suggested it was just one part of the administration's multipronged approach to the crisis. It would also be useful, he said, if they supported his tax proposals, youth employment initiatives, mass transit job creation programs, and extensions to area development legislation.[52]

Ahead of a gathering of 250 religious leaders on June 17, Ralph Dungan told the president that religious leaders could be especially instrumental in developing "community solidarity and mutual respect." Kennedy agreed and called upon them to preach a message of racial harmony from their pulpits, and "recognize the conflict between racial bigotry and the Holy Word." Robert Kennedy then urged the priests, rabbis, and ministers to form biracial committees. "I would think that the best way to prevent the most violent situations," the attorney general suggested, "would be the closest co-ordination between the clergy of both Negro and white in each community." The new legislation hardly received a mention. On June 19, Kennedy asked a meeting of educators to establish biracial conferences between parents and teacher. Two days later he asked a group of 250 leading lawyers to join biracial conferences. Their negotiating skills, he noted, would be particularly useful in mediating local disputes.[53]

The discussion was even more expansive at a White House meeting on June 4 for representatives of the Business Council, an organization of blue-ribbon corporations. Speaking first, Vice President Johnson called for the business leaders to help address the school dropout problem and to sponsor after-school training programs that would help black youths become more self-supporting. Robert Kennedy called upon them to voluntarily desegregate their businesses, before new legislation compelled them to do so. The president himself then spoke and honed in on the economic and social means by which business leaders could help to heal the racial fracture in America. Businessmen could help by actively trying to recruit black workers, he said, and by joining biracial commissions. "Our concern is that we do not have a battle in the streets of America in the coming months," said the president.[54]

These White House meetings have generally been viewed solely as attempts to build public support on behalf of the civil rights bill. But in fact most of the meetings were rather secretive affairs, conducted on a strictly off-the-record basis. Afterwards, Salinger revealed few details to reporters. Instead, the primary aim of every meeting was to encourage participants to either join or form local biracial committees after returning home from Washington, and to take or support economic action to tackle the sources of racial discord. They were not mere exercises in public relations; rather, they were carefully considered efforts at long-term social and economic reengineering.[55]

CHAPTER 24

∾

"Fires of Frustration"

The president moved from crisis to crisis. Within hours of returning from his trip to Hawaii, Kennedy took personal charge of the looming standoff at the University of Alabama in Tuscaloosa, which was due to reach a climax on Tuesday, June 11. Seven years earlier, in February 1956, the university had admitted Autherine Lucy as its first black student. But Lucy immediately became the target of violent demonstrations when she attempted to attend class and had to run the gauntlet of a jeering mob shouting: "Keep 'Bama White" and "Hit the nigger whore." On February 4, just three days after she had first set foot on campus, university officials ordered her to stop attending classes, purportedly for her own safety. The following month Lucy was permanently expelled on the specious grounds that she had made defamatory remarks against the University Board (she had in fact suggested that the board had suspended her on account of race). In the summer of 1963, two more black students, Vivian Malone and James Hood, had won a federal court order to bring about the desegregation of the university. Handed down on May 21, the ruling threatened to bring another collision between the state and federal government, with echoes of the Battle of Ole Miss.[1]

Governor George C. Wallace had staked his reputation on maintaining the university's reputation as a citadel of segregation. Taking his oath of office in January, on the very spot where Jefferson Davis had been inaugurated, Wallace had sounded the battle cry: "Segregation now . . . segregation tomorrow . . . segregation forever." Appearing on *Meet the Press* on June 2, Wallace renewed his pledge to defy the federal court order. "I shall stand at the door as I stated in my campaign for Governor," he said, but added, "The confrontation will be handled peacefully and without violence." But Wallace had a volatile personality, and it was difficult to take him at his word.[2]

The administration had learned from its mistakes at Ole Miss and was much better prepared this time around. Robert Kennedy had traveled to Montgomery in late April so he could directly inform George Wallace of the federal government's determination to uphold the law, and to secure the entry of Malone and Hood. "I just don't want it to get in the streets," said the attorney general. "I don't want to have another Oxford, Mississippi. That is all I ask," Kennedy told Wallace.[3]

For weeks, Deputy Attorney General Nicholas Katzenbach had also been working full-time on the crisis. A battle-hardened veteran of the Ole Miss riot, Katzenbach had conducted his own postmortem into the events of the previous September and was determined not to repeat the same missteps. Above all, Katzenbach had urged the president to adopt an uncompromising stance, the central failure in dealings with Ross Barnett. "Under the circumstances if we move too quickly with too much force we will be subject to criticism," Katzenbach noted on May 31. "If we fail to do so we run a greater risk of genuine resistance and mob violence."[4]

Throughout the spring, Burke Marshall had conducted a series of discreet discussions with local publishers, newspaper editors, ministers, businessmen, and community leaders in an attempt to isolate the governor. It was part of an impressively coordinated lobbying effort that also involved cabinet members, who were handed an "Alabama Notebook" listing 375 of the state's leading corporate executives. The cabinet officials were asked to contact them one by one. Air Force reconnaissance planes had even taken aerial photographs to provide the kind of critical intelligence that had been unavailable at Ole Miss. Katzenbach had also managed to procure a set of keys to the dormitories where he wanted Malone and Hood to stay after they arrived on campus.[5]

On June 4, Justice Department lawyers secured a federal injunction against Wallace. It allowed him to appear on campus on June 11 so he could mount a one-man protest but prevented him from interfering with Malone and Hood or blocking their entry. The order had a chastening effect. Though Wallace continued to spout defiance publicly, in private he admitted to being frightened of imprisonment. The governor passed word to the Kennedy brothers through Senator Lister Hill of Alabama that there would be no violence on campus and certainly no rerun of the Battle of Ole Miss. He wanted a phony confrontation rather than a real one. To that end, on June 8 Wallace put in place strict security measures on the borders of the Tuscaloosa campus, and brought in 825 state troopers to keep troublemakers at bay.[6]

By Monday, June 10, Katzenbach was installed at his makeshift command post in the Army Reserve Building about half a mile from campus. He had choreographed the entire showdown. Soldiers based close to Tuscaloosa had even rehearsed a possible maneuver, whereby the diminutive Wallace would be grabbed by the wrists and one arm, then gently shunted to one side if he stood in the schoolhouse door. The president, though mildly amused, had deep misgivings about placing "federal hands" on Wallace. He feared that even a gentle display of force could be interpreted as an act of aggression. "Try to walk round him," Kennedy told Katzenbach via speakerphone during a meeting with his civil rights team that Monday afternoon.[7]

Before the discussion came to an end, Sorensen raised the question of the broader impact of the showdown and suggested the president consider a nationwide television address, similar to his Ole Miss speech. At first, the president demurred. But Bobby Kennedy was strongly in favor. He thought it "would be helpful," even if the confrontation passed off peaceably. "I think there is reason to do it, I think you don't have to talk about the legislation, but talk about employment and talk about education. I don't think you can get by without it."

"Well I suppose I could do it," said the president, slowly warming to the idea.

Fearing its impact on southern lawmakers, Lawrence O'Brien was fiercely opposed. So before making a final decision the president decided to see how events in Alabama unfolded.[8]

Robert Kennedy arrived for work early the next morning, Tuesday, June 11, accompanied by three of his young children, who played at his feet as he poured over four maps of the Tuscaloosa campus. Shortly after 10:15 A.M., Wallace emerged from his Tuscaloosa hotel, to the applause of the supporters who lined the sidewalk. He then set off for the Foster Auditorium, a basketball arena with a classical façade that Wallace considered the perfect backdrop for the showdown. The stage directions were in place—workmen had painted a blue semicircle on the concrete pathway to indicate precisely where Katzenbach and the black students should stand. The governor himself planned to remain directly in front of the entrance, behind a wooden lectern borrowed from a nearby classroom.

After a sleepless night, Katzenbach set off in a heavily armored convoy from Birmingham, where Hood and Malone had been billeted. About twenty miles east of Tuscaloosa, he received a radio message from Washington that Robert Kennedy wanted to speak. With his radio phone malfunctioning, Katzenbach stopped at a pay phone and called the Justice Department. "What are you gonna say to the Governor?" Kennedy inquired.

"Oh, I don't know exactly," Katzenbach replied.

"Well, the President says it's important to make him look silly," Kennedy deadpanned.[9]

Shortly after 10:45 A.M., the convoy drew to a halt outside the Foster Auditorium. Wallace was already positioned behind his lectern, with an unwieldy television microphone draped from his neck. There were also 150 state troopers on hand, with an even bigger number of journalists, photographers, and cameramen. Unlike Oxford, there was no baying mob, and no prospect of violence. Leaving Malone and Hood in the car for the time being, Katzenbach strode purposely toward the lectern. He ignored both the blue lines painted on the concrete floor and Wallace's order to "Stop." With a presidential proclamation stuffed into his suit pocket, Katzenbach came to a halt just three yards short. In response, the five-foot-seven-inch governor placed his arms behind his back, puffed out his bantam-weight chest, and thrust his jaw into the air.

Six feet two inches tall, Katzenbach towered over Wallace but nonetheless looked awkward. The temperature had already reached ninety-five degrees, and sweat poured from his body and soaked through his suit. Not quite knowing what to do with his hands, he folded them in front of him and then leaned uncomfortably towards the governor, with most of his weight on one foot. His knees were visibly shaking. Katzenbach began by asking Wallace to step aside. "No," said Wallace firmly, before launching into his prepared speech that droned on for a full seven minutes. Katzenbach listened carefully.

"I take it from the statement that you are going to stand in the door and that you are not going to carry out the orders of the court," said Katzenbach.

"I stand according to my statement," snapped Wallace.

Katzenbach returned to the car, and then escorted Vivian Malone to a dormitory on campus. Wallace went back into the Foster Auditorium and awaited the federal government's next move.[10]

At 1:34 P.M., Kennedy signed the necessary papers federalizing the Alabama National Guard, which brought local troops under presidential control. Within four hours, Wallace passed word through the Alabama National Guard to the Pentagon that he would be prepared to end his protest if he was allowed to take part in one last standoff and make one last speech. Since there was no sign of any disorder on campus, and no danger of a repeat of the Battle of Ole Miss, Robert Kennedy agreed.[11]

The sham confrontation quickly unfolded. Shortly after three o'clock, three troop carriers rumbled onto campus, disgorging 100 rifle-carrying Alabama National Guardsmen, who formed up on the grass verges surrounding the Foster Auditorium. Fifteen minutes later, General Henry Graham, who had accompanied the freedom riders out of Montgomery, pulled up in a green command car. Graham briefly conferred with Katzenbach and then strode purposefully toward the entrance. Five feet from Wallace, Graham drew to a halt and saluted. Wallace, who seemed slightly taken aback by the general's formality, shot a desultory salute back. "It is my sad duty to ask you to step aside, on order of the President of the United States," said the general, who had the Confederate flag of the 31st Dixie division stitched onto his breast pocket. After reading a brief statement bemoaning "the trend toward military dictatorship in this country," Wallace did just that. His resistance had crumbled within the space of five hours. There was now no state in the union without an integrated university.[12]

The Tuscaloosa showdown demonstrated the value of the administration's conviction and careful planning. Unlike Ole Miss, where the president and his brother had shown almost continual flexibility, this time they were firm with Wallace, as the decision to seek a federal injunction against him aptly demonstrated. The early decision to federalize the Alabama National Guard was also important. Again, it signaled firm resolve. In contrast to Mississippi, where Barnett and his henchman found it easy to defy a small group of poorly armed U.S marshals, the administration confronted Wallace with a formidable display of force within hours, not weeks, of mounting his protest. That night, Katzenbach and Edwin Guthman, the attorney general's press spokesperson, returned to their hotel and celebrated with a stiff drink. They had made the governor look ridiculous. More importantly, they handled the showdown in a manner that avoided any violence on campus and averted any need for the insertion of federal troops.

∽

All day, the president had toyed with the idea of delivering a televised address. But with the crisis averted, O'Brien, O'Donnell, and Sorensen now considered it unnecessary. After watching the television replay of "the showdown in Tuscaloosa," Kennedy decided to disregard his aides' advice and personally contacted executives at the three television networks to request airtime at eight o'clock that very evening. He did not explain his reasoning. Perhaps he felt emboldened by the fact that his administration had finally *managed* a crisis rather than merely reacted to it. Perhaps he was so worried by the angry mood of black protesters that he had come to believe presidential leadership, asserted in the form of a high-profile nationwide address, offered the only hope of restoring calm. "The situation was rapidly reaching a boil," Sorensen later reflected, "which the President felt the federal government should not permit if it was to lead and not be swamped." Perhaps he wanted to prove his critics wrong—that morning, King had been quoted in the *New York Times* accusing Kennedy of timid leadership. Kennedy himself had told Commerce Secretary Luther Hodges in June: "There comes a time when a man has to take a stand and history will record that he has to meet these tough situations and ultimately make a decision."[13]

Only a month earlier, Kennedy had told the ADA representatives that he had no faith in his own power to convince the nation on national television of the injustice of segregation. But for whatever reason, he had now changed his mind. Notably, he made the decision under no duress—the immediate crisis had been averted. In the wake of the administration's coordinated management of the Tuscaloosa standoff, Kennedy had clearly realized that he could take a more proactive role in shaping public opinion. He would offer something more than a response to a racial crisis—this time, he would offer moral leadership and appeal to the conscience of white America.

The task of writing the speech fell to Sorensen, who was still basking in the success of the so-called Peace Speech, the president's foreign policy address at American University the day before. Sorensen now had just six hours to finalize the script for what was arguably the most important speech of the Kennedy presidency. Soon, Marshall and Robert Kennedy joined Sorensen in the Cabinet Room to work up a draft. At the request of Robert Kennedy, Louis Martin helped, too. It was an indication that the address was targeted at blacks, unlike the Ole Miss speech, which was written with the sensibilities of a southern white audience in mind.[14]

With only minutes to go before airtime, the speech was a muddle—a jumble of typed pages, with almost indecipherable handwritten notes scribbled in the margins and between the lines. Evelyn Lincoln, the president's secretary, had no time to type out a clean draft. And given the impossibly tight deadline, Sorensen and his writing team had not even decided what the president should say in conclusion. As airtime approached, Kennedy thought he might "have to go off the cuff." With only six minutes to go, the president left the chaos of the Cabinet Room and walked into the Oval Office. As technicians made the final adjustments, he asked for the camera to be brought closer to his desk and a pillow was placed on his office chair to improve his posture. Recognizing the historic import of his speech, Kennedy was edgy, and nervously shuffled the pages of his speech between his fingers. It was almost eight o'clock. Kennedy inched forward in his seat and launched into his speech.[15]

"Good evening, my fellow Americans. This afternoon, following a series of threats and defiant statements, the presence of Alabama National Guardsmen was required on the University of Alabama to carry out the final and unequivocal order of the United States District Court of the Northern District of Alabama. That order called for the admission of two clearly qualified young Alabama residents who happen to have been born Negro." The events in Tuscaloosa and other related incidents, he continued, should make every American, regardless of whether they lived in the North or South, "stop and examine his conscience" and recall the majestic first principle of the Declaration of Independence "that all men are created equal, and that the rights of every man are diminished when the rights of one are threatened." Not only were those words rooted in history, he said, but of immense modern-day import, especially in the context of the ongoing Cold War. "Today we are committed to a worldwide struggle to promote and protect the rights of all who wish to be free. And when Americans are sent to Vietnam or West Berlin, we do not ask for whites only." Echoing language which he had used to such devastating effect during the 1960 campaign to address the Catholic question, Kennedy went on: If blacks were expected to fight for their country, then they should be able to attend any university, to receive equal treatment in hotels, restaurants, and movie theaters, and "to vote in a free election without interference or fear of reprisal." Then came a simple statement of moral principle: "It ought to be possible, in short, for every American to enjoy the privileges of being American without regard to his race or his color. In short, every American ought to have the right to be treated as he would wish to be treated, as one would wish his children to be treated but this is not the case."

"We are confronted with primarily a moral issue," he went on. "It is as old as the scriptures and it is as clear as the American Constitution. The heart of the question is whether all Americans are to be afforded equal rights and equal opportunities, whether we are going to treat our fellow Americans as we want to be treated."

Then, using stark language, Kennedy tried to convey both the scale and intensity of the racial crisis. "The fires of frustration and discord are burning in every city, North and South, where legal remedies are not at hand. Redress is sought in the streets, in demonstrations, parades, and protests which create tensions and threaten violence and threaten lives." It would be impossible to solve the crisis by "repressive police action" or "token moves." New legislation was essential. "A great change is at hand, and our task, our obligation, is to make that revolution, that change, peaceful and constructive for all. Those who do nothing are inviting shame as well as violence." His legislative proposals would give blacks the right to be served in hotels, restaurants, theaters, stores, and other establishments; enable the federal government to "participate more fully" in lawsuits integrating public schools; and offer greater protections for blacks seeking to vote.

For the remaining four minutes of the speech, the president looked up from his script and spoke extemporaneously. He echoed phrases used during the 1960 campaign, the February civil rights message, and his Honolulu address. Shorn of Sorensen's eloquence, Kennedy was at times rambling and repetitive. But he spoke with rare passion. "We have a right to expect that the Negro community will be responsible, will uphold the law, but they have the right to expect that the law will be fair, that the Constitution will be color blind, as Justice Harlan said at the turn of the century. This is what we are talking about and this is a matter which concerns this country and what it stands for, and in meeting it I ask for the support of all our citizens. Thank you very much."[16]

The speech was the most courageous of Kennedy's presidency. After two years of equivocation on the subject of civil rights, Kennedy had finally sought to mobilize that vast body of Americans, who had long considered segregation immoral, and who were certainly unprepared to countenance the most extreme forms of discrimination. By speaking to the issues in such a forceful manner—something he had never attempted before—he tried, however belatedly, to mold public opinion and to mobilize the pro–civil rights majority behind his bill.

The speech met with broad acclaim. Watching in Atlanta, Martin Luther King, Jr. thought it "one of the most eloquent, profound and unequivocal pleas for justice and freedom by any President." Jackie Robinson was almost stupefied and called it the most forthright presidential statement in history and one of the "finest declarations ever issued in the cause of human rights." If the election were held tomorrow, said Robinson, he would have no hesitation in voting "Kennedy." In a congratulatory telegram to the White House, Wilkins called it "a clear, resolute exposition of basic Americanism."[17]

Members of the Southern Caucus reacted fiercely. Russell said he was "shocked" and claimed that the proposals to outlaw discrimination in public accommodations amounted to a step toward communism. He was angry, too, at the president's warning that the failure to enact legislation could foment violence in black communities, calling it a "threat" that would only frighten "a few weak-kneed people." It was the Georgian's most vitriolic attack on the president to date, which revealed the newfound fear within southern ranks. A president long considered weak and ineffectual now posed a genuine threat.[18]

Not long after midnight, Medgar Evers pulled his station wagon into the driveway of his home in the black section of Jackson, Mississippi. Evers, a veteran of the D-Day landings and one of James Meredith's key confidants before the Battle of Ole Miss, was the NAACP's only full-time organizer in the state. Rather than staying with his family to watch the president's speech, Evers had spent the evening plotting further demonstrations. He arrived home with a bundle of white T-shirts emblazoned with the slogan "Jim Crow Must Go," which he planned to distribute the following morning.

Crouched in honeysuckle bushes 150 feet away, a fertilizer salesman named Byron De La Beckwith gripped a 30.06 bolt-action Winchester in his hands. Beckwith watched through the crosshairs of his Golden Hawk telescopic sight, as Evers locked the car door and walked toward the door of his house. Then he pulled the trigger. The steel-cased bullet entered Evers's back, passed between his ribs, exited through his sternum, and then pierced a window and wall before finally coming to a rest beneath a watermelon on the kitchen counter.[19]

Evers's wife, Myrlie, had spent part of the evening watching the president's televised address. Hearing the crack of gunfire, she shouted to her three small children to lie on the floor and then ran outside. She found her husband lying on the doorstep in a pool of blood. Evers was pronounced dead within the hour. The assassination was not linked to the president's speech, but it nonetheless provided a tragic and violent coda.

By three A.M., news of Evers's murder had reached the White House. Aides decided against waking the president. Kennedy was informed at breakfast and instructed Hatcher to tell reporters he was "appalled by the barbarity of this act." In the days afterwards, he told Arthur Schlesinger how the murder had once again challenged his long-held views on Reconstruction. "I don't understand the South," he admitted. "I'm coming to believe that Thaddeus Stevens was right. I had always been taught to regard him as a man of vicious bias. But when I see this sort of thing, I begin to wonder how else you can treat them."[20]

Kennedy became even more enraged later that afternoon when House Majority leader Carl Albert contacted him with news that southern Democrats had exacted revenge for his speech the night before by defeating a routine funding bill for the Area Redevelopment Administration. The agency had been set up in 1961 with a lopsided majority of 251–167. Kennedy was disconsolate. "Oh, no, well, you know Christ," he spluttered, "Christ, you know, it's like they shoot this guy in Mississippi, and they shoot somebody, uh, I mean it's just in everything. I mean, this has become everything."

"It's overwhelming the whole, the whole program," Albert replied. "I couldn't do a damn thing with them, you know."

"Civil rights did it," the president said heavily.[21]

Sometime that day, Kennedy composed a condolence letter to Myrlie Evers. "Although comforting thoughts are difficult at a time like this," he wrote, "surely there can be some solace in the realization of the justice of the cause for which your husband gave his life." After signing the typed letter, he added in handwriting at the bottom: "Mrs. Kennedy joins me in extending her deepest sympathy."[22]

Partly in reaction to Evers's murder, there were further demonstrations that week in thirty-nine separate cities, some of which escalated into violence. In Harlem, blacks fought street battles with police. Oxford, North Carolina, witnessed two consecutive nights of "rock and knife fights" between black and white youths. The escalation of violence prompted G. Mennen "Soapy" Williams, the assistant secretary of state, to issue the direst of warnings on June 15. "We still have a situation of crisis proportions," he cautioned the president. "The grass roots of the Negro population is clearly aroused. . . . Unless there is a satisfaction of legitimate Negro aspirations the situation will be fraught with danger." The time for appeasing southern Democrats was over, he warned. "At this time of crisis, the President should be guided not by what appears to be the common denominator of the Congress," he went on, "but by what the President knows the country needs and must have. . . . Temporizing will only lose the confidence and support of the responsible Negro and give the extremists on both sides a chance to seize the initiative." In a memorandum to Sorensen, Williams struck an even more desperate tone, noting "there is the possibility that the inter-action of fervent demonstration and brutal repression would reach such a pitch that public peace and safety would be endangered beyond reasonable control."[23]

There were warnings, too, that violence might soon erupt in the nation's capital, where Evers's body was due to be buried later that week. "The Washington situation is more critical than generally realized," Dr. Franklin Jackson, the president of the Washington NAACP, wrote in a telegram to the White House.

Franklin added that there was an "imminent danger" that protests marking Evers's death could "easily develop into another Birmingham." Tensions increased in the capital. On Friday, June 14, two days after the Evers assassination, some 2,500 angry protesters besieged the Justice Department on Pennsylvania Avenue, carrying a variety of homemade signs: "Let Negroes Work in the Justice Department" and "Why an Almost Lily White Justice Department? It's Not Easter." After twenty minutes, Robert Kennedy decided to address the crowd, standing on a makeshift wooden platform with bullhorn in hand. "There is no discrimination here at Justice," he bellowed, to boos from his audience. "Any individual can come in here and get a job if he is qualified." When a heckler pointed out how few blacks had entered and left the Justice Department during the course of the protest, Kennedy lost his cool. "Individuals will be hired according to their ability, not their color," he barked, an admonition met by loud jeers.[24]

Robert Kennedy's performance neatly distilled so many aspects of his character and his ideology on the subject of civil rights. He was pugnacious—even brave—in confronting the protesters. He stood firm in his commitment to increasing black employment. But he was prickly and defensive when faced with criticisms of the administration's record and frustrated by what he considered the naïveté of black protesters. RFK was capable of enormous warmth and great empathy. But the crowd on Pennsylvania Avenue had seen the uncompromising aspect of his character that Jerome Smith had witnessed in New York.

The mood was even angrier in Jackson, Evers's hometown. On Tuesday, June 18, in temperatures nudging over 100 degrees, 3,000 mourners marched behind Evers's hearse, with Roy Wilkins, Martin Luther King, and Ralph Bunche at the head of the procession. But almost as soon as the funeral liturgy finished, frustrations boiled over, as 500 enraged black youths pelted police with stones and rocks and shouted, "Where's the killer? We want the killer!" Just as the local police started to bring in dogs and order up fire hoses, Justice Department official John Doar charged into the center of the mob and pleaded for order. "Medgar Evers would not have wanted it this way," he shouted, asking the black rioters to take his hand and retreat. "Rocks and bottles won't solve anything." After he and several black leaders repeated their appeals, the mob finally dispersed.[25]

On Wednesday, June 19, in a burial attended by some 2,000 mourners, Evers's body was laid to rest with full military honors at Arlington National Cemetery. Local police were placed on heightened alert, but fears the event would be marred by unruly demonstrations proved groundless. For security reasons, the president decided against attending the burial in person and asked his brother to represent him. After the ceremony, Kennedy had Myrlie Evers and her two eldest children brought back to the White House in a government limousine. As the family waited in the Cabinet Room, Evelyn Lincoln told them a West Wing fable of how, if you sat in the president's chair and made a wish, it would one day come true. Evers's son, Darrell prayed his father had not died in vain. A short while later, they were ushered into the Oval Office, where Kennedy offered words of comfort, handed them PT109 tie-clasps and bracelets, and then posed for a photograph.[26]

Kennedy's gestures demonstrated his growing empathy for the civil rights movement. It was the first time he had invited a victim of racist violence to the White House. And the simple fact that he had allowed a White House photographer to record the event showed that he was happy now to publicly display his concern. Robert Kennedy offered practical assistance. He gave his personal telephone numbers to Charles Evers, Medgar's brother, and told him to get in contact at any time of the day or night.[27]

☙

The mood of the country was fractious and uncertain, and Kennedy needed desperately to arrest its slide toward disorder. On June 19, the 880th day of his presidency and a week after Evers's murder, the president sent up his civil rights message to Congress. It restated the risks of inaction. "Last week I addressed to the American people an appeal to conscience," it began. "In the days that have followed, the predictions of increased violence have been tragically borne out. The 'fires of frustration and discord' have been hotter than ever." The bill included measures boosting voting rights in federal elections through the appointment of government referees and the abolition of literacy tests. It prohibited discrimination in places of public accommodations, including hotels, restaurants, places of amusement, and retail establishments. It allowed the attorney general to initiate school desegregation suits—in cases where black citizens filed written complaints to prove that they could not bring cases on their own—though it stopped short of the universal Part III powers sought by black leaders. It called for the establishment of a Community Relations Service to assist individuals and communities in racial disputes, and relieve the burden on the Justice Department. It extended the CRC for a further four years, granted statutory authority to the PCEEO, and prevented discrimination in federally assisted programs. The main omission was any commitment to create a statutory Fair Employment Practices Committee, a central demand of liberal Democrats. The White House knew its inclusion would alienate Republicans and therefore jeopardize the entire bill. By way of compromise, Kennedy endorsed a FEPC measure already pending before the Senate. On June 19, Majority Leader Mike Mansfield introduced the bill onto the floor, and then joined Minority Leader Everett Dirksen in sponsoring a bipartisan measure identical in every aspect, with the exception of the public accommodations title.[28]

Even now, the president harbored doubts. "Do you think we did the right thing in sending the legislation up?" he asked his brother, momentarily worried again about the potential political costs of introducing such a far-reaching bill. "Look at the trouble it has got us into," the president added. Robert Kennedy offered reassurance and told him it was a problem that "really had to be faced up to." RFK was forced to prop his brother up repeatedly over the coming weeks— he later recalled that the president would ask the same question every four or so days. Robert Kennedy was a man of much firmer conviction and sterner resolve than his brother. He was far less plagued by ambivalence and prepared to make braver judgments.[29]

The response of the Southern Caucus to the new proposals was predictably vociferous. Eastland described the bill as a "complete blueprint for the totalitarian state" and claimed it would make the attorney general "as great a czar as the world has ever known." Mississippi Senator John Stennis warned that "Bobby Kennedy could ultimately have federal marshals at every crossroads" and could "become the private attorney of every member of the NAACP." Congressman Carl Vinson of Georgia complained the measures destroyed "the last vestige" of states rights. Richard Russell called them "a threatened crime against the whole philosophy of liberty."[30]

Russell eschewed calls for a campaign of "massive resistance," however, fearing it would harden public opinion against segregationists. He planned instead to fight a campaign of attrition in Congress in hopes that Kennedy's enthusiasm for the bill would dwindle over time, especially with the presidential campaign looming the following year. Even so, Russell looked with great foreboding at the legislative battle ahead. "It is next to impossible to realize the extent to which feeling against the South on the racial issue has been generated throughout the country," he had told a constituent in May. While they could "slow down" the civil rights bill, he told another, they "could not stop legislation." "As you know, we have lost some of our Southern group," he noted in the early summer, reflecting on how the Southern Caucus had dwindled from twenty-two members to eighteen since the end of the 1950s, "and some of those who remaind [sic] are rather lukewarm in their opposition."[31]

The Kennedy administration had anticipated the response from the Southern bloc; they were surprised, however, that the revised bill also failed to mollify civil rights activists. On June 24, five days after the civil rights bill arrived on Capitol Hill, King complained Kennedy had not provided the leadership "that the enormity of the problem demands," adding, "I think both [the Kennedy brothers] are men of genuine goodwill, but I think they just understand more about the depths and dimensions of the problem, and I think there is a necessity now to see the urgency of the moment." Four weeks later, on July 28, King put his name to a joint statement from the leaders of the Big Six civil rights groups, complaining that the administration's proposals were "not enough." Black leaders wanted stronger Part III powers for the attorney general, partly so the federal government could instigate a greater number of school integration suits, and partly so the Justice Department could offer greater physical protection to civil rights protesters. Protection from police brutality and segregationist violence had by now become one of the movement's foremost demands. It was also an area where protesters believed that the federal government had been derelict.[32]

In his written message to Congress, Kennedy had asked for civil rights leaders to "do their utmost to lessen tensions and to exercise restraint." But black leaders rejected this thinly veiled call for a truce in antisegregation demonstrations. "We do not intend to call off demonstrations," announced James Farmer, "and we would not if we could." The following week, more than 100,000 activists participated in thirty large-scale demonstrations across nineteen different states. In Savannah, where blacks were demanding the complete desegregation of motels, restaurants, and lunch counters, a SNCC activist predicted that "the dark cloud of the tornado is about to descend." Even Richard Russell was afraid—in a telegram to Governor Carl Sanders he warned that if demonstrations were to continue unchecked "we will have a situation of anarchy in some Georgia cities."[33]

The NAACP annual convention held in Chicago from July 1 to July 6 provided stark evidence of the angry mood of the black activists. On July 2, delegates adopted a resolution calling the administration's proposals "inadequate to meet the minimum demands of the existing situation." Wilkins urged delegates to "accelerate, accelerate, accelerate" the civil rights struggle. The Reverend J. H. Jackson, the "Negro Pope," was chased off the stage when he signaled his opposition to plans for the March on Washington. Even James Meredith received a hostile reception after delivering a speech attacking the indiscipline of black youth leaders.[34]

At the CORE convention in Dayton, Ohio, held June 27–30, activists belittled the White House bill, bemoaning its failure to tackle police brutality and the problem of Kennedy's racist judicial appointees. The organization adopted a resolution on June 30 that criticized the administration for failing to appreciate "the immediacy of the impending retaliation and mass violence on the part of the Negro community . . . as evidenced by the fact that Negroes are increasingly arming themselves for the purpose of self-defense against continued oppression and violence." CORE also decided to withdraw support from biracial commissions, which it derided as "meaningless." Northern members pledged to expand their direct-action campaigns to protest slum housing conditions in urban ghettoes, while southern delegates warned black volunteers were arriving for mass meetings and demonstrations armed with knives and revolvers.[35]

The civil rights movement had been completely transformed over the course of only a few weeks. Prior to Birmingham, black protesters tried to project an air of respectability by wearing suits and ties, and neat dresses; by midsummer jeans and T-shirts had become the uniform of the street. Once orderly picket lines, where smoking and talking was often banned, became raucous affairs, with singing, clapping, and chanting. Many direct-action campaigns now involved civil disobedience—protesters forced themselves under the wheels of police cars, chained themselves to buildings, and resisted arrest by falling to the floor rather than willingly being taken into custody. Protests were bigger and activists' demands were growing broader by the day. Civil rights groups targeted discriminatory housing, racist employment practices, inequitable housing policies, de facto school segregation in the North, and discrimination by banks. Radicalism was becoming increasingly seductive. Reflecting on the sudden rise in membership and the addition of twenty-six new affiliate chapters, Farmer noted how new recruits were attracted "by CORE's militancy rather than its non-violent philosophy."[36]

Black leaders became more aggressive, partly because they did not wish to be supplanted by more youthful firebrands. Now they not only called for racial justice but demanded special treatment to bring it about. Addressing the annual conference of the National Urban League, Whitney Young, the most corporate-friendly black leader, argued that blacks should receive preferential treatment and special privileges for a limited period of time in order to help them catch up with whites. Young also raised the idea of a "compensatory effort" to overcome "the heavy aftermath of past neglect." Soon there was talk within the National Urban League of granting reparations to the ancestors of former slaves, and of a Marshall Plan for black Americans. At the beginning of July, CORE passed a resolution demanding compensation and preferential treatment. The idea of meeting strict racial quotas also started take hold. In Hollywood, the NAACP planned fresh demonstrations against the movie industry and insisted on a quota of at least one black employee in every film and television production. When the president of the NAACP Hollywood–Beverly Hills chapter suggested that was unreasonable, he was unceremoniously removed by the organization's more zealous members. In Harlem, community leaders demanded that blacks make up a quarter of the workforce on all jobs performed for the city by private contractors.[37]

The president had not yet been confronted in person by this militant mood. He had shied away from meeting King, Wilkins, or any other black protest leader in the immediate aftermath of the Birmingham crisis. Finally, on June 22, seven weeks into the crisis, he convened thirty of the country's black leaders for the first summit concentrating exclusively on domestic civil rights of his entire presidency. Three specific issues were uppermost in Kennedy's mind: the passage of his civil rights proposals; the March on Washington planned for late August; and the strong possibility that the civil rights movement had been infiltrated by communists.

The Kennedy brothers were particularly worried about charges that communists had hijacked the civil rights movement. It was an allegation southern lawmakers could easily exploit as they began to mobilize against the civil rights bill. James Eastland, the chairman of the Internal Security Subcommittee, had close connections with J. Edgar Hoover, who had long believed that the civil rights movement was a communist front and that King was being manipulated by the KGB. The administration's concerns centered on two of King's close allies: Stanley Levison, a bespectacled New York lawyer who had first befriended King during the Montgomery bus boycott, whom J. Edgar Hoover suspected of being a Soviet spy; and Jack O'Dell, a high-ranking member of the SCLC and one-time member of the Communist Party. Ever since late 1961, Robert Kennedy and Burke Marshall had tried unsuccessfully to persuade King to sever his ties with the two men. Then, in February 1962, the attorney general authorized wiretaps on Levison's New York office after being told by Hoover that he was a member of the Communist Party and "allegedly a close advisor" to King. Just over a year later, in March 1963, Hoover was handed incontrovertible evidence from a FBI informer showing Levison had cut off completely his ties with the Communist Party. Hoover failed to disclose this vital detail to either Robert Kennedy or his brother, however. He wanted the Kennedy brothers to continue believing that King was being influenced by a Soviet spy so that he could step up his surveillance of the civil rights movement.[38]

Now the president decided to confront King himself. Before his meeting on June 22, Kennedy personally urged King to sever ties with Levison and O'Dell. The public disclosure of the two men's communist links, he argued, would have a destructive impact on the civil rights bill. Kennedy ushered King into the Rose Garden, and spoke in a conspiratorial tone. Somewhat taken aback, King thought that Hoover might even have planted listening devices in the Oval Office. Kennedy did not mince his words. "I assume you know that you're under very close surveillance," he said, adding that the FBI had incontrovertible evidence incriminating Levison and O'Dell. "Get rid of them," he said. "They're communists."

King demanded evidence to prove their guilt. But the president claimed the information was "too classified." He did, however, reveal that O'Dell was being handled by Levison, who he claimed was the fifth most senior communist operating in the United States. "You've read about Profumo in the papers?" Kennedy added, a reference to the recent Westminster scandal in which John Profumo, the British Secretary for War, had admitted to having an affair with Christine Keeler, a high-class prostitute who was also known to be sleeping with a suspected KGB spy. "Macmillan is likely to lose his government because he had been loyal to a friend," Kennedy warned. "You must be careful not to lose your cause for the same reason. . . . If they shoot you down, they'll shoot us down, too. So we're asking you to be careful." After the meeting, King agreed to stop communicating directly with Levison, although he reserved the right to consult him on a casual basis.[39]

Their private conversation complete, Kennedy and King moved back inside, where Wilkins, Randolph, Farmer, Young, and John Lewis, the newly elected chairman of SNCC, were waiting. With his guests seated around the Cabinet table, Kennedy delivered a short preamble. He claimed his support had plummeted since coming out so forcefully in favor of civil rights. Then he pulled a scrap of paper from his coat pocket purportedly showing how his approval ratings had dropped from 60 to 47 percent—though the origin of these polling numbers remain a mystery to this day. "I may lose the next election because of this," Kennedy claimed, "[but] I don't care." The passage of new legislation had become his urgent priority, and this meant defeating the southern filibuster. Initial head counts suggested that fifty senators were firm supporters of the administration's proposals, and twenty-two were vigorously opposed. Thirty-eight wavering moderates would determine the civil rights bill's fate. At one point, Kennedy shocked his audience by commenting, "You may be too hard on Bull Connor. After all, Bull has probably done more for civil rights than anyone else"—a flippant remark that drew sharp intakes of breath, until everyone grasped his deliberate irony.

One of the main purposes of the Oval Office meeting was to try to persuade the black leadership to cancel plans for the March on Washington. Kennedy made his pitch: "We want success in the Congress, not a big show on the Capitol. Some of these people are just looking for an excuse to oppose us. I don't want to give them the chance to say 'Yes, I'm for the bill—but not at the point of a gun.'" At this point, Randolph, whose plans for a similar mass protest in 1941 had spurred action from Franklin Roosevelt, interrupted. "The Negroes are already in the streets," he said. "There will be a march." Others insisted the march should proceed, if only to validate the strategy of nonviolent direct action and give black moderates a much-needed chance to reassert their leadership. The only area of possible compromise, they said, concerned the choice of venue. Under the present plan, protesters intended to gather on Capitol Hill in order to lobby congressmen directly. But that could be changed. At this point, Lyndon Johnson spoke up for the first time. Far from being swayed by a mass demonstration outside Congress, he said, lawmakers would be enraged by one.

King was adamant that some sort of mass protest should take place. "It may seem ill-timed," said King. "Frankly, I have never engaged in a direct-action movement that did not seem ill-timed. Some people thought Birmingham was ill-timed."

"Including the attorney general," joked the president.

Wilkins and Young shared the administration's concerns that the demonstration might be impossible to police, but the other black leaders refused to yield. They argued that even a postponement of the March on Washington would represent a humiliating retreat. The president finally admitted defeat. "Well, we all have our problems," Kennedy sighed. "You have your problems, I have my problems." With that, he brought the meeting to a speedy end, and reemphasized what he hoped was their common goal: that the freedom struggle should remain a peaceful enterprise. Then Kennedy left the South Lawn by helicopter for a brief stopover at Camp David. From there, he left for a four-country visit to Europe, a trip that White House officials hoped would help defuse the present crisis, not the least by shifting the focus of reporters.[40]

∾

By the beginning of August the number of demonstrations showed a small decline. Kennedy believed it was a direct consequence of the introduction of the civil rights bill. The proposals had helped restore faith in government and bolstered the standing of what he called the "responsible Negro leadership." At a press conference on August 1, Kennedy warned against complacency and stressed it would be foolish to "go to sleep and forget the problem." He also urged civil and business leaders to use the "period of quiet" to explore long-term solutions.[41]

Louis Martin thought the president had been wholly mistaken in using the phrase "period of quiet." That week alone there were seventy-nine protests in places as far flung as Gadsden, Alabama, Torrance, California, Athens, Georgia, and Chicago. In a sharply worded memorandum to Robert Kennedy, Martin called for the CRC to convene a series of emergency meetings in racial trouble spots "to put brakes on the extremists." He also complained that the CRC was underutilized. "I also agree that they have not shown the greatest wisdom in some of their operations in the past," he wrote. "Nevertheless, I feel that some of the heat of the current crisis could be deflected their way." Others in the administration also disagreed with the president's optimistic assessment. Burke Marshall was particularly worried by the situation in Cambridge, Maryland, where the governor had reimposed martial law on July 12 and sent 500 National Guardsmen to enforce a ban on demonstrations. "[T]he Negro community does not follow the leadership in terms of non-violence or in demonstrations," he reported in July, and there was "no control at all." Worse still, the situation would very likely deteriorate. "There is a very serious danger of violence, as everyone must admit," he predicted. "If the violence breaks out the violence could be very severe, since everyone also agrees that there are a good many firearm[s] in the possession of both Negroes and whites in this area."[42]

The debate within the administration over whether the racial crisis was subsiding provided the backdrop for one of Robert Kennedy's most controversial decisions as attorney general. At the beginning of August, he came under mounting pressure from lawyers in the Justice Department's Criminal Division to authorize prosecutions against a group of black protesters in Albany, Georgia. The defendants, who included William G. Anderson, the former head of the Albany Movement, were accused of obstruction of justice and perjury after picketing a grocery store back in April. The store was owned by a white juror who had voted to acquit "Gator" Johnson, a notorious local sheriff, who had allegedly shot a black man in his custody at point-blank range on July 4, 1961. Black demonstrators had retaliated against the juror following Johnson's acquittal in April 1963.

The Criminal Division had dispatched over fifty FBI agents to investigate the claims of obstruction of justice, and the local U.S. attorney believed there had been a blatant violation of the law. But lawyers in Burke Marshall's Civil Rights Division considered it unfair to charge black demonstrators for participating in a peaceful picket in a city where segregationist violence commonly went unpunished. Robert Kennedy had enough power to crush the prosecution but decided to back the local U.S. attorney, Wilbur D. Owens, Jr., who had devoted enormous energy into building a case against the Albany protesters.[43]

At a press conference on August 10, Katzenbach announced the prosecution of the black protesters, who were soon dubbed the "Albany Nine." "Peaceful protest demonstrations and picketing are not forbidden or discouraged by Federal law," he announced. "The charges here, however, involve retaliation against a juror for his vote in a Federal case. Such conduct must become a matter of serious Federal concern." The attorney general never publicly explained his motives for letting the case proceed. Robert Owen, a lawyer in the Civil Rights Division, claimed that Robert Kennedy decided the case first and foremost as a lawyer determined to strictly interpret the letter of the law.[44]

But it is hard to disentangle the decision from the politics of the moment. Now that the administration was pushing so strongly for civil rights, the prosecution might have been intended to show white southerners that the administration was not in the thrall of the civil rights movement. (As the *Washington Star* editorialized on August 14, the attorney general had demonstrated that he did not stand "with the Negro against the white man.") The attorney general might have hoped the prosecutions would deter violence at the impending March on Washington by sending a clear message to black activists that they were not above the law.[45]

It is also possible that Robert Kennedy took such an aggressive position on the Albany Nine because the administration was desperate to deflect charges that it was lending support to communist sympathizers within the civil rights movement. But in an effort to destroy the civil rights bill, the Southern bloc was trying ever more desperately to connect the two issues in the mind of the public. On July 12, during congressional hearings before the Senate Commerce Committee on the administration's civil rights bill, Governor Ross Barnett claimed that Martin Luther King stood at the head of a communist conspiracy. As proof, he brandished a photograph taken in 1957 at the Highlander Folk School, a retreat in the East Tennessee Cumberland Mountains that ran workshops for civil rights activists, which Barnett claimed was in fact a "communist training school." Appearing before the committee on July 15, George Wallace repeated the same allegations and held up the same picture.[46]

Just as the Kennedy administration was trying to court moderates within the civil rights movement, the Albany prosecutions risked inflaming its radical fringe. Some of Kennedy's most loyal supporters were outraged. Paul Freund and Mark DeWolfe Howe, Kennedy's legal advisers during the 1957 civil rights battle, believed the prosecutions would undercut black moderates and radicalize black militants. "They must have the sense that the country at large sustains them," they wrote of the SNCC leadership in a letter of complaint to Marshall, "and that the federal government is sympathetic to their efforts."[47]

King was flabbergasted by the announcement. "I was really shocked when I read this," he told Slater King, one of the Albany Nine, who had lost an unborn child after his pregnant wife was beaten to the ground by police in Camilla—a case of police brutality that was never prosecuted by the FBI or the Justice Department. "I just couldn't conceive it. . . . But I do feel they really overstepped their political and moral boundaries." If the attorney general did not drop the case, said King, he would ensure "pressures will come from everywhere." Wiretaps revealed that King thought the administration was making a terrible political mistake and had started laying plans for a "national protest." King also complained to John Doar, "we are not going to take this lying down." Almost immediately, SNCC mounted a round-the-clock protest outside the Justice Department.[48]

The Albany prosecutions also threatened to change the tenor of the March on Washington, scheduled for August 28. SNCC leader John Lewis intended to use his nationwide platform to launch an excoriating attack on the Kennedy administration. In a final draft, punctuated at least eight times with the word "revolution," Lewis decried the administration's civil rights bill as being "too little, too late." He also decided to highlight the Albany Nine indictments. Lewis planned to deliver an incendiary message at the end of his speech: "We won't stop now. All of the forces of Eastland, Barnett, Wallace, and Thurmond, won't stop this revolution. The time will come when we will not confine our marching to Washington. We will march through the South, through the heart of Dixie, the way Sherman did. We shall pursue our own 'scorched earth' policy and burn Jim Crow to the ground—non-violently."[49]

Lewis's rhetoric was so fiery that it threatened to undo much of the meticulous planning that had preceded the March on Washington. Bayard Rustin, the chief planner, had wanted the event to have a strong biracial and ecumenical feel and had invited leading churchmen to take a prominent part. But after reading an advance copy of Lewis's speech, Washington's Catholic Archbishop Patrick O'Boyle, who was due to deliver the opening invocation, threatened to boycott the event. Lewis also came under strong pressure from King, Rustin, and Burke Marshall, who feared the speech could incite violence. Lewis backed down and softened some of the most bellicose language. He even agreed to strike from the speech its most trenchant question: "I want to know: which side is the federal government on?"[50]

On August 28, John Lewis delivered his heavily edited speech before a crowd estimated to be over 200,000 people strong. But it was completely overshadowed not just by King's soaring freedom anthem but by the spirit and carnival trappings of the day. Many of the Kennedy's administration's elaborate security preparations—including the mobilization of so many troops and FBI agents— were entirely superfluous. And rather than mob violence, the protest's most memorable images included a young folk singer named Joan Baez singing "O Freedom Over Me"; of Bob Dylan performing a ballad written to commemorate the life of Medgar Evers—"a pawn in a white man's game"; and of Marlon Brando sauntering onto the stage twirling a four-foot long electric cattle prod, the exact model used by policemen in Mississippi to corral black demonstrators into jail. Russell Baker of the *New York Times* summed up the mood. "Instead of the emotional horde of angry militants that many had feared, what Washington saw was a vast army of quiet, middle-class Americans who had come in the spirit of the church outing."[51]

Afterwards, the president was in buoyant mood when he met the leaders of the march at the White House. "You did a superb job in making your case," he said, ushering the march leaders into the Oval Office. He ordered up sandwiches, milk, and coffee as soon as he discovered they had skipped lunch. According to Wilkins, he was "bubbling over with the success of this event" and obviously relieved that fears of Washington being invaded "by a horde of rowdies and vigilantes" had proved groundless. Kennedy lavished most attention on King, the undoubted star of the afternoon's event. Taken aback by the president's extravagant praise, King tried to deflect some of the glory onto Walter Reuther, who had told the crowd: "We cannot defend freedom in Berlin so long as we deny freedom in Birmingham," a reference to Kennedy's famed "Ich bin ein Berliner" speech delivered only a few weeks before.

"Oh, I've heard him plenty of times," Kennedy replied, offhandedly.[52]

The pleasantries over, Wilkins tried to steer the discussion back toward politics. "I feel it my lot, sir, in this afternoon of superlative oratory, to be the one to deal rather pedantically and pedestrianly with the hard business of legislation." Wilkins demanded changes to the civil rights bill, most notably an even tougher Part III, which would grant the attorney general more sweeping powers to initiate school desegregation cases.

The president wanted to inject a shot of political realism into the conversation. O'Brien provided it by breaking down the intentions of lawmakers on Capitol Hill. In the House alone, the administration would require the support of at least sixty Republicans. And that would not be easy.

Wilkins suspected that the president and O'Brien were colluding in their pessimism as part of an effort to convince black leaders to suspend further demonstrations. Wilkins turned the argument around by explaining that, given the resistance on Capitol Hill to the civil rights bill, Kennedy would have to demonstrate bold presidential leadership to secure its passage. "From the description you have made of the state of affairs in the House and Senate, it is going to take nothing less than a crusade to win approval of the civil rights measures," said Wilkins. "It is going to be a crusade that, I think, nobody but you can lead."[53]

The legislative battle had to be a bipartisan effort, Kennedy replied, rather than a personal struggle. He also claimed that the politics of civil rights had changed over the course of the summer. While he still expected moderate Republicans to support the civil rights bill, he pointed out that the Goldwater wing of the party was trying to "play to the South—with some success." Conservative Republicans had calculated that blacks would support the Democrats, and that their best chance of winning the presidential election in 1964 was to appeal to discontented whites. The message was unmistakable: If the civil rights leadership stepped up their demonstrations, the civil rights bill would be much harder to enact.

The next morning, after finding the upbeat newspaper coverage of the March on Washington much to his liking, Kennedy contacted Rustin and Randolph at their hotel. He did so partly to apologize for having called initially for the cancellation of the protest. Now that the demonstration had passed off so successfully, the mood at the White House was more relaxed. The polls were looking reasonably healthy, as well. Kennedy's approval ratings in the South had taken a predictable hit—dropping from 60 percent in March to 44 percent in September. But his nationwide rating remained steady at 62 percent. More gratifying still, a series of polls taken in August, pitting him against the three most frequently mentioned Republican hopefuls (Governor George Romney of Michigan, Arizona Senator Barry Goldwater, and Rockefeller), suggested he was heading for a comfortable victory. "There is no Republican candidate for the Presidency today who is even within hailing distance of seriously challenging John F. Kennedy in the 1964 elections," concluded a bullish Louis Harris. Since the introduction of the civil rights bill and his televised address to the nation, Kennedy's approval ratings among blacks had skyrocketed. Polls showed that he was likely to receive support from 95 percent of blacks, a huge improvement on 1960.[54]

As the summer faded into fall, there were more indications that, in certain states, southerners were finally coming to terms with the prospect of racial assimilation. At the beginning of September, schools in Tennessee, Louisiana, South Carolina, Texas, Georgia, and Florida quietly complied with federal court rulings ordering their integration. At his weekly press conference on September

12, Kennedy commended the districts where integration had taken place, which he called "really impressive." On the more general question of the racial crisis, he was also upbeat: "this Nation is passing through a very grueling test, and with the exception of a few aberrations, I think we are meeting it."[55]

Some hard-line segregationists remained recalcitrant, however. At the beginning of September, Governor Wallace used Alabama state troopers to prevent the court-ordered integration of nine schools in Birmingham, Tuskegee, Mobile, and Huntsville. The Kennedy administration believed that Wallace was attempting to engineer another showdown, this time more violent than the Tuscaloosa standoff. It was therefore reluctant to forcibly intervene and for the moment left the matter in the hands of the federal courts. On September 8 five federal district court judges ruled against Wallace and placed the enforcement of the court in the hands of the Justice Department. On September 10, the president responded to Wallace's continued defiance by federalizing the Alabama National Guard and by ordering its men to return to their barracks. Later on, twenty black students entered the previously all-white schools. As with the Tuscaloosa standoff, firm and speedy federal action had forced the governor into a humiliating retreat from his posture of massive resistance. As Wallace himself noted, "I can't fight bayonets with my bare hands."[56]

For the president, September 10 was proving to be one of the most satisfying days of a troubled year. Wallace had capitulated, and the administration's tax proposals, which had been stalled since January, passed the House Ways and Means Committee. The administration was still celebrating the success of the March on Washington, which had buttressed support within the movement for moderate leaders such as King and vindicated the strategy of nonviolent protest. The administration and moderate black leadership were working more closely together than at any time since the launch of the Voter Education Project in 1961. They had shared political goals, namely the passage of the civil rights bill, and enjoyed a new mutual understanding. Alas, it would prove to be a fleeting moment of accord.

CHAPTER 25

❧

The "New South"

Youth Day at the Sixteenth Street Baptist Church promised to be a joyous celebration—particularly this year, coming as it did just six days after the desegregation of three Birmingham schools. Standing at the intersection of the black and white communities, the yellow-brick building at the northwest corner of Kelly-Ingram Park had played a vital role in the Birmingham movement. From its sanctuary, many thousands of black protesters had poured onto the streets. From its pulpit, Martin Luther King and Fred Shuttlesworth had given the campaign its spiritual impetus. For local blacks, it had become a landmark of hope; for diehard segregationists, a target of hatred. In preparation for the eleven o'clock service on Sunday, September 15, the local pastor, the Reverend John Cross, had chosen a passage from Matthew chapter 5. "You have heard it said, 'Love your neighbor and hate your enemy.' But I tell you: Love your enemies and pray for those who persecute you."[1]

Early that morning, while the downtown area was shrouded in darkness, four Klansmen drove to the church in a turquoise Chevrolet, flying two Confederate flags on its rear antenna. Robert "Dynamite Bob" Chambliss was the planner and perpetrator of many of the city's fifty-five unsolved bomb attacks. He was accompanied in the car by three colleagues from Klavern 13, the most murderous chapter of the local KKK. Outside the basement entrance at the front of the church, they placed twenty sticks of dynamite. The explosives were connected by a thin strand of wire to a crude timing device fashioned from a fishing float and a bucket full of water with a tiny hole punctured in the bottom. As the water level dropped, the float gradually lowered. It would eventually complete an electrical circuit some eight hours later. Then the explosives would ignite.

By ten o'clock the following morning, the church brimmed with life. In the basement Ladies Lounge, five young girls primped themselves in front of the mirror and adjusted each other's sashes. Young choristers milled around in the corridor before heading to the upstairs sanctuary for the main service. At 10:22 A.M. a thunderous explosion ripped through the church, blasting shards of stained glass into the sanctuary, shredding pews and collapsing rafters. At the northeast entrance, where the bomb detonated, a thirty-inch brick and stone wall caved in on the Ladies Lounge below. After digging away through a foot-and-a-half of masonry and rubble, rescuers discovered the bodies of eleven-year-old Denise McNair, and three fourteen-year-olds, Cynthia Wesley, Carole Robertson, and Addie Mae Collins. The only child to emerge alive from the Ladies Lounge was twelve-year-old Sarah Collins. Her eyes were partially blinded and her body was shredded with twenty-one pieces of glass. As she was pulled from the rubble, Sarah could be heard mumbling the words, "Addie Mae, Addie Mae"—the name of her murdered elder sister.[2]

Soon, a mob of black youths gathered outside, pelting firemen and police with rocks and debris. In the maelstrom of violence that followed, two more black youngsters were killed. Sixteen-year-old Johnny Robinson was shot in the back by a Birmingham police officer, after ignoring an order to halt. Thirteen-year-old Virgil Ware was murdered by two white Eagle Scouts on their way home from a segregationist rally. Only eighteen days earlier, King had looked forward to the day when black children would grow up in a country where they were judged not by the color of their skin but the content of their character.[3]

The bombing sparked national outrage. "How long can such barbaric abuses go on without a mass uprising by men and women who see in the forces of law and order only a shield for their bloodstained oppressors?" asked the editorial writers in the *New York Times*. "This outrageous and disgraceful occurrence is a great tragedy for the whole country as well as Birmingham," said Senator J. William Fulbright, the only southern senator to comment publicly in the immediate aftermath of the bombing. There was an international outcry, as well. "Murder in Church" ran the headline in Britain's *Daily Worker*. "Race Hate Blast Kills Girls in Church" noted the *Daily Mirror* in huge black letters. In Rome, *L'Osservatore Romano* simply noted: "The manner, the place, the victims of the crime, the cynical brutality which cannot be attenuated by any ideological pretext, cry out for condemnation."[4]

There was dismay at the Justice Department, for it seemed that much of the good work of the previous ten weeks had been obliterated. Fearing the worst, Burke Marshall flew immediately to Birmingham, where he discovered guntoting gangs of whites and blacks roaming the streets at will. Marshall wanted to confer with King, who had arrived that evening. But he was told by local police and FBI agents that it was too dangerous for whites to venture into black communities. Eventually, after insisting that the meeting had to take place, Marshall was picked up from the downtown federal building by a group of local blacks wearing Civil Defense uniforms and then bundled into the back of a car.

He was taken to a safe house in "Dynamite Hill," where King was being protected by bodyguards openly brandishing guns.[5]

King immediately demanded the deployment of federal troops to protect the black community. Marshall strongly suspected the president would not sanction a troop deployment, and tried to placate King with assurances that FBI explosive specialists would apprehend the bombers. King was adamant. The very next day, Monday, September 16, King wired the president to warn of the "worst racial holocaust this nation has ever seen" if the federal government failed to intervene forcefully. At a rally in the city, Fred Shuttlesworth made an impassioned plea: "There is a breakdown of law and order in Birmingham and we need Federal troops." Marshall sympathized with King and Shuttlesworth's request. He told Robert Kennedy that the situation in Birmingham was even more precarious than in May. But Robert Kennedy firmly believed that the military occupation of Birmingham would raise tensions even further.[6]

The president responded to the bombing by cutting short his weekend visit to Newport, Rhode Island, and returned to the White House. But he waited until Monday to issue a presidential statement. Rather than deliver the statement personally in the form of a televised address to the nation, he left Salinger to read it to reporters. The statement was severe. The president laid blame squarely on Governor Wallace for inciting the bombers. "It is regrettable that public disparagement of law and order has encouraged violence which has fallen on the innocent," said the president, an unmistakable reference to Wallace's opposition to the integration of Birmingham's schools. The statement announced the return of Burke Marshall and said that FBI bomb specialists were also in the city. Missing from the statement, however, was any commitment to deploy federal troops, the central demand of blacks in the city. Administration officials privately told reporters that the president hoped that the quick arrest of the bombers would soon soothe tensions.[7]

In response to the Birmingham riot in May, Kennedy had stationed troops on the edge of the city, ready to be deployed if trouble flared up again. But this time the president was firmly opposed to sending in the military. Even though a military reconnaissance team arrived in the city in the immediate aftermath of the bombing to lay the groundwork for a deployment, Kennedy hoped that local law enforcement agencies would maintain order. In reaching this decision, the president was influenced by Justice Department lawyer Louis Oberdorfer, a Birmingham native and the first federal official to arrive on the scene. Oberdorfer advised the president that there was no legal basis for federal intervention and suggested that security in the city was best left to the local police and FBI. Fearful that the insertion of federal troops would exacerbate an already tense situation, Oberdorfer strongly urged against bringing in the Pentagon. Alabama Senator John Sparkman also cautioned Kennedy against the use of troops. The president agreed with their analysis, even though there was in fact a clear basis for federal intervention. Title 10, Section 333 of the U.S. Code entitled the president to use the armed forces to "suppress any domestic violence." Indeed, the president had cited Title 10 to justify the deployment of troops to the outskirts of Birmingham in May, and the insertion of U.S. marshals into Montgomery during the freedom rides crisis.[8]

The president's stance was manifestly inconsistent. In his statement on the bombings, Kennedy implied that Alabama officials had incited the bombers. Now he placed the protection of Birmingham's black community in their hands. George Wallace immediately dispatched Colonel Al Lingo, the Alabama public safety director, whose savage tactics during the May riot had made him hated by Birmingham's blacks. A local black commented, "Sending Lingo in here was like spitting in our face."[9]

The death of four young schoolgirls in such an unconscionable act of violence sparked outrage both in the North and South. But on Tuesday evening, when Kennedy delivered a nationwide radio and television address on the nuclear test ban treaty with the Soviet Union and his administration's planned tax cuts, he did not even mention the bombing. He did not attend any of the funerals of the four black schoolgirls. Nor did he proclaim a day of national mourning. The wording of his presidential statement, and its condemnation of Wallace, suggested that Kennedy had been outraged by the bombing. But he did not express himself publicly. Indeed, the president's reserved reaction to the death of the four schoolgirls seemed all the more inexplicable given that he was still mourning the death of his own second son. In early August, Jackie Kennedy had given birth prematurely to a five-pound baby. The infant died just thirty-nine hours after his birth. The president was profoundly affected by Patrick's death and had traveled to Newport on the weekend of the bombing to spend time with Jackie and mark their tenth wedding anniversary together.

Why his reserve? Perhaps he thought that the tough written statement had sufficiently expressed his outrage. After all, he had come close to accusing Wallace of complicity in the bombing. Perhaps he wanted to see how the situation developed. Perhaps he was conscious that on two of the three previous occasions when he addressed the nation on civil rights, he had announced the mobilization of troops—a step that on this occasion he was unprepared to take. He might even have been concerned that a fourth televised address on civil rights might overshadow his planned address to the nation on the test ban treaty and tax cuts.

Kennedy's apparent detachment in the aftermath of the Birmingham bombing suggested that he had not yet fully evolved his thinking about America's racial crisis. Throughout the country, blacks and whites had responded with outrage to the tragedy, but Kennedy seemed unable to muster a similar level of emotion. Over the course of the summer of 1963, Kennedy had come to realize that he could not longer ignore the rage and alienation of black Americans. But his public silence now implied that he still did not fully comprehend what blacks were up against in pockets of fierce segregationist resistance, like Birmingham.

Given the monstrous nature of the crime, many black leaders considered the president's response woefully inadequate. Fred Shuttlesworth was bitterly disappointed at the president's refusal to dispatch troops and on September 16 threatened renewed street protests. That same day, James Farmer called for the president to address the nation, and Roy Wilkins argued for a stronger package of legislative reforms. "Anything less than a strongly reinforced civil rights bill," he wired the president on September 16, would be "a confession that the Federal Government is willing to occupy a spectator role." James Baldwin, who by now had emerged almost as the unofficial spokesman for the country's disillusioned blacks, was much harsher: "It is certainly time to ask why a sovereign people should continue so abjectly to choose between the interchangeable mediocrities with which Washington continually confronts us." On September 15, an FBI wiretap picked up Stanley Levison complaining: "The administration did nothing. . . . This is so barbaric that some real feeling can be aroused to cause the government to do something."[10]

On Thursday, September 19, Kennedy convened a meeting at the White House, to which King, Shuttlesworth, Ralph Abernathy, and other black leaders from Birmingham were invited. King pressed once more for the deployment of troops in Birmingham. "There is a great deal of frustration and despair and confusion in the Negro community," he stressed. "And there is a feeling of being alone and not being protected." Beforehand, the president had been briefed by Robert Kennedy that there was no legal basis for ordering in troops or even a contingent of U.S. marshals. The situation, said the president, was beyond his control. "Now it's tough for the Negro community," he explained. "And I know that this bombing is particularly difficult. But if you look at any, as you know, of these struggles over a period, across the world, it's a very dangerous effort. So everybody just has to keep their nerve."[11]

Kennedy had decided already on an alternative to troops. He planned to dispatch two personal emissaries: Kenneth Royall, a sixty-nine-year-old North Carolinian who had served as secretary of war in the Truman administration, and Earl "Red" Blaik, the legendary West Point football coach (though his preferred candidate was the eighty-year-old retired General Douglas MacArthur). As Kennedy explained to King, they were men of great standing with a strong chance of opening a constructive biracial dialogue. He then asked King to help forestall further violent outbreaks and demonstrations. Kennedy said they could adversely affect the civil rights bill, a reiteration of the same argument he had made to civil rights leaders after the March on Washington. "I can't do very much," said Kennedy, "Congress can't do very much, unless we keep the support of the white community throughout the country. Once that goes, then we're pretty much down to a racial struggle." Afterwards the president issued a second written statement on the bombings, which called for the situation to be handled locally.[12]

The decision to appoint two presidential emissaries rather than send in troops was also met with almost universal black fury; and the choice of Blaik and Royall seemed especially insensitive. During his tenure at West Point, Blaik had maintained all-white football teams. Royall had resisted demands for military integration during the Truman administration. At a New York rally on September 22, Baldwin called for a nationwide campaign of civil disobedience and described the appointment of Blaik and Royall as an "insult to the Negro race." Bayard Rustin urged a nonviolent "uprising" in 100 cities. Farmer, who had just been released from a jail in Plaquemine, Louisiana, accused the Kennedy administration of complicity in the Birmingham bombing because of its policy of "inaction."[13]

Kennedy first spoke out publicly about the bombings on Friday, September 20, when he addressed the 18th General Assembly of the United Nations. He placed the bombing in the context of the global struggle for human rights: "Those rights are not respected when a Buddhist priest is driven from his pagoda, when a synagogue is shut down, when a Protestant church cannot open a mission, when a Cardinal is forced into hiding, or when a crowded church is bombed." They were stirring words, but the decision to deliver them at the United Nations did little to silence his black critics. Throughout the summer, Kennedy had viewed the racial tumult primarily as a domestic crisis rather than a foreign policy concern. That remained the case. But by making his first public remarks about the September bombing at the United Nations before an audience of international diplomats he gave the impression that he regarded them more as a national embarrassment than a national tragedy. A week later, on September 27, King complained that the president had failed to fully recognize the "atmosphere of urgency" and threatened once more to lead demonstrations in Birmingham. The church bombing marked "a turning point in the civil rights movement," he said, "which is becoming a third American revolution."[14]

Black leaders soon started to lay plans for further demonstrations, citing the president's inadequate response to the September church bombing as justification. At an SCLC convention in Richmond in late September, Wyatt Tee Walker spoke of an "all-out war against racism" and called for massive acts of civil disobedience involving shutdowns of major airports and train and bus stations. Wyatt chided Kennedy for his "kid glove treatment of the . . . Barnetts and the Wallaces." From the same platform, King spoke of the need to expand direct action campaigns into northern communities. Jackie Robinson, who had rejoiced in the president's June address, now turned against him. "Mr. President, this nonviolence and calm is not going to last much longer," he warned in early October, "unless the government finds some way, somehow to halt the reign of terror which is threatening the Negro."[15]

The president took a more central role in the crisis on September 23, having invited a delegation of leading Birmingham businessmen to the White House. He had called from the start for a localized settlement, and now he sought to help engineer it. Kennedy presented the Birmingham delegation with a list of demands, which included the recruitment of a greater number of black sales clerks in downtown stores and the token desegregation of the Birmingham police department. "Now isn't it possible to do something?" asked the president. "I'm just trying to think of two or three things that could be done. . . . Is there anything that you can do now?"

At that point, the president turned to Frank Newton, the president of Southern Bell Telephone and Telegraph and one of Birmingham's famed "Big Mule" businessmen. Newton threw the question straight back in Kennedy's face. If administration officials could force "outside agitators" like King to leave the city, said Newton, progress could be made more easily.

"There seems to be a belief on the part of your people," Kennedy responded, "that we can move these people in and out. I am just telling you flatly that we cannot."

Newton shot back. Granting concessions to the Birmingham movement would only encourage them to protest more. "A lot of people . . . think you've been giving those people encouragement," Newton went on.

Kennedy said he did not understand why there was so much resistance in Birmingham to the token integration of the police and the employment of more black sales staff. "We're talking about some things which are rather limited," he said.

But Frank Newton fought back: "I think your public accommodations, your public accommodations goes a lot further than that."

"Public accommodations is nothing!" Kennedy insisted. "Public accommodations is nothing! My God, it's whether you can go into a store or a hotel. They don't go into Statler," the glitzy Washington hotel, where he suspected the delegation of businessmen had probably stayed. "And they won't be coming into the hotel in Birmingham."

Newton demanded once more that the president drive King out of town. But Kennedy explained that King would only be replaced by SNCC activists, whose tactics were more militant. "King has got a . . . terrific investment in non-violence," he pointed out, "and SNCC has got an investment in violence, and that's the struggle."[16]

The president's anger simmered for weeks, and, thereafter, he referred to Newton as "that son-of-a-bitch who sat there." In private, Kennedy had displayed the kind of anger that civil rights leaders dearly wanted him to show in public.[17]

The meeting drew together various strands of the president's thinking: his frustration with the irrational intransigence of southern segregationists; his fear that SNCC could usurp the SCLC; and his prickliness at having his civil rights policies questioned. But it also underlined his continued wariness of federal intrusion in the South. The president's main aim, after all, was to persuade the Birmingham businessmen to reach a voluntary agreement, which would obviate the need for further federal involvement. Afterwards, administration officials steered reporters in that direction. As the *New York Times* noted the following morning: "Kennedy says Birmingham Can Solve Its Own Problems."[18]

Blaik and Royall encountered the same obduracy on their mission, and it ended in failure. They had never been given a clear mandate by the president, and they did not get along with each other personally. When they presented their interim findings at the White House on October 10, Blaik spent most of the time discussing football with the president. But the meeting is perhaps best remembered for mention of a bumper sticker which Blaik and Royall had observed in Birmingham: "Goldwater for President, Kennedy for King." In their interim report, Blaik and Royall concluded that the problems of Birmingham were best rectified by "its own citizens" rather than the federal government, a viewpoint that did not chime with the feelings of black leaders in the city. Blaik and Royall also believed that they had extracted a pledge from civic leaders to employ the city's first black policeman. But the promise was never carried out. (Their final report was due on November 25. But in the aftermath of Kennedy's assassination, Johnson told them it would no longer be required.[19])

∾

Robert Kennedy had been more sure-footed than the president in responding to the Birmingham bombings. As well as dispatching Burke Marshall to Birmingham, the attorney general exerted enormous pressure on J. Edgar Hoover and the FBI to find and arrest the bombers. Hoover assigned 231 agents to the investigation, and by late September, Robert Chambliss, the main ringleader, was under twenty-four-hour surveillance. But the investigation was deliberately sabotaged by Al Lingo. On September 30, Lingo ordered Chambliss's arrest on the lesser charge of the illegal possession of explosives so that the FBI would find it impossible to build up enough evidence to mount a prosecution. Pleading guilty to the charge, Chambliss was fined $100 and sentenced to six months in jail. (It was not until 1977 that Chambliss was found guilty of the church bombing.)[20]

Partly in response to the Birmingham bombings, the Justice Department also started treating the problem of police brutality with much greater seriousness. Burke Marshall's Civil Rights Division had always been reluctant to investigate allegations against southern law enforcement officials accused of victimizing black protesters. There was the practical problem of securing convictions from southern juries, and the political problem of angering southern lawmakers. Neither did Marshall want black protesters to believe that they would receive protection from the federal government if they targeted communities where there was a strong possibility that local law enforcements would respond violently. Three days after the Birmingham bombing, however, Robert Kennedy and Marshall decided to take a firmer line.[21]

On September 18, the Justice Department brought charges in Oxford, Mississippi, against a police chief and sheriff in connection with a vicious assault on Fannie Lou Hamer in June. Hamer, a black activist from Indianola, Mississippi, had been beaten up with leather whips and nightsticks by prison guards in Winona. On September 18, Marshall also considered pursuing a police brutality suit in Plaquemine, where officers had used brutal tactics against black protesters during the summer demonstrations. Here, though, Marshall was concerned that a prosecution would stir up racial tensions in the town. Before reaching his decision, he had been warned by a Justice Department official in the town that there was potential for very serious violence between the black and white communities, and that young blacks had started to arm themselves.[22]

Three weeks after the church bombing, Robert Kennedy also faced what turned out to be one of his most controversial decisions of his entire attorney generalship: whether or not to authorize wiretaps on King. Convinced that King had come under the influence of two alleged leading communists, Stanley Levison and Jack O'Dell, Hoover had been pressing for months to step up surveillance. On July 23, the FBI made the first formal request for wiretaps on King's home and SCLC office in Atlanta, citing King's links with Levison. But Robert Kennedy raised objections. He explained to Courtney Evans, the bureau's liaison with the Justice Department, that there was little to be gained from the wiretaps, since King spent so little time in Atlanta, and much to lose. He was particularly worried that the wiretaps would be discovered and that their public exposure would cause great political embarrassment for the administration—both with blacks, who might react angrily, and southern Democrats, who would likely step up their attacks on King.[23]

In July, Robert Kennedy was prepared, however, to authorize wiretaps on Clarence Jones, a New York attorney who worked closely with King. Here his reasoning was clear-cut. The FBI had presented evidence that, days after the Rose Garden meeting at which Kennedy had told King to sever ties with Levison, Jones had become a "telephonic intermediary" to maintain communications between them. Over the summer, the wiretaps on Jones's office and home harvested a welter of evidence about King's protest plans, strategizing, and sexual recklessness. Equally important, the wiretaps provided incontrovertible proof that King was still communicating with Levison.

On October 7, Hoover made a second attempt to get the attorney general's authorization for wiretaps on King, and cited his ongoing relationship with Levison. It has been claimed that Hoover used blackmail to gain the attorney general's authorization (specifically a threat to reveal the president's affair with

Ellen Rometsch, the wife of a soldier stationed at the West German embassy, also believed to be working as an East Germany spy). But it is more likely that Robert Kennedy was simply angered by King's duplicity. King had told the president he would sever his ties with Levison and had then broken his word. On October 10, RFK gave Courtney Evans the go-ahead to wiretap King's home phone in Atlanta. A few days later, the SCLC office in the city was wire-tapped, as well.[24]

∾

On Capitol Hill, liberal Democrats had hoped to translate the wave of public revulsion at the Birmingham bombing into support for tougher measures. They responded by strengthening Kennedy's civil rights bill. On the House side, Congressman Emanuel Celler added amendments granting the Attorney General universal Part III powers to sue over the alleged infringement of any civil rights. Celler also broadened the public accommodations section, and pressed for a tougher fair employment section.

Back in the summer, Ted Sorensen had designed the original civil rights bill so that it would attract the support of moderate Republican support. By loading the bill with controversial amendments, Celler threatened to shatter the bipartisan coalition forged in June. Republicans were already in an uproar. Congressman William McCulloch, a key Republican whom the White House hoped would help deliver the sixty GOP votes needed for victory, called the proposed amendments a "pail of garbage." When Kennedy learned on September 30 that McCulloch might withdraw his support for the measure, he was livid. "Without him it can't be done," the president snapped at an Oval Office meeting. "Once McCulloch is mad, then it ceases to be bipartisan."[25]

The Kennedy brothers shared McCulloch's unease over the content of the strengthened bill. They were especially worried at the proposed changes to Part III, which would have handed the attorney general power to intervene in any civil rights matter and which raised the specter of the creation of a national police force (a proposal that Marshall later described as a "desperate measure"). The possible withdrawal of Republican support was even more perturbing for the president. It meant the White House would never overcome the opposition of southern lawmakers. The politics were also complicated by McCulloch's refusal to take personal blame for weakening Celler's maximal bill. On October 8, he passed word to the president that he would only continue to support the administration's civil rights bill if the White House came out publicly against Celler's proposals. The deal was soon put into effect.[26]

On October 15, Robert Kennedy appeared before a private session of Subcommittee 5 of the House Judiciary Committee, the body charged with marking up the civil rights bill. He immediately started tearing into Celler's amendments. Much of Robert Kennedy's ire was directed at the bolstered Title III, which he argued would undermine the federal system. "One result might be that state and local authorities would abdicate their law enforcement responsibilities," the attorney general argued, "thereby creating a vacuum in authority which could be filled only be federal force." After the attorney general's testimony was over, Celler announced, through clenched teeth, that he would set aside his own ambitious proposals. Given "the urgency for bipartisan legislation," Celler agreed to support the administration's more modest proposals.[27]

Black leaders saw only treachery in the deal between the president and Republicans, even though the bill now had a much greater chance of passage. Clarence Mitchell of the NAACP called it a "sellout," and was especially annoyed that Robert Kennedy had appeared before the subcommittee behind closed doors. "Everybody in there is a white man," Mitchell grumbled, "and what they are doing affects 10 per cent of the population that is black." James Farmer commented that this "kind of political expedience brought me to the point of nausea." Roy Wilkins, whom Malcolm X had taken to calling "Kennedy's nigger," complained that the revised proposals were "inadequate to meet the needs of 1963." The Leadership Conference on Civil Rights described them as "a cause for keen disappointment," adding that it was "almost as if Birmingham hadn't happened."[28]

∾

Southern Democrats had long realized that the weaker the bill, the stronger were its chances of passage. Segregationists on the House Judiciary Committee had been prepared to support Celler's maximal draft, knowing that it would be unpalatable to moderate Republicans. The deal between McCulloch and the White House therefore marked a major setback. An air of defeat now clung to Richard Russell and his "embattled little group of southern Constitutionalists," as he had taken to calling them. Russell was confronted now by a fearful trifecta: a president who had staked his reputation on ramming through legislation; a bipartisan coalition seemingly with the votes necessary to overcome a southern filibuster; and a public sympathetic toward reform. "We are in deep trouble here," Russell wrote a constituent on October 25. "The political power play by the leaders of both parties at the demands of the minority blocs is almost inconceivable." "I would be less than frank if I did not say that the odds seem to grow greater each day," Russell wrote a week later.[29]

Russell also knew that he could no longer rely on the loyalty of fellow southerners. By October, J. William Fulbright had started secretly colluding with the White House, tipping off Lee White on the strategy of the southern Democrats. Southern senators had concluded "their best approach to the civil rights legislation rests in delaying consideration as long as possible, since they detect a steadily growing disenchantment with civil rights throughout the country." Ful-bright dropped unmistakable hints of his readiness to offer further assistance to Mike Manatos, a member of the White House congressional liaison office. "Just a reminder that Senator Fulbright was deeply shocked by the bombing which killed the four girls in Birmingham," Manatos wrote O'Brien in early October. "You will recall his offer to help carry out some sort of scheme which would re-solve Civil Rights after a very short debate. Fulbright has indicated that he would be willing to discuss this with the President or with you if there is a feel-ing it would be helpful." The president, however, never took him up on his offer. Earlier in the summer, Kennedy had hoped a modern-day Arthur Vandenberg would emerge, who would be prepared to break from the Southern Caucus. Yet when a potential Vandenberg presented himself, neither Kennedy nor O'Brien did anything to encourage his defection.[30]

For Lee White, the president's failure to orchestrate the inglorious defeat of the Southern Caucus was part of a broader problem. In October, he feared the president's sense of urgency was slowly draining away. His worries only inten-sified in November when Kennedy predicted the civil rights bill might be "an eighteen month delivery" and suggested his proposed tax cut was the adminis-tration's most urgent priority (back in the summer he had said that civil rights was "the most pressing business"). Immediately, black activists seized upon this gloomy assessment, suspecting the White House had ordered a "go-slow" strategy to delay the final vote until after the 1964 election in the interests of party unity.

Kennedy's attention was also drifting toward Asia. With South Vietnamese generals secretly plotting a coup attempt against the Diem-Nhu regime, the situ-ation in Saigon occupied a large portion of his time. Kennedy had spent much of the fall engaged in a lively correspondence with the new U.S. ambassador, Henry Cabot Lodge, Jr., and in late September had dispatched Defense Secretary Robert McNamara and General Maxwell Taylor to the city to conduct an overview of U.S. policy. On October 30, Kennedy had even taken the extraordinary step of or-dering that he be given every single cable on the subject of Vietnam that came from the State and Defense Department, the Joint Chiefs of Staff, the CIA, and the United States Information Agency. On November 2, word reached the White House that the Washington-backed coup had succeeded and that South Viet-nam's prime minister, Ngo Dinh Diem, had been assassinated. The Cold War had displaced the race war as Kennedy's chief concern.[31]

Black leaders made plans for further demonstrations to maintain pressure on the president and to refocus national attention on the subject of civil rights. Midway through October, Bob Moses launched a new Freedom Vote campaign in Mississippi. SNCC also targeted Selma, Alabama, which provided an ideal backdrop for demonstrations. According to an internal SNCC field report, "po-lice brutality, shots in the night, beatings and economic reprisals" had raised tensions in the city. And the presence of Sheriff Jim Clark, whose policing methods were not unlike Bull Connor's, gave it precisely the kind of explosive brew that SNCC could exploit. After spending two weeks in the Dallas County jail, John Lewis enthused at how more aggressive voter registration campaigns offered a radical way forward. "SNCC is no longer a spontaneous movement, but an *Organized Revolution,"* he wrote in an internal report. Activists should be unyielding in pursuit of their goals. "I think it cannot be overstressed," he affirmed, "there are times 'flexibility' is not the word." No wonder the *Chicago Defender* carried the prescient headline: "Expect Violence to Explode in Selma."[32]

SNCC started to plan an even bolder crusade in the fall. It formulated a draft "Battle Plan" with the aim of cutting off Montgomery from the outside world. "Non-violent battle-groups," with their own flags and insignia, would lie on railway tracks and bus driveways, blockade the airport, shut down local power plants, and lay siege to the State Capitol. Afraid of being bested by SNCC, Shuttlesworth raised the idea of a 40,000-strong march between Birmingham and Montgomery for early the next spring. Bayard Rustin called for a "new dimension of Direct Action" in Birmingham and offered SNCC help in organizing its Montgomery battle plan. The administration had not put its full weight behind the civil rights bill, Rustin told King. Further demonstrations were therefore essential.[33]

King was under mounting pressure to take a tougher line against the White House and to adopt more militant tactics. Adam Clayton Powell wanted King to become the leader of a "black revolution," and to co-opt the support of the ninety percent of blacks not currently involved in the struggle, as he put it. On September 19, James Baldwin even warned Clarence Jones, one of King's closest aides, that "Negroes are thinking seriously of assassinating King" because they considered him too conservative. By late October, King sensed that a fresh round of demonstrations might now be needed. On October 22, King informed Jones that he would have "to sit down and develop a planned attack on Alabama and Governor Wallace." He also agreed to mount demonstrations in Danville, Virginia, largely to reassert his leadership of the nonviolent struggle. As an FBI surveillance report put it, "if he loses Danville he will lose all of Virginia." Plans were soon put in place for Operation Showdown, a new direct-action campaign that he hoped would rival the Birmingham protests both in size and impact. King started laying plans for repeat demonstrations against the Boutwell administration in Birmingham, and in particular its refusal to employ black police officers. In late November, Wyatt Tee Walker plotted a boycott of Christmas shopping, which he hoped would "throw the business world into shock." On November 2, in a conversation recorded by the FBI, King told Jones that the nation needed "another dramatic push."[34]

Four months after the introduction of the civil rights bill, the fires of frustration were burning again. In the three weeks leading up to November 22, there were demonstrations in fifty-one cities, more than at the height of the summer. They targeted a luncheonette in Wilmington, Delaware, a roller rink in Baltimore, a school board meeting in Los Angeles, a gas and electric plant in San Diego, all-white Methodist churches in Jackson, Mississippi, and Senator Strom Thurmond during a speaking engagement in Champaign, Illinois. The offices of ABC-TV in New York were also targeted because the network had broadcast an interview with George Wallace. At the start of November, Roy Wilkins complained that the Kennedy administration had "underestimated the depth of feelings of Americans over" civil rights and warned black activists were "bewildered and disillusioned by the 'politics as usual' approach to human rights." Relations between black leaders and the administration reached a new low.[35]

∾

In the final month of his presidency, Kennedy was much less concerned by the sharp rise in black radicalism than by his bid for reelection in 1964. This raised the obvious question of how his handling of civil rights would likely affect the race. Writing in the summer, conservative columnists Rowland Evans and Robert Novak identified what they dubbed a "white backlash" among socially conservative blue-collar workers, a direct response to the racial upheaval of the previous six months. "Mr. Kennedy would survive the white reaction," wrote Evans and Novak in late August, "but his forces in Congress would be so badly depleted that he would enter his second term with incomparably less authority than he has today." Democratic leaders had already spotted "danger signals" in Philadelphia and Chicago, which right-wing Republican strategists were determined to exploit. "These circumstances have raised the unhappy prospect of the race question becoming an open issue for the first time in Northern political campaigns," wrote New York Times reporter Anthony Lewis on October 30.[36]

Theodore White, the dean of Washington political correspondents and one of the Kennedy brothers' favorite journalists, called the phenomenon "Negrophobia." "The black revolt in 1963 is pushing the white liberal leadership in the north further away from the white working class," White observed in November, "and the working class itself toward the temptation offered by anti-Negro demagoguery." White had based his findings on a trip to Dearborn, Michigan, where Mayor Orville Hubbard had started to tap this white resentment by committing himself to "complete segregation one million per cent on all levels."[37]

In Boston, too, there was mounting evidence of an emerging white backlash. In the fall, Louise Day Hicks, a local white activist, had stepped up her campaign against Ruth Batson and the local NAACP, which had been demanding an end to the de facto segregation of many of Boston's schools. Hicks received her strongest support from blue-collar white families. Many working-class whites had started to equate black advancement with lawlessness and a threat to their own livelihoods. The climate was ripe for racial demagogues to prosper. Demands for preferential treatment from black activists only aggravated the situation, for they reinforced the sense that blacks were becoming "too pushy."[38]

On October 30, in a trip to Philadelphia, Kennedy's motorcade passed through near-deserted streets in an Italian-American neighborhood, which heightened speculation that blue-collar workers in traditional Democratic strongholds had withdrawn their support for his presidency. *New York Times* journalist Tom Wicker noticed the sparse crowds on the thirteen-mile route from the airport and reported on how the president received a "cool reception" when he toured the racially troubled districts of South Philadelphia. Wicker claimed it was "one of the poorest receptions Mr. Kennedy has had in a major city since he became President." The visit, along with Wicker's account of it, was quickly cited as proof of the "white backlash."[39]

Governor George Wallace tried to harness this growing white unrest. Wallace had become something of a national celebrity after the showdown at Tuscaloosa, and in the fall he started testing the waters for a possible presidential bid. In October, Wallace announced plans for a northern speaking tour, and deliberately targeted Ohio, Michigan, Wisconsin and Maryland. They were states with a heavy concentration of traditionally Democratic, blue-collar voters, whom he believed were particularly receptive to his racial demagoguery.[40]

Senator Barry Goldwater, the hard-core Arizona conservative, had his eye on the same constituency. Goldwater avoided the kind of race-baiting that had propelled Wallace to political stardom. But he knew that he could benefit from white disillusionment over Kennedy's civil rights policies. Already strong in the West, Goldwater believed that if he could make inroads into the South then he could mount a serious presidential challenge. By November, Draft Goldwater Committees had been set up in thirty-two states, and some of his strongest support came from the South (in South Carolina, the State Republican Committee decided to formally rename itself the Draft Goldwater Committee).[41]

Nelson Rockefeller, meanwhile, had seen his challenge fade. On May 4, 1963, just eighteen months after announcing his separation from his first wife, Rockefeller married "Happy" Murphy, the wife of a talented young scientist at the Rockefeller Institute in New York, and the mother of four children. The wedding received prominent newspaper coverage, as did pictures of the smiling couple on their honeymoon at the Rockefeller ranch in Venezuela. Commentators raised the "morality question" and asked whether Rockefeller was fit to be president. Ex-Senator Prescott Bush, a long-time friend of the Rockefeller family, came out publicly against the governor, accusing him of destroying American families. By the end of May, Goldwater had edged past him in the polls. On November 7, Rockefeller declared his candidacy for the Republican nomination. But by that stage, most commentators had written off his chances.[42]

Kennedy always knew that his support for a strong civil rights bill would cost him political support in the South, and that the Republicans would be the main beneficiaries. Back in May, Kennedy had told the ADA delegation: "I would be surprised if the Democratic Party carries two or three southern states," especially since the GOP was likely to mount a strong challenge. When Gallup published a poll in mid-June suggesting fifty percent thought the administration was pushing "too fast" on civil rights, Kennedy did not seem overly concerned. He seemed to take comfort in the fact that forty percent considered the pace of reform "more or less right." If anything, Kennedy was surprised that not more people opposed his reforms given the turbulence of the previous six months. "Change always disturbs," he commented on September 12, three days before the Birmingham church bombing. "I was surprised that there wasn't greater opposition. I think we are going at about the right tempo."[43]

A number of polls offered further succor to the president and suggested that the white backlash had been exaggerated. A poll in mid-June by the American Institute of Public Opinion (AIPO) showed only thirty-five percent thought he was moving "too fast." Fifty-two percent thought his policies were "about right." In July, a further poll from AIPO showed that fifty-five percent of northern whites favored the new public accommodations proposals, compared to thirty-four percent against. Studies by the National Opinion Research Center (NORC) at the University of Chicago suggested that seventy-five percent of northern whites now supported school integration and seventy percent were prepared to accept the integration of their neighborhoods. "In the minds and hearts of the majority of the Americans," NORC analysts concluded in July, "the principle of integration seems already to have been won." A *Newsweek* poll in October showed that eighty percent of whites favored equal treatment for blacks. In the south, the figure was sixty percent. A poll conducted by the *Saturday Evening Post* on the eve of the Birmingham church bombing suggested more deep-rooted support. Sixty-three percent of respondents supported the civil rights bill, and sixty percent backed the president's overall performance in office.[44]

Louis Harris interpreted the data not as evidence of white backlash but rather an indication of a countervailing phenomenon, which later came to be known as the "white frontlash": moderate Republicans who defected to the Democrats in disgust at Goldwater's racial conservatism. Harris estimated that the president had lost 4.5 million supporters largely because of his civil rights stance. But he confidently predicted that eleven million Nixon supporters would vote for Kennedy in 1964, which would more than compensate for the loss. (Following the death of President Kennedy, Johnson's pollsters latched onto much the same trend, after learning that thirty-nine percent of New York Republicans who voted for Nixon in 1960 intended to vote for Johnson in 1964. Soon "frontlash" became one of the new president's favorite expressions.[45])

Harris also believed that black voters would carry Kennedy to victory in the North. Despite the fractious mood of black civil rights activists, black voters continued to support the president. They were also suspicious of Goldwater's growing popularity. In July, a *Newsweek* poll suggested that in a presidential race against Goldwater, Kennedy would get ninety-one percent of the black vote. In the final months of his presidency, Kennedy's approval ratings among black voters ranged between eighty and ninety percent.[46]

Harris spotted a strategic opening: the opportunity to isolate die-hard segregationists and appeal directly to southern moderates. Now that Goldwater seemed determined to target disenchanted white Democrats, a potentially seismic electoral realignment was slowly underway. Harris urged Kennedy to help carve that new political landscape. "It is commonly assumed that the main stream of southern politics today is segregationist, states rights, and right wing conservatism," Harris told Kennedy on September 3. "The fact is that the outstanding developments in the South today do not directly concern the race question." Harris spoke enthusiastically of an "industrial explosion" and "comparable educational awakening," and argued that "a new South is in the making right now, but is hidden mostly from view over the surface manifestations of segregation and the pratings about states rights and super-conservatism."[47]

"You can well go into the South throughout 1964 not to lay down the gauntlet on civil rights," Harris continued, "but rather to describe and encourage the new industrial and educational explosion in the region. . . . But you can also stick it to the Republicans and the renegade Democrats by saying that it is your view that the main stream of the new South is not states rights, not bitter end segregationists, not ultra-conservative. And that you are willing to take your chances with this new South. . . . Such a tack will not only help you in the rest of the country, but will also pay handsomely in the South itself."

Harris's ideas began to imprint themselves on the president during the fall and emerged forcefully during a speech Kennedy delivered at the state fairground in Little Rock, Arkansas, on October 3. "The old South has its problems and they are not over," said Kennedy, referring to the events of the summer. "But there is rising every day, I believe, a new South, a new South of which Henry Grady spoke about eighty years ago, and I have seen it in your universities, in your cities, in your industries." There was something almost evangelical about the climax to his speech, and it was given added resonance since Governor Orval Faubus of Arkansas was seated on the same platform: "This great new South contributes to a great new America, and you particularly, those of you who are young, I think, can look forward to a day when we shall have no South, no North, no East, no West, but 'one nation under God, indivisible, with liberty and justice for all.'"[48]

It was the first time Kennedy had used the phrases "old" and "new South" during a major address above or below the Mason-Dixon line. And his audience responded warmly to the speech. In contrast, Governor Faubus had received only a smattering of applause at a dam opening ceremony earlier in the day, when, in front of the president, he brandished the administration's civil rights proposals as "civil wrongs." The success of the Arkansas visit showed that the president still remained politically viable in the South. The seeds of his 1964 electoral strategy, which would be based on an explicit appeal to southern moderates, had been sown.[49]

This nascent "New South" strategy came into sharper relief at a meeting in the Cabinet Room on November 13. It was the first time that Kennedy's top political strategists had assembled to lay plans for the 1964 campaign. Goldwater now seemed likely to emerge as the Republican nominee, which meant the Republicans were almost certain to improve on Nixon's performance in the South four years earlier. Polls showed seventy percent of southerners thought the president was pushing too hard for racial integration, and Richard Russell had even predicted that Goldwater would win the Democratic stronghold of Georgia. Before the November strategy meeting, Robert Kennedy had even suggested stepping down as attorney general because "it was such a burden to carry in the 1964 election." As Robert Kennedy had learned during his trip to Alabama in April, hard-line segregationists detested him. In some quarters, the name "Bobby" had become a curse. But the president would have none of it, and told his brother that his resignation would make it appear that the administration was "running out on civil rights." The president also realized that he needed to maintain his high levels of support among blacks, because they would offset the losses from southern whites.[50]

At the November strategy meeting, Kennedy appeared supremely confident of winning reelection and could not quite believe his good fortune that Goldwater had emerged as the Republican front-runner. "Give me Barry," he said. "I won't even have to leave the Oval Office." Pollster Richard Scammon warned that Kennedy's unpopularity in the South had dragged his overall approval rating down to fifty-nine percent. But there was no great sense of alarm. The expected windfall among black voters meant Kennedy was especially well-placed to win California, the richest Electoral College prize of all, which Nixon had taken by just 35,000 votes. With the Democratic National Committee already planning a massive voter registration drive in black communities, Harris gleefully predicted that an additional 580,000 black voters would support Kennedy, enabling him to sweep the North. Just as important, Kennedy believed that he could win Texas and Florida. These states harbored the most Electoral College votes in the South and boasted a moderately inclined electorate, which would respond to a message of economic, educational, and racial change. Whereas Goldwater intended to pursue a crude southern strategy, Kennedy was leaning toward a "New South strategy."[51]

The president now sought to target moderate white voters more aggressively. Earlier in the year, in the aftermath of the Birmingham demonstrations, Robert

Kennedy had suggested a tour of the region to appeal to racial moderates. Back then, the president considered a speaking tour impractical, given the intensity of racial tensions. In November, he warmed to the scheme. Bobby Troutman was even summoned from his self-imposed political exile to implement it.[52]

Lyndon Johnson, however, was not consulted as the administration plotted its new campaign strategy. He was not even invited to the meeting on November 13. In fact, the vice president had almost disappeared from view by the fall. In October, Bobby Baker, one of Johnson's closest intimates on Capitol Hill, had become the subject of an explosive Senate corruption probe. So it was just as well for Johnson to maintain a low profile. Johnson's withdrawal from public view heightened speculation that he might be dumped from the ticket—a suggestion that Kennedy privately described as "preposterous" given the need to carry Texas in 1964. Prickly as ever, Johnson suspected the rumors had come from his old nemesis, Robert Kennedy.[53]

Though still in embryonic form, the New South strategy came into almost immediate effect during Kennedy's southern tour. During a speech before the Florida Chamber of Commerce in Tampa on November 18, Kennedy emphasized the twin virtues of economic growth and educational opportunity and suggested that Florida could emulate the stunning success of California in technology and engineering. During a question-and-answer session afterwards, he also defended his civil rights proposals. "No country has ever faced a more difficult problem than attempting to bring 10 percent of the population of a different color, educate them, give them a chance of a job, and give them a chance for a fair life," said Kennedy. "That is my objective and I think it is the objective of the United States as I have always understood it."[54]

During his trip to Texas, which began on November 21, Kennedy intended to appeal to southern moderates once more. His undelivered speech at the Trade Mart in Dallas on the afternoon of November 22 offered proof of that. The speech argued that only "an America which practices what it preaches about equal rights and social justice will be respected by those whose choice affects our future," and that "only an America which is growing and prospering economically can sustain the worldwide defenses of freedom, while demonstrating to all concerned the opportunities of our system and society." The speech was all the more salient given an ongoing fight within the Texas Democratic Party, between a conservative faction under Governor John Connally, and a liberal bloc under Senator Ralph Yarborough. Civil rights was one of their main points of convergence.[55]

The last words ever penned for the president, which were slated for delivery at a meeting of the Texas Democratic State Committee on November 22, were nobler still: "Let us stand together with renewed confidence in our cause—united in our heritage of the past and our hopes for the future—and determined that this land we love shall lead all mankind into new frontiers of peace and abundance." The inference of "all mankind" was unmistakable.[56]

During the president's trip to Texas, the bipartisan civil rights bill was formally reported out of the House Judiciary Committee (though Judge Howard Smith's Rules Committee had yet to clear it for floor action). On November 21, Senate Minority leader Everett Dirksen boosted the bill's prospects further still by predicting Congress would be ready to act within a few months. With Republican backing, there was a strong likelihood it would become law before the 1964 election and that the president would take much of the political credit.

During these visits south, Kennedy did not champion his civil rights bill. But neither did he shy away from the question of civil rights. And the public response to his trips to Arkansas, Florida, and Texas showed the New South strategy unquestionably had potential. In Arkansas he received a warm reception, while his visit to Florida had the feel of a "full-scale election campaign," in the words of one reporter. Bands played and hawkers did a thriving trade in Kennedy buttons. In Texas, the streets of San Antonio, Houston, Fort Worth, and Dallas were teeming with well-wishers. As the president's open-topped limousine turned into Dealey Plaza, Nellie Connally, the wife of the Texas Governor, John Connally, turned round and commented: "Mr. President, you can't say Dallas doesn't love you."

"That's obvious," replied the president.

Just as he was reaching out to southern moderates, Kennedy's political journey came to a horrifying end.[57]

∽

Blacks felt the loss of their president just as strongly as whites, and arguably more so. Of the 300,000 mourners who filed past his casket in the Capitol Rotunda, *Jet* estimated a third were black—a disproportionately high number. In keeping with the national mood, even strident black critics of the president now paid him generous tributes. James Farmer commented: "I think historians will agree that President Kennedy's civil rights program was the strongest of any of the Presidents in the nation's history, a beautiful legacy." On November 22, Leslie Dunbar, the head of the Southern Regional Council, had to rip up a speech lambasting the administration's civil rights policies, which he had planned to deliver that very day.[58]

On the day of the assassination, Stanley Levison urged King to describe the killing as "political," and to use it to advance the black cause. So even though there was no evidence of a racial motive behind the assassination, King sought to portray Kennedy as a martyr for the struggle. King traced a line from the Sixteenth Street Baptist Church to the Texas Book Depository. "We have seen children murdered in church, men shot down from ambush in a manner so similar to the assassination of President Kennedy," he said, "that we must face the fact that we are dealing with a social disease that can no longer be neglected or avoided." Kennedy's vitriolic critics also interpreted the assassination in the context of the civil rights struggle. Malcolm X claimed that Kennedy's death was a case of "the chickens coming home to roost . . . that the hate in white men had not stopped with the killing of defenseless black people, but that hate, allowed to go unchecked, finally had struck down this country's Chief of Staff."[59]

Kennedy's elaborately choreographed state funeral on Monday, November 25, spoke of the racial changes that the late president helped engineer. The elite ceremonial guard that accompanied the flag-draped coffin included a black soldier, and there were black faces as well in the formal contingents of other arms of the military. And Simeon Booker joined the small pool of journalists covering the somber event.

But the funeral arrangements also attested to the late president's difficult relationship with the civil rights movement. Martin Luther King, Jr. watched the procession from the sidewalk; the Kennedy family had not invited him to attend. Roy Wilkins and Whitney Young had been overlooked as well and were only sent invitations after President Lyndon Johnson learned they had been snubbed.[60]

"A Dear, Dear Friend Is Dead" ran the headline in the *Chicago Defender* the day after the assassination: "Kennedy, like Lincoln, Killed." A. Philip Randolph echoed the same refrain: "his place in history will be next to Abraham Lincoln." On December 22, a month after his death, a flame from the late president's grave at Arlington National Cemetery was taken to the Lincoln Memorial for a candlelight vigil to mark his passing. In January 1964, the southern journalist Harry Golden published *Mr. Kennedy and the Negroes,* the first book devoted to Kennedy and civil rights. It described Kennedy as "our second 'Emancipator President'," a characterization with which tens of thousands of blacks wholeheartedly agreed. President Kennedy had started the year desperate to escape Lincoln's long shadow. In death, he found himself cloaked in the mantle of the Great Emancipator.[61]

CONCLUSION

The morning after President Kennedy's death, Johnson had told aides that the enactment of the civil rights bill was his top priority. Four days later, on November 27, 1963, President Lyndon Johnson announced to a joint session of Congress that the passage of new civil rights legislation would stand as the most powerful memorial to his slain predecessor. "We have talked long enough in this country about equal rights," declared Johnson, echoing his Gettysburg address in May. "We have talked for one-hundred years or more. It is now time to write the next chapter—and to write it in the books of law." The next day, he delivered a nationally televised address to build public support.[1]

Over the next two weeks, he held a series of one-on-one meetings with the leaders of the main civil rights groups—SNCC being the only exception—to personally demonstrate his commitment to the issue. During those meetings, Johnson provided assurances that there would be no compromises, dilutions, or sellouts when it came to fighting for the bill. At a meeting with the ADA's Joseph Rauh and the NAACP's Clarence Mitchell on January 21, 1964, Johnson unveiled his legislative strategy to ensure that the entire process would be as transparent as possible. In a further attempt to forge trust between the White House and blacks, Johnson made Hubert Humphrey the floor manager for the bill. It was all part of his carefully orchestrated campaign to assemble a pro–civil rights coalition that could defeat the Southern Caucus.[2]

By far the most important meeting took place on December 7. Johnson summoned Richard Russell to the Executive Mansion of the White House because he wanted to convey to Washington's most powerful southern oligarch that he was determined to force through legislation, whatever the cost might be to his popularity in the South. During the meeting, Johnson edged so close to the Georgian that their noses almost touched. His intimidating physicality was intended to underscore its political message. "Dick, you've got to get out of my way," said Johnson. "I'm going to run over you. I don't intend to cavil or compromise. I don't want to hurt you, but don't stand in my way."

461

"You may do that," a defiant Russell replied, "but, by God, it's going to cost you the South and cost you the election."[3]

Russell knew that resistance was futile. Asked shortly afterwards if the civil rights bill would be watered down, Russell responded, "No, the way that fellow operates, he'll get the whole bill, every last bit of it." Less than seven months later, on July 2, 1964, Johnson signed the civil rights bill into law, after a coalition of liberal Democrats and moderate Republicans overcame a fifty-seven-day southern filibuster, the longest in Senate history.[4]

Four months after that, in the presidential election, Johnson won a landslide victory against Barry Goldwater. It was spectacular proof that a politician could take a bold position on civil rights reforms and still achieve electoral success. A Gallup poll in February 1964 had indicated that seventy-two percent of whites living outside the South thought that Johnson was pushing civil rights "about right" or "not fast enough." Only twenty-eight percent thought he was moving "too fast."[5]

In the Deep South, Johnson unquestionably suffered as a result of his pro–civil rights stance. Goldwater won Alabama, Louisiana, Georgia, Mississippi, and South Carolina, the states where resistance to integration was strongest. But Johnson took Arkansas, Texas, Florida, Tennessee, Virginia, and North Carolina. Johnson also amassed 48.9 percent of the southern white popular vote, compared with Goldwater's forty-nine percent, a remarkable achievement given that his eleven-month-old administration had been defined by its fight to dismantle segregation. Nationally, Johnson beat Goldwater in all but sixty of the country's 435 congressional districts.

The Democrats also triumphed in the congressional elections. The party achieved a sixty-eight-to-thirty-two margin in the Senate, and a 295-to-140 advantage in the House, a net gain of two seats in the Senate and thirty-six in the House. Johnson found himself in a commanding position, and one from which he could implement further civil rights reforms, most notably the 1965 Voting Rights Act. Russell, by contrast, cut an increasingly forlorn figure. The southern lawmaker whom Kennedy had revered and feared in almost equal measure truly had become the leader of a lost cause.

∾

Had Kennedy lived, he would almost certainly have secured passage of the 1964 Civil Rights Act. The key to the passage of the bill, after all, was the support of moderate Republicans, and Kennedy had already received firm assurances from Senate Minority Leader Everett Dirksen that they would stand with the president. "This program was on its way before November 22," Dirksen commented after its passage. "Its time had come." Senate Majority Leader Mike Mansfield agreed that the civil rights bill would still have passed, but "might have a taken a little longer"—a reference perhaps to Kennedy's deficiencies as a legislative strategist as well as the skills with which Johnson had transformed national grief over Kennedy's murder into support for the civil rights bill. But Kennedy had proposed the legislation, and he deserved much of the credit when it became law.[6]

At the time of his death, however, Kennedy had only a small record of accomplishment in civil rights. Progress had been agonizingly slow in voting rights and employment reform, the areas where his administration had devoted most of its energy. By 1963, black registration had increased from five percent to just 8.3 percent of eligible voters in the 100 counties targeted by the Justice Department. Between 1961 and 1964, the number of blacks employed by the federal government had inched from 12.9 percent to 13.2 percent. The Plans for Progress, meanwhile, remained an embarrassment. Between May 1961 and January 1963, black employment in participating companies rose from 5 percent to 5.1 percent. The black share of white-collar jobs showed only a negligible gain, from 1.5 percent to 1.6 percent. Even so, the president continued to encourage new firms to sign up. In other areas of policy, too, the picture was much the same. The long-delayed housing order had proved to be a glaring failure in practice. After Kennedy's death, Robert Weaver estimated the order had covered less than three percent of existing housing. Most African diplomats continued to look on Washington as a hardship posting, because of their difficulties in finding adequate housing.[7]

The administration had also adhered to a distinctly southern timetable in the implementation of *Brown*. By 1963, one hundred and sixty-six school districts had been integrated, compared to just seventeen in 1960. But in Mississippi, Alabama, and South Carolina, not a single school district had been entirely desegregated. Georgia and Louisiana could claim just one. King estimated that if integration continued at the current pace, it would take until 2054 for southern schools to be completely desegregated. After all, by 1964 just one in a hundred black schoolchildren attended integrated schools in the south.[8]

The Kennedy administration had made greater strides in less readily quantifiable areas. The White House became more welcoming to blacks, which in turn encouraged greater racial integration in much of American society. Kennedy's ease in the company of blacks, combined with his public denunciations of the capital's all-white gentlemen's clubs, helped to establish an unwritten code of racial acceptance. Washington hostesses adorned their cocktail and dinner parties with more black faces. It was now unthinkable to plan a major national event without guaranteeing the participation of blacks. Through his own powerful personal example, Kennedy had made it unfashionable to be racist. Up until the summer of 1963, it was arguably his greatest contribution to the struggle for equality.

Kennedy's inclusiveness represented a genuine paradigm shift in American racial politics. Franklin Delano Roosevelt, a far more aloof politician, had earned the love of blacks through his success in ameliorating black poverty. Kennedy offered blacks something quite different, but no less empowering: a sense of acceptance. As his consistently high poll numbers among blacks demonstrated, and the thousands of black mourners at his funeral confirmed, many blacks felt a tremendously powerful connection to Kennedy. Some considered him to be the Great Emancipator of the twentieth century.

Of course, Kennedy's symbolic approach to the race problem meant that many of the changes he ushered in were largely cosmetic. And often they were restricted to the capital—where segregation had troubled him since his earliest days in Congress. Kennedy certainly had a keen eye for racial detail—as he demonstrated on his first day in office when he complained that the Coast Guard Academy honor guard did not include any blacks. But the episode was also emblematic of Kennedy's tendency to respond to examples of racial inequity that were directly in front of him, while he ignored the broader problems that fell outside of his limited range of vision. Far too often, Kennedy was content as long as problems simply disappeared from view. Sometimes, it was what he saw with his own eyes that disturbed him—as with the whites-only gentlemen's clubs in Washington. Other times, he wanted to hide segregation from the sight of others—African diplomats, the Kremlin, newspaper photographers.

Perhaps not surprisingly, given his privileged upbringing, Kennedy identified far more easily with middle-class blacks, who were more concentrated in the North, than with the far poorer blacks who populated the South. Middle-class blacks had already achieved a degree of financial success and longed primarily for social acceptance—something Kennedy could bestow through his highly publicized gestures of black outreach. Southern blacks still needed basic civil rights—access to jobs, education, voting booths. These demands were far harder to fulfill—particularly because in many cases whites would have to pay the price for black advancement. And so Kennedy shied away from more controversial policy areas, such as schooling and public accommodations, which would be successfully implemented only with substantial white support. Instead, Kennedy steered his administration toward areas such as voting rights and employment reform, which emphasized black self-improvement and self-empowerment.

When it came to emotionally charged issues, such as school integration, Kennedy always advocated piecemeal reform. But his timetable was completely misaligned with that of the black leadership. In 1961, black leaders were initially prepared to accept the administration's nonlegislative strategy but expected other civil rights reforms to come at a quicker pace. By 1963, civil rights activists demanded "Freedom Now," and adopted more militant tactics in the hope of spurring the administration to act more quickly.

What if Kennedy had moved faster? In 1961, his administration could have dealt with many black demands—such as accelerated school integration, fair housing, greater employment opportunities, and greater presidential leadership on race—with only a relatively mild readjustment of policies. Had the administration released the housing order at an earlier date, pushed for a more active PCEEO, launched a greater number of voting rights suits, or sought to enforce the ICC ruling on interstate travel, it probably could have channeled the civil rights movement in a more peaceful direction. Instead, the most violent clashes—the Freedom Rides, Ole Miss, and the Birmingham crisis—all ignited as a result of the frustration of protesters, who wanted to jolt the administration into action. Had Kennedy done more, earlier, then many of these crises—along with the southern backlash they provoked—might have been averted.

Certainly, the race crisis would not have melted away—after all, the civil rights movement was trying to reverse the effects of an American institution that had endured for over 250 years. But bolder federal policies would almost certainly have had a calming effect and could have led to a sincere collaboration between black activists and white policymakers. When civil rights rose to the top of the presidential agenda in the summer of 1963, Kennedy finally helped to engineer a multipronged assault on southern segregation and northern discrimination that blacks had been demanding since the end of World War II. But it was too late for black leaders. Even Kennedy's civil rights bill, the boldest proposals ever put by a president before Congress, was not enough to satisfy black demands. Civil rights leaders attacked the administration for the absence of stronger Part III powers and a commitment to create a fair employment practices committee. And they raised the stakes far higher—now they called for quotas, affirmative action, reparations, and other compensatory governmental programs. Kennedy had lost so much credibility through his years of equivocation that there was now little he could do to appease black activists.

After Kennedy's death, black leaders plotted more aggressive protest campaigns. They did so partly to safeguard their own leadership positions within an increasingly radicalized movement but mainly to maintain pressure on the federal government. In 1964, CORE, SNCC, the SCLC, and the NAACP joined forces to mount the Mississippi Freedom Summer Project, a voter registration campaign that resulted in another upsurge of racial violence. Segregationists firebombed thirty buildings and razed twelve churches. A thousand protesters were arrested by police, and civil rights activists James Chaney, Andrew Goodman, and Michael Schwerner were murdered. In January 1965, the SCLC launched a bold new voting rights campaign in Selma, in hopes of provoking a violent white backlash. Martin Luther King intended to "arouse the federal government," as he put it, into proposing new voting rights legislation. King was merely applying the central lesson that black activists had learned during the

Kennedy years: that provoking racist violence was the best way to secure presidential attention.[9]

By the mid-1960s, the movement had gained such momentum that it was now largely beyond presidential control. Legislative remedies held only limited value. On August 6, 1965, Johnson signed the Voting Rights Act into law. Five days later, rioting erupted in the Watts section of Los Angeles, during which thirty-four people were killed, hundreds injured, and almost 4,000 people arrested. In the years after Kennedy's death, there was an explosion of racial violence on the streets of the country's worst black slums—Rochester, Harlem, and Philadelphia erupted in 1964, and later Washington, Baltimore, San Francisco, Detroit, Cleveland, and Chicago.

In July 1967, President Johnson appointed a commission headed by Illinois Governor Otto Kerner to investigate the racial disorders in American cities. The Kerner Commission, as it became known, reported back the following year. The commissioners discussed urban violence—and the sense of disillusionment from which it sprang—in the context of broader national trends. They pointed out that the great judicial and legislative victories of the civil rights era had produced a new form of resentment as blacks realized that it would take far more comprehensive reforms to ensure genuine black equality. They also cited the "white terrorism directed against nonviolent protesters" as a precipitating factor in the riots, along with a prevailing sense of alienation and powerlessness among young black Americans, which had led many to believe that there was no effective alternative to violence. In many communities, the commissioners also noted, the police had come to symbolize "white power, white racism and white repression." Every one of these trends cited in the report had been in evidence at various stages of the Kennedy presidency—from police brutality to white terrorism. But the Kennedy administration had done little to address these underlying problems. If anything, it had exacerbated them through its own inaction.[10]

∾

There are a number of explanations—political and temperamental—for Kennedy's distracted and often excessively and unnecessarily cautious approach to the civil rights agenda. But perhaps the most obvious explanation lies in Kennedy's own successes as a lawmaker and as a political candidate. From his very first congressional campaign, Kennedy had learned how to gain electoral advantage through manipulation—sometimes cynical, sometimes sincere—of black opinion. He had drawn on the same skills during his years in Congress— had it not been for his adroit, and at times brilliant, handling of civil rights, Kennedy would never have risen so fast in the 1950s. Throughout his political career, up until and including his 1960 presidential campaign, Kennedy had reached out to black voters (as well as white liberal sympathizers) through symbolic gestures and tokenistic measures.

Kennedy believed he could enjoy much the same political success as president—and to some extent, he was right. At the very moment that SNCC activists were formulating their Montgomery Battle Plan, Kennedy enjoyed black approval ratings above eighty percent. Kennedy had good reason to believe that his policies were in step with the expectations of blacks nationwide. His sense that black activists such as King and Wilkins had gone beyond the constituency they claimed to represent was not entirely unjustified.

But over the long term, Kennedy's reliance on opinion polls proved to be politically myopic. High black approval ratings validated lackluster policies. Kennedy marginalized advisers like Harris Wofford and Louis Martin who tried to draw attention to the disaffection of black leaders and civil rights activists. He kept his distance from those who tried to confront him with less rosy assessments of the race problem—including members of the Civil Rights Commission. When criticized, Kennedy would lurch to the defensive. All too often, he would justify any perceived complacency by comparing his record on civil rights to that of his predecessors. But given the turbulent and rapidly changing political climate of the early 1960s, and the heightened expectations of civil rights activists, the comparison was meaningless.

There were other reasons for Kennedy's shortcomings when it came to civil rights. He was temperamentally averse to confrontation, which partly explained his preference for voluntary solutions to intractable problems of segregation and discrimination. He was chronically unwilling to endorse punitive action, particularly in the realm of employment reform and school integration.

Kennedy's convivial leadership style also meant that he was unwilling to do anything that would antagonize members of the Southern Caucus—he was afraid of souring his cordial personal relationships by conducting what he considered pointless arguments over race. He was endlessly ingratiating even when it came to negotiating with diehard segregationists—a tendency that proved particularly disastrous at the height of the Ole Miss crisis.

Kennedy could have accomplished a great deal by taking on the Southern Caucus early in his presidency. Had he done so, and thereby exposed their diminishing political power, radical figures such as George Wallace and Ross Barnett would never have had the confidence to defy the federal government so brazenly. But Kennedy's deference toward southern lawmakers emboldened diehard segregationists. It contributed to a culture of impunity in the Deep South, in which the most virulent proponents of segregation—Wallace, Barnett, and their ilk—were able to commit flagrant violations of basic civil rights on behalf of their shrinking constituency.

Kennedy was also emotionally limited—in many ways a product of his highly regimented Boston family and the exclusive schools he had attended. He took great pride in his coolness under pressure, and this detachment came to define his style of presidential leadership. At times, such as the Cuban missile crisis, it was a tremendous asset. But when it came to civil rights, it meant that he was notoriously unresponsive even when confronted by the most heinous acts of racial violence. Images that affected most Americans on a visceral level—from the Birmingham photograph to Martin Luther King's "I Have a Dream" speech—elicited purely pragmatic responses from the president.

Kennedy's extraordinary personal charisma and the idealistic promise of his young administration often masked his cynicism and conservatism. His restless campaign rhetoric had created the false impression that he intended to usher in an era of fervent reform. The reality was less stirring. Kennedy could be an inspiring speaker, but he was no political visionary. As his congressional record demonstrated, he was an incrementalist with only limited ambitions in domestic policy. The Kennedy campaign had invented the phrase "New Frontier" specifically to tap into the deep well of American nostalgia for the presidency of Franklin Delano Roosevelt. But when it came to civil rights Kennedy had no intention of offering the nation a genuinely new deal.

Kennedy had immense skill when it came to crafting his own image. But he was largely unwilling to lend this skill to the cause of civil rights. As the columnist James Reston once so aptly pointed out, Kennedy was much better at dramatizing himself than the issues. In the spring of 1963, when a delegation from the ADA suggested a series of fireside chats to help defuse the civil rights crisis, Kennedy demurred on the grounds that he did not have Roosevelt's voice. The response spoke less of humility than of Kennedy's timid governing philosophy.[11]

Kennedy compounded his deficiencies by surrounding himself with advisers who reinforced his instinctively conservative nature. Political operatives like Kenneth O'Donnell and Larry O'Brien shared not only Kennedy's cautious political instincts but also his contempt for moralizing liberals. During the summer of 1963, Kennedy started to rely more and more on the advice of his brother and Burke Marshall, who were pushing him to embrace reform. Nonetheless, O'Donnell and O'Brien repeatedly tried to restrain him.

By the time of his death, Kennedy had unquestionably become more sympathetic to the plight of black Americans. He had grown in office. He had started to question the version of southern history that had underpinned much of his thinking on federal power and had grown increasingly impatient with die-hard segregationists, who seemed ever more irrational to Kennedy and in some cases even deranged. He also showed some signs of increased emotional engagement—evident in his extemporaneous remarks during his nationwide television address on June 11, and his response to the death of Medgar Evers.

But Kennedy never seemed able to sustain this level of empathy for the black cause. Days after he invited Myrlie Evers to the White House, Kennedy spoke scornfully of how the black demonstrators who were arriving in the capital might "shit" on the Washington monument. He vacillated in much the same way in the aftermath of the Birmingham bombing. He released a fiercely worded statement on the Monday after the bomb attack but failed even to mention the murders when he addressed the nation the very next evening.

Martin Luther King was right to draw attention to Kennedy's "schizophrenic tendency" when it came to civil rights. There was, however, something of a pattern to Kennedy's fluctuations. He tended to be cold and calculating when organized civil rights protesters tried to pressure him into taking a political stand. He was much more sympathetic to individuals who had suffered directly from the violent outrages of segregation. He offered no public support to King and the Birmingham protesters in April 1963, for instance, but hastened to offer private reassurances to Coretta King over the telephone. That same month, Kennedy publicly criticized the CRC for its interim report on the racial crisis in Mississippi but made a point of calling to the attention of journalists his revulsion at the murder of William Moore. The CRC was an abstract political entity that both criticized Kennedy and demanded of him an overtly political response. Moore's protest, by contrast, was far more understated. While he had also sought to focus attention on Mississippi, Moore did so by making a solitary march toward Jackson, with only a simple placard: "Equal Rights for All (Mississippi or Bust)." Because little in Moore's actions challenged Kennedy or his administration directly, the president was able to respond in purely human terms to this appalling murder.

Perhaps there is something more to Kennedy's pattern of response. At times, it seemed almost as if Kennedy found in these individual victims a means of expiating his guilt for his failure to speak and act more forcefully on the public stage. From his earliest days as a congressman, Kennedy had been personally committed to the cause of black equality—but he constantly made excuses for failing to push for it politically. Perhaps on some level, Kennedy wanted to be something more than he was—a stronger president, a more virtuous man.

Civil rights could certainly bring out the best in Kennedy—his personal warmth, his lack of prejudice, his gallantry, his natural skill as a speaker, and—belatedly—his extraordinary ability to inspire. But the issue also brought out the weaker side of his personality—his indecisiveness, his political cautiousness, his instinctive defensiveness in the face of criticism, and, above all, his lack of moral conviction.

In the final summer of his life, Kennedy seemed to be trying to resurrect the nobler ideals that motivated him in the early years of his career, when his views on civil rights were less corrupted by politics. But would that dedication have endured into his second term? Perhaps. By the time of his assassination, Kennedy had considerable support for civil rights reform throughout the country. And he was beginning to experiment with this new southern strategy, which had already shown early promise. But it is all too easy to imagine a real retrenchment. Throughout his political career, Kennedy had been willing—even eager—to abandon the cause of reform when he sensed it might lead to any sort of unpleasant confrontation. There is no way, of course, to know what Kennedy would have done in the next five years of his presidency. But his political history demonstrates that, at least when it came to civil rights, he almost always allowed the voice of political expedience to drown out the better angels of his nature.

∽

More so than any other issue, civil rights brought to the surface the stark differences in character between Jack and Bobby Kennedy. RFK was more passionate than his brother, and more ethically doctrinaire. He was much less forgiving of southern racism than his brother and refused to make excuses for the intransigence of southern segregationists. He was far more curious about the problem of race than his brother, and far more thoughtful about possible solutions. And he was willing to learn. When Burke Marshall was asked later in the decade how Robert Kennedy's understanding of civil rights had developed during his years as attorney general, his arm shot high into the air to illustrate the steep learning curve. (Asked to describe the president's reaction to the racial turbulence, Marshall was much more circumspect: "He didn't like it at all. It was politically unpleasant for him.") As a consequence, RFK was far more attuned than his brother to the growing disenchantment of black Americans over the course of the early 1960s.[12]

Ultimately, RFK outstripped his brother in his dedication to the cause of black equality. Tensions between the brothers first surfaced at the end of the 1961, when RFK started to press his brother to push for new voting rights laws. Their differences of opinion intensified twelve months later, when he mounted a more determined lobbying campaign to persuade the president to support new legislation. But up until the summer of 1963, the president was reluctant to lend his active backing for a new voting rights bill that would have expedited the Justice Department's work. As a consequence, the Justice Department moved slowly and achieved only piecemeal reform. Robert Kennedy was never able to deliver "Freedom Now" or even freedom soon.

Of course, enfranchisement was not the sole—or even the most important— demand of civil rights leaders. If anything, the Kennedy administration's nearly monomaniacal focus on voting rights angered civil rights leaders, who rightly complained that insufficient attention was being paid to school integration and public accommodations. But Robert Kennedy's faith that the expansion of the black franchise would transform southern politics over the long run was ultimately borne out. From 1964 to 1972, the number of eligible black voters in the South increased from 10.3 million to 13.5 million; and by the end of 1975, there were eighteen black representatives in Congress and 135 black mayors. In 1979, the citizens of Birmingham voted in Richard Arrington, Jr., as their first black mayor; in 1986, John Lewis won election to Congress representing Georgia's fifth congressional district. But the greatest strides in this area came not under Kennedy but with the passage of Lyndon Johnson's 1965 Voting Rights Act.[13]

Despite their differences over civil rights, however, RFK remained fiercely loyal to his brother and always yielded to the president's will. He was an extremely disciplined politician and never put his own interests above those of his family and his party. Even when a clear rift opened up between the White House and Justice Department over whether to introduce a voting rights bill at the beginning of 1963, he never allowed the conflict to burst into the open. And it was only after his brother's assassination that RFK revealed the president's ongoing vacillations about whether or not to introduce the 1963 civil rights bill. He did so in a series of interviews with the journalist Anthony Lewis in December 1963, to whom he stoutly defended the administration's performance on civil rights. But he was also surprisingly candid about his own failures, as well as those of his brother's administration. On reflection, Robert Kennedy acknowledged that he had personally "botched things up" during the Ole Miss crisis. He also suggested, albeit obliquely, that the president could have been firmer in his handling of the Southern Caucus. Anthony Lewis asked RFK a question about the Birmingham church bombing in September 1963, which prompted a discussion about the president's comments in which he had blamed Wallace for the atrocity. "It's just an editorial comment," RFK interjected. "But I think that all the smiles and graciousness of Dick Russell and Herman Talmadge and Jim Eastland and George Smathers and [Spessard] Holland—in fact, none of them really made any effort to counter this. And they're the ones, really, who have the major responsibility, rather than these stupid figures who think that they become national heroes by taking on these tasks. They [Russell et al.] are to blame, obviously. Great blame, in my judgment."[14]

∾

John Kennedy had never set out—as a legislator or as president—to dramatically overhaul race relations in the American South. For him, the defining struggle of the postwar era was not civil rights but the Cold War, and he not unreasonably believed that his presidency would be judged by his handling of the threat from the Soviet Union. From the outset of his career, Kennedy was primarily interested in foreign relations, and as president during the hottest years of the Cold War, he trained his gaze on Moscow far more often than on Birmingham or Atlanta. Consequently, Kennedy was almost perpetually distracted from civil rights issues. Even on the day of the momentous March on Washington, Kennedy spent more time chairing discussions on South Vietnam than he did with King and other march leaders.

But Kennedy's approach to civil rights was also deeply intertwined with his foreign policy. To a large extent, Kennedy's early interest in the problem of segregation derived from his fear that it would embarrass the United States on the international stage and provide the Soviets with a crucial propaganda tool in their battle for supremacy in the developing world. Kennedy spoke out vocally against segregation in many of his early speeches specifically for this reason, and his early presidential efforts to promote integration in both the federal government and the clubs and restaurants of the capital were all part of the broader Cold War strategy.

Because his anticommunism drove so much of his thinking about civil rights, however, Kennedy could also quickly turn against the black cause when it suited the exigencies of international politics. During the Freedom Rides, Kennedy was almost paralyzed by his fear of handing Khrushchev a public relations victory, which partly explained why his personal role during the first civil rights crisis of his presidency was so very limited. He later infuriated civil rights leaders when it became clear that his early support for black nationalist movements in Africa had given way to purely strategic geopolitical considerations. Even in the final year of his presidency, Kennedy continued to refer to civil rights in the context of the Cold War. But the rhetoric began to sound hollow. Transfixed by the fierce spiritual energy of Martin Luther King, a new generation of black Americans needed a president who spoke with the same kind of moral force.

Kennedy was all too often tone deaf when it came to civil rights. He was never able to provide the kind of principled leadership that black activists so desperately needed. Instead, the president leaned heavily on his highly effective strategy of association—a strategy that his successors quickly learned to imitate. The Kennedy administration taught Washington an ugly political lesson: that politicians could win black support through grand symbolic gestures, which obviated the need for truly substantive reforms.

Kennedy's strategy ultimately transformed the politics of race in America. Lyndon Johnson pressed for fresh civil rights legislation, but he also acutely understood the value of symbolic change. He awarded Roy Wilkins, Whitney Young, and A. Philip Randolph the Presidential Medal of Freedom, elevated Thurgood Marshall to the Supreme Court, and made Robert Weaver the head of the Department of Housing and Urban Development (HUD). Jimmy Carter relied more heavily on this tactic. In the absence of a forceful civil rights program, he appointed Andrew Young as his ambassador to the United Nations, made a pilgrimage to Martin Luther King's tomb at the Ebenezer Baptist Church in Atlanta, and even had a White House adviser who was nicknamed the "Secretary for Symbolism." The strategy also worked in reverse, of course. When Richard Nixon wanted to court the George Wallace constituency during the 1972 election campaign, he asked Alexander Haig, his chief of staff, to explore of possibility of securing federal funding for a statute of Robert E. Lee and a memorial to Confederate soldiers. Kennedy had demonstrated that racial politics could be played out at the level of spectacle—it was far less dangerous than a serious battle of ideas.[15]

Kennedy had become president at a turning point in American history. By the end of the 1950s, many segregationists had come to accept the vulnerability of their position. Southern blacks looked forward to the day—just around the corner it seemed—when they would finally enjoy first class citizenship. An optimistic civil rights movement remained resolutely committed to the idea of nonviolent, peaceful change. A majority of Americans were favorably disposed toward racial reform.

At the time of his presidential victory, Kennedy had a unique opportunity to secure a peaceful transition toward a more integrated and equitable society. Instead, Kennedy stood aside. The battle for the revision of Rule XXII in 1960, the New Orleans school crisis, the Freedom Rides, the Battle of Ole Miss, D-Day in Birmingham—all were opportunities for Kennedy to hasten the downfall of southern segregation. But up until the Birmingham riot in 1963, when the crisis in race relations finally threatened to overwhelm the country, Kennedy abdicated his responsibility to lead the great social revolution of his age. And by then it was too late. At the time of his death, America was already moving inexorably toward what the Kerner Commission would later vividly describe as "two societies, one black, one white—separate and unequal." For far too long, Kennedy had remained a bystander.[16]

ACKNOWLEDGMENTS

My eight-year-old niece, Ellie Selkirk, has long been mystified why her uncle has taken her entire lifetime to complete just one single "story." The true answer, I am ashamed to admit, is that it has taken considerably longer.

The origins of *The Bystander* are found in my schooldays at Wellsway School on the outskirts of Bristol, where a history teacher named Lawrence Wilmshurst nourished a nascent interest in postwar American politics and then helped ease my passage into Cambridge. There, I was lucky enough to come under the tutelage of Marciel Echenique, who had the good grace to admit me; Mike Sewell, who vastly increased my knowledge of U.S. history; and Vic Gatrell, who encouraged me to study the country at greater depth as a doctoral student. At Oxford, I was taught by Byron Shafer, whose insights and passion for U.S. politics I hope found expression in the doctoral thesis he so generously supervised.

During my years as a doctoral student, Professor Bruce Mazlish helped engineer a year-long study trip to the Massachusetts Institute of Technology, so I could conduct research at the John F. Kennedy Presidential Library. At the Kennedy Library, I was lucky to encounter Maura Porter, June Payne, and Sharon Kelly, the most helpful of a phalanx of librarians and archivists in repositories across the country, whose names are too numerous to mention.

As my student career ended, Mary Dejevsky of *The Independent* not only helped launch me on the journalistic path but inadvertently brought this book into being. My first article for the newspaper, marking the thirtieth anniversary of the March on Washington, was read–on a beach, no less–by Robert Baldock of Yale University Press. He helpfully suggested I contact Lara Heimert. Lara is an astonishingly gifted editor and has become a trusted friend. With great humor, patience, and grace, she has made an extraordinary contribution.

On both sides of the Atlantic, I have been grateful for the kindnesses of many dear friends: from Mary Watkins, who offered a roof over my head on numerous occasions in Boston, to Justin Muston, who helpfully proofread my thesis; from Fiona Ward, who was always a source of great love and encouragement, to

Jeanette Thomas, my former BBC colleague, who was kind enough to read an early draft.

Former members of the Kennedy administration, civil rights activists, and associates of Jack Kennedy were generous with their time and insights. They include Burke Marshall, Ted Sorensen, Arthur M. Schlesinger, Jr., Lee White, Richard Donahue, Ruth Batson, Harold Vaughan, Louis F. Oberdorfer, Harris Wofford, Charlayne Hunter-Gault, Louis Harris, Sam Beer, Mary McGrory, Herbert Tucker, Roger Wilkins, John Douglas, Joseph Lowery, James Farmer, Joseph Rauh, and John Lewis.

Professors David J. Garrow, Tony Badger, and Irwin F. Gellman read drafts of the manuscript and offered a stream of helpful thoughts and ideas.

I am grateful for the guidance and professionalism of the staff at Perseus Books, in particular Carol Smith and Norman MacAfee.

At the BBC, many fellow correspondents, producers, and cameramen in both Washington and Delhi have worked far harder than they should really have had to so that I could concentrate on the book. Of those, I will always be most grateful to Shelley Thakral, Karina Rozentals, Sara Halfpenny, Sharon Blanchet, Beth Miller, Joni Mazer Field, Dorry Gundy-Rice, Shilpa Kannan, Melissa Anderson, Rob Magee, Ron Skeans, Linda Seeley, Adam Mynott, Martin Turner, Paul Danahar, Vivek Raj, Nik Millard, Richard Lister, Sanjeev Srivastava, Philippa Thomas, Lou Kerslake, Jon Jones, Andrew Roy, Tom Carver, Rob Watson, Stephen Sackur, Martin Turner, Philippa Tarrant, Phil Goodwin, and Paul Reynolds. Close friends, like James Helm, Charlotte Coleman-Smith, Paul Kalra, Sian Holiday, Anna Magee, Graham Croft, David Kershaw, Kate Soldan, Claire Flynn, Kimberley Jackson, John Hanshaw, Mark and Rachel Egan have been an abundant source of encouragement, support, and fun.

My family has been outstanding. Sarah and Rod Selkirk have offered me countless kindnesses, their legendary hospitality foremost among them. Ellie, Katie, Millie and Rory have been a wonderful distraction. But I owe the greatest debt to my parents, Colin and Janet Bryant, for their faith, their example, their optimism and their wisdom. They truly know how long it has taken to write this story, and have been steadfast in their love from beginning to end.

ABBREVIATIONS

AGGC   Attorney General General Correspondence.

AGPC   Attorney General Personal Correspondence.

AMSP   Arthur M. Schlesinger Jr. Papers.

BBP   Berl Bernhard Papers.

BC   *Boston Chronicle.*

BG   *Boston Globe.*

BMP   Burke Marshall Papers.

CBP   Chester Bowles Papers.

CR   *Congressional Record.*

CRDKA   Civil Rights during the Kennedy Administration Microfilm Collection.

DFPP   David F. Powers Papers.

DNCF   Democratic National Committee Files.

FOCKS   Freedom of Communications: Speeches of John F. Kennedy during 1960 presidential campaign.

FOCNS   Freedom of Communications: Speeches of Richard M. Nixon during 1960 presidential campaign.

HWP   Harris Wofford Papers.

JFKL   John F. Kennedy Library.

JFKOHP   John F. Kennedy Library Oral History Program.

JFKPPP   John F. Kennedy Pre-presidential Papers.

JFKPPP 1961   John F. Kennedy Public Papers of the President, 1961.

JFKPPP 1962   John F. Kennedy Public Papers of the President, 1962.

JFKPPP 1963   John F. Kennedy Public Papers of the President, 1963.

JFKPOF   John F. Kennedy President's Office Files.

LBJL   Lyndon Baines Johnson Library.

LBJOHP   Lyndon Baines Johnson Oral History Program

LBJVPCR   Lyndon Baines Johnson Vice-Presidential Files: Civil Rights.

LWP   Lee White Papers.

MLKC   Martin Luther King Jr. Center for Nonviolent and Social Change, Atlanta, Georgia.

NR   *New Republic.*

NSF   National Security Files, John F. Kennedy Library.

NYT   *New York Times.*

PC   *Pittsburgh Courier.*

RFKPAP   Robert F. Kennedy Pre-administration Papers

RRML   Richard Russell Memorial Library.
RRP   Richard Russell Papers.
SEP   Sam Ervin Papers.
TSP   Theodore Sorensen Papers.
USNWR   *US News and World Report.*
WES   *Washington Evening Star.*
WHSF   White House Staff Files.
WP   *Washington Post.*

NOTES

INTRODUCTION

1. Memorandum from Edwin Guthman to RFK, August 23, 1963. BMP Box 31; *Baltimore Afro-American* July 20, 1963.

2. Memorandum from St. John Barrett to Burke Marshall, June 19, 1963. BMP Box 31; telephone call from Thelton Henderson to Justice Department, June 13, 1963. BMP Box 31; *NYT* July 28, 1963; *Time* August 30, 1963.

3. *Newsweek* May 27, 1963; *NYT* July 5, 1963.

4. *Time* August 30, 1963.

5. FBI transcript of conversation between MLK and Clarence Jones, November 23, 1963. NY100–7350–1c 6a; telegram from MLK to JFK, May 30, 1963. BMP Box 8; *NYT* June 16, 1963; *Time* June 21, 1963; MLK speech at Tufts University, Boston, June 9, 1963. MLKP Box 9; *Time* August 30, 1963.

6. *Time* May 6, 1963; *CBS Eyewitness Report Special* June 14, 1963.

7. Hugh Sidey, *John F. Kennedy, President* p. 331; memorandum from G. Mennen Williams to Theodore Sorensen, June 15, 1963. TSP Box 30; Berl Bernhard speech to Central State College, Wilberforce, Ohio, June 2, 1963. BBP Box 14; minutes of the Alabama Advisory Committee to the CRC, May 22, 1963. BMP Box 17; letter from J. K. Galbraith to RFK, June 11, 1963. BMP Box 31.

8. LBJ address at Capital Press Club, Washington, May 18, 1963. BBP Box 4; memorandum from George Reedy to LBJ, May 24, 1963. LBJVPCR Box 6; memorandum from Louis Martin to RFK, May 13, 1963. WHSF Box 365a.

9. Transcript of Oval Office meeting, May 20, 1963. Presidential recording #88.4.

10. JFKPPP 1963 pp. 458, 455; JFKPPP 1963 p. 469.

11. Transcript of meeting between JFK and corporate leaders, June 4, 1963. CRDKA #3; transcript of phone conversation between JFK and Jimmie Davis, June 3, 1963. Presidential recording tape 21.4.

12. *Look* September 10, 1963; *WP* August 18 1963.

13. John Lewis interview with author; Arthur M. Schlesinger, Jr., *A Thousand Days: John F. Kennedy in the White House* pp. 968–972; John Lewis, *Walking with the Wind: A Memoir of the Movement* p. 206; Roy Wilkins, *Standing Fast: The Autobiography of Roy Wilkins* p. 291.

14. *WP* August 28, 1963; Walter Tobriner JFKOHP p. 4; Alan Raywid JFKOHP p. 2.

15. FBI memorandum from Mr. Belmont to A. Rosen, July 30, 1963; FBI memorandum from SAC, Richmond to director, August 8, 1963, FBI memorandum from name deleted to

A. Rosen, August 20, 1963; FBI memorandum from C. A. Evans to Mr. Belmont, August 26, 1963; FBI memorandum from SAC, Washington to director, August 26, 1963.

16. Memorandum from SAC, Baltimore to director, August 27, 1963; Drew Hansen, *The Dream: Martin Luther King, Jr. and the Speech That Inspired a Nation* p. 31.

17. FBI memorandum from W. C. Sullivan to D. J. Brennan, August 26, 1963; FBI Memorandum from Mr. Belmont to C. A. Evans, July 23, 1963.

18. FBI memorandum from Mr. Belmont to A. Rosen, August 22, 1963.

19. Thomas Gentile, *March on Washington: August 28, 1963* pp. 63–64; letter from Bayard Rustin to Robert Murray, [undated]. Bayard Rustin Papers Reel #7; Charles Horsky JFKOHP p. 75.

20. *WP* August 25, 1963; FBI memorandum from Mr. Belmont to A. Rosen, August 22, 1963.

21. John Douglas interview with the author; Lee White interview with the author.

22. Memorandum from Arthur Caldwell to Burke Marshall, July 11, 1963. BMP Box 31.

23. John Douglas interview with the author.

24. Ibid.; Victor Navasky, *Kennedy Justice* p. 183; Bayard Rustin quoted in memorandum from Rodney Clurman to Charles Horsky, July 11, 1963. Charles A. Horsky White House Staff Files Box 3.

25. "Notes of meeting between march organizers and police" from Rodney Clurman to Charles Horsky, July 11, 1963. Charles A. Horsky White House Staff Files Box 3.

26. FBI memorandum from C. A. Evans to Mr. Belmont, August 26, 1963; James Farmer interview with the author.

27. Memorandum from Major General B. E. Powell to Major General Philip Wable, undated, AGPC Box 11.

28. FBI memorandum from Mr. Belmont to A. Rosen, August 22, 1963; *Jet* September 12, 1963; *New York Courier* September 7, 1963.

29. Letter from Captain Tazewell Shepard to Charles Horsky, August 29, 1963. Charles A. Horsky White House Staff Files Box 3.

30. Memorandum for Secretary of Army, unsigned and undated. AGPC Box 11; memorandum from Norbert Schlei to Myer Feldman, August 23, 1963. AGPC Box 11; memorandum from Norbert Schlei to Myer Feldman, August 23, 1963. AGPC Box 11; letter from Major General B. K. Powell to Major General Philip Wable, undated. AGPC Box 11.

31. John Douglas interview with author; Lee White interview with author; Roy Wilkins, *Standing Fast* 292.

32. *NYT* August 29, 1963.

33. Lee White interview with author.

34. JFKPPP 1963 p. 469.

35. *Report of the National Advisory Commission on Civil Disorders* p. 1.

36. *WP* August 29, 1963; John Douglas interview with author.

CHAPTER 1

1. *BG* April 23, 1946.

2. John F. Kennedy, ed., *As We Remember Joe* p. 5.

3. Doris Kearns Goodwin, *The Fitzgeralds and the Kennedys* p. 709; Ralph G. Martin and Ed Plant, *Front Runner, Dark Horse* p. 133; John H. Davis, *The Kennedys: Dynasty and Disaster 1848–1984* p. 125.

4. Nigel Hamilton, *JFK: Restless Youth* p. 774; 1946 Campaign Platform, [undated], JFKPPP Box 98.

5. 1946 Campaign Platform, [undated], JFKPPP Box 98; 1946 Campaign Platform, Additional Statement [undated]. JFKPPP Box 94.

6. Harold Vaughan interview with author.

7. "Remember the Man, John F. Kennedy," campaign brochure, June 1946. DFPP Box 24; "The New Generation offers a leader," campaign brochure, June 1946. DFPP Box 24; George Taylor JFKOHP p. 10; the story came from Paul Pennoyer, a campaign aide, and was quoted in Herbert Parmet, *Jack: The Struggles of John F. Kennedy* p. 111.

8. "Some Elements of the American Character," Independence Day Oration, 1946 (Boston: City of Boston, 1946).

9. George Taylor JFKOHP p. 10.

10. *NYT* June 19, 1946; *Time* July 1, 1946.

11. Gunnar Myrdal, *An American Dilemma: The Negro Problem and Modern Democracy*.

12. *The Report of the National Advisory Commission on Civil Disorders* p. 226.

13. Kenneth O'Reilly, *Nixon's Piano: Presidents and Racial Politics from Washington to Clinton* pp. 109–144.

14. Dewey Grantham, *The South in Modern America, A Region at Odds* p. 175; Manning Marable, *Race, Reform and Rebellion: The Second Reconstruction in Black America, 1945–1982* p. 14.

15. David P. Colley, *Blood for Dignity: The Story of the First Integrated Combat Unit in the U.S. Army* p. 22; James T. Patterson, *Grand Expectations: The United States, 1945–1974* p. 23.

16. John Gunther, *Inside USA* p. 704.

17. Letter from JFK to Lem Billings, February 14, 1942. K. LeMoyne Billings letters in Nigel Hamilton Papers, Massachusetts Historical Society. LeMoyne Billings Papers; Edwin Guthman and Jeffrey Shulman, *Robert Kennedy: In His Own Words* p. 68.

18. Belford Lawson JFKOHP p. 3.

19. *Sea Breeze*, July 1964 p. 11; Doris E. Saunders, *The Kennedy Years and the Negro* p. x.

20. Harold Vaughan interview with author.

21. *BC* November 6, 1948; John F. Kennedy, ed. *As We Remember Joe* p. 31; the claim is made by James N. Giglio in *The Presidency of John F. Kennedy* p. 159.

22. Theodore Sorensen, *Kennedy* p. 471; Arthur Krock, *Memoirs: Sixty Years in the Firing Line* p. 339; Guthman and Shulman, *Robert Kennedy* p. 66.

23. "Record of Senator John F. Kennedy on Civil Rights and Race Relations," [undated], TSP Box 9.

24. *To Secure These Rights: The Report of the President's Committee on Civil Rights* p. 149.

25. "Record of Senator John F. Kennedy on Civil Rights and Race Relations," [undated], TSP Box 9.

26. *To Secure These Rights* p. 89.

27. *BG* January 28, 1960.

28. JFK speech, March 3, 1950. *John F. Kennedy: A Compendium of Speeches, Statements, and Remarks Delivered During His Service in the Congress of the United States* pp. 51–53.

29. "Record of Senator John F. Kennedy on Civil Rights and Race Relations," [undated], TSP Box 9.

30. JFK speech, June 8, 1948. *John F. Kennedy: A Compendium* pp. 21–22; JFK speech, March 28, 1949. *John F. Kennedy: A Compendium* p. 43; *WES* March 15, 1949; *Washington Daily News* March 16, 1949.

31. Absentee record of Jack Kennedy, undated. JFKPPP Box 98.

32. Joe Alsop JFKOHP pp. 74, 98.

33. *BG* July 15, 1948.

34. CBS News, Presidential Countdown: "Mr. Kennedy: A Profile," September 19, 1960.

35. "Some Elements of the American Character," Independence Day Oration, 1946; *NYT* September 27, 1960.

36. *Time* November 7, 1960.

37. *Saturday Evening Post* June 13, 1953; Sam Beer interview with author; Sorensen, *Kennedy* p. 471.

CHAPTER 2

1. Kenneth P. O'Donnell and David F. Powers, *"Johnny, We Hardly Knew Ye"* p. 91.

2. Lawrence O'Brien, *No Final Victories: A Life in Politics from John F. Kennedy to Watergate* p. 29.

3. *New York Herald Tribune* January 4, 1952; *BC* January 26, 1952.

4. Memorandum to research staff from JFK, [undated]. JFKPPP Box 104; Poll of 1946 State Election, [undated]. JFKPPP Box 1041.

5. Memorandum from JFK to research staff, [undated].

6. JFK speech, "Kennedy fights for civil rights," undated. JFKPPP Box 93.

7. Ibid.

8. Press Release from JFK Senate Office, July 18, 1951. JFKPPP Box 98.

9. Harold Vaughan interview with author.

10. Ruth Batson interview with author; Herbert Tucker JFKOHP p. 2.

11. Harold Vaughan interview with author.

12. *BC* November 1, 1952; Poster "Kennedy, Champion of Human Rights," [undated]. JFKPPP Box 103; "Lodge vs. Lodge," JFKPPP, Box 112.

13. *BC* August 9, 1952.

14. Harold Vaughan interview with the author.

15. *Atlanta Daily World* August 13, 1952.

16. *BC* October 18, 1952.

17. Ruth Batson interview with author.

18. Ruth Batson JFKOHP p. 2; *BC* October 25, 1952.

19. Harold Vaughan interview with author.

20. Letter from Rheable Edwards to JFK, March 19, 1951. JFKPPP Box 70; letter from JFK to Rheable Edwards, March 19, 1951. JFKPPP Box 70; Harold Vaughan interview with author; Herbert Tucker JFKOHP pp. 4–5.

21. *Afro-American Colored Weekly* October 25, 1952.

22. *Afro-American Colored Weekly* November 1, 1952.

23. O'Donnell and Powers, *"Johnny, We Hardly Knew Ye"* p. 104.

24. "1952 election statistics," undated. JFKPPP Box 758.

CHAPTER 3

1. William S. White, *Citadel: The Story of the U.S. Senate* p. 72.

2. Richard Polenberg, *One Nation Divisible: Class, Race, and Ethnicity in the United States Since 1938* p. 119; Jack Bass and Marilyn W. Thompson, *Strom: The Complicated Personal and Political Life of Strom Thurmond* p. 111; Robert Sherrill, *Gothic Politics in the Deep South: Stars of the New Confederacy* p. 263.

3. Gilbert C. Fite has written the most authoritative biography on the life and work of Senator Russell, *Richard B. Russell, Jr., Senator from Georgia.*

4. Hubert H. Humphrey, *The Education of a Public Man* p. 124.

5. Ibid. p. 135.

6. JFK speech to the NAACP at Howard University, January 29, 1954. JFKPPP Box 758.

7. Press release: Record of Senator John F. Kennedy on Civil Rights and Race Relations, undated. TSP Box 9.

8. Arthur M. Schlesinger, Jr. *Robert Kennedy and His Times* pp. 105–106.

9. Parmet, *Jack: The Struggles of John F. Kennedy* pp. 288–291 and 300–311.

10. O'Donnell and Powers, *"Johnny, We Hardly Knew Ye"* p. *99: Civil Rights Campaign Bulletin* October 31, 1960.

11. John F. Kennedy, *Profiles in Courage* p. 18.

12. Ibid. p. 139.

13. Ibid. p. 147.

14. Ibid. pp. 133–134.

15. Ibid. pp. 140–141, p. 115, p. 151.

16. These works included C. Vann Woodward, *Origins of the New South, 1877–1913* (Baton Rouge: Louisiana State University Press, 1951); Vernon L. Wharton, *The Negro in Mississippi, 1865–1890* (Chapel Hill: University of North Carolina Press, 1947); Pauli Murray, *State Laws on Race and Color* (Cincinnati: Women's Division, Christian Service, 1952).

17. For a riveting overview of the intellectual legacy of the Civil War see David W. Blight, *Race and Reunion: The Civil War in American Memory.*

18. Arguably the finest account of the deliberations which led to the *Brown* decision is found in Michael J. Klarman, *From Jim Crow to Civil Rights: The Supreme Court and the Struggle for Black Equality.*

19. *NYT* February 8, 1956.

20. *NYT* March 12, 1956.

21. Robert A. Caro, *The Years of Lyndon Johnson Vol. 3: Master of the Senate* pp. 786–788.

22. *NYT* March 14, 1956.

23. *NYT* March 22, 1956; *NYT* March 27, 1956.

24. Numan V. Bartley, *The Rise of Massive Resistance: Race and Politics in the South during the 1950s* pp. 116–117; Dewey Grantham, *The South in Modern America* p. 208.

25. *Liberation* April, 1956.

26. Transcript of *Face the Nation* July 1, 1956. TSP Box 12.

27. Ibid.

28. Ibid.

29. Letter from JFK to Joe Kennedy, June 29, 1956. TSP Box 9.

30. *NYT* August 14, 1956.

31. *NYT* August 15, 1956.

32. The best accounts of the ensuing battle for the nomination are found in Sorensen, *Kennedy* pp. 87–91; Schlesinger, *Robert Kennedy* pp. 130–133; Martin and Plaut, *Front Runner, Dark Horse* pp. 90–103; John Barlow Martin, *Adlai Stevenson and His World* pp. 347–354; O'Donnell and Powers, *"Johnny, We Hardly Knew Ye"* pp. 118–128.

33. O'Donnell and Powers, *"Johnny, We Hardly Knew Ye"* p. 122.

34. Harry Golden, *Mr. Kennedy and the Negroes* pp. 127–128; *NYT* August 18, 1957.

35. Doris Kearns Goodwin, *The Fitzgeralds and the Kennedys* p. 780; *NYT* August 18, 1956.

36. James MacGregor Burns, *Kennedy: A Political Profile* p. 190; letter from Arthur M. Schlesinger to JFK, August 21, 1956. JFKPPP Box 534.

37. Letter from Edgar Stephens to JFK, [undated]. JFKPPP Box 950; Carl M. Brauer, *John F. Kennedy and the Second Reconstruction* p. 20; letter from J. P. Coleman to JFK, September 11,

1956. JFKPPP Box 534; letter from JFK to J. P. Coleman, November 1, 1956. Adlai Stevenson Papers Box 9; *NYT* August 18, 1956.

38. Parmet, *Jack: The Struggles of John F. Kennedy* p. 384; telegram from Robert Troutman to JFK, August 17, 1956. JFKPPP Box 933.

39. Arthur Krock, *Memoirs* p. 359; O'Donnell and Powers, *"Johnny, We Hardly Knew Ye"* p. 146.

CHAPTER 4

1. JFK speech at the University of Georgia, Athens, Georgia, June 10, 1957. JFKPPP Box 897; Robert Troutman OHP RRML p. 20.

2. Herbert Parmet, *Jack: The Struggles of John F. Kennedy* p. 409; JFK speech, Bristol, Virginia, March 7, 1958. JFKPPP Box 897; *Birmingham Post Herald* October 25, 1956.

3. Robert Mann, *The Walls of Jericho: Lyndon Johnson, Hubert Humphrey, Richard Russell, and the Struggle for Civil Rights* p. 178; *NYT* November 7, 1956.

4. Letter from JFK to Paul Butler, February 7, 1957. TSP Box 9; Theodore Sorensen interview with author.

5. *NYT* January 5, 1957.

6. *Chicago Defender* March 2, 1957.

7. Letter from Sargent Shriver to Theodore Sorensen, March 5, 1957. TSP Box 13; letter from JFK to John Sengstacke, March 8, 1957. TSP Box 13; Harold Vaughan interview with author.

8. *Montgomery Advertiser* March 24, 1957.

9. *NYT* March 12, 1956; Rowland Evans and Robert Novak, *Lyndon B. Johnson: The Exercise of Power* p. 121.

10. Doris Kearns, *Lyndon Johnson and the American Dream* p. 148.

11. For accounts of the legislative battle to win enactment of the 1957 Civil Rights Act see Mann, *The Walls of Jericho* pp. 121-224; Robert Caro, *The Years of Lyndon Johnson Vol. 3: Master of the Senate* pp. 894-1012.

12. Paul Douglas, *In the Fullness of Time: The Memoirs of Paul H. Douglas* p. 255; letter from Clarence Mitchell to JFK, June 10, 1957. TSP Box 9.

13. *John F. Kennedy: A Compendium* pp. 503-504.

14. Letter from Herbert Tucker to JFK, June 21, 1957. JFKPPP Box 664; letter from Ruth Batson to JFK, June 24, 1957. JFKPPP Box 664; letter from Robert S. Moore to JFK, June 26, 1957. JFKPPP Box 664.

15. Letter from JFK to Herbert Tucker, June 24, 1957. JFKPPP Box 664.

16. Letter from JFK to Ruth Batson, June 29, 1957. JFKPPP Box 664; "Civil Rights Fights," J. M. Burns Personal Papers; letter from JFK to Roy Wilkins, July 10, 1957. DFPP Box 23.

17. *Chicago Defender* July 20, 1957.

18. *BC* July 13, 1957.

19. *Birmingham Post-Herald* June 27, 1957; letter from JFK to John Temple Graves, July 11, 1957, Microfilm reel #2, Pre-presidential Clippings; Parmet, *Jack: The Struggles of John F. Kennedy* p. 409.

20. *CR* July 2, 1957 p. 11350; *NYT* July 3, 1957.

21. *NYT* July 18, 1957.

22. *BC* July 20, 1957; *BG* July 22, 1957.

23. *BG* July 24, 1957.

24. JFK speech, July 23, 1957, *John F. Kennedy: A Compendium* pp. 535-537.

25. *NYT* July 26, 1957; *BG* July 23, 1957; *BC* July 27, 1957.

26. *NYT* August 2, 1957.

27. *NYT* August 1, 1957.

28. Telegram from JFK to Ruth Batson, July 10, 1957. JFKPPP Box 664; letter from JFK to Alfred Lewis, July 13, 1957. JFKPPP Box 664; Roy Wilkins, *Standing Fast* p. 273.

29. Memorandum from Theodore Sorensen to JFK, July 26, 1957. TSP Box 1.

30. Letter from Arthur Sutherland to JFK, July 23, 1957. JFKPPP Box 536; letter from Arthur Sutherland to JFK, July 26, 1957. JFKPPP Box 536.

31. Letter from Paul Freund to JFK, July 23, 1957. JFKPPP Box 536; statement of JFK on Civil Rights Legislation [undated]; letter from Mark DeWolfe Howe to JFK, August 1, 1957. JFKPPP Box 536; JFK speech, August 1, 1957, *Kennedy: A Compendium* pp. 537-541.

32. Telegram from Marvin Griffin to JFK, July 26, 1957. JFKPPP Box 664; letter from JFK to Thomas Upton Sisson, July 24, 1957. JFKPPP Box 664; telegram from Luther Hodges to JFK, July 28, 1957. JFKPPP Box 664; letter from Robert Troutman to JFK, July 26, 1957. JFKPPP Box 536.

33. *Newsweek* August 12, 1957.

34. Evans and Novak, *Lyndon B. Johnson* p. 136; Joseph Rauh JFKOHP p. 14.

35. Ruth Batson interview with author.

36. JFK speech, August 1, 1957. *CR* pp. 13305–13307.

37. *WES* August 2, 1957; *CR* August 1, 1957 p. 13330; *CR* August 1, 1957 pp. 13312–13313.

38. *CR* August 1, 1957 pp. 13356.

39. *NYT* August 2, 1957; Mann, *The Walls of Jericho* p. 217; Frank Church JFKOHP p. 4.

40. Letter from JFK to Ruth Batson, August 1, 1957. JFKPPP Box 664; letter from JFK to Herbert Tucker, August 2, 1957. JFKPPP Box 664.

41. Letter from JFK to Sam Beer, August 3, 1957. TSP Box 9; letter from Sam Beer to JFK, August 5, 1957. TSP Box 9.

42. *BC* August 10, 1957; *BC* August 17, 1957; *BC* August 31, 1957.

43. *NYT* August 3, 1957; *NYT* August 4, 1957; *NR* July 15, 1957.

44. Telegram from James Gray to JFK, August 2, 1957. JFKPPP Box 536; letter from Griffin Smith to JFK, August 2, 1957. JFKPPP Box 664; letter from JFK to Thomas Upton Sisson, August 2, 1957. JFKPPP Box 664; letter from JFK to D. M. Nelson, August 10, 1957. JFKPPP Box 664; letter from JFK to Mrs. Clifford Lamar, August 1, 1957. J. M. Burns personal papers.

45. Harry Vaughan interview with author; "Civil Rights Fight, 1957," J. M. Burns personal papers.

46. Roy Wilkins LBJ OHP pp. 3-4; letter from JFK to Roy Wilkins, August 2, 1957. JFKPPP Box 536.

47. *NYT* August 29, 1957.

CHAPTER 5

1. *The Nation* October 4, 1965.

2. *NYT* September 5, 1957.

3. Kenneth O'Reilly, *Nixon's Piano: Presidents and Racial Politics from Washington to Clinton* pp. 180–182.

4. *Washington Afro-American* September 24, 1957; *Time* October 7, 1960; Associated Press wire copy, September 23, 1957.

5. Sherman Adams, *First-Hand Report: The Story of the Eisenhower Administration* p. 355.

6. *NYT* September 26, 1957.

7. *USNWR* October 4, 1957.

8. "Kennedy statement on Little Rock," September 27, 1957. TSP Box 9.

9. Letter from Lloyd Bell to JFK, September 29, 1957. TSP Box 9; letter from JFK to Lloyd Bell, October 14, 1957. TSP Box 9.

10. *Newsweek* October 14, 1957; *WP* October 24, 1957.

11. Letter from Theodore Sorensen to Frank Smith, October 1, 1957. TSP Box 9.

12. JFK speech at Young Democrats dinner, Jackson, Mississippi, October 17, 1957. JFKPPP Box 898.

13. Ibid.; Senator Kennedy Press Release, October 18, 1957. TSP Box 9.

14. *Time* October 28, 1957; Senator Kennedy Press Release, October 18, 1957. TSP Box 9; *Clarion Ledger* October 20, 1957.

15. *Clarion Ledger* October 17, 1957.

16. Senator Kennedy Press Release, October 18, 1957. TSP Box 9.

17. Letter from Adam Clayton Powell to JFK, November 5, 1957. TSP Box 9; *Time* October 28, 1957; *Providence Journal* November 2, 1957.

18. Letter from Leroy Augenstine to JFK, January 10, 1958. JFKPPP box 687; letter from JFK to Leroy Augenstine, January 18, 1958. JFKPPP Box 687.

19. Letter from JFK to Anthony Silveira, August 23, 1958. JFKPPP Box 687; letter from JFK to Thomas Bennet, September 19, 1958. JFKPPP Box 687.

20. Fite, *Richard B. Russell* p. 344.

21. *Look* August 6, 1957; *Saturday Evening Post* September 7, 1957.

22. *Berkshire Eagle* April 28, 1958.

23. Roy Wilkins, *Standing Fast* p. 273.

24. Letter from JFK to Roy Wilkins, May 6, 1958. TSP Box 9.

25. Letter from Roy Wilkins to JFK, May 29, 1958. TSP Box 9; letter from JFK to Roy Wilkins, June 6, 1958. TSP Box 9.

26. Ruth Batson interview with author.

27. Letter from JFK to Roy Wilkins, July 18, 1958. TSP Box 9.

28. Wilkins, *Standing Fast* p. 274; Louis Harris, "A Study of the Election for United States Senator in Massachusetts," June, 1958. JFKPPP Box 594.

29. Belford Lawson JFKOHP p. 6.

30. Lewis H. Weinstein, *Masa: Odyssey of an American Jew* p. 235; letter from JFK to Lewis Weinstein, August 14, 1958. TSP Box 13; Press release from Kennedy Reception Committee, June 9, 1958. JFKPPP Box 758.

31. Harold Vaughan interview with author; telegram from JFK to Herbert Tucker, July 18, 1958. TSP Box 9; Ruth Batson JFKOHP pp. 5–6.

32. Letter from JFK to Ruth Batson, July 18, 1958. TSP Box 9.

33. Ruth Batson JFKOHP p. 6; memorandum from Marjorie Lawson to JFK, November 26, 1958. TSP Box 9.

34. Letter from JFK to P. L. Prattis et al., August 21, 1958. TSP Box 13.

35. Letter from P. L. Prattis to JFK, August 18, 1958. TSP Box 13; *Philadelphia Afro-American* August 30, 1958.

36. Michal Belknap, *Federal Law and Southern Order: Racial Violence and Constitutional Conflict in the Post-Brown South* p. 54.

37. Ibid. p. 54; statement by JFK in Senate on Explosions Bill, May 28, 1958. JFKPPP Box 762.

38. Senator Kennedy Press Release, October 13, 1958. JFKPPP Box 122; telegram from JFK to Lyndon Johnson, October 13, 1958. TSP Box 19.

39. Senator Kennedy Press Release, [undated]. TSP Box 9; memorandum from Marjorie Lawson to JFK, November 26, 1958. TSP Box 9.

40. Harold Vaughan interview with author.

41. Civil rights record of John F. Kennedy, undated. TSP Box 9; *Pittsburgh Courier* May 22, 1954; *BC* May 25, 1957; *Roxbury Citizen* May 16, 1957.

42. Howard Shuman JFKOHP p. 163; Harold Vaughan interview with author.

43. Douglas, *In the Fullness of Time* p. 256; memorandum from Marjorie Lawson to JFK, November 26, 1958. TSP Box 9; Ruth Batson interview with author; letter from Roy Wilkins to Herbert Tucker, October, 1958. DFPP Box 23; *PC* November 1, 1958; Wilkins, *Standing Fast* p. 274.

44. Speech by JFK at Statler hotel, Boston, October 18, 1958. JFKPPP Box 122.

45. *BC* October 25, 1956; *BC* November 1, 1958.

46. List of polls, undated. TSP Box 20.

47. *Albany Herald* November 24, 1958; letter from Robert Troutman to JFK, November 7, 1958. JFKPPP Box 933; *Atlanta Journal* November 5, 1958; letter from Strom Thurmond to JFK, November 10, 1958. JFKPPP Box 537.

48. Letter from JFK to Roy Wilkins, December 9, 1958. TSP Box 9.

CHAPTER 6

1. Dominic Sandbrook, *Eugene McCarthy: The Rise and Fall of Postwar American Liberalism* p. 92.

2. *Reporter* May, 1956; Arthur M. Schlesinger, Jr., *A Thousand Days* pp. 17–18; John Kenneth Galbraith, *The Affluent Society*.

3. Mann, *Walls of Jericho* p. 237.

4. Letter from Sam Ervin to Durham E. Allen, December 29, 1958. SEP Box 35.

5. Press statement from Sam Ervin, December 18, 1958. SEP Box 44; press statement, January 13, 1959. DFPP Box 31.

6. Letter from Marjorie Lawson to JFK, December 27, 1958. JFKPPP Box 991.

7. *NYT* November 7, 1956.

8. *Baltimore Afro-American* January 24, 1959; letter from JFK to Herbert Tucker, January 24, 1959. TSP Box 9; letter from Herbert Tucker to the *Baltimore Afro-American* February 14, 1959. JFKPPP Box 930.

9. JFK speech before United Negro College Fund, Indianapolis, Indiana, April 12, 1959. JFKPPP Box 902.

10. Burns, *John Kennedy: A Political Profile* p. 278.

11. JFK speech, "Imperialism–the Enemy of Freedom," July 2, 1957. *John F. Kennedy: A Compendium* p. 511.

12. "The United States and Africa: A New Policy for a New Era," June 28, 1959. DFPP Box 31; JFK speech at Wesleyan University, Lincoln, Nebraska, on October 13, 1959. *CR1960* p. 17567; "Negro press releases," undated. JFKPPP Box 530.

13. John Patterson JFKOHP pp. 1–2.

14. *Montgomery Advertiser* July 26, 1959.

15. Howell Raines, *My Soul Is Rested: The Story of the Civil Rights Movement in the Deep South* p. 306.

16. Letter from Aubrey Williams to Paul Butler June 17, 1959. JFKPPP Box 536.

17. Letter from Jackie Robinson to JFK, May 25, 1959. TSP Box 9; Belford Lawson, JFKOHP p. 4; letter from Chester Bowles to Jackie Robinson August 20, 1959. CBP #628, Box 215; letter from Jackie Robinson to Chester Bowles, August 26, 1959. CBP #628 Box 215.

18. Letter from Marjorie Lawson to JFK, August 4, 1959. JFKPPP Box 930.

19. Memorandum from Marjorie Lawson to JFK, July 29, 1957. TSP Box 23.

20. Ibid.

21. Memorandum from Marjorie Lawson to JFK, August 3, 1959. JFKPPP Box 930.

22. Ibid.

23. Theodore White, *The Making of the President, 1960* p. 43.

24. Memorandum from Theodore Sorensen to JFK, August 9, 1959. TSP Box 1.

25. Lawrence Fuchs, JFKOHP p. 17; Abram Chayes JFKOHP pp. 36–53; JFK speech at the National Civil Liberties Clearing House, April 16, 1959. JFKPPP Box 902.

26. Chester Bowles, *Promises to Keep: My Years in Public Life (1941–1969)* p. 288.

27. Letter from James MacGregor Burns to Theodore Sorensen, October 14, 1959. TSP Box 6; memorandum from Theodore Sorensen to James MacGregor Burns, October 6, 1959. TSP Box 6.

28. Burns, *Kennedy* pp. 202–204; letter from James MacGregor Burns to JFK, November 1, 1959. TSP Box 6; letter from Theodore Sorensen to James MacGregor Burns, December 13, 1959. TSP Box 6.

29. John F. Kennedy, *The Strategy of Peace*.

30. Harris Wofford, *Of Kennedys and Kings: Making Sense of the Sixties* pp. 37–38.

31. Notes on meeting at Hyannis Port, October 28, 1959, [unsigned]. RFKPAP Box 39.

32. Memorandum from Marjorie Lawson to RFK, December 29, 1959. RFKPAP Box 39; Notes of Hyannis Port meeting, October 28, 1959. RFKPAP Box 39.

33. Memorandum from Marjorie Lawson to RFK, October 29, 1959. JFKPPP Box 930.

34. Memorandum from RFK to files, November 11, 1959. RFPAP Box 39; Sorensen, *Kennedy* p. 121.

35. *Time* October 19, 1959.

36. *Washington Afro-American* November 3, 1959; *Jet* December 10, 1959; *PC* November 28, 1959; *Washington Afro-American* November 24, 1959; *Chicago Defender* November 28, 1959; memorandum from Lawrence O'Brien and Kenneth O'Donnell, November 13, 1959. JFKPOF Box 39; letter from Marjorie Lawson to JFK, October 7, 1959. JFKPPP Box 930.

37. Letter from Kivie Kaplan to JFK, August 13, 1959, JFKPPP Box 745.

38. Letter from JFK to MLK, November 10, 1959. Martin Luther King Papers Box 90.

39. Louis Harris, "A Proposal for Survey research," December 29, 1959. TSP Box 25.

40. Pierre Salinger, *With Kennedy* pp. 30–31.

CHAPTER 7

1. Evelyn Lincoln, *My Twelve Years with John F. Kennedy* p. 105; *NYT* January 3, 1960.

2. *Time* January 11, 1960.

3. *Jet* January 21, 1960.

4. O'Donnell and Powers, *"Johnny, We Hardly Knew Ye"* p. 150; letter from Theodore Sorensen to Patrick Lucey, March 19, 1960. TSP Box 26.

5. JFK remarks at Wisconsin NAACP convention in Milwaukee, Wisconsin, October 17, 1959. DFPP Box 32.

6. Louis Harris Poll, "Preferences in the Democratic Primary in Wisconsin," February 23, 1960. RFKPAP Box 45; Louis Harris Poll, "The Democratic Presidential Primary in Wisconsin," March 7, 1960. RFKPAP Box 45; memorandum, unsigned, February 1, 1960. JFKPPP Box 535.

7. JFK speech, "Protecting the Right to Vote," Milwaukee, Wisconsin, March 20, 1960. JFKPPP Box 907.

8. Louis Harris, "A Study of Wisconsin's Second, Twelfth and Fifth Congressional Districts in the 1960 Democratic Primary," March 21, 1960. JFKPPP Box 598; Arnold Rampersad, *Jackie Robinson: A Biography* p. 344.

9. JFK remarks at Jewish Community Center, Milwaukee, Wisconsin, March 23, 1960. JFKPPP Box 907.

10. Ibid.

11. JFK speech at Democratic Midwest Conference, Detroit, Michigan, March 26, 1960. JFKPPP Box 907.

12. *Milwaukee Journal* March 27, 1960.

13. Vel Phillips JFKOHP p. 7.

14. Memorandum from Marjorie Lawson to JFK, September 25, 1959. JFKPPP Box 930; Vel Phillips Moorland-Spingarn OHP p. 48; letter from Patrick Lucey to Theodore Sorensen, December 22, 1959. TSP Box 26; Vel Phillips Moorland Spingarn OHP pp. 40–47.

15. Pierre Salinger, *With Kennedy* p. 33.

16. *Time* April 18, 1960.

17. O'Donnell and Powers, *"Johnny, We Hardly Knew Ye"* p. 184.

18. Ibid. p. 186; letter from Arthur Schlesinger Jr. to Hubert Humphrey, April 2, 1960. Arthur Schlesinger Papers Box P 16.

19. O'Donnell and Powers, *"Johnny, We Hardly Knew Ye"* pp. 166–167; Schlesinger, *Robert Kennedy and His Times* p. 199; Notes on West Virginia Strategy Meeting, [undated]. RFK-PAP Box 39; *NYT* April 29, 1960; Sorenson, *Kennedy* p. 138.

20. *Charleston Gazette* May 5, 1960.

21. Sorensen, *Kennedy* p. 146; Richard Goodwin, *Remembering America* pp. 82–83; O'Brien, *No Final Victories* p. 69.

22. *Boston Globe* May 11, 1960.

23. *Time* May 30, 1960; Humphrey, *Education of a Public Man* pp. 217–218.

24. Letter from JFK to Harris Wofford, January 3, 1960. TSP Box 21.

25. *CR* March 10, 1960 p. 5110.

CHAPTER 8

1. *Time* May 16, 1960; see also Michael R. Beschloss, *Mayday: Eisenhower, Khrushchev and the U-2 Affair* (New York: Harper and Row, 1986).

2. *NYT* May 6, 1960.

3. *Time* May 16, 1960; *Time* May 23, 1960.

4. *Chicago Daily News* May 20, 1960.

5. *Time* May 30, 1960.

6. *Time* June 13, 1960.

7. Letter from Arthur Schlesinger, Jr. to Adlai Stevenson, May 16, 1960. JFKPOF Box 33.

8. Memorandum from Theodore Sorensen to RFK, [undated]. RFKPAF Box 34.

9. Harris Wofford JFKOHP p. 8; Edwin Guthman and Jeffrey Shulman eds., *Robert Kennedy* p. 69.

10. JFK speech in Baltimore, Maryland, May 13, 1960. JFKPPP Box 909.

11. Taylor Branch, *Parting the Waters: America in the King Years, 1954–1963* pp. 307–308.

12. Ibid.

13. Memorandum from Marjorie Lawson to JFK, June 6, 1960. DNC 1960 Campaign Files Box 144.

14. *New York Post* June 3, 1960.

15. JFK speech at Jefferson-Jackson Day Dinner, Minneapolis, Minnesota, June 4, 1960. JFKPPP Box 909.

16. Ibid.

17. Memorandum from Harris Wofford to JFK, June 11, 1960. DNCF Box 223.

18. Ibid.

19. JFK speech to National Democratic Club Luncheon, New York, New York, June 17, 1960. JFKPPP Box 910.

20. *NYT* June 16, 1960; *NYT* June 18, 1960.

21. "An Important Message of Interest to All Liberals," June 27, 1960. DNCF Box 140; Joseph Rauh JFKOHP p. 7; Joseph Rauh interview with author.

22. Clifton Brock, *Americans for Democratic Action: Its Role in National Politics* p. 177; *Jet* June 23, 1960.

23. Herbert Tucker JFKOHP p. 15; John Feild Moorland-Spingarn OHP pp. 31–32.

24. "Summary of the Washington meeting on Civil Rights." JFKPPP Box 1044; Harris Wofford JFKOHP pp. 9–10; Wofford, *Of Kennedys and Kings* pp. 47–48; *NYT* July 2, 1960.

25. *Time* July 4, 1960.

26. Letter from George Reedy to LBJ, June 21, 1960. LBJ Senate Files Box 430.

27. John Barlow Martin, *Adlai Stevenson and the World: The Life of Adlai E. Stevenson* p. 496; "1960 Democratic Convention delegate headcount," undated. DFPP Box 25.

28. *PC* June 22, 1960.

29. Adam Fairclough, *To Redeem the Soul of America: The Southern Christian Leadership Conference and Martin Luther King Jr.* p. 72; MLKOHP p. 1; *NYT* June 25, 1963.

30. Letter from MLK to Chester Bowles, June 24, 1960. CBP Box 257; letter from Chester Bowles to MLK, June 29, 1960. CBP Box 211; letter from G. Mennen Williams to JFK, June 25, 1960. JFKPPP Box 536.

31. JFK speech to New York State Liberal Party, June 23, 1960. JFKPPP Box 910.

32. *PC* June 22, 1960; *NYT* June 24, 1960.

33. *NYT* June 24, 1960; letter from Joseph Rauh to Abram Chayes, July 25, 1960. AMSP Box P21.

34. JFK speech at luncheon in honor of African Diplomatic Corps, Washington, June 24, 1960. JFKPPP Box 1044; *NYT* June 25, 1960.

35. Memorandum from RFK to JFK, June 24, 1960. RFK Papers campaign and transition Box 7; memorandum from Theodore Sorensen to RFK, June 27, 1960. TSP Box 25.

36. *NYT* June 28, 1960; Carl M. Brauer, *John F. Kennedy and the Second Reconstruction* p. 34; *NYT* June 28, 1960.

37. Rampersad, *Jackie Robinson* p. 345.

38. *NYT* July 2, 1960; *NYT* July 2, 1960.

39. *NYT* July 5, 1960.

40. Brian Urquhart, *Ralph Bunche: An American Life* p. 303; *Minneapolis Morning Tribune* June 24, 1960.

41. *NYT* July 7, 1960; *NYT* July 13, 1960.

42. Schlesinger, *A Thousand Days* p. 31.

43. *Chicago Daily News* May 14, 1960.

CHAPTER 9

1. *Time* July 18, 1960.

2. *Newsweek* July 4, 1960; Benjamin C. Bradlee, *Conversations with Kennedy* pp. 30–31.

3. *NYT* July 6, 1963.

4. *NYT* July 9, 1960; *NYT* July 10, 1960.

5. Sorensen, *Kennedy* p. 155; *Washington Afro-American* July 16, 1960.

6. Memorandum from Marjorie Lawson to JFK, June 6, 1960. DNC 1960 campaign Files Box 144.

7. Ibid.

8. Ibid.

9. Memorandum from Harris Wofford to JFK, July 1, 1960. JFKPPP Box 931.

10. Vel Phillips JFKOHP p. 8.

11. Ibid. pp. 8–9.

12. Wilkins, *Standing Fast* p. 276; Branch, *Parting the Waters* p. 317; *WES* July 11, 1960; JFK speech to the NAACP Rally, Los Angeles, California, July 10, 1960. JFKPPP Box 1028.

13. *WES* July 11, 1960; *NYT* July 11, 1960; Dave Powers, "Notes on Democratic National Convention, July 9 to July 15," undated. DFPP Box 25; *NYT* July 11, 1960.

14. Schlesinger, *A Thousand Days* p. 34; Joseph Rauh interview with author.

15. "Democratic Platform Draft II," [undated and unsigned]. CBP Series 628 Box 259; letter from Chester Bowles to Eleanor Roosevelt, June 23, 1960. CBP Series 628 Box 215; "Democratic Platform Draft VI," [undated and unsigned]; "Democratic Platform Draft VIII," [undated and unsigned]. CBP Series 628 Box 256.

16. Wofford, *Of Kennedys and Kings* p. 51; *NYT* July 5, 1960; *NYT* July 10, 1960.

17. Letter from Sam Rayburn to Chester Bowles, August 4, 1960. CBP Series 628 Box 214.

18. LeRoy Collins JFKOHP p. 23.

19. *NYT* July 13, 1960.

20. John Seigenthaler JFKOHP pp. 146–148.

21. *Washington Afro-American* July 16, 1960.

22. Theodore White, *The Making of the President, 1960* pp. 163–164.

23. Schlesinger, *A Thousand Days* p. 39.

24. Memorandum from Theodore Sorensen to RFK, June 28, 1960. RFKPAP Box 28; *Washington Afro-American* July 16, 1960.

25. *NYT* July 14, 1960.

26. O'Donnell and Powers, *"Johnny, We Hardly Knew Ye"* pp. 186–187.

27. *Montgomery Advertiser* June 4, 1960; Raines, *My Soul Is Rested* pp. 307–308.

28. *Los Angeles Times* July 13, 1960.

29. Ibid.; Harris Wofford interview with author.

30. Jeff Shesol, *Mutual Contempt: Lyndon Johnson, Robert Kennedy, and the Feud That Defined a Decade* p. 41.

31. The best descriptions of the confusion surrounding Lyndon Johnson's selection are found in Theodore White, *The Making of the President, 1960* and Jeff Shesol, *Mutual Contempt.*

32. Shesol, *Mutual Contempt* p. 54.

33. Ernest Vandiver JFKOHP p. 19; memorandum from Theodore Sorensen to JFK, June 29, 1960. TSP Box 21; memorandum from Harris Wofford to Chester Bowles, [undated]. CBP Series 628 Box 210; memorandum from Arthur M. Schlesinger to JFK and RFK, [undated]. RFKPPP Box 26; Charles Bartlett JFKOHP; Evan Thomas, *Robert Kennedy: His Life* p. 98.

34. Frank Reeves LBJOHP p. 35; Frank Reeves JFKOHP p. 13.

35. Ruth Batson interview with author; Herbert Tucker JFKOHP p. 23.

36. Joseph Rauh interview with author.

37. *WES* July 15, 1960; *Washington Afro-American* July 16, 1960.

38. *WES* July 15, 1960.

39. Roy Wilkins LBJOHP p. 14; Frank Reeves JFKOHP p. 13.

40. Press Release from DNC, July 15, 1960. DNCF Box 142.

41. Ibid.

42. *The Afro-American* July 30, 1960; Ernest Vandiver JFKOHP p. 26.

43. *The Afro-American* July 30, 1960.

44. *New York Post* August 8, 1960; *WP* August 8, 1960; *NYT* August 8, 1960.

45. Memorandum to JFK, July 28, 1960 unsigned. JFKPPP Box 1044; *Time* August 1, 1960.

46. Memorandum from Harris Wofford to JFK, undated. JFKPPP Box 536; letter from Arthur M. Schlesinger to JFK, August 2, 1960. JFKPOF Box 32.

47. Memorandum to RFK, unsigned and undated. RFKPA Box 34.

48. DNC press statement, August 3, 1960. DNCF Box 142.

49. *NYT* August 10, 1960; JFK statement on August 8, 1960. FOCKS p. 961.

50. Memorandum to JFK, July 28, 1960, unsigned. JFKPPP Box 1044.

51. Memorandum from Louis Martin to the CRS, August 11, 1960. DNC Box 144; *New York Post* August 10, 1960.

52. Draft of statement at press conference with members of Congressional Drafting Committee, [undated]. JFKPPP Box 536.

53. *NYT* August 14, 1960.

54. *NYT* August 20, 1960.

55. Harris Wofford JFKOHP pp. 47–48; Harris Wofford interview with author.

56. Ibid.

57. Letter from Arthur M. Schlesinger to JFK, August 26, 1960. JFKPOF Box 32.

58. Minutes of National Board Meeting, ADA, August 27, 1960. Sam Beer Papers Box 1; letter from Sam Beer to JFK, August 30, 1960. Sam Beer Papers, Box 5; memorandum from Chester Bowles to JFK, August 24, 1960. JFKPOF Box 533.

59. Wofford, *Of Kennedys and Kings* p. 59.

60. FOCKS pp. 68–69.

61. *NYT* September 2, 1960.

62. Memorandum from George Reedy to LBJ, [undated]. Office Files of George Reedy Box 426, LBJL; memorandum from Harris Wofford to JFK, [undated]. JFKPPP Box 536.

CHAPTER 10

1. *Time* August 29, 1960.

2. Richard Nixon speech in Birmingham, Alabama, August 26, 1960. FOCNS p. 40; Theodore H. White, *The Making of the President, 1960* p. 271.

3. Memorandum from Marjorie Lawson to JFK, June 6, 1960. DNC 1960 Campaign Files Box 144; *Ebony* November, 1960; memorandum from Marjorie Lawson to RFK, September 30, 1960. DNCF Box 140.

4. Memorandum from Theodore Sorensen to JFK, undated. RFKPA Box 34.

5. Ibid.

6. "Public Opinion and the 1960 Elections," by George Belknap, May, 1960. JFKPPP Box 1044.

7. Memorandum from Marjorie Lawson to JFK, June 6, 1960. DNC 1960 Campaign Files Box 144.

8. Herbert Tucker interview with author; E. Frederic Morrow, Eisenhower's black adviser, had called himself "Exhibit A" during his speech at the Republican convention (*Washington Afro-American* July 30, 1960); Vel Phillips Moorland-Spingarn OHP p. 43, p. 47.

9. White, *The Making of the President, 1960* p. 252.

10. Richard Reeves, *President Kennedy: Profile of Power* p. 62; Pierre Salinger, *With Kennedy* p. 38; *Jet* October 27, 1960.

11. Memorandum from Louis Martin to Frank Reeves, undated. DNCF Box 149; memorandum from Marjorie Lawson to CRS staff, August 15, 1960. DNCF Box 144.

12. Herbert Tucker interview with author; Simulmatics Report No 1: Negro Voters in Northern Cities, May 5, 1960. DNC Research Box 212.

13. Wofford, *Of Kennedys and Kings* p. 61; John Seigenthaler JFKOHP p. 242.

14. Louis Martin in Kenneth W. Thompson, ed., *The Kennedy Presidency: Seventeen Intimate Perspectives of John F. Kennedy* pp. 86–87; Louis Martin JFKOHP p. 10.

15. Nicholas Lemann, *The Promised Land: The Great Black Migration and How It Changed America* p. 113; John Seigenthaler JFKOHP p. 120.

16. Branch, *Parting the Waters* p. 343; Lemann, *The Promised Land* p. 114; John Seigenthaler JFKOHP p. 196.

17. Memorandum from Marjorie Lawson to JFK, June 6, 1960. DNC 1960 Campaign Files Box 144; Simeon Booker, JFKOHP p. 15.

18. *Ebony* November, 1960.

19. "A Leader in the Tradition of Roosevelt." DNCF Box 143.

20. "FEPC Ball Game." DNCF Box 143.

21. Richard Nixon, *Six Crises* p. 421; E. Frederic Morrow, *Black Man in the White House* pp. 295–296.

22. Background memorandum prepared for JFK, August 1960. FOCKS pp. 1275–1285.

23. *USNWR* August 8, 1960; Tom Mboya JFKOHP p. 65; Background memorandum, undated and unsigned. DNC 1960 Campaign Files Box 145.

24. JFK speech in New York, October 12, 1960. FOCKS pp. 567–571.

25. Giglio, *The Presidency of John F. Kennedy* p. 221; JFK speech in Buffalo, September 28, 1960. FOCKS p. 398; JFK speech in Los Angeles, November 1, 1960. FOCKS p. 846.

26. JFK speech in Los Angeles, November 1, 1960. FOCKS p. 846; JFK speech in San Francisco, November 2, 1960. FOCKS p. 846.

27. JFK speech in Cleveland, Ohio, September 25, 1960. FOCKS p. 361.

28. JFK speech at Howard University, Washington D.C., October 7, 1960. FOCKS pp. 517–520; Louis Martin JFKOHP p. 26; Louis Martin JFKOHP p. 26.

29. Question and answer session in Minneapolis, Minnesota, October 1, 1960. FOCKS p. 432.

30. Louis Harris, "The Presidential Election in Texas," September 9, 1960. RFKPAP Box 45; Sorensen, *Kennedy* p. 187; Ernest Vandiver JFKOHP p. 33.

31. *Time* October 24, 1960.

32. *Time* September 9, 1960; *Time* October 3, 1960; *Atlanta Journal* October 14, 1960.

33. Richard Russell speech draft, January 14, 1961. Richard Russell Papers Series III Box 19; Fite, *Richard B. Russell* p. 379; *Time* July 11, 1960.

34. Memorandum from Harris Wofford to JFK, September 23, 1960. DNCF Box 146.

35. Ibid.

36. *Freedom of Communications: Televised Debates between Richard M. Nixon and John F. Kennedy* p. 74.

37. Roy Wilkins, *Standing Fast* pp. 278–279; *Washington Afro-American* October 1, 1960.

38. *NYT* September 26, 1960.

39. White, *The Making of the President, 1960* p. 295; JFK speech at Greater Houston Ministerial Association, Houston, September 12, 1960. FOCKS p. 206.

40. *Freedom of Communications: Televised Debates* p. 150.

41. Ibid. p. 151.

42. Louis Harris, "Survey of Presidential Race in Louisiana, October 20, 1960. RFKPAP Box 44; Louis Harris, "The Presidential Election in South Carolina," November 4, 1960. RFKPAP Box 45.

43. *NYT* October 13, 1960.

44. Ibid.

45. *NYT* October 14, 1960; *NYT* October 14, 1960; *Amsterdam News* October 29, 1960.

46. John Seigenthaler JFKOHP p. 240; *NYT* October 18, 1960.

47. Campaign Bulletin: CRS, DNC, October 31, 1960. HWP Box 2.

48. Memorandum from Harris Wofford to RFK, undated. RFKPA Box 32.

49. Memorandum from James Rowe to RFK, September 26, 1960. RFKPAP Box 26.

50. Campaign Bulletin, CRS, October 31, 1960. HWP Box 2; Press statement, [undated]. DNCF, Box 144.

51. *NYT* October 12, 1960.

52. JFK speech at National Conference on Constitutional Rights, New York, October 12, 1960. FOCKS p. 576.

53. Ibid. p. 576.

54. JFK speech in Harlem, October 12, 1960. FOCKS p. 581.

CHAPTER 11

1. Branch, *Parting the Waters* p. 219.

2. Wofford, *Of Kennedys and Kings* pp. 12–13.

3. MLK JFKOHP pp. 4–5.

4. Branch, *Parting the Waters* p. 349.

5. Frank Reeves JFKOHP p. 16; Frank Reeves Moorland Spingarn OHP p. 32.

6. Wofford, *Of Kennedys and Kings* p. 14.

7. William Hartsfield JFKOHP pp. 2–7.

8. Wofford, *Of Kennedys and Kings* p. 15.

9. Ibid.

10. Ibid. p. 16.

11. Jack Bass, *Taming the Storm: The Life and Times of Judge Frank M. Johnson, Jr., and the South's Fight over Civil Rights* p. 170; *Atlanta Constitution* May 10, 1961.

12. Wofford, *Of Kennedys and Kings* p. 16; Clifford M. Kuhn, "'There's a Footnote to History': Memory and the History of Martin Luther King's October 1960 Arrest and Its Aftermath" in *Journal of American History* September 1997.

13. Bass, *Taming the Storm* pp. 170–171; Louis Martin quoted in Thompson, ed., *The Kennedy Presidency* p. 87; John Seigenthaler JFKOHP p. 93.

14. Wofford, *Of Kennedys and Kings* p. 17.

15. Ibid.

16. Coretta King, *My Life with Martin Luther King* p. 180.

17. Wofford, *Of Kennedys and Kings* p. 18.

18. Ibid. pp. 18–19.

19. King, *My Life with Martin Luther King* p. 180.

20. Louis Martin JFKOHP p. 55; Louis Martin Moorland Spingarn OHP p. 10.

21. JFK comments at Idlewild airport, October 26, 1960. FOCKS p. 1201; Wofford, *Of Kennedys and Kings* p. 20; *NYT* November 1, 1960; *Time* November 7, 1960.

22. Bass, *Taming the Storm* p. 171; Wofford, *Of Kennedys and Kings* p. 22.

23. Louis Martin JFKOHP p. 52; *Washington Afro-American* October 29, 1960; *New York Post* October 28, 1960; *USNWR* November 7, 1960.

24. Wofford, *Of Kennedys and Kings* p. 23.

25. Ibid. p. 28.

26. *NR* November 21, 1960; *NYT* November 27, 1960; "Post-election analysis," undated; DNCF Box 149.

27. *NR* November 21, 1960; *NYT* November 27, 1960; *NR* November 21, 1960.

28. *NYT* November 11, 1960.

29. *WP* November 10, 1960; *USNWR* November 21, 1960; *NR* November 21, 1960; *Time* November 21, 1960.

30. *USWNR* November 21, 1960; Sorensen, *Kennedy* p. 215; J. K. Galbraith, *Ambassador's Journal* p. 6.

31. Memorandum from Jesse Unruh to RFK, October 6, 1960. DNCF Box 140; *NYT* October 30, 1960; Louis Harris, "The Presidential Election in Ohio," October 19, 1960; Louis Harris, "The Presidential Election in Ohio," November 4, 1960. RFKPAP Box 45; Louis Harris, "The Presidential Election in Pennsylvania," October 12, 1960; Louis Harris, "The Presidential Election in Pennsylvania," November 3, 1960. RFKPAP Box 45.

32. Wofford, *Of Kennedys and Kings* p. 65; *Amsterdam News* November 5, 1960; "Kennedy's Call to King" JFKOHP p. 65; *Atlanta Daily World* November 10, 1960.

CHAPTER 12

1. *NYT* November 10, 1960; *WES* November 9, 1960.

2. *Time* December 19, 1960; *Newsweek* January 2, 1961.

3. *NYT* December 21, 1960; Sorensen, *Kennedy* pp. 475, 476; O'Brien, *No Final Victories* p. 104.

4. Sorensen, *Kennedy* pp. 475–476.

5. Ralph McGill JFKOHP pp. 4–5; *NYT* December 1, 1960; *NYT* December 2, 1960.

6. Fite, *Richard B. Russell* p. 377.

7. Ibid.

8. *NYT* November 10, 1960; *Newsweek* November 14, 1960.

9. *Newsweek* December 5, 1960.

10. *Washington Afro-American* November 12, 1960; *NYT* March 6, 1961; *Newsweek* November 21, 1960.

11. *Newsweek* December 5, 1960.

12. White, *The Making of the President, 1960* p. 353.

13. Sean J. Savage, *JFK, LBJ, and the Democratic Party* p. 392.

14. *NYT* November 14, 1960.

15. Thomas D. Clark, *The Emerging South* p. 272.

16. McGill, *The South and the Southerner* pp. 237–238; Clark, *The Emerging South* p. 275.

17. Memorandum from Chester Bowles to RFK, September 21, 1960. RFKPAP Box 4.

18. Adam Fairclough, *Better Day Coming: Blacks and Equality, 1890–2000* p. 244.

19. The most detailed account of the New Orleans schools crisis is found in Liva Baker, *The Second Battle of New Orleans: The Hundred Year Struggle to Integrate the Schools.*

20. *NYT* November 21, 1960.

21. *Atlanta Constitution* January 12, 1961; *Atlanta Constitution* January 13, 1961.

22. Ernest Vandiver JFKOHP p. 13; Klarman, *From Jim Crow to Civil Rights* p. 405; LeRoy Collins JFKOHP p. 23; Herman Talmadge, *Talmadge: A Political Legacy, A Politician's Life* p. 186; *PC* January 14, 1961.

23. "Terry Sanford: A Political Gambler," *NYT* January 19, 1963; Bass and DeVries, *The Transformation of Southern Politics* p. 289.

24. George Belknap, "Political Behavior report: 'People are more liberal than you think',"
May, 1960. RFKPAP Box 39.

25. George H. Gallup, *The Gallup Poll: Public Opinion 1935–1971 Volume III* pp. 1687, 1655.

26. James L. Sundquist, *Politics and Policy: The Eisenhower, Kennedy and Johnson Years* pp. 448ñ450; *The Gallup Poll* pp. 1700–1701.

27. Poll on school integration, March 13, 1959. *The Gallup Poll* p. 1598; "Public Opinion and the 1960 elections" by George Belknap, undated. JFKPPP Box 1044; *The Gallup Poll* p. 1705; Klarman, *From Jim Crow to Civil Rights* p. 401.

28. *NYT* July 29, 1960; Anthony Lewis, *Portrait of a Decade* p. 114.

29. *NYT* November 13, 1960.

30. *Mademoiselle* August, 1960; *Progressive* 24, May 1960.

31. *NYT* January 12, 1961.

32. Memorandum from Harris Wofford to JFK, December 30, 1960. AGPC Box 12.

33. Memorandum from Harris Wofford to JFK, November 20, 1960. HWP Box 9; letter from Arthur M. Schlesinger to JFK, November 14, 1960. JFKPOF Box 65; *Newsweek* January 2, 1961; *NYT* January 5, 1961; memorandum from Joseph Clark to JFK, undated. JFKPOF Box 49.

34. *NYT* December 12, 1960; *WP* December 12, 1960; *NYT* December 21, 1960.

35. *CR* Volume 107 (January 10, 1961) p. 520; *NYT* January 12, 1961.

36. *WES* January 13, 1961; Brock, *Americans for Democratic Action* p. 201.

37. *NYT* February 1, 1961; *WP* February 1, 1961.

38. Ralph M. Goldman, *The National Party Chairmen and Committees: Factionalism at the Top* p. 475; *NYT* March 12, 1961.

39. Joe Alsop JFKOHP pp. 74, 98; Frank Church JFKOHP p. 7.

40. *NYT* December 30, 1960; Roy Wilkins LBJOHP pp. 7–8; Wilkins, *Standing Fast* p. 280.

41. Memorandum from Harris Wofford to JFK, December 30, 1960. HWP Box 8.

CHAPTER 13

1. *PC* January 28, 1961; *Jet* February 2, 1961.

2. *WP* January 20, 1961.

3. JFKPPP 1961 p. 1.

4. Memorandum from Harris Wofford and Louis Martin to JFK, January 18, 1960. JFKPOF Box 34.

5. *Time* January 27, 1961; Fite, *Richard B. Russell* p. 381; Brock, *Americans for Democratic Action* p. 194; *PC* January 28, 1961.

6. Booker, *Black Man's America* p. 21; Branch, *Parting the Waters* p. 384; *Jet* February 2, 1961.

7. *PC* January 28, 1961; *Jet* February 2, 1961; *Ebony* February 1961.

8. *Ebony* January 1961.

9. *WES* March 7, 1961; Goodwin, *Remembering America* p. 4.

10. Memorandum from Douglas Dillon to Fred Dutton, March 5, 1961. CRDKA reel #1; Speech by Douglas Dillon to Anti-Defamation League of B'nai B'rith, October 17, 1962. AGGC Box 16.

11. *Jet* March 23, 1961.

12. Memorandum from Carlisle Runge to Fred Dutton, April 10, 1961. CRDKA reel #5.

13. Sorensen, *Kennedy* p. 473; letter from JFK to Chester Bowles, January 26, 1961. CBP Box 297.

14. Letter from Chester Bowles to JFK, January 31, 1961. JFKPOF Box 97.

15. Memorandum from Fred Dutton to JFK, February 9, 1961. CRDKA reel #1; Cabinet Agenda, February 13, 1961. JFKPOF Box 92.

16. Wofford, *Of Kennedys and Kings* p. 141.

17. Memorandum from Fred Dutton to L. D. Battle, April 11, 1961. CRDKA reel # 5; letter from RFK to Dean Eugene Rostow, May 9, 1961. AGCP Box 9.

18. Summary of Present Civil Rights Programs, undated, JFKPOF Box 97; memorandum from Harris Wofford to Fred Dutton, April 11, 1961. HWP Box 7; Minutes of PCEEO meeting on June 28, 1962. Willie Day Taylor Papers Box 420; Charles Bartlett JFKOHP p. 79.

19. Guthman and Shulman, *Robert Kennedy in His Own Words* pp. 115–116.

20. Dean Rusk JFKOHP pp. 328–335; Louis Martin quoted in Kenneth Thompson, *The Kennedy Presidency* p. 89.

21. Louis Martin JFKOHP p. 86.

22. *Jet* April 29, 1961; Herbert Tucker interview with author; Louis Martin JFKOHP p. 91; Vel Phillips Moorland Spingarn OHP p. 58; *PC* February 25, 1961.

23. Sorensen, *Kennedy* pp. 251–252.

24. *NYT* December 16, 1960; Sorensen, *Kennedy* p. 252; Lester Tanzer, *The Kennedy Circle* p. 261.

25. *Jet* February 23, 1961; *NYT* February 8, 1961.

26. *Jet* March 9, 1961; *Chicago Daily Defender* January 5, 1961.

27. Louis Martin JFKOHP p. 94.

28. Frank Reeves JFKOHP pp. 28–30; *Jet* February 16, 1961.

29. *Jet* July 13, 1961; *Jet* August 3, 1961.

30. Memorandum from Harris Wofford to JFK, December 30, 1960. RFKPAF Box 52; letter from Harris Wofford to JFK, December 30, 1960. AGGC Box 12.

31. *Jet* April 6, 1961; *Jet* March 16, 1961.

32. Guthman and Shulman, *Robert Kennedy* p. 37; *Ebony* January 1961.

33. *NYT* January 11, 1961; letter from Harris Wofford to JFK, December 30, 1960. AGGC Box 12; *NYT* January 5, 1961; Ernest Vandiver JFKOHP p. 46.

34. *WES* March 7, 1961.

35. Roger Wilkins interview with author.

36. Richard D. Mahoney, *JFK: Ordeal in Africa* p. 23; *NYT* July 7, 1961.

37. "Report of the First Nine Months of the Special Protocol Service Section," undated. Pedro Sanjuan MS Box 3; Pedro Sanjuan JFKOHP pp. 26–55.

38. *The Reporter* October 26, 1961; Minutes of Second Meeting with representatives of State Governors, June 16, 1961. Pedro Sanjuan Papers MS Box 2.

39. *NYT* July 7, 1961.

40. Harris Wofford JFKOHP p. 61; Wofford, *Of Kennedys and Kings* pp. 127, 128.

41. Mary Dudziak, *Cold War and Civil Rights: Race and the Image of American Democracy* p. 168; Thomas Borstelmann, *The Cold War and the Color Line: American Race Relations in the Global Arena* p. 167.

42. Letter from Dean Rusk to RFK, January 31, 1961. HWP Box 2; *Jet* March 2, 1961; Dean Rusk JFKOHP p. 341.

43. "Report of the First Nine Months of the Special Protocol Service Section," undated. Pedro Sanjuan MS Box 3; Pedro Sanjuan JFKOHP p. 92.

44. Brauer, *John F. Kennedy* p. 78.

45. James Giglio, "Kennedy," in *American Visions* Volume 10 Issue 1; Donald A. Ritchie, *Reporting from Washington: The History of the White House Press Corps* p. 45.

46. Booker, *Black Man's America* pp. 19–20; *Jet* April 27, 1961.

47. Carl T. Rowan, *Breaking Barriers: A Memoir* p. 205; Arthur Krock, *Memoirs* p. 357.

48. *Newsweek* January 29, 1962; *Newsweek* October 1, 1962.

49. Memorandum from Louis Harris to JFK, March 22, 1961. TSP Box 54; *Jet* June 29, 1961.

50. Letter from Roy Wilkins to Harris Wofford, April 4, 1961. HWP Box 11.

CHAPTER 14

1. Memorandum from Harris Wofford to JFK, December 30, 1960. RFKPAP Box 52.

2. Ibid.

3. Theodore Hesburgh JFKOHP p. 8; memorandum from Carlisle Runge to Theodore Sorensen, October 26, 1961. TSP Box 30.

4. Memorandum from Roy Wilkins and Arnold Aronson, February 6, 1961. TSP Box 30; Summary Memorandum of Executive Action on Civil Rights, undated. TSP Box 30; memorandum from Fred Dutton to JFK, February 9, 1961. CRDKA reel #1.

5. JFKPPP 1961 p. 33; JFKPPP 1961 p. 157.

6. Brauer, *John F. Kennedy* p. 127.

7. JFKPPP 1961 pp. 256–257.

8. Evans and Novak, *Lyndon Johnson* p. 308.

9. Letter from James Rowe to LBJ, December 22, 1960. LBJVPCR Box 2.

10. Johnson recounted this conversation to his black associate, Hobart Taylor. Hobart Taylor LBJOHP Tape 1 p. 14.

11. Memorandum from Nicholas Katzenbach to Robert Kennedy, February 15, 1961. AGPC Box 13; Hugh Davis Graham, *The Civil Rights Era: Origins and Development of National Policy, 1960–1972* p. 39; memorandum from Nicholas Katzenbach to RFK, February 15, 1962. AGPC Box 12.

12. Transcript of conversation between Richard Goodwin and LBJ (undated). LBJVPCR Box 2; memorandum from George Reedy to LBJ, February 28, 1961. LBJVPCR Box 8.

13. Nicholas Katzenbach JFKOHP p. 41.

14. JFKPPP 1961 p. 150; JFKPPP 1961 pp. 256–257; *NYT* March 7, 1961.

15. Jerry Holleman LBJOHP p. 44; letter from LBJ to Russell Long, May 3, 1961. LBJVPCR Box 2.

16. Memorandum from Berl Bernhard to Burke Marshall, March 30, 1961. CRDKA reel #6.

17. JFKPPP 1961 p. 10; Wofford, *Of Kennedys and Kings* p. 136; memorandum from Frank Reeves to John Doar, May 2, 1961. CRDKA reel #4; *Jet* March 30, 1961.

18. JFKPPP 1961 p. 22.

19. Ibid. p. 69.

20. *PC* February 18, 1961; *NYT* February 9, 1961; *Washington Afro-American*, February 11, 1961.

21. JFKPPP 1961 p. 125l; Wofford, *Of Kennedys and Kings* p. 135; Harris Wofford interview with the author.

22. JFKPPP 1961 p. 790.

23. Memorandum from Arthur M. Schlesinger to JFK, March 16, 1961. JFKPOF Box 65; letter from Chester Bowles to JFK, March 13, 1961. JFKPOF Box 28.

24. Memorandum from Harris Wofford to JFK, March 14, 1961. AGGC Box 6; *NYT* March 18, 1961; *NYT* March 22, 1961.

25. JFKPPP 1961 p. 217.

26. Wofford, *Of Kennedys and Kings* p. 149.

27. *NYT* April 15, 1961; Charles V. Hamilton, *Adam Clayton Powell, Jr.: The Political Biography of an American Dilemma* pp. 340–341.

28. Memorandum from JFK to Myer Feldman, February 16, 1961. JFKPOF Box 63.

29. Memorandum to JFK, undated and unsigned, JFKPOF Box 50; John Seigenthaler JFKOHP pp. 500–501.

30. Memorandum from Harris Wofford to JFK, April 18, 1961. CRDKA reel #8.

31. *NYT* January 12, 1961; memorandum from Mike Manatos to Lawrence O'Brien, March 29, 1961. Lawrence O'Brien Papers Box 17.

32. *Atlanta Constitution* May 10, 1961; letter from Hubert Humphrey to Lawrence O'Brien, March 24, 1961. CRDKA reel #8; unsigned memorandum to Hubert Humphrey, March 27, 1961. CRDKA reel #18; *WP* May 9, 1961; Wofford, *Of Kennedys and Kings* p. 150; *NYT* May 18, 1961.

33. *NYT* May 9 1961; *NYT* May 11, 1961.

34. Memorandum from Louis Martin to Theodore Sorensen, May 10, 1961. TSP Box 30.

35. Berl Bernhard JFKOHP p. 5.

36. Wofford, *Of Kennedys and Kings* pp. 131–133; Harris Wofford JFKOHP pp. 34–36.

37. Letter from Harris Wofford to LBJ, April 21, 1961. LBJVPCR Box 1.

38. Memorandum from Harris Wofford to Pierre Salinger, July 18, 1961. HWP Box 14.

39. Minutes of the Sub-cabinet Group on Civil Rights, April 14, 1961. HWP Box 14; memorandum from Fred Dutton to JFK, May 26, 1961. CRDKA reel # 6.

40. Memorandum from Roswell Gilpatric to the Secretary of the Army, June 19, 1961. BMP Box 34; letter from Carlisle Runge, Assistant Secretary of Defense, to Murray Gross, November 29, 1961. JFKPOF Box 97.

41. Memorandum from Stewart Udall to Fred Dutton, August 26, 1961. LBJVPCR Box 1; the story is told in Thomas G. Smith, "Civil Rights on the Gridiron: The Kennedy Administration and the Desegregation of the Washington Redskins," *Journal of Sport History* 14 (Summer 1987).

42. Wofford, *Of Kennedys and Kings* p. 148.

43. *Jet* January 25, 1961.

44. Memorandum, unsigned, December 11, 1961. HWP Box 1; *Jet* May 18, 1961.

45. *NYT* May 23, 1961.

46. *PC* April 29, 1961; *PC* May 13, 1961.

47. Letter from Harris Wofford to Walter Karatz, November 20th, 1961. HWP Box 4; Fite, *Richard B. Russell* p. 395.

48. Wofford, *Of Kennedys and Kings* p. 148; Harris Wofford interview with author.

CHAPTER 15

1. John Seigenthaler JFKOHP pp. 183–201.

2. Guthman and Shulman, *Robert Kennedy* p. 73; Arthur M. Schlesinger, Jr. *Robert Kennedy and His Times* p. 233.

3. *NR* December 26, 1960; Joseph Rauh interview with author.

4. Bobby Baker, *Wheeling and Dealing: Confessions of a Capitol Hill Operator* pp. 120–140.

5. Letter from Sam Ervin to T. G. Willis, January 13, 1961. SEP Box 62.

6. Helen O'Donnell, *A Common Good: The Friendship of Robert F. Kennedy and Kenneth P. O'Donnell* p. 67.

7. Guthman and Shulman, *Robert Kennedy* JFKPPP 1961 p. 66.

8. *WES* January 13, 1961; *NYT* January 14, 1961.

9. *NYT* January 14, 1961.

10. Schlesinger, *Robert Kennedy* p. 234; *NYT* January 14, 1961; Robert Sherrill, *Gothic Politics* p. 259; Guthman and Shulman, *Robert Kennedy* pp. 77–78.

11. *Look* March 28, 1961.

12. Guthman and Shulman, *Robert Kennedy* p. 57.

13. John Seigenthaler JFKOHP p. 210; Burke Marshall JFKOHP pp. 42–43; Edwin Guthman, *We Band of Brothers* pp. 95–96.

14. RFK Memorandum, February 9, 1961 RFK Papers, quoted in Schlesinger, *Robert Kennedy* p. 288.

15. Hearings of the Senate Judiciary Committee, March 2, 1961.

16. Letter from Burke Marshall to Leslie Dunbar, February 26, 1963. BMP Box 1; Burke Marshall, *Federalism and Civil Rights* p. 46; Michal Belknap, *Federal Law and Southern Order* p. 74.

17. Notes on civil rights meeting held in RFK's office on March 6, 1961. Edwin Guthman Personal Papers Box 1.

18. Ibid.

19. Ibid.

20. Guthman and Shulman, *Robert Kennedy* p. 107; Schlesinger, *A Thousand Days* p. 853.

21. John Seigenthaler JFKOHP p. 334.

22. Guthman and Shulman, *Robert Kennedy* p. 78.

23. Steven Lawson, *Black Ballots: Voting Rights in the South, 1944–69* p. 271.

24. RFK press conference, April 6, 1961. Edwin Guthman Personal Papers Box 1.

25. Memorandum from Harris Wofford to JFK, December 30, 1960. RFKPAF Box 52.

26. *Newsweek* November 28, 1960; Victor Navasky, *Kennedy Justice* p. 220.

27. Guthman and Shulman, *Robert Kennedy* p. 82; Wofford, *Of Kennedys and Kings* p. 135.

28. Liva Baker, *The Second Battle of New Orleans: The Hundred-Year Struggle to Integrate the Schools* pp. 462–463; Navasky, *Kennedy Justice* p. 273; *NYT* February 17, 1963.

29. Schlesinger, *Robert Kennedy and His Times* p. 289.

30. Transcript of WDSU-TV news. April 26, 1961. Edwin Guthman Personal Papers, Box 1.

31. Letter from Bill Monroe to Ed Guthman, May 3, 1961. Edwin Guthman Personal Papers, Box 1.

32. *Look* March 28, 1961.

33. *WP* April 27, 1961.

34. *WES* April 26, 1961.

35. *WP* April 27, 1961; *WES* May 8, 1961.

36. *WP* May 8, 1961; Bob Smith, *They Closed their Schools: Prince Edward County, Virginia, 1955–1964* pp. 192–193.

37. JFKPPP 1961 p. 572; *Ebony* Volume 17 1961.

38. Memorandum from Burke Marshall to RFK, September 6, 1961. BMP Box 8.

39. Michael Klarman, *From Jim Crow to Civil Rights* p. 360.

40. Memorandum from Fred Dutton to JFK, February 14, 1961, JFKPOF Box 97; memorandum from Burke Marshall to RFK, August 1961. BMP Box 3; David Halberstam, *The Fifties* p. 685; memorandum from Harris Wofford to JFK, December 12, 1960. RFKPPP Box 52; Halberstam, *The Fifties* p. 685.

41. Klarman, *From Jim Crow to Civil Rights* p. 363.

42. John Seigenthaler, quoted in Thompson, eds., *The Kennedy Presidency* pp. 117–118.

43. *WP* May 7, 1961; *NYT* May 7, 1961; *WP* May 7, 1961.

44. *NYT* May 7, 1961; Charlayne Hunter-Gault, interview with author; Edwin Guthman, *We Band of Brothers* p. 160.

45. *WP* May 7, 1961; *NYT* May 7, 1961; *Atlanta Constitution* May 8, 1961.

46. Charlayne Hunter-Gault, interview with author.

47. Letter from Theodore Hesburgh to RFK, May 15, 1961. AGPC Box 2; *Atlanta Constitution* May 8, 1961; *Pittsburgh Courier* May 20, 1961; *Jet* May 25, 1961; letter from Louis Martin to RFK, May 9, 1961. AGGC Box 35.

48. *WP* May 7, 1961.

49. *Atlanta Constitution* May 8, 1961; *WP* May 7, 1961.

CHAPTER 16

1. Letter from Roy Wilkins to Theodore Sorensen, February 6, 1961. TCS, Civil rights file; *PC* January 14, 1961.

2. Branch, *Parting the Waters* p. 404; letter from James Farmer to JFK, April 26, 1961. CRDKA reel #7. Harris Wofford, *Of Kennedys and Kings* p. 216.

3. Branch, *Parting the Waters* p. 406.

4. MLK JFKOHP pp. 14–16; *Jet* May 4, 1961.

5. Henry Hampton, *Voices of Freedom: An Oral History of the Civil Rights Movement from the 1950s through the 1980s* p. 75; Edwin Guthman, *We Band of Brothers* p. 167; Howell Raines, *My Soul Is Rested* p. 110.

6. Simeon Booker later recounted this conversation to Taylor Branch, *Parting the Waters* p. 413.

7. Compelling accounts of the Freedom Rides crisis are found in August Meier and Elliott Rudwick, *CORE: A Study in the Civil Rights Movement, 1942–1968*; John Lewis, with Michael D'Orso, *Walking with the Wind*; and Raines, *My Soul Is Rested*.

8. Gary Thomas Rowe, Jr., *My Undercover Years with the Ku Klux Klan* pp. 39–44.

9. Guthman *We Band of Brothers* pp. 167–168; Wilkins, *Standing Fast* p. 283; Burke Marshall JFKOHP p. 11.

10. *NYT* May 16, 1961; Gerald Strober, *Let Us Begin Anew: An Oral History of the Kennedy Presidency* p. 294; Wofford, *Of Kennedys and Kings* p. 153; p. 125.

11. Guthman, *We Band of Brothers* pp. 167–168; Wilkins, *Standing Fast* p. 283.

12. *Jet* June 1, 1961; Branch, *Parting the Waters* p. 426.

13. Guthman, *We Band of Brothers* p. 168; *Clarion Ledger* May 15, 1961.

14. Transcript of phone conversation between RFK and George Cruit, May 15, 1961. AGGC Box 10.

15. Wilkins, *Standing Fast* p. 283.

16. John Seigenthaler JFKOHP p. 433.

17. Lewis, *Walking with the Wind* p. 148.

18. *NYT* May 17, 1961; Burke Marshall JFKOHP pp. 5–8.

19. Nicholas Katzenbach JFKOHP p. 17.

20. Raines, *My Soul Is Rested* p. 118.

21. Schlesinger, *Robert Kennedy and His Times* p. 296; John Seigenthaler JFKLOHP p. 449.

22. Raines *My Soul Is Rested* p. 119.

23. Guthman, *Band of Brothers* p. 171.

24. Memorandum from John Seigenthaler to RFK, November 14, 1961. AGGC Box 53.

25. Jean Stein, *American Journey: The Times of Robert Kennedy* p. 103.

26. *Time* May 26, 1961; John Seigenthaler JFKOHP pp. 325–333.

27. Burke Marshall JFKOHP p. 25; Nicholas Katzenbach JFKOHP p. 25.

28. Brauer, *John F. Kennedy and the Second Reconstruction* p. 102; *NYT* May 21, 1961; *NYT* May 21, 1961.

29. *Time* May 26, 1961.

30. Branch, *Parting the Waters* p. 452.

31. JFKPPP 1961 p. 391; *NYT* May 21, 1961.

32. Transcript of phone conversation between RFK and John Patterson, May 20, 1961. AGGC Box 10.

33. *NYT* May 21, 1961; Nicholas Katzenbach JFKOHP pp. 22–23; Nicholas Katzenbach JFKOHP p. 10.

34. "Status Report on availability of troops," May 22, 1961. AGGC Box 10; Raines, *My Soul Is Rested* p. 309.

35. Louis Oberdorfer interview with author.

36. *Time* May 26, 1961.

37. Guthman, *We Band of Brothers* pp. 172–178; *Time* May 26, 1961; Taylor Branch, *Parting the Waters* pp. 462–463.

38. MLK sermon at First Baptist Church in Montgomery, May 21, 1961. MLK Papers Speeches 1961.

39. Edwin Guthman kept handwritten notes of the conversation, which formed the basis for his account in his 1971 memoir, *We Band of Brothers* pp. 177–178; MLK JFKOHP pp. 15–16; RFK Volume 2 pp. 20–21; reporter Harold B. Meyers was also party to these conversations, which formed the basis for his report in *Time* on May 26, 1961.

40. John Patterson JFKOHP p. 36; Guthman, *We Band of Brothers* p. 178; *Time* May 26, 1961.

41. William Orrick JFKOHP p. 92; *NYT* May 23, 1961.

42. Belknap, *Federal Law and Southern Order* p. 85; *Montgomery Advertiser* May 23, 1961.

43. Letter from RFK to Alabama Congressional Delegation, May 23, 1961. LBJVPCR Box 1; *NYT* May 24, 1961; *NYT* May 23, 1961.

44. Harris Wofford JFKOHP pp. 66–68.

45. Ibid.

46. Transcript of telephone conversation between Burke Marshall and John Patterson, May 22, 1961. AGGC Box 10; RFK JFKOHP Volume 3 p. 11; transcript of telephone conversation between RFK and Ross Barnett, May 23, 1961. AGGC Box 10.

47. *Newsweek* June 5, 1961; *Clarion Ledger* May 25, 1961.

48. *Newsweek* June 5, 1961; Brauer, *John F. Kennedy and the Second Reconstruction* p. 111; Burke Marshall JFKOHP p. 41.

49. Justice Department Press Release, May 24, 1961. AGGC Box 10; *Jackson Daily News* May 25, 1961.

50. Justice Department Press Release, May 24, 1961. AGGC, Box 10; letter from Sam Ervin to William Reasonover, May 24, 1961. SEP Box 64; *Bailey v. Patterson* 368 U.S. 346 (1961).

51. *Time* June 2, 1961; Wofford, *Of Kennedys and Kings* p. 156; *NYT* May 25, 1961.

52. *Time* June 2, 1961; *NYT* May 16, 1961.

53. Meier and Rudwick, *CORE* p. 139; Guthman, *We Band of Brothers* pp. 154–155.

54. Guthman, *We Band of Brothers* pp. 154–155; Wofford, *Of Kennedys and Kings* p. 155.

55. Wofford, *Of Kennedys and Kings* p. 156; *WP* May 25, 1961.

56. *Newsweek* June 5, 1961.

57. JFKPPP 1961 pp. 396–406; Wofford, *Of Kennedys and Kings* p. 157.

58. Wofford, *Of Kennedys and Kings* p. 158; memorandum from Harris Wofford to JFK, May 29, 1961. JFKPOF Box 67.

59. Letter from Harris Wofford to JFK, June 6, 1961. JFKPOF Box 67; JFKPPP 1961 p. 517.

60. *The Gallup Poll: Public Opinion 1935–1971 Volume III* p. 1723.

61. Victor Navasky, *Kennedy Justice* p. 23; Burke Marshall JFKOHP pp. 52–53.

62. Wofford, *Of Kennedys and Kings* p. 156.

63. Telegram from John Patterson to RFK, August 28, 1961. AGGC Box 9; Timothy B. Tyson, *Radio Free Dixie: Robert F. Williams and the Roots of Black Power* pp. 262–286.

64. *Atlanta Journal* December 19, 1961; *New York Herald Tribune* December 19, 1961; *NR* July 20, 1963.

65. *Time* June 2, 1961; *NYT* May 26, 1961; telegram from John Patterson to RFK, August 28, 1961. AGGC Box 9.

66. RFK JFKOHP pp. 578–580.

CHAPTER 17

1. *Jet* July 6, 1961; *Commentary* April 1961; Marable, *Race, Reform and Rebellion* pp. 70, 74.

2. Minutes of Sub-cabinet Meeting, June 16, 1961. HWP Box 14; Wofford, *Of Kennedys and Kings* pp. 158–160.

3. Quoted in Belknap, *Federal Law and Southern Order* p. 107.

4. Branch, *Parting the Waters* p. 480; James Farmer, *Lay Bare the Heart: An Autobiography of the Civil Rights Movement* pp. 219–220; Raines, *My Soul Is Rested* pp. 245–246.

5. Meier and Rudwick, *CORE* pp. 174–175.

6. Raines, *My Soul Is Rested* p. 250.

7. Ibid. p. 231.

8. *NYT* May 20, 1961.

9. Giglio, *The Presidency of John F. Kennedy* p. 43; Bass, *Unlikely Heroes* p. 165; Guthman and Shulman, *Robert Kennedy in His Own Words* pp. 106–108.

10. Wilkins, *Standing Fast* p. 284; telegram from Roy Wilkins to JFK, June 22, 1961. HWP Box 11; Alexander Bickel, "Impeach Judge Cox," *NR* September 4, 1965.

11. Watters and Cleghorn, *Climbing Jacob's Ladder: The Arrival of Negroes in Southern Politics* p. 219.

12. Navasky, *Kennedy Justice* p. 266; Louis Oberdorfer interview with author.

13. Bass, *Unlikely Heroes* p. 168; Watters and Cleghorn, *Climbing Jacob's Ladder* p. 220.

14. Louis Martin JFKOHP p. 83.

15. Robert Sherrill, *Gothic Politics in the Deep South* p. 212; *Washington Afro-American* September 9, 1961; *Chicago Defender* September 23, 1961.

16. *1961 United States Commission on Civil Rights Report: 1. Voting* (Washington, D.C.: U.S. Government Printing Office, 1961).

17. *1961 United States Commission on Civil Rights Report: 2. Education* (Washington, D.C.: U.S. Government Printing Office, 1961).

18. *1961 United States Commission on Civil Rights Report: 5. Justice* (Washington, D.C.: U.S. Government Office, 1961).

19. Navasky, *Kennedy Justice* p. 116; memorandum from Burke Marshall to Byron White, December 12, 1961. BMP Box 1A.

20. *WES* April 18, 1961; *NYT* August 31, 1961.

21. "Report of the Attorney General to the President of the United States on the Department of Justice's Activities in the Field of Civil Rights," December 29, 1961.

22. JFKPPP 1961 p. 703; "Major Foreign Policy Measures Taken by the Kennedy administration," September 19, 1961. TSP Box 34.

23. "Report of the Attorney General," December 29, 1961.

24. Joseph Rauh JFKOHP pp. 102–103; Joseph Rauh interview with author; Sam Beer interview with author; Abe Fortas LBJOHP pp. 13–14.

25. Transcript of *Meet the Press* September 24, 1961; Wofford, *Of Kennedys and Kings* p. 161.

26. Burke Marshall JFKOHP p. 64; Guthman and Shulman, *Robert Kennedy in His Own Words* p. 148; memorandum from Harris Wofford to Lee White, September 29, 1961. CRDKA reel #7; Reeves, *President Kennedy* p. 270; Burke Marshall JFKOHP p. 60.

27. *Jet* June 29, 1961; *USNWR* November 20, 1961.

28. *Ebony* Volume 17, 1961.

29. Wilkins, *Standing Fast* p. 284; statement by Bishop Stephen G. Spottswood, July 12, 1961. HWP Box 5.

30. Wilkins, *Standing Fast* p. 285.

31. Simeon Booker, *Black Man's America* p. 24.

32. *Jet* October 26, 1961; *Look* November, 1964; Stewart Burns, *To the Mountaintop: Martin Luther King's Sacred Mission to Save America, 1955–1968* p. 172.

33. James Farmer interview with author.

34. *Newsweek* January 29, 1962.

35. Giglio, *The Presidency of John F. Kennedy* pp. 99–104.

36. *Clarion Ledger* May 19, 1961; Randall Ripley, *Kennedy and Congress* (New York: General Learning Press, 1972) p. 22.

37. Press Release, ADA, October 2, 1961. Sam Beer Papers Box 2; Wilkins, *Standing Fast* p. 279; Allen Ellender JFKOHP p. 14; Wilbur Mills JFKOHP p. 82.

38. Fite, *Richard B. Russell* p. 394.

39. Reeves, *President Kennedy* p. 274.

CHAPTER 18

1. Memorandum from Lee White to JFK, November 13, 1961. TSP Box 30.

2. Ibid.

3. JFKPPP 1962 p. 8.

4. *NYT* January 12, 1962.

5. Ibid.; *Washington Afro-American* January 20, 1961.

6. JFKPPP 1962 p. 21; *Washington Afro-American* January 20, 1962.

7. *NYT* January 25, 1962.

8. JFKPPP 1962 pp. 60–61.

9. *Newsweek* March 5, 1962; *Washington Afro-American* January 27, 1962; *NYT* January 25, 1962; telegram from Roy Wilkins to JFK, undated, TSP Box 30; letter from Charles Abrams to Burke Marshall, March 5, 1962. BMP Box 4; memorandum from Louis Martin to RFK, April 10, 1962.

10. *WES* February 20, 1962.

11. *NYT* February 21, 1962.

12. *WES* February 22, 1962.

13. Memorandum from Mike Manatos to Lawrence O'Brien, January 19, 1962. WHSF: Mike Manatos Box 1.

14. Burke Marshall JFKOHP p. 64; *WP* April 13, 1962.

15. The five states were Alabama, Arkansas, Mississippi, Texas, and Virginia.

16. The House approved the poll tax amendment on August 27, and within two years it was ratified as the Twenty-Fourth Amendment to the Constitution.

17. Memorandum from Lawrence O'Brien to JFK, April 16, 1962. JFKPOF Box 64.

18. Memorandum, unsigned and undated. JFKPOF Box 50.

19. Letter from Burke Marshall to Paul Freund, March 7, 1962. BMP Box 1A; Burke Marshall interview with author.

20. *WP* March 16, 1962; *WP* March 30, 1962.

21. *WP* April 11, 1962.

22. *WP* April 14, 1962.

23. *NYT* May 9, 1962; *WP* May 9, 1962.

24. JFKPPP 1962 pp. 382–383.

25. *NYT* May 10, 1962; *NYT* May 15, 1963.

26. *Congressional Quarterly Almanac, 1962* p. 377; *CR* May 15, 1962 p. 8416; *Time* May 18, 1962; David J. Garrow, *Bearing the Cross: Martin Luther King, Jr., and the Southern Christian Leadership Conference* p. 199; Burke Marshall interview with author.

27. *NYT* May 10, 1962.

28. Memorandum from Lawrence O'Brien to JFK, July 23, 1962. JFKPOF Box 51.

29. *PC* April 15, 1961.

30. Troutman memorandum quoted in Hugh Davis Graham, *The Civil Rights Era* p. 51.

31. Evans and Novak, *Lyndon Johnson* p. 317.

32. *NYT* April 6, 1962; letter from C. Sumner Stone to LBJ, March 9, 1962. George Reedy Papers, LBJL, Box 7.

33. Letter from RFK to LBJ, May 8, 1962. Whfn-rfk, LBJL, Box 6.

34. Graham, *The Civil Rights Era* p. 56.

35. Letter from Bobby Troutman to JFK, June 30, 1962. JFKPOF Box 65; memorandum from JFK to LBJ, August 22, 1962. TSP Box 30.

36. Memorandum from JFK to LBJ, August 22, 1962. TSP Box 30.

37. *NYT* May 9, 1962.

38. *NYT* March 31, 1962.

39. Memorandum from Lee White to JFK, November 13, 1961. WHSF Box 358; Berl Bernhard JFKOHP p. 42.

40. Letter from Whitney Young to Gerhard Gesell, August 27, 1962.

41. *Washington Afro-American* April 14, 1962; *Jet* April 26, 1962.

CHAPTER 19

1. Wofford, *Of Kennedys and Kings* p. 166; memorandum from Harris Wofford to Kenneth O'Donnell, October 4, 1961. CRDKA reel #1.

2. Memorandum from Harris Wofford to JFK, January 20, 1962. JFKPOF Box 67; memorandum from Harris Wofford to JFK, January 23, 1962. JFKPOF Box 67.

3. Memorandum from Harris Wofford to JFK, March 7, 1962. JFKPOF Box 67.

4. Wofford, *Of Kennedys and Kings* p. 125.

5. Ibid. p. 167; letter from Sargent Shriver to Harris Wofford, October 4, 1962. Sargent Shriver Papers Series 1 Box 12; *Washington Afro-American* April 14, 1962.

6. Reese Cleghorn, "Epilogue in Albany, Were the Mass Marches Worthwhile?" in *NR* July 20, 1963.

7. Garrow, *Bearing the Cross* p. 201.

8. *The Nation* March 3, 1962; Garrow, *Bearing the Cross* p. 197.

9. Ralph Abernathy, *And the Walls Came Tumbling Down* p. 214.

10. *NYT* July 12, 1962.

11. Ibid.; Burke Marshall JFKOHP pp. 69–70.

12. Branch, *Parting the Waters* p. 603.

13. Ibid. p. 604.

14. Ibid. p. 606.

15. *Atlanta Journal* July 12, 1962; *NYT* July 12, 1962.

16. *CR* July 20, 1962 p. 14248.

17. *NYT* July 21, 1962.

18. *NYT* July 22, 1962.

19. Andrew Young, *An Easy Burden: The Civil Rights Movement and the Transformation of America* p. 180; memorandum from J. Edgar Hoover to RFK, August 8, 1962. FBI Files: MLK Papers; MLK JFKOHP p. 25; Branch, *Parting the Waters* pp. 610–611.

20. MLK JFKOHP p. 25; Branch, *Parting the Waters* pp. 610–611; *NYT* July 22, 1962.

21. Telegram from Burke Marshall to MLK, July 26, 1962. BMP Box 16.

22. *NYT* July 25, 1962.

23. *Time* August 3, 1962.

24. Garrow, *Bearing the Cross* p. 211.

25. William G. Anderson, *Meet the Press* July 29, 1962.

26. Telegram from Roy Wilkins to JFK, July 30, 1962; telegram from James Farmer to JFK, July 30, 1962; telegram from Walter Reuther to JFK, August 1, 1962. CRDKA Reel #5; *CR* August 1, 1962 p. 15215.

27. *NYT* July 28, 1962.

28. Garrow, *Bearing the Cross* p. 212.

29. *NYT* July 27, 1962.

30. *NYT* July 29, 1962; *The Nation* December 1, 1962.

31. *NYT* July 27, 1962; John Doar recounted the story to the author Taylor Branch. Branch, *Parting the Waters* p. 620; memorandum from Burke Marshall to RFK, August 29, 1962. BMP Box 16.

32. JFKPPP 1962 pp. 592–593.

33. Telegram from MLK to JFK, August 2, 1962. CRDKA reel #4; Garrow, *Bearing the Cross* p. 212; telegram from A. Philip Randolph to JFK, August 2, 1961. CRDKA Reel #2; telegram from Roy Wilkins to JFK, August 2, 1961. CRDKA reel #2; *The Nation* December 1, 1962.

34. *Albany Herald* August 10, 1962.

35. William M. Kunstler, *Deep in My Heart* pp. 118–119.

36. Ibid.

37. *NYT* August 9, 1962.

38. Ibid.

39. Ibid.

40. News Release from Jackie Robinson, August 15, 1962, MLK Papers Series 1 Box 20; *NYT* August 7, 1962; memorandum from William Taylor to Lee White, August 15, 1962, LWP Box 21.

41. *NYT* August 11, 1962; *NYT* August 16, 1962.

42. Telegram from MLK to JFK, August 31, 1962. CRDKA #5.

43. SNCC press please, September 10, 1962, SNCC Papers.

44. *NYT* September 13, 1962.

45. JFKPPP 1962 pp. 378–379.

46. Brauer, *John F. Kennedy* pp. 145–146; *NYT* February 28, 1963.

47. Fairclough, *To Redeem the Soul of America* p. 108.

CHAPTER 20

1. JFKPPP 1962 p. 497; *Jet* May 31, 1962.

2. Letter from Fred Schwengel to Kenneth O'Donnell, August 24, 1962. Arthur M. Schlesinger White House Papers Box 15; Lee White interview with author.

3. JFKPPP 1962 p. 702.

4. *NYT* September 22, 1962.

5. Letter from Pierre Salinger to William Burn, May 25, 1962. CRDKA reel #2; *NYT* September 23, 1962; Berl Bernhard JFKOHP p. 55; *Jet* September 27, 1962.

6. William Doyle, *An American Insurrection: The Battle of Oxford, Mississippi, 1962* pp. 29–30; James Meredith, *Three Years in Mississippi* p. 294.

7. James Silver, *Mississippi: A Closed Society* p. 6.

8. Jack Bass and Walter DeVries, *The Transformation of Southern Politics: Social Change and Political Consequences since 1945* p. 195.

9. William Doyle, *An American Insurrection* p. 28.

10. *NYT* September 11, 1962.

11. Guthman and Shulman, *Robert Kennedy* p. 195.

12. Ibid. p. 160; Schlesinger, *Robert Kennedy and His Times* p. 318.

13. Sorensen, *Kennedy* p. 483; Norbert Schlei JFKOHP p. 13.

14. Doyle, *An American Insurrection* p. 65.

15. Schlesinger, *Robert Kennedy and His Times* p. 318; Lord, *The Past That Would Not Die* p. 143.

16. *Clarion Ledger* September 15, 1962.

17. *New Orleans Times-Picayune* September 21, 1962.

18. *Wall Street Journal* September 27, 1962; *NYT* September 24, 1962.

19. Conversation between RFK and Ross Barnett, September 24, 1962. BMP Box 20.

20. Conversation between RFK and Ross Barnett, at 12:20 P.M., September 25, 1962. BMP Box 20.

21. Ibid.

22. *NYT* September 26, 1962.

23. Conversation between RFK and Ross Barnett at 6:10 P.M., September 25, 1962. BMP Box 20.

24. *Time* September 29, 1962; conversation between RFK and Ross Barnett at 7:25 P.M., September 25, 1962. BMP Box 20.

25. Guthman, *We Band of Brothers* pp. 191–192.

26. Memorandum from Burke Marshall to RFK, September 27, 1962. BMP Box 20.

27. Conversation between RFK and Ross Barnett at 2:50 P.M., September 26, 1962. BMP Box 20.

28. Conversation between RFK and Ross Barnett at 4:20 P.M., September 26, 1962. BMP Box 20.

29. Conversation between RFK and Ross Barnett at 6:35 P.M., September 26, 1962. BMP Box 20.

30. *NYT* September 29, 1962; Schlesinger, *Robert Kennedy and His Times* p. 320.

31. *NYT* September 27, 1961.

32. Burke Marshall JFKOHP p. 73; memorandum from Theodore Sorensen to JFK, September 28, 1962. JFKPOF Box 97.

33. *NYT* September 27, 1962; *NYT* September 28, 1962.

34. Telegram from James E. Folsom to JFK, September 19, 1962. AGPC Box 11; unsigned note detailing James Coleman's telephone call, undated. AGPC Box 11.

35. *Wall Street Journal* September 26, 1962; *NYT* September 27, 1962; telegram from John Patterson to JFK, September 27, 1962. CRDKA reel #4.

36. Doyle, *An American Insurrection* p. 104; Schlesinger, *A Thousand Days* p. 942.

37. Lord, *The Past That Would Not Die* p. 159; Doyle, *An American Insurrection* p. 98.

38. *Look* December 31, 1962.

39. Doyle, *An American Insurrection* pp. 107–108.

40. Schlesinger, *Robert Kennedy and His Times* p. 320.

41. Conversation between JFK and Ross Barnett, September 29, 1962. BMP Box 20; Schlesinger, *Robert Kennedy and His Times* p. 321.

42. Conversation between JFK, RFK and Ross Barnett, September 29, 1962. BMP Box 20.

43. *NYT* September 30, 1962; *Time* October 5, 1962.

44. Wilkins, *Standing Fast* p. 286.

45. Norbert Schlei JFKOHP pp. 14–15.

46. Conversation between RFK and Ross Barnett, September 30, 1962. BMP Box 20.

47. Nicholas Katzenbach JFKOHP pp. 98–99.

48. Lord, *The Past That Would Not Die* pp. 215–217.

49. Unpublished memoirs of Max Jacobson quoted in Richard Reeves, *President Kennedy* p. 364; Sorensen, *Kennedy* p. 484.

50. Doyle, *An American Insurrection* p. 144.

51. *NYT* October 1, 1962; Doyle, *An American Insurrection* p. 146.

52. Lord, *The Past That Would Not Die* p. 202; Burke Marshall JFKOHP p. 79; memorandum from Jack Rosenthal to Burke Marshall, undated. BMP Box 19.

53. JFKPPP 1962 pp. 726–728.

54. Transcript of White House Audiotape Tape 26, September 30, 1962; RFK, undated notes. AGPC Box 11.

55. Ibid.

56. Dictabelt recording 4F.4 of conversation between JFK and Ross Barnett, September 30, 1962.

57. Dictabelt recording 4F.5 of conversation between JFK and Ross Barnett, September 30, 1962.

58. Transcript of White House Audiotape Tape 26, September 30, 1962.

59. *NYT* October 3, 1962.

60. Transcript of White House Audiotape Tape 26, September 30, 1962.

61. Ibid.; Schlesinger, *Robert Kennedy and His Times* p. 324.

62. Hugh Sidey, *John F. Kennedy, President* p. 265.

63. Dictabelt recording 4G.3 of conversation between JFK and Ross Barnett, October 1, 1962; *NYT* October 2, 1962; Doyle, *An American Insurrection* pp. 273–278.

64. Burke Marshall JFKOHP p. 83.

65. Burke Marshall memorandum to file, January 1, 1963. BMP Box 9.

66. *Nashville Tennessean* October 3, 1962; FIND in notebook; notes from Dean Markham, October 9, 1962. AGPC Box 11.

67. Telegram from Strom Thurmond to JFK, September 30, 1962; telegram from John Bell Williams to JFK, October 12, 1962. CRDKA reel #4; letter from Richard Russell to Waldo McCook, October 17, 1962. RRP Series X Box 154.

68. *NYT* October 1, 1962.

69. Bobby Baker, with Larry L. King, *Wheeling and Dealing: Confessions of a Capitol Hill Operator* p. 100; letter from Sam Ervin to Franklin Smith, October 5, 1962. SEP, SHC, Box 79; letter from Sam Ervin to Allen Gwyn, Jr., October 17, 1962. SEP, SHC, Box 79; *Wall Street Journal* October 4, 1960.

70. Brauer, *John F. Kennedy* p. 202.

71. Ibid.; *Amsterdam News* October 6, 1962.

72. Telegram from A. Philip Randolph to JFK, October 2, 1962. CRDKA reel #4; *Look* November 17, 1964; *Buffalo Evening News* January 31, 1963.

73. Guthman, *We Band of Brothers* p. 205.

74. Memorandum from Major General C.V. Clifton to JFK, October 4, 1962. JFKPOF Box 98; memorandum from Major General C.V. Clifton to JFK, October 5, 1962. JFKPOF Box 98; memorandum from Major General C.V. Clifton to JFK, October 2, 1962. JFKPOF Box 98; memorandum from Burke Marshall to RFK, April 23, 1963. BMP Box 8; memorandum from Cyrus Vance to Robert McNamara, May 7, 1963. BMP Box 19.

75. Doyle, *An American Insurrection* p. 290; *Freedomways* Spring 1965; Louis Martin JFKOHP p. 107; Department of Defense Press Release, February 26, 1963. BMP Box 9.

76. Guthman and Shulman, *Robert Kennedy in His Own Words* p. 167.

77. Notes of Dean Markham, October 9, 1962; RFK notes, undated. AGPC Box 11; "Shell Mississippi roadmap" AGPC Box 11.

78. Letter from RFK to Mrs. John Stennis, March 29, 1963. AGGC Box 8; JFKPPP 1962 pp. 893–894.

79. *Time* October 12, 1962.

80. Memorandum from Louis Martin to RFK, September 24, 1962. BMP Box 9; memorandum from Burke Marshall to RFK, October 19, 1962, BMP Box 9.

81. Sorensen, *Kennedy* p. 491.

CHAPTER 21

1. Schlesinger, *Robert Kennedy and His Times* p. 545.

2. *The Gallup Poll* p. 1800; memorandum from Louis Martin to Robert Kennedy, September 24, 1962. AGPC Box 12.

3. Letter from Martha Griffiths to Lawrence O'Brien, September 18, 1962. LWP Box 21; memorandum from Lawrence O'Brien to Lee White, September 11, 1962. LWP Box 21; memorandum from Bill Welsh to Lee White, October 4, 1962. LWP Box 21; memorandum from Lawrence O'Brien to Lee White, September 11, 1963. LWP Box 21; memorandum from Theodore Sorensen to files, October 16, 1962. TSP Box 59.

4. Memorandum from Louis Harris to JFK, November 19, 1962. JFKPOF Box 30; DNC press statement, November 8, 1962. AGPC Box 12; DNC press statement, November 8, 1962. AGPC Box 12; *Time* January 25, 1963.

5. Frank E. Smith, *Congressman from Mississippi* pp. 284–286.

6. *USNWR* November 19, 1962; *Newsweek* January 28, 1963.

7. *Time* January 25, 1963.

8. Memorandum from Louis Harris to JFK, November 19, 1962. JFKPOF Box 30.

9. Letter from Leonard Frank to JFK, November 9, 1962. CRDKA reel #7; Norbert Schlei JFKOHP pp. 30–32.

10. Brauer, *John F. Kennedy* p. 208.

11. JFKPPP 1962 pp. 831–832.

12. Telegram from A. Philip Randolph to JFK, November 21, 1962. CRDKA reel #7; telegram from Roy Wilkins to JFK, November 21, 1962. CRDKA reel #7; telegram from MLK to JFK, November 20, 1962. CRDKA reel #7; *Amsterdam News* December 13, 1962; *PC* December 22, 1962.

13. Memorandum from Roger Wilkins to Ralph Dungan, November 19, 1962. WHSF Box 358.

14. Oliver Hill JFKOHP p. 51; David Lawrence JFKOHP p. 18.

15. Thomas Borstelmann, *The Cold War and the Color Line: American Race Relations in the Global Arena* pp. 135–171.

16. *WP* December 18, 1962; *Jet* January 3, 1963.

17. *PC* December 18, 1962; *Jet* January 3, 1963.

18. Garrow, *Bearing the Cross* p. 225.

19. *WP* December 18, 1962; Booker, *Black Man's America* pp. 30–31.

20. Booker, *Black Man's America* pp. 30–31.

21. Memorandum from RFK to JFK, January 24, 1963. JFKPOF Box 80; memorandum from Burke Marshall to RFK, October 4, 1963. BMP Box 6.

22. *NYT* January 13, 1963.

23. Schlesinger, *Robert Kennedy and His Times* p. 397.

24. JFKPPP 1962 p. 890.

25. Memorandum from Berl Bernhard to Lee White, June 19, 1962. LWP Box 20; Berl Bernhard JFKOHP p. 55; *Jet* September 27, 1962.

26. Memorandum from William Taylor to Lee White, July 9, 1962. LWP Box 20; memorandum from Berl Bernhard to Arthur M. Schlesinger, December 13, 1962. LWP Box 20; memorandum to from Berl Bernhard and Louis Martin to Theodore Sorensen and Lee White, August 14, 1962. BBP Box 5.

27. Memorandum from Lee White to Pierre Salinger, December 26, 1962. LWP Box 20.

28. Speech by LBJ at Wayne State University, Detroit, Michigan, January 7, 1963. BBP Box 4.

29. Letter from Hubert Humphrey to JFK, January 8, 1963. WHSF Box 363.

30. MLK JFKOHP p. 17.

31. JFKPPP 1963 p. 14; *NYT* January 15, 1963.

32. Report from RFK to JFK, January 24, 1963. BMP Box 16.

33. *NYT* January 18, 1963; Schlesinger, *Robert Kennedy and His Times* pp. 398–401.

34. Letter from Paul Douglas to JFK, January 26, 1963. BMP Box 5; *NYT* February 1, 1963.

35. Memorandum from Louis Martin to Theodore Sorensen, January 30, 1963. TSP Box 30; memorandum from JFK, January 28, 1963; memorandum from JFK, January 31, 1963. JFKPOF Box 62.

36. *WP* February 13, 1962.

37. Booker, *Black Man's America* p. 34.

38. *Newsweek* February 22, 1963; *WP* February 13, 1962.

39. *WP* February 13, 1962; *Chicago Daily Tribune* February 13, 1963; *NYT* February 13, 1963.

40. *Newsweek* February 25, 1963.

41. Speech by Chester Bowles, Lincoln University, Oxford, Pennsylvania, February 15, 1963. AGGC Box 6.

42. Ibid.

43. *Jet* March 22, 1962; letter from Jackie Robinson to MLK, October 9, 1962. King Papers Series 1 Box 20.

44. Roy Wilkins speech in New York, January 7, 1963. AGCP Box 67; *USNWR* May 29, 1963.

45. *NYT* January 2, 1963; *Time* February 15, 1963; Reeves, *President Kennedy* p. 465.

46. Memorandum from Lee White to JFK, February 25, 1963, TSP Box 30.

47. Memorandum from Lawrence O'Brien and Theodore Sorensen to JFK, February 26, 1963. JFKPOF Box 52; Lee White, JFKLOHP p. 101.

48. JFKPPP 1963 pp. 221–222.

49. Ibid. pp. 222–225.

50. Ibid. pp. 225–226.

51. Ibid. p. 230.

52. Memorandum from Mike Manatos to Lawrence O'Brien, February 15, 1963. Mike Manatos Papers Box 1.

53. *The Nation* March 30, 1963.

54. JFKPPP 1963 p. 239; *NYT* March 7, 1963; telephone conversation between JFK and Nicholas Katzenbach, March 7, 1963. Dictabelt recording 11A5; memorandum from Joe Dolan to Theodore Sorensen, April 23, 1964. TSP Box 30.

55. Brauer, *John F. Kennedy* p. 223.

56. *NYT* February 28, 1963; *NYT* March 4, 1963.

57. Telegram from Roy Wilkins to JFK, March 7, 1963; telegram from A. Philip Randolph to JFK, March 27, 1963; telegram from James Forman to JFK, March 25, 1963, CRDKA reel #5.

58. *NYT* April 3, 1963.

59. Memorandum from Lawrence O'Brien to JFK, March 25, 1963. JFKPOF Box 52; *NYT* March 29, 1963; *NYT* March 29, 1963.

60. Department of Justice press conference, April 2, 1963, BMP Box 8.

61. Telegram from MLK to JFK, March 28, 1963. Martin Luther King Papers Box 14 folder 5; telegram from Walter Reuther to JFK, Aril 1, 1963. WHCF Box 24.

62. JFKPPP 1963 p. 311.

63. Adam Fairclough, *Better Day Coming* p. 256.

64. *Atlanta Journal* April 17, 1963; *Atlanta Journal* April 14, 1963.

65. Memorandum from Lee White to Lawrence O'Brien, April 17, 1963. LWP Box 22; Garrow, *Bearing the Cross* p. 233.

66. Memorandum from Lee White to JFK, February 25, 1963. TSP Box 30; letter from John Hannah to Kenneth O'Donnell, December 28, 1962, BBP Box 5; letter from Kenneth O'Donnell to John Hannah, December 17, 1962, BBP Box 5.

67. Letter from RFK to John Hannah, December 15, 1962. NAACP papers, transfile 2, LC.

68. Berl Bernhard JFKOHP pp. 24–26.

69. *United States Commission on Civil Rights, Interim Report* (Mimeo, April 16, 1963).

70. Memorandum from Burke Marshall to JFK, April 8, 1963. BMP Box 2; memorandum from Lee White to JFK, April 10, 1963. LWP Box 23.

71. Wofford, *Of Kennedys and Kings* p. 164.

72. *USNWR* April, 1963; *NYT* April 19, 1963; *PC* May 4, 1963.

73. JFKPPP 1963 pp. 334–335; letter from JFK to John Hannah, April 19, 1963. JFKPOF Box 97; *NYT* April 20, 1963.

74. Foster Rhea Dulles, *The Civil Rights Commission: 1957–1965* p. 181.

75. Report of the Mississippi General Legislative Investigating Committee, April 24, 1963; *NYT* May 9, 1963.

76. Justice Department press statement, April 24, 1963. BMP Box 20; Kennedy, *Profiles in Courage* p. 151; Guthman and Shulman, *Robert Kennedy in His Own Words* p. 161.

77. Brauer, *John F. Kennedy* p. 153.

78. Ibid. p. 240.

CHAPTER 22

1. *NYT* April 4, 1960; *Atlanta Inquirer* April 14, 1962.

2. Telegram from MLK to JFK, December 15, 1962 White House Central Files; David J. Garrow, *The FBI and Martin Luther King, Jr.: From "Solo" to Memphis* p. 58.

3. The literature on the Birmingham demonstrations is extensive. The best accounts are found in Garrow, *Bearing the Cross* pp. 231–286; Glenn T. Eskew, *But for Birmingham: The Local and National Movements in the Civil Rights Struggle*; Diane McWhorter, *Carry Me Home: Birmingham, Alabama, the Climactic Battle of the Civil Rights Revolution* pp. 303–454; Taylor Branch, *Parting the Waters* pp. 708–845.

4. Letter from David Vann to Burke Marshall, January 19, 1963; letter from David Vann to Burke Marshall, January 22, 1963. BMP Box 17.

5. *Birmingham News* April 3, 1963; Eskew, *But for Birmingham* p. 216; Branch, *Parting the Waters* p. 725.

6. Burke Marshall JFKOHP pp. 95–96; McWhorter, *Carry Me Home* p. 323.

7. Eskew, *But for Birmingham* p. 226.

8. *NYT* April 13, 1963.

9. *NYT* April 17, 1963; Eskew, *But for Birmingham* p. 260.

10. *NYT* April 14, 1963; McWhorter, *Carry Me Home* p. 347.

11. Branch, *Parting the Waters* p. 735.

12. King, *My Life with Martin Luther King* p. 209; Schlesinger, *Robert Kennedy and His Times* p. 328.

13. King, *My Life with Martin Luther King* pp. 210–211.

14. *Birmingham News* April 13, 1963.

15. JFKPPP 1963 pp. 347–348.

16. Eskew, *But for Birmingham* p. 261.

17. *Newsweek* May 13, 1963; *NYT* May 3, 1963.

18. *NYT* May 3, 1963; *NYT* May 4, 1963.

19. Statement by RFK, May 3, 1963. BMP Box 19.

20. *NYT* May 4, 1963; *NYT* May 5, 1963; Klarman, *From Jim Crow to Civil Rights* p. 436.

21. Recording of meeting between JFK and ADA leaders, May 4, 1963. Presidential Recording #85.

22. Schlesinger, *A Thousand Days* p. 959.

23. *NYT* May 5, 1963.

24. Memorandum from Theodore Sorensen to JFK, May 7, 1963. TSP Box 59.

25. Recording of meeting between JFK and ADA leaders, May 4, 1963. Presidential Recording #85.

26. *NYT* May 8, 1963.

27. JFKPPP 1963 p. 372, p. 378.

28. Branch, *Parting the Waters* p. 787.

29. King, *My Life with Martin Luther King* p. 215.

30. Raines, *My Soul Is Rested* p. 152.

31. *NYT* May 13, 1963.

32. Anthony Lewis, *Portrait of a Decade: The Second American Revolution* pp. 202–203.

33. *NYT* May 13, 1963.

34. Transcript of Oval Office meeting, May 12, involving JFK, RFK, Burke Marshall, Robert McNamara and Nicholas Katzenbach. Presidential recording #86.2.

35. Transcript of Oval Office meeting, May 12. Presidential recording #86.2; draft of presidential statement, undated. JFKPOF Box 96.

36. Drafts of presidential statements May 12, 1963. JFKPOF Box 96; McWhorter, *Carry Me Home* p. 463.

37. JFKPPP 1963 pp. 397–398.

38. *NYT* May 14, 1963; Situation Report "Oak Tree" (Alabama) May 15, 1963. JFKPOF Box 96.

39. Raines, *My Soul Is Rested* p. 291.

40. Navasky, *Kennedy Justice* p. 218; *Newsweek* May 27, 1963.

CHAPTER 23

1. *NYT* May 15, 1963; *NYT* May 17, 1963; *Newsweek* May 6, 1963; memorandum or meeting with Congressman Diggs, May 9, 1963. Lawrence O'Brien Papers Box 4.

2. *NYT* May 13, 1963; *NYT* May 14, 1963; *NYT* May 15, 1963; *NYT* May 16, 1963; *NYT* May 17, 1963; *NYT* May 18, 1963; *NYT* May 19, 1963.

3. JFKPPP 1963 p. 407.

4. Ibid. pp. 408–409.

5. *NYT* May 19, 1963.

6. Memorandum from Norbert Schlei to Lee White, May 17, 1963. JFKPOF Box 96; McWhorter, *Carry Me Home* p. 448.

7. JFKPPP 1963 p. 411.

8. Memorandum prepared by Pierre Salinger, May 17, 1963. JFKPOF Box 96.

9. Memorandum from Theodore Sorensen and Lawrence O'Brien to JFK, May 14, 1963. TSP Box 59.

10. Transcript of Oval Office meeting, May 20, 1963 involving JFK, RFK, Lawrence O'Brien, Burke Marshall, Theodore Sorensen, Lee White, and Kenneth O'Donnell. Presidential recording #88.4. For a more complete transcript of the meeting see Jonathan Rosenberg and Zachary Karabell, *Kennedy, Johnson, and the Quest for Justice: The Civil Rights Tapes* pp. 117–127.

11. Navasky, *Kennedy Justice* p. 113.

12. JFKPPP 1963 p. 423.

13. Navasky, *Kennedy Justice* p. 113; *Newsweek* June 3, 1963; Hugh Sidey, *John F. Kennedy, President* p. 331.

14. Louis Oberdorfer interview with the author; Guthman and Shulman, *Robert Kennedy in His Own Words* p. 198.

15. *NYT* May 29, 1963.

16. *NYT* June 1, 1963; *NYT* June 2, 1963.

17. Memorandum from J. Edgar Hoover to RFK, May 31, 1963. FBI Papers MLK File #3; phone conversation between MLK and Stanley Levison, June 1, 1963. FBI recording 100–106670.

18. Speech by LBJ at Wayne State University, Detroit, Michigan, January 7, 1963. BBP Box 4.

19. Robert Dallek, *Lyndon Johnson and His Times Vol. 2: Flawed Giant, 1961–1973* p. 36.

20. LBJ speech at Capital Press Club, May 18, 1963. BBP Box 4.

21. Memorandum from William Orrick to RFK, May 29, 1963. AGGC Box 10.

22. Berl Bernhard JFKOHP p. 38.

23. Minutes of 7th meeting of the PCEEO, May 29, 1963. LBJ Vice-Presidential Papers: Civil Rights Box 10, LBJL.

24. *NYT* May 19, 1963; Dallek, *Lyndon Johnson and His Times Vol. 2: Flawed Giant, 1961–1973* p. 26.

25. Memorandum from George Reedy to LBJ, May 24, 1963. LBJVPCR Box 6.

26. LBJ Memorial Day speech at Gettysburg, May 30, 1963. BBP Box 4.

27. Johnson reiterated this theme on June 9, in a speech at Tufts University in Boston. "We are now learning that no moral issue can be postponed indefinitely," he noted. "Now we find we must settle it with turmoil and agony." BBP Box 4.

28. *NYT* May 31, 1963.

29. Transcript from Oval Office meeting on June 1, 1963, involving JFK, RFK, Burke Marshall, Theodore Sorensen, LBJ, Lee White, Lawrence O'Brien, and Willard Wirtz. Presidential Recording #90.3.

30. Transcript of conversation between Theodore Sorensen and LBJ, June 3, 1963. TSP Box 30.

31. Letter from JFK to Dwight D. Eisenhower, June 10, 1963 TSP Box 30; transcript of Oval Office meeting, May 20, 1963. Presidential recording #88.4.

32. *NYT* June 11, 1963; Sorensen, *Kennedy* p. 499.

33. Sorensen, *Kennedy* p. 501.

34. Lee White LBJOHP p. 19; Lee White interview with author.

35. Memorandum from Norbert Schlei to RFK, June 4, 1963. AGGC Papers Box 11.

36. Transcript of conversation between Theodore Sorensen and LBJ, June 3, 1963. TSP Box 30.

37. Ibid.

38. Guthman and Shulman, *Robert Kennedy* p. 180.

39. Justice Department memorandum, Demonstrations for period June 1 thru 6, June 7, 1963, BMP Box 31; JFKPPP 1963 pp. 455–56.

40. *NYT* June 10, 1963; *BC* June 10, 1963.

41. *Southern School News* September, 1963 p. 18.

42. *Harper's* September 1963.

43. *NYT* July 27, 1963; Lee White LBJOHP pp. 163–164; Lee White interview with author.

44. *NYT* July 22, 1963.

45. John Macy JFKOHP pp. 70–73; Lyndon Johnson, speech in St. Louis, Missouri, June 26, 1963. Willie Day Taylor Papers, Box 421, LBJL.

46. JFKPPP 1963 p. 488; memorandum from Anthony Celebrezze to JFK, June 10, 1963. TSP Box 30; memorandum from Willard Wirtz to JFK, June 10, 1963. TSP Box 30.

47. Recording of meeting between JFK and ADA leaders, May 4, 1963. Presidential Recording #85.

48. Allen J. Matusow, *The Unravelling of America: A History of Liberalism in the 1960s* pp. 119–121.

49. Memorandum from RFK to JFK, undated. BMP Box 8.

50. Memorandum from Berl Bernhard to Theodore Sorensen, May 15, 1963. BMP Box 17.

51. Memorandum from Lee White to JFK, undated, LWP Box 21.

52. Memorandum from Lee White to JFK, June 4, 1963. JFKPOF Box 97.

53. Memorandum from Ralph Dungan to JFK, June 14, 1963. JFKPOF Box 97; Sorensen, *Kennedy* p. 502; statements of JFK and RFK at meeting with religious leaders, June 17, 1963. JFKPOF Box 97.

54. Transcript of meeting between JFK and business leaders, June 4, 1963, CRDKA reel #3.

55. The historian Hugh Davis Graham called the meetings "sales pitches" for the civil rights bill; Carl Brauer said they were intended "to enhance the legislation's prospects for passage." Hugh Davis Graham, *The Civil Rights Era* p. 76; Brauer, *John F. Kennedy* p. 273.

CHAPTER 24

1. The most complete accounts of the Tuscaloosa stand-off are found in E. Culpepper Clark, *The Schoolhouse Door: Segregation's Last Stand at the University of Alabama* and Dan T. Carter, *The Politics of Rage: George Wallace, the Origins of the New Conservatism, and the Transformation of American Politics.*

2. *NYT* June 3, 1963.

3. Transcript of conversation between RFK and George Wallace, April 25, 1963. AGPC Box 11.

4. Memorandum from Nicholas Katzenbach to RFK, May 31, 1963. AGGC Box 10.

5. Memorandum from Burke Marshall to cabinet members, May 21, 1963. BMP Box 17; Sidey, *John F. Kennedy, President* p. 332.

6. Dan Carter, *The Politics of Rage* p. 139.

7. Television documentary, *Crisis: Behind a Presidential Commitment*, Drew Associates, a remarkable fly-on-the-wall account of the Tuscaloosa stand-off.

8. Ibid.

9. Raines, *My Soul Is Rested* p. 342.

10. *Crisis: Behind a Presidential Commitment; NYT* June 12, 1963.

11. Raines, *My Soul Is Rested* p. 341.

12. Ibid.

13. Burke Marshall JFKOHP p. 108; Brauer, *John F. Kennedy* p. 246; *NYT* June 11, 1963; Luther Hodges JFKOHP p. 92.

14. *Crisis: Behind a Presidential Commitment.*

15. Sorensen, *Kennedy* p. 495; Sidey, *John F. Kennedy, President* p. 334.

16. JFKPPP 1963 pp. 468–471.

17. Telegram from MLK to JFK, June 11, 1963. Martin Luther King Papers Box 14; Jackie Robinson statement, June 13, 1963. JFKPOF Box 97; Mark Stern, *Calculating Visions: Kennedy, Johnson and Civil Rights* p. 88.

18. *NYT* June 13, 1963.

19. See Myrlie Evers and Manning Marable, *The Autobiography of Medgar Evers.*

20. Sidey, *John F. Kennedy, President* p. 335; Schlesinger, *A Thousand Days* p. 966.

21. Conversation between JFK and Carl Albert, June 12, 1963. Dictabelt 22A2.

22. Letter from JFK to Myrlie Evers, June 13, 1963. BMP Box 8.

23. Justice Department memorandum, demonstrations for period June 14 thru 20, June 21, 1963. BMP Box 32; memorandum from G. Mennen Williams to JFK, June 15, 1963. TSP Box 30; memorandum from G. Mennen Williams to Theodore Sorensen, June 15, 1963. TSP Box 30.

24. Telegram from Franklin Jackson to JFK, June 12, 1963. Charles Horsky White House Staff Files Box 2; *NYT* June 15, 1963.

25. *Newsweek* June 24, 1963.

26. Lincoln, *My Twelve Years with John F. Kennedy* p. 283; *WP* June 21, 1963.

27. Schlesinger, *A Thousand Days* p. 966.

28. JFKPPP 1963 p. 483; *NYT* June 20, 1963.

29. Robert Kennedy JFKOHP Volume 5 p. 3.

30. *NYT* June 20, 1963; Richard Russell, Speech in Jasper, Georgia, July 4, RRP Series X Box 127.

31. Letter from Richard Russell to Charles Block, May 22, 1963. RRP Series X Box 154; letter from Richard Russell to J. Harris Morton, August 10, 1963. RRP Series 1 Box 16; letter from Richard Russell to Eleanor Dudley, May 28, 1963. RRP Series 1 Box 16.

32. *WP* July 27, 1963.

33. *NYT* June 20, 1963; Justice Department memorandum, demonstrations for period June 21 through 27. BMP Box 32; memorandum from Frank Dunbaugh to RFK, July 9, 1963. BMP Box 31; telegram from Richard Russell to Carl Sanders, [undated], Richard Russell Papers Series 1 Box 16.

34. *NYT* July 2, 1963; *NYT* July 3, 1963; *NYT* July 5, 1963.

35. *NYT* July 2, 1963; *NYT* June 28, 1963; *NYT* July 1, 1963.

36. Meier and Rudwick, *CORE* pp. 225–250, 255.

37. *Time* June 21, 1963; *NYT* July 2, 1963; *NYT* July 20, 1963; *NYT* August 1, 1963; *NYT* June 25, 1963.

38. David J. Garrow, "The FBI and Martin Luther King," *Atlantic Monthly* July/August 2002.

39. Guthman and Shulman, *Robert Kennedy* pp. 143–146; Schlesinger, *Robert Kennedy* pp. 357–358; Garrow, *Bearing the Cross* pp. 272–273; Branch, *Parting the Waters* pp. 835–837.

40. Schlesinger, *A Thousand Days* pp. 968–972; John Lewis interview with author; Joseph Rauh interview with author; Lewis, *Walking with the Wind* p. 206; Wilkins, *Standing Fast* p. 291.

41. JFKPPP 1963 p. 617.

42. Memorandum from Edwin Guthman to RFK, August 13 1963. JFKPOF Box 97; memorandum from CRC: Civil Rights Calendar 1–15, August, 1963. BBP Box 2; memorandum from Edwin Guthman to RFK, August 13 1963. JFKPOF Box 97; memorandum from Louis Martin to RFK, August 1, 1963. TSP Box 30; memorandum from Burke Marshall to RFK, undated, AGC Box 10.

43. Navasky, *Kennedy Justice* pp. 121–123.

44. *NYT* August 11, 1963; Navasky, *Kennedy Justice* p. 122.

45. *Washington Star* August 14, 1963.

46. *NYT* July 13, 1963; *NYT* July 16, 1963.

47. Letter from Paul Freund et al. to Burke Marshall, October 4, 1963, BMP Box 6.

48. Conversation between MLK and Slater King, August 15, 1963. FBI NY 100–7350–1c 6a; FBI memorandum from C.L. McGowan to Mr. Rosen, August 28, 1963; summary of conversation between MLK and John Doar, August 16, 1963 and summary of MLK phone call, August 14, 1963, FBI NY 100–7350–1c 6a.

49. Draft of Lewis speech, August 28, 1963. AGPC Box 11.

50. Lewis, *Walking with the Wind* pp. 219–230.

51. *NYT* August 29, 1963.

52. Wilkins, *Standing Fast* p. 293; Wilkins LBJ OHP p. 10.

53. Meeting between JFK, MLK, Roy Wilkins et al., August 28, 1963. Presidential recording # 108.2.

54. Bayard Rustin undated interview, Bayard Rustin Papers reel #4; *WP* August 16, 1963; Stern, *Calculating Visions* p. 111.

55. JFKPPP 1963 p. 678.

56. *NYT* September 11, 1963.

CHAPTER 25

1. *NYT* September 16, 1963.

2. *Time* September 30, 1963; *Newsweek* September 30, 1963; *NYT* September 16, 1963; *Jet* October 3, 1963.

3. *NYT* September 16, 1963.

4. Ibid.; *Daily Worker* September 16, 1963; *Daily Mirror* September 16, 1963; *L'Osservatore Romano* September 16, 1963.

5. Branch, *Parting the Waters* pp. 891–892.

6. *USNWR* September 30, 1963; *NYT* September 16, 1963; *Newsweek* September 30, 1963; Louis Oberdorder interview with author.

7. JFKPPP 1963 pp. 681–682; *NYT* September 17, 1963.

8. Louis Oberdorfer interview with author.

9. *Newsweek* September 30, 1963.

10. *NYT* September 17, 1963; *NYT* September 18, 1963; telegram from James Farmer to JFK, September 16, 1963; telegram from Roy Wilkins to JFK, September 16, 1963. CRDKA # 4; Statement by James Baldwin, September 16, 1963. Bayard Rustin Papers Reel reel #8; FBI transcript of conversation between Stanley Levison and Clarence Jones, September 15, 1963, NY100–7350-Ic 6a.

11. Transcript of meeting between JFK, MLK, and Birmingham black leaders, September 19, 1963. Presidential recording #112.1.

12. Ibid. JFKPPP 1963 pp. 692–693.

13. *Newsweek* September 30, 1963; *NYT* September 23, 1963.

14. JFKPPP 1963 pp. 696–697; *Richmond News Leader* September 25, 1963.

15. *Richmond Times Dispatch* September 26, 1963; FBI memorandum re: National Convention SCLC, September 26, 1963; *NYT* September 28, 1963; *Chicago Defender* October 4, 1963.

16. White House meeting, September 23, 1963. Presidential recordings #112.6 and #113.1.

17. Burke Marshall OHP p. 100.

18. *NYT* September 24, 1963.

19. Interim report from Kenneth Royall and Earl Blaik to JFK, October 20, 1963, BMP Box 19; letter from Kenneth Royall to RFK, March 12, 1964. BMP Box 19; Memorandum, undated and unsigned. BMP Box 19.

20. *NYT* October 1, 1963.

21. Belknap, *Federal Law and Southern Order* p. 126.

22. Ibid.; memorandum from St. John Barrett to Burke Marshall, undated. BMP Box 32.

23. Garrow, *The FBI and Martin Luther King, Jr.* pp. 65–66.

24. Garrow, "The FBI and Martin Luther King," *Atlantic Monthly* July/August 2002.

25. Charles and Barbara Whalen, *The Longest Debate: A Legislative History of the 1964 Civil Rights Act* p. 38; White House Audiotape log 113.2. September 30, 1963.

26. Burke Marshall, *Federalism and Civil Rights* pp. 61–63.

27. Whalen and Whalen, *The Longest Debate* p. 45.

28. *WP* October 17, 1963; Brauer, *John F. Kennedy* p. 306; memorandum to Arnold Aronson, [unsigned], September 20, 1963. Bayard Rustin Papers reel #1; Whalen and Whalen, *The Longest Debate* p. 66.

29. Letter from Richard Russell to J. Henry Howard, October 25, 1963. RRP Series I, Box 16; letter from Richard Russell to F. M. McDaniel, November 2, 1963. RRP Series I, Box 16.

30. Memorandum from Lee White to Larry O'Brien, October 30, 1963. LWP Box 22; memorandum from Mike Manatos to Larry O'Brien, October 1, 1963. Larry O'Brien papers Box 18.

31. Lawrence Freedman, *Kennedy's Wars: Berlin, Cuba, Laos and Vietnam* pp. 356–397.

32. SNCC six-month report, December 12, 1963. SNCC papers reel #2; *Chicago Defender* October 12, 1963.

33. Memorandum from Thelton Henderson to Burke Marshall, undated. BMP Box 8; Fairclough, *To Redeem the Soul of America* p. 160; quoted in Stern, *Calculating Visions* p. 111.

34. FBI serial "Report on SCLC Conference," September 28, 1963; conversation between James Baldwin and Clarence Jones, September 19, 1963, NY100–7350-Ic 6a; FBI transcripts of conversation between MLK and Clarence Jones, October 22, 1963; summary of conversa-

tion between MLK and Clarence Jones, November 2, 1963, NY100–7350-Ic 6a; Fairclough, *To Redeem the Soul of America* p. 160; *Richmond Times Dispatch* September 26, 1963; FBI transcript of conversation between MLK and Clarence Jones, November 2, 1963, NY100–7350-Ic 6a.

35. Demonstrations for period 11/4/63 through 11/21/63: BMP Box 32; *Chicago Defender* November 9, 1963.

36. *WP* August 23, 1963; *NYT* October 30, 1963.

37. *Life* November 29, 1963; *Life* November 22, 1963.

38. Ronald P. Formisano, *Boston Against Busing: Race, Class, and Ethnicity in the 1960s and 1970s* pp. 28–31.

39. *NYT* October 31, 1963.

40. Carter, *The Politics of Rage* pp. 195–216.

41. Theodore White, *The Making of the President, 1964* pp. 114–122.

42. Ibid. pp. 99–105.

43. Meeting between JFK and members of the ADA, May 4, 1963. Presidential recording #85; *The Gallup Poll* pp. 1823, 1827; JFKPPP 1963 p. 678.

44. American Institute of Public Opinion press release, June 16, 1963; American Institute of Public Opinion press release, July 10, 1963; Sundquist, *Politics and Policy* p. 485; *Newsweek* October 21, 1963; *Saturday Evening Post* September 7, 1963.

45. *Newsweek* October 26, 1963; *Life* October 16, 1964.

46. *Newsweek* July 29, 1963; quoted in Stern, *Calculating Visions* p. 111.

47. Memorandum from Louis Harris to JFK, September 3, 1963, JFKPOF Box 34.

48. JFKPPP 1963 pp. 763–765.

49. *NYT* October 4, 1963.

50. Guthman and Shulman, *Robert Kennedy in His Own Words* pp. 75, 392.

51. Sidey, *John F. Kennedy, President* p. 352; Brauer, *John F. Kennedy* p. 298; O'Donnell and Powers, *"Johnny, We Hardly Knew Ye"* pp. 383–384; Schlesinger, *Robert Kennedy and His Times* pp. 650, 651; Reeves, *President Kennedy* pp. 656–657.

52. Guthman and Shulman, *Robert Kennedy in His Own Words* pp. 383, 391.

53. Dallek, *Lyndon Johnson and His Times Vol. 2: Flawed Giant, 1961–1973* pp. 43–44.

54. JFKPPP 1963 pp. 862–865.

55. Ibid. p. 477.

56. Ibid. p. 478.

57. *NYT* November 19, 1963; *President's Commission on the Assassination of John F. Kennedy* Volume 4 p. 147.

58. Nick Kotz, *Judgment Days: Lyndon Baines Johnson, Martin Luther King, Jr., and the Laws That Changed America* pp. 7–8.

59. FBI memorandum from director to SAC, New York, 100–73250-sub 2, November 20, 1963; *Jet* December 12, 1963; Marable, *Race, Reform and Rebellion* p. 98.

60. Kotz, *Judgment Days* p. 18.

61. *Chicago Defender* November 23, 1963; Schlesinger, *A Thousand Days* p. 1027; Harry Golden, *Mr. Kennedy and the Negroes* p. 7.

CONCLUSION

1. *NYT* November 28, 1963.

2. Whalen and Whalen, *The Longest Debate* p. 63; *NYT* November 29, 1963; Stern, *Calculating Visions* p. 169.

3. *NYT* July 2, 1989; Stern, *Calculating Visions* p. 162.

4. Evans and Novak, *Lyndon B. Johnson* p. 380; a thorough account of the legislative battle is found in Whalen and Whalen, *The Longest Debate*.

5. James L. Sundquist, *Dynamics of the Party System* p. 388.

6. Schlesinger, *A Thousand Days* p. 1030.

7. Memorandum from Clarence Ferguson to Berl Bernhard, September 17, 1963. Papers of U.S. Civil Rights Commission, microfilm; Harold Fleming, *The Federal Executive and Civil Rights* p. 934; State Department Minority Employment Program, October 7, 1963, AGGC Box 58; Richard Nathan, *Jobs and Civil Rights* pp. 134–135; Allen Matusow, *The Unraveling of America* p. 69.

8. Information on school desegregation, undated, BMP Box 2; Martin Luther King, *Why Can't We Wait* p. 18; Klarman, *From Jim Crow to Civil Rights* p. 363.

9. Marable, *Race, Reform and Rebellion* p. 91; Sitkoff, *The Struggle for Black Equality* p. 188.

10. *Report of the National Advisory Commission on Civil Disorders* pp. 10–11.

11. *NYT* July 29, 1962.

12. Navasky, *Kennedy Justice* pp. 96–97; Dan Carter, *The Politics of Rage* p. 134.

13. Marable, *Race, Reform and Rebellion* p. 134.

14. RFK's interviews with Anthony Lewis were conducted on December 4 and December 22, 1963. They were conducted for the John F. Kennedy Library oral history project and published in Guthman and Shulman, *Robert Kennedy in His Own Words* pp. 161, 230.

15. O'Reilly, *Nixon's Piano* pp. 241, 342–343, 322.

16. *Report of the National Advisory Commission on Civil Disorders* p. 1.

BIBLIOGRAPHY

MANUSCRIPT COLLECTIONS

Sam Beer Papers, JFKL.

Berl Bernhard Papers, JFKL.

Chester Bowles Papers, Sterling Memorial Library, Yale University, New Haven.

Emanuel Celler Papers, Library of Congress.

Democratic National Committee Files, JFKL.

Sam Ervin Papers, Southern Historical Collection, Chapel Hill, North Carolina.

FBI Papers, J. Edgar Hoover Building, Washington D.C.

John Kenneth Galbraith Papers, JFKL.

Gerhard Gesell Papers, JFKL.

Edwin Guthman Papers, JFKL.

Charles A. Horsky Papers, JFKL.

Lyndon Baines Johnson Vice-Presidential Files: Civil Rights, LBJL.

John F. Kennedy Pre-presidential Papers, JFKL.

John F. Kennedy President's Office Files, JFKL.

Robert F. Kennedy Papers: Attorney General General Correspondence, JFKL.

Robert F. Kennedy Pre-administration Papers.

Robert F. Kennedy Papers: Attorney General Personal Correspondence, JFKL.

Martin Luther King, Jr. Papers, King Center for Nonviolent and Social Change, Atlanta, Georgia.

Mike Manatos Papers, JFKL.

Burke Marshall Papers, JFKL.

Burke Marshall Papers, National Archive, Washington.

NAACP Papers, Library of Congress.

National Security Files, JFKL.

David F. Powers Papers, JFKL.

George Reedy Papers, LBJL.

Richard Russell Papers, Richard B. Russell Memorial Library, University of Georgia, Athens, Georgia.

Arthur M. Schlesinger, Jr. Papers, JFKL.

Sargent Shriver Papers, JFKL.

Theodore C. Sorensen Papers, JFKL.

Southern Christian Leadership Conference papers, King Center for Nonviolent and Social Change, Atlanta, Georgia.

Student Nonviolent Coordinating Committee Papers, Library of Congress.

Herman Talmadge Papers, Richard B. Russell Memorial Library, University of Georgia, Athens, Georgia.

Willie Day Taylor Papers, LBJL.

Lee White Papers, JFKL.

White House Staff Files, JFKL.

Henry Wilson Papers, JFKL.

Harris Wofford Papers, JFKL.

ORAL HISTORY COLLECTIONS

Civil Rights Documentation Project, Moorland-Spingarn Research Center, Howard University, Washington, D.C.

John F. Kennedy Oral History Program, JFKL.

Lyndon Baines Johnson Oral History Program, LBJL.

Robert F. Kennedy Oral History Program, JFKL.

Oral History Collection, Richard B. Russell Memorial Library, Athens, Georgia.

SELECTED BIBLIOGRAPHY

Ralph Abernathy, *And the Walls Came Tumbling Down* (New York: Harper and Row, 1989).

Sherman Adams, *First-Hand Report: The Story of the Eisenhower Administration* (New York: Harper and Brothers, 1961).

Stephen Ambrose, *Nixon: The Education of a Politician, 1913–1962* (New York: Simon and Schuster, 1987).

J. W. Anderson, *Eisenhower, Brownell and the Congress: The Tangled Origins of the Civil Rights Bill of 1956–1957* (Montgomery: University of Alabama Press, 1964).

Bobby Baker, with Larry L. King, *Wheeling and Dealing: Confessions of a Capitol Hill Operator* (New York: W. W. Norton, 1978).

Liva Baker, *The Second Battle of New Orleans: The Hundred-Year Struggle to Integrate the Schools* (New York: HarperCollins, 1996).

James Baldwin, *The Fire Next Time* (New York: Dell Publishing, 1963).

Numan V. Bartley, *The Rise of Massive Resistance: Race and Politics in the South during the 1950's* (Baton Rouge: Louisiana State University Press, 1969).

Numan V. Bartley and Hugh Davis Graham, *Southern Politics and the Second Reconstruction* (Baltimore: Johns Hopkins University Press, 1975).

Jack Bass, *Unlikely Heroes* (Tuscaloosa: University of Alabama Press, 1981).

Jack Bass, *Taming the Storm: The Life and Times of Judge Frank M. Johnson, Jr., and the South's Fight over Civil Rights* (New York: Doubleday, 1993).

Jack Bass and Marilyn W. Thompson, *Strom: The Complicated Personal and Political Life of Strom Thurmond* (New York: PublicAffairs, 2005).

Michal R. Belknap, *Federal Law and Southern Order: Racial Violence and Constitutional Conflict in the Post-Brown South* (Athens: University of Georgia Press, 1987).

William C. Berman, *The Politics of Civil Rights in the Truman Administration* (Columbus: Ohio State University Press, 1970).

Irving Bernstein, *Promises Kept: John F. Kennedy's New Frontier* (New York: Oxford University Press, 1991).

Roger Biles, *Crusading Liberal: Paul H. Douglas of Illinois* (DeKalb: Northern Illinois University Press, 2002).

David W. Blight, *Race and Reunion: The Civil War in American Memory* (Cambridge: Belknap Press, 2002).

Jack M. Bloom, *Class, Race, and the Civil Rights Movement* (Bloomington: Indiana University Press, 1987).

Simeon Booker, *Black Man's America* (Englewood Cliffs: Prentice-Hall, 1964).

Thomas Borstelmann, *The Cold War and the Color Line: American Race Relations in the Global Arena* (Cambridge: Harvard University Press, 2001).

Chester Bowles, *Promises to Keep: My Years in Public Life (1941–1969)* (New York: Harper and Row, 1971).

Benjamin Bradlee, *Conversations with Kennedy* (New York: W. W. Norton, 1975).

Taylor Branch, *Parting the Waters: America in the King Years, 1954–1963* (New York: Simon and Schuster, 1988).

Taylor Branch, *Pillar of Fire: America in the King Years, 1963–1965* (New York: Simon & Schuster, 1998).

Carl M. Brauer, *John F. Kennedy and the Second Reconstruction* (New York: Columbia University Press, 1977).

Clifton Brock, *Americans for Democratic Action: Its Role in National Politics* (Washington, D.C.: Public Affairs Press, 1962).

Thomas Brown, *JFK: History of an Image* (London: I. B. Tauris and Co., 1988).

David Burner and Thomas R. West, *The Torch Is Passed: The Kennedy Brothers and American Liberalism* (New York: Atheneum, 1984).

James MacGregor Burns, *John Kennedy: A Political Profile* (New York: Harcourt, Brace, and World, 1961).

Stewart Burns, *To the Mountaintop: Martin Luther King Jr.'s Sacred Mission to Save America, 1955–1968* (San Francisco: Harper, 2004).

Robert F. Bush, *The Eisenhower Administration and Black Civil Rights* (Knoxville: University of Tennessee Press, 1984).

Robert A. Caro, *The Years of Lyndon Johnson Vol. 3: Master of the Senate* (New York: Knopf, 2002).

Clayborne Carson, *In Struggle: SNCC and the Black Awakening of the 1960s* (Cambridge, Mass.: Harvard University Press, 1981).

Dan T. Carter, *The Politics of Rage: George Wallace, the Origins of the New Conservatism, and the Transformation of American Politics* (New York: Simon and Schuster, 1995).

E. Culpepper Clark, *The Schoolhouse Door: Segregation's Last Stand at the University of Alabama* (New York: Oxford University Press, 1993).

Thomas D. Clark, *The Emerging South* (New York: Oxford University Press, 1961).

Thurston Clarke, *Ask Not: The Inauguration of John F. Kennedy and the Speech That Changed America* (New York: Henry Holt, 2004).

David P. Colley, *Blood for Dignity: The Story of the First Integrated Combat Unit in the U.S. Army* (New York: St. Martin's Press, 2003).

Peter Collier and David Horowitz, *The Kennedys* (New York: Summit Books, 1984).

Robert Dallek, *Lyndon Johnson and His Times Vol. 2: Flawed Giant, 1961–1973* (New York: Oxford University Press, 1998).

Robert Dallek, *An Unfinished Life: John F. Kennedy, 1917–1963* (New York: Little, Brown and Company, 2003).

John H. Davis, *The Kennedys: Dynasty and Disaster 1848–1984* (New York: McGraw Hill, 1984).

John D'Emilio, *Lost Prophet: The Life and Times of Bayard Rustin* (New York: Free Press, 2003).

Dwight D. Dorough, *Mr. Sam* (New York: Random House, 1962).

Paul H. Douglas, *In the Fullness of Time* (New York: Harcourt Brace Jovanovich, 1971).

William Doyle, *An American Insurrection: The Battle of Oxford, Mississippi, 1962* (New York: Doubleday, 2001).

Mary Dudziak, *Cold War Civil Rights: Race and the Image of American Democracy* (Princeton: Princeton University Press, 2000).

Foster Rhea Dulles, *The Civil Rights Commission: 1957–1965* (East Lansing: Michigan State University Press, 1968).

Thomas Byrne Edsall, with Mary D. Edsall, *Chain Reaction: The Impact of Race, Rights, and Taxes on American Politics* (New York: W. W. Norton, 1991).

Glenn T. Eskew, *But for Birmingham: The Local and National Movements in the Civil Rights Struggle* (Chapel Hill: University of North Carolina Press, 1997).

Rowland Evans and Robert Novak, *Lyndon B. Johnson: The Exercise of Power* (New York: New American Library, 1966).

Myrlie Evers and Manning Marable, *The Autobiography of Medgar Evers* (New York: Basic Books, 2005).

Adam Fairclough, *To Redeem the Soul of America: The Southern Christian Leadership Conference and Martin Luther King, Jr.* (Athens: University of Georgia Press, 1987).

Adam Fairclough, *Better Day Coming: Blacks and Equality, 1890–2000* (New York: Viking, 2001).

Henry Fairlie, *The Kennedy Promise: The Politics of Expectation* (Garden City: Doubleday, 1973).

James Farmer, *Lay Bare the Heart: An Autobiography of the Civil Rights Movement* (New York: Arbor House, 1985).

Gilbert C. Fite, *Richard B. Russell, Jr.: Senator from Georgia* (Chapel Hill: University of North Carolina Press, 1991).

Michael Foley, *The New Senate: Liberal Influence on a Conservative Institution 1959–1972* (New Haven: Yale University Press, 1980).

James Forman, *The Making of Black Revolutionaries* (New York: Macmillan, 1972).

Ronald P. Formisano, *Boston Against Busing: Race, Class, and Ethnicity in the 1960s and 1970s* (Chapel Hill: University of North Carolina Press, 1991).

Marshall Frady, *Wallace* (New York: World, 1970).

Lawrence Freedman, *Kennedy's Wars: Berlin, Cuba, Laos and Vietnam* (New York: Oxford University Press, 2000), pp. 356–397.

John Kenneth Galbraith, *The Affluent Society* (Boston: Houghton Mifflin, 1958).

John Kenneth Galbraith, *Ambassador's Journal: A Personal Account of the Kennedy Years* (New York: Paragon House, 1988; 1969).

George H. Gallup, *The Gallup Poll: Public Opinion, 1935–1971*, 3 volumes (New York: Random House, 1972).

David J. Garrow, *Protest at Selma: Martin Luther King, Jr. and the Voting Rights Act of 1965* (New Haven: Yale University Press, 1978).

David J. Garrow, *The FBI and Martin Luther King, Jr.: From "Solo" to Memphis* (New York: W. W. Norton, 1981).

David J. Garrow, *Bearing the Cross: Martin Luther King, Jr., and the Southern Christian Leadership Conference* (New York: Vintage, 1987).

Thomas Gentile, *March on Washington: August 28, 1963* (Washington, D.C.: New Day, 1983).

James N. Giglio, *The Presidency of John F. Kennedy* (Lawrence: University of Kansas Press, 1991).

Steven M. Gillon, *Politics and Vision: The ADA and American Liberalism, 1947–1985* (New York: Oxford University Press, 1987).

Harry Golden, *Mr. Kennedy and the Negroes* (New York: World Publishing Company, 1964).

Richard N. Goodwin, *Remembering America: A Voice from the Sixties* (Boston: Little, Brown, 1988).

Joseph Bruce Gorman, *Kefauver: A Political Biography* (New York: Columbia University Press, 1971).

Hugh Davis Graham, *The Civil Rights Era: Origins and Development of National Policy, 1960–1972* (New York: Oxford University Press, 1990).

Dewey W. Grantham, *The South in Modern America, A Region at Odds* (New York: Harper-Collins, 1984).

John Gunther, *Inside USA* (New York: Harper and Brothers, 1947).

Edwin Guthman, *We Band of Brothers: A Memoir of Robert F. Kennedy* (New York: Harper and Row, 1971).

Edwin Guthman and Jeffrey Shulman, *Robert Kennedy: In His Own Words* (New York: Bantam, 1988).

David Halberstam, *The Fifties* (New York: Villard, 1993).

David Halberstam, *The Children* (New York: Random House, 1998).

Alonzo L. Hamby, *Liberalism and its Challengers: FDR to Reagan* (New York: Oxford University Press, 1985).

Charles V. Hamilton, *Adam Clayton Powell, Jr.: The Political Biography of an American Dilemma* (New York: Atheneum, 1991).

Nigel Hamilton, *JFK: Restless Youth* (New York: Random House, 1992).

Henry Hampton, *Voices of Freedom: An Oral History of the Civil Rights Movement from the 1950s through the 1980s* (New York: Bantam Books, 1990).

Drew Hansen, *The Dream: Martin Luther King, Jr. and the Speech that Inspired a Nation* (New York: HarperCollins, 2003).

Michael Harrington, *The Other America: Poverty in the United States,* revised edition (Baltimore: Penguin, 1971).

Jim F. Heath, *Decade of Disillusionment: The Kennedy-Johnson Years* (Bloomington: Indiana University Press, 1975).

Paul Hendrickson, *Sons of Mississippi: A Story of Race and Its Legacy* (New York: Vintage, 2004).

Seymour M. Hersh, *The Dark Side of Camelot* (Boston: Little, Brown, 1997).

Lance Hill, *The Deacons for Defense: Armed Resistance and the Civil Rights Movement* (Chapel Hill: University of North Carolina Press, 2004).

Hubert H. Humphrey, *The Education of a Public Man: My Life and Politics* (Garden City: Doubleday, 1976).

Lyndon Baines Johnson, *The Vantage Point: Perspectives of the Presidency, 1963–1969* (New York: Holt, Rinehart, and Winston, 1971).

Gilbert Jonas, *Freedom's Sword: The NAACP and the Struggle Against Racism in America, 1909–1969* (New York: Routledge, 2005).

Doris Kearns, *Lyndon Johnson and the American Dream* (New York: Harper and Row, 1976).

Doris Kearns Goodwin, *The Fitzgeralds and the Kennedys* (New York: Simon and Schuster, 1987).

John F. Kennedy, ed., *As We Remember Joe* (privately printed).

John F. Kennedy, *Profiles in Courage* (New York: Harper and Brothers, 1956).

John F. Kennedy, *The Strategy of Peace,* Allan Nevins, ed. (New York: Harper and Brothers, 1960).

John F. Kennedy: A Compendium of Speeches, Statements, and Remarks Delivered during his Service in the Congress of the United States (Washington, D.C.: U.S. Government Printing Office, 1964).

Coretta King, *My Life with Martin Luther King,* revised (New York: Henry Holt, 1993).

Martin Luther King, Jr., *Why Can't We Wait* (New York: Harper and Row, 1963).

Michael J. Klarman, *From Jim Crow to Civil Rights: The Supreme Court and the Struggle for Racial Equality* (New York: Oxford University Press, 2004).

Arthur Krock, *Memoirs: Sixty Years in the Firing Line* (New York: Funk and Wagnalls, 1968).

William M. Kunstler, *Deep in My Heart* (New York: Morrow, 1966).

Steven F. Lawson, *Black Ballots: Voting Rights in the South, 1944–69* (New York: Columbia University Press, 1976).

Nicholas Lemann, *The Promised Land: The Great Black Migration and How It Changed America* (New York: Alfred A. Knopf, 1991).

Anthony Lewis, *Portrait of a Decade: The Second American Revolution* (New York: Random House, 1964).

David L. Lewis, *King: A Critical Biography* (Chicago: University of Illinois Press, 1970).

John Lewis, with Michael D'Orso, *Walking with the Wind: A Memoir of the Movement* (New York: Harcourt, Brace, 1998).

Evelyn Lincoln, *My Twelve Years with John F. Kennedy* (New York: David McKay, 1965).

Louis E. Lomax, *The Negro Revolt* (New York: Harper, 1962).

Walter Lord, *The Past That Would Not Die* (New York: Harper and Row, 1965).

Richard D. Mahoney, *JFK: Ordeal in Africa* (New York: Oxford University Press, 1983).

Robert Mann, *The Walls of Jericho: Lyndon Johnson, Hubert Humphrey, Richard Russell, and the Struggle for Civil Rights* (New York: Harcourt Brace and Company, 1996).

Manning Marable, *Race, Reform and Rebellion: The Second Reconstruction in Black America, 1945–1982* (Jackson: University Press of Mississippi, 1984).

Burke Marshall, *Federalism and Civil Rights* (New York: Columbia University Press, 1964).

John Frederick Martin, *Civil Rights and the Crisis of Liberalism: The Democratic Party 1945–1976* (Boulder: Westview Press, 1979).

John Barlow Martin, *Adlai Stevenson and the World: The Life of Adlai E. Stevenson* (New York: Doubleday, 1976).

Ralph G. Martin and Ed Plaut, *Front Runner, Dark Horse* (Garden City, N.Y.: Doubleday, 1960).

Christopher Matthews, *Kennedy and Nixon: The Rivalry that Shaped Postwar America* (New York: Simon and Schuster, 1996).

Donald R. Matthews and James Prothro, *Negroes and the New Southern Politics* (New York: Harcourt Brace and World, 1966).

Allen J. Matusow, *The Unraveling of America: A History of Liberalism in the 1960's* (New York: Harper and Row, 1984).

David McCullough, *Truman* (New York: Simon and Schuster, 1992).

Ralph McGill, *The South and the Southerner* (New York: Little Brown, 1963).

Porter McKeever, *Adlai Stevenson: His Life and Legacy* (New York: William Morrow and Co., 1989).

Diane McWhorter, *Carry Me Home: Birmingham, Alabama, the Climactic Battle of the Civil Rights Revolution* (New York: Simon and Schuster, 2001).

August Meier and Elliott Rudwick, *CORE: A Study in the Civil Rights Movement, 1942–1968* (Urbana: University of Illinois Press, 1973).

James Meredith, *Three Years in Mississippi* (Bloomington: Indiana University Press, 1966).

Merle Miller, *Lyndon: An Oral Biography* (New York: Putnam, 1980).

Bruce Miroff, *Pragmatic Illusions: The Presidential Politics of John F. Kennedy* (New York: David McKay, 1976).

E. Frederic Morrow, *Black Man in the White House* (New York: Coward-McCann, 1963).

Gunnar Myrdal, *An American Dilemma: The Negro Problem and Modern Democracy* (New York: Harper, 1944).

Richard Nathan, *Jobs and Civil Rights* (Washington, D.C.: Brookings Institution, 1969).

Victor Navasky, *Kennedy Justice* (New York: Atheneum, 1972).

Richard M. Nixon, *Six Crises* (Garden City, N.Y.: Doubleday, 1962).

Richard M. Nixon, *RN: The Memoirs of Richard Nixon* (New York: Grosset and Dunlop, 1978).

Lawrence O'Brien, *No Final Victories: A Life in Politics from John F. Kennedy to Watergate* (Garden City, N.Y.: Doubleday, 1974).

Helen O'Donnell, *A Common Good: The Friendship of Robert F. Kennedy and Kenneth P. O'Donnell* (New York: William Morrow, 1998).

Kenneth P. O'Donnell and David F. Powers, *"Johnny, We Hardly Knew Ye"* (Boston: Little, Brown, 1970).

Kenneth O'Reilly, *"Racial Matters": The FBI's Secret File on Black America, 1960–1972* (New York: Free Press, 1989).

Kenneth O'Reilly, *Nixon's Piano: Presidents and Racial Politics from Washington to Clinton* (New York: Free Press, 1995).

Lewis Paper, *John F. Kennedy: The Promise and the Performance* (New York: Da Capo Press, 1979).

Herbert S. Parmet, *The Democrats: The Years After FDR* (New York: Macmillan, 1976).

Herbert S. Parmet, *Jack: The Struggles of John F. Kennedy* (New York: Dial, 1980).

Herbert S. Parmet, *JFK: The Presidency of John F. Kennedy* (New York: Dial, 1983).

James T. Patterson, *Grand Expectations: The United States, 1945–1974* (New York: Oxford University Press, 1996).

Joseph E. Persico, *The Imperial Rockefeller: A Biography of Nelson A. Rockefeller* (New York: Washington Square Press, 1982).

Richard Polenberg, *One Nation Divisible: Class, Race, and Ethnicity in the United States since 1938* (New York: Penguin, 1980).

Howell Raines, *My Soul Is Rested: The Story of the Civil Rights Movement in the Deep South* (New York: Penguin, 1983).

Arnold Rampersad, *Jackie Robinson: A Biography* (New York: Knopf, 1997).

Richard Reeves, *President Kennedy: Profile of Power* (New York: Simon and Schuster, 1993).

Thomas C. Reeves, *A Question of Character: A Life of John F. Kennedy* (New York: Macmillan, 1991).

David W. Reinhard, *The Republican Right Since 1945* (Lexington: University Press of Kentucky, 1983).

Report of the National Advisory Commission on Civil Disorders (Washington, D.C.: U.S. Government Printing Office, 1968).

Donald A. Ritchie, *Reporting from Washington: The History of the White House Press Corps* (New York: Oxford University Press, 2005).

Jonathan Rosenberg and Zachary Karabell, *Kennedy, Johnson, and the Quest for Justice: The Civil Rights Tapes* (New York: W. W. Norton, 2003).

Carl T. Rowan, *Breaking Barriers: A Memoir* (New York: HarperPerennial, 1991).

Gary Thomas Rowe, Jr., *My Undercover Years with the Ku Klux Klan* (New York: Bantam Books, 1976).

Dean Rusk and Richard Rusk, *As I Saw It* (New York: W. W. Norton, 1990).

Pierre Salinger, *With Kennedy* (Garden City: Doubleday, 1966).

Dominic Sandbrook, *Eugene McCarthy: The Rise and Fall of Postwar American Liberalism* (New York: Alfred A. Knopf, 2004).

Doris E. Saunders, *The Kennedy Years and the Negro* (Chicago: Johnson Publishing, 1964).

Sean J. Savage, *JFK, LBJ, and the Democratic Party* (Albany: State University of New York Press, 2004), p. 392.

Arthur M. Schlesinger, Jr., *Kennedy or Nixon: Does it Make Any Difference?* (New York: Macmillan, 1960).

Arthur M. Schlesinger, Jr., *A Thousand Days: John F. Kennedy in the White House* (Boston: Houghton Mifflin, 1965).

Arthur M. Schlesinger, Jr., *Robert Kennedy and His Times* (Boston: Houghton Mifflin, 1979).

Arthur M. Schlesinger, Jr., *The Cycles of American History* (Boston: Houghton Mifflin, 1986).

Robert Sherrill, *Gothic Politics in the Deep South: Stars of the New Confederacy* (New York: Ballantine Books, 1968).

Jeff Shesol, *Mutual Contempt: Lyndon Johnson, Robert Kennedy, and the Feud that Defined a Decade* (New York: W. W. Norton, 1997).

Steven A. Shull, *The President and Civil Rights Policy: Leadership and Change* (New York: Greenwood Press, 1989).

Hugh Sidey, *John F. Kennedy, President* (New York: Atheneum, 1964).

James W. Silver, *Mississippi: The Closed Society* (New York: Harcourt Brace and World, 1966).

Harvard Sitkoff, *The Struggle for Black Equality, 1954–1992* (New York: Hill and Wang, 1993).

Bob Smith, *They Closed their Schools: Prince Edward County, Virginia, 1955–1964* (Chapel Hill: University of North Carolina Press, 1965).

Frank E. Smith, *Congressman from Mississippi* (New York: Pantheon Books, 1964).

Carl Solberg, *Hubert H. Humphrey: A Biography* (New York: Norton, 1984).

Theodore C. Sorensen, *Kennedy* (New York: Harper and Row, 1965).

Theodore C. Sorensen, *The Kennedy Legacy* (New York: Macmillan, 1969).

Southern Regional Council, *The Federal Executive and Civil Rights* (Atlanta: Southern Regional Council, 1964).

Jean Stein, with George Plimpton, *American Journey: The Times of Robert Kennedy* (New York: Harcourt, Brace, 1970).

Mark Stern, *Calculating Visions: Kennedy, Johnson and Civil Rights* (New Brunswick, N.J.: Rutgers University Press, 1992).

Scott Stossel, *Sarge: The Life and Times of Sargent Shriver* (Washington: Smithsonian Books, 2004).

Gerald Strober and Deborah H. Strober, *Let Us Begin Anew: An Oral History of the Kennedy Presidency* (New York: HarperCollins, 1993).

James L. Sundquist, *Politics and Policy: The Eisenhower, Kennedy and Johnson Years* (Washington, D.C.: Brookings Institution, 1968).

James L. Sundquist, *Dynamics of the Party System* (Washington, D.C.: Brookings Institution, 1983).

Herman E. Talmadge, *Talmadge: A Political Legacy, A Politician's Life* (Atlanta: Peachtree, 1987).

Lester Tanzer, *The Kennedy Circle* (Washington, D.C.: Luce, 1961).

Evan Thomas, *Robert Kennedy: His Life* (New York: Simon and Schuster, 2000).

Kenneth W. Thompson, ed., *The Kennedy Presidency: Seventeen Intimate Perspectives of John F. Kennedy* (Lanham, Md.: University Press of America, 1985).

Paul Tillett, ed., *Inside Politics: The National Conventions, 1960* (Dobbs Ferry, N.Y.: Oceana Publications, 1962).

Timothy B. Tyson, *Radio Free Dixie: Robert F. Williams and the Roots of Black Power* (Chapel Hill: University of North Carolina Press, 1999).

Brian Urquhart, *Ralph Bunche: An American Life* (New York: W. W. Norton, 1993).

Francis R. Valeo, *Mike Mansfield, Majority Leader: A Different Kind of Senate, 1961–1976* (Armonk, N.Y.: M. E. Sharpe, 1999).

Richard J. Walton, *Cold War and Counter-Revolution: The Foreign Policy of John F. Kennedy* (New York: Viking Press, 1972).

Pat Watters and Reese Cleghorn, *Climbing Jacob's Ladder: The Arrival of Negroes in Southern Politics* (New York: Harcourt Brace and World 1967).

Lewis H. Weinstein, *Masa: Odyssey of an American Jew* (Boston: Quinten Press, 1989).

Nancy J. Weiss, *Whitney Young, Jr., and the Struggle for Civil Rights* (Princeton: Princeton University Press, 1989).

Charles and Barbara Whalen, *The Longest Debate: A Legislative History of the 1964 Civil Rights Act* (Washington, D.C.: Seven Locks, 1985).

Richard J. Whalen, *The Founding Father: The Story of Joseph P. Kennedy* (New York: New American Library, 1964).

Theodore H. White, *The Making of the President, 1960* (New York: Atheneum, 1961).

Theodore H. White, *The Making of the President, 1964* (New York: Atheneum, 1965).

William S. White, *Citadel: The Story of the U.S. Senate* (New York: Harper and Brothers, 1956).

Tom Wicker, *JFK and LBJ: The Influence of Personality upon Politics* (Baltimore: Penguin, 1962).

Roy Wilkins, with Tom Mathews, *Standing Fast: The Autobiography of Roy Wilkins* (New York: Viking Press, 1982).

J. Harvie Wilkinson III, *Harry Byrd and the Changing Face of Virginia Politics, 1946–1966* (Charlottesville: University Press of Virginia, 1968).

J. Harvie Wilkinson III, *From Brown to Bakke: The Supreme Court and School Integration, 1954–78* (New York: Oxford University Press, 1979).

Harris Wofford, *Of Kennedys and Kings: Making Sense of the Sixties* (Pittsburgh: University of Pittsburgh Press, 1992).

C. Vann Woodward, *The Strange Career of Jim Crow*, 2nd edition (New York: Oxford University Press, 1966).

Andrew Young, *An Easy Burden: The Civil Rights Movement and the Transformation of America* (New York: HarperCollins, 1996).

Howard Zinn, *The New Abolitionists* (Boston: Beacon Press, 1965).

INDEX